THE BILL OF RIGHTS

ORIGINAL MEANING AND CURRENT UNDERSTANDING

THE BILL OF RIGHTS

Original Meaning and Current Understanding

Edited by
EUGENE W. HICKOK, JR.

UNIVERSITY PRESS OF VIRGINIA
CHARLOTTESVILLE AND LONDON

THE UNIVERSITY PRESS OF VIRGINIA

Third paperback printing 1996

Library of Congress Cataloging-in-Publication Data
The Bill of Rights : original meaning and current understanding /
edited by Eugene W. Hickok, Jr.
p. cm.
"This book is the result of eight separate conferences conducted
by the Center for Judicial Studies between 1985 and 1987"—Foreword.
Includes index.
ISBN 0-8139-1297-0 (cloth)
ISBN 0-8139-1336-5 (paper)
1. Civil rights—United States—Interpretation and construction.
2. United States—Constitutional law—Amendments—1st–10th—
Interpretation and construction. 3. United States—Constitutional
history. I. Hickok, Eugene W. II. Center for Judicial Studies
(U.S.)
KF4749.A2B56 1990
342.73′085—dc20
[347.30285] 90-19945
CIP

Printed in the United States of America

Contents

Foreword

This book is the result of eight separate conferences conducted by the Center for Judicial Studies between 1985 and 1987 under a grant from the National Endowment for the Humanities. The Center for Judicial Studies, which maintains offices in Virginia and Washington, D.C., is a nonprofit educational organization established in 1983 for the advanced study of the Constitution and the courts. The Center publishes *Benchmark* (a quarterly journal), books, and monographs. It also conducts educational seminars on the Constitution for both state and federal judges and for high school civics teachers. More than thirty constitutional scholars are associated with the work of the Center.

John Baker, Professor of Law at Louisiana State University, Eugene Hickok, Associate Professor of Political Science at Dickinson College, and Dan Peterson, the Center's Executive Director, assisted me in organizing these conferences. Professor Hickok also took charge of editing the papers that were presented by the participants and are published here. Limitations on space made it impossible for us to publish all of the papers that were delivered at these conferences; nor was there room to publish the remarks of the discussants. The proceedings of each conference are available on tape cassettes, however, and may be obtained through the Center. We owe a special debt of gratitude to the Dean and faculty of Claremont McKenna College and seven law schools—the University of Virginia, Marquette University, Vanderbilt University, Loyola University (New Orleans), the University of Texas, Washington University in St. Louis, and the University of California, Berkeley—who gave generously of their time and resources as conference hosts.

The first conference, which was held at the University of Virginia School of Law, focused on the origin and general purpose of the Bill of Rights as a states'-rights document strengthening the principle of federalism. This opening session also examined the impact of the Fourteenth Amendment on the Bill of Rights and the controversy surrounding the Supreme Court's nationalization of the Bill of Rights through the so-called doctrine of incorporation. The remaining conferences took up a specific guarantee or amendment, beginning with a historical inquiry into its original meaning and concluding with a discussion of its current interpretation by the Supreme Court.

That there is now an ever-expanding gulf between the original meaning and current understanding of the Bill of Rights is the principal finding of this book. This is not a particularly novel or revolutionary discovery, for it is no secret that freedom of speech and press, the right to assistance of counsel, the guarantee against cruel and unusual punishments, and indeed most other provisions of the Bill of Rights are interpreted much more loosely today than two hundred years ago. What makes this book an original contribution to the literature on the Constitution is the fact that it is the first to offer a comprehensive account, amendment by amendment, clause by clause, of the radical transformation of the Bill of Rights that has taken place in recent years. With so many authors, representing so many diverse points of view, addressing so many different areas of the law, this book does not purport to present a unified picture or consistent analysis of constitutional development. In this sense, the book is exploratory and invites further inquiry. At the very least, however, it confirms the suspicions of the critics of judicial activism and suggests that the provisions of the Bill of Rights have been subjected to much greater interpretive revision by the Supreme Court than other parts of the Constitution. This, at least, would seem to be the case in light of the essays presented here.

The authors have not been indifferent to the question of whether these changes have been good or bad, legitimate or illegitimate; but that question was not assigned to the participants of these conferences, and this book claims only that substantive changes, whatever their merits, have indeed occurred. Accordingly, *The Bill of Rights: Original Meaning and Current Understanding* is a prolegomenon to further study of our constitutional guarantees of liberty that will serve as a stimulus, we hope, for a more critical appraisal of the Supreme Court's interpretive skills respecting our fundamental liberties.

Many individuals devoted countless hours to the planning and administration of the symposia and the publication of this volume. Special mention should be made of Joyce Pfeiffer, Victoria Kuhn, Elaine Mellen, Sylvia Kierszenbaum, Daniel Heisey, and the many students of law, politics, and the Constitution who have contributed in a variety of ways to this project.

James McClellan
President of the Center for Judicial Studies
and John M. Olin Professor of Government
Claremont McKenna College

Contributors

JAMES McCLELLAN is the President of the Center for Judicial Studies in Cumberland, Virginia, and the Editor of *Benchmark*, a quarterly journal on the courts and the Constitution.

EUGENE W. HICKOK, JR., is associate professor of political science at Dickinson College in Carlisle, Pennsylvania, and adjunct professor of law at the Dickinson School of Law, also in Carlisle.

RONALD J. ALLEN is professor of law at Northwestern University.

ALBERT W. ALSCHULER is professor of law at the University of Chicago School of Law.

MORRIS S. ARNOLD is United States District Judge for the Western District of Arkansas.

JOHN S. BAKER, JR., is professor of law at Louisiana State University.

RAOUL BERGER was for years the Charles Warren Senior Fellow in American Legal History at Harvard University.

PAUL BREST is the Kenneth and Harle Montgomery Professor of Clinical Legal Education at Stanford University Law School.

KATHLEEN F. BRICKEY is professor of law at Washington University's law school in St. Louis.

STANLEY C. BRUBAKER is associate professor of political science at Colgate University.

CHARLES J. COOPER is a partner with Shaw, Pitman, Potts, and Trowbridge in Washington, D.C.

EDWARD J. ERLER is Chairman of the Department of Political Science at California State University in San Bernardino.

WILLIAM GANGI is professor of government and politics at St. John's University, Queens, N.Y.

JULES B. GERARD is professor of law at Washington University in St. Louis.

JACK GREENBERG is a professor of law at the Columbia University School of Law.

STEPHEN P. HALBROOK, an attorney, is the author of *Let Every Man Be Armed* (Albuquerque: University of New Mexico Press, 1984).

DON P. KATES, Jr., is a partner with Beneson & Kates in San Francisco.

BARRY W. LYNN is legislative counsel for the Washington, D.C., office of the American Civil Liberties Union.

MICHAEL W. McCONNELL is assistant professor of law at the University of Chicago School of Law.

MELODY B. McCUTCHEON is an attorney in Seattle, Washington.

PAUL J. MISHKIN is professor of law at the University of California, Berkeley.

WILLIAM E. NELSON is professor of law at the New York University School of Law.

WILLIAM BRADFORD REYNOLDS, formerly Assistant Attorney General of the United States, is currently resident scholar at the National Legal Center for the Public Interest and a partner with Ross and Hardies.

CHARLES RICE is professor of law at the University of Notre Dame Law School.

RALPH ROSSUM is Alice Tweed Twohy Professor and Chairman, Department of Government at Claremont McKenna College and the Director of the Henry Salvatore Center there.

HARRY N. SCHEIBER is professor of law at the University of California, Berkeley.

STEPHEN J. SCHULHOFER is Greenberg Professor of Law and the Director of the Center for Studies in Criminal Justice at the University of Chicago School of Law.

WILLIAM B. STOEBUCK is professor of law at the University of Washington in Seattle.

JAMES E. VIATOR is assistant professor of law at Texas Tech University School of Law.

LLOYD L. WEINREB is professor of law at Harvard University.

BRADFORD P. WILSON is Deputy Director of the John M. Ashebrook Center at Ashland University in Ohio and professor of political science.

RALPH K. WINTER is Judge of the United States Court of Appeals for the Second Circuit.

CHRISTOPHER WOLFE is associate professor of political science at Marquette University.

THE BILL OF RIGHTS

ORIGINAL MEANING AND CURRENT UNDERSTANDING

EUGENE W. HICKOK, JR.

Introduction

For many Americans, the Bill of Rights is the Constitution. Ask a citizen where he can find in the Constitution provisions outlining the powers of the president, or the Congress, or the federal courts, and more often than not you will confront a blank stare. But it seems almost everyone is willing to assert that he or she enjoys freedom of speech, the virtues of a separation between church and state, the right to bear arms, and the right to be protected against unreasonable searches and seizures. It's all right there, in the Constitution.

One can only conjecture how those men who framed the original document over two hundred years ago might react to contemporary popular understanding of their work. But there is little doubt that during the summer of 1787 and during the formative years of the early Republic, there was considerable disagreement over the idea of appending a bill of rights to the new Constitution, as there was controversy over the Constitution itself.

The Constitution that was signed in Philadelphia on September 17, 1787, contained no bill of rights. Indeed, the issue of a bill of rights was hardly raised during the summer, until George Mason of Virginia asserted toward the end of the deliberations that a listing of rights might be needed to ensure that the new government created by the Constitution posed no threat to the citizens in the several states.[1] His concerns were almost completely ignored, however, and the Constitution was sent to the states for ratification without a bill of rights.

James Madison, who along with James Wilson of Pennsylvania was most influential in the deliberations that produced the Constitution, saw no need for a bill of rights. Writing months later for the newspapers of New York, he asserted that a bill of rights was almost superfluous to good government. "Is a bill of rights essential to liberty?" he asked. "The Confederation has no bill of rights." How could those who opposed the Constitution on this basis not also oppose the system of government under the Articles of Confederation?[2]

But it was Alexander Hamilton, Madison's collaborator in that exercise in editorializing that became *The Federalist Papers*, who produced the more complete response to critics seeking a bill of rights. Turning their argument against them, Hamilton asserted that while the citizens of New York seemed bothered by the absence of a bill of rights, the Constitution of New York contained no bill of rights either. If New Yorkers looked to "various provisions [in the state constitution] in favor of particular privileges and rights which, in substance, amount to the same thing" as a bill of rights, then they could find similar provisions in the new federal Constitution. After listing several such provisions, Hamilton remarked that "it may well be a question whether these are not, upon the whole, of equal importance with any which are to be found in the constitution of this State."[3]

Hamilton objected to a bill of rights on the level of principle as well. According to the influential New Yorker, bills of rights had their origin in stipulations between kings and their subjects. They were regarded as "reservations of rights not surrendered to the prince." A bill of rights would seem inapplicable in the American context, therefore, because the Constitution under consideration was "founded upon the power of the people and executed by their immediate representatives and servants." Hamilton continued:

> Here, in strictness, the people surrender nothing; and as they retain everything they have no need of particular reservations, "We, The People of the United States, to secure the blessings of liberty to ourselves and our posterity, do ordain and establish this Constitution for the United States of America." Here is a better recognition of popular rights than volumes of those aphorisms which make the principal figure in several of our State bills of rights and which would sound much better in a treatise of ethics than in a constitution of government.[4]

Hamilton asserted that a bill of rights was not only unnecessary but dangerous. "For why declare that things shall not be done which there is no power to do?" The new Constitution created a government of limited and enumerated powers. It had no power to regulate speech or the press. Why then, asked Hamilton, say it shall not regulate speech or press. Moreover, the danger in explicitly stating the limitations on governmental power was not to be dismissed lightly. Any bill of rights "would contain various exceptions to powers which are not granted; and, on this very account, would afford a colorable pretext to claim more than were granted."[5] Hamilton saw the possibility that a bill of rights aimed at keeping government in its place might provide the vehicle for the exercise of governmental power in areas beyond those delegated to it by the Constitution.

Hamilton continued his attack on the critics of the Constitution, arguing that a bill of rights would be, at best, only a parchment barrier against governmental action. And it would be a problematical barrier at that. Any rights listed would need interpretation, after all: "What is the liberty of the press? Who can give it any definition which would not leave the utmost latitude for evasion?"[6]

For Hamilton, the greatest argument against adding a bill of rights to the Constitution was the fact that the Constitution is itself, "in every rational sense, and to every useful purpose, A Bill of Rights."[7] The very structure of the system of government created by the Constitution—of separated powers checking one another, of the need for election and reelection, a government of enumerated and limited powers—meant that the rights so jealously guarded by the citizens of the Republic would not be threatened by that government.

Arguments such as those mounted by Madison and Hamilton in the newspapers of New York appeared in the press among the thirteen states and provided much of the fuel for deliberations during the ratification conventions that convened in the states.

At one such convention, in the spring of 1788, delegates gathered in Richmond, Virginia, to debate the new Constitution. Among those present were George Mason, still concerned about the new charter, Patrick Henry, the most able orator of his time and a staunch opponent of the Constitution, and James Madison, who by now enjoyed a reputation as the "Father" of the Constitution—a reputation he himself frowned upon. In Richmond, as in every state ratification convention, the issue of amendments came up time and again. Many delegates favored "conditional ratification": approving the Constitution on the condition that it be amended. Others argued that "conditional ratification" offered no real guarantee that amendments would be forthcoming from the new Congress. Still others argued that it was foolhardy to go about changing the document before it had even been implemented. One might as well call for a new convention and start from scratch.

In Richmond, Madison opposed amendments and was able to carry the debate—in spite of Mason and Henry. Virginia had been a pivotal state; it was the tenth state to ratify the Constitution. There would be a new constitution, and a new government.[8]

While the Constitution was ratified, there was less than a general consensus of support for the new government. Those who were elected to the First Congress, meeting in New York in 1789, understood this. Two states had withheld their support for the Constitution. Proposals for amendments had come from every state. There was still a relatively strong and vocal opposition to the new government. On June 8 James Madison offered a series of revisions to the Constitution, hoping that they would satisfy those who seemed most opposed to the Constitution without offending its supporters. He wrote his good friend Thomas Jefferson, "A bill of rights, incorporated in the constitution will be proposed, with a few other alterations most called for by the opponents of the Government and least objectionable to its friends."[9]

That Madison came to the position of recommending a bill of rights after having opposed one for so long can be attributed to the vicissitudes of politics. After the ratification struggle in Virginia, Patrick Henry made it his business to end the public career of James Madison. In the legislature Henry was able to make sure that Madison was not chosen as a senator to the new Congress. Madison then sought a seat in the House of Representatives.

His victory would have been easily secured save for the fact that Patrick Henry was able to prevail upon James Monroe to contest the seat. Monroe was Madison's friend. Moreover, Madison disliked campaigning. He hit upon a strategy aimed at securing the support of those who remained wary of the new government—he would admit that he had changed his mind and that he now felt a bill of rights was needed as a means of "satisfying the minds of well-meaning opponents, and of providing additional guards in favor of liberty." Writing during the campaign, Madison asserted: "it is my sincere opinion that the Constitution ought to be revised, and that the first Congress meeting under it, ought to prepare and recommend to the States for ratification, the most satisfactory provisions for all essential rights, particularly the rights of Conscience in the fullest latitude, the freedom of the press, trials by jury, security against general warrants etc."[10]

The strategy worked. Madison was elected by a comfortable margin. Between his election and the day he offered his constitutional revisions to his colleagues in Congress, he attempted to determine what sorts of changes were most desired by the opponents of the government and were most appropriate.

The Bill of Rights that Americans hold so dear today differs markedly from the list of constitutional revisions that Madison recommended to the Congress in 1789. Madison wanted to incorporate the changes into the text of the Constitution, rather than appending them to the document. He would have added as a prefix to the Constitution a declaration that "all power is originally vested in, and consequently derived from, the people," and he would have included in the preamble of the Constitution language reminiscent of the Declaration of Independence: "That Government is instituted and ought to be exercised for the benefit of the people; which consists in the enjoyment of life and liberty, with the right of acquiring and using property, and generally of pursuing and obtaining happiness and safety."

These additions would be followed by eight revisions, most of which were to appear in Article I of the Constitution—that article which pertains to the powers of the Congress. Interestingly, Madison recommended that there be incorporated into the document a statement saying, "No State shall violate the equal rights of conscience, or the freedom of the press, or trial by jury in criminal cases." He also sought to emphasize separation of powers with a recommendation for a new article: "The powers delegated by this Constitution are appropriated to the departments to which they are respectively distributed: so that the Legislative Department shall never exercise the powers vested in the Executive or Judicial, nor the Executive exercise powers vested in the Legislative or Judicial, nor the Judicial exercise the powers vested in the Legislative or Executive Departments." Madison also recommended changes relating to the size of congressional districts and salaries for members of Congress.[11]

Madison's recommendations failed to arouse much debate. Indeed, they were dismissed rather quickly and assigned to a committee, on which Madison served. Evidently the members of the House remained somewhat ambivalent about the wisdom of proposing changes to the Constitution, even though most admitted that Madison was correct in asserting the need to make good on promises and appease those who opposed the government. Moreover, the congressmen were eager to get on with the important business of passing a revenue-raising bill.

Reaction in Virginia to Madison's proposal was hardly overwhelming either. George Mason wrote to a friend that he held out little hope for important and substantial amendments. Patrick Henry bristled with anger, directed at the changes Madison proposed and at Madison as well. In the Senate, South Carolina's Pierce Butler referred to the revisions as "milk and water amendments."[12]

The proposals were not debated in the House of Representatives until August. Many of the recommendations were adopted by the House by the two-thirds needed and sent to the Senate. There some changes were made in the format and wording of the revisions. What emerged from the conference between the House of Representatives and the Senate were twelve amendments. Congress proposed that they be added to the Constitution rather than incorporated into the original document itself. In September, the twelve amendments to the Constitution were sent to the states for ratification. Ten of these twelve were ratified and became the Bill of Rights to the Constitution in 1791.

Determining the original meaning of the Bill of Rights is no easy task. There is no record of the deliberations that took place in the Senate. The proceedings of the House of Representatives are recorded in the *Annals of Congress*, but, surprisingly, there was relatively little debate over the proposed amendments. There was some discussion over whether or not members of the House of Representatives should receive instructions from their constituents. But most of the debate focused on the wisdom of taking up the House's time with the proposals, especially when the Congress needed to get on with creating a government and funding it.

It is not an oversimplification to say that by the time the members of the First Congress got down to the business of drafting the amendments, a general consensus existed regarding just what sorts of things should be included in a bill of rights. And there was general agreement over what was meant by such ideas as freedom of speech and of the press and the right to bear arms. There was a need to refine the terms and clarify their meaning. The discussions reflected a desire to limit the possible ambiguities of interpretation, as well as a need to clarify, as much as possible, the nature of the relationship between the national government and the states. But for the most part, the deliberations demonstrate remarkable consensus, especially when compared with the sort of controversy that typically surrounds contemporary debate over similar issues.

Of course, most of the issues addressed in the first ten amendments to the Constitution had a rich history rooted in British law and the political experience of colonial America and government under the Articles of Confederation. The amendments were not born in the Congress in 1789 and were not the brainchild of James Madison. Madison had collected proposals from all over the Republic, many of them having been offered during the various ratification conventions. Scholars can turn to *Elliot's Debates* for the records of those conventions. Madison himself turned to the Virginia Declaration of Rights, which had been written by George Mason, for direction. In addition, many state constitutions contained bills of rights or provisions that secured individual rights. These were not new ideas.

The chapters presented here explore two dimensions of the debate over the Bill of Rights. Many of the chapters explore the history, theory, and practice behind the rights protected in the Bill of Rights. These chapters, because they discuss the animating ideas and principles behind the Bill of Rights, provide a unique and appropriate context in which to approach the analysis of contemporary jurisprudence surrounding the amendments. For too long now, such a context has been missing from the study of constitutional law and politics.

Considered together, the chapters presented here represent a constitutional dialogue of sorts. They are premised on the assumption that in order to understand the Bill of Rights today, it is necessary to attempt to understand the original meaning of the amendments; to understand the Bill of Rights the way those who wrote the amendments understood them. It is important to get beyond the latest opinions of the Supreme Court in order to analyze and evaluate critically those opinions. Lawyers and students of law and politics need to remember that long before the process of "incorporating" the Bill of Rights into the Fourteenth Amendment was begun in *Gitlow v. New York*,[13] John Marshall in *Barron v. Baltimore*[14] had asserted that the protections of the first ten amendments to the Constitution did not secure citizens against actions by state governments. They need to understand how the system of trial by jury has changed over time. They need to become reacquainted with (or perhaps introduced to) the debate surrounding religious freedom at the time of the adoption of the Bill of Rights so to better determine the way the contemporary Supreme Court understands that concept. In order to decide whether flag burning is a protected form of symbolic speech, it might be fitting and proper to determine just what freedom of speech meant to those who ratified the Bill of Rights. The purpose of these essays, in sum, is to contribute to the ongoing debate over constitutional interpretation and the proper role of "original intent" in determining what the Constitution means and in resolving contemporary constitutional questions. At a time when national attention is focused on how to understand the Constitution and the Bill of Rights, the chapters presented here help to shed light on that question and are a reminder of just how important it is that the debate continue.

Notes

1. J. Madison, *Notes of Debates in the Federal Convention of 1787*, ed. A. Koch (Athens: Ohio Univ. Press, 1966), p. 651.

2. A. Hamilton, J. Madison and J. Jay, *The Federalist Papers*, ed. C. Rossiter (New York: New American Library, 1961), No. 38, p. 238.

3. Ibid., No. 84, pp. 510, 511.

4. Ibid., pp. 512, 513.

5. Ibid., p. 513.

6. Ibid.

7. Ibid., p. 515.

8. R. Rutland, *James Madison, the Founding Father* (New York: Macmillan, 1987), pp. 23–49.

9. James Madison to Thomas Jefferson, May 27, 1789, cited in ibid., p. 60.

10. James Madison to George Eve, Jan. 2, 1789, cited in ibid., p. 47.

11. *Annals of Congress*, vol. 1 (Washington, D.C.: Gales & Seaton, 1834), pp. 424–49.

12. Rutland, *James Madison*, pp. 51–72.

13. *Gitlow v. New York*, 268 U.S. 652 (1925).

14. *Barron v. Baltimore*, 7 Pet. 243 (1833).

I.

UNDERSTANDING THE BILL OF RIGHTS

CHARLES RICE

1. The Bill of Rights and the Doctrine of Incorporation

The Constitution of the United States is the first instance in all history of the creation of a government possessing only limited powers. The Magna Charta, the Petition of Right, the English Bill of Rights, and all the other previous efforts to restrain government had merely imposed restrictions on the otherwise unlimited power of government. The framers of the Constitution, however, created a new government which would possess only the powers delegated to it. To be sure, some implied powers were delegated, and some of the delegated powers, such as the power to regulate interstate commerce, were subject to elastic interpretation. Nevertheless, the federalism ordained by the Constitution rested upon the essential principle that the federal government was given only the powers delegated and that all other governmental power remained with the states. This principle was embodied in the Constitution even before the adoption of the Tenth Amendment. Thus, Article I, Section 1 provides: "All legislative powers herein granted. . . ." The Tenth Amendment merely reaffirmed the principle, as if to say, "And we really mean it."

Various factors have contributed to the erosion of federalism in constitutional theory and practice—the changed character of the economy, the conferral on the federal government by the Sixteenth Amendment of an unlimited power to tax income, the direct election of senators provided by the Seventeenth Amendment, the effect of four major wars in seven decades, and others. This chapter, however, will focus on a little-noticed but decisive reason for the shift in governmental power from the states to Washington in matters affecting basic aspects of local government and community life. Consider a few examples.

When a twelve-year-old girl was shot and killed not long ago in the crossfire of a gang fight in Chicago's Cabrini-Green housing project, why could the police not respond to the demands of residents and columnists that they search the project, seize all the illegal weapons, and arrest their possessors?

When a small midwestern city finds that the newest addition to its downtown business district is a bar featuring totally nude dancing, why are the authorities unable to close the place down?

When a public school teacher responds to the requests of all the parents of her kindergarten class by allowing the children to recite the Romper Room grace—"God is great, God is good, Let us thank Him for our food"—before their cookies and milk, why is that teacher subject to injunction as a violator of the First Amendment to the U. S. Constitution?

Why are public high schools and colleges required to recognize a homosexual club on the same basis as they recognize other student clubs such as a stamp club or a history club?

Why are unborn human beings killed each year in this country in numbers equivalent to the combined populations of Boston, Denver, and Seattle, with the states unable to do anything effective to prevent it?

Why is a public figure who is financially destroyed by a falsehood published by a newspaper unable to recover a dime unless he proves the falsehood was published with actual malice?

These are questions about which many Americans are concerned. The answer in each case is that the states and communities are prevented from doing anything because of the incorporation doctrine. This has nothing to do with corporations. It is, rather, an invention of the Supreme Court of the United States by which that Court, contrary to the intent of the Constitution, has succeeded in binding the states uniformly by every requirement of the first eight amendments of the Bill of Rights as those requirements are interpreted by the Supreme Court.

The first eight amendments to the Bill of Rights were intended by the First Congress and by the states that approved them to protect the specified rights against invasion by the federal government. The state governments were not bound by those provisions. For protection of their rights against invasion by state governments, the people relied primarily upon state constitutions.

The Fourteenth Amendment, adopted in 1868, provides that "No State shall . . . abridge the privileges or immunities of citizens of the United States; nor shall any State deprive any person of life, liberty, or property, without due process of law; nor deny to any person within its jurisdiction the equal protection of the laws." In a line of decisions beginning more than six decades ago, the Supreme Court has held that virtually all of the protections of the first eight amendments of the Bill of Rights are included in the "liberty" protected by the Fourteenth Amendment due process clause and that therefore the states are as fully obliged to comply with them as is the federal government. Therefore, in the view of the Court, "The Fourteenth Amendment has rendered the legislatures of the states as incompetent as Congress to enact" laws in violation of, for example, the clause of the First Amendment, which provides, "Congress shall make no law respecting an establishment of religion."[1]

The Court has interpreted the Bill of Rights so as to include also rights not specified therein, which rights, arising from its own interpretation, it has proceeded to apply against the states. For example, in 1965 the Supreme Court struck down as unconstitutional a Connecticut law prohibiting the use of contraceptives. To accomplish this, the Court had to find a right of reproductive privacy in the Bill of Rights so as to hold that the due process clause of the Fourteenth Amendment forbids Connecticut to violate it. Less resourceful jurists might have said, as Justice Black did in dissent, that the framers did not have reproductive privacy in mind when they proposed the Bill of Rights and that therefore the Connecticut law did not violate the Fourteenth Amendment. The majority of the Court, however, discovered such a right of privacy in the "penumbras formed by emanations from the Bill of Rights."[2] This ruling was the precursor of *Roe v. Wade*,[3] in which the Supreme Court held that the unborn child is not a person for purposes of the Fourteenth Amendment and that the right of privacy prevents the states from prohibiting abortion. Even in the third trimester the state cannot prohibit abortion in any case where it is sought for the physical or mental health of the mother. In view of the elasticity of mental health as a criterion, the rulings are thus a warrant for elective abortion at every stage of pregnancy, right up to the time of birth. As a result, every year we kill by legalized abortion more than 1.5 million babies. The point here is not to analyze the abortion issue itself. Rather, the purpose is to discuss the error involved in the Supreme Court's holding that the first eight amendments of the Bill of Rights are strictly applied against the states through the Fourteenth Amendment. This error affects areas as diverse as defamation, school prayer, search and seizure, self-incrimination, capital punishment, pornography, and homosexual activity.

The legislative history of the Fourteenth Amendment demonstrates that the application by the Supreme Court of the Bill of Rights to the states fits Justice Holmes's description, in another context, of "an unconstitutional assumption of powers by courts of the United States which no lapse of time or respectable array of opinion should make us hesitate to correct."[4] In his definitive analysis of that legislative history, Charles Fairman exhaustively analyzes the "mountain of evidence" from the congressional debates, the state ratifying proceedings, and other original sources in support of his conclusion that the framers and ratifiers of the Fourteenth Amendment did not intend to make the Bill of Rights applicable against the states. He contrasts this "mountain of evidence" with "the few stones and pebbles that made up the theory that the Fourteenth Amendment incorporated Amendments I to VIII."[5]

Nor can it be soundly argued that the Fourteenth Amendment applied some but not all of the provisions of the first eight amendments against the states. This selective incorporation theory, as Louis Henkin wrote, "finds no support in the language of the amendment, or in the history of its adoption, and it is truly more difficult to justify than Justice Black's position that the Bill of Rights was wholly incorporated."[6]

In this matter, the Supreme Court prefers its own fictional version to the actual meaning of the Constitution. A central feature of the Constitution is the division of powers between the federal and state governments. The Supreme Court's erroneous application of the Bill of Rights against the states has imposed an artificial uniformity which obliterates that division of powers in important areas. It is also counterproductive in that it frustrates that capacity for innovation and local diversity which is itself a significant safeguard of liberty.

This erroneous application of the Bill of Rights against the states is a major contribution to the congestion on the docket of the Supreme Court itself. Various proposed remedies for that congestion, such as higher standards for counsel and a new intermediate court of appeals, miss the point that an essential cause of the Supreme Court's overload is the Court's own misinterpretation of the Fourteenth Amendment's guarantee of due process of law; the Court interprets that guarantee so as to make every state and local subdivision uniformly subject to the prohibitions contained in the Bill of Rights in matters of speech, religious expression, admissibility of illegally seized evidence against a criminal defendant, and the like. Since the Court mandates one uniform rule in these matters, there must be one interpreter, which is, of course, the Supreme Court itself. Hence the avalanche of appeals to the Court. And the problem is compounded because the Court is wont to invent rights that are not in the Bill of Rights; for example, the right of reproductive privacy, which the Court uses as a justification for killing unborn babies. In short, the overload of cases is primarily due to the Court's own activism.

Respect for the intent of the Constitution requires that the Supreme Court abandon its erroneous doctrine that applies the Bill of Rights against the states. But a proper interpretation of the Fourteenth Amendment would not leave the states free from all federal restraint in the matter of individual rights. The Supreme Court has misconstrued the due process clause of the Fourteenth Amendment so as to bind the states strictly by the Supreme Court's interpretations of the Bill of Rights. But another clause of that amendment, the privileges and immunities clause, was intended to require the states to protect basic rights, including the rights to life, property, personal security, and mobility. Unfortunately, the Supreme Court in the *Slaughter-House Cases*, in 1873, interpreted the privileges or immunities clause so as to render it ineffectual. Under a proper interpretation of the privileges or immunities clause, federal courts would have a limited power to declare state laws unconstitutional. This judicial power would be limited by the power of Congress to enforce the Fourteenth Amendment, which power is explicitly conferred by Section 5 of that amendment. And a further check is provided by the power of Congress under Article III, Section 2 to limit the appellate jurisdiction of the Supreme Court as well as the jurisdiction of lower federal courts.

The privileges or immunities clause was intended to confirm the constitutionality of the Civil Rights Acts of 1866. The "fundamental" rights that the framers were anxious to secure were those described by Blackstone—personal security and the freedom to move about and to own property. They had been picked up in the "privileges and immunities" of Article IV, Section 2; the incidental rights necessary for that protection were "enumerated" in the Civil Rights Act of 1866; that enumeration, according to the framers, marked the bounds of the grant; and at length those rights were embodied in the "privileges or immunities" of the Fourteenth Amendment.[7] The "original design" of the Fourteenth Amendment

> was to make the "privileges or immunities" clause the pivotal provision in order to shield the "fundamental rights" enumerated in the Civil Rights Act from the Black Codes. Intertwined with that enumeration was repeated emphasis on the enjoyment of the "same rights," and "equal benefit of all laws and proceedings for the security of person and property." . . . In lawyer's parlance, the privileges or immunities clause conferred *substantive* rights which were to be secured through the medium of two *adjective* rights: the equal protection clause outlawed statutory, the due process clause judicial, discrimination with respect to those substantive rights.[8]

In the *Slaughter-House Cases*,[9] the Supreme Court drained the privileges or immunities clause of meaning by holding that it protected only a limited category of privileges of "a citizen of the United States." This error has been compounded by the Supreme Court's erroneous interpretation of the due process clause of the Fourteenth Amendment as a guarantee of virtually every right, substantive as well as procedural, protected by the first eight amendments to the Bill of Rights against infringement by the federal government.

The errors discussed here are fundamental. So are the consequences in terms of the erosion of federalism. And the remedy should likewise be fundamental. What is needed is a reversal of the incorporation doctrine and a reversal of the *Slaughter-House Cases* so as to restore the three clauses of the Fourteenth Amendment—privileges or immunities, equal protection, and due process—to their proper functions. The amendment was serviceable as conceived by its framers. And it can be made serviceable again, whether through corrective action by Congress in the exercise of its Section 5 power to enforce the amendment by "appropriate legislation" or through the recovery by the Supreme Court of a sense of its own responsibility to interpret the Constitution rather than to amend it.

Notes

1. *Abington School District v. Schempp*, 374 U.S. 203, 215 (1963).

2. *Griswold v. Conn.*, 381 U.S. 479, 484 (1965).

3. *Roe v. Wade*, 410 U.S. 113 (1973).

4. *Black & White Taxicab Co. v. Brown & Yellow Taxicab Co.*, 276 U.S. 518, 533 (1928) (Holmes, J., dissenting).

5. Fairman, *Does the Fourteenth Amendment Incorporate the Bill of Rights?*, 2 Stan. L. Rev. 5, 134 (1949).

6. Henkin, *"Selective Incorporation" in the Fourteenth Amendment*, 73 Yale L.J. 74, 77 (1963); *see also* R. Berger, *Death Penalties: The Supreme Court's Obstacle Course* (Cambridge: Harvard Univ. Press, 1982), pp. 15–16.

7. R. Berger, *Government by Judiciary: The Transformation of the Fourteenth Amendment* (Cambridge: Harvard Univ. Press, 1977), p. 36.

8. Ibid., pp. 208–9.

9. *Slaughter-House Cases*, 83 U.S. (16 Wall.) 36 (1872).

Paul Brest

2. The Intentions of the Adopters Are in the Eyes of the Beholder

Constitutional interpretation proceeds by reading the text of a provision in the light of its general purpose and in the light of precedent (that is, the history of previous interpretations). The text, rather than the adopters' subjective states of mind, is the primary guide to the purpose of a provision. The evolution of doctrine through precedent generates a tradition which Justice John M. Harlan aptly described as "a living thing."[1] The tradition provides stability while also allowing constitutional change.

I will call this the "classical" approach, because it describes how the Constitution usually has been interpreted during its two-hundred-year history, and also because its focus on text rather than intentions is how the adopters themselves interpreted state statutes and constitutions.[2]

From time to time this approach to the Constitution has come under attack from people who urge so-called strict construction, by which they usually mean focusing on the adopters' specific intentions. We are in such a time again. During the recent past Edwin Meese repeatedly urged this view from his platform as attorney general of the United States.[3]

Much of the impetus for strict construction has been the hope that it will restrain "judicial activism"—that strict adherence to the intentions of the adopters can prevent judges from reading their own views into the Constitution. In fact, strict construction cannot achieve this end. Because it is based on mistaken views of language, intentionality, history, and law itself, it invites—even encourages—interpreters to read their own predispositions into the Constitution. This tendency is exacerbated because strict construction gives relatively little weight to precedent as compared to supposed new insights into the adopters' intentions; it therefore forgoes the moderating forces of tradition. Let me emphasize that none of this occurs because strict constructionists act in bad faith. It occurs because of limitations inherent in the enterprise.

Before going into this at greater length, let me make a collateral point, just to set the matter to rest. People often equate classical construction with an interventionist judicial stance—that is, a readiness to strike down legislation—and strict construction with an approach which gives more deference to legislative decisions. In fact, whether judges are interventionist or deferential has nothing to do with whether they are strict constructionists.

For example, Justice Frankfurter was anything but a strict constructionist. He believed that the due process clause had substantive content; that it incorporated so-called fundamental values. It embodied, in his words, "a system of rights based on moral principles so deeply embedded in the traditions and feelings of our people as to be deemed fundamental to a civilized society as conceived by our whole history."[4] But Frankfurter was the quintessential noninterventionist, believing that the Court should only strike down a law which was egregiously inconsistent with these fundamental values. On the other hand, Justice Sutherland often was a strict constructionist: "The whole aim of construction, as applied to a provision of the Constitution," he wrote, "is . . . to ascertain and give effect to the intent of its framers, and the people who adopted it." That was written in dissent in the *Blaisdell* case, where the majority deferred to the judgment of the Minnesota legislature and upheld a mortgage moratorium during the depression. Sutherland, joined by justices Van Devanter, McReynolds, and Butler, would have struck down the law.[5] These were the so-called four horsemen who did battle against the New Deal. Not infrequently, they rode under the banner of strict construction.

The issue between classical and strict constructionists might be posed this way: On what level of generality should an interpreter try to ascertain and apply the adopters' intentions? Should the interpreter try to learn precisely how the adopters would have applied the provision to the case at hand (what we might call their "specific intent"—assuming that they had intentions about the case at hand), or should the interpreter focus on their more "general purposes"?

Let me use as an example the familiar text of the equal protection clause of the Fourteenth Amendment: "No state shall deny anyone within its jurisdiction the equal protection of the laws." A strict constructionist would ask: How would the adopters of the Fourteenth Amendment have decided the case at bar, for example, *Brown v. Board of Education*.[6]

Raoul Berger tries to do just this in his book *Government by Judiciary*.[7] He uses congressional debates and other sources to conclude that those who adopted the Fourteenth Amendment intended only to provide blacks minimum civil rights, such as holding property, entering into contracts, and the like. They would not have wanted their children to go to school with blacks and did not intend to outlaw segregation. Under Berger's reading, the Court was not faithful to the adopters' intentions when it prohibited school segregation in *Brown*.

This strict constructionist venture faces some troublesome historiographic problems. Let me outline a few of them.

First, what ultimately matters are the intentions not of the relatively few members of Congress who framed the equal protection clause or the even fewer who publicly talked about their intentions, but rather the intentions of those who adopted the Fourteenth Amendment. What theoretically matters are the commonly held intentions of two-thirds of the members of both houses of Congress and the legislators in three-quarters of the states. It is plausible to describe the general aims of these multitudes of people. But it is obviously impossible to describe their specific intentions. It was partly for this reason that in describing the task of statutory construction, Justice Frankfurter wrote:

> All these years I have avoided speaking of the "legislative intent." . . . Legislation has an aim; it seeks to obviate some mischief, to supply an inadequacy, to effect a change of policy, to formulate a plan of government. That aim, that policy is not drawn . . . out of the air; it is evinced in the language of the statute, as read in the light of other external manifestations of purpose. That is what the judge must seek and effectuate, and he ought not to be led off the trail by tests that have overtones of subjective design. We are not concerned with anything subjective. We do not delve into the mind of legislators or their draftsmen, or committee members.[8]

Second, is the relevant question, (a) how would the adopters have applied the equal protection clause to the issue if it had arisen in 1868, or (b) how would they apply it today? Either approach requires that we put ourselves in the adopters' heads; imagine how they understood the relevant part of their social, political, or economic world, and then imagine how they intended the clause to affect (or not affect) it.

Answering either question requires going beyond the ordinary task of the historian, for it requires changing the adopters or their world in a speculative, hypothetical way—for their world and worldview are not the same as ours. The problem is easiest to grasp if you think of technological change: for example, how would the adopters of the commerce clause have dealt with the regulation of the interstate transmission of electromagnetic signals? The problem is far more difficult when the changes have been social: Consider, as Chief Justice Warren noted in *Brown*, the vastly different role of public education in 1868 and in 1954.

None of this means that history is useless in constitutional interpretation. But it does impose significant limits on the level of specificity with which one can discern the adopters' intentions.

Third, if we really care about the adopters' intentions regarding the application of a provision, we need to distinguish these from various other mental states they may have had—such as their hopes, fears, and expectations—and sometimes even from how they themselves would have applied the provision. Let me focus on the last of these, for it seems strange to imagine that the adopters of a provision could intend that others might apply it differently than they would.

The point is nicely made by the great British legal philosopher H. L. A. Hart. In describing the inevitable "open texture" of legal provisions, Hart explains why "we should not cherish, even as an ideal, the conception of a rule so detailed that the question whether it applied or not to a particular case was always settled in advance, and never involved, at the point of actual application, a fresh choice between open alternatives." He goes on to say:

> Put shortly, the reason is that . . . we are men, not gods. It is a feature of the human predicament (and so of the legislative one) that we labour under two connected handicaps whenever we seek to regulate, unambiguously and in advance, some sphere of conduct by means of general standards to be used without further official direction on particular occasions. The first handicap is our relative ignorance of fact; the second is our relative indeterminacy of aim. . . .
>
> [H]uman legislators [cannot know] all the possible combinations of circumstances which the future may bring. This inability to anticipate brings with it a relative indeterminacy of aim. When we are bold enough to frame some general rule of conduct (e.g. a rule that no vehicle may be taken into the park), the language used in this context fixes necessary conditions which anything must satisfy if it is to be within its scope, and certain clear examples of what is certainly within its scope may be present to our minds. They are the paradigm, clear cases (the motor-car, the bus, the motor-cycle); and our aim in legislating is so far determinate because we have made a certain choice. . . . On the other hand, until we have put the general aim of peace in the park into conjunction with those cases which we did not, or perhaps could not, initially envisage (perhaps a toy motor-car electrically propelled) our aim is, in this direction, indeterminate. We have not settled, because we have not anticipated, the question which will be raised by the unenvisaged case when it occurs: whether some degree of peace in the park is to be sacrificed to, or defended against, those children whose pleasure or interest it is to use these things. When the unenvisaged case does arise, we confront the issues at stake and can then settle the question by choosing between the competing interests in the way which best satisfies us.[9]

What Hart suggests is that adopters may intend to delegate discretion to subsequent decisionmakers. Indeed, the adopters have no choice but to delegate, for as the distinguished American lawyer Charles Curtis wrote: "Words in legal documents are simply delegations to others of authority to give them meaning by applying them to particular things or occasions."[10]

Fourth, Hart's and Curtis's observations suggest some other features of the relationship between intention and language: That which is voted on and adopted is not a set of intentions but a set of words. Although the words don't mean much—or else they mean too many different things—without our having some understanding of the adopters' general aims, the words also provide an important clue about how closely the adopters intended to bind future interpreters. Curtis noted that "the more imprecise the words are, the greater is the delegation, simply because then they can be applied or not to more particulars. This is the only important feature of words in legal draftsmanship or interpretation." And Justice Frankfurter wrote in *National Mutual Insurance Co. v. Tidewater Transfer Co.*:

> The precision which characterizes [the jurisdictional provisions] of Article 3 is in striking contrast to the imprecision of so many other provisions of the Constitution dealing with other very vital aspects of government. This was not due to chance or ineptitude on the part of the Framers. The differences in subject-matter account for the drastic differences in treatment. Great concepts like "Commerce . . . among the several States," "due process of law," "liberty," "property," were purposely left to gather meaning from experience. For they relate to the whole domain of social and economic fact, and the statesmen who founded this nation knew too well that only a stagnant society remains unchanged.[11]

Or, as Professor Paul Freund once remarked in a class, "We ought not read the Constitution like a last will and testament lest it become one."

An interpreter faced with almost any clause, and especially one as broad as the equal protection clause, must posit a theory or principle for the clause. The starting point for this enterprise is the language of the clause and our understanding of the adopters' purposes. But the principle inevitably will be more general than anything that one can describe as the adopters' "intentions." And the choice of the principle will necessarily force the interpreter to exercise discretion or judgment.

Continuing with the previous example, what theory or principle might underlie the equal protection clause? Let me mention four contenders:

1. the clause forbids discrimination against blacks;
2. the clause forbids discrimination based on race—whether against blacks or whites;
3. the clause forbids discrimination against any group that is systematically disadvantaged by those in power;
4. the clause forbids discrimination against any group.

The first of these is the "narrowest" in terms of the adopters' intentions. If the equal protection clause only forbids discrimination against blacks, then *Brown* is correct, but the justices in *Bakke*[12] and more recent decisions overreached in thinking that the Fourteenth Amendment had anything at all to say about reverse discrimination. Also, all the decisions extending the equal protection clause beyond blacks—for example, to Chinese, Mexican-Americans, or women—would be wrong.

This seemed to be Judge Bork's position in an important article he wrote in 1971. He said that the Fourteenth Amendment "was intended to enforce a core idea of black equality against governmental discrimination."[13] In the same article, however, he asserted that in order for the Court to be "neutral," it should "choose a general principle of equality that applies to all cases." This might suggest the fourth and broadest possible interpretation of the equal protection clause: no discrimination against any group—whites, women, men, homosexuals. Of course, Judge Bork does not adopt this position. Like former Attorney General Meese and most other conservative lawyers, he seems to choose a much narrower principle, which would prohibit all racial classifications but would not be concerned with most other classifications.

You may or may not agree with this stopping place. My own view is that the language of the equal protection clause suggests a more general principle of equality: In what must surely have been a self-conscious decision, the adopters did not even mention race but prohibited denying equal protection of the laws to "any person."

What is important for present purposes, however, is not the particular choice that Judge Bork, Attorney General Meese, or you, or I, or even the Court ends up making. The point is, first, that a choice must be made; and second, that though the adopters' language and purposes can be suggestive, they cannot determine the choice—the right "level of generality" on which to interpret the clause.

This does not mean that the choice is based on the justices' personal whim. For the justices operate in an environment of legal, social, and political values and against the background of a tradition which constrains these choices. Let me quote from Judge Bork again—this time from a lecture, in which he drew a parallel between law and theology: "Both . . . fields purport to rest upon sacred texts, and it seemed odd that in both the main bulwark against heresy should be only tradition. Law is certainly like that. . . . As Alexander Bickel observed, all we ever had was a tradition, and in the last thirty years that has been shattered. Now we need theory, theory that relates the framers' values to today's world."[14]

I agree with Judge Bork about the centrality of tradition. But I disagree with the suggestion that it has been shattered or that tradition can ever be replaced by mere theory. For better or worse, our traditions are quite resilient. More importantly, one can only think of them as being "shattered" in the last three decades if we imagine tradition as something static and unchangeable by those who participate in it. But that's to confuse tradition with orthodoxy. To quote Justice Harlan again, our constitutional tradition is a "living" one.

To be sure, that tradition has not been smoothly continuous. To use Bruce Ackerman's term, we have had two major "constitutional moments"—two significant changes in the tradition—since the founding. One was the adoption of the Fourteenth Amendment; the second, the changes occasioned by the New Deal—an "informal" amendment, if you will.[15] The last thirty years have seen considerable constitutional activity. But, as someone who teaches constitutional law and organizes his course in a chronological fashion, I have no sense of an abandonment of tradition.

The claim that tradition has been shattered lends itself to a radical form of activism in the form of ignoring well-established precedents under the guise of returning to the original understanding. I doubt that Judge Bork intends this. However, this view has been urged by Attorney General Meese, who, for example, would have the Court reject the long-standing series of decisions holding that the Bill of Rights applies to the states through the Fourteenth Amendment.[16] Our tradition of giving considerable weight to the interpretations of earlier courts tends to assure that constitutional doctrine is relatively stable, and equally important, it provides a safeguard against the justices' importing their own ideologies into the Constitution by claiming to have new insights into the intentions of the adopters. For one fact that history, or more precisely the history of doing history, has taught us is that our view of the "true" meaning of a provision can never be free from our own preconceptions. No matter how pure our motives, we tend to see what we expect or want to see.

Let me close by quoting again from Charles Curtis, who sums up eloquently what I have been trying to say:

> [S]hould we not pay the authors the compliment of believing that they meant no more than they said? What they left unsaid, they left open for *us* to decide. What then are the judges looking for, if it is not the intent of those who made the Constitution? They are engaged in doing something, not looking for anything. . . . The Court is not dealing with the men who made the Constitution, but what they made.
>
> The Constitution has become something in its own right. It is an integral part of what men do with it. It has long ceased to be no more than what other men hoped they would do or intended them to do. The Constitution, together with the Court's work, is not so much pushed by the plans of the past as pulled by hopes of the future. It is not stuffed, but pregnant with meaning.
>
> The intent of the framers when it is not expressed is only that we, the Congress, the President, and the Court, should be allowed to make good on their best hopes and cash in on their boldest bets. What our forefathers said, they said. What they didn't say, they meant to leave to us, and what they said ambiguously, indefinitely, equivocally, or indistinctly, is in so far not said.[17]

Notes

1. *Poe v. Ulmann*, 367 U.S. 497, 542 (1961) (dissenting opinion).

2. Powell, *The Original Understanding of Original Intent*, 98 Harv. L. Rev. 885 (1985).

3. *See, e.g.*, Speech before the American Bar Association (July 9, 1985), and Speech before the District of Columbia Chapter of the Federalist Society Lawyers Division (Nov. 15, 1985), in Edwin Meese III, *The Great Debate: Interpreting Our Written Constitution* (Washington, D.C.: Federalist Society, 1986).

4. *Solesbee v. Balkcom*, 339 U.S. 9, 16 (1950) (dissenting opinion).

5. *Home Building & Loan Association v. Blaisdell*, 290 U.S. 398, 453 (1934).

6. *Brown v. Board of Education*, 347 U.S. 483 (1954).

7. R. Berger, *Government by Judiciary: The Transformation of the Fourteenth Amendment* (Cambridge: Harvard Univ. Press, 1977).

8. *Some Reflections on the Reading of Statutes*, 1947 Colum. L. Rev. 527, 538–39 (1947).

9. H. L. A. Hart, *The Concept of Law* (Oxford: Clarendon, 1961), pp. 125–26.

10. C. Curtis, *A Better Theory of Legal Interpretation*, 3 Vand. L. Rev. 407, 422 (1950).

11. *National Mutual Insurance Co. v. Tidewater Transfer Co.*, 337 U.S. 582, 646 (1949).

12. *Regents of the University of California v. Bakke*, 438 U.S. 265 (1978).

13. Bork, *Neutral Principles and Some First Amendment Problems*, 47 Ind. L.J. 1, 14 (1971).

14. R. Bork, *Tradition and Morality in Constitutional Law* (Washington, D.C.: American Enterprise Institute, 1984).

15. Ackerman, *The Storrs Lectures: Discovering the Constitution*, 93 Yale L.J. 1013 (1984).

16. *See, e.g.*, Speeches, *supra* note 3.

17. C. Curtis, *Lions under the Throne* (Boston: Houghton Mifflin, 1947), pp. 2–3, 7–8.

RALPH K. WINTER

3. Constitutional Adjudication: The Interpretive View

Under the interpretive view, courts are dispute-settling tribunals and are confined to traditional legal methods in constitutional adjudication. Many of those who dispute the interpretive view actually are attacking a caricature. They deride the interpretive view on the one hand as a snipe hunt, a search for a historic intent which never existed in a form sufficiently concrete to be used to decide today's cases, and on the other hand as a charade, a thinly transparent use of irrelevant historical materials to conceal resort to personal whim.

The interpretive view of the judicial role, however, is not a vulgarized version of strict constructionism. Rather, it is a complex set of concepts relating to whether a constitutional question should be judicially resolved, how the resolution should be achieved, when it should be done, and what effect it will have. It embodies both a methodology of constitutional interpretation and techniques of enforcement that reduce the role of judicial subjectivity and the tension between judicial review and the democratic political process.

The interpretive view consists of the following propositions. First, a genuine dispute between parties with a personal stake in the litigation must exist before courts will render a decision interpreting the Constitution. Second, resolution of that dispute must be based on values or principles rooted in the Constitution that embody judicially manageable standards. Third, the courts must make a full explanation of that resolution. Fourth, the courts must be aware that validating the acts of other branches is as important as invalidating them. Fifth, the courts also must bear in mind that the power to avoid a constitutional issue is as important as the power to resolve it. Sixth and finally, the coercive effect of a ruling is limited to the parties to the dispute, although the ruling as precedent may affect the decisions of future courts in future cases.

A Dispute Must Exist between Parties with a Personal Stake in the Outcome of the Litigation

Every legal order needs tribunals to enforce governmental policies in particularized instances. Without such tribunals, government policy is no more than an exhortation, freely ignored by those who flout or misunderstand it.

The nature of dispute-settling tribunals is determined by the nature of the government itself. A totalitarian government may have one tribunal for nonpolitical disputes, perhaps courts, and another for political crimes, perhaps a secret police. A more random and less predictable totalitarian government may make up policy as it goes along and enforce it swiftly and violently as it pleases.

In a democratic society, distinct kinds of tribunals are normally provided. In the United States, at the federal level, courts are staffed exclusively by persons with professional training in case law and statutory law and who have life tenure. They are the tribunals empowered to resolve disputes among individuals and groups to which established federal legal rules are relevant.

The characteristics of our courts are directly related to the democratic nature of our government. Professional adjudicators without direct political accountability are needed, first, to insure that a particular policy has been adopted through mandated democratic processes (for example, passage in a Congress by both houses or by constitutional amendment) and, second, to resolve disputes over the effect of that policy on the parties to litigation.

No general policy-making function is given to courts, however. Indeed, courts are expected to reflect not their wills but the wills of others. That interstitial or inferential judgments entailing considerable discretion are often required in the course of decision making is, of course, true. That important and controversial policy matters sometimes are determined by such judgments is also true. It is also unavoidable because drafters simply cannot fashion codes that cover every conceivable eventuality and compromises among drafters may lead to deliberate ambiguities. Leaving interstitial or inferential judgments to professional adjudicators without direct political accountability seems the best of several bad solutions, because it reduces the chance that such judgments will be used as a facade to conceal the circumvention of the democratic process. The apparent freedom of the judiciary is thus purposely designed to implement democratic political processes, not to replace them.

Because adjudication raises the danger that judges may apply their personal policy values, however, judicial power in a democracy should be called upon only where necessary, that is where genuine disputes involving tangible parties and tangible interests result in litigation. The resolution of hypothetical issues or policy ambiguities that do not directly and concretely affect parties to litigation is unnecessary and should be left to the elected policy-making branches of government.

The rule that courts not act absent an actual dispute that has culminated in litigation finds a textual base in the "Cases" or "Controversies" language of Article III of the Constitution. This has been fashioned into a legal requirement that any party seeking to raise a constitutional issue must have "standing to sue," that is, a personal stake in the outcome of the controversy other than a general ideological interest.[1]

Resolution of Disputes Must Be Governed by Values or Principles Rooted in the Constitution That Embody Judicially Manageable Standards

Central to the interpretive view is the requirement that courts, in resolving disputed constitutional issues, utilize principles rooted in the Constitution. The independence of the judiciary is designed to insulate dispute settling from transitory whim and to insure the application of legal standards resulting from a process which itself is basically democratic. In the case of the Constitution, this process is the adoption and amendment provisions. If the Constitution may be ignored by courts or if it is viewed as authorizing courts to impose the purely personal values of judges, then judicial decisions will lack democratic legitimacy.

This is not to suggest that subjectivity has no place in constitutional interpretation or that there is available a strict constructionism which transforms judicial methods into a computerized set of mechanical formulae. Particularly where constitutional provisions are concerned, no such formulae exist. Rather, the Constitution embodies very general theories and principles of government that gain content both from examination of underlying intent and from actual use.

The separation of government into relatively independent branches, for example, inevitably raises issues without a textual solution, such as to what extent one branch may defy the demands of another, as in the case of the assertion of an executive privilege.[2] The words "nor shall any State . . . deny to any person . . . the equal protection of the laws"[3] on their face have no obvious impact at all but must be given meaning from the history of their adoption and elaboration through years of adjudication.

It would be ridiculous to suggest that such issues can be resolved wholly without reference to the personal outlook of judges. The executive privilege issue, for example, demands an honest, informed, yet personal judgment as to whether the executive branch can function efficiently and independently if certain internal matters are subject to disclosure.[4] The impact of the equal protection clause on school segregation turns on a similar judgment as to whether such a segregated school system imposes inequality on a racial basis. Judges cannot resolve such questions without making some personal judgments. To suggest that the executive privilege issue is fully resolved by a reference to obscure English precedents in a parliamentary system[5] or that the segregation issue is settled by occasional remarks by senators debating the Fourteenth Amendment in an age when free public education was a novelty[6] is to reduce constitutional interpretation to arbitrary judgment based largely on accidents of historical record keeping.

The interpretive view, therefore, must be based on methodologies of constitutional interpretation that permit the personal judgment necessary to sensible decision making yet circumscribe it sufficiently to keep within bounds the tension between discretion and democratic rule.

The first such methodology relies not on textual analysis and explication but, in the words of Charles L. Black, Jr., on "the method of inference from the structures and relationships created by the constitution in all its parts or in some principal part."[7] To take one of Professor Black's examples, the Supreme Court for years has wrestled with the problem of state regulation or taxation that appears to burden commerce among the states. The Court's doctrinal discussions have for the most part focused on the implications of the Article I commerce clause. Because that clause empowers Congress only to regulate commerce and any claim that states have no power over interstate commerce is ridiculous—consider speed limits on interstate highways—the text of the Constitution seems less than a complete answer to the danger of states engaging in economic discrimination against each other. Professor Black, on the other hand, reconciles good sense and the document by noting

> that what sense the subject has finally received . . . has come precisely from its transmutation from a problem in textual construction and single-text implication into a problem about the economic structure of nationhood—about the implications of the fact that we are one people, commercially as otherwise. . . . The sense of the matter seems to come from a concept of economic interdependence which is not so much implied logically or legally in the commerce clause as it is evidenced by that clause as well as by other things, including even the Preamble. . . . [A]ll that is good (in the cases) about the commerce clause negative inference would have been attained if the Court had said forthrightly in the very beginning: "We are, in commerce, a single nation. That nationhood imposes important disabilities on the states. They may do whatever is consonant with it, but may not regulate or tax in any way which jars with it."[8]

Inferences from structure and relation also aid in giving content to explicit textual provisions. The First Amendment employs the general, undifferentiated term "speech." The facts that the structure of the government established by the Constitution relies on free elections and such elections are informed by political debate, however, give rise to the inference that explicit political argument should be at the core of protected speech.

The second methodology of interpretation is the search for constitutional intent. We use the word "intent" in two very distinct senses. First, there are the specific, immediate expectations of the drafters as to the effect a constitutional provision will have on the laws and practices of the day. The search for, and application of, such an intent is, of course, familiar to lawyers since it is the common stuff of statutory interpretation.

However, in a second sense constitutional intent often transcends the specifically articulated goals of the drafters. When language of great generality is used in a constitutional provision, the framers may have intended to achieve or authorize far more than the immediate ends that came to mind in the legislative discussions of the measure. The nature of a written constitution with difficult amendment procedures is itself such that the body politic is strongly encouraged to add to the document only declarations on matters of great import to the society. The document as framed leaves room for growth and change in the light of history and the perspective afforded by a deliberate, case-by-case elaboration. General language in a constitutional amendment, therefore, may be taken as a signal that a general principle or theory of government transcending the immediate political expectations of the drafters is involved.

This general principle or theory may be as legitimately spoken of as "intended" as the immediate expectations of the drafters. In the tradition of John Marshall's opinion in *McCulloch v. Maryland*, we may—and should—view the Constitution as a statement of general principles rather than as a catalogue of specifically defined and narrow purposes. As he argued in that decision, were the Constitution to go beyond marking the "great outlines" and designating its "important objects," it "would partake of the prolixity of a legal code, and could scarcely be embraced by the human mind. It would, probably, never be understood by the public."[9] The benefits of simplicity and public understanding, of course, are achieved at the cost of considerable doubt regarding the application of particular provisions in particular cases.

Interpretation must seek to extrapolate from all the data the core principles of government underlying the provision and to elaborate those principles in a case-by-case process of adjudication. That is no easy task, to be sure. But often the "great outline" and "important objects" provide significant guidance. For example, the First Amendment tells us little more than that some speech may not be abridged. It takes no great feat of logic for an honest judge to conclude that explicit political advocacy is entitled to the highest protection afforded by the amendment. Debate over the precise protection afforded and the extension of protection to other forms of speech ought not obscure what a major piece of guidance this is.

As the generalized purposes of a constitutional provision are elaborated over time, in particular factual contexts, the need for courts to override an apparent expectation of the framers may arise. There are three circumstances in which this may occur: (1) where changed conditions call for a particular result not contemplated by the drafters; (2) where one established constitutional norm conflicts with another; and (3) where a specific expectation of the framers is inconsistent with the "line of growth" or core purpose of the constitutional provision.

As to the first circumstance, when presented with a situation which simply could not have been foreseen by the drafters, a court's responsibility is to apply the underlying policies of a constitutional provision in light of the unanticipated circumstances and not to concern itself with the framers' failure to provide a specific resolution of the issue. The fact that Article I, Section 7 makes no mention of an air force surely does not compel a court to put that branch of the services on a different constitutional level than the army and navy. Nor are the Fourth Amendment's provisions protecting the "right of the people to be secure in their persons, houses, papers, and effects, against unreasonable searches and seizures" wholly irrelevant to the use of elaborate communication technology and correspondingly elaborate interception devices simply because its framers could not have contemplated the existence of such technology.[10] In all such cases, the judicial function is not to abandon history but to apply principles derived from it in light of the new technology or other changed conditions. Although disputes may arise as to whether there has been a relevant change in circumstances or as to the proper application of the underlying principle in light of the change, the legitimacy of this mode of analysis is not seriously disputed.

As to the second, when constitutional norms conflict in a particular case—for example, where a defendant's right to a fair trial conflicts with the right to a free press[11]—courts are called upon to accommodate or, if necessary, to choose between the norms. In such a case, a court should strive to narrow the conflict by requiring that other branches choose means to their ends which minimize the clash of constitutional norms. Thus, rules on overbreadth or least restrictive means have been developed in the First Amendment area.[12] Conflict may persist, however, and a court then must weigh one constitutional value against another and reach a result which may seem to violate an expectation of the framers, who failed to foresee, or at least to resolve, irreconcilable constitutional goals. While such decisions often generate heated debate, it is difficult to see how a court can avoid such hard choices, at least where the constitutional goals are truly irreconcilable in the context of a particular case.

Finally, when an articulated expectation is overridden to pursue a provision's line of precedential growth or core purpose, it may appear that courts are applying values derived from nonconstitutional sources. There is, however, a sense in which a line of growth legitimately derived from history may well lead a court to contradict specific expectations of the framers. In the course of elaborating a constitutional provision on a case-by-case basis, actual experience may demonstrate that in practice a goal originally believed by the framers to be consistent with their core purpose is, in fact, in conflict with it. In such circumstances, courts are faced with a choice which entails overriding legislative purpose one way or the other and should choose coherence in effectuating what they find to be the core purpose, even against an inconsistent specific expectation of the drafters.

For example, the framers of the Fourteenth Amendment apparently expected that segregated schools would not be outlawed by the equal protection clause. Although the *Plessy* Court did not rely upon this history, a plausible historical case for the result has been made.[13] By 1954, however, and indeed much earlier, it was clear that the core purpose of equal protection—the ending of legal discrimination against blacks—was flagrantly at odds with the practice of segregated education. The separation almost universally resulted in gross inequality in educational resources, so that wasteful and expensive litigation was necessary under the "separate but equal" doctrine to prove what every sensate being knew was inequality in each school district. Additionally, the Jim Crow laws were in every form they took an important state-sponsored stimulus for racism. Matched against this self-evident frustration of the core purpose of the equal protection clause were the statements of a few legislators in the debate over the Fourteenth Amendment that the amendment would not end segregated education. At the time of the amendment, however, free public education was just beginning in many areas, including the South, and was not the major institution it is today. To have permitted these expectations, which had been shown over time and in practice to be inconsistent with the basic policy underlying the equal protection clause, to undermine that basic policy would have been a manifest perversion of constitutional intent.

Precedent is, of course, a vital but not exclusively determinative factor in constitutional interpretation. Under the interpretive view, inferences drawn from structure and relation and policies derived from constitutional intent produce constitutional principles by which courts decide litigated cases. Precedent is a means by which courts can avoid rethinking interpretive issues every time they arise and can treat like litigants alike. If every case treated the legal issue involved as one of first impression, courts would face the task of relentlessly deciding the same issue again and again. Moreover, inevitable differences in conclusions would be simply unfair and would create opportunities for outright corruption.

Precedent is instructive as well as efficient. The development of a principle will be more orderly and informed if it occurs through a series of adjudications that reflect the full range of factual patterns in which the problem arises. In the case of segregation, cases in the Supreme Court prior to *Brown* were evidence that "separate but equal" was not working and that segregation was not consistent with the guarantee of equal protection of the laws.[14]

That a constitutional principle ought not be reexamined whenever and wherever it arises does not mean that constitutional principles ought never be reexamined. Neither efficiency nor fairness justifies the use of precedent as invariably dispositive. A court may well reexamine a previous decision and determine in light of structure or relation or of constitutional intent that it was wrongly decided. More likely, it may come to believe that a decision has not in practice worked to bring about designated constitutional ends. The overruling of prior decisions, however, ought not occur unless the court decides that the prior decision is both wrong and a continuing source of injury to individuals, the political process, or the nation.

In the interpretive view, not all constitutional provisions provide an occasion for the exercise of judicial power and not every syllable of the Constitution is a source of judicial power. When rhetorical phrases do not choose between alternative principles or policies, when certain issues are committed exclusively to another branch, or when empowerments call for the kind of policy decisions for which courts are unsuited, courts should decline to exercise the judicial power. This notion has found a potent doctrinal existence in the so-called political question doctrine.[15]

Unless the Constitution itself makes a choice between cogent policy alternatives, courts can at best only define the responsibilities of other branches for the issue. Where constitutional language makes no such policy choice, courts have no business using it to impose law on the country. Legislative acts ought not be struck down because a court believes they will lead to a less "perfect Union" or will not "promote the General Welfare." So too the Ninth Amendment, which reads, "The enumeration in the Constitution, of certain rights, shall not be construed to deny or disparage others retained by the people," does not represent a policy choice between alternatives which permits courts to restrict the power of state legislatures to regulate.

Among the powers likely to be unreviewable by this analysis are the president's power to receive ambassadors and to extend diplomatic recognition. The executive power as commander in chief to make military decisions about the use of force or the deployment of the armed forces also seems beyond direct judicial control, notwithstanding Justice Douglas's contrary view,[16] at least where no use of the system of military justice or attempted displacement of domestic civil authority is involved. So, too, Congress's power to declare war or to impeach officers of the United States seems unreviewable.

In each of these cases, there is a textual commitment which seems on its face complete but which lacks an explicit declaration of exclusivity. Nevertheless, the view that the exercise of such powers is unreviewable is eminently correct, because, unlike other provisions, these powers do not include, in the Court's phrase, "judicially discoverable and manageable standards."[17] The executive power in foreign or military affairs and the congressional power to expel members, to declare war, or to impeach officers of the United States imply a choice between concrete policy alternatives to be made only by that particular branch to which the issue is committed.

The danger is not simply judicial decisions inconsistent with constitutional intent but judicial intrusions into areas in which other institutions are far more competent. Courts clearly have no business reviewing decisions to bomb one target rather than another or stating that a declaration of war is invalid because national security is better protected by neutrality.

The Requirement of an Explanation for Judicial Decision

Because the interpretive view requires that constitutional decisions be made on the basis of principles, values, or policies expressed in the Constitution or in precedent, it emphasizes the need for a formal, written explanation of judicial decisions. Of course, explanatory statements are not unique to judicial decisions. Any system in which democratic responsibility exists will entail some form of public explanation of important decisions by those exercising that responsibility. Nevertheless, the explanations provided by courts are unique. Explanations by elected officials occur when the political circumstances call for them, that is to say, when they involve issues of political visibility among particular constituents. Moreover, the explanations of elected officials may appeal to a universe of considerations bounded only by notions of political viability. Courts, on the other hand, must explain decisions as a matter of routine in each case, even if to say only that a particular prior decision governs. One reason for this is the need for monitoring an institution which is subject only derivatively and somewhat remotely to democratic control and is also expected to act according to certain specified criteria. If no explanations were required, judicial decisions would be, for the most part, inscrutable, and even incessant departure from permissible criteria would be difficult to detect.

Moreover, regular explanations of judicial decisions are essential if a system of precedents is to operate effectively. Because there are always several grounds available to justify a particular decision, one cannot know what a decision "stands for" unless one knows which grounds were decisive. Without an explanation of prior decisions, in short, reexamination of constitutional principles would be essential in almost every case.

Statements of judicial reasoning also educate other judges, legal commentators, and the public. Explanations expose wrong decisions, promote the orderly progression of constitutional principles, foster informed commentary, and, to some extent, generate public consent. Judicial explanations thus are critical in the interpretive mode of adjudication.

Validating the Acts of Other Branches of Government Is as Important as Invalidating Them

In *The Federalist* No. 78, Hamilton spoke of the courts as an "intermediate body between the people and the legislature,"[18] implying that the court's function is not simply to protect the people against the unconstitutional exercise of power by elected officials but also to protect those officials in the exercise of power from the claim that they are usurpers. This suggestion much later became an important insight into the role of judicial review when elaborated by Professor Black.[19]

In a government of limited powers, debates over the wisdom or lack of wisdom of governmental acts inevitably spill over into debates over constitutional legitimacy. A governmental structure which limits power but lacks a means of testing claims about legitimacy may encounter grave problems of instability. People will more quickly consent to distasteful laws conceded to be legitimately enacted than to laws insistently and sincerely challenged as beyond government's power. Challenges to the legitimacy of particular actions, if unresolved for a long period of time, at best distract; at worst they create sullen resentment, which hampers law enforcement. The accumulation of such claims among particular groups is the stuff of which revolution and civil war are made.

The courts provide a forum for testing and resolving claims about the legitimacy of governmental acts. Upholding acts as within the legitimate power of government is fully as significant as striking them down, because it eliminates—or is a major first step in the direction of eliminating—from the political arena a range of potentially dangerous arguments about usurpation of power.

The idea that legitimating acts of government is as important as invalidating them has an important implication for the nature of judicial review. To the extent that some mean by "judicial restraint" a posture of passivity toward the acts of other branches that can be overcome only in egregious or flagrant cases—in effect a call to judges to ignore a sincere conviction that a law is beyond the power of Congress on the grounds that courts must approach constitutional issues timidly and with fear and trembling—the judicial restraint position is invalid. As Professor Black noted, once a court betrays an unwillingness to adopt a correct constitutional principle because it would invalidate an act of another branch, its approval of such acts will be considerably less effective in eliminating debates over legitimacy.[20]

The Power Not to Decide a Constitutional Issue Is Essential to Judicial Review

The proposition that legitimating is as important a judicial function as invalidating leads to a paradoxical conclusion: The courts must have the power not to decide. As Alexander Bickel noted, legitimating the acts of government does more than give those acts a final stamp of approval. It also increases the political impetus for them. Removing doubt as to the legitimacy of certain acts disarms their opponents and eliminates residues of doubt among proponents. The political viability of such measures increases, as does the likelihood that government will enact and expand them.

We are accustomed to appreciating the high stakes in the invalidation of governmental acts on constitutional grounds. We are less likely to realize that the stakes are quite as high in upholding those acts because of the political ripple effect resulting from the elimination of doubts as to legitimacy. A most forceful example is *Plessy v. Ferguson.*[21] At the time of the decision, segregation was in its infancy, and while it is easy today to say that the Court got the constitutional principle backwards, the greatest error of the *Plessy* Court was, as Bickel noted, in reaching the constitutional issue at all. Once the Court had lent "its affirmative sanction to the practice of segregation in the nineteenth century, and doing so on principle, across the board,"[22] it insured the political victory of Jim Crow in the southern and border states.

Judicial caution is necessary, therefore, not to avoid conflicts with other branches but because the cost of judicial error is potentially so great, whether in upholding or invalidating the acts of other branches of government. Courts thus should avoid major constitutional decisions when litigation can be disposed of on grounds of lesser magnitude. Courts also should avoid major constitutional decisions until the dimensions of an issue have crystallized, have become "ripe" in the lexicon of the trade, and a substantial debate beyond the confines of the briefs of the parties to litigation has taken place.

A Constitutional Decision Is Coercive Only as to the Parties to the Litigation

Judicial review exists not because of judicial omnicompetence but because settling disputes is a necessary function of government. It follows that judicial rulings apply only to the parties to the particular dispute and that the doctrine or reasoning of a case is law only to the extent the courts are prepared to apply it to parties involved in subsequent litigation. The Supreme Court's authority as the ultimate interpreter of the Constitution is the authority only to rule on a particular dispute to which the Constitution is relevant. To the extent the decision in one case controls another, it is because courts are expected to explain their decisions and to treat like cases alike. Precedent, however, may not control when a court determines that a prior decision is erroneous and is visiting serious and continuing harm upon the people and the government. Further, that harm must outweigh the damage that will be done to the general principle that like cases shall be treated alike when a court declines to follow a controlling precedent.

The most explicit exposition of this view was by a political candidate on the stump. Running for the Senate against Stephen Douglas, Abraham Lincoln had to answer the charge that because he was quite prepared to vote against the extension of slavery—one such law having been struck down as unconstitutional in *Dred Scott*—he was defiant of the Constitution. Answering that in no sense was he calling for the overturning of the decision as to Dred Scott himself or any other person declared to be a slave by final court order, Lincoln argued that he was nevertheless free to resist the underlying principle as a "political rule." Lincoln said:

> We oppose the Dred Scott decision in a certain way. . . . We do not propose that when Dred Scott has been decided to be a slave by the court, we, as a mob, will decide him to be free. We do not propose that, when any other one, or one thousand, shall be decided by that court to be slaves, we will in any violent way disturb the rights of property thus settled; but we nevertheless do oppose that decision as a political rule which shall be binding on the voter, to vote for nobody who thinks it wrong, which shall be binding on the members of Congress or the President to favor no measure that does not actually concur with the principles of that decision. We propose so resisting it as to have it reversed if we can, and a new judicial rule established upon this subject.[23]

Like the rules regarding standing, this narrow view of the judicial power to declare constitutional law is derived both from prudential considerations and from the theory used to justify judicial review. Court decisions, unlike statutes, do not come into being as a result of electoral processes that give them legitimacy in a democratic society. Judicial acts must rely on the moral authority of courts and on the ultimate consent of the people. Viewing decisions on matters of constitutional law as directly affecting only the parties to the particular litigation and not inexorably controlling in future cases gives the kinds of leeway judicial review needs in a democratic society.

Those who dispute a decision can test its scope and challenge it on the merits. The Supreme Court is insulated but not isolated from political forces, and its opponents can have their day in the court of public opinion. This is a necessary, albeit not major, intrusion on the stability of constitutional law, for those who would challenge the Court bear a heavy burden at "the bar of politics."[24] Opponents of the *Dred Scott* decision won their struggle only after the decision's supporters abandoned the federal Constitution and put the issues to the test of civil war. Where opponents of other decisions have been unsuccessful in reversing the tide of constitutional doctrine, the fact that they have actively sought to do so and failed has usually strengthened rather than weakened most of the principles involved.

The Lincolnian posture on the *Dred Scott* issue is, of course, another manifestation of judicial review as an aspect of dispute settlement. In the interpretive view, the only function of courts is to decide disputes to which the Constitution is relevant. It thus is the heavily qualified doctrine of stare decisis, rather than some special lawmaking power of courts, that creates the appearance of courts as makers of law.

Notes

1. *See Flast v. Cohen*, 392 U.S. 83, 94–100 (1968); *Baker v. Carr*, 369 U.S. 186, 204 (1962).

2. *See United States v. Nixon*, 418 U.S. 683, 703–13 (1974).

3. U.S. Constitution, Amendment XIV, Section 1.

4. *See* Winter, *The Seedlings for the Forest* (Book Review), 83 Yale L.J. 1730, 1740 (1974) (reviewing R. Berger, *Executive Privilege: A Constitutional Myth* [1974]).

5. *See* R. Berger, *Executive Privilege: A Constitutional Myth* (Cambridge: Harvard Univ. Press, 1974), pp. 15–31, 169–71.

6. *See* R. Berger, *Government by Judiciary: The Transformation of the Fourteenth Amendment* (Cambridge: Harvard Univ. Press, 1977), pp. 117–33.

7. C. Black, *Structure and Relationship in Constitutional Law* (Baton Rouge: Louisiana State Univ. Press, 1969), p. 7.

8. Ibid., pp. 20–21.

9. 17 U.S. (4 Wheat.) 316, 407 (1819).

10. *See Katz v. United States*, 389 U.S. 347, 352–53 (1967).

11. *See Nebraska Press Ass'n v. Stuart*, 427 U.S. 539, 561, 570 (1976).

12. *See, e.g., City of Lakewood v. Plain Dealer Publishing Co.*, 468 U.S. 750 (1988) (unbridled discretion in municipal regulation of free speech is unconstitutional); *United States v. Robel*, 389 U.S. 258 (1967) (statute that is overbroad and does not represent least drastic impact on First Amendment freedoms is unconstitutional).

13. *See* A. Bickel, *Politics and the Warren Court* (New York: Harper and Row, 1965), pp. 211–61.

14. *See Brown v. Board of Educ.*, 347 U.S. 483, 491–92 (1954) (noting cases finding inequality).

15. *See Baker v. Carr*, 369 U.S. at 210–11.

16. *See Mora v. McNamara*, 389 U.S. 934, 935 (1967) (Douglas, J., dissenting from denial of certiorari).

17. *Baker v. Carr*, 369 U.S. at 217.

18. A. Hamilton, J. Madison, and J. Jay, *The Federalist Papers*, ed. C. Rossiter (New York: New American Library, 1961), No. 78, p. 467.

19. *See* C. Black, *The People and the Court: Judicial Review in a Democracy* (New York: Macmillan, 1960).

20. *See* ibid., chaps. 2, 7; *see also* A. Bickel, *The Least Dangerous Branch: The Supreme Court at the Bar of Politics* (Indianapolis: Bobbs-Merrill, 1962), pp. 29–31 (discussing legitimating function of judicial review).

21. 163 U.S. 537 (1896).

22. Bickel, *The Least Dangerous Branch*, p. 71.

23. P. Angle, ed., *Created Equal? The Complete Lincoln-Douglas Debates of 1858* (Chicago: Univ. of Chicago Press, 1958), p. 333 (Lincoln's opening speech at Quincy, Illinois).

24. *See* Bickel, *The Least Dangerous Branch*, p. 244 (final chapter discussing "the Supreme Court at the Bar of Politics").

II.

ORIGINAL INTENT AND THE FIRST AMENDMENT

JOHN S. BAKER, JR.

4. The Establishment Clause as Intended: No Preference among Sects and Pluralism in a Large Commercial Republic

Until recently the historical interpretation of the establishment clause had been considered infallibly settled, at least by the Supreme Court. In *Everson v. Board of Education*, 330 U.S. 1 (1947), both the majority and the dissenting opinions took a strict separationist position on matters of church-state and made that position applicable to the states through the Fourteenth Amendment due process clause. By 1963 the Court was characterizing its view of the establishment clause as "long established" and was dismissing challenges to it as "entirely untenable and of value only as academic exercises."[1] The then-accepted history of the original understanding of the establishment clause focused not on the actual drafting of the religious clauses but on earlier events surrounding the struggle over establishment in the state of Virginia. The Court relied on the statements of Thomas Jefferson and James Madison and assumed that Madison must have had the same intention when he proposed the First Amendment. Even though Jefferson was not even in the country at the time the amendment was drafted, his metaphor about a "wall of separation" between church and state, written years later,[2] became the touchstone for interpreting the establishment clause. Although the Court itself found it impossible to adhere to a doctrine of strict separation, the myth and the metaphor determined what was doctrinally orthodox and accepted in argument.

Then in 1983 heresy rang out from within the ranks when Judge Brevard Hand, a federal district judge in Mobile, Alabama, declared that the "Supreme Court has erred in its reading of history."[3] Although Judge Hand was rebuked when the high Court ruled in the case of *Wallace v. Jaffree*, 105 S. Ct. 279 (1985), the Court was no longer relying on the intent of the framers. In striking down Alabama's statute providing a moment of silence for meditation or prayer, the Court found its authority in something called "the crucible of litigation." Justice Stevens did acknowledge that the establishment clause had a different meaning "At one time." Justice Stevens's retreat from the historical record to relatively recent cases that themselves relied on the previously assumed historical record was for good reason. In dissent, Justice Rehnquist gave the most complete review of the historical record ever given in a Supreme Court opinion as to the intent of the framers of the First Amendment's religion clauses. In words similar to those of Judge Hand, Justice Rehnquist challenged the Court's history as "totally incorrect."

As you might expect from the losing attorney in *Wallace v. Jaffree*, I am in agreement with Justice Rehnquist's view on the original understanding, and hopefully future interpretation, of the establishment clause. I am therefore fond of using Justice Rehnquist's words, rather than my own, wherever possible. Indeed, after reading Justice Rehnquist's opinion, I think there is little left that need be said, at least about historical events.

No Preference among Sects

Justice Rehnquist's review of the history led him to conclude

> that the Establishment Clause of the First Amendment had acquired a well-accepted meaning: it forbade establishment of a national religion, and forbade preference among religious sects or denominations. . . . The Establishment Clause did not require government neutrality between religion and irreligion nor did it prohibit the federal government from providing non-discriminatory aid to religion. There is simply no historical foundation for the position that the Framers intended to build the "wall of separation" that was constitutionalized in Everson. (105 S. Ct. at 2516, Rehnquist, J., dissenting)

As Professor Michael McConnell has observed, Justice Rehnquist was the first member of the Court ever to analyze the debates in Congress concerning the adoption of the religion clauses.[4] Rehnquist demonstrated from the debates that Madison was not attempting in the First Amendment to accomplish for the nation what he and Jefferson had accomplished in Virginia with the Statute on Religious Liberty. To begin with, as Rehnquist states, Madison's words of introduction to the proposed Bill of Rights were "less those of a dedicated advocate of the wisdom of such measures than those of a prudent statesman seeking the enactment of measures sought by a number of his fellow citizens which could surely do no harm and might do a great deal of good."[5] Madison's comments on the floor of the House, according to Rehnquist, show "that he saw the amendment as designed to prohibit the establishment of national religion, and perhaps to prevent discrimination among sects."[6]

By going first to what must be considered the most authoritative discussion of the original intent of the religion clauses, Rehnquist showed that other actions of the early Congresses, in particular the first, and the early presidents, except Jefferson, followed from this view of the original intent as generally well understood. He referred to the joint resolution by Congress in its first session calling on President Washington to issue a Thanksgiving

Day proclamation and the issuance of such proclamations by presidents Washington, Adams, and Madison. He noted that the First Congress re-enacted the Northwest Ordinance, which provided: "[r]eligion, morality, and knowledge, being necessary to good government and the happiness of the mankind, schools and the means of education are forever encouraged." He pointed to Congress's appropriation of funds to support sectarian education of Indians. About the only significant action at the federal level that he did not directly mention was the action of the First Congress in providing for House and Senate chaplains paid at public expense. But see *Marsh v. Chambers*, 463 U.S. 783 (1983).

Although Justice Rehnquist was the first justice in recent times to adopt the "no-preference" understanding of the establishment clause,[7] his was not an original view. He relied on modern scholarship by Professor Robert Cord in *Separation of Church and State* (1982) and Antieau, Downey, and Roberts in *Freedom from Federal Establishment* (1964). He could have also cited Michael Malbin's *Religion and Politics* (1978) and Professor Corwin's "The Supreme Court as a National School Board" (14 Law & Contemporary Problems 3 [1949]). But by quoting from the nineteenth-century writings of two of the greatest treatise writers in American legal history, Justice Joseph Story and Thomas Cooley, he convincingly established the continuity of the original understanding over a considerable period of our history.

Justice Rehnquist's references to Story and Cooley are worth quoting as he gave them because they characterize the establishment clause as nothing more than a prohibition against preferring one sect over another.

> Joseph Story, a member of this Court from 1811 to 1845, and during much of that time professor at the Harvard Law School, published by far the most comprehensive treatise on the United States Constitution that had then appeared. Volume 2 of Story's Commentaries on the Constitution of the United States 630–632 (5th ed. 1981) discussed the meaning of the Establishment Clause of the First Amendment this way:
>
> "Probably at the time of the adoption of the Constitution, and the amendment to it now under consideration [First Amendment], the general if not the universal sentiment in America was, that Christianity ought to receive encouragement from the State so far as was not incompatible with the private rights of conscience and the freedom of religious worship. An attempt to level all religions, and to make it a matter of state policy to hold all in utter indifference, would have created universal disapprobation, if not universal indignation. . . .
>
> "The real object of the [First] Amendment was not to countenance, much less to advance, Mahometanism, or Judaism, or infidelity, by prostrating Christianity; but to exclude all rivalry among Christian sects, and to prevent any national ecclesiastical establishment which should give to a hierarchy the exclusive patronage of the

national government. It thus cut off the means of religious persecution (the vice and pest of former ages), and of the subversion of the rights of conscience in matters of religion, which had been trampled upon almost from the days of the Apostles to the present age. . . ." [Footnotes omitted.]

Thomas Cooley's eminence as a legal authority rivaled that of Story. Cooley stated in his treatise entitled Constitutional Limitations that aid to a particular religious sect was prohibited by the United States Constitution, but he went on to say:

"But while thus to establish, protect, and defend religious freedom and equality, the American constitutions contain no provisions which prohibit the authorities from such solemn recognition of a superintending Providence in public transactions and exercises as the general religious sentiment of mankind inspires, and as seems meet and proper in finite and dependent beings. Whatever may be the shades of religious belief, all must acknowledge the fitness of recognizing in important human affairs the superintending areas and control of the Great Governor of the Universe, and of acknowledging with thanksgiving his boundless favors, or bowing in contrition when visited with the penalties of his broken laws. No principle of constitutional law is violated when thanksgiving or fast days are appointed; when chaplains are designated for the army and navy; when legislative sessions are opened with prayer or the reading of the Scriptures, or when religious teaching is encouraged by a general exemption of the houses of religious worship from taxation for the support of the state government. Undoubtedly the spirit of the Constitution will require, in all these cases, that care be taken to avoid discrimination in favor of or against any one religious denomination or sect; but the power to do any of these things does not become unconstitutional simply because of its susceptibility to abuse. . . ." *Id.*, at 470–471. Cooley added that,

"[t]his public recognition of religious worship, however, is not based entirely, perhaps not even mainly, upon a sense or what is due to the Supreme Being himself as author of all good and of the law; but the same reasons of state policy which induce the government to aid institutions of charity and seminaries of instruction will incline to also foster religious worship and religious institutions, as conservators of the public morals and valuable, if not indispensable, assistants to the preservation of the public order." *Id.*, at 470.[8]

After Justice Rehnquist's discussion of the congressional debates on the religion clauses, the republicizing of Justice Joseph Story's writing has been, in my opinion, the most devastating blow to the mythical history created by *Everson v. Board of Education*, 330 U.S. 1 (1947). Until 1984 Justice Story's discussion of the religion clauses had been referred to in only one modern Supreme Court case, and then only obliquely.[9] Whether or not members of the Court chose to overlook his considerable authority, the fact is that the briefs in major religion cases simply made no reference to Story's work. Story was important if for no other reason than that he was the first justice to write for the Court on the issues of church-state relationships, in *Terrett v. Taylor*, 9 Cranch 42 (1815); see also, *Vidal v. Girard's Executors*, 2 Howard 127 (1844).

In *Terrett v. Taylor*, Justice Story, writing for a unanimous Court, specifically addressed the Virginia experience. Story ruled that the legislature of the state of Virginia lacked the authority to expropriate land formerly granted to the Church of England. Jefferson had carried the logic of strict separation to the point of influencing the Virginia legislature to pass a statute in 1801 which, asserting the state's right to all the property of the Episcopal churches in the state, had directed that church property be sold and the proceeds given to the poor.[10] Speaking for the Court, Justice Story said:

> although it may be true that "religion can be directed only by reason and conviction, not by force or violence," and that "all men are equally entitled to the free exercise of religion according to the dictates of conscience," as the bill of rights of Virginia declares, yet it is difficult to perceive how it follows as a consequence that the legislature may not enact laws more effectively to enable all sects to accomplish the great objects of religion by giving them corporate rights for the management of their property, and the regulation of their temporal as well as spiritual concerns. Consistent with the constitution of Virginia the legislature could not create or continue a religious establishment which should have exclusive rights and prerogatives, or compel the citizens to worship under a stipulated form or discipline, or to pay taxes to those creeds they could not conscientiously believe. But the free exercise of religion cannot be justly deemed to be restrained by aiding with equal attention the votaries of every sect to perform their own religious duties, or by establishing funds for the support of ministers, for public charities, for the endowment of churches, or for the sepulture of the dead.[11]

Story was first quoted in a modern religion case by the majority in *Lynch v. Donnelly*, 104 S. Ct. 1355, 1361 (1984), allowing a city to have a Nativity scene as part of a Christmas display. That quote was taken verbatim from the Justice Department's brief (which I suspect the Justice Department became aware of from Judge Hand's opinion, January 14, 1983). Unlike legislative chaplains, which had been found not to violate the establishment clause the year before in *Marsh v. Chambers*, 463 U.S. 783 (1983), *Lynch* did not involve a practice initiated by the First Congress. Story's writings, however, provided the basis for generalizing a historical understanding of the religion clauses. Finally, in *Wallace v. Jaffree* not only Justice Rehnquist but the majority seriously considered the references in Story's treatise. Faced with Story's lengthy discussion, the Court acknowledged it had departed from the earlier understanding of the establishment clause.[12]

Justice Stevens, however, distorted the earlier understanding by misrepresenting what Story had written. Stevens stated: "At one time it was thought that this right [to choose one's creed] merely prescribed the preference of one Christian sect over another, but would not require equal *respect for the conscience* of the infidel, the atheist, or the adherent of a non-Christian faith such as Mohammedism or Judaism."[13] In a footnote, Stevens included the same two passages from Story quoted above and taken from Rehnquist's opinion. But Stevens did not quote other passages from Story (some of which were quoted in my brief in anticipation of this very objection). Quite to the contrary of what Stevens said was the earlier understanding, Story clearly stated that the purpose of the religion clauses was to protect the consciences of all and that that purpose was not inconsistent with promoting religion: "But the duty of supporting religion, and especially the Christian religion, is very different from the right to force the consciences of other men, or to punish them for worshipping God in the manner which they believe their accountability to him requires."[14]

Story then quoted John Locke on the rights of conscience. After further discussion, including one of the two passages now twice referred to, he stated:

> It is under a solemn consciousness of the dangers from ecclesiastical ambition, the bigotry of spiritual pride, and intolerance of the sects, thus exemplified in our domestic, as well as in foreign annals, that it was deemed advisable to exclude from the national government all power to act upon the subject. The situation, too, of the different states equally proclaimed the policy, as well as the necessity of such an exclusion. In some of the states, episcopalians constituted the predominant sect; in others, presbyterians; in others, congregationalists; in others, quakers; and in others again, there was a close numerical rivalry among the contending sects. It was impossible, that there not arise perpetual strife and perpetual jealousy on the subject of ecclesiastical ascendancy, if the national government were left free to create a religious establishment. The only security was in extirpating the power. But this alone would have been an imperfect security, if it had not been followed up by a declaration of the right of the free exercise of religion, and a prohibition (as we have seen) of all religion tests. Thus the whole power over the subject of religion is left exclusively to the state governments, to be acted upon according to their own sense of justice, and the state constitutions; and the Catholic and the Protestant, the Calvinist and the Arminian, the Jew and the Infidel, may sit down at the common table of the national councils without any inquisition into their faith, or mode of worship.[15]

Having conceded that they are abandoning the historical meaning of the establishment clause, the majority in *Jaffree* had to have some justification for doing so. By characterizing the previous understanding as he did, Stevens implicitly stated that it would be unjust and intolerable to return to the original understanding. Properly understood, however, the original meaning was not unjust or intolerable. After all, religious toleration increased over the approximately one hundred and fifty years that the original understanding held sway. Until forty years ago, the federal courts had little occasion to rule on the religion clauses and thus had very little directly to do with these developments. Without being forced to do so by any federal court, those states which had establishments at the time of the adoption of the First Amendment had eliminated them before the Civil War. By the end of the nineteenth century, Congress had on its own stopped funding sectarian education of Indians. In other words, religious liberty spread without the involvement of the federal courts.

The Large Commercial Republic and the Spread of Religious Liberty

With Professor McConnell, I hold (as I argued in *Jaffree*) that the religion clauses are to be read together in light of the common underlying principle of religious liberty. I need not devote too much time to a discussion of the free exercise of religion to make some historically oriented observations about religious liberty that bear on the continued viability of the original understanding of the establishment clause. But before doing so, I wish to address the irrelevance of the issue of incorporation to the continued viability of the original understanding of the religion clauses.

The usual argument against accepting the original view of the religion clause as binding today has been that the adoption of the Fourteenth Amendment and the later incorporation of the First Amendment as well as most other provisions of the Bill of Rights to the states make that view no longer applicable. Certainly, as stated in the last of the above-quoted passages, Story took for granted that the religion clauses had no application to the states: "Thus, the whole power over the subject of religion is left exclusively to the state governments, to be acted upon according to their own sense of justice and the state constitutions." Here Story was in agreement with Jefferson, with whom Story disagreed on many issues including matters of establishment. In a statement from his second inaugural as president, which is not quoted by strict separationists who otherwise have searched out every quote by Jefferson about religion, Jefferson declared that religion was a matter better left to the states and local authorities: "In matters of religion I have considered that its free exercise is placed by the Constitution independent of the powers of the General Government. I have therefore undertaken on no occasion to prescribe the religious exercises suited to it, but have left them, as the Constitution found them, under the direction and discipline of the Church or State authorities acknowledged by the several religious societies."[16]

Debate over incorporation has clouded the basic issue concerning the continuing validity of the no-preference interpretation of the establishment clause. As long as it did not apply to the states, the establishment clause's meaning did not present many problems because most governmental practices related to religion had been state practices. Given the application of the establishment clause to the states, however, it did not necessarily follow that state practices, in particular those related to schools, violated the establishment clause. In other words, incorporation has not invalidated the no-preference understanding of the establishment clause. In *Wallace v. Jaffree*, when it noted probable jurisdiction, the Court precluded argument on the issue of incorporation. Justice Rehnquist, who elsewhere has questioned the incorporation of the religion clauses as applicable to the states,[17] did not do so in his dissenting opinion in *Jaffree*. ("Given the 'incorporation' of the Establishment Clause as against the States via the Fourteenth Amendment in *Everson*, States are prohibited as well from establishing a religion or discriminating between sects." 105 S. Ct. at 2520.) Nevertheless, Justice Rehnquist defended the applicability of the no-preference doctrine.

Any fears that return to the original understanding would mean a return to the established churches of the eighteenth century are unfounded. It is not merely that Americans have become more religiously tolerant, but that the more farseeing of the Founders understood that the structure of the new government would bring that about in time. It is clear that Madison especially realized the relationship between a large commercial republic and the protection of liberty, especially religious liberty. Madison's involvement both in the drafting of the Northwest Ordinance and in the writing of *The Federalist Papers* evidences this understanding. These two documents, one a statute and the other a series of essays, both written at the moment of the Constitution's creation (1787–89), shed considerable light on how Madison and others intended indirectly to mitigate religious and other intolerances in the states.

The Northwest Ordinance was largely the work of Nathan Dane of Massachusetts, with whom Joseph Story became closely associated. Story, who praised the ordinance "for its masterly display of the fundamentals of civil and religious liberty," said that "[t]he third [section] provides for the encouragement of religion, and education, and schools."[18] Until Justice Rehnquist mentioned it, the Northwest Ordinance has been virtually overlooked in this Court's modern discussion of the religion clauses. Other than a passing reference in *Jones v. City of Opelika*, 316 U.S. 584, 622 (Murphy J., dissenting) (1962), the only other reference was by Justice Douglas concurring in *Engel v. Vitale*, 370 U.S. 421 (1962), noting that the Northwest Ordinance "antedated the First Amendment" (370 U.S. at 443, n.9). As a result there has been the uncritical assumption that the Founders had not given much thought to religion and public education. See *Schempp*, 374 U.S. at 238 (Brennan, J., concurring). See also Justice O'Connor's concurring opinion in *Wallace v. Jaffree*.

Of the six articles in the Northwest Ordinance, two related to religion. In addition to Article 3, the provision relating schools and religion quoted above, Article 1 provided for religious freedom: "No person demeaning himself in a peaceable and orderly manner, shall ever be molested on account of his mode of worship or religious sentiments, in said territory." These were two of the six conditions for admitting states into the Confederacy (see *The Federalist* No. 38) and later into the Union. Article 1 guaranteed religious freedom in the new states, beginning with the admission of Ohio in 1803. Typically, the enabling acts for states admitted pursuant to the Northwest Ordinance provided that the state's constitution was to conform to the Northwest Ordinance. Congress had the power to refuse states if their proposed constitutions did not so conform (*Permoli v. 1st Municipality of New Orleans*, 3 Howard 589, 609 [1845]; *Coyle v. Smith*, 221 U.S. 559, 568 [1910]). Although the states were free to change their constitutions after admission to the Union (*Permoli*, *supra*, at 609; *Coyle*, *supra*, at 568), the fact that these states were settled on the basis of religious freedom effectively guaranteed the continuation of such practices and may well have influenced the movement toward disestablishment in the original states.

It would seem difficult to argue that the First Congress, which proposed the religion clauses of the First Amendment and which by reenacting the Northwest Ordinance extended religious freedom to the territories, acted unconstitutionally by promoting religion, morality, and knowledge in public education and setting aside land "for the purposes of religion." Nevertheless, the leading advocate of strict separation, Professor Leo Pfeffer, has found these practices inconsistent with the First Amendment. However, he had not had to confront the conflict between the historical facts and his theory. Relying on a secondary source, he had erroneously stated "that after the Constitution and the First Amendment were adopted no more public land was granted for the support of religion under the Ordinance." Again, apparently relying on a secondary source, he erroneously suggested that James Madison opposed any grants of land for purposes of religion because Madison was opposed to the unsuccessful attempt in 1785 to dedicate lands for those purposes.[19]

The facts were not as Professor Pfeffer related them. The 1785 proposal, which Madison opposed and which was not adopted, differed from later successful provisions. The 1785 provision would have set apart a district of land in each township "for the support of religion . . . of the majority of male residents." Later provisions simply set apart land "for purposes of religion." The proceeds from the sale of the land were to be distributed equally among the various sects. Most significantly, Madison was a member of the committees that in fact set aside lands for purposes of religion, without reference to the will of the majority. Given the actions of the First Congress as well as those of Madison, there must be an extremely strong presumption that those practices of Congress which directly promoted religion were not unconstitutional.

In all the discussions of Madison's understanding of the religion clauses, relatively little attention has been paid to his writings in *The Federalist Papers*. *Larson v. Valente*, 456 U.S. 228, 245 (1982), mentioned Madison's discussion in *The Federalist* No. 51 of a "multiplicity of interests" as a protection for religious rights, but without reference to Madison's discussion in *The Federalist* No. 10, which concerns the danger of factions. Madison's solution to the problem of factions, including religious factions, was to promote a multiplicity of interests dispersed throughout a large commercial republic. Religious pluralism developed not by accident but by design.

Madison defined a "faction" as "a number of citizens, whether amounting to a majority or a minority of the whole, who are united and actuated by some common impulse of passion, or of interest, adverse to the rights of other citizens, or to the permanent and aggregate interests of the community," in *The Federalist* No. 10 at 54 (Mod. Lib. ed.). He clearly included religious groups in this definition. Nevertheless, his approach when dealing with the Constitution differed in part from his support of the Declaration of Rights for his own state of Virginia. His solution to the dangers posed by religious and other factions as a national and therefore a constitutional problem was to eliminate the "effects," rather than the "causes." Pluralism would be achieved by multiplying factions dispersed throughout a large commercial republic. Madison summarized the solution to factionalism as something which is more subtle than today's popular notion of pluralism:

> The influence of factious leaders may kindle a flame within their particular States, but will be unable to spread a general conflagration through the other States. A religious sect may degenerate into a political faction in a part of the Confederacy; but the variety of sects dispersed over the entire face of it must secure the national councils against any danger from that source. . . .
>
> In the extent and proper structure of the Union, therefore, we behold a republican remedy for the diseases most incident to republican government. And according to the degree of pleasure and pride we feel in being republicans, ought to be our zeal in cherishing the spirit and supporting the character of Federalists. (*The Federalist* No. 10 at 61–62 [Mod. Lib. ed.])

It would not have been at all inconsistent for Madison to support Congress's promotion of religion without discrimination among sects as a means of diluting the influence of the majority religious sects in each locale. The "secular purpose" would have been both the protection of religious minorities and political stability. The rationale clearly stated for confining religious matters to the states has nothing to do with states' rights, but rather with protecting the national government from religious pressures.

As indicated in the last quote from Madison, he and other Federalists placed considerable reliance on the "proper structure." For lawyers, who today at least are as a group more comfortable analyzing specific phrases in isolation, structural interpretation of the Constitution, of the kind in which Chief Justice Marshall engaged in *McCulloch v. Maryland*, 17 U.S. (4 Wheat.) 316 (1819), has been difficult to comprehend. Thus while lawyers understand specific cases involving Congress's power over "commerce among the states," few have probably ever thought of that power as related to the overall plan described in *The Federalist Papers* to protect liberty (but see *Heart of Atlanta Motel, Inc. v. U.S.*, 379 U.S. 241 [1964]). Yet Madison also understood that the more people became engaged in a lively commerce, the less they could afford to be intolerant, especially on the basis of religion.

The Federalists favored a large republic not only because that would facilitate a growing commerce but because that in turn would unite the pursuit of self-interest to the protection of liberty. They were opposed by those known as the Anti-Federalists, who favored small republics that promoted virtue by limiting commerce and protecting agriculture. After adoption of the Constitution, some Anti-Federalists "urged that the new rulers should turn their attention to the task, which surpasses the framing of constitutions, of fostering religion and morals, thereby making government less necessary by rendering 'the people more capable of being *a Law to themselves*.' Such self-government was possible, however, only if the center of American government remained in the States."[20] The Federalists, and increasingly all Americans, became more interested in commerce and, for better or worse, less concerned about public virtue.

Madison's discussion of factions was tied to the development of a large commercial republic. In *The Federalist* No. 51 he again discussed the problem of factions and the need for an extended republic.

> In the extended republic of the United States, and among the great variety of interests, parties, and sects which it embraces, a coalition of a majority of the whole society could seldom take place on any other principles than those of justice and the general good; whilst there being thus less danger to a minor from the will of the major party, there must be less pretext, also, to provide for the security of the former, by introducing into the government a will not dependent on the latter, or in other words, a will independent of the society itself. It is no less certain than it is important, notwithstanding the contrary opinions which have been entertained, that the larger the

> society, provided it lie within a practical sphere, the more duly capable it will be for self-government. And happily for the republican cause, the practical sphere may be carried to a very great extent, by a judicious modification and mixture of a federal principle.

Conclusion

I consider the adherence to the original intent of the religion clauses, in particular the establishment clause, not only constitutionally compelled but also quite prudent. The best evidence, for me, of the continuing wisdom and utility of the original understanding of the religion clauses, as expressed by Madison speaking in *The Federalist Papers* and acting in Congress and confirmed by Story, has been the intense controversy generated by the Supreme Court's well-intentioned but naive rewriting of the establishment clause. Both Madison in *The Federalist* No. 10 and Story in his *Commentaries* were concerned that religious zealotry not dominate and incapacitate the federal government. Given incorporation of the establishment clause, the Supreme Court's abandonment of the original understanding of the establishment clause has meant decisions in the area of religion that have generated tremendous popular reaction. The school prayer issue has often paralyzed the federal government with proposals to amend the Constitution or to restrict the Court's jurisdiction because the vast majority of the American people disagree with the Court on this issue and a sizable minority of them have been ignited to create the kind of faction that Madison feared.

Notes

1. *Abington School Dist. v. Schempp*, 374 U.S. 203, 217 (1963).

2. Thomas Jefferson to Messrs. Nehemiah Dodge, Ephraim Robbins, and Stephen S. Nelson, Committee of the Danbury Baptist Association in the State of Connecticut, Jan. 1, 1902, cited in S. Padover, *The Complete Jefferson Notes*, 2d ed. (Freeport, N.Y.: Libraries Press, 1969), pp. 518–19.

3. *Jaffree v. Board of School Comm. of Mobile Co.*, 554 F. Supp. 1104, 1128 (1983).

4. McConnell, *Accommodation of Religion*, 1985 Sup. C. Rev. 1, 20 n.73.

5. 105 S. Ct. at 2510.

6. *Id.* at 2512.

7. See also Justice Reed, dissenting in *McCollum v. Board of Education*, 333 U.S. 203, 247 (1948).

8. 105 S. Ct. at 2515–16.

9. *McGowan v. Maryland*, 336 U.S. 240, 441 (1961).

10. *See* J. McClellan, *Joseph Story and the American Constitution* (Norman: Univ. of Oklahoma Press, 1971), p. 129.

11. 9 Cranch at 48–49.

12. *See Wallace v. Jaffree*, 105 S. Ct. at 2488.

13. *Id.*

14. J. Story, *Commentaries on the Con-*

stitution of the United States, 2d ed., vol. 2 (Boston: C. C. Little and J. Brown, 1851), p. 664.

15. Ibid., pp. 666–67.

16. Jefferson's Second Inaugural Address, March 4, 1905, in *Inaugural Addresses of the Presidents of the United States* (Washington, D.C.: GPO, 1965), pp. 17, 18.

17. *Thomas v. Review Board*, 450 U.S. 707, 720 (1981) (Rehnquist, J., dissenting).

18. Story, *Commentaries on the Constitution* 2: 191, 192.

19. L. Pfeffer, *Church, State, and Freedom*, rev. ed. (Boston: Beacon, 1967), p. 108.

20. H. Storing, *What the Anti-Federalists Were For*, vol. 1 (Chicago: Univ. of Chicago Press, 1981), p. 23.

MICHAEL W. MCCONNELL

5. Free Exercise As the Framers Understood It

The free exercise clause of the First Amendment passed the First Congress and the ratifying states with little controversy. In marked contrast, the establishment clause was the most hotly debated of all the provisions of the Bill of Rights. Perhaps this was because the thirteen states had evolved institutional relationships between religion and government that differed dramatically one from another. The free exercise clause was barely discussed, perhaps again because the states at that time were nearly unanimous that religious conscience was inviolable.

Until quite recently, much the same difference in consensus between free exercise and establishment issues existed in modern constitutional law. Interpretation of the establishment clause has been a source of continual and often acrimonious public dispute—not just in the courts but in the scholarly journals and books, the churches and synagogues, the popular electoral campaigns and even the streets. There are few more heated subjects of debate and few more muddled areas of legal doctrine. By contrast, while individual cases sparked disagreement, the interpretation of the free exercise clause had settled into a basic framework and remained essentially undisturbed for more than twenty-five years—until 1990, in *Employment Division v. Smith.*[1] Under the law as it stood before *Smith*, if the plaintiff could show that a law or governmental practice inhibited the exercise of his religious beliefs, the burden shifted to the government to demonstrate that it was necessary to the accomplishment of some important (or "compelling") secular objective and that it was the least restrictive means of achieving that objective. If the plaintiff met his burden, and the government did not, the plaintiff was entitled to be relieved of the burden on his religious exercise.[2]

In *Smith* the Supreme Court abandoned the compelling governmental interest test and held instead that a law or government practice is constitutional under the free exercise clause if it applies to religion and nonreligion alike and does not discriminate against religion.[3] Thus, in *Smith* itself the Court held that an Oregon law against the use of hallucinogenic drugs raised no constitutional issue as applied to outlaw the sacramental use of peyote in religious ceremonies of the Native American Church. Under the prior doctrine, the government would have had to demonstrate that application of the law in those circumstances was necessary to satisfy a compelling purpose—a close question on which advocates of a strong free exercise clause might well disagree.[4] Under the new doctrine announced in *Smith*, the government bore no burden of demonstrating any significant interest; the fact that the antidrug law was neutral on its face was sufficient to satisfy the free exercise clause. Under this view, the sole function of the free exercise clause is to prevent the government from singling out religious practice for peculiar disability. So long as everyone is subject to the same generally applicable law, the religious person or institution has no constitutional ground for complaint if the law happens to make his religious practice difficult or illegal.

This view is a throwback to the law as it stood a generation ago. It was most pointedly articulated by Justice Frankfurter:

> The constitutional protection of religious freedom terminated disabilities, it did not create new privileges. It gave religious equality, not civil immunity. Its essence is freedom from conformity to religious dogma, not freedom from conformity to law because of religious dogma. . . . Otherwise each individual could set up his own censor against obedience to laws conscientiously deemed for the public good by those whose business it is to make laws.[5]

The revival of this view on the Court and among some thoughtful scholars[6] warrants reconsideration of the principle of free exercise as the Founders understood it. Surprisingly—even shockingly—the *Smith* Court reversed course on free exercise protection without so much as a glance at the history or original understanding. If it had consulted the historical record, it would have found substantial evidence that the compelling governmental interest test accorded with the original understanding.

Consideration of the issue requires analysis of two seemingly opposite but in practice complementary objections to the religiously compelled free exercise exemptions: (1) that no one should be excused on religious or other personal grounds from compliance with generally applicable laws, and (2) that if there are to be exemptions, they must be extended to persons who have conscientious but nonreligious claims. I believe it can be demonstrated that the fundamental purpose of the free exercise clause contradicts both of these propositions. I will then discuss the more theoretical unifying argument underlying these objections—that a liberal state is necessarily a secular state—and show that this was not the vision held by the most forceful advocates of religious freedom at the time of the founding. But first some background is in order.

The original Constitution drafted by the Constitutional Convention in 1787 and ratified by the states in 1788 contained no provision protecting the freedom of religion, save only the prohibition in Article VI that "no religious Test shall ever be required as a Qualification to any Office or public Trust under the United States." The prevailing view among the Federalists, the supporters of the new Constitution, was that explicit guarantees of individual liberty were not necessary, since the new federal government was not given the power to invade them. Indeed, some argued that such guarantees might even be counterproductive, since the express mention of some liberties might be taken to disparage the existence of others.[7] Other participants in the debate, less trustful of the institutional checks and balances of the constitutional scheme, pressed for a bill of rights and were sufficiently persuasive (or sufficiently numerous) to extract the promise of a bill of rights as the price for ratification of the rest of the Constitution. Among the rights proposed for inclusion was the "free exercise of religion."[8]

New York, for example, ratified the Constitution but proposed a bill of rights including the following provision: "That the people have an equal, natural, and unalienable right freely and peaceably to exercise their religion, according to the dictates of conscience."[9] Virginia proposed a similar provision, using the phrase "free exercise of religion";[10] Rhode Island and North Carolina made proposals virtually identical to Virginia's.[11] Only New Hampshire, of the states that proposed a federal bill of rights, used a markedly different formulation: "Congress shall make no laws touching religion, or to infringe the rights of conscience."[12] To the extent that this proposal would have had a different meaning than the others (and I think it would), it is significant that the New Hampshire formulation was considered by the House of Representatives, briefly adopted, and then rejected in favor of a formulation similar to today's free exercise clause.[13]

James Madison's initial draft of the free exercise clause did not follow the language of the state proposals. Rather, he suggested that it read: "The Civil Rights of none shall be abridged on account of religious belief or worship, nor shall any national religion be established, nor shall the full and equal rights of conscience be in any manner, nor on any pretext infringed."[14] Two observations might be made about this proposal. First, the formulation "full and equal rights of conscience" implies that the liberty has both a substantive and an equality component. That is to say, the liberty of conscience is entitled not only to equal protection but also to some absolute measure of protection apart from mere governmental neutrality. Second, the formulation that the rights in question shall not "in any manner, nor on any pretext" be infringed suggests protection from infringements in any form—even those not expressly directed at religious practice.

But let us not linger on Madison's proposal, which was never publicly debated. The Select Committee proposed a much shorter version: "[N]o religion shall be established by law, nor shall the equal rights of conscience be infringed."[15] Madison's reference to "Civil Rights" was deleted, probably because it was redundant, and his "full and equal rights of conscience" was shortened to "equal rights of conscience." If this change was more than stylistic, it suggests a move toward a neutrality view of free exercise, rather than protection for a substantive liberty.

The debates in the House over this proposal cast little light on the meaning of the "rights of conscience." The controversy was over establishment. Daniel Carroll, a Roman Catholic from Maryland, commented that "the rights of conscience are, in their nature, of peculiar delicacy, and will little bear the gentlest touch of governmental hand."[16] He also indicated that the political pressure for a religious liberty provision had come from "many sects." This comment indicates that the prime movers behind the First Amendment were religious sects, rather than exponents of the secularistic Enlightenment.

The Select Committee language ran into trouble in the House, largely because of concern that its establishment provision might interfere with the ability of the states to support religion—an issue especially important to those states with established churches. After a brief flirtation with the New Hampshire language, already discussed, the House adopted a formulation proposed by Fisher Ames of Massachusetts: "Congress shall make no law establishing religion, or to prevent the free exercise thereof, or to infringe the rights of conscience."[17] Note that this version used the formulation "free exercise of religion," which had been present in many state proposals. It also used the phrase "rights of conscience," without the modifiers "full" or "equal." The latter change suggests that the deletion of "full" by the committee was probably stylistic and that the word "equal" was deleted so as not to create a negative inference. The House of Representatives adopted the amendment as proposed by Ames without further recorded debate, but a slightly different version was sent to the Senate (whether there was an unrecorded additional amendment to the amendment or whether the unofficial report was garbled is unknown). The Senate received and acted upon the following proposal: "Congress shall make no law establishing Religion, or prohibiting the free exercise thereof, nor shall the rights of conscience be infringed."[18]

In the Senate (where the debate was not recorded), various versions of the religion clauses were adopted and rejected in succession. Each of these used either the phrase "rights of conscience" or the phrase "free exercise of religion." The Senate finally settled upon "free exercise of religion."[19]

One final point about the debate in the First Congress deserves mention. In addition to the provision already discussed, which applied expressly and unmistakably only to the federal government, Madison proposed an amendment which would have been applicable to the states. It read: "[N]o state shall infringe the equal rights of conscience, nor the freedom of speech or of the press, nor of the right of trial by jury in criminal cases."[20] This Madison said he conceived to be "the most valuable amendment in the whole list. If there was any reason to restrain the Government of the United

States from infringing upon these essential rights, it was equally necessary that they should be secured against the State Governments."[21] Significantly, Madison did not propose that the establishment clause be made applicable to the states. With minor editorial change, Madison's proposal was adopted by the House.[22] Later it was rejected by the Senate, thus leaving the Bill of Rights solely as limitations against the federal government, as they were to remain until the Supreme Court held that they had been selectively "incorporated" pursuant to the Fourteenth Amendment.[23]

At no point in the recorded debates is there any definition or substantive discussion of the phrase "free exercise of religion." Nonetheless, the term "exercise" or "free exercise" of religion had a rich history in preconstitutional America. Each of the thirteen states, with only one exception (Connecticut), guaranteed religious liberty in its constitution, often using the terminology "free exercise of religion." It is reasonable to assume that those who drafted and adopted the First Amendment used the term in the then-accustomed manner. It is to these we should turn for enlightenment on our questions.

What, then, was the understanding of free exercise in the states during this period? New York's 1777 Constitution was typical: "the free exercise and enjoyment of religious profession and worship, without discrimination or preference, shall forever hereafter be allowed, within the State, to all mankind: *Provided*, That the liberty of conscience, hereby granted, shall not be so construed as to excuse acts of licentiousness, or justify practices inconsistent with the peace or safety of this State."[24] Or New Hampshire: "Every individual has a natural and unalienable right to worship God according to the dictates of his own conscience, and reason; and no subject shall be hurt, molested, or restrained in his person, liberty or estate for worshipping God, in the manner and season most agreeable to the dictates of his own conscience, . . . provided he doth not disturb the public peace, or disturb others, in their religious worship."[25] Or Georgia: "All persons whatever shall have the free exercise of their religion; provided it be not repugnant to the peace and safety of the State."[26]

There are two common elements in these provisions. The first is that the scope of the free exercise right, in the first instance, depends on the conscience of the individual believer—not on a judgment by the state about the appropriate forms of worship. The believer's right is to worship "according to the dictates of his own conscience and reason," in the New Hampshire formulation. The Virginia Declaration is especially clear on this point: it protects the "free exercise of religion" and defines "religion" as "the duty which we owe to our Creator, and the manner of discharging it."[27] (The Virginia Declaration of Rights has always been considered especially important in interpreting the First Amendment, because the fight for it was led by James Madison, the same legislator who was the principal exponent of the First Amendment in Congress.) Massachusetts, home state of Fisher Ames, who first proposed using the language "free exercise" in the federal Constitution, had a provision to similar effect. It defined the right as "worshipping God in the manner and season most agreeable to the dictates of [one's] own conscience."[28]

The free exercise right, therefore, cannot be evaluated from the secular perspective of the state. Its scope is not defined by what the state views as religious or worthwhile, but what the believer views as his duty toward God. The precise content of the right depends on the beliefs of the individual claiming the right. And since those beliefs differ from person to person, the practical consequence is that individuals will be claiming different privileges or immunities. The specific rights claimed cannot be universalized. That Roman Catholics must be permitted to discriminate on the basis of sex in the hiring of priests, for example, does not mean that there can be no sex discrimination laws. Or, to take another example, special provision for kosher meat slaughtering does not mean that commercial slaughterhouses can deviate from uniform quality standards. The state may, quite properly, view "employment discrimination" or "meatpacking standards" as within its civil jurisdiction. That does not mean that they are not also "religious" for free exercise purposes.

The second common element in these free exercise provisions is that the right is limited. Nine of the twelve states with free exercise of rights of conscience provisions expressly added a proviso which limited the exercise of the right when it would interfere with the peace or safety of the state. This is revealing. It means, first, that the free exercise right was not understood to be confined to beliefs or expression of beliefs. As Thomas Jefferson pointedly stated: "it does me no injury for my neighbor to say there are twenty gods, or no God. It neither picks my pocket nor breaks my leg."[29] Obviously, the state free exercise provisions were understood to encompass religiously motivated conduct, or it would have been unnecessary to limit the right in this manner. More significantly, it means that free exercise was understood to include religiously compelled exceptions from generally applicable laws—precisely the interpretation rejected in *Smith*. The peace and safety provisos were the eighteenth-century equivalent of the modern compelling governmental interest test. If there were no right to exemptions, then there would be no need to protect against extreme practices that might endanger public peace.

This conclusion is borne out by an examination of the actual free exercise controversies in the preconstitutional period. By far the most common source of friction, other than that resulting from established churches, was the issue of oaths. The oath requirement is a neutral, generally applicable means of ensuring that the person taking the oath is telling the truth. The difficulty is that Quakers and certain other Protestant sects, relying on scriptural evidence, are conscientiously opposed to taking oaths. There are, logically speaking, three possible solutions to this difficulty.

First, the government could eliminate the oath-taking requirement for everyone, making oath taking purely voluntary. Second, the government could continue to insist on the oath requirement, making it impossible for dissenters to give evidence in court or participate in any civic activity involving an oath. Third, the government could continue the oath requirement for the majority, while allowing those with religious scruples to comply by an appropriate alternative procedure. But the first possibility is disruptive of the entire judicial system, and the second is unnecessarily harsh to the dissenters.

The third alternative—to create a religious exception to the oath requirement—was in fact adopted in most states. For example, as early as the seventeenth century the proprietors of the Carolina colony permitted Quakers to enter pledges in a book in lieu of swearing an oath. This liberal provision was made pursuant to the proprietors' charter authority to allow "such Indulgences and Dispensations" as they "shall, in their discretion, think fit and reasonable." Similarly, New York passed a law in 1691 permitting Quakers to testify by affirmation in civil cases and in 1734 passed a law permitting Quakers to qualify for the vote by affirmation instead of oath. In 1743 Massachusetts, one of the states with a strong established church tradition, substituted an affirmation requirement for "Quakers [who] profess to be in their consciences scrupulous of taking oaths."[30]

Another example was exemption from military service. As early as 1688 the Quakers in New York asserted unsuccessfully that liberty of conscience exempted them from bearing arms. But in Rhode Island, North Carolina, and Maryland (not coincidentally, three of the five colonies with strong free exercise provisions in their seventeenth-century charters) the exemptions were granted; most other colonies followed suit in the eighteenth century.[31] Later, the Continental Congress was to grant such exemptions, a policy which was continued by the First Congress and continues to this day. This is a particularly telling example, for two reasons. First, the requirement of military service is of extraordinary importance to preservation of the state, and the granting of exemptions imposes high costs on others. If the government determines to grant religious exemptions, it is evidence of a highly sympathetic view toward free exercise.

Second, the issue of religious military exemptions was debated by the First Congress in the context of the Bill of Rights. These were the same legislators who also adopted the free exercise clause, and thus their opinions carry weight. The Select Committee draft of what is now the Second Amendment included a clause that "no person religiously scrupulous shall be compelled to bear arms."[32] The proposal was quite controversial; it passed the House by a mere 24–22 vote and was rejected by the Senate. For our purposes, however, what is important are the reasons offered by opponents of the provision. They did not oppose the proposal on the theory that religious scruples cannot form the basis for exemption from civic obligations. Rather, they argued that the exemption should be left to "the discretion of the Government."[33] There is no support in any statement made in the debate for the view that religiously compelled exemptions from generally applicable laws are illegitimate as a matter of principle. Nor is there any statement that suggests that judicially enforceable constitutional exemptions would be inappropriate in other contexts.

A third historical example of the types of religious exception honored under the preconstitutional free exercise clauses of the states is found only in states with established churches. Such states often required the citizens to make payments for the support of ministers either of the favored church or of their own denomination. Not uncommonly, however, these states made provision for members of sects conscientiously opposed to compelled tithes. For example, from 1727 on, Massachusetts and Connecticut exempted Baptists and Quakers from ministerial taxes. This exception was expressly, if grudgingly, made in recognition of the "alleged scruple of conscience" of these sects.[34] In sum, the history of the application of free exercise provisions shows that the provisions were understood to imply some exemptions from generally applicable laws for the benefit of dissenters.

It remains to be seen how broad the scope for religious exemptions is. The Virginia debate over the 1776 Declaration of Rights provides the best evidence of the range of opinion over how far the free exercise right should go. George Mason, the author of the religious liberty clause of the declaration, proposed the following: "that all men should enjoy the fullest toleration in the exercise of religion, according to the dictates of conscience, unpunished and unrestrained by the magistrate, unless under color of religion any man disturb the peace, the happiness, or safety or society."[35]

Madison objected to the proposal on two grounds. First, he criticized the use of the word "toleration," which implies an act of legislative grace. He offered a substitute which read that "all men are entitled to the full and free exercise of [religion]."[36] This change was accepted, with minor alteration. Second, he criticized the breadth of Mason's proposed state interest limitation. Madison proposed instead that free exercise be protected "unless under color of religion the preservation of equal liberty, and the existence of the State be manifestly endangered." This is obviously a much narrower state interest exception than Mason's.

The legislature ultimately passed a religious liberty guarantee which did not spell out the nature of the state interest that could outweigh a free exercise claim. Apparently, the legislature could not decide between the Mason and Madison formulations and compromised through silence. It is fair to assume, however, that the state's interest would fall somewhere between "the peace, the happiness, or safety of society"—Mason's broad formulation—and "manifest danger" to the "preservation of equal liberty, and existence of the State"—Madison's more limited formulation. The

Supreme Court's now-discarded "compelling" governmental interest test was close to the mark.[37]

Underlying this concept of religiously compelled exemptions is a theory about the respective jurisdictions of religion and government. As articulated by John Locke, the civil and ecclesiastical authorities have different and distinct functions: "the one attending only to the worldly welfare of the commonwealth, the other to the salvation of souls." Each should stay within its proper "bounds."[38] This understanding is reflected in the free exercise provisions we have examined: the dictates of conscience are the province of religion, and the peace and safety of the public are the province of government. The difficulty is in drawing the boundary. While there may be wide, even universal agreement that some activities are "religious" in nature and others purely civic, there will inevitably be an overlap. Who is to judge? According to the free exercise provisions, the believer is the judge of his own manner of discharging his duties to God. Presumably the state must be the judge of peace and safety.

Locke was content to leave the boundary drawing to the government; to the civil "magistrate." "For the private judgment of any person concerning a law enacted in political matters, for the public good, does not take away the obligation of that law, nor deserve a dispensation."[39] Our constitutional system, however, is based on the premise that the political branches of government are not to be judges in their own case. The institution of judicial review places the courts between the believer and the magistrate, to determine the boundary. Accordingly, it is the task of the courts to determine, independently of the legislature, whether granting a religious exception would impair the public peace and safety or, in modern language, a "compelling governmental interest." While deference may be due the political branches, an automatic acquiescence in their determinations is not.

In summary, it is not sufficient under the free exercise clause that a law be neutral and generally applicable. The free exercise provisions at the time of the founding were predicated on the understanding that the obligations of religion are entrusted to the individual conscience of the believer, just as the obligations of the state are entrusted to the government. Where the two come into conflict—that is, where generally applicable laws would inhibit the discharge of religious duties—the solution was to allow the believer to exercise his religion, unless the religious exercise is so injurious to others that it would injure the public peace and safety.

Criticisms of the Supreme Court's doctrine of religiously compelled exceptions are not confined to those who claim that the exceptions are illegitimate. There are others who assert that while religious exceptions may be required, such exceptions must be extended to a broader class of claimant. Their argument is that the First Amendment protects a broad liberty of conscience, and that to allow an exemption to persons whose conflict with civic obligations is religious in nature, without also allowing it to persons who entertain a conscientious objection on secular grounds, would be to favor religion over nonreligion. It would, they say, amount to an establishment of religion.

Perhaps the clearest example of this argument is Justice Harlan's decisive fifth vote in *Welsh v. United States*,[40] a Vietnam era military conscientious objection case. Elliott Ashton Welsh II was a young man conscientiously opposed to war, whose views were shaped by a secular form of moral philosophy. He could not claim that his views were "religious" in any sense of that term. The conscientious objection provision of the Selective Service Act, however, was expressly limited to those whose objection was "by reason of religious training and belief." Four justices were willing to stretch the language of the statute far enough to encompass Welsh. Justice Harlan, however, after a painstaking analysis of the statute and legislative history, concluded that Welsh simply did not qualify under the statute. He nonetheless concurred in the decision granting Welsh conscientious objector status on the theory that the First Amendment precludes drawing the line "between theistic or nontheistic religious beliefs on the one hand and secular beliefs on the other." This, he said, "accords a preference to the 'religious'" and thereby "offends the Establishment Clause."[41] Justice Douglas has taken substantially the same position.[42]

The Supreme Court subsequently moved away from the Douglas-Harlan position, most notably in *Wisconsin v. Yoder*.[43] In that decision, which exempted members of the Old Order Amish faith in Wisconsin from sending their children to school beyond the eighth grade, the Court stated: "A way of life, however virtuous and admirable, may not be interposed as a barrier to reasonable state regulation . . . if it is based on purely secular considerations; to have the protection of the Religion Clauses, the claims must be rooted in religious belief."[44] But it remains a common view in some circles that exemptions cannot be limited to religious claimants. The American Civil Liberties Union, for example, has brought suit claiming that special provisions respecting the rights of churches conducting religious preschool education for young children are unconstitutional since the same provisions have not been extended to secular day-care centers.[45]

Even on its own terms, I do not find this argument persuasive. If the operative principle is that the government may not distinguish between one form of conscience and another, it follows that the Douglas-Harlan position is itself too restrictive. The exemption, under the Douglas-Harlan view, would be extended to all those with an intense moral objection to war. But does this not reward those with an intense moral objection over persons with an equally intense objection based on other grounds, such as self-interest or cowardice? Liberty of conscience, if it means anything, must include egoistic as well as other-regarding forms of morality. If government cannot prefer one form of conscience over another, it must either deny exemptions to everyone or make conscription essentially voluntary.

The Douglas-Harlan position is especially troubling when coupled, as it often is, with the modern misconstruction of the establishment clause under which government action is unconstitutional if a significant effect, even if incidental and unintended, is to "advance religion." Under this notion, a neutral and generally applicable law, such as one providing public subsidy for private as well as public education, may be struck down to the extent that it "benefits religion."[46] The combination of these two views is to prevent the government from "singling out" religion for special protection, even when enforcement of neutral rules would burden free exercise; but also to require the government to "single out" religion when neutral rules might benefit religion. This serves neither neutrality nor liberty.

But in addition, the Douglas-Harlan view is quite inconsistent with both the language and the history of the free exercise clause. The clause reads, after all: "Congress shall pass no law . . . prohibiting the free exercise [of religion]." It is linguistically absurd to say that religion cannot be the basis for line drawing under a constitutional provision protecting the free exercise of religion.

The Douglas-Harlan argument might have had more force if the amendment had been passed in another form. As first proposed by Madison and the Select Committee, the amendment would have protected the "equal rights of conscience." The word "conscience" is susceptible to a broader construction than the word "religion." Even here it must be noted, however, that the phrase "liberty of conscience" was used in preconstitutional times in a predominantly, if not exclusively, religious sense. Nonetheless, the argument has some plausibility in the case of Fisher Ames's proposal, which would have prohibited Congress from making any law "to prevent the free exercise [of religion], or to infringe the rights of conscience."[47] Given the disjunctive, the "rights of conscience" would appear to be something different from the "free exercise of religion" in this version.

However, in the final version adopted by Congress and ratified by the states, the reference to "rights of conscience" was dropped and only the free exercise clause remained. There are two possible explanations for this, and the historical record does not establish which is true. First, the reference to conscience could have been dropped because it was redundant. This would have been consistent with the widespread usage of the term as apparently synonymous with religious freedom. Or second, the reference could have been dropped because conscience was understood to have a broader meaning than religion, and the framers deliberately intended to confine the protections of the free exercise clause to religion. Under either interpretation, the view that exemptions must be extended to secular moral conflicts is impossible.

The very situation involved in *Welsh* was debated by the framers. The proposal, which I have already discussed, for an express constitutional exemption from the draft read: "no person religiously scrupulous shall be compelled to bear arms."[48] No one suggested that this proposal be broadened to include secular objections. Indeed, one representative was worried lest the provision somehow be used by "those who are of no religion" as a "pretext to get excused from bearing arms."[49] The Congress was divided between those who believed this exemption should be made part of the Constitution and those who believed that it should be enacted by statute. The notion that it is illegitimate to draw lines between religious and secular objections was altogether foreign to the framers of the Bill of Rights.

Justice Brennan is correct. "Under the Free Exercise Clause," as he has stated, "religiously motivated claims of conscience may give rise to constitutional rights that other strongly-held beliefs do not."[50]

It has been argued thus far that the historical background of the free exercise clause provides support for pre-1990 Supreme Court doctrine on two counts: that the free exercise right was understood to entail, on appropriate occasions, exemptions from generally applicable laws or governmental practices, and that such exemptions need not be extended to purely secular claims. In a sense, the contrary arguments are opposites: one holds that the Supreme Court has gone too far and granted too many exemptions from neutral laws, while the other holds that the Supreme Court has not gone far enough and should broaden the exemptions. In another sense, however, the contrary arguments share the view that religion is not entitled to a special place among our constitutional values. The underlying assumption is that the framers of the First Amendment intended to create a secular state.

Justice Frankfurter, in the statement quoted at the beginning, was quite straightforward. The "essence" of the religion clauses, he said, "is freedom from conformity to religious dogma, not freedom from conformity to law because of religious dogma."[51] Walter Berns has been equally straightforward: "Congress does not have to grant an exemption to someone who follows the command of God rather than the command of the law because the Congress established by the Constitution denied . . . *that God issues any such commands*."[52] "Liberalism," Professor Berns goes on to say, "began in the effort to subordinate religious opinion to the law."[53]

With all due respect, Frankfurter and Berns have mistaken the impulse for religious liberty in America with the Enlightenment desire for freedom from religion. Locke and Jefferson may well have been animated, in Frankfurter's words, by the "freedom from conformity to religious dogma." They may have intended, in Berns's words, to "subordinate religious opinion to the law." But that is not what the Baptists, Quakers, and Presbyterians who provided the political muscle for religious liberty in America had in mind.

Who were the advocates of religious liberty in preconstitutional America? The atheists and agnostics, if any, were an invisible force. The deists and Unitarians, like Jefferson, were few in number and (unlike Jefferson) tended to support the religious establishment and oppose religious freedom for what they considered to be fanatical and irrational sects. In the Virginia struggle over religious assessments, Madison's *Memorial and Remonstrance*, with its mixed religious and secular arguments, garnered thousands of signatures. But over twice as many Virginians subscribed to petitions arguing against the assessment in frankly religious terms—stating, among other things, that the bill violated "the Spirit of the Gospel."[54] The decisive political event in the struggle was the decision of the Virginia Presbyterians to desert the assessment cause and join the opposition. Later, it was potential Baptist opposition to his election to Congress that induced Madison to embrace the cause of a religious liberty guarantee in the federal Constitution.[55]

Religious proponents of the First Amendment did not do so in order to free themselves from religious "dogma" but to ensure their right to follow religious dogma, and their right to choose for themselves what dogma to follow. This means, inevitably, that those indifferent or hostile to religion are freed from dogma as well. This is a commendable incident to religious liberty; but it should not be mistaken for its core.

The notion that a liberal society is a secular society—or, in Professor Berns's striking formulation, that the Constitution denies that God issues commands—is, I think, a misconception. It is more accurate to say that the liberal state takes no position as to whether God issues commands, or what God it is, or what commands He issues. The liberal state can no more deny that God issues commands than it can affirm that He issues commands. That is why it must honor the beliefs of its citizens (when it can do so without sacrificing the public peace and safety) that the commands of God can conflict with the dictates of the state. To take the position, in principle, that the dictates of the state must always prevail over religious scruple is to deny in principle the possibility of the existence of an authority higher than the state. That a liberal government cannot do.

Tocqueville, writing half a century after passage of the First Amendment, came much closer to an accurate understanding of the relation between religion and the liberal state. "Religion," he wrote, while not intervening directly in the government of American society, is nonetheless "the first of their political institutions."[56] "Despotism may be able to do without faith, but freedom cannot. Religion is much more needed in the republic they advocate than in the monarchy they attack, and in democratic republics most of all."[57] The reason is that the liberal state is unable in itself to foster a sense of morality and justice in the people. Despotism, whether by the monarchs of Tocqueville's day or the totalitarians of our own, can maintain social order through fear; a democratic republic requires consent. The liberal state, by its nature, is dependent upon free associations, such as churches and synagogues, to develop and transmit social values, which are necessary to civil life. In the absence of such associations the liberal community cannot help but degenerate into selfish and self-destructive Hobbesian individuals. It would be the gravest of errors for liberalism to set itself up as opponent of the claims of faith.

Tocqueville also came much closer to understanding the effect—the intended effect of the First Amendment on the vitality of religion and religious institutions. In his chapter entitled "The Main Causes That Make Religion Powerful in America," he explains that the American constitutional scheme is "the main reason for the quiet sway of religion over their country."[58] The multiplicity of religious sects in the United States is a great source of energy, in contrast to the deadened monopolies of established churches in Europe.

The free exercise clause guarantees the widest possible scope for religious activity, consistent with public peace and safety, and the establishment clause ensures that religious activity is purely voluntary. The result is a religiously pluralistic society, with a religious tradition stronger than that of virtually any other Western nation. Jefferson would not be happy; he hoped that Americans would all become Unitarians. But the religious dissenters who were the true authors of religious freedom in America were proved right.

Notes

1. *Employment Division v. Smith*, 110 S. Ct. 1595 (1990).

2. *See, e.g., United States v. Lee*, 455 U.S. 252, 257–58 (1982); *Thomas v. Review Board*, 450 U.S. 707, 718 (1981); *Goldman v. Weinberger*, 106 S. Ct. 1310, 1324–25 (1986) (O'Connor, J., dissenting).

3. 110 S. Ct. 1595.

4. For example, of the four justices in *Smith* who adhered to the compelling governmental interest test, one concluded that the law satisfied the test and three concluded that it did not.

5. *West Virginia Bd. of Education v. Barnette*, 319 U.S. 624, 653 (1943) (dissenting opinion).

6. W. Berns, *The First Amendment and the Future of American Democracy* (New York: Basic Books, 1976), pp. 35–55; M. Malbin, *Religion and Politics: The Intentions of the Authors of the First Amendment* (Washington, D.C.: American Enterprise Institute, 1978), pp. 19–40; Tushnet, *"Of Church and State and the Supreme Court": Kurland Reunited*, 1989 Sup. Ct. Rev. 373. This view has long been maintained by Professor Kurland. *See* P. Kurland, *Religion and the Law* (Chicago: Aldine, 1962); Kurland, *The Irrelevance of the Constitution: The Religion Clauses of the First Amendment and the Supreme Court*, 24 Vill. L. Rev. 3 (1978).

7. *See, e.g.*, A. Hamilton, J. Madison, and J. Jay, *The Federalist Papers*, ed. C. Rossiter (New York: New American Library, 1961), No. 84; *Annals of Congress*, vol. 1 (Washington, D.C.: Gales & Seaton, 1834), pp. 449, 757 (Madison).

8. Each of the states which proposed a free exercise provision also proposed a nonestablishment provision.

9. J. Elliot, *The Debates in the Several State Conventions on the Adoption of the Federal Constitution* (Washington, D.C.: U.S. Congress, 1854), 1:327.

10. Ibid., 3:659.

11. Ibid., 1:334 (North Carolina), 3:244 (Rhode Island).

12. Ibid., 1:326.

13. *Annals of Congress* 1:759 (Aug. 15, 1789).

14. Ibid., p. 434 (June 8, 1789).

15. Ibid., p. 758 (Aug. 15, 1789).

16. Ibid., p. 757.

17. Ibid., p. 766 (Aug. 20, 1789).

18. L. DePauw, ed., *Documentary History of the First Federal Congress of the United States of America* (Baltimore: Johns Hopkins Univ. Press, 1972), 1: 136.

19. Ibid., pp. 151, 166.

20. *Annals of Congress* 1:783 (Aug. 17, 1789).

21. Ibid., p. 784.

22. Ibid.

23. *See Wallace v. Jaffree*, 105 S. Ct. 2479, 2486–89 (1985).

24. B. Poore, ed., *The Federal and State Constitutions, Colonial Charters, and Other Organic Law of the United States*, 2d ed., 2 vols. (New York: B. Franklin, 1973), p. 1338 (Art. XXXVIII).

25. Ibid., p. 1281 (Const. of 1784, Art. V of Bill of Rights).

26. Ibid., p. 383 (Const. of 1777, Art. LVI).

27. Ibid., p. 1909 (Bill of Rights of 1776, Section 16).

28. Ibid., p. 957 (Const. of 1780, Pt. I, Art. II).

29. T. Jefferson, *Notes on Virginia* (Philadelphia: Wilson & Blackwell, 1803), Query XVII.

30. I am grateful to T. Curry, *The First Freedoms: Church and State in America to the Passage of the First Amendment* (New York: Oxford Univ. Press, 1986), for the historical evidence for these examples.

31. *See* McConnell, *The Origins and Historical Understanding of Free Exercise of Religion*, 103 Harv. L. Rev. 1409, 1468 (1990).

32. *Annals of Congress* 1:778 (Aug. 17, 1789).

33. Ibid., p. 780 (Benson); *see also* ibid., p. 796 (Aug. 20, 1789; Scott). This account of the debate is necessarily somewhat truncated in the interest of brevity.

34. Curry, *The First Freedoms*, pp. 89–90.

35. Hunt, *Madison and Religious Liberty*, in American Historical Association Annual Report, 163, 166 (1901).

36. Ibid., pp. 166–67.

37. This is not, of course, to endorse the Supreme Court's applications of the compelling governmental interest test, prior to *Smith*, in such cases as *Goldman v. Weinberger* (475 U.S. 503 [1986]), *United States v. Lee* (455 U.S. 252 [1982]), or *Bob Jones University v. United States* (461 U.S. 574 [1983]). This chapter is not the occasion for criticism of specific decisions, but it must be said, in defending the Court's articulated doctrine, that its deeds recently fell short of its words.

38. J. Locke, *A Letter concerning Toleration* (Indianapolis: Bobbs-Merrill, 1955).

39. Ibid., p. 48.

40. *Welsh v. United States*, 398 U.S. 333 (1970).

41. *Id.* at 356, 357.

42. *Wisconsin v. Yoder*, 406 U.S. 205, 247–49 (1972) (dissenting in part).

43. *Id.* at 205, 215–16 (1972).

44. *Id.* at 215–16.

45. *Child Day Care Ass'n v. O'Hara*, No. 864–00228 (Mo. Cir. Ct., filed May 2, 1986).

46. *See, e.g., Committee for Public Education & Religious Liberty v. Nyquist*, 413 U.S. 756 (1973).

47. *See* note 17, *supra*.

48. *See* note 32, *supra*.

49. *Annals of Congress* 1:796 (Scott).

50. *Marsh v. Chambers*, 103 S. Ct. 3330, 3346 (1983) (dissenting opinion).

51. *Barnette*, 319 U.S. at 653.

52. Berns, *The First Amendment*, p. 48.

53. Ibid., p. 50.

54. *See* T. Buckley, *Church and State in Revolutionary Virginia, 1776–1782* (Charlottesville: Univ. Press of Virginia, 1977), pp. 148–50; Curry, *The First Freedoms*, pp. 143–44.

55. *See* Curry, *The First Freedoms*, pp. 198–99.

56. A. de Tocqueville, *Democracy in America* (New York: Anchor/Doubleday, 1969), p. 292.

57. Ibid., p. 294.

58. Ibid., p. 295.

Barry W. Lynn

6. The Sad State of Free Exercise in the Courts

There are many "absolutists" when it comes to most provisions of the First Amendment. For example, in regard to the guarantees of freedom of speech and press, there are those so unswerving in their commitment they would permit the publication of troop movement schedules in wartime and the shouting of "Fire" in a crowded theater simultaneously. However, I have never encountered a true "free exercise of religion" absolutist. That is, I have found no one who seriously believes the Constitution should be read to sanction the unfettered release of all religious impulses, even if that includes, for example, the eradication of nonbelievers.

The First Amendment language providing that "Congress shall make no law respecting an establishment of religion, or prohibiting the free exercise thereof" is, like most provisions of the Bill of Rights, a majestic generality. Even were it dispositive, there is no way to obtain through the historical record any clear sense of either what the Congress that adopted this language or the state legislatures that ratified it thought was being protected within the generality. However, the Supreme Court, no slavish follower of the mythology of "original intent," has, over the past century, ascribed several broad meanings to the phrase. First, it guarantees that Americans can believe any religious dogma they can imagine, even though they cannot always act upon it. Second, it mandates religious, and not governmental, resolution of conflicts that are essentially theological. Third, it warrants that under some circumstances there must be exemptions from laws (or other regulations) of general applicability for those who cannot abide by those laws because of religious scruples.

Early Supreme Court decisions made it clear that religious belief could not be circumscribed by federal action (as if it could, regardless of the position on the subject taken by the Court), but that actions based on such religious belief could be regulated. Mormons were free to believe they were sometimes required to engage in polygamy, but they could not actually take the second wife in light of a federal statute barring the practice.[1] An individual could believe that compulsory vaccination was prohibited by God, but the state could use the needle anyway because of the state interest in public health.[2] In *Cantwell v. Connecticut*, which clarified that the guarantees of the First Amendment were applicable to the states, the Court noted in now ubiquitous dicta in religion cases: "Thus the [First] Amendment embraces two concepts,—freedom to believe and freedom to act. The first is absolute but, in the nature of things, the second cannot be."[3]

The general trend of Supreme Court jurisprudence in regard to doctrinal disputes (often connected to property claims) has been quite healthy. Since the late 1800s the Court has been deferring to the authority of ecclesiastical tribunals where a religion is hierarchical and allowing local (generally majoritarian) control where independent congregational polity or property was in dispute.[4]

In more recent cases, the Court has invalidated legislative and judicial efforts to vest independent power in a part of the hierarchical Russian Orthodox church which claimed to seek autonomy from the misguided central church in Moscow;[5] refused inquiry into whether a denomination had deviated from its faith sufficiently to withdraw the legal protection of a property trust from a local church;[6] and refused to review claims that a hierarchical church had arbitrarily violated its internal rules of governance.[7] In a somewhat more controversial decision, the Court permitted Georgia authorities to apply so-called neutral principles of property law to determine whether title in church property resided in a local congregation, a majority of whose members sought to align it with a new denomination.[8] Although discontented parishioners still seek judicial intervention in a variety of intrachurch disputes with some regularity, the manner in which these cases are generally resolved is reasonably clear.

The real heart of free exercise litigation today rests in conflicts between governmental regulation and the actual practice of religious ritual or other activity with a religious motivation. Although this is the heart, it is a relatively constricted organ. In fact, relatively little litigation occurs that implicates a free exercise claim. Moreover, only a minuscule proportion of that is successful for the First Amendment litigant. When successfully invoked, courts generally view it as an appendage to constitutional guarantees of "freedom of speech" or "equal protection of the laws," and not as a sufficient and independent basis for resolving a clash between governmental regulation and personal or corporate religious desire.

It is of importance to note that even those cases which are considered to be the genesis of modern free exercise claims ultimately turned more on the principle of content neutrality than religious motivation. Supreme Court decisions that involved Jehovah's Witness plaintiffs seeking to solicit funds without a municipal license,[9] distribute handbills on a city street,[10] make door-to-door solicitations,[11] and refuse to salute the American flag in a public school classroom[12] are most properly read as free speech cases that happened to be brought by religious persons, and not as recognitions of special constitutional claims based on religious purposes. In 1982 the Court invalidated a Minnesota law imposing record-keeping and reporting requirements only on religious organizations that solicited over half of their funds from nonmembers, based on the discriminatory effect it had favoring more established religions.[13] It did not suggest that the state had no authority to insist on the reporting of income by religious groups.

The relative dearth of litigation could, of course, be plausibly explained because the state of religious freedom in the nation is so high that there is little need to litigate in order to vindicate it. The obverse could also be true: that religion in America has become so placid that its activities are not worth the attention of government regulators or law enforcers and are therefore not burdened by state action. There is a certain amount of truth to both these propositions.

In the main there is no war between religion and government today. Certainly the Christian majority, at least, has little to fear from governmental interference in the practice of their religion. On the other hand, it rarely challenges the action of government. This is hardly an era where prophetic pronouncements are sounded daily, calling for the destruction of the nation and its leaders because of their individual or collective sins. Even in regard to smaller or newer religious movements, there is no general conflict. The relative calm, however, does not fully explain the low level of litigation. The more discouraging reality is that many attorneys potentially representing religious groups or individuals realize that litigation against the state to vindicate religious interests is largely fruitless because of the substantial impediments erected by judicial analyses of free exercise claims.

A threshold issue of no small significance is just what qualifies as the exercise of religion, in contrast to the exercise of some secular belief system. In 1944 in *Ballard v. U.S.* the Supreme Court appeared to give some guidance when it examined the criminal prosecution of leaders of the "I Am" movement for allegedly fraudulent mail solicitations.[14] The Court's majority quite properly concluded that juries could give no consideration to the "truth or falsity" of religious belief (in this instance, the regular visitations of a prophetic angel who gave information to the defendants on how to heal disease) in their considerations of guilt or innocence. However, it concluded that the jury could be instructed that the "sincerity" of the defendants' religious beliefs was a proper inquiry. Justice Jackson, in dissent, argued that even an inquiry into what amounted to the "good faith" of the religious believer could have a chilling effect on constitutional freedom. He argued that demonstrating "that one knowingly falsified is best proved by showing that what he said happened never did happen" and that this analysis drew courts into examining matters of religious doctrine. Jackson's ringing pronouncement, however, leaves little room for any inquiry at all and develops no test to uncover even deliberate fraud. On the proof question, at least another adequate way to demonstrate falsification is to show that a defendant never really believed something had happened. As a practical matter, in current litigation, often in reliance on *Ballard*, courts take an extremely deferential view of what is religious, generally acknowledging that a belief system is religious if the litigant asserts it to be so.

In fact, lower courts are sometimes criticized about the level of scrutiny of the religious nature of claims, by reference to a comment of Justice Burger that "the resolution of that question is not to turn upon a judicial perception of the particular belief or practice in question; religious beliefs need not be acceptable, logical, consistent, or comprehensible to others to merit First Amendment protection."[15] For example, the Eighth Circuit overruled a lower court's assertion that a white Christian could be barred from a prison because the racist doctrines he espoused were generally viewed as secular political viewpoints.[16] The appeals court noted that nothing barred an idea from being grounded in both secular and religious considerations.

Courts are usually less than Jesuitical when they do attempt to delve into exactly what considerations make a claim religious. Thus, a member of the Philadelphia group MOVE who asserted special dietary needs (specifically, all raw food) while in prison was denied relief when the Third Circuit concluded MOVE's views were not in fact religious.[17] They reached this conclusion because any "ultimate" views held by the defendant were concerned with secular matters and not religious principles, "MOVE cannot lay claim to be a comprehensive, multi-faceted theology," and MOVE "lacks the defining structural characteristics of a traditional religion." If the "One True Faith" isn't already on our shores, it best not come in a less than full-blown fashion to any locale within the jurisdiction of the Third Circuit. Notwithstanding the few cases like this one, however, courts are as reluctant to reject the religious nature of the claims of the sincere Satanist or Scientologist as of those of the sincere Episcopalian.

Courts also have not had any great difficulty with framing how to proceed with "sincerity" inquiries. In one recent example, the "Dare to Be Rich" program of the Church of Hakeem was deemed fraudulent when it was demonstrated that the head of the church, who represented to potential "ministers" that their financial "gifts" were to provide for foreign investments in gold, oil, and diamonds, knew that he had never made and was never planning to make such investments.[18]

In several major decisions from 1963 to 1981, the Supreme Court seemed to be developing a serious effort to infuse real life into the free exercise concept. In 1963 it ruled in *Sherbert v. Verner* that a Seventh-Day Adventist could not be denied state unemployment benefits because she refused to accept jobs that would require Saturday work in violation of her religious beliefs.[19] The Court rejected the state's claimed compelling interest in defeating false financial claims and noted that even if spurious religious claims were a problem, there was no evidence that any less restrictive alternatives to this system of denials had been explored.

Even more dramatically, in 1972 in *Wisconsin v. Yoder* the Court essentially granted to Old Order Amish church members immunity from criminal prosecution under a state compulsory education law when they refused to permit children of their community to attend public schools beyond the eighth grade.[20] The Amish viewed high school attendance as contrary to their religion because it exposed their children to "worldly" values and interfered with their development in the Amish community during their crucial adolescent period. The majority viewed carefully the factual setting of the case and obviously was impressed by the strong, lengthy, and pervasive influence the religious belief system of the Amish had on its community adherents. It noted the "law abiding" nature and "self sufficiency" of the group. Justice Burger stated for the Court: "The essence of all that has been said or written on the subject is that only those interests of the highest order and those not otherwise served can overbalance legitimate claims to the free exercise of religion." He concluded that the "inescapable" impact of Wisconsin's law was that it "affirmatively compels them, under threat of criminal sanction, to perform acts at odds with fundamental tenets of their religious beliefs." This was "precisely the kind of objective danger to the free exercise of religion which the First Amendment was designed to prevent" because it "would gravely endanger if not destroy" the exercise of Amish beliefs. The state's asserted educational interest was not sufficiently compelling, given the life-style the Amish needed to have their children prepared to lead.

Justice Douglas, in dissent, viewed the decision as too deferential to parental religious views, and thus possibly infringing on the rights of young people to obtain the kind of education they would need in the larger society were they to leave the Amish community. Douglas was also troubled by references to the "law and order" record of the Amish, implying not only that there was some doubt about its accuracy but also that it was irrelevant in determining the strength of the religious claim.

In 1981 the Court in *Thomas v. Review Board* repudiated a state's denial of unemployment benefits to a Jehovah's Witness plaintiff who quit his job after he was transferred to a position which would have required production of weapons parts in violation of his religious belief.[21] This was true notwithstanding that this view was not a doctrinal part of the denomination's belief system and that the plaintiff admitted to "struggling" over his personal views. Justice Burger, writing for the Court, viewed the state's position as a substantial burden on "free exercise" even though the Indiana law "does not compel a violation of conscience." He noted: "Where the state conditions receipt of an important benefit upon conduct proscribed by a religious faith, or where it denies such a benefit because of conduct mandated by religious belief, thereby putting substantial pressure on an adherent to modify his behavior and to violate his beliefs, a burden on religion exists." This burden was unjustified by the government's interest in either preventing high unemployment or avoiding probes into job applicants' religious beliefs. Justice Rehnquist, in lone dissent, noted that the opinion disposed too quickly of the "tension" between "free exercise" and "establishment" generated by such exemptions.

To this point, the Court's analysis seemed to be that any substantial burden on a religious practice would be upheld only if there was a compelling governmental interest of the highest order to counterbalance it and no less restrictive alternative existed. Then something began to change.

In 1982 the Court in *U.S. v. Lee* rejected an Amish employer's claim that he should be exempt from paying Social Security taxes on his all-Amish work force of carpenters.[22] The Court acknowledged that the system interfered with free exercise rights of the Amish, who do not believe they should participate in governmentally supported insurance funds because a religiously based obligation to provide such assistance exists within their community. The governmental interest in a national system was held sufficiently compelling to overcome the objection, however, because the Court felt it "would be difficult to accommodate the comprehensive social security system with myriad exceptions flowing from a wide variety of religious beliefs." Justice Stevens, in concurrence with the result, pointed out, however, that as a fiscal matter, the exemption would probably benefit the system since the nonpayment would be more than offset by the elimination of the employees' right to collect benefits. He also viewed the fear of a "myriad" of other religious claimants as largely speculative. His agreement with the disposition rested essentially on the difficulty in evaluating other claims to tax exemptions on religious grounds.

The Court has also recognized several constitutionally based limitations on free exercise. In 1983, in *Bob Jones University v. U.S.*, the Court found unavailing the free exercise claim for a tax exemption by a racially discriminatory private school because of the compelling governmental interest in ending race discrimination, a goal of the highest order.[23] During the 1984–85 term it invalidated a Connecticut statute which required private employers to honor every employee's desire to avoid work on his or her Sabbath, asserting that such a broad requirement advanced religion in violation of the establishment clause.[24] Even the most recent religious solicitation case before the Court upheld a nondiscretionary system by Minnesota state fair officials where distribution of literature and sale of materials of all kinds were confined to a fixed location at booths on the fairgrounds for the purpose of maintaining the orderly flow of patrons.[25] The case had been brought by the International Society for Krishna Consciousness (ISKCON), which argued that the system inhibited the practice of Sankirtan, a ritual in which members go into public places to distribute religious literature and seek donations to support the Krishna faith. Justice White in his opinion stated:

> None of our cases suggest that the inclusion of peripatetic solicitation as part of a church ritual entitles church members to solicitation rights in a public forum superior to those of members of other religious groups that raise money but do not purport to ritualize the process. Nor for present purposes do religious organizations enjoy rights to communicate, distribute, and solicit on the fairgrounds superior to those of other organizations having social, political, or other ideological messages to proselytize.

Justice Brennan, in partial dissent, indicated that since ISKCON was willing to base its case on general free speech principles, he did not understand why Justice White needed to "disparage" the significance of the ritualistic Sankirtan duty by asserting that it had no "special" protection under the First Amendment.

A more recent term of the Court resulted in two new and quite significant rejections of free exercise claims. In *Goldman v. Weinberger*, a 5-4 majority rejected a Jewish air force chaplain's claim that he be allowed to wear a yarmulke even though service regulations ordinarily prohibited all headwear.[26] Although the decision noted that the special nature of the military mission and the need to subordinate individual desires to service needs "do not, of course, render entirely nugatory in the military context the guarantees of the First Amendment," it is hard to imagine a more unobtrusive and noninterfering claim than that of Chaplain Goldman. The Court found sufficiently compelling the air force assertion that standardized attire "encourages the subordination of personal preferences and identities in favor of the overall group mission." It deemed the interest "vital" even in peacetime because military personnel "must be ready to provide an effective defense on a moment's notice." The underlying wisdom of the conclusion that morale was bolstered by conformity was not up for judicial interference by review. Justice Stevens's concurrence contained the additional argument that if a yarmulke was approved, subsequent claims by Sikhs or Rastafarians would need to be evaluated, drawing matters of "character and integrity" into decision making. *Goldman* clearly supports the many appeals courts decisions that find virtually any claimed military need sufficient to overcome free exercise assertions.[27]

At first blush it was possible to relegate the *Goldman* decision to the heap of other cases that grant extraordinary judicial deference to military decisions in areas like equal protection and free expression. It is perversely consistent with one of the most poorly reasoned Vietnam War cases to reach the Court, *Gillette v. U.S.*, in which a draft resister unsuccessfully invoked a free exercise argument against the failure of the government to provide exemptions from military service for those conscientiously opposed only to "unjust" wars.[28] After noting in dicta that the Court had never indicated that the grant of conscientious objection to anyone, even those who opposed war in all forms, was constitutionally required, it reviewed why the governmental interest in obtaining personnel through the draft was extremely significant. It then asserted that conscription laws applied to "selective" objectors and others "are not designed to interfere with any religious ritual or practice, and do not work a penalty against any theological position." This appalling decision prompted Justice Douglas's single most notable exposition about the exercise of religion: "I had assumed that the welfare of the single human soul was the ultimate test of the vitality of the First Amendment." By refusing to recognize the need to accommodate within a system of compulsion created by the government a religious belief consistent with the mainstream of American theological thought and of central religious significance to the claimant, the Court had seriously diminished the significance of the free exercise clause in the military and elsewhere.

Although *Goldman* was itself damaging, a few months later the vitality of free exercise was struck another blow in *Bowen v. Roy.*[29] In this case a Native American asserted, among other things, a free exercise right not to have his daughter obtain a Social Security number in order to apply for certain welfare benefits because use of this number would "rob" her of her uniqueness and her spiritual power. In rejecting the claim, Justice Burger noted for three members of the Court that the requirement of a number being provided by an applicant for benefits was different than other regulations: "A government requirement that indirectly and incidentally calls for a choice between securing a government benefit and adherence to religious beliefs is wholly different from governmental action or legislation that criminalizes religiously inspired activity or inescapably compels conduct that some find objectionable for religious reasons." *Sherbert* and *Thomas* were deemed inapplicable because to Burger they represented instances where a government had decided to permit persons to quit jobs for "good cause" and the failure to consider a religious motivation such a "cause" tended to exhibit hostility to religion, rather than neutrality. *Yoder* was also deemed inapposite, because the program to be administered is so large that government must have broad latitude to run it. A restriction on religion in such a context should be upheld because it is "a reasonable means of promoting a legitimate public interest."

Justice O'Connor, in dissent on this issue, characterized the Burger decision as "a new standard to be applied to test the validity of government regulations under the Free Exercise Clause," which "relegates a serious First Amendment value to the barest level of minimal scrutiny that the Equal Protection Clause already provides." For her, under the proper standard of "especially important governmental interests pursued by narrowly tailored means," an exemption would not diminish the ability to combat fraud. She also pointed out that five members of the Court believed *Sherbert* and *Thomas* controlled the case to the extent it was not moot (Justices Stevens and Blackmun felt the case moot).

During the previous term, an equally divided court, with Justice Powell absent, upheld an Eighth Circuit decision supporting the right of a Nebraska resident to refuse to have her photograph placed on her driver's license because of her belief that the requirement was violative of the Second Commandment's injunction against "graven images."[30] Since Justice Powell had no problem with the Burger-announced standard in *Bowen v. Roy*, one can speculate that this case would have been disposed of differently with Powell present.

In a footnote to the decision in *Lee*, Justice Stevens expressed the view that the most accurate characterization of the standard for consideration of free exercise claims is that it "places an almost insurmountable burden on any individual who objects to a valid and neutral law of general applicability on the ground that the law proscribes (or prescribes) conduct that his religion prescribes (or proscribes)." This was, of course, before *Roy* and its possible further erosion of the free exercise principle by reference to the "reasonableness" of regulation. Sadly, in virtually every clash between governmental policy and religious principle, principle is the loser.

The historic *Yoder* decision is largely anomalous. No case in the Supreme Court or any federal appellate court since has come close to accepting such a sweeping claim of exemption. In fact, it is difficult to believe, given the intense scrutiny of the factual situation in the Amish community, that either then or now the same flexibility in education would have been accorded a newer or more controversial religious group. Even *Sherbert* and *Thomas* are, I believe, of limited precedential value and can be successfully invoked only in regard to exemptions affecting minuscule numbers of persons.

When the exercise of some religious belief is discriminatorily regulated, or where the exercise of religion as well as of other protected activities is burdened, religious litigants remain successful in appellate decisions. Curfew ordinances which are so restrictive that they prohibit minors from attending "religious or school meetings" will not pass constitutional muster.[31] Religious meetings in areas opened as genuine public forums, such as many state government buildings and the Ellipse behind the White House, may not be prohibited.[32] In prisons, rough parity of worship opportunities must be accorded inmates of various religious persuasions.[33] As indicated above, though, there is no sense in these and similar cases that the asserted free exercise claim would have been alone sufficient for success.

A review of free exercise claims at the appellate level provides a catalogue of noble and ignoble failures, often showing remarkable creativity. Native American claims regarding the religious nature of certain government lands or the desire to collect sacred articles there will not block their sale or development.[34] Interest in constructing religious buildings will not negate zoning limitations.[35] The religious status of a corporate or individual target of an IRS or FCC probe has no effect in preventing investigation, even where the free exercise claim is that governmental investigation and its attendant publicity make it harder to gain converts.[36] A school system may prohibit the wearing of headgear, including a yarmulke attached with bobby pins during sports, because of the fear that the article could fall off and cause someone to trip.[37] In prisons almost any administrative or security claim is held to counterbalance significant free exercise claims under a variety of articulated standards.

Not surprisingly, religious objection to criminal laws is even less availing. Opposition to the American currency system does not negate federal counterfeiting statutes.[38] In cases where marijuana use has been asserted as a defense to criminal prosecution (usually involving members of the Ethiopian Zion Coptic church), courts uniformly find an overriding interest in regulating the drug to protect the health of individuals and the social welfare.[39] Any exemption is usually held to nullify criminal possession statutes by making enforcement impossible. It is interesting to note that courts reject equal protection claims based on the administrative decision to exempt from Schedule I drug classification peyote used for the benefit of the Native American church, arguing that this effort toward accommodation for a readily identifiable narrow category of persons in unique legal status has minimal enforcement impact. This equal protection argument does not succeed when other not-strictly-Indian churches wish to use peyote in religious rituals.[40]

Justice Douglas once warned: "Freedom to differ is not limited to things that do not matter much. . . . The test of its substance is the right to differ as to things that touch the heart of the existing order."[41] If courts do not begin to reassess the kind of governmental claims which will vitiate free exercise arguments, the free exercise clause will represent an empty promise. Let me propose a few steps toward that end.

First, it is time to admit that the most polite thing one can say about the relationship between the two religion clauses in the First Amendment is that there is some tension between them. It would, however, be more accurate to acknowledge that they are essentially in direct conflict when it comes to religious exemptions from laws of general applicability, which is at the core of contemporary litigation. Every exemption amounts to a grant of preferential treatment to a group in apparent violation of the establishment clause, at least if that guarantee is read as prohibiting aid to any or all religions. Moreover, such an exemption at least indirectly encourages such persons who wish to engage in the otherwise prohibited activity to become an adherent of the exempted religion and thus gain similar benefit. Where a court acknowledges that members of the Native American church can use the otherwise prohibited hallucinogenic peyote cactus, there would at least be some incentive to all would-be users to start doing a quick theological reevaluation.

Rather than develop any talismanic method of resolving this conflict, courts should engage in a balancing test which would raise the following kinds of questions. To what extent would the grant of exemption be perceived as a grant of state imprimatur to the religious activity? To what degree would it interfere with the right of others to exercise their religion or keep a distance from all religion? To what extent are the competing constitutional claims jeopardized in the historical setting in which the conflict arises? Similar issues arise when the claim competing with that of free exercise implicates another constitutional right such as the nonpromotion of invidious discrimination.

In the event that a practice under this standard does not abridge another constitutional value, the inquiry might then be appropriately focused on the imminence and degree to which the exercise of religion has an adverse effect on the government interest in public safety and order. This would provide more explicitly for a kind of "clear and present danger" test for free exercise.[42]

The rhetorical significance of a guarantee that governments not abridge the right of Americans to put their religious faith into practice is not insignificant. However, the special rights enumerated in the First Amendment deserve more than a general tip of the hat. In regard to the free exercise clause, courts must acknowledge that they must ensure that every claim of government power will not be permitted to trample on every troublesome challenge posed by the religious activities of the citizens.

Notes

1. *Reynolds v. U.S.*, 98 U.S. (8 Otto) 145 (1879).

2. *Jacobsen v. Massachusetts*, 197 U.S. 11 (1905).

3. *Cantwell v. Connecticut*, 310 U.S. 296 (1940).

4. *See, e.g.*, *Watson v. Jones*, 80 U.S. (13 Wall.) 679 (1872); *Bouldin v. Alexander*, 82 U.S. (15 Wall.) 131 (1872).

5. *Kedroff v. St. Nicholas Cathedral*, 334 U.S. 94 (1952); *Kreshik v. St. Nicholas Cathedral*, 363 U.S. 190 (1960), *reh'g denied* 364 U.S. 855 (1960).

6. *Presbyterian Church v. Mary Elizabeth Blue Hull Memorial Presbyterian Church*, 393 U.S. 440 (1969).

7. *Serbian Eastern Orthodox Church v. Milivojevich*, 426 U.S. 696 (1976).

8. *Jones v. Wolf*, 443 U.S. 595 (1979), *on remand* 260 S.E. 2d 84 (1979), cert. denied 444 U.S. 1080 (1980).

9. *Cantwell v. Connecticut*, 310 U.S. 296 (1940).

10. *Jamison v. Texas*, 318 U.S. 413 (1943).

11. *Murdock v. Pennsylvania*, 319 U.S. 105 (1943).

12. *West Va. State Board of Education v. Barnette*, 319 U.S. 624 (1943).

13. *Larson v. Valente*, 456 U.S. 228 (1982), *reh'g denied* 457 U.S. 111 (1982).

14. *Ballard v. U.S.*, 332 U.S. 78 (1944).

15. *Thomas v. Review Board*, 450 U.S. 707, 714 (1981).

16. *Wiggins v. Sargent*, 753 F.2d 663 (8th Cir. 1985).

17. *Africa v. Com. of Pa.*, 662 F.2d 1025 (3d Cir. 1981).

18. *U.S. v. Rasheed*, 663 F.2d 843 (9th Cir. 1981).

19. *Sherbert v. Verner*, 374 U.S. 398 (1963).

20. *Wisconsin v. Yoder*, 406 U.S. 205 (1972).

21. *Thomas*, *supra* note 15.

22. *U.S. v. Lee*, 455 U.S. 252 (1982).

23. *Bob Jones University v. U.S.*, 461 U.S. 574 (1983).

24. *Estate of Thornton v. Caldor, Inc.*, 472 U.S. 703 (1985).

25. *Heffron v. International Society for Krishna Consciousness*, 452 U.S. 640 (1981), *on remand* 311 N.W. 2d 843 (Minn. 1981).

26. *Goldman v. Weinberger*, 475 U.S. 503 (1986).

27. *See, e.g., Sherwood v. Brown*, 619 F.2d 47 (9th Cir. 1980) (Sikh cannot wear turban); *U.S. v. Mowat*, 582 F.2d 1194 (9th Cir. 1978) (religious ceremony cannot be held on island sometimes used for military target practice).

28. *Gillette v. U.S.*, 401 U.S. 437 (1971), *reh'g denied* 402 U.S. 934 (1971).

29. *Bowen v. Roy*, 476 U.S. 693, (1986).

30. *Quaring v. Peterson*, 728 F.2d 1121 (8th Cir. 1984) 472 U.S. 478, *aff'd by evenly divided court*; *Jensen v. Quaring*, 472 U.S. 478 (1985) (per curiam).

31. *Johnson v. City of Opelousas*, 658 F.2d 1065 (5th Cir. 1981).

32. *See, e.g., Jaffe v. Alexis*, 659 F.2d 1018 (9th Cir. 1981); *O'Hair v. Andrus*, 613 F.2d 931 (D.C. Cir. 1979).

33. This litigation is based on *Cruz v. Beto*, 405 U.S. 319 (1972).

34. *See, e.g., Wilson v. Block*, 708 F.2d 735 (D.C. Cir. 1983).

35. *Lakewood, Ohio, Cong. of Jehovah's Witnesses, Inc. v. Lakewood Ohio*, 699 F.2d 303 (6th Cir. 1983).

36. *See, e.g., Scott v. Rosenberg*, 702 F.2d 1263 (9th Cir. 1983); *U.S. v. Norcutt*, 680 F.2d 54 (8th Cir. 1982) (per curiam).

37. *Menora v. Ill. High School Ass'n.*, 683 F.2d 1030 (7th Cir. 1982).

38. *U.S. v. Grismore*, 564 F.2d 929 (10th Cir. 1977).

39. *See, e.g., U.S. v. Rush*, 738 F.2d 497 (1st Cir. 1984).

40. *Peyote Way Church of God, Inc. v. Smith*, 742 F.2d 193 (5th Cir. 1984).

41. *Supra* note 12, at 642.

42. *Schenck v. United States*, 249 U.S. 47 (1919) (speech regulation).

STANLEY C. BRUBAKER

7. Original Intent and Freedom of Speech and Press

The topic of this chapter, "Original Intent and the Free Speech and Press Clauses," entails three related questions: What do we mean by original intent? What was that original intent regarding the free speech and press clauses? To what extent, if any, is this intent or some other intent authoritative? I understand my primary task to concern the second question, though to make this inquiry intelligible I must adopt a preliminary answer to the question of what "original intent" means, and to make it significant, I must address the question of what authority original intent has.

The meaning of "original intent," quite apart from what role it should play in constitutional interpretation, has become a closely analyzed and warmly disputed area of constitutional theory,[1] so I think it is necessary at the outset to make explicit, without becoming overly technical, what I mean when I use the term. For a preliminary definition, I will use the term in a way which I think will do violence neither to the sense urged by advocates of a jurisprudence of original intention[2] nor to the conventions of contemporary language philosophers. That is, I will define it as the meaning of the clauses in question as understood by the adopters. By "adopters" I mean all who cast a vote which would determine whether or not the words should become part of the Constitution. By "meaning"—this, of course, is the trickier part—I mean what the linguists call "utterance meaning," that is, the combination of semantics (meaning of the words) and pragmatics (the context in which the words were used). And finally, by "semantics," I again will follow contemporary linguists and say that we understand the meaning of words through other words. Thus, we are looking for the sort of criteria that the adopters had in mind[3] in 1789 when they spoke of a freedom of speech and the press, that is, the conditions *a*, *b*, and *c* that would need to be met if they were to call a press free. There remains the problem that only individuals, not groups, have concrete semantic intentions in an "utterance meaning," but we shall look for the core criteria that allowed the legislators to believe that they understood each other when they spoke of free speech and press.

Unfortunately for devotees of exacting notions of original intent, but fortunately for ease of summation, we do not have access to the minds of each of the adopters. I will consider, as a proxy, what was said by those who were spokesmen in the debate and the sources upon which these spokesmen seem to have relied. To simplify things further, I will not distinguish between speech and press (except when necessary), and I will focus on what is usually agreed to be of central importance, the original intent regarding political speech, especially concerning the doctrine of seditious libel: the crime of defaming the government, its officers, or its policies.[4]

There exists what we might call a romantic understanding of the original intent of the First Amendment's speech and press clauses. We usually hear a version of this from our students when we ask them what the First Amendment means. We are told that the First Amendment was given pride of place in the Bill of Rights in order to emphasize the bedrock importance of free speech in the country; and this bedrock importance, we discover, amounts to the principle that one should be free to do whatever he wants to do just so long as he doesn't hurt anybody—with "hurt" meaning a palpable harm, not just an offense—and as a corollary that no one should be allowed to impose his values on another, and, certainly, the government shouldn't be allowed to impose its values on anybody. And if we ask if liberty of speech is distinct from license of speech, we are likely to be told that the clause was intended to abolish such distinctions. From scholars and justices of the twentieth century, we have heard a more sophisticated version of this same understanding. Professor Chafee told us that the framers' intent was "to wipe out the common law of sedition, and make further prosecutions for criticism of the government, without any incitement of law-breaking, forever impossible in the United States of America";[5] that with the Sedition Act of 1798, small-minded men choked the expansive protection of free speech with wicked doctrines; that Holmes breathed new life into the document, reviving its original spirit with his eloquent dissents, the general thrust of which constitutes today's law. Perhaps the most exemplary of these dissents is that of *Gitlow v. New York*, where he wrote: "If in the long run the beliefs expressed in proletarian dictatorship are destined to be accepted by the dominant forces of the community, the only meaning of free speech is that they should be given their chance and have their way."[6]

We probably will continue to hear versions of original intent such as these from beginning students, and we will no doubt continue to hear such ideas put forward by scholars and justices as the central meaning of free speech. But since 1960, none has been able to claim plausibly that if this is the only meaning of free speech, it is the one intended by those who wrote and ratified the First Amendment. That year was when Leonard Levy published *Legacy of Suppression.*[7] Drawing largely upon this work by Levy, as he has revised it in his 1985 edition,[8] we have a reasonably clear idea of what the adopters must have had in mind when they used the term "freedom of speech and press."

To begin, we should consider the pragmatics, or the context of the free speech and press clause. For the framers there was no intention of emphasizing a firstness of the speech and press clauses by placing them in the First Amendment. In Madison's original submission of a bill of rights, free press protections were listed twice—one protecting the press against state government, the other against national government—but in neither case was speech protection first. In fact, Madison did not really intend for these amendments to be listed as a distinct bill of rights but rather to be interspersed in appropriate places in the Constitution. These amendments, seventeen in number, as slightly revised by the special House committee and on the House floor, were sent to the Senate. There the restriction on state infringement of freedom of the press was dropped and the restriction on the federal government, apparently for stylistic reasons only, was combined with those protecting religious liberty, forming what was returned to the House as the Third Amendment, in which position it remained when submitted to the states, emerging as our First Amendment only when the original first two failed to secure the support of three-quarters of the states. Perhaps it should come as no great surprise that a free press clause was not first when we consider that of the twelve states ratifying the Constitution before the Bill of Rights was considered, only three recommended such a provision.[9]

As for the primary intention behind these clauses, and the Bill of Rights generally, it seems that ratifying a bill of rights was merely incidental to other political intentions. Anti-Federalists pointed to the absence of a bill of rights in order to drum up further opposition to the Constitution that they would have rejected in any case. The Federalists responded that a bill of rights was unnecessary as the Constitution authorized only the enumerated powers and thus the federal government had no authority to abridge such rights in the first place. Only when it seemed that the Constitution would fail if pledges were not made to adopt a bill of rights did leading Federalists make such pledges. But here, too, the motivation was less the bill of rights than how it would affect the strength of the new government. Madison and others believed, no doubt correctly, that if Congress did not approve a bill of rights, the Federalists might not be able to halt the move for a new constitutional convention which would significantly curtail the authority of the new Constitution. Since a new convention was exactly what the Anti-Federalists wanted, they voiced no great enthusiasm for this bill of rights, the want of which they had so shrilly decried during the ratification debates. In the midst of this struggle, against the unremitting apathy of the Federalists and the baffled opposition of the Anti-Federalists, Madison confided to a colleague his principal motivation in urging the amendments. Though he thought there was nothing "improper" in the amendments, and perhaps they might produce some good, he found the project of gaining support for the amendments was "nauseous." But the amendments "will kill the opposition everywhere, and by putting an end to disaffection to the Government itself, enable the administration to venture on measures not otherwise safe."[10] As Levy writes: "Our precious Bill of Rights, at least in its immediate background, resulted from the reluctant necessity of certain Federalists to capitalize on a cause that had been originated, in vain, by the Anti-Federalists for ulterior party purposes. The party that had first opposed the Bill of Rights inadvertently wound up with the responsibility for its framing and ratification, while the party that had first professedly wanted it discovered too late that it not only was embarrassing but disastrous for those ulterior purposes."[11]

In so describing the motivations of the Federalists and Anti-Federalists, I do not mean to denigrate their concern for the liberties that we find in the Bill of Rights. Rather, I mean to emphasize that both saw the form of government, more than any parchment barrier appended to it, as the guarantor of rights. As Hamilton said in *The Federalist* No. 84, the Constitution itself is a bill of rights. And for the Anti-Federalists, following classical republicanism, only in a small republic could liberties remain secure. Still, beyond their pragmatic intention, the framers and adopters had a semantic intention, and it is to this we now turn.

The debates in Congress concerning the speech and press clauses shed scant light on the question of meaning. The Senate kept no records of its debates, so that we can only make sketchy inferences from motions accepted and rejected. We do know, for instance, that the Senate rejected a motion to specify the protection of free speech as "as ample . . . as hath at any time been secured by the common law." But we cannot infer much from this. The Senate might have thought it too narrow or too confusing a definition of free speech, or it might simply have regarded the phrase as unnecessary. And for reasons that remain a mystery, the Senate changed the House restriction on the federal government generally to a restriction on Congress alone: "Congress shall make no law . . . ." On the House floor, where Madison introduced his bill of rights, there was only a brief exchange concerning free speech. This occurred when the Federalists fought back a move to insert into the right of assembly the doctrine of instructions. Madison simply affirmed that the free speech clause would encompass the right of the people "to express and communicate their sentiments and wishes" to their representatives.[12]

Nor do we find enlightening comments in the state legislatures that considered the amendments or the local newspapers or pamphlets of the time. To be sure, there was lavish praise for freedom of speech, but, according to Levy, "no one seems to have cared enough to clarify what he meant by the subject upon which he lavished praise."[13] But in a way this very lack of debate on the scope of meaning of free speech is helpful, for it suggests that there was a commonly shared understanding of what was meant, and if so, that understanding is almost certainly the one existing in the common law as it had been applied in the states.[14] If the free speech clause had deviated from what was the established law, surely there would have been some debate about it. This common-law understanding is given in a well-known passage from Blackstone (echoes of which resounded throughout America in the colonial, Revolutionary, and founding eras):

> The liberty of the press is indeed essential to the nature of a free state; but this consists in laying no *previous* restraints upon publications, and not in freedom from censure for criminal matter when published. Every freeman has an undoubted right to lay what sentiments he pleases before the public: to forbid this is to destroy the freedom of the press: but if he publishes what is improper, mischievous, or illegal, he must take the consequences of his own temerity. . . . [T]o punish (as the law does at present) any dangerous or offensive writings, which, when published, shall on a fair and impartial trial be adjudged of a pernicious tendency, is necessary for the preservation of peace and good order, a government and religion, the only solid foundations of civil liberty. Thus the will of the individuals is still left free; the abuse only of that free-will is the object of legal punishment. Neither is any restraint hereby laid upon freedom of thought or enquiry: liberty of private sentiments is still left; the disseminating, or making public, of bad sentiments, destructive of the ends of society, is the crime which society corrects.[15]

And this scope of free press does not differ in any significant way from that advocated by the major theorists who might have influenced the framers—Locke, Spinoza, Trenchard and Gordon, Milton.

There exist some indications that the adopters intended to go beyond the Blackstonian statement of the common law. Four are worthy of consideration. First, the Zenger trial of 1735 had gained some support for the notion that truth should serve as a defense against a libel charge and that juries rather than the judges should determine whether the words in question were libelous. And, loosely tied to these developments, there was some support for the proposition that, contrary to the common-law tradition, good motives could exculpate one from a charge of libel. Yet, as Levy notes, during the era of the American Revolution, "no state, despite its new freedom, adopted the Zengerian reforms," and at the time of the founding "Zengerian principles had few open advocates."[16]

Second is the possibility of literalism, suggesting that the words "no law" meant that the federal government should have nothing to do with the freedom of the press. That it would not, except for copyright, was, of course, the response of the Federalists to the contention of the Anti-Federalists that the Constitution was defective in lacking a bill of rights. Pursuing the logic of this position, the Federalists argued that it would be dangerous to have such a limit where there was never intended to be any authority. A bill of rights, wrote Hamilton in *The Federalist* No. 84, "would contain various exceptions to powers which are not granted; and, on this very account, would afford a colorable pretext to claim more than were granted. For why declare that things not be done which there is not power to do? Why, for instance, should it be said that the liberty of the press shall not be restrained when no power is given by which restrictions may be imposed?" At least with hindsight, the Federalist claim appears patently defective, for clearly in the name of several of the enumerated powers—commerce, tax, raising an army—it is possible to abridge freedom of the press. And further, it is no doubt necessary for the federal government to restrict speech. As Robert Bork asks rhetorically, "Is Congress forbidden to prohibit incitement to mutiny aboard a naval vessel engaged in action against an enemy, to prohibit shouted harangues from the visitors gallery during its own deliberations or to provide any rules for decorum in the federal courtrooms?"[17] But that the federal government would have no power over speech and the press was a stated position and a repeated one, and perhaps it was believed by some.

Still, even if the no power at all interpretation of the clause is true, it does little to forward an expansive free speech doctrine. For no one doubted that the press needed to be restrained, and thus such a reading would carry the corollaries (a) that the business of press restriction is emphatically the business of the state, and if so, then (b) incorporating the First Amendment into the Fourteenth becomes a logical impossibility. I doubt, however, that this is an accurate understanding of the intentions of the adopters, for the more the proposed constitution was considered, the less plausible the Federalist argument seemed. Further, many of the states had wording similar to that of the First Amendment, and they were not understood to have the absolute meanings suggested here.

Pursuing the claim of literalism, what about the opening words, "Congress shall make no law . . ."? Did the adopters intend this literally? Possibly, but the observation seems most likely to count for a common-law scope of freedom of the press. As mentioned above, there was a move in the Senate to define the freedom of the press as identical to that of the common law. That failed. But perhaps its proponents did not stop there and carried their efforts into the committee where the broad language of the House, affirming the freedom of the press against all aspects of the federal government, was narrowed at "Congress." James Wilson thought that the Constitution affirmed a common-law cognizance of criminal cases in the federal courts, and so did every member of the Supreme Court before whom the question was raised before 1812, save Samuel Chase in 1798, who within a year changed his position to affirm that of his fellow justices, and these cases included a case of seditious libel.[18] That also is the conclusion of Charles Warren's exemplary study of the Judiciary Act of 1798.[19] Whether this was intended to be a federal common law or state common law is, of course, a matter of continuing controversy, but on the question of the protection afforded freedom of speech the controversy has little bearing, for on this point the common law was virtually the same in all the states.

The third possibility for an understanding broader than that at common law focuses on press practices of the time. These were indeed more expansive than press law and press theories of the time, and this observation forms the basis for Levy's somewhat more liberal conclusions in his revised study. "When the framers of the First Amendment provided that Congress shall not abridge the freedom of the press they could only have meant to protect the press with which they were familiar and as it operated at the time. They constitutionally guaranteed the practice of freedom of the press." But as he admits in his preface, practice does not dictate the meaning of the concept. "In our own time, obscenity is still illegal, though we live in a society saturated by it and witness few prosecutions; their paucity does not illumine the meaning of obscenity. So, too, the rarity of prosecutions for seditious libel, and the existence of an unfettered press do not illumine the scope and meaning of freedom of the press or the law on freedom of the press."[20]

Finally, in favor of a more expansive interpretation, commentators turn to the resistance to the Sedition Act, which involved several men we count as framers, including James Madison. And here we do find arguments for a more liberal interpretation of the First Amendment's free speech and press clauses than that which existed at the common law. But two points need to be made. First, as Walter Berns has convincingly demonstrated[21]—and Levy has not effectively refuted him—the primary concern of the opponents of the Sedition Act was not freedom of the press but freedom of the states, which included a freedom to regulate the press and punish libel as they saw appropriate. And second, in looking to these comments we have shifted our focus from original intent to the evolving intent of the originators. Comments made in the heat of the controversy of 1798–1800 provided little insight about the thinking of 1789.

On the intentions of the adopters, we can say in summation, that while there are areas of ambiguity, if we are looking for the criteria meaning that the adopters had in their minds, one cannot possibly claim that it followed the romantic vision mentioned above, and one cannot possibly disclaim that it simply embraced the common-law understanding of free press.

A rather striking conclusion is thus forced on us. Between the most generous interpretation of this original intent and the most restrictive view that we find expressed by justices and scholars today, there lies a gulf. What then lies between us and them that leads to such incompatible conclusions when we look to the same words? Do we know something that they did not know? Did they know something that we've forgotten? To the latter two questions, I think that the answer is yes and yes. We do know something that they didn't. For one thing, the distinction between opposition to a regime and opposition to policies or leaders within a regime as the basis for a political party is so clear to us today that Washington's Farewell Address warning us "in the most solemn manner against the baneful effects of the spirit of party" seems almost quaint. Animadversion directed toward throwing the rascals out is now easier to distinguish from animadversion directed toward overthrowing the regime, and far easier to tolerate. And when this distinction is coupled with the realization that the regime is in a sense the people themselves, the place for a doctrine of seditious libel becomes more narrowly defined. Of course, the framers knew these things in the abstract, but they had to be proved as historical facts—and more significantly as historical possibilities—before they could supply a knowledgeable foundation for the expansion of free speech. Upon them can comfortably rest our familiar arguments: that speech must be expansively protected if we are to have informed voting, if public affairs will be genuine affairs of the public, if public officials can be held responsible for their actions, if abuses of power are to be discovered. Only upon the knowledge that a people can govern itself can one sensibly argue that freedom of speech is the very matrix of all our other liberties.

But the adopters also knew some things that we seem to have forgotten. For one thing, they understood the sense in which freedom of speech is meaningless unless tied to self-government, using that term in both its public and personal sense. That is, they understood that a coherent sense of self, an identity, must logically precede freedom, for an act is free only if it is self-generated. In short, freedom presupposes character, and character presupposes self-discipline or self-government. But self-discipline is not self-acquired. It is virtually impossible without cultivation by family, society, and, at least indirectly, government.

Similarly, the action of the government is free only if it proceeds from a coherent identity of the public self. It was this very lack of coherence that had moved Madison and the other key actors to form the Constitution; repeatedly one finds in the writings of the leading framers concern with the inconstancy of the state governments, the mutability of their laws. Thus the primary concern of the framers with the form of government—structuring, as is necessary with individual identity, its elements in a proper, stable, and coherent fashion—and their relative inattention to parchment statements of rights. And the framers were probably correct in their judgment that a press which inflamed the passions, exciting fear, jealousy, or hatred of the government and its leaders, could not help the cause of deliberative identity and thus could not aid the cause of free government.

Self-government for the framers entailed the distinction—repeated in virtually all pre-twentieth-century discussions of freedom of speech—between liberty and license. Without that distinction, the cultivation of individual identity and the structuring of the elements of political power are both utterly arbitrary; all restraints on the individual become tyrannical, and obedience to the laws becomes servility.[22] In sum, they realized that liberty is worthless unless there is some good and truth to be pursued.

One major lesson we should learn from the framers, then, is that many common expressions of support for an expansive interpretation of freedom of speech and press invoke not a philosophy of self-government but one of nihilistic relativism. Consider Holmes's famous obiter dictum in *Gitlow* quoted above: "If in the long run the beliefs expressed in proletarian dictatorship are destined to be accepted by the dominant forces of the community, the only meaning of free speech is that they should be given their chance and have their way." Free speech stands on the same status as dictatorship of the proletariat; whatever time brings is right. Or consider the philosophical reflections that open Levy's exhaustive work: "Neither freedom of speech nor of press could become a civil liberty until people believed that the truth of their opinions, especially their religious opinions was relative rather than absolute."[23] If all opinions are relative, then the opinion in favor of freedom of speech is itself relative. At this point, where liberty is indistinguishable from license, it suddenly transforms to nihilism, for if all opinions are relative, then nothing is forbidden and all is permitted.

This reflection suggests another question. If we are not bound by original intent, are we unbound? Is everything, as a matter of constitutional interpretation, permitted? Can we add to the things that the adopters knew the things that they didn't know, without abandoning all ground of authority? Again, we must return to the questions that I dealt with perfunctorily at the outset: What do we mean by "original intent"? and, Is there a conception of it that is authoritative?

A theory of the Constitution which takes seriously a theory of original intent must give careful attention to the adopters' interpretive intent:[24] How did they intend the document to be interpreted? In this regard, we should note the approach that Madison took in regard to the free press clause. A decade after the adoption of the First Amendment, Madison advocated a meaning of free press which it is hard to imagine was in the minds of most Americans, including his own, in 1789.[25] As part of the Jeffersonian response to the Sedition Act of 1798, Madison repudiated a significant component of the common-law understanding of seditious libel, libel of the government itself.[26] Arguing from the form of government, he maintained that the Blackstonian understanding of free speech, appropriate for a country based on sovereignty of the legislature, is not appropriate for a country based on sovereignty of the people. Where in Britain the sovereign Parliament maintains rights against the prerogative of the king, in America, the sovereign people must maintain their rights against the government. Intelligent selection of representatives and informed judgment of their conduct are utterly dependent on a free press, Madison maintained, and "the right of electing the members of the Government constitutes . . . the essence of free and responsible government."[27] That is to say, Madison did not base his interpretation of free speech, either at the federal or state level, on the specific intentions of the adopters but on his best understanding of the true meaning of free speech in a democratic republic.

We should note as well that the authority sought and won by *The*

Federalist Papers rests upon a similar sort of claim. The authority and respect accorded to Publius's explication of the Constitution derives not from his intimate knowledge of specific intentions—which was never claimed[28]—but from his patriotism, comprehension of America's historical situation, and, most important, his profound understanding of the nature of republican government. If the identity of Publius had never been revealed, I think we would be foolish to regard his arguments as any less persuasive or authoritative than we do today.

It follows from this observation that my preliminary definition of "original intent" is defective, at least upon its own terms.[29] This definition accepted the "criteria" understanding of meaning, following the apparent sense of some advocates of original jurisprudence and contemporary language philosophy. For most of the latter, how we divide up the world and the names we attach to those divisions are merely matters of convention. For the framers, the adopters, and I think for a coherent theory of the Constitution, on the other hand, there is a nature to the divisions,[30] a nature to republican government, and a nature to freedom of speech. Original intent, properly understood, should entail not an intention to render the contemporaneous definitions of the words authoritative, but to indicate the "thing" whose nature, in light of our collective experience, we as interpreters must try to comprehend. In place of a "criteria" meaning of original intent, this approach would focus on "natural" meaning.[31]

No doubt, it will be objected that such an understanding of original intent undermines one strong rationale for this form of jurisprudence, that is, to confine the discretion of the interpreter. And without further elaboration of the concept, the charge is certainly understandable, for it might seem to open the door to interpretations wildly divergent from what the framers intended by any reasonable understanding of "intent." Here, I can only point to *The Federalist Papers* and aspects of Tocqueville's *Democracy in America* as examples of the sort of "natural" interpretation I have in mind.[33]

Finally, I should make clear that as I understand original intent here in this revised form, the task of discovering the true meaning of the things indicated by the words of the Constitution is a task not intended for the judges alone. Indeed, on questions concerning the constitutionality of statutory law, their judgment is a secondary one, the primary one being vested with the legislators. And to avoid duplicating the legislative function, courts should follow the rule articulated by James Bradley Thayer, to declare an act of the legislature unconstitutional only if it involves a clear mistake of constitutional meaning. If my conclusion in favor of "natural" interpretation alarms conservatives, my conclusion in favor of judicial restraint is certain to do no less for the liberals. But in both cases I think the concern is unfounded. For the reluctance of the Federalists to enact a bill of rights was not entirely unwarranted, and it remains true that the form of government is itself our strongest bill of rights.

Notes

1. *See, e.g.*, Brest, *The Misconceived Quest for the Original Understanding*, 60 B.U.L. Rev. 204 (1980); Dworkin, *The Forum of Principle*, 56 N.Y.U. L. Rev. 20 (1981); Moore, *A Natural Law Theory of Interpretation*, 58 S. Cal. L. Rev. 279 (1985).

2. *See, e.g.*, R. Berger, *Government by Judiciary: The Transformation of the Fourteenth Amendment* (Cambridge: Harvard Univ. Press, 1977), chap. 20.

3. In conceptualizing original intent this way, I am drawing on the splendid article by Michael Moore, *A Natural Law Theory of Interpretation*. I am also indebted to this article for the idea of "natural meaning," which is discussed below.

4. Obviously, I am not reaching for precision in this definition. For further elaboration of the concept, *see* W. Blackstone, *Commentaries on the Laws of England* (London, 1765-69), vol. 4, chap. 11, sec. 13; J. Stephen, *A History of the Criminal Law of England*, vol. 2 (London, 1883), pp. 304–5.

5. Z. Chafee, *Free Speech in the United States* (Cambridge: Harvard Univ. Press, 1941), chap. 21.

6. *Gitlow v. New York*, 268 U.S. 652, 673 (1925).

7. L. Levy, *Legacy of Suppression* (New York: Oxford Univ. Press, 1960).

8. L. Levy, *The Emergence of a Free Press* (New York: Oxford Univ. Press, 1985).

9. Ibid., p. 253.

10. Madison to Richard Peters, Aug. 19, 1789, quoted in ibid., p. 261.

11. Ibid., p. 266.

12. B. Schwartz, ed., *The Bill of Rights: A Documentary History*, vol. 2 (New York: Chelsea House, 1971), pp. 1149, 1096.

13. Levy, *The Emergence of a Free Press*, p. 267.

14. Levy reported that "twelve of the thirteen original states, all but Connecticut, expressly adopted the common-law system after separating from England." And "[n]o state abolished or altered the common law of criminal defamation in general or seditious libel in particular, and no state court ruled that the free press clause of its state constitution rendered void the prosecution of a libel" (ibid., p. 183).

15. Blackstone, *Commentaries*, chap. 2, sec. 13.

16. Levy, *The Emergence of a Free Press*, pp. 177, 269.

17. Bork, *Neutral Principles and Some First Amendment Problems*, 47 Ind. L.J. 1, 21 (1971).

18. Levy, *The Emergence of a Free Press*, pp. 204, 277–78.

19. Ibid., p. 275, n. 132.

20. Ibid., pp. 272, xvi.

21. W. Berns, *The First Amendment and the Future of American Democracy* (New York: Basic Books, 1976), chap. 3.

22. A. de Tocqueville, *Democracy in America* (New York: Harper and Row, 1969).

23. Levy, *The Emergence of a Free Press*, p. 5.

24. *See* Brest, *The Misconceived Quest for the Original Understanding*, p. 215.

25. Levy, *The Emergence of a Free*

Press, pp. 323–24. Accepting for the sake of argument that Madison did intend in 1789 the absolute bar to legislation restricting the press that he advocated in 1799–80, we should note that a theory of original intent as I have defined it above would bind him to the prevailing intention. I.e., after ratification he would have had to abandon his understanding of what freedom of speech means in favor of the common sentiment.

26. Berns, *The First Amendment*, p. 113. On whether he meant to repudiate as well criminal libel for defamation of public officials, compare Berns with Levy, *Legacy of Suppression*, pp. 321–22.

27. Quoted in Berns, *The First Amendment*, p. 119.

28. Nor, of course, could it have been in reference to the adopters.

29. This is a fairly common observation, and the debate deserves more attention than I can give it here. For a spirited defense of interpretive intent as a specific intent, what I have called "criteria," *see* R. Berger, *Death Penalties: The Supreme Court's Obstacle Course* (Cambridge: Harvard Univ. Press, 1982).

30. *See* Moore, *A Natural Law Theory of Interpretation*, pp. 280–300.

31. The distinction made here bears some obvious resemblance to Dworkin's influence distinction between concepts and conceptions (R. Dworkin, *Taking Rights Seriously* [Cambridge: Harvard Univ. Press, 1977], p. 134). I've chosen distinct language because Dworkin's theory of meaning is one of deep and shallow contentions rather than of nature. More significantly, his deep conventionalism leads him to reject the concept of a human good; thus his jurisprudence cannot possibly comprehend what the framers pointed to when they spoke of "liberty," as that term was understood in distinction to license.

32. Of contemporary works pertaining to particular clauses, I would cite F. Schauer, *Free Speech* (New York: Cambridge Univ. Press, 1982) and W. Berns, *For Capital Punishment* (New York: Basic Books, 1979) as engaging in the sort of "nature of the thing" analysis that I have in mind. For a work dealing with constitutional interpretation more broadly, I would cite C. Wolfe, *The Rise of Modern Judicial Review* (New York: Basic Books, 1986).

JULES B. GERARD

8. May Society Preserve a Modicum of Decorum in Public Discourse?

Suppose a federal judge in a criminal trial has just overruled the defense attorney's effort to exclude a critical piece of incriminating evidence. Suppose the attorney, overcome by the emotion of the moment, exclaims, "You God-damned, motherfucking, fascist son of a bitch, you are railroading my client into jail in violation of his constitutional rights." And further suppose that the judge holds the lawyer in contempt of court for his outburst. What would the U.S. Supreme Court do if it agreed to review the lawyer's conviction?

A number of things are clear on the basis of precedent. First, if the lawyer had addressed the language to a school board at a meeting attended by women and children, the First Amendment would preclude punishing him. Second, if he had embroidered the words on the back of his coat and worn the coat into the courthouse, the First Amendment would preclude punishing him. Third, if he had uttered the words at a student assembly in a college chapel, the First Amendment would preclude punishing him. Fourth, if he had uttered the words to a police officer who was arresting his client, the First Amendment would preclude punishing him. But, fifth, since he addressed the words to a judge in a courtroom, the Supreme Court will sustain his conviction—and it won't even mention the First Amendment!

The current state of the law is troublesome not because the lawyer may be held in contempt but because society may not protect itself in the other situations. Before reviewing the events that led to this aberration, two preliminary matters may be laid aside.

First, the idea contained in the lawyer's outburst (criticism of the judge's ruling), as distinguished from the vulgar words used to express it, is entitled to constitutional protection. The issue is whether those words ought to be protected.

Second, the exclusive focus of this chapter is on expletives uttered in public, in places where other people have a right to be, and under circumstances that make it impossible for others to avoid them. It does not deal with private conversation or with language printed in newspapers, magazines, or books.[1]

Cohen v. California was the first step on the road to the present.[2] Cohen wore a jacket emblazoned with the words "Fuck the Draft" into a courthouse where others were present. He was convicted of violating a statute which prohibited "maliciously and willfully disturb[ing] the peace or quiet of any neighborhood or person . . . by . . . offensive conduct." In a 5–4 decision written by Justice Harlan, the Supreme Court reversed.

Harlan began by observing that the conviction rested on the words Cohen used, not on the underlying message. Focusing on the words, he rejected three arguments the state offered to justify regulating offensive language. Preserving "an appropriately decorous atmosphere in the courthouse" was inadequate because the statute was not limited to certain designated places but was applicable everywhere. Nor did the case fall within the relatively few categories, such as "fighting words" and obscenity, in which the Supreme Court had previously approved bans on certain forms of speech. Finally, the conviction could not be upheld on the ground that those who were offended by the words were a captive audience; they "could effectively avoid further bombardment of their sensibilities simply by averting their eyes."[3]

Having identified what the case did not involve, Harlan then defined the issue as whether states, "acting as guardians of public morality, may properly remove this offensive word from the public vocabulary . . . in order to maintain what they regard as a suitable level of discourse within the body politic."[4] He held the states could not do so.

He began by emphasizing that "most situations where the state has a justifiable interest in regulating speech will fall within one or more of the established [categories]," such as obscenity and "fighting words," that he had just held were not applicable. "The usual rule," he said, was that "governmental bodies may not prescribe the form or the content of individual expression."[5] He found three reasons why that "rule" should govern the outcome of this case.[6]

The first reason was the "stopping point" argument. "No readily ascertainable general principle exists," Harlan argued, by which to distinguish one offensive word from another. Here Harlan used language that has become a virtual First Amendment proverb as well as his epitaph: "one man's vulgarity is another's lyric."[7]

The second reason, illustrated by this very case, was that words frequently are chosen for the emotion they convey as well as for their meaning. "We cannot sanction the view that the Constitution, while solicitous of the cognitive content of individual speech, has little or no regard for that emotive function which, practically speaking, may often be the more important element of the overall message."[8]

The third reason offered by Harlan was that permitting states to censor particular words ran a substantial risk of permitting them to suppress ideas in the process. "Indeed, governments might soon seize upon the censorship of particular words as a convenient guise for banning the expression of unpopular views."[9]

Harlan then was able to state the Court's holding in a sentence: "Absent a more particularized and compelling reason for its actions, the State may not . . . make the simple public display . . . of this single four-letter expletive a criminal offense."[10]

The Court took its second step toward the present one year later in *Gooding v. Wilson.*[11] When police attempted to stop Wilson from blocking the entrance to a government building, he said to them, "White son of a bitch, I'll kill you"; "You son of a bitch, I'll choke you to death"; and "You son of a bitch, if you ever put your hands on me again, I'll cut you all to pieces." He was convicted of violating a statute which made it a crime for anyone, without provocation, to "use to or of another, and in his presence, . . . opprobrious words or abusive language, tending to cause a breach of the peace." In an opinion written by Justice Brennan, the Court held that the statute, as construed by the state courts, was not limited to the category of "fighting words." Hence the statute was susceptible of being applied to protected speech and therefore was unconstitutionally overbroad. The Court affirmed a judgment overturning Wilson's conviction.

A few months later, the Court vacated and remanded three cases. Two of the cases, *Rosenfeld v. New Jersey*[12] and *Brown v. Oklahoma,*[13] were to be reconsidered in light of both *Cohen* and *Gooding*. The other, *Lewis v. City of New Orleans,*[14] was returned for reconsideration in light of *Gooding* only. Rosenfeld had spoken at a public school board meeting attended by approximately 150 people, 25 of whom were women and 40 of whom were children. During his speech, he used the adjective "motherfucking" four times, variously describing the teachers, the school system, the school board, the town, the county, and the country. Brown had spoken before a college audience of both genders in a chapel. During a question-and-answer period, he twice referred to some police officers as "motherfucking fascist pig cops." Lewis was arrested after she called police officers who were arresting her son "God damned motherfucking police." She was convicted of violating a city ordinance reading, "It shall be unlawful . . . for any person wantonly to curse or revile or to use obscene or opprobrious language toward . . . any member of the city police while in the actual performance of his duty."

The *Lewis* case returned to the Court two years later.[15] On remand, the Louisiana Supreme Court had construed the ordinance to be limited to the category of "fighting words" and had reaffirmed its earlier judgment sustaining Lewis's conviction. The Supreme Court reversed in an opinion by Justice Brennan. Even though the state court had said the ordinance was limited to "fighting words" and could be used only against them, it had not given a limiting definition to the adjective "opprobrious" in the ordinance.

Not all "opprobrious" words were "fighting words." Therefore the statute was susceptible of being applied to protected speech and was unconstitutionally overbroad, despite the state court's attempt to narrow it.

A review of the contempt of court cases may usefully begin with *Mayberry v. Pennsylvania*,[16] which was decided one year before *Cohen*. Mayberry and two codefendants were on trial in a state court for attempted prison break and holding a hostage. The defendants rejected appointed attorneys and elected to proceed *pro se*. All were convicted. At their sentencing, the trial judge also held them in contempt of court for eleven episodes that had occurred during the trial and imposed additional sentences of from eleven to twenty-two years. Three examples are enough to provide the flavor and the range of these episodes. (1) At a side-bar conference, Mayberry said to the judge, "It doesn't appear that I am going to get [a fair trial] the way you are overruling all our motions . . . being like a hatchet man for the State." When the judge announced, "This side bar is over," Mayberry replied, "You dirty son of a bitch." (2) When the judge sustained the prosecutor's objection to one of his questions, Mayberry said, "You ought to be Gilbert and Sullivan the way you sustain the district attorney every time he objects." (3) On a similar occasion, Mayberry said, "Now, I am going to produce my defense in this case and not be railroaded into my life sentence by any dirty, tyrannical old dog like yourself." The state supreme court affirmed the contempt sentences.

A unanimous Supreme Court left no doubt that Mayberry could be convicted of contempt of court for his utterances. The opinion of the Court, written by Justice Douglas, characterized them as "brazen efforts to denounce, insult, and slander the court," as "downright insults of a trial judge," and, most interesting of all, as "tactics taken from street brawls and transported to the courtroom."[17] Douglas's righteous indignation jumps right off the page! The Court went on to reverse the contempt convictions, however, on the ground that due process under the circumstances required the contempt charges to be tried by a different judge. Nowhere did the Court mention the First Amendment.

The petitioner in *In re Little* attempted to defend himself when the judge refused to grant him a continuance even though his retained attorney was engaged in another trial.[18] In his summation to the jury, Little said that the judge was biased, had prejudged his case, and that he was a political prisoner. The judge held him in contempt for these statements. In a per curiam opinion, the Supreme Court reversed on due process grounds.

Little bears on this discussion for another reason. As Little was being led from the courtroom after being held in contempt, he called the judge a "motherfucker." None of the state courts had relied on that explosion to justify the contempt conviction, however, and the Supreme Court therefore did not consider it. But the per curiam opinion commented, "This language in a courtroom is, of course, reprehensible and cannot be tolerated."[19] That quotation was in an opinion delivered less than a year after *Cohen* and devoid of any mention of the First Amendment!

The final contempt case is *Eaton v. City of Tulsa*.[20] Eaton was on trial for violating a city ordinance. While being cross-examined, he referred to a person who had allegedly assaulted him as a "chicken shit." The trial judge promptly held him in contempt of court. The Supreme Court summarily reversed in another per curiam opinion, again on due process grounds. This sentence appears toward the beginning of the opinion: "This single isolated usage of street vernacular, not directed at the judge or any officer of the court, cannot constitutionally support the conviction of criminal contempt."[21] The clear implication, of course, was that the result would have been different had the language been directed at the judge.

Society's effort to preserve a modicum of decorum in public discourse raises two issues. One is the Supreme Court's use of overbreadth doctrine on behalf of undeserving[22] litigants to invalidate laws enacted in good faith to protect a decent and civilized community. A comparison of the contempt of court cases with the other cases reveals that the Court's use of overbreadth doctrine in this area is an exercise in hypocrisy. One agency of government—the judiciary—is empowered by the Court to punish offensive language directed at its officers without being required even to hint in advance at the kind of language that might be considered offensive. That is overbreadth run amok. But every other agency of government is required by the Court to define the language that it considers offensive with such rigorous punctilio that drafting legislation becomes a practical impossibility. That is overbreadth doctrine run amok.

Overbreadth doctrine aside, the fundamental issue is whether the First Amendment permits government to regulate the public utterance of words universally regarded as offensive in order to foster an environment of decency and civility, to promote the orderly administration of public affairs, and to protect the sensibilities of individual citizens from unprovoked and despicable abuse. In *Cohen v. California*, the Supreme Court gave a negative answer to that question.

Central to Harlan's thesis in *Cohen* was the argument that the words prohibited by the California statute did not fall within any of the "established categories" of permissible content regulation.[23] He mentioned two such categories: obscenity and "fighting words." The words prohibited by the statute clearly were not "obscene" as the Supreme Court has defined that term.[24] The other category requires closer examination.

The notion that "fighting words" may be banned stems from *Chaplinsky v. New Hampshire*, a case decided in 1942.[25] Chaplinsky was a Jehovah's Witness who was distributing literature and denouncing organized religion as a racket. Citizens complained to the city marshal, Bowering, who told them Chaplinsky was within his rights but also warned Chaplinsky that the crowd was getting restless. A disturbance occurred later, and a traffic officer on the scene began escorting Chaplinsky to the police station, although he apparently had not arrested him. On the way they met Bowering, who had been told a riot was in progress. Chaplinsky admitted saying to Bowering (except he denied invoking the Deity), "You are a God damned racketeer," and "a damned fascist and the whole government of Rochester are fascists." Chaplinsky was convicted of violating a statute which provided: "No person shall address any offensive, derisive or annoying word to any other person who is lawfully in any street or other public place, nor call him by an offensive or derisive name, nor make any noise or exclamation in his presence and hearing with intent to deride, offend or annoy him, or to prevent him from pursuing his lawful business or occupation."[26]

In affirming Chaplinsky's conviction, the state supreme court said,

> The word "offensive" [in the statute] is not to be defined in terms of what a particular addressee thinks. . . . The test is what men of common intelligence would understand would be words likely to cause an addressee to fight. . . . The English language has a number of words and expressions which by general consent are "fighting words" when said without a disarming smile. . . . The statute . . . does no more than prohibit the face-to-face words plainly likely to cause a breach of the peace by the addressee.[27]

The U.S. Supreme Court held the statute constitutional as so construed. Up to this point Harlan's opinion in *Cohen* is again correct. The words on Cohen's jacket were not addressed to anyone in particular, nor were they uttered in a face-to-face situation; hence they were not the kind of "fighting words" that were at issue in *Chaplinsky*. But that is not the whole story.

The issue, as Harlan himself defined it, was not whether Cohen's utterance was "fighting words," but whether it fell into any "established category" of speech that could be banned because of the words used. On that point, the *Chaplinsky* opinion, which was written by Justice Murphy, a known champion of the First Amendment,[28] delivers a message quite different from the one Harlan drew from it. Before analyzing the terms of the New Hampshire statute, Murphy had said:

> There are certain well-defined and narrowly limited classes of speech, the prevention and punishment of which have never been thought to raise any constitutional problem. These include the lewd and obscene, the profane, the libelous, and the insulting or "fighting" words—those which by their very utterance inflict injury or tend to incite an immediate breach of the peace. It has been well observed that such utterances are no essential part of any exposition of ideas, and are of such slight social value as a step to truth that any

> benefit that may be derived from them is clearly outweighed by the social interest in order and morality.[29]

Murphy plainly said that among the categories of public speech that may be punished without raising constitutional problems are the lewd and the profane, "those which by their very utterance inflict injury." That he used the disjunctive in his summary—"those which by their very utterance inflict injury or tend to incite an immediate breach of the peace"—proves that he was speaking of more than just "fighting words."[30] Harlan simply ignored the obvious meaning of Murphy's statement.

Nor can it be doubted that Murphy's conclusion—that the public utterance of lewd and profane words may constitutionally be punished—was correct at the time he stated it. When the First Amendment was proposed and ratified and when the Fourteenth Amendment was ratified, laws forbidding such public utterances were common.[31] Until *Cohen*, indeed, no one seems to have doubted society's authority to ban them.

Uncharacteristically, Harlan made no investigation of the historical background. Thus Harlan's conclusion that Cohen's utterance did not fall within an "established category" of speech that may be banned because of the words used is at best dubious—as a matter of stare decisis or of constitutional history.

Harlan then moved to the three "particularized considerations" that he argued required the reversal of Cohen's conviction. The first of these was the stopping point. "How is one to distinguish this from any other offensive word?" he asked rhetorically.[32] One answer is to point out that the comedian George Carlin, in his "Filthy Words" monologue, seemed to have little trouble identifying "the cuss words and the words that you can't say."[33] When I was growing up, the word "fuck" wasn't in even the unabridged dictionary. The editors of that work apparently did not find it impossible to distinguish that word from others. Surely if comedians and dictionary editors can distinguish the unspeakable from the merely offensive, judges and lawyers can too. "Even a dog distinguishes between being stumbled over and being kicked," Justice Holmes once remarked.[34]

"It is nevertheless often true," Harlan continued, "that one man's vulgarity is another's lyric."[35] I confess I have been puzzling over that sentence for more then fifteen years and still am uncertain what Harlan meant by it. Assuming he intended it to be taken literally, it is meaningless, for it tells us nothing at all. With equal force and equivalent grace, one could say, "One man's obscenity is another's lyric." It has been known for some time that many people find obscenity attractive and stimulating. But so what? That surely would not be accepted as a legitimate reason for invalidating obscenity regulations. As an explanation for overturning regulations of offensive speech in public, Harlan's beguiling epigram is a nullity.

Perhaps he meant only that some people are unaware that others regard certain words as profane. That is true. As a teenager I worked on a railroad section gang which employed a father and his son who were recent immigrants from West Virginia. I remember collapsing with laughter when the father once ordered his son to "stop that shitten cussing." Later, upon reading Chaucer in college, I discovered that "shitten" is an Old English word that meant "dirty" or "filthy."[36] And I learned that scholars believe that longtime residents of isolated rural and mountainous areas still retain aspects of Elizabethan or earlier English in their speech.[37] But if that is all he meant, Harlan could have waited for a case in which the speaker was genuinely surprised that others considered his words to be offensive.

Harlan's second "particularized consideration" was that the Constitution protects the emotive as well as the cognitive element of speech. "We cannot sanction the view that the Constitution, while solicitous of the cognitive content of individual speech, has little or no regard for that emotive function which, practically speaking, may often be the more important element of the overall message."[38] Here again Harlan overstated the case.[39] The issue was not whether the Constitution "has little or no regard" for the emotive element of speech. The issue, rather, was whether society must tolerate the indignity of being confronted by words deliberately chosen for their offensiveness just because Cohen found that to be the easiest way to communicate his emotions.

Consider a hypothetical variation on this theme. Suppose an advocate is arguing an abortion case before the Supreme Court. Suppose the advocate is one who sincerely believes that abortion is murder, and that the justices who held it to be a constitutional right were literally God-damned baby killers.[40] Could he call the justices that with impunity in oral argument? And reconsider the hypothetical that began this chapter. Are the depth of the lawyer's emotions and the accuracy with which they are conveyed constitutional justifications for his language?

Harlan tells us in *Cohen* that, absent more particularized and compelling reasons than that the audience is captive and contains women and children, "the simple public display . . . of this four-letter expletive" may not be made a crime. That must mean that "Fuck the Draft" could also be displayed on bumper stickers, placards carried on sidewalks, and even on billboards. If "Fuck the Draft" cannot be banned, then neither can "Fuck Earl Warren." (Not many years ago, you will recall, billboards and matchbook covers all over the nation carried the slogan "Impeach [Chief Justice] Earl Warren.") If the word cannot be banned, presumably neither could a cartoon depicting Warren raping a beautiful woman symbolizing the Constitution.[41] In 1980 a minor-party candidate for president of the United States used a radio commercial describing the platforms of the two major political parties as "bullshit." Hearing that word issue from radio loudspeakers gave many people an unpleasant jolt. I have seen a bumper sticker while driving on a street in St. Louis, a city not known as a hotbed of trendy radicalism. Its message was in two lines:

Have A Nice Day
Fuck Somebody.

Language like this is chosen solely for its offensive value. Its ideological content is not intended to be taken literally. These two features distinguish it from other sorts of offensive words. Compare, for example, the words "motherfucker" and "fascist" in the hypothetical that opened this essay. Both are offensive because of their ideological content. But "fascist" has some factual denotations and connotations that are, or at least may be, related to the criticism of the judge's ruling. The factual element of "motherfucker," on the other hand, is entirely unrelated to that criticism. The word is used not because it has some relevance to the factual context in which it is uttered but solely because of its quality as an insult. It is, in other words, devoid of legitimate cognitive content. Moreover, the use of these words is unnecessary even when their factual component has some relevance. Sophocles' *Oedipus Rex*, for example, could accurately be described as "a play about a motherfucker." But no one who was not intent on shocking his audience would characterize it that way. Alternative means of communicating the same message are always available.

If offensive language is constitutionally immune from regulation, is conduct that is intended to convey the same offensive message similarly immune?[42] As a result of another line of Supreme Court decisions, desecration or misuse of the American flag is now regarded as protected speech.[43] Suppose a critic of this nation carries a flag into a public park and, before a sizable crowd of picnickers, sun worshipers, and joggers of both sexes and all ages, drops his pants and defecates on it. Does the First Amendment immunize him from punishment? *Cohen* makes it obvious that he could not be punished for proclaiming "Shit on the United States" in the identical circumstances. The substitute conduct would be intended to communicate the same message, and doubtless would do so. It also would communicate the message with an appropriate degree of emotional fervor. It would do so in a needlessly offensive manner, of course, but that is clearly irrelevant after *Cohen*. If other users of the park are offended, they have merely to avert their eyes, according to the *Cohen* logic. Is it arguable that there is a constitutionally significant difference in public offensiveness between seeing someone defecate and hearing words like "motherfucker"? Whence comes the calculus to make distinctions like that?[44]

I see no "readily ascertainable general principle," as Harlan required in *Cohen*, to distinguish these situations one from another. I therefore believe the balance should be struck the other way. I believe society's interest in protecting its citizens from unwanted public confrontations with gutter language is substantial. I believe the interest in protecting the emotive element of speech, by comparison, is trivial when it takes the form of choosing language solely because it is known to be offensive to most people, and when it takes that form solely because that is the easiest way of communicating emotion. The ideological content of the message would not be affected. Only this deliberately rude way of transmitting it would be regulated.

Harlan's final "particularized consideration" addressed this point of suppressing ideas under the guise of regulating offensive language. "Governments might soon seize upon the censorship of particular words as a convenient guise for banning the expression of unpopular views," he suggested. I suppose it is theoretically possible that allowing government to forbid the public utterance of a few specific words might result in suppressing ideas. I concede, for example, that banning the display of the swastika makes it harder to communicate all of the evil messages associated with that hated symbol.[45] Like the swastika, words are only symbols. But it will take more than unsupported assertions, even by someone as revered as Harlan, to persuade me that the danger is more than trivial. I grew up—as did Harlan—in a generation in which those words were never used in public and were rarely used in print. I cannot think of a single idea to which I was denied access by the fact that these words were not used. Nor can I think of a single idea I have learned since, my understanding of which depended on, or was even facilitated by, the use of offensive language.

Some examples from another area may make the point more effectively. They come from movies that are on virtually everyone's list of all-time great films. Consider two scenes from *The Treasure of the Sierra Madre*. In one scene, Humphrey Bogart attempts to kill Tim Holt. What we see on the screen is Bogart, pistol in hand, following Holt into dense underbrush. We hear a shot and see Bogart reemerge from the brush. A few scenes later we see Holt, obviously injured, crawling along a path. In a scene toward the end of the movie, Bogart is hacked to death with machetes by a band of outlaws. All we see on the screen, however, are three mules in the foreground standing in front of men who are chopping at something with their weapons. Imagine how that movie would be composed today in color. Blood and gore would cover the screen. We probably would be treated to a close-up view of a severed carotid artery pumping out blood in great spurts and to the pitiful sounds of a human being dying a ghastly death.

Consider the episode of what feminists today would call marital rape in *Gone with the Wind*. Clark Gable seizes Vivien Leigh and carries her in his arms up the giant staircase, two steps at a time. The next scene is the following morning and shows Leigh in bed—alone. If that sequence were remade today, I have no doubt we would be offered all of the sounds and most of the sights of copulation.[46]

Neither of these movies would be one whit more comprehensible if the scenes I have suggested were added to them. The failure to include them did not interfere significantly with the communication of their messages. I think it is even arguable that they are in every way better movies without them.

Of course, it is possible that the ideological content of a message might be jeopardized by an impermissibly expansive view of what language is offensive. But it will be time enough for the Court to decide that case when—and if—it arises.

In contrast to *Cohen*, which is merely unpersuasive,[47] the Court's opinions in *Gooding* and the cases relying on it are indefensible. Whether one compares the words used[48] or the legislation involved[49] in *Chaplinsky* with the same feature of the later cases, the resulting differences are either trivial or nonexistent and cut in favor of sustaining the convictions rather than reversing them. The later decisions amount simply to a deceitful and covert overruling of *Chaplinsky*. They do not address the issues discussed in *Chaplinsky* or attempt to explain why that unanimous opinion by a known advocate of free speech values was defective.

Whether or not *Cohen*, *Gooding*, and their progeny were correctly decided, they clearly are not followed in the contempt of court cases. Instead, they are ignored. The Court's application of the free speech principles they represent, in other words, is decidedly not neutral.[50] The question is whether this discrepancy in the application of principle can be justified.

One possibility is that judges are entitled to some special status among the ranks of government officials that requires them to be shielded from offensive language that may be directed at all other officials and citizens. But why should that be so? Surely not because the tasks they perform are more important to society than those of mayors, prosecutors, governors, legislators, or, indeed, police officers. Even in this litigious age, only a small percentage of citizens ever have direct contact with the judicial system. And it would be hard to keep a straight face if one were forced to argue that judges' sensibilities are more tender than those of other human beings.

Another possibility is that the judicial process itself is so fragile that the interjection into it of offensive language dangerously weakens it. That is obviously ridiculous. Society's garbage is a staple of the judicial diet, as virtually any criminal case will attest.

Perhaps the argument should be that permitting open disrespect for judges in the courtroom runs the grave risk of bringing the whole judicial process into disrepute, since, as everyone knows, if people believe that officials are contemptible, they are likely to believe the processes those officials administer are contemptible too. This is closer to the mark. But it still doesn't explain why the judicial process, alone among governmental instrumentalities, is entitled to such sacrosanct treatment.

The answer, of course, is that there is no convincing justification for giving the judiciary and the judicial system such peculiarly favorable consideration. But that does not necessarily mean the *Cohen-Gooding* principles should be applied in the contempt of court cases. Rather, it suggests that a proper interpretation of the First Amendment would not deny society at least some of the same protection that the Supreme Court provides for its own turf.

Viewed in this light, the Court's refusal to apply the *Cohen-Gooding* principles to contempt of court cases is of major significance. It confirms two truths that refuse to stay buried beneath the Court's libertarian rhetoric. First, the free speech interests in offensive language cases are not nearly as important as the Court pretends they are everywhere outside the courtroom. Second, society's interests in protecting its institutions and citizens from unprovoked verbal abuse are substantially more important than the Court admits they are everywhere except inside the courtroom.

Justice Douglas was outraged that the *Mayberry* defendants engaged in "tactics taken from street brawls and transported [them] to the courtroom."[51] Neither he nor the Court has ever convincingly explained why "tactics taken from street brawls" are any more appropriate in school board meetings and college assemblies than they are in courtrooms, or why all members of society must risk confronting them every time they venture outside their homes.

If the proper conduct of judicial business requires that rules of decorum be observed, why may society not conclude that the efficient and orderly conduct of other kinds of public business requires the observance of similar norms of civilized behavior? If maintaining the integrity of the judicial process requires people to refrain from publicly insulting judges while they are engaged in their duties, why may society not conclude that maintaining the integrity of other governmental processes also demands a ban on profane aural aggression in public? Indeed, why may society not protect the dignity and sensibilities of every one of its citizens from indecent public abuse?

Society's interests are substantial. With regard to the individual, personal dignity and the right to be free from the intentional infliction of emotional distress are both implicated.[52] One commentator has suggested that *Chaplinsky* is "a quaint remnant of an earlier morality that has no place in a democratic society dedicated to the principle of free expression."[53] The argument made here certainly is a "remnant of an earlier morality." But so are laws against murder and rape. Are they also "quaint"? That *Chaplinsky* should be thought to have "no place in a democratic society dedicated to the principle of free expression" is astounding. That decision was by a unanimous Supreme Court more than a century and a half after the Constitution was adopted. Until *Cohen*, no one—not Madison, not Jefferson, no justice of the Court—ever realized that suppressing the kinds of language discussed in *Chaplinsky* violated "the principle of free expression" and had "no place in a democratic society."

It can be argued with greater force that banning profane public abuse directly advances the democratic interests protected by the First Amendment.[54] To begin with, this kind of speech is a form of bullying.[55] It discourages many people from taking part in democratic processes, such as school board meetings, simply to avoid the humiliation of being assaulted by profane loudmouths. In *Cohen*, Justice Harlan rejected the argument that offensive words could be banned from public places because the audience was captive and could not avoid exposure to them. His response, that people who were offended "could effectively avoid further bombardment of their sensibilities simply by averting their eyes,"[56] is fatuous. The justices have made rules that protect themselves and their colleagues from this kind of abuse, so it is perhaps not surprising that they don't appreciate the degradation it inflicts on others. Their very isolation may explain why their decisions reflect such a shocking disdain for public decency. But in the real world outside the fortress of the courtroom, the inclination to avoid bullies rather than confront them is surely not unusual.

Individual dignity, moreover, is as much a matter of concern for democracy as it is for the individual.[57] "Kings may speak haughtily and tyrants cruelly, insultingly, or even contemptuously, but men who share a legislative duty because they recognize the principle of the equality of all men must adopt a mode of address that reflects a disposition to respect the interests of others."[58] Government by consent requires everyone to abide by decisions made by the majority even when one is on the losing side. The assumption that this will be done rests on mutual trust and respect. Insults and abuse are inappropriate to this enterprise because they treat the enterprise as contemptible.

Finally, there is the governmental interest in avoiding violence. Writing for three dissenters in the *Rosenfeld* trio of cases, Chief Justice Burger expressed the concern in these words:

> It is barely a century since men in parts of this country carried guns constantly because the law did not afford protection. In that setting, the words used in these cases, if directed toward such an armed civilian, could well have led to death or bodily injury. When we undermine the general belief that the law will give protection against fighting words and profane and abusive language . . . we take steps to return to the law of the jungle. . . . If continued, this permissiveness will tend further to erode public confidence in the law—that subtle but indispensable ingredient of ordered liberty.[59]

The modern tendency is to scoff at such arguments. But this is an age when a subway rider who believes he is about to be mugged can receive substantial approbation for shooting his alleged assailants; when the father of a rape victim shoots the accused rapist; when abortion clinics and ROTC buildings are bombed, all because of firmly held convictions that the law offers inadequate protection to vital interests. In such an age, scorning this argument is folly.

Moreover, Burger's dissent raised another issue in addition to potential violence. Surely it is not fanciful to believe that public skepticism about the law's ability to protect vital interests will undermine democratic government. Two vital interests arguably are at stake. One is the transformation of illegitimate speech into legitimate discourse. For in the process of holding that it may not be suppressed in public, *Cohen* teaches that vulgar verbal abuse is an acceptable manner of communicating.[60] Society may be willing to tolerate the acquittal of a few aural bullies, as it will tolerate the failure to convict all murderers, if it has confidence that unprovoked verbal aggression will be regulated most of the time. But I believe it will resist the notion, as it would the repeal of statutes against homicide, that profane assaults may not be regulated at all.

There is, in addition, the link between speech and conduct. The total environment is likely to become as coarse and uncivilized as the speech that pervades it. If there is a difference between billboards displaying the words "Fuck President X" and ones exhibiting a cartoon of President X raping the Statue of Liberty, it is only slight. The step between constitutionalizing the words "Shit on the United States" and validating the act of defecating on the flag is a short one. Alexander Bickel marveled that anyone should be surprised that pimps and prostitutes, muggers and pickpockets, congregated in areas infested by bookstores and movie theaters purveying so-called sexually explicit but nonobscene fare. In his felicitous phrase, "Where nothing is unspeakable, nothing is undoable."[61]

Against these substantial interests must be balanced whatever interests are implicated in banning profane public assaults on sensibilities. Those interests cannot be weighty, if for no other reason than that alternative language is always available to communicate both the message and the emotion underlying it.[62] At a time when society is distressed at what seems to be a growing rate of illiteracy in the nation, it hardly makes sense to discourage literacy.

The remaining question is whether this subcategory of unprotected speech[63] can be defined with enough precision as to avoid the risk of endangering communications that ought to be included within the "freedom of speech" protected by the First Amendment. I believe that it can be, if appropriate allowances are made for the inevitable uncertainties that are inherent in the use of words to convey meaning.[64] The Supreme Court itself has recognized the need to make these allowances in speech cases: "Condemned to the use of words, we can never expect mathematical certainty from our language. The words of the Rockford ordinance are marked by 'flexibility and reasonable breadth, rather than meticulous specificity,' . . .

but we think it is clear what the ordinance as a whole prohibits."[65] The test, then, is whether a regulation can be drafted which would make clear what words are prohibited.[66]

The first consideration, one that I have tried to emphasize throughout this chapter, is that everybody already knows what those words are. In *Chaplinsky*, the decisions of both the state court and the Supreme Court were explicitly based on this consideration.[67] Moreover, until the *Cohen-Gooding* line of cases cast doubt on the utility of their enterprise, the drafters of the *Model Penal Code* believed it was possible to define the words with sufficient precision to pass constitutional muster. Their suggested formulation was: "A person is guilty of disorderly conduct if, with purpose to cause public inconvenience, annoyance or alarm, or recklessly creating a risk thereof, he: . . . (b) makes . . . offensively coarse utterance, gesture or display, or addresses abusive language to any person present."[68] "Offensively coarse utterance" would seem to be an adequate description of the kind of language that ought to be prohibitable.

A contrary argument would be that statutes like this ought to be unconstitutional because free speech is such a fragile commodity that it must be overprotected; that is, unprotected speech must be protected to safeguard protected speech from suppression. Arguably, in other words, statutes like this must be prohibited because insensitive or manipulative lower court judges might sometimes apply them to protected speech, and any such improper application is a greater danger to democratic government than requiring society to tolerate unprotected profane public abuse.[69]

That argument is not persuasive. If broad prophylactic measures that shelter unprotected speech are required, they would seem more appropriate in the contempt cases than in the offensive public speech cases. First, the Supreme Court has developed no First Amendment guidelines at all in the contempt cases; the power to hold someone in contempt for speech in the courtroom remains essentially arbitrary. Second, if insensitive or manipulative judges are to be feared, it seems obvious that they pose a greater danger when they themselves feel insulted than when they are merely construing a statute in a situation where they have no personal involvement. Finally, case-by-case adjudication is what occurs now in the contempt of court cases. There is no reason to suppose it would be less adequate to protect essential free speech values in the public offensiveness cases.

The Court itself has on occasion departed from its *Cohen-Gooding* principles outside the courtroom. In *FCC v. Pacifica Foundation*,[70] it held that a radio station could be disciplined for broadcasting an "indecent but not obscene" monologue during the daytime. In the recent *Fraser* case,[71] the Court sustained the punishment of a high school student for making a lewd speech before an assembly. Chief Justice Burger said for a majority: "The undoubted freedom to advocate unpopular and controversial views in schools and classrooms must be balanced against society's countervailing interest in teaching students the boundaries of socially appropriate behavior. Even the most heated political discourse in a democratic society requires consideration for the personal sensibilities of the other participants and audiences."[72]

Perhaps *Pacifica* and *Fraser* are straws in the wind, indications that the Court may sometime soon return to the path so clearly and correctly marked years ago by *Chaplinsky*.

Notes

1. Hence *Papish v. Board of Curators*, 410 U.S. 667 (1973) (expulsion of college student for distributing periodical containing a cartoon depicting police officers raping the Statute of Liberty and an article using the word "motherfucker" overturned) is of no direct concern.

2. *Cohen v. California*, 403 U.S. 15 (1971).

3. *Id.* at 19, 21.

4. *Id.* at 22–23.

5. *Id.* at 24.

6. The Supreme Court applies different standards of constitutionality to regulations of speech. The most stringent standard is applied to regulations that are based on the content of the speech. That is the rule quoted by Harlan in the text. A regulation of speech aimed at certain words is, on its face at least, one based on "content" as that word is normally understood. However, the Court's antipathy for content regulations originally was designed to block governments from censoring ideas, or "viewpoints"; was intended, in other words, to prevent governments from favoring one side of an argument by suppressing the other side(s). In this sense, a regulation of the use of certain words arguably is not a content regulation at all because it regulates all points of view evenhandedly and is thus "viewpoint neutral." *See generally* Stone, *Content Regulation and the First Amendment*, 25 Wm. & Mary L. Rev. 189 (1983).

The Court has been erratic, to put it mildly, in its willingness to distinguish viewpoint- from content-based regulations and to reserve the application of its stringent standard for the former. *E.g., compare Metromedia, Inc. v. City of San Diego*, 453 U.S. 490 (1981) (stringent standard applied to overturn a viewpoint-neutral regulation of billboards with certain content) *with Heffron v. International Society for Krishna Consciousness*, 452 U.S. 640 (1981) (stringent standard not applied to viewpoint-neutral regulation of solicitation—manifestly a content-based classification—on state fairgrounds). *See* Stone, *Content Regulation and the First Amendment*.

7. 403 U.S. at 25. Even short biographical sketches of Harlan include it. *See, e.g.*, G. Stone, L. Seidman, C. Sunstein, and M. Tushnet, *Constitutional Law* (Boston: Little, Brown, 1986), p. lxi.

8. 403 U.S. at 26.

9. *Id.*

10. *Id.*

11. *Gooding v. Wilson*, 405 U.S. 518 (1972).

12. *Rosenfeld v. New Jersey*, 408 U.S. 901 (1972).

13. *Brown v. Oklahoma*, 408 U.S. 914 (1972).

14. *Lewis v. City of New Orleans*, 408 U.S. 913 (1972).

15. *Lewis v. City of New Orleans*, 415 U.S. 130 (1974).

16. *Mayberry v. Pennsylvania*, 400 U.S. 455 (1970).

17. *Id.* at 462.

18. *In re* Little, 404 U.S. 553 (1972).

19. *Id.* at 554.

20. *Eaton v. City of Tulsa*, 415 U.S. 697 (1974).

21. *Id.* at 698.

22. By "undeserving" I mean litigants who have used offensive language that is devoid of meaningful ideological content in the context where employed, that was deliberately chosen solely because of its offensiveness, and that the Court itself appears to concede could be punished if only the statute forbidding it had been drafted more narrowly.

23. *See* text at note 5, *supra*.

24. *See Miller v. California*, 413 U.S. 15 (1973).

25. *Chaplinsky v. New Hampshire*, 315 U.S. 568 (1942).

26. *Id.* at 569.

27. As quoted in *id.* at 573.

28. *See, e.g.*, Stone et al., *Constitutional Law*, p. lxv, or any other biography of Murphy.

29. 315 U.S. at 571–72. The last sentence is a quotation from *Cantwell v. Connecticut*, 310 U.S. 296, 309–10 (1940).

30. I recognize, of course, that Murphy may have been using "lewd" and "obscene" as synonyms to cover only one category. But the Court's first effort to define obscenity came more than fifteen years after Murphy's opinion in *Chaplinsky*, in *Roth v. United States*, 354 U.S. 476 (1957). And it was only with Harlan's opinion in *Cohen* itself that the gloss on the Court's definition—that obscenity "must be, in some significant way, erotic" (403 U.S. at 20)—was added. Thus it is arguable that, at the time Murphy wrote, the public utterance of simple sexual expletives could be punished even if they did not meet the Court's subsequently announced criteria for obscenity. I believe this to be the more persuasive reading of *Chaplinsky*, and it justifies the textual statement that lewd words constitute a distinct category. *Accord* Stone et al., *Constitutional Law*, p. 1146. And *see* note 31, *infra*.

31. *See Roth v. United States*, 354 U.S. 476, 482–83(1957): "The guarantees of freedom of expression in effect in 10 of the 14 States which by 1792 had ratified the Constitution gave no absolute protection to every utterance. Thirteen of the 14 States provided for the prosecution of libel, and all of those States made either blasphemy or profanity, or both, statutory crimes. As early as 1712, Massachusetts made it criminal to publish 'any filthy, obscene, or profane song, pamphlet, libel or mock sermon.' . . . Thus, profanity and obscenity were related offenses. [Footnotes omitted.]"

32. 403 U.S. at 25.

33. As quoted in *FCC v. Pacifica Foundation*, 438 U.S. 726, 751 (1978).

34. O. Holmes, *The Common Law* (Boston: Little, Brown, 1881), p. 3.

35. 403 U.S. at 25.

36. In modern translation, lines 503–4

of the "Prologue" to the *Canterbury Tales* read: "And shame it is to see—let priests take stock— / A shitten shepherd and a snowy flock." G. Chaucer, *The Canterbury Tales*, trans. N. Coghill [Baltimore: Penguin Classics, 1952], p. 38. In the original, they appear: "And shame it is, if a prest take keep, / A shiten shepherde and a clene sheep" (F. Robinson, ed., *The Poetical Works of Chaucer* [Boston: Houghton Mifflin, 1933], p. 24).

37. H. Mencken, *The American Language*, 4th ed. (New York: Knopf, 1947), pp. 124–29.

38. 403 U.S. at 26.

39. "Surely the State has no right to cleanse public debate to the point where it is grammatically palatable to the most squeamish among us" (403 U.S. at 25). But *Cohen* obviously had nothing to do with grammatical squeamishness.

If society had the power to regulate on the basis of grammatical squeamishness, radio and television sports programs would be eliminated for the atrocities they regularly commit on the English language. My current favorite example comes from KMOX radio in St. Louis: "Stay tuned for Mike and I's sports open line." (Spelled phonetically, what he said was, "Mike and Eyes sports open line.")

40. For an instructive example of non-neutral, result-oriented application of alleged free speech doctrine in exactly this context, *see* the Washington Supreme Court's decision in *Bering v. SHARE*, 106 Wn.2d 212, 721 P.2d 918 (Wash. en banc 1986).

41. *Cf.* note 1, *supra.*

42. Constitutional scholars call the problem addressed here "symbolic conduct" or "symbolic speech." *See generally* J. Nowak, R. Rotunda, and J. Young, *Constitutional Law*, 3d ed. (St. Paul: West, 1986), sec. 16.48–16.49.

43. *Texas v. Johnson*, 109 S. Ct. 2533 (1989), is the last case in the line. It was preceded by *Spence v. Washington*, 418 U.S. 405 (1974), *Street v. New York*, 394 U.S. 576 (1969), and *Smith v. Goguen*, 415 U.S. 566 (1974).

44. I do not mean to suggest that current doctrine provides no tools at all for distinguishing the two situations. The Court might invoke the speech-conduct distinction and treat the flag abuse hypothetical solely as conduct, not speech. But that distinction could hardly be described as a "readily ascertainable general principle," as *Cohen* requires. In the first place, too much conduct has already been held to be protected speech for the Court to be able to argue persuasively that it always distinguishes verbal from nonverbal communications. *See, e.g., Texas v. Johnson, supra* note 43. In the second place, the Court has been unprincipled in determining when to invoke the distinction and when to ignore it. *See, e.g., Haig v. Agee*, 453 U.S. 280 (1981).

45. The Skokie controversy is usefully summarized in Stone et al., *Constitutional Law*, pp. 1015–17.

46. Perhaps I should add, for the benefit of younger readers, that the movie did cause something of a scandal when it was released in 1939. That was because of Gable's final bit of dialogue: "Frankly, my dear, I don't give a damn." "Damn" was a word one just did not then use in public. There was at least one exception, based, not surprisingly, on patriotism: "Damn the torpedoes; full speed ahead."

47. *Contra, e.g.*, Farber, *Civilizing Public Discourse: An Essay on Professor Bickel, Justice Harlan, and the Endur-*

ing Significance of Cohen v. California, 1980 Duke L.J. 283.

48. For the language used in *Chaplinsky*, *see* text before note 26, *supra*; for that used in *Gooding*, *see* text following note 11, *supra*; for the other cases, *see* text after note 14, *supra*.

49. For the statute in *Chaplinsky*, *see* text at note 26, *supra*; for that in *Gooding*, *see* text following note 11, *supra*; for that in *Lewis*, *see* text after note 14, *supra*. *Compare* the ordinance upheld in *Grayned v. City of Rockford*, 408 U.S. 104 (1972), *infra* note 65.

50. *See* Bork, *Neutral Principles and Some First Amendment Problems*, 47 Ind. L.J. 1 (1971).

51. 400 U.S. at 462.

52. *See, e.g.*, W. Keeton, D. Dobbs, R. Keeton, and D. Owen, *Prosser and Keeton on the Law of Torts*, 5th ed. (New York: Foundation Press, 1984), pp. 54–66, which does not necessarily support the position taken in the text.

53. Gard, *Fighting Words as Free Speech*, 58 Wash. U.L.Q. 531, 536 (1980).

54. The various interests that have been argued to be protected by the First Amendment are canvassed in M. Nimmer, *Freedom of Speech* (New York: Melville Nimmer, 1984), chap. 1.

55. *See* A. Bickel, *The Morality of Consent* (New Haven: Yale Univ. Press, 1975), pp. 72–75: "There is such a thing as verbal violence, a kind of cursing, assaultive speech that amounts to almost physical aggression, bullying that is not less punishing because it is simulated. Thus there is a difference . . . between a publication that vigorously criticizes the police and one that depicts them in a cartoon as raping the Statue of Liberty. . . . This sort of speech constitutes an assault. More, and equally important, it may create a climate, an environment in which conduct and actions that were not possible before become possible. . . .

". . . Where nothing is unspeakable, nothing is undoable. . . . Perhaps each of us can, if he wishes, effectively avert the eye and stop the ear. Still, what is commonly read and seen and heard and done intrudes upon us all, wanted or not, for it constitutes our environment."

56. 403 U.S. at 21.

57. Most of the thoughts in these paragraphs were inspired by W. Berns, *The First Amendment and the Future of American Democracy* (New York: Basic Books, 1976), pp. 180–205.

58. Ibid., p. 202.

59. 408 U.S. at 902.

60. Berns, *The First Amendment*, p. 204.

61. Bickel, *The Morality of Consent*, pp. 74, 73. *See Young v. American Mini-Theatres*, 427 U.S. 50 (1976).

62. Additional reasons why this interest is not weighty have been canvassed in the text at notes 23–46, *supra*.

63. *See generally* Schauer, *Categories and the First Amendment: A Play in Three Acts*, 34 Vand. L. Rev. 265 (1981).

64. *Contra, e.g.*, ibid., pp. 292–96.

65. *Grayned v. City of Rockford*, 408 U.S. 104, 110 (1972), which upheld, against a claim of unconstitutional vagueness, an ordinance that provided: "No person, while on public or private grounds adjacent to any building in which a school or any class thereof is in session, shall willfully make . . . any noise or diversion which disturbs or

tends to disturb the peace or good order of such school session or class."

66. A regulation of offensive speech is more like a "manner" regulation than a "content" restriction. It therefore should be tested by the more relaxed standard of constitutionality applied to "time, place, and manner" regulations rather than the stringent standard applied to "content" restrictions. *See* Stone, *Content Regulation and the First Amendment*, pp. 242–44. *See* note 6, *supra*.

67. *See* text at note 27, *supra*.

68. Model Penal Code Sec. 250.2, and comment 4 (Official Draft and Revised Comments 1980).

69. *Cf.* L. Tribe, *American Constitutional Law* (Mineola, N.Y.: Foundation Press, 1978), pp. 583–84; Stone, *Content Regulation and the First Amendment*, pp. 225–26.

70. 438 U.S. 726 (1978); *see* text at note 33, *supra*.

71. *Bethel School Dist. No. 403 v. Fraser*, 478 U.S. 675 (1986).

72. *Id.* at 3164. *Fraser* concerned a high school; *Papish v. Board of Curators*, *supra* note 1, concerned a university. Otherwise the cases are difficult if not impossible to distinguish. None of the various opinions in *Fraser* even mentioned *Papish*.

III.

THE SECOND AMENDMENT AND THE RIGHT TO KEEP AND BEAR ARMS

STEPHEN P. HALBROOK

9. The Original Understanding of the Second Amendment

Like other provisions of the federal Bill of Rights, the Second Amendment guarantee that "the right of the people to keep and bear Arms, shall not be infringed" was intended to prevent recurrence of the British acts of oppression that sparked the American Revolution. A written testimonial in plain English understandable by the average person would encourage the people to stand up for their right to own and carry firearms and other implements suitable for defense of self, family, community, and nation.

All of the colonies suffered to some degree from an increasingly intransigent British policy, but the worst excesses were executed upon the people of Boston, whose bad experiences created the impetus for the War for Independence and, a decade and a half later, the adoption of the Bill of Rights. The perceived need for written recognition of the right to keep and bear arms stemmed directly from the Redcoats' somewhat successful attempt to disarm the citizens of Boston.

Lobsterbacks sent by General Sir Thomas Gage to disarm rebellious patriots at Lexington and Concord on April 19, 1775, served only to provoke a "shot heard 'round the world." Three days later Gage represented to the selectmen of Boston that "there was a large body of men in arms" hostilely assembled and that the inhabitants could be injured if the soldiers attacked.[1] The next day a town committee met with Gage, who promised "that upon the inhabitants in general lodging their arms in Faneuil hall, or any other convenient place, under the care of the Selectmen, marked with the names of the respective owners, that all such inhabitants as are inclined, may depart from the town. . . And that the arms aforesaid at a suitable time would be return'd to the owners."[2]

The committee swallowed the bait, recommending "that the town accept of his excellency's proposal, and will lodge their arms with the selectmen accordingly."[3] "The town unanimously accepted of the foregoing report, and desired the inhabitants would deliver their arms to the Selectmen as soon as may be."[4] The agreement was coerced, in that Boston suffered from poor food supplies, troops bullied people on the streets and lodged in their homes, and most people were desperate to leave the town.

Accordingly, "on the 27th of April the people delivered to the selectmen 1778 fire-arms, 634 pistols, 973 bayonets, and 38 blunderbusses."

Thousands applied for passes to leave the city, but each pass Gage issued mandated: "No arms or ammunition is allowed to pass."[5] The surrendered muskets, pistols, and short-barreled shotguns totaled 2,624, which is 1 for every 5.6 inhabitants of that city of 15,000.[6] Probably a lot of junk was turned in, and the best arms were hidden with the intention of smuggling them out of the town.

The committee continued to meet with Gage through April 30, when it optimistically reported to the town: "The committee waited on his Excellency General Gage with the papers containing the account of the arms delivered to the selectmen, and the return made to them by the constables of the town relative to the delivery of the arms in their respective wards."[7] On the same date the Provincial Congress naively resolved:

> Whereas, an agreement hath been made, between General Gage and the inhabitants of the town of Boston, for the removal of the persons and effects of the inhabitants of the town of Boston, as may be so disposed, excepting their fire arms and ammunition, into the country.
>
> Resolved, That any of the inhabitants of this colony, who may incline to go into the town of Boston with their effects, fire-arms and ammunition excepted, have toleration for that purpose. . . .
>
> P.S. Officers are appointed for the giving of permits for the above purposes.[8]

A newspaper account described the background in more detail and told the predictable result. The Sunday after the battle at Lexington, a town meeting chose a committee of selectmen to meet with Gage. "The General convenanted with them—that if the inhabitants of Boston would give up their arms and ammunition, and not assist against the King's troops, they should immediately be permitted to depart with all their effects, merchandise included; finally, the inhabitants gave up their arms and ammunition—to the care of the Selectmen: the General then set a guard over the arms." Gage was then in a position to, and did, refuse the passage of both merchandise and people.[9] On announcing that no Bostonian could leave, "the same day a town meeting was to be held in Boston, when the inhabitants were determined to demand the arms they had deposited in the hands of the select men, or have liberty to leave town."[10]

The Continental Congress adopted an address on May 10 to the people of Ireland which complained that "the citizens petitioned the General for permission to leave the town, and he promised, on surrendering their arms, to permit them to depart with their other effects; they accordingly surrendered their arms, and the General violated his faith."[11] An anonymous patriot was less restrained in addressing outrage "to the perfidious, the truce-breaking Thomas Gage":

> But the single breach of the capitulation with them [the people of Boston], after they had religiously fulfilled their part, must brand your name and memory with eternal infamy. The proposal came from you to the inhabitants by the medium of one of your officers, through the Selectmen, and was, *that if the inhabitants would deposit their fire-arms in the hands of the Selectmen, to be returned to them after a reasonable time, you would give leave to the inhabitants to remove out of town with all their effects, without any lett or molestation.* The town punctually complied, and you remain an infamous monument of perfidy, for which an Arab, a Wild Tartar or Savage would dispise you!!![12]

On June 12 Gage proclaimed martial law and offered a pardon to all who would lay down their arms except Samuel Adams and John Hancock.[13] A patriot with a sense of humor responded with a poem entitled "Tom Gage's Proclamation," which told how the general had sent an expedition "the men of *Concord* to disarm" and how he afterwards reflected:

> Yet e'er I draw the vengeful sword,
> I have thought fit to send abroad,
> This present gracious Proclamation,
> Of purpose mild the demonstration;
> That whoseoe'er keeps gun or pistol,
> I'll spoil the motion of his systole;
> Or, whip his breech, or cut his weapon
> As has the measure of his Treason:
> —But every one that will lay down
> His hanger bright, and musket brown,
> Shall not be beat, nor bruis'd, nor bang'd,
> Much less for past offenses, hang'd,
> But on surrendering his toledo,
> Go to and fro unhurt as we do:
> —But then I must, out of this plan, lock
> Both Samuel Adams and John Hancock;
> For those vile traitors (like debentures)
> Must be tuck'd up at all adventures;
> As any proffer of a pardon,
> Would only tend those rogues to harden:
> —But every other mother's son,
> The instant he destroys his gun,
> (For thus doth run the King's command)
> May, if he will, come kiss my hand.—
>
> . . . . .
>
> Meanwhile let all, and every one
> Who loves his life, foresake his gun:[14]

Gage's seizures and attempts to seize the guns, pistols, Brown Bess muskets, and swords known as hangers and toledos of the individual citizens of Boston who were not even involved in the hostilities sent a message to all of the colonies that the right to keep and bear private arms was in a perilous condition. Indeed, the following item datelined London, April 24, was published throughout the colonies in June: "It is reported, that on the landing of the General Officers, who have sailed for America, a proclamation will be published throughout the colonies inviting the Americans to deliver up their arms by a certain stipulated day; and that such of the colonists as are afterwards proved to carry arms shall be deemed rebels, and be punished accordingly."[15]

British plans to disarm the colonists of their private arms were the last straw. The final break came when the Continental Congress adopted the Declaration of Causes and Necessity of Taking Up Arms on July 6, 1775, which had been drafted by John Hancock and Thomas Jefferson and which complained: "It was stipulated that the said inhabitants having deposited their arms with their own magistrates, should have liberty to depart. . . . They accordingly delivered up their arms, but in open violation of honor, in defiance of the obligations of treaties, which even savage nations esteem sacred, the governor ordered the arms deposited as aforesaid, that they might be preserved for the owners, to be seized by a body of soldiers."[16]

The violation of the right of individual citizens of Boston to keep and bear their private arms and the actual or feared violation of this right throughout the colonies generally sparked the American Revolution. The events of 1775 would be well remembered in 1787 when a federal constitution without a bill of rights was proposed.

In 1776 some of the newly independent states began to pass bills of rights to guard against recently experienced abuses. The Virginia Declaration of Rights of 1776, written by George Mason, included the provision "that a well regulated Militia, composed of the body of the people, trained to Arms, is the proper, natural, and safe Defence of a free State."[17] Thomas Jefferson proposed that the Virginia Constitution contain the provision, "No freeman shall be debarred the use of arms,"[18] and in the Declaration of Independence he vindicated the imperative of an armed uprising of the people, in times of oppression, against the standing army and the established government.

The Pennsylvania Declaration of 1776 stated "that the people have a right to bear arms for the defence of themselves and the state; and as standing armies in the time of peace are dangerous to liberty, they ought not to be kept up."[19] North Carolina's Declaration of Rights, adopted the same year, asserted "that the people have a right to bear arms, for the defense of the State"[20]—a subtle way of claiming not only the individual right to personal defense but also the right to overthrow the established (British) government by protecting the state against it. The Vermont Declaration of

Rights of 1777 maintained "that the people have a right to bear arms for the defence of themselves and the state."[21]

The Massachusetts Declaration of Rights of 1780 provided that "the people have a right to keep and bear arms for the common defence."[22] The phrase "common defence" precluded any construction that arms could be used only for individual self-defense but not for common defense against governmental despotism. Both private and general defense had already been recognized in Article I of the declaration, which included among the unalienable rights those of "defending their lives and liberties; . . . and protecting property." Even so, because Massachusetts had felt the impact of British disarmament measures more than the other colonies, some objected to the clause as too narrow. The town of Williamsburg proposed the following alteration:

> Upon reading the 17th Article in the Bill of Rights. Voted that these words their Own be inserted which makes it read thus; that the people have a right to keep and to bear Arms for their Own and the Common defence.
>
> Voted Nemine Contradic.
>
> Our reasons gentlemen for making this Addition Are these. 1st that we esteem it an essential privilege to keep Arms in Our houses for Our Own Defense and while we Continue honest and Lawful subjects of Government we Ought Never to be deprived of them.
> Reas. 2 That the legislature in some future period may Confine all the fire Arms to some publick Magazine and thereby deprive the people of the benefit of them.[23]

The objection to including what some believed could be construed as a limitation on the right to keep and bear arms explains why, nine years later, the U.S. Senate rejected a proposal to add "for the common defense" at the end of what became the Second Amendment.[24] However, the framers of the Massachusetts declaration never intended a narrow construction. In fact, it was drafted by John Adams, who had defended the right to carry arms for self-defense and, in his study of American state constitutions, wrote that "arms in the hands of citizens [may] be used at individual discretion . . . in private self-defence."[25]

When the federal Constitution was proposed in 1787, critics immediately objected that it would create a standing army and diminish the militia composed of all able-bodied males and that it contained no bill of rights. Alexander Hamilton sought to allay these fears in *The Federalist* No. 29, where he argued that the government should not require

> the great body of yeomanry and of the other classes of citizens to be under arms for the purpose of going through military exercises and evolutions, as often as might be necessary to acquire the degree of

> perfection which would entitle them to the character of a well regulated militia.
>
> Little more can reasonably be aimed at with respect to the people at large than to have them properly armed and equipped. . . . This will not only lessen the call for military establishments, but if circumstances should at any time oblige the government to form an army of any magnitude that army can never be formidable to the liberties of the people while there is a large body of citizens, little if at all inferior to them in discipline and the use of arms, who stand ready to defend their rights and those of their fellow citizens.[26]

In *The Federalist* No. 46, James Madison argued that against an abusive federal army "would be opposed a militia amounting to near half a million citizens with arms in their hands." Alluding to "the advantage of being armed, which the Americans possess over the people of almost every other nation," Madison continued: "Notwithstanding the military establishments in the several kingdoms of Europe, which are carried as far as the public resources will bear, the governments are afraid to trust the people with arms."[27]

Similarly, Noah Webster, an influential Federalist who would compose the first American dictionary, pointed out: "Before a standing army can rule, the people must be disarmed; as they are in almost every kingdom in Europe. The supreme power in America cannot enforce unjust laws by the sword; because the whole body of the people are armed, and constitute a force superior to any band of regular troops that can be, on any pretence, raised in the United States."[28]

The most influential pamphlet against ratification of the Constitution without a bill of rights was Richard Henry Lee's *Letters from the Federal Farmer*. He concluded that at that time "the yeomanry of the country possess the lands, the weight of property, possess arms, and are too strong a body of men to be openly offended—and, therefore, it is urged, they will take care of themselves, that men who shall govern will not dare pay any disrespect to their opinions."[29] A few years of legislation by Congress on taxes and armies, Lee maintained, would shift power away from the people.

Lee urged adoption of written guarantees protecting a free press, the right to petition, religious freedom, and speedy trial by jury; forbidding unreasonable search and seizure and quartering soldiers in homes; and insuring that "the militia ought always to be armed and disciplined, and the usual defense of the country."[30] He argued for a general militia, which "are in fact the people themselves," and against a "select militia" composed of "distinct bodies of military men."[31]

> But, say gentlemen, the general militia are for the most part employed at home in their private concerns, cannot well be called out, or be depended upon; that we must have a select militia; that is, as I

> understand it, particular corps or bodies of young men, and of men who have but little to do at home, particularly armed and disciplined in some measure, at the public expense, and always ready to take the field. These corps, not much unlike regular troops, will ever produce an inattention to the general militia; and the consequence has ever been, and always must be, that the substantial men, having families and property, will generally be without arms, without knowing the use of them and defenseless; whereas to preserve liberty, it is essential that the whole body of the people always possess arms, and be taught alike, especially when young, how to use them; nor does it follow from this, that all promiscuously must go into actual service on every occasion. The mind that aims at a select militia, must be influenced by truly anti-republican principle; and when we see many men disposed to practice upon it, whenever they can prevail, no wonder true republicans are for carefully guarding against it.[32]

A host of Anti-Federalists echoed the same sentiments. John Dewitt predicted that Congress "at their pleasure may arm or disarm all or any part of the freemen of the United States, so that when their army is sufficiently numerous, they may put it out of the power of the freemen militia of America to assert and defend their liberties."[33] One "Common Sense" noted "that the chief power will be in the Congress, and that what is to be left of our government is plain, because a citizen may be deprived of the privilege of keeping arms for his own defence, he may have his property taken without a trial by jury."[34]

In the debates in the state conventions over the ratification of the Constitution, the existence of an armed citizenry was presumed by Federalists and Anti-Federalists alike as essential to prevent despotism. Issues that divided the delegates included whether a written bill of rights guaranteeing the right to keep and bear arms among other individual rights should be added to the Constitution and whether a provision guarding against standing armies or select militias was necessary. In the Pennsylvania convention John Smilie warned:

> Congress may give us a select militia which will, in fact, be a standing army—or Congress, afraid of a general militia, may say there shall be no militia at all.
>
> When a select militia is formed; the people in general may be disarmed.[35]

Theodore Sedwick in the Massachusetts convention found the fear of standing armies to be groundless, doubting that "if raised, whether they could subdue a nation of freemen, who know how to prize liberty, and who have arms in their hands?"[36] But in the North Carolina convention, William Lenoir worried that Congress could "disarm the militia. If they were armed, they would be a resource against great oppressions. . . . If the laws of the Union were oppressive, they could not carry them into effect, if the people were possessed of proper means of defence."[37]

In the Virginia convention, Patrick Henry argued that "the great object is, that every man be armed. . . . Everyone who is able may have a gun."[38] George Mason buttressed Henry's arguments by pointing out that pro-British strategists resolved "to disarm the people; that it was the best and most effectual way to enslave them . . . by totally disusing and neglecting the militia."[39] Mason also clarified that under prevailing practice the militia included all men, rich and poor. "Who are the militia? They consist now of the whole people, except a few public officers."[40] Madison emphasized that a standing army would be unnecessary because of the existence of militias[41]—in short, that the people would remain armed. Zachariah Johnston argued that the new Constitution could never result in religious or other oppression because "the people are not to be disarmed of their weapons. They are left in full possession of them."[42]

To address these concerns, Samuel Adams proposed in the Massachusetts convention "that the said Constitution be never construed to authorize Congress to infringe the just liberty of the press, or the rights of conscience; or to prevent the people of the United States, who are peaceable citizens, from keeping their own arms."[43] Similarly, the Pennsylvania minority proposed: "That the people have a right to bear arms for the defense of themselves, their state, or the United States, and for killing game, and no law shall be enacted for disarming the people except for crimes committed or in a case of real danger of public injury from individuals."[44]

While the majority in the above two states failed to recommend a written bill of rights, five state conventions did so and proposed recognition of the right to have arms. New Hampshire proposed that "Congress shall never disarm any citizen, unless such as are or have been in actual rebellion."[45] Virginia recommended the following language: "That the people have a right to keep and bear arms; that a well-regulated militia, composed of the body of the people trained to arms, is the proper, natural, and safe defence of a free state; that standing armies, in time of peace, are dangerous to liberty, and therefore ought to be avoided."[46] Similar language was adopted by the conventions of New York, Rhode Island, and North Carolina.[47]

The Reverend Nicholas Collin of Philadelphia published a series under the pen name "A Foreign Spectator" (from Sweden) entitled "Remarks on the Amendments to the Federal Constitutions" proposed by the state conventions. If the Constitution contained "a scrupulous enumeration of all the rights of the states and individuals, it would make a larger volume than the Bible."[48] Further, an army was no danger "especially when I am well armed myself." "While the people have property, arms in their hands, and only a spark of noble spirit, the most corrupt Congress must be mad to form any project of tyranny."[49]

Collin further held that "a good militia is the natural, easy, powerful and honorable defense of a country." Identifying "a citizen, as a militia man," he referred to "that noble art, by which you can defend your life, liberty and property; your parents, wife and children!"[50]

Collin then considered "those amendments which particularly concern several personal rights and liberties." Attacking a proposal that the privilege of habeas corpus should not be suspended for more than six months, he supported his position by referring to two of the proposed arms guarantees:

> What is said on this matter, is a sufficient reply to the 12th amend. of the New-Hampshire convention, *that congress shall never disarm any citizen, unless such as are or have been in actual rebellion*. If, by the acknowledged necessity of suspending the privilege of *habeas corpus*, a suspected person may be secured, he may much more be disarmed. In such unhappy times it may be very expedient to disarm those, who cannot conveniently be guarded, or whose conduct has been less obnoxious. Indeed to prevent by such a gentle measure, crimes and misery, is at once justice to the nation, and mercy to deluded wretches, who may otherwise, by the instigation of a dark and bloody ringleader, commit many horrid murders, for which they must suffer condign punishments. . . .
>
> The minority of Pennsylvania seems to have been desirous of limiting the federal power in these cases; but their conviction of its necessity appears by those very parts of the 3d and 7th amendments framed in this view, to wit, *that no man be deprived of his liberty except by the law of the land, or the judgment of his peers—and that no law shall be passed for disarming the people, or any of them, unless for crimes committed, or real danger of public injury from individuals*. The occasional suspension of the above privilege [of habeas corpus] becomes pro tempore the law of the land, and by virtue of it dangerous persons are secured. Insurrections against the federal government are undoubtedly real dangers of public injury, not only from individuals, but great bodies; consequently the laws of the union should be competent for the disarming of both.[51]

Collin was the only writer in the ratification period who discussed the limited power of Congress to disarm any person or group under the two proposed amendments. Since persons involved in an insurrection could be arrested, Collin reasoned, they could certainly also be disarmed. This argument reflected the experiences of the Revolution, in that a Tory who could be tarred and feathered could be disarmed first and a Redcoat who could be shot could surrender his person and weapons instead. There is no hint in Collin's discussion that Congress could pass any law restricting firearms ownership by law-abiding citizens.

Arguments against a bill of rights did not prevail, and on June 8, 1789, James Madison proposed to the House of Representatives a bill of rights which included the following provision: "The right of the people to keep and bear arms shall not be infringed; a well armed, and well regulated militia being the best security of a free country: but no person religiously scrupulous of bearing arms shall be compelled to render military service in person."[52] Ten days later, Federalist leader Tench Coxe published his "Remarks on the First Part of the Amendments to the Federal Constitution," under the pen name "A Pennsylvanian," in the Philadelphia *Federal Gazette*. The most complete exposition of the Bill of Rights to be published during its ratification period, the "Remarks" stated: "As civil rulers, not having their duty to the people duly before them, may attempt to tyrannize, and as the military forces which must be occasionally raised to defend our country, might pervert their power to the injury of their fellow-citizens, the people are confirmed by the next article in their right to keep and bear their private arms."[53]

Coxe sent a copy of his article to Madison along with a letter of the same date. "It has appeared to me that a few well tempered observations on these propositions might have a good effect. . . . It may perhaps be of use in the present turn of the public opinions in New York state that they should be republished there." Madison wrote back, acknowledging "your favor of the 18th instant. The printed remarks inclosed in it are already I find in the Gazettes here [New York]." Far from disagreeing that the amendment protected the possession and use of "private arms," Madison explained that ratification of the amendments "will however be greatly favored by explanatory strictures of a healing tendency, and is therefore already indebted to the co-operation of your pen."[54]

Coxe's defense of the amendments was widely reprinted,[55] and his interpretation that what became the Second Amendment protected the right of the people "to keep and bear their private arms" was never contradicted. Indeed, one writer interpreted the proposal as identical in meaning to the language of Samuel Adams, that the Constitution would never be "construed to authorize congress . . . to prevent the people of the United States, who are peaceable citizens, from keeping their own arms."[56]

The Senate reworded and passed the proposal in the form that would become part of the Bill of Rights: "A well regulated Militia, being necessary to the security of a free State, the right of the people to keep and bear Arms, shall not be infringed." The Senate rejected a proposal to word the passage "to keep and bear arms *for the common defense*," thereby insuring that individuals could have arms for personal as well as collective defense.[57]

As adopted, the Bill of Rights uses the term "the people" in the First, Second, Fourth, Ninth, and Tenth Amendments. It is "the people" who are guaranteed the rights to free speech, press, religion, and assembly; to keep and bear arms; against unreasonable searches and seizures; and to exercise unenumerated rights and the powers not delegated to the United States or the individual states.

The first major legal commentary on the Second Amendment was published in 1803 by St. George Tucker, a longtime friend of Jefferson and Madison who had smuggled arms into the colonies during the Revolution.[58] Now a judge on Virginia's highest court, Tucker interpreted the Second Amendment to guarantee that "the right of the people to keep and bear arms shall not be infringed . . . and this without any qualification as to their condition or degree, as is the case in the British government."[59] As to the value of enumerating this and other rights in the Constitution, Tucker wrote:

> The want of a bill of rights was among the objections most strongly urged against the constitution in its original form. The author of the Federalist undertakes to show, that a bill of rights was not only unnecessary, but would be dangerous. *A bill of rights may be considered*, not only as intended to give law, and assign limits to a government about to be established, but *as giving information to the people*. By reducing speculative truths to fundamental laws, *every man of the meanest capacity and understanding may learn his own rights, and know when they are violated*; a circumstance, of itself, sufficient, I conceive, to counterbalance every argument against one.[60]

Hamilton had argued in *The Federalist Papers* that a bill of rights would be dangerous because no matter how it was worded, artful misconstruction would be used to destroy the very rights intended to be protected.[61] While his prediction has come true, so too has Tucker's explanation of the purpose of the Bill of Rights as giving information to the people been served. No amount of history rewriting will ever convince the simplest citizen who can read that he is not one of "the people" whose right to keep and bear arms is secured by the Second Amendment.

Notes

1. Attested Copy of Proceedings between Gage and Selectmen, April 22, 1775, in *Hartford Connecticut Courant*, July 17, 1775, p. 1, col. 3, p. 4, col. 1. Many of the items quoted from this source also were printed in numerous other colonial newspapers.

2. Ibid., p. 4, col. 2 (April 23, 1775).

3. Ibid.

4. Ibid., col. 3.

5. R. Frothingham, *History of the Siege of Boston*, 6th ed. (New York: Da Capo, 1970), p. 95.

6. D. Freeman, *George Washington: A Biography* (New York: Scribner, 1948–57), 3:576.

7. Attested Copy of Proceedings between Gage and Selectmen, April 30, 1775, in *Hartford Connecticut Courant*, p. 4, col. 3.

8. Ibid., May 8, 1775, p. 2, col. 1.

9. Worcester, May 3, ibid., p. 3, col. 1.

10. New London, May 12, in *Connecticut Journal and New-Haven Post-Boy*, May 19, 1775, p. 6, col. 2.

11. *Hartford Connecticut Courant*, Aug. 21, 1775, p. 1, col. 3.

12. From the *Boston Gazette*, by "Massachusettsensis," in *Hartford Connecticut Courant*, June 19, 1775, p. 4, col. 2.

13. Gage's Proclamation of June 12, in *Connecticut Journal and New-Haven Post-Boy*, June 21, 1775, p. 3, cols. 1–2.

14. *Hartford Connecticut Courant*, June 17, 1775, p. 4, col. 1.

15. *Maryland Gazette*, June 22, 1775, p. 1, col. 1; *Virginia Gazette*, June 24, 1775, p. 1, col. 1.

16. *Hartford Connecticut Courant*, June 17, 1775, p. 2, col. 1. The declaration was published in virtually every colonial newspaper. A reading of the declaration at Cambridge on July 21 excited "great applause" (ibid., July 24, 1775, p. 2, col. 1).

17. Va. Declaration of Rights, Art. XIII (1776).

18. J. Boyd et al., eds., *The Papers of Thomas Jefferson* (Princeton, N.J.: Princeton Univ. Press, 1950—), 1:344.

19. Pa. Declaration of Rights, Art. XIII (1776).

20. N.C. Declaration of Rights, Art. XVII (1776).

21. Vt. Declaration of Rights, Art. XV (1777).

22. Mass. Declaration of Rights, Art. XVII (1780).

23. O. and M. Handlin, eds., *The Popular Sources of Political Authority: Documents on the Massachusetts Constitution of 1780* (Cambridge: Belknap, 1966), p. 624.

24. *Infra* note 57.

25. J. Adams, *A Defense of the Constitution of Government of the United States of America*, vol. 3 (Philadelphia: Budd & Bartram, 1787), p. 475.

26. J. Madison, A. Hamilton, and J. Jay, *The Federalist Papers* (Arlington House ed., n.d.), No. 29, pp. 184–85.

27. Ibid., No. 46, p. 299.

28. N. Webster, *An Examination into the Leading Principles of the Federal Constitution* (1787), in P. Ford, ed., *Pamphlets on the Constitution of the United States* (1888; rept. New York: Da Capo, 1968), p. 56.

29. R. Lee, *Letters of a Federal Farmer* (1787–88), in ibid., pp. 305–6.

30. R. Lee, *Additional Letters from the Federal Farmer* (1788; rept. Chicago: Quadrangle, 1962), p. 53.

31. Ibid., p. 169.

32. Ibid., p. 170.

33. M. Borden, ed., *The Antifederalist Papers* (East Lansing: Michigan State Univ., 1965), p. 75.

34. *New York Journal and Daily Advertiser*, April 21, 1788, p. 2, col. 2. This quotation was recently located by David T. Hardy.

35. M. Jansen, ed., *The Documentary History of the Ratification of the Constitution*, vol. 2 (Madison: State Historical Society of Wisconsin, 1976), p. 509.

36. J. Elliot, *The Debates in the Several State Conventions on the Adoption of the Federal Constitution*, 2d ed. (Philadelphia: J. B. Lippincott, 1836), 2:97.

37. Ibid., 4:203.

38. Ibid., 3:386.

39. Ibid., p. 380.

40. Ibid., pp. 425–26.

41. Ibid., p. 413.

42. Ibid., p. 646.

43. B. Schwartz, ed., *The Bill of Rights: A Documentary History*, vol. 2 (New York: Chelsea House, 1971), p. 681.

44. Jensen, *Documentary History of the Ratification of the Constitution* 2:597–98, 623–24.

45. Schwartz, *The Bill of Rights* 2:761.

46. Elliot, *Debates* 3:659.

47. Ibid., 1:327–35, 4:244.

48. "Remarks," No. II, *Philadelphia Federal Gazette*, Oct. 24, 1788.

49. No. IV, *Fayetteville (N.C.) Gazette*, Oct. 12, 1789, p. 1, col. 2–3, p. 2, col. 1–2.

50. No. VIII, *Philadelphia Federal Gazette*, Nov. 14, 1788.

51. No. XI, ibid., Nov. 28, 1788. Collin also opposed amendments guaranteeing a free press and jury trial, a prohibition on general warrants and cruel and unusual punishment, and all other proposed amendments (No. XII, ibid., Dec. 2, 1788, and No. XXVIII, ibid., Feb. 16, 1789).

52. *Annals of Congress*, vol. 1 (Washington, D.C.: Gales & Seaton, 1834), p. 434.

53. *Philadelphia Federal Gazette*, June 18, 1789, p. 2, col. 1.

54. Coxe to Madison, June 18, 1789, Madison to Coxe, June 24, 1789, in Charles F. Hobson and Robert A. Rutland, eds., *The Papers of James Madison*, vol. 12 (Charlottesville: Univ. Press of Virginia, 1979), pp. 239–40, 257.

55. *E.g.*, *New York Packet*, June 23, 1789, p. 2, col. 1–2; *Boston Massachusetts Centinel*, July 4, 1789, p. 1, col. 2. The latter was a special Independence Day issue.

56. From the *Boston Independent Chronicle*, in the *Philadelphia Independent Gazetteer*, Aug. 20, 1789, p. 2, col. 2.

57. *Senate Journal*, Sept. 9, 1789, attested by Sam A. Otis, secretary of the Senate, Executive Communications, box 13, p. 1, Virginia State Library and Archives.

58. Halbrook, *St. George Tucker: The American Blackstone*, 32 Va. Bar News 45, 47 (Feb. 1984).

59. S. Tucker, *Blackstone's Commentaries*, vol. 1 (Philadelphia, 1803), p. 143 n. 40.

60. Ibid., (App.) p. 308.

61. "Bills of rights . . . would contain various exceptions to powers not granted; and, on this very account, would afford a colorable pretext to claim more than were granted" (*The Federalist*, No. 84, p. 513).

DON B. KATES, JR.

10. Minimalist Interpretation of the Second Amendment

Although a new minimalist interpretation of the Second Amendment has recently appeared,[1] the traditional and best-known is states'-right minimalism, the theory that the amendment guarantees nothing to individuals, but only the states' now obsolete right to arm their militias. Since its initial appearance early in this century, states'-right minimalism has been expounded in law review articles[2] and endorsed by the American Bar Association and the American Civil Liberties Union[3] and by dicta or actual holdings of a number of lower federal court cases.[4] Although nineteenth-century Supreme Court cases referring to the Second Amendment treated it as an individual right, they also held it subject to the nonincorporation doctrine that held the restrictions of the Bill of Rights applicable to the federal government alone, not to the states.[5] Nonincorporation has long been abandoned, but in none of the twentieth-century Supreme Court cases enunciating the new selective incorporation doctrine has the Second Amendment been specifically involved. The old nineteenth-century Supreme Court holdings on the Second Amendment having never been overruled, they are (at least technically) still binding on state and lower federal courts, which duly continue to follow them.[6] To add confusion, gun control advocates commonly cite the nonincorporation holdings as if they had denied there is any Second Amendment right to own a gun.[7] The truth is the reverse: the nonincorporation holdings do not support states'-right minimalism, but that minimalism can provide them the needed rationale to survive the erosion of their original doctrinal basis. For if what the Second Amendment protects really is only a right of the states, it obviously would not apply against the states (and in favor of individuals) even under the modern selective incorporation doctrine.[8]

For reasons which this chapter will explore, states'-right minimalism has become a veritable truism, the only interpretation of the Second Amendment even mentioned in the leading modern texts.[9] This requires exploration if only because the truism is manifestly untrue; to deny that the amendment assures responsible adults a right to handguns and other ordinary civilian firearms in their own homes requires almost herculean indifference to every kind of evidence.[10] Of course, recognition for the right as just limned does not justify the gun lobby's obnoxious habit of assailing all forms of regulation on Second Amendment grounds.[11] But the evidence so clearly renders states'-right minimalism untenable that the latest minimalist analysis virtually abandons it in favor of a different minimalist position which is, however, no more tenable.[12]

Both Professor Sanford Levinson and Professor Franklin Zimring have recently criticized the inconsistency between the grudging, hostile spirit in which minimalists approach the Second Amendment and the respectful deference most of them deem appropriate to the interpretation of constitutional rights.[13] I suggest that this inconsistency derives from an emotional inability to comprehend the concepts that motivate the amendment: Minimalist analysts' ambivalence (at best) about self-defense and their deep antipathy toward guns render them not only unwilling but unable to come to grips with the diametrically opposite views of the Founding Fathers. Such emotions and derivative misconceptions about the Founders' views simply blind some modern Americans to the armed citizenship ideal of civic virtue that was so basic in the school of republican philosophy to which the Founders were heir.[14]

Exemplifying the myopic view of the Second Amendment such antigun sentiments induce is one of the responses to my analyses of the general effect of such sentiment on the gun debate: From a distinguished law professor and ACLU national board member I received a postcard bearing a picture of the library at Monticello; in emphasizing his horror of "an armed society" he asked rhetorically, "what would Thomas Jefferson have thought?" So extreme is the misconception thereby projected back onto the Founders that it is almost embarrassing to set out their actual views. "One loves to possess arms," Thomas Jefferson wrote to George Washington on June 19, 1796.[15] Jefferson's life and writings epitomize what an intellectual historian has described as the "almost religious" veneration of the Founders generally for "the relationship between men and arms."[16] Jefferson felt every boy of ten should be given a gun as he had been; an accomplished gunsmith, he stocked Monticello with an extensive armory and brought to the New World the idea of manufacturing guns with interchangeable parts.[17]

That Jefferson saw gun ownership as a right is clear from the guarantee in a model state constitution he drafted that "no free man shall be debarred the right to arms."[18] But understanding the full meaning of such a guarantee to the Founders requires considering not only violent uses of arms but their nonviolent aspects, and particularly their moral dimension, as emphasized in republican philosophy. Minimalist analyses of the Second Amendment reflect the utter incomprehensibility of such a moral dimension to people who see guns and the desire to have them for family defense as immoral and atavistic. In contrast, the states'-right view naturally appeals to people who view guns this way: for, in the unlikely event that they themselves would ever have written a constitutional guarantee of gun ownership, it would have been only for governments, not individuals. Likewise, they conceptualize the reasons an individual right to gun ownership might be guaranteed in disturbingly violent images of self-defense, revolution, etc.: i.e., the brutal, actual use of arms, which is repellent even when just and necessary.[19]

But paramount to eighteenth- (and many twentieth-) century Americans were (are) two nonviolent aspects of arms possession: to shape the character necessary to republican citizens and to reduce violence by deterring usurpations that tend to provoke it. Of course, occasions for the actual use of defensive arms were not lacking in eighteenth century American life.[20] Yet, even per capita, such occasions were probably less frequent then than now,[21] as also was the incidence of actual defensive use.[22] And an important tenet of republican philosophy was the belief (which persists today) that arming the good citizen minimized the likelihood of violence by deterring the wrongs that would provoke it. As Thomas Paine put it, "[T]he supposed quietude of a good man allures the ruffian; while; on the other hand, arms like laws discourage and keep the invader and plunderer in awe and preserve order in the world as well as property."[23]

This belief was important to Locke, Sidney, and their followers because they were accused of promoting disorder and bloodshed by advocating the right of revolution against tyranny. The deterrent theory allowed them to throw back the same charge, claiming an armed citizenry peacefully deterred ministerial usurpation, whereas unarmed people would suffer progressive abuse until bloody revolt became unavoidable.[24] "[T]here is no end to observations on the difference between the measures likely to be pursued by a minister backed by a standing army, and those of a court awed by the fear of an armed people," wrote James Burgh, the English philosopher, "most attractive to Americans," in a book whose first colonial edition was edited by Franklin and purchased by Washington, Jefferson, Hancock, John Adams, and John Dickinson.[25]

Thus, the Second Amendment rests on a profound faith in the nonviolent deterrent effect of an armed people, whether "against the Ambition of their Governours . . . , the Domestick Affronts of any of their own [criminals, or] against the Foreign Invasions of ambitious and unruly neighbors. . . . [E]nabled to stand upon their own Defence [the people] shall never be put upon in but [their] Swords will grown rusty in their hands; . . . a Man that hath a sword by his side, shall have least occasion to make use of it."[26]

Believing occasions for violence minimized by the deterrent effect of arms, the next importance that republican philosophers saw in popular arms possession was the promotion of civic virtue. In this school of thought, "[c]ivic virtue came to be defined as the freeholder bearing arms in defense of his property and his state. . . . [James Burgh] clearly articulated the idea that the very character of the people—the cornerstone and strength of a republican society—was related to the individual's ability and desire to arm and defend himself against threats to his person, his property and his state."[27] Republican theorists from Machiavelli through the Founders and beyond believed popular government could survive only so long as the populace remained virtuous. This model of virtuous citizenship was drawn from the ancient Greek and Roman republics where every free man was armed—instantly ready both to spring to his family's defense and to the city walls at the tocsin's warning of approaching enemies. Thus, even though arms might never be used, their possession signified the good citizen's commitment both to his private and public responsibilities.

Constant suspicion of government, an almost ascetic disdain for wealth, scrupulousness, honor, intrepidity, manly independence, and self-reliance—these were the "'Republican virtues,' brought into the eighteenth century from the ancient world, via Machiavelli."[28] Likewise, from Machiavelli the Founders received the view that "to be disarmed is to be contemptible"—not simply to be held in contempt but to deserve it, for by disarming men tyrants render them at once brutish and cowardly.[29] Disarmament, wrote Madison's friend the late eighteenth-century political philosopher Joel Barlow, "palsies the hand and brutalizes the mind: an habitual disuse of physical force totally destroys the moral; and men lose at once the power of protecting themselves, and of discerning the cause of their oppression."[30]

The Revolution—and the lessons the Founders took from its success—can be understood only in the context of their belief that disarmament destroys the people's moral as well as physical capacity to resist tyranny. From fiery philippics by radical English republicans like Burgh, the colonials believed the English people had been deliberately corrupted by a combination of insidious ministerial policies, including the banning of guns.[31] They believed themselves directly threatened by what they saw as the further purpose of extending these and cognate policies to corrupt all free people throughout the English empire. Thus, all America reacted to the attempt to confiscate arms at Lexington and Concord, not as an isolated event in New England but as a step in a long-standing, nefarious plot against them all.[32] As the Virginian George Mason put it: "Forty years ago when the resolution of enslaving America was formed in Great Britain, the British Parliament was advised by an artful man [Sir William Keith, newly returned from his service as royal governor of Pennsylvania] to disarm the people—that was the most effectual way to enslave them—but that they should not do it openly; but to weaken them and let them sink gradually."[33] Yet, ironically enough the Founders believed, the very plot that caused the Revolution assured its success: Despite its enormously greater resources, Britain had been unable to suppress the Americans; having undermined its own people's moral fiber, Britain had to hire mercenaries who had inevitably failed, being at once too few and too degraded to conquer a free people.[34]

Is it any wonder that deeming their theory of the role of arms in civic virtue confirmed by their own experience, the Founders forbade laws that would sap the citizen's moral fiber by depriving him of the means of defending his family, liberty, and nation? It was in this tradition that Thomas Jefferson wrote his fifteen-year-old nephew: "A strong body makes the mind strong. As to the species of exercises, I advise the gun. While this gives a moderate exercise to the body, it gives boldness, enterprise and independence to the mind. Games played with the ball, and others of that nature, are too violent for the body and stamp no character on the mind. Let your gun therefore be the companion of your walks."[35]

Though this theory of civic virtue may seem archaic—given the language and examples in which the Founders and their school expressed it—many Americans still accept it. Indeed, the extreme bitterness of our present gun debate has been ascribed to its representing a broader dispute between these Americans and those others who reject the Founders' worldview.

> [U]nderlying the gun control struggle is a fundamental division in our nation. The intensity of passion on this issue suggests to me that we are experiencing a sort of low-grade war going on between two alternative views of what America is and ought to be. On the one side are those who take bourgeois Europe as a model of a civilized society: a society just, equitable, and democratic; but well ordered, with the lines of responsibility and authority clearly drawn, and with decisions made rationally and correctly by intelligent men for the entire nation. To such people, hunting is atavistic, personal violence is shameful, and uncontrolled gun ownership is a blot upon civilization.
>
> On the other side is a group of people who do not tend to be especially articulate or literate, and whose world view is rarely expressed in print. Their model is that of the independent frontiersman who takes care of himself and his family with no interference from the state. They are "conservative" in the sense that they cling to America's unique pre-modern tradition—a non-feudal society with a sort of medieval liberty writ large for everyman. To these people, "sociological" is an epithet. Life is tough and competitive. Manhood means responsibility and caring for your own.[36]

The similarity between the "conservative" views just described and those of the Founders is obvious. But it is unclear, and certainly unwelcome, to the other side. The attempt of Professor Beschle to obfuscate the meaning of Jefferson's advice to his nephew as evidence of the Founders' affirmative desire for an armed citizenry provides ample evidence of this. He slyly asks whether the alleged fact that Jefferson "hated dogs, and suggested that they all be exterminated" explains why "he would urge that a gun be a constant companion on one's walks?"[37]

In evaluating the real significance of this query, it is important to recognize that on its face it is not only wrong but plainly irrelevant to what it is supposedly addressing. It gratuitously obtrudes Jefferson's alleged view of dogs on a piece of advice whose actual subject was his views on the gun—"it gives boldness, enterprise and independence to the mind." Now Professor Beschle should have had no difficulty seeing that this language expressed not Jefferson's singular view of dogs but an ideal common to all the Founders, the "ideal of republican virtue [as] the armed freeholder, scrupulously honest, self-reliant and independent—defender of his family, home and property."[38] This description of that ideal appears not four pages away in the very article to which Professor Beschle cites Jefferson's advice. Also quoted in that article is Patrick Henry's declamation, "The great object is that every man be armed," and, on the same page as Jefferson's advice, Professor Asbury's description of the Founders' "almost religious" veneration for "the relationship between men and arms."[39]

Indeed, on or near that same page are other quotations lauding gun ownership as a basic individual right from John Adams, Sam Adams, Fisher Ames, Tench Coxe, Hamilton, Richard Henry Lee, Madison, Mason, Monroe, Washington, Noah Webster, and many lesser figures.[40] Professor Beschle does not claim they all hated dogs. Yet that is the least he would have to prove to gainsay the importance for interpreting the Second Amendment of Jefferson's—of all the Founders'—faith in the civic virtue of gun possession.

The gratuitousness of Professor Beschle's reference to Jefferson's view of dogs illustrates the psychodynamics of minimalist interpretation no less than did the postcard from the ACLU board member. For those Americans who find gun ownership abhorrent, the Founders' moral vision is both absurd and repellent. Revering Jefferson, the ACLU board member could not imagine that he would have held such views. Knowing better, Professor Beschle is driven to the other extreme of traducing Jefferson by accusing him of other views that most of us would dismiss as absurd and repellent.[41]

But it would be unjust to dismiss Professor Beschle's innovative approach to the amendment (indeed to the Bill of Rights generally) on the basis of one regrettable comment. Says Professor Beschle: Though the Constitution seems to guarantee all rights equally, differences can and should be drawn between "primary" rights and those, like the right to arms, which he pronounces "functional," i.e., guaranteed only for the purpose of securing some primary value. From these premises he proceeds (by reasoning which I must admit I find obscure) to a remarkable conclusion: Functional rights are not rights at all in the sense of protections for individual decisionmaking; rather they are only admonitions that government promote the underlying primary value by whatever means may be reasonable—even means forbidden by the constitutional guarantee in question. For instance, the primary value he considers the Second Amendment to be implementing is the "security" of the populace; so, he concludes, if the state may reasonably think individuals wrong in believing that their families are more secure armed than disarmed, it may overrule their judgment and confiscate all guns.[42]

The full flavor of his approach is best derived by quoting him directly:

> [Primary] freedoms or entitlements are essential to human existence, or at least an existence granting human beings the dignity they deserve [and] require no further elaboration beyond their mere enunciation to justify their existence. It is obvious that such rights, which would include the right to be free from arbitrary deprivations of life, liberty and property, the right to have and express one's own beliefs, religious and otherwise, and the right to be free from torture or cruel and unusual punishments, are fundamental to human dignity. While considerable dispute may exist over the precise scope of such rights, and the means necessary to implement them, no significant controversy exists as to their existence in some basic, unadorned form. To a person who shares basic Western political and philosophical values even a request to explain why such rights are recognized will seem strange. [Professor Beschle footnotes this to an acknowledgment that "[i]n other cultures the existence of such rights are doubtful," citing cross-cultural analyses.]
>
> The right to possess firearms is not this type of right. It is by no means evident that a life without access to firearms is lacking in some fundamental way. Nations which share a basic commitment to Western values vary widely in their attitudes toward private ownership of firearms.[43]

Though this double standard approach is innovative, certain difficulties may occur to those of us who value civil liberty—as well as logic and consistency. First, it is hopelessly simplistic to label constitutional rights either wholly "functional" or wholly "primary" (particularly if one airily dismisses any need to examine or explain the right being labeled). In fact, when examined, many, if not most, constitutional rights turn out to involve both primary and functional aspects, insofar as such labels have meaning at all. For instance, a full and fair examination of the Second Amendment shows that it inextricably combines at least four different things: (1) a basic "human right,"[44] (2) a right the Founders deemed essential to good citizenship, (3) a means of avoiding bloody revolution by deterring usurpations that might occasion it, and (4) the ultimate means of self-defense against outlaws or domestic or foreign tyranny. Having addressed only one of the arguments, Professor Beschle classifies the amendment as merely functional. But what about the others, of which the first is clearly primary (in the Founders' eyes, if not Professor Beschle's), and the second is probably so?

To evaluate Professor Beschle's double standard approach, it must instead be applied to a right like free speech, which is far closer than the Second Amendment to being purely functional. Though primary explanations for free speech may be possible, the traditional and accepted ones are all functional, e.g., Meikeljohn's (free speech is central to the function of republican government),[45] Brandeis's and Holmes's (full debate is necessary to ascertainment of truth),[46] and Hughes's (free speech averts revolution by providing alternative means of altering government or its policies).[47] Note that, though in a different way, this last function serves the same value as that served by the Second Amendment (popular arms possession averts revolution by deterring usurpations that provoke it).

This makes especially appropriate the following question as to the Beschle double standard in the First Amendment context. Suppose as to some particular topic the state could reasonably conclude that debate thereon is not central to government, that debate has already established the truth, and that any dissenters from that truth are either too disorganized or too weak or pusillanimous to rebel (or too determined on revolution to be diverted by the alternative of free debate). Since free speech on this particular topic would apparently no longer further any of the primary values the First Amendment is supposed to serve, may the state forbid further debate on it?[48]

The short and obvious answer is that even if a guaranteed right may properly be described as only functional, its terms are binding until altered or repealed by the deliberately cumbersome process of constitutional amendment.[49] Of course, function (if ascertainable) may be an important issue in deciding whether new conditions require expanding a right's scope beyond its literal words to effectuate its full intent today. But it is never appropriate to contract our Constitution, using methods it forbids on the theory that it does not disserve (or even that it actually better serves) some supposedly primary purpose.

The foregoing by no means exhausts the problems with this new minimalist analysis of the Second Amendment. Even if the entire approach were not repugnant to the concept of constitutional liberty, and even if the functional/primary dichotomy were not hopelessly simplistic, the criterion by which Professor Beschle applies it against the amendment is both conceptually and factually wrong. As to factual error, suffice it to say that no matter how one defines "Western," the rights Beschle deems primary have not consistently prevailed in Western nations for any appreciable length of time.[50] When none of his own candidates for a primary right meet his own test, what weight can be given Professor Beschle's assertion that the Second Amendment does not do so?

Moreover, Professor Beschle's culture-bound test (purely Western values) is plainly inadequate to identifying such rights. Remember that he is not simply attempting to explain why rights like speech, arms, etc., are guaranteed in our Constitution. Rather, he postulates major differences in how seriously we should take those guarantees on the claim that some of them are so "fundamental to human dignity," "essential to human existence" as to "require no further elaboration or explanation beyond their mere enunciation to justify their existence." Of course, reasonable people may disagree both as to the existence of such transcendent rights and whether they can be deduced from the fact of acceptance in human societies rather than by some other criterion. But if that is to be the standard, reference must at least be had to consistent acceptance across the broad range of present human cultures, if not the whole history of mankind.

The most likely candidate for a cross-cultural right, as well as one that is "essential to human existence," is what Professor Wechsler calls "the universal judgment that there is no social interest in preserving the lives of the aggressors at the cost of those of their victims."[51] This is ironic, for it is the discomfort many modern Americans feel about this judgment—and their loathing for the only practical means most victims have for implementing it—that explains minimalist interpretations of the Second Amendment. As one of America's foremost liberal constitutional theorists has recently noted: "I cannot help but suspect that the best explanation for the absence of the Second Amendment from the legal consciousness of the elite bar, including the component found in the legal academy, is derived from a mixture of sheer opposition to the idea of private ownership of guns and the perhaps subconscious fear that altogether plausible, perhaps even 'winning' interpretations of the Second Amendment would present hurdles to those of us supporting prohibitory regulation."[52]

Notes

1. Beschle, *Reconsidering the Second Amendment: Constitutional Protection for a Right of Security*, 9 Hamline L. Rev. 69. To avoid confusion, I shall describe the older reductive analysis as "states'-rights minimalism" and Professor Beschle's approach as "functional minimalism."

2. *See, e.g.* Feller and Gotting, *The Second Amendment, A Second Look*, 61 Nw. U.L. Rev. 46 (1966); Rohner, *The Right to Bear Arms*, 16 Cath. U.L. Rev. 53 (1966); Levin, *The Right to Bear Arms: The Development of the American Experience*, 48 Chi.[-]Kent L. Rev. 148 (1971); Weatherup, *Standing Armies and Armed Citizens: An Historical Analysis of the Second Amendment*, 2 Hast. Const. L.Q. 961 (1972); Riley, *Shooting to Kill the Handgun: Time to Martyr Another American "Hero,"* 49 J. of Urban L. 51 (1974); Note, *Right to Keep and Bear Arms*, 26 Drake L. R. 423 (1977), Jackson, *Handgun Control: Constitutional and Critically Needed*, 8 N.C. Cent. L.J. 867 (1977).

3. *See* references cited in Kates, *Handgun Prohibition and the Original Understanding of the Second Amendment*, 82 Mich. L. Rev. 203, 207 (1983) (hereafter cited as Mich. L. Rev.). A Feb. 27, 1986, letter to me from Ira Glasser, the ACLU's executive director, states: "As to current ACLU policy, we no longer support legislation to prohibit handguns. However we do not believe the Second Amendment prohibits such legislation and therefore would not oppose it."

4. *E.g.*, *United States v. Oakes*, 564

F.2d 384, 387 (10th Cir. 1977); *Stevens v. United States*, 440 F.2d 144, 149 (6th Cir. 1971), *Cases v. United States*, 131 F.2d 916 (1st Cir. 1942); *United States v. Tot*, 131 F.2d 261, 266 (3d Cir. 1942), *rev'd on other grounds*, 319 U.S. 463 (1943).

5. *See* cases cited and analyzed at pp. 245–47 and n. 183 of my Mich. L. Rev. article.

6. In addition to the cases cited in ibid., p. 251, n. 201, *see Commonwealth v. Davis*, 343 N.E.2d 847, 850, 369 Mass. 886 (1976).

7. *See* discussion in Kates, *The Second Amendment: A Dialogue*, 49 Law & Contemporary Problems 143 at 144, n. 8.

8. J. Nowak, R. Rotunda, and J. Young, *Constitutional Law*, 2d ed. (St. Paul: West, 1983).

9. *E.g.* ibid., and L. Tribe, *American Constitutional Law* (Mineola, N.Y.: Foundation Press, 1978), p. 266, n. 6. But see my discussion of the Second Amendment in K. Karst and L. Levi, eds., *Encyclopedia of the American Constitution* (New York: Macmillan, 1986).

10. Kates, *The Second Amendment*, pp. 144–45 summarizes the evidence as follows: "The states'-right concept is a twentieth-century invention which was totally unknown to courts and commentators from the time of the amendment's enactment through the end of the nineteenth century; the two written interpretations available to Congress before it voted on the amendment described the amendment as confirming in 'the people of the United States who are peaceable citizens' the right to keep 'their own arms,' 'their private arms'; contemporary materials show congressmen, and others among the Founding Fathers, describing the right to arms as an elementary 'human right,' 'respected personal liberty,' 'essential and sacred,' and referring to it interchangeably with such other 'private rights' as freedom of religion and expression; the entire corpus of political philosophy known to the Founding Fathers taught them to promote an armed citizenry as the hallmark of, and indispensable precondition for, maintaining individual liberty and republican institutions; the writings of the Founding Fathers themselves reveal what one intellectual historian has described as an 'almost religious' veneration for 'the relationship between men and arms'; the 'right' referred to in the Second Amendment was that which the Founders knew from their own law and from Blackstone's characterization of the right to arms as one of the five preeminent and 'absolute rights of individuals' at common law; 'militia,' as used in the amendment and in the eighteenth century generally, referred not to some kind of military unit but to a system under which virtually every male of military age was legally required to possess his own arms for personal defense, crime prevention, and community defense; and interpreting the amendment as guaranteeing a state right to possess armed forces produces a gratuitous conflict with Article I, Section 10, Clause 3 of the U.S. Constitution, which forbids the states from doing so without express congressional consent.

"More telling yet is the grotesque inconsistency of the states' right interpretation with the actual text of the Bill of Rights:

"To accept such an interpretation requires the anomalous assumption that the Framers ill-advisedly used the phrase 'right of the people' to describe what was being guaranteed when what they actually meant was 'right of the states.' In turn, that assumption leads to a host of further anomalies. The phrase 'the people' appears in four other provisions of the Bill of Rights, always denoting rights pertaining to individuals. Thus, to justify an exclusively states' right view, the following set of propositions must be accepted: (1) when the first Congress drafted the Bill of Rights it used 'right of the people' in the first Amendment to denote a right of individuals (assembly); (2) then, some sixteen words later, it used the same phrase in the Second Amendment to denote a right belonging exclusively to the states; (3) but then, forty-six words later, the Fourth Amendment's 'right of the people' had reverted to its normal individual right meaning; (4) 'right of the people' was again used in the natural sense in the Ninth Amendment; and (5) finally, in the Tenth Amendment the first Congress specifically distinguished 'the states' from 'the people,' although it had failed to do so in the Second Amendment."

11. Mich. L. Rev., pp. 257–67, argues that neither handgun nor all gun ownership may be banned to the responsible adult populace but that controls (registration, licensing, etc.) are constitutional. In addition to informal negative comments from various NRA directors and officials, this part of my article has been denounced in the official National Rifle Association magazine as "Orwellian Newspeak" (Halbrook, *To Bear Arms for Self-Defense: Our Second Amendment Heritage*, Am. Rifleman, Nov. 1984 at 28). A subsequent debate with a leading NRA theorist is Kates, *The Second Amendment*, and Halbrook, *What the Framers Intended: A Linguistic Analysis of the Right to Bear Arms*, 49 Law & Contemporary Problems 151 (1986).

12. Beschle, *Reconsidering the Second Amendment*. Professor Beschle's innovative attempt to turn the Second Amendment on its head is addressed in the final section of this chapter.

13. Levinson, *The Embarrassing Second Amendment*, 99 Yale Law Journal 637 (1989). Professor Zimring's comments, which were initially made in a speech, are substantially replicated in F. Zimring and G. Hawkins, *The Citizen's Guide to Gun Control* (New York: Macmillan, 1987), p. 146.

Professor Zimring did not accuse the NRA of any such hypocrisy, and in fairness (not to mention desire to avoid yet another NRA outburst) I emphasize that it cannot be so accused. Unlike some who stereotype it as arch-conservative, the NRA stands foursquare behind the entire Bill of Rights. A paper presented at the 1984 annual meeting of the American Society of Criminology by the NRA research coordinator described "[c]onservatives, including leaders in law enforcement" who attacked the criminal procedure decisions of the Warren Court as "blatant in their disregard for traditional liberties" and denounced the Reagan administration and Burger Court for having "turned the ideas of the Founding Fathers on their heads" (H. Blackman, Civil Liberties and Gun Law Enforcement: Some Implications of Expanding the Powers of Police to Enforce a "Liberal" Victimless Crime).

14. *See* discussion *infra* at notes 31–44. The republican school can be traced back to Aristotle. Principal contributors include Machiavelli, Harrington, Sidney, Locke, Trenchard, Gordon, Moyle, and Burgh. *See generally* Shalhope, *Republicanism and Early American Historiography* 39 Wm. & Mary Q. 334 (1982). The armed citizenry aspects of republicanism are summarized in Mich. L. Rev., pp. 230–35, and Levin-

son, *The Embarrassing Second Amendment*. They are more thoroughly treated in S. Halbrook, *That Every Man Be Armed: The Evolution of a Constitutional Right* (Albuquerque: Univ. of New Mexico Press, 1984), chap. 1, and Shalhope, *The Ideological Origins of the Second Amendment*, 69 J. Am. Hist. 599 (1982). Detailed discussion of Machiavelli, Harrington, and a number of the less well known Continental and seventeenth- and eighteenth-century English republicans appears in J. Pocock's *The Machiavellian Moment: Florentine Political Thought and the Atlantic Republican Tradition* (Princeton, N.J.: Princeton Univ. Press, 1975), pp. 199–213, 290–92, and *The Political Works of James Harrington* (Cambridge: Cambridge Univ. Press, 1977), pp. 42–54.

Note: This is not to say that Americans, 50 percent of whose households contain guns, are generally antipathetic to gun ownership. Two quite different sentiments are involved, as I have suggested in discussing the gun lobby's phenomenal success in frustrating the overwhelming American consensus for many kinds of gun controls. Though not "antigun," most Americans, emphatically including most gun owners, favor regulation for pragmatic purposes like crime reduction. If the "control" leadership were only procontrol, the problem would only be the (still) complex one of tailoring laws to serve such pragmatic goals without unduly infringing the right—which most Americans also support—of responsible citizens to keep handguns for family defense. But to those most prominent in the gun-control lobby pragmatic goals are subordinate to the symbolic one of laws endorsing their perspective that gun ownership is an immoral atavism. By intruding this perspective into the discussion of every gun-control proposal—even those otherwise acceptable to all but the gun lobby—they so alarm and offend gun owners as to destroy the consensus for moderate pragmatic control. As debate over even modest controls produces fiery denunciation of gun owners, millions of them are driven to the gun lobby out of the conviction that control is motivated by, and betokens, utter hostility to them.

Illustrative of the virulence with which antigun sentiments are expressed are Garry Wills's "Handguns That Kill," *Washington Star*, Jan. 18, 1981, and "John Lennon's War," *Chicago Sun Times*, Dec. 12, 1980 (calling gun owners "anti-patriots," "traitors" arming "against their own neighbors"); Braucher, "Gun Lunatics Silence [the] Sound of Civilization" and "Handgun Nuts Are Just That—Really Nuts," *Miami Herald*, July 19, 1982, Oct. 29, 1981; Grizzard, "Bulletbrains and the Guns That Don't Kill" *Atlanta Constitution*, Jan. 19, 1981. The length to which this virulence is taken is evident from Marianne Means's nationally syndicated column "Gun Happy" (*San Francisco Examiner*, May 14, 1986). Without even suggesting crime reduction as a rationale, she actually argued in favor of banning ownership of fully automatic weapons by movie companies that such a "ban might mean that no more jungle warrior movies like Rambo could be produced. Great. There are those of us who think that's a wonderful reason for a ban." The beleaguered minority syndrome such columns produce among gun owners (and how important this effect is to the gun lobby) is evidenced by the faithful summaries provided gun owners of such denunciamento in such publications as *Gun Week*.

15. A. Lipscomb, ed., *Writings of Thomas Jefferson*, vol. 9 (Washington,

D.C.: Thomas Jefferson Memorial Foundation, 1904), p. 341.

16. C. Asbury, "The Right to Keep and Bear Arms in America: The Origins and Application of the Second Amendment to the Constitution" (Ph.D. diss., U. of Mich., 1974), p. 88.

17. Mich. L. Rev., p. 229. It may surprise those who envision intellectuals in modern stereotypes that Jefferson, the greatest intellectual of his day in this country, if not the world, was a lifelong vigorous hunter and outdoorsman and an outstanding horseman. In addition to his political importance, his contributions as naturalist, botanist, agronomist, horticulturalist, inventor (the moldboard for a plow), and architect were substantial. For Jefferson's major contributions as a natural historian, *see generally* H. Savage, Jr., *Discovering America, 1700–1875* (New York: Harpers, 1979), pp. 70, 72, 78ff.

The modern stereotype of the intellectual more closely fits James Madison, though he was enough of a man of his time to exult at his ability to shoot a target the size of a man's head at 100 paces (R. Ketcham, *James Madison: A Biography* [New York: Macmillan, 1971], p. 64).

18. J. Foley, ed., *The Jefferson Cyclopedia* (New York: Russell and Russell, 1967), p. 51.

19. *See, e.g.*, Beschle, *Reconsidering the Second Amendment*, who addresses what he deems its purposes in such narrow terms only, without even considering either the deterrent effect of civilian gun ownership on putative military despots (compare Mich. L. Rev., pp. 270–71, and *see* notes 23–26 *infra* and accompanying text), and the moral dimension so important in the Founders' thought (compare Mich. L. Rev., pp. 231–34 and notes 27–35, *infra* and accompanying text).

20. Eighteenth-century Americans, having no police and, under ordinary circumstances, no standing army to rely upon, combined in themselves the functions of defender of their families and their communities from criminals, Indians, and soldiers (Kates, *The Second Amendment*, p. 147, n. 24). From the 1730s on colonial Americans regularly resisted individual soldiers or groups of soldiers with arms in a variety of disputes (P. Maier, *From Resistance to Revolution: Colonial Radicals and the Development of American Opposition to Britain, 1765–76* [New York: Knopf, 1976], chap. 1).

Of course, modern Americans tend to conceptualize occasions for the defensive use of arms in terms merely of repelling attacks by criminals until the police arrive. But as civil rights workers and political dissenters have learned, there are some people whom the police may be unwilling to defend. *See, e.g.*, Kessler, *Gun Control and Political Power* 5 L. and Pol'y Q. 381 (1983), Kates, *Why a Civil Libertarian Opposes Handgun Prohibition*, Civil Liberties Review, June/July and Aug./Sept. 1976. For a foreign example, *see New York Times*, Aug. 10, 1976, "British M.P. Holds Mob at Bay," recounting how police failure to respond to his nine frantic calls for help obliged the leader of the Irish Catholic moderate party to hold off a mob which broke into his home ("If I hadn't had a gun, I am sure I would be dead by now . . . they would have kicked me to death.").

21. The lack of anything comparable to the highly sophisticated statistical basis that exists today makes it impossible to even estimate crime rates (much less those for violent crime or any particular form thereof) in eighteenth-century

America. But it is clear that crime, including violent crime, existed and was perceived as a social problem; there were even organized gangs operating across state lines and probable instances of officials being bribed to allow jailbreaks by crime leaders. D. Greenberg, *Crime and Law Enforcement in the Colony of New York, 1691–1776* (Ithaca, N.Y.: Cornell Univ. Press, 1974); Brown, *Historical Patterns of Violence in America*; and Brooks, *Domestic Violence and America's Wars: An Historical Interpretation*, in the Eisenhower Commission's Staff Report entitled *Violence in America: Historical and Comparative Perspectives* (Washington, D.C.: GPO, 1969). *See also* Gurr, *Historical Trends in Violent Crime: A Critical View of Evidence*, 3 Annual Review of Crime and Justice (1981).

Inconclusive as it is, the eighteenth-century evidence does not suggest anything remotely approaching modern American crime: survey data indicate 9 percent of American households suffer burglary or violent felony each year; thus, all other things being equal, over a ten-year period 90 percent of American households would suffer such a crime (Wright, *Firearms Ownership for Self-Defense*, p. 316, in D. Kates, ed., *Firearms and Violence: Issues of Public Policy* (Cambridge: Ballinger, 1984). Note, however, that all things are not equal since the poor and disadvantaged are disproportionately subject to criminal victimization. Indeed, one explanation for the concentration of antigun activism among well-to-do whites is that though their class suffers occasional criminal victimization, it is too idiosyncratic to make defensive gun possession a realistic precaution. The opposite is true for those who live or work in high crime areas. *See* ibid.; Kates, *The Battle over Gun Control*, 84 Public Interest 42, 45, 46–47 (1986).

22. Again, it cannot be determined how many eighteenth-century Americans actually used guns defensively (*see* n. 21 *supra*). Indeed, until national figures became available in the last few years, the extent of such uses even today was greatly underestimated through reliance on truncated figures from a few unrepresentative cities which were specially selected for partisan reasons. *See* Kleck, *Guns and Self-Defense: Crime Control through the Use of Force in the Private Sector*, 35 Social Problems 1 (1988).

23. M. Conway, ed., *Writings of Thomas Paine*, vol. 1 (New York: Putnam, 1894), p. 56.

24. *See* Maier, *From Resistance to Revolution*, chap. 2.

25. J. Burgh, *Political Disquisitions: An Enquiry into Public Errors, Defects, and Abuses* (rept. New York: Da Capo, 1971), p. 476; the characterization of Burgh's attractiveness of the Founders is from Shalhope, *The Ideological Origin of the Second Amendment*, p. 604; as to Burgh's publication in colonial America, *see* Hardy, *Armed Citizens, Citizen Armies: Toward a Jurisprudence of the Second Amendment*, 9 Harv. J. L. & Pub. Pol'y 559, 587 (1986).

26. Trenchard and Moyle (1697), as quoted in Shalhope, *The Ideological Origin of the Second Amendment*, pp. 603–4.

27. Ibid.

28. P. Maier, *The Old Revolutionaries: Political Lives in the Age of Samuel Adams* (New York: Knopf, 1980), p. 38 (and detailing the virtues at p. 32ff.); Shalhope, *The Armed Citizen in the Early Republic*, 49 Law and Contemporary Prob. 125, 127–28 (1986) (emphasizing the importance of arms possession in building and maintaining civic

virtue). *See* Pocock, *Machiavelli, Harrington, and English Political Ideologies in the Eighteenth Century*, 22 Wm. & Mary Q. 442, 553–54 (1965) (the virtuous republican citizen's "independence being in the last analysis measured by his ability to bear arms and use them in his own quarrels").

29. N. Machiavelli, *The Prince*, trans. and ed. M. Ruso (New York: St. Martin's, 1952). Machiavelli's central contribution to republican philosophy was the view that fatal "corruption" of the republic would stem from loss of "the individual citizen's autonomy" and that "the test of that autonomy is his willingness and ability to bear arms" (Pocock, *The Machiavellian Moment*, p. 204ff).

30. J. Barlow, *Advice to the Privileged Orders in the Several States of Europe* (London, 1792, Ithaca: Great Seal Books, rept. 1956), pp. 16–17.

31. Shalhope, *The Ideological Origins of the Second Amendment*, pp. 604–6.

32. Ibid. *See* also Pocock, *The Machiavellian Moment*, pp. 507–8, and Maier, *The Old Revolutionaries*, pp. xv–xvi: "Given [the colonists'] political assumptions, and given the events that occurred in the previous decade, [revolution] made great sense. British action not just in America but also in Ireland, Corsica, the West Indies, and England itself contributed to the colonists' conclusion that they had no future as 'free Britons' within the empire, that to remain under the Crown would be to accept for themselves and their children the status of the oppressed Irish."

33. Quoted in J. Elliot, ed., *The Debates in the Several State Conventions on the Adoption of the Federal Constitution* (Washington, D.C., U.S. Congress, 1836), p. 380. For discussion of Keith's recommendation of disarming the colonials, *see* Asbury, *The Right to Keep and Bear Arms in America*, p. 65.

34. Republican theorists despised professional armies and disparaged their fighting abilities vis-à-vis those of armed citizens. *See* Halbrook, *That Every Man Be Armed*, pp. 9, 23, 30, and Pocock, *The Machiavellian Moment*, pp. 89, 357. For express avowal of these views by American and English liberals in predicting that the Revolution would succeed and, later, in analyzing its success, *see* Shalhope, *The Ideological Origins of the Second Amendment*, pp. 604–6, and Hardy, *Armed Citizens, Citizen Armies*, pp. 585, 593.

35. *The Jefferson Cyclopedia*, p. 318.

36. Bruce-Briggs, *The Great American Gun War*, Public Interest, Fall 1976 at 61.

37. Beschle, *Reconsidering the Second Amendment*, p. 89, n. 99, citing for these alleged views the biography by Fawn Brodie whose inaccuracy has been assailed by historians. I must admit my skepticism on this point is fueled by a combination of reverence for Jefferson and diametrically contrary feelings about dogs.

38. Mich. L. Rev., p. 232. *See also* notes 23–35 *supra* and accompanying text.

39. Ibid., p. 229; for pertinent quotations *see generally* pp. 221–25, 228–30, 235.

40. I do not mean to imply that Professor Beschle here (or anywhere) directly confronts the republican theory of civic virtue. In denying that the amendment guarantees a positive right to possess arms, he considers only the destructive actual use of arms in war, revolution, and personal defense without ever acknowledging the Founders' paramount concern with nonviolent as-

pects of arms. *See* n. 23 *supra* and accompanying text.

41. Professor Beschle adds another irrelevant and derisive ad hominem to the effect that "hot air balloons [were] among Jefferson's favorite things" (*Reconsidering the Second Amendment*, p. 89, n. 99).

42. *See, e.g.*, ibid., p. 97: "a state decision which determines that individually-owned firearms are irrelevant to the individual's right against government oppression is rational and should be considered constitutional. . . . If the people, acting through their elected federal representatives, decide that individual firearms possession is unnecessary, then in light of the existence of other means of protection available their decision poses no substantial threat to the individual's right of security . . . [and thus does not violate the Second Amendment]." *See also* ibid., pp. 92–93, 98, 99. In short, Professor Beschle assures us that since government can be trusted to want to maximize the people's "security," banning guns is rational, a decision (to use Bruce-Briggs's words—*see* text accompanying n. 36 *supra*) "made rationally and correctly by intelligent men for the entire nation." It is trite but necessary to remark that if the Founders had reposed such confidence in government they would not have enacted the Second Amendment—or, probably, the rest of the Bill of Rights.

43. Ibid., p. 85; *see also* pp. 86–87, 88–89.

44. For this, James Monroe's description, and similarly effusive contemporary references to the right to arms, *see* n. 10 *supra*. *See* generally the exhaustive quotations in Halbrook, *That Every Man Be Armed*, chap. 3.

45. A. Meikeljohn, *Free Speech and Its Relation to Self Government* (New York: Harper, 1948).

46. *Abrams v. United States*, 250 U.S. 616, 630–31 (1919) (Holmes and Brandeis dissenting), *Whitney v. California*, 274 U.S. 357, 375–76 (1927) (Brandeis and Holmes concurring).

47. *Stromberg v. California*, 283 U.S. 359 (1931). In addition to the similarity between Hughes's argument here and the Second Amendment theory that arms avert bloodshed by deterring the usurpations that provoke it, consider the similarity between the promotion of the civic virtue theory of arms possession and Professor Emerson's justification of free speech on the ground that a self-governing society maximizes input by its individual members. *See generally* T. Emerson, *The System of Free Expression* (New Haven: Yale Univ. Press, 1970).

48. But a moment's reflection will suggest any number of such particular topics (i.e., a long-debated issue of some social or other generally nonpolitical significance as to which rational argument is no longer possible) to the imagination of any reader. One topic that occurs immediately to me is creationism, the pseudoscientific argument for the biblical theory of creation; another is the *Protocols of the Elders of Zion*, the long-discredited fabrication of a purported secret document emanating from a Jewish conspiracy for world domination. Under Professor Beschle's functionalist approach, a law prohibiting believers in these things from arguing for their genuineness would seem not inconsistent with freedom of speech. (Of course, freedom of religion might protect creationist arguments and even the Protocols, albeit proponents of both emphatically deny making a religiously based argument.)

49. As Justice Frankurter said in refuting calls for judicial abrogation of the right against self-incrimination: "If it be thought that the privilege is outmoded in the conditions of this modern age, then the thing to do is take it out of the Constitution, not to whittle it down by subtle encroachments of judicial opinion." *Uhlmann v. United States*, 350 U.S. 422, 427–28 (1956).

50. The elusiveness of whatever "Western" is supposed to connote reveals how slipshod the argument is. Even if, contrary to both logic and usage, Professor Beschle thinks this word includes no other countries but the United States and those of Western Europe, it would still encompass Nazi Germany, Fascist Italy, and Spain and Portugal under Franco and Somosa respectively.

Moreover, the most natural understanding of "Western" would refer to the Western Hemisphere alone. I assume Professor Beschle would not cite the countries of Central and South America as models of respect for his "primary" rights. A more limited (indeed illogically so) use of "Western" would limit it to North America. But that would still include Mexico where torture is widely used by police, prison conditions often constitute cruel and unusual punishment, and, earlier in this century, Catholics were subjected to savage official persecution.

Note that the term "Western nations" is generally used to distinguish the United States and its (mostly) allied nations from those of the Eastern or Communist bloc. It is significant that, far from defining nations that share the values Professor Beschle deems primary, this usage is preferred precisely because it is a less inaccurate alternative to the older phrase "Free World" nations.

51. Wechsler, *A Rationale of the Law of Homicide*, 27 Colum. L. Rev. 701, 736 (1937).

Note: Included in the critique of this chapter Professor Daniel Polsby was kind enough to give me is an alternative explanation of minimalist interpretation. Although I do not fully concur in that explanation, it is so insightful and forceful that I append it here with his permission:

"Professor Beschle recognizes that the treatment given to the Second Amendment by Nowack et al. and Tribe won't cut it, and in this he's correct—but the version he then advances is no better. What is the underlying problem you see with all these authors? Although they do not want to repudiate the classical liberal assumptions on which the Constitution was premised, they really do not share its values. To classical liberals, an armed citizenry was part of the republic.

"Modern liberals do not share that ideal, and it is not simply that they are phobic about guns. They are uncomfortable about individuals exercising initiatives about lots of things that have an impact on the public. Their idea is that the right way to get collective goods (like public security, generalized prosperity, unspoiled wildernesses—etc. and etc.) is through collective mechanisms. They think this about the decisions of markets no less than about decisions about when and where to employ deadly force. How could anyone prefer the disorderly, wasteful, and dehumanizing world of economic competition to the rational, orderly, humane world of central planning? Or letting individuals rather than cops (experts, we are always told—picked, trained, subjected to public supervision under public standards) exercise the power to decide when to destroy life?

"My point is that beneath the values dissonance, there is a lurking empirical question: how do you get more public welfare: is it really true that collective mechanisms are superior? At least in the sphere of political economy, we have a tentative answer. The hard paddle of History has dealt the collectivists a smartening generation of whacks. A legitimate question remains, however, as to how far this experience generalizes into theory.

"So far as weapons policy is concerned, however, we need not allow the issue to become clouded with theory: there is an imposing threshold fact. It is this: there aren't enough cops to secure the state's monopoly of deadly force. The Hobbesian bargain requires everybody, not just the good guys, to submit to Leviathan's will; if not everybody submits, then we're discussing 'what if' and not 'what.' "

52. Levinson, *The Embarrassing Second Amendment*, p. 642.

IV.

ORIGINAL INTENT AND THE FOURTH AMENDMENT

BRADFORD P. WILSON

11. The Fourth Amendment as More Than a Form of Words: The View from the Founding

Justice Frankfurter once remarked, "The course of true law pertaining to searches and seizures . . . has not—to put it mildly—run smooth."[1] The most frequent apologia offered by legal commentators for this imperfect state of the art of Fourth Amendment jurisprudence rests on the terms of the amendment itself. For example, it is said by one scholar that although the Fourth Amendment has the virtue of brevity, it is stained with "the vice of ambiguity."[2] Another commentator writes, "The fifty four words which make up the Fourth Amendment are not particularly illuminating."[3] From this view emerges a particular perspective toward the judicial function: "The work of giving concrete and contemporary meaning to that brief, vague, general, unilluminating text written nearly two centuries ago is inescapably judgmental. In the pans of judgment sit imponderable weights."[4]

The interpretation of such words and phrases does indeed call for more than logical prowess. Yet, are not the interpretive difficulties besetting the judge's task qualitatively the same in regard to all of the rights secured in the first ten amendments? Freedom of speech, due process of law, just compensation, a speedy trial, excessive bail: in all of these instances, saying what the law is is "inescapably judgmental." As Herbert Storing has argued, "[I]t is impossible in any interesting case to define the rights protected in the amendments with sufficient exactness to permit their automatic application. A bill of rights cannot eliminate the need for political judgment, and therewith the risk of abuse."[5]

The necessity of ambiguity in the expression of constitutional rights provided the Federalists with one of their most powerful arguments against including a bill of rights in the Constitution. It was argued in defense of the unamended Constitution that expressions such as "cruel and unusual punishments," or, it might just as well have been said, "unreasonable searches and seizures," would have been "too vague to have been of any consequence, since they admit of no clear and precise signification." Nor, it was argued, could the problem be resolved by substituting a "labyrinth of detail" specifying the content of the more general terms, as that would be unbefitting an original charter of government and would leave no room for prudential changes "as must be in the power of every Legislature that is rationally formed."[6]

In light of this now ancient attack on the Bill of Rights, it is curious that contemporary scholars of the Fourth Amendment believe, contrary to the Federalists, in the necessity of the Fourth Amendment for the preservation and fostering of civil liberty yet do not hesitate to place the blame for the undisciplined development of Fourth Amendment doctrine primarily on the general terms of the amendment and not on the amendment's chief interpreter. Such a posture serves neither to encourage responsible criticism of contemporary Fourth Amendment adjudication nor to increase respect for the Fourth Amendment right. Instead, it points one in the direction of Justice Iredell's argument against the wisdom of having such an amendment.

The impossibility of exhaustive particularization of the scope of the rights given constitutional protection increases rather than diminishes the responsibility of the Supreme Court for the rough course run by Fourth Amendment law. For "what is a reasonable or an unreasonable search or seizure is 'purely a judicial question and in determining it the court must look to all the circumstances.' "[7] In choosing to have a Fourth Amendment, with its necessarily sweeping terms, the American people placed in the hands of the judiciary the task of refuting the charge that the amendment would be a mistake. This task called from the start for a judicial statesmanship which, with clarity and consistency and with faithfulness to the intention of those who framed and ratified the amendment, would render its terms not only consequential but beneficial.

To attribute a role for judicial statesmanship to the plan of the Constitution is not to imply that judicial judgment does not differ from political judgment, or that by virtue of judicial review, the judicial branch of the government is supreme vis-à-vis the other branches. As stated quite adequately by Herbert Wechsler, "Federal Courts, including the Supreme Court, do not pass on constitutional questions because there is a special function vested in them to enforce the Constitution or police the other agencies of government. They do so rather for the reason that they must decide a litigated issue that is otherwise within their jurisdiction and in doing so must give effect to the supreme law of the land."[8] That is the teaching of *Marbury v. Madison*. Judicial review over governmental actions having a constitutional dimension was there justified as a necessary incident to the normal judicial activity of applying governing law to particular circumstances. The application of laws, in their nature general, to singular circumstances comprises the judicial duty. It is this activity that the Supreme Court has executed in an erratic and often contradictory manner in its interpretation of the Fourth Amendment.

This chapter is concerned with an area of Fourth Amendment jurisprudence in which the defects of inconstancy and intellectual confusion have been most apparent: the question of the legal consequences of an unreasonable search and seizure. The burgeoning of Fourth Amendment case law in the twentieth century has rested on the judicial assertion of the so-called exclusionary rule: A rule of evidence prohibiting a judge from admitting evidence in a criminal trial if law enforcement officers acquired it in a manner which violated the defendant's right to be secure from arbitrary searches and seizures. While there are certain important exceptions to that rule, they are few in number and limited in scope.

Since the inception of the exclusionary rule, nearly every search and seizure case that has reached the Supreme Court has addressed the question: Was the evidence that was introduced at trial obtained in violation of the requirements of the Fourth Amendment, thereby rendering it inadmissible in the court proceeding? To answer this question, the Court dutifully scrutinizes the Fourth Amendment in search of the constitutional standard governing the circumstances in the case before it. Thus, the invocation of the exclusionary rule results in an additional construction of the Fourth Amendment. As Jacob Landynski has noted, "Without the exclusionary rule, the illegality of the search would be immaterial to the admission of the evidence, and the judicial *development* of the Fourth Amendment as we know it would have proved impossible."[9]

This special dependence of the modern history of the construction of the Fourth Amendment right upon the rule of exclusion has encouraged many friends of Fourth Amendment liberties to favor the exclusionary rule as the method of enforcement most in harmony with the ends served by the amendment. I have elsewhere examined and found wanting the juridical origins of the rule of exclusion and the various Supreme Court opinions defining its legal status.[10] My purpose here remains to apply, in the parlance of our time, the "jurisprudence of original intent" to the enforcement of the Fourth Amendment.

When the Supreme Court excluded the exclusionary rule from certain good-faith situations a few years ago, one of the dissenting justices wrote: "It now appears that the Court's victory over the Fourth Amendment is complete."[11] Yet, the Constitution had been in effect for nearly a century before the Supreme Court found in it any support for the exclusion of evidence procured in violation of the Fourth Amendment. This fact is significant for understanding the revolution in constitutional interpretation achieved by the Court's adoption of the exclusionary rule. It implies that before 1886 when the Fourth Amendment was first invoked to reverse a court-imposed penalty based on unconstitutionally seized evidence,[12] another view of the consequences of an unreasonable search and seizure reigned in American legal thought.

In *Marbury v. Madison*, Chief Justice Marshall wrote: "The government of the United States has been emphatically termed a government of laws, and not of men. It will certainly cease to deserve this high appellation, if the laws furnish no remedy for the violation of a vested legal right."[13] As Marshall readily acknowledged, he was saying nothing that the common lawyer did not know from his Blackstone. Blackstone had analyzed the law into four parts: the declaratory, the directory, the remedial, and the vindicatory. For our purposes, his discussion of remedies is most relevant: "The REMEDIAL part of the law is so necessary a consequence of the former two [i.e., declaratory and directory], that laws must be very vague and imperfect without it. For in vain would rights be declared, in vain directed to be observed, if there were no method of recovering and asserting those rights, when wrongfully withheld or invaded. This is what we mean properly, when we speak of the protection of the law."[14] As the later Justice Harlan observed, the Founding generation, following Blackstone, "link[ed] 'rights' and 'remedies' in a 1:1 correlation."[15] What light does this shed on the original understanding of the Fourth Amendment?

The Fourth Amendment consists of two clauses. The first clause prohibits the violation of "[t]he right of the people to be secure in their persons, houses, papers, and effects, against unreasonable searches and seizures." The second clause establishes certain conditions for the lawful issuance of a warrant. Although it is not obvious from the language alone, the antecedent history of the amendment makes clear that the second clause was intended by the framers to provide a standard, though not an exhaustive one, of what constitutes a reasonable or an unreasonable search or seizure. Thus the language of the Fourth Amendment is both declaratory and directory: it declares rights and wrongs and directs their observance.

A problem arises, however, when we inquire into the remedial branch of the law. No express provision for the enforcement of the right declared in the Fourth Amendment can be found either in the words of the amendment or in any other clause of the Constitution. On the face of it, then, there is an affirmation of a right with no provision for a corresponding remedy.

It would therefore seem that the Fourth Amendment in its terms is an incomplete law: Given the common understanding of the nature of law at the time of the amendment's ratification, it is inconceivable that its framers intended to establish a right without at the same time requiring that a method, remedial or punitive, exist for its enforcement. Yet in regard to its own enforcement, the Fourth Amendment is silent.

One possible solution to this problem of the apparent incompleteness of the Fourth Amendment is that the amendment implies an obligation on the part of the national legislature, and perhaps on the parts of the legislatures of the states, to act as auxiliaries in the enforcement of the right by providing remedies and sanctions for its violation.

What Justice Story had to say with respect to the fugitive slave clause (Art. IV, Sec. 2) is relevant here. In *Prigg v. Pennsylvania* he stated for the Supreme Court:

> If . . . the Constitution guarantees the right, . . . the natural inference certainly is, that the national government is clothed with the appropriate authority and functions to enforce it. The fundamental principle applicable to all cases of this sort, would seem to be, that where the end is required, the means are given. . . . The clause is found in the national Constitution. . . . It does not point out any state functionaries, or any state action to carry its provisions into effect. The states cannot, therefore, be compelled to enforce them; and it might well be deemed an unconstitutional exercise of the power of interpretation, to insist that the states are bound to provide means to carry into effect the duties of the national government, nowhere delegated or entrusted to them by the Constitution. On the contrary, the natural, if not the necessary conclusion is, that the national government, in the absence of all positive provisions to the contrary, is bound, through its own proper departments, legislative, judicial or executive, as the case may require, to carry into effect all the rights and duties imposed upon it by the Constitution. The remark of Mr. Madison, in the Federalist, (No. 43,) would seem in such cases to apply with peculiar force. "A right (says he) implies a remedy; and where else would the remedy be deposited, than where it is deposited by the Constitution?" meaning as the context shows, in the government of the United States.[16]

According to Justice Story, then, the Constitution, being national in character, obliges the federal government to provide, presumably through legislation, remedies for the violation of constitutionally guaranteed rights; the Constitution does not, however, compel a like obligation on the part of the states, unless it explicitly provides for it.

It must nonetheless be observed that the federal Constitution is properly called national, not in the sense that it is the fundamental law of the nation as distinct from the states, but rather in the sense that it is the fundamental law for every part of the Union, including the states. Each one of its provisions is a part—a paramount part—of the laws of every state. This fact suggests that it is contrary only to Justice Story and not to the plan of the Constitution to hold that an authority devolves upon the people of the United States to use their state legislatures, as well as their national Congress, to pass laws aiding in the enforcement of the fundamental compact binding them one to another. The supremacy clause (Art. VI, para. 2) protects against any attempt by a state to establish remedies for the violation of federal constitutional rights that conflict with remedies provided by the Constitution itself or created by the national legislature.

Was this the solution for the problem of enforcing the Fourth Amendment that was contemplated by its framers? Was it generally understood that, upon ratification of the amendment, the state or national legislatures, or both, would promptly legislate remedies, to be implemented through civil actions in the courts or through sanctions to be enforced in criminal courts, in protection of the Fourth Amendment right?

To maintain this position, one would have to concede that the framers had left the right asserted in the Fourth Amendment in an extraordinarily vulnerable condition. Perhaps the Fourth Amendment could be read as obliging Congress or state legislatures to create legal consequences for its violation, but in the absence of such remedial legislation, the amendment would, in this view, exist only as a form of words.

I have suggested that such an understanding is in tension with the founding generation's notion of law. It does not conform to the view that consequences of noncompliance are as much a part of law as are declarations and directives.

To understand what the Founders had in mind for the enforcement of constitutional rights, it is necessary to recall that they understood themselves to be building upon the English legal institutions that had been transplanted to the colonies. With equity existing only in a rudimentary form at the time of the founding, these legal institutions were primarily those of the common law. It was generally accepted that where no positively enacted law held otherwise, the common law governed rights and duties.

This circumstance is highly significant for our coming to grips with the peculiar "incompleteness" of those constitutional provisions that pronounce the law regarding certain rights but are silent as to the legal consequences that result from their violation. As one commentator has argued, "There is no reason to believe that the draftsmen of the Constitution gave specific attention to the problems of implementation. . . . [T]he Constitution was to be implemented in accordance with the remedial institutions of the common law."[17] Although the framers surely did not intend to prohibit legislative action aiding in the enforcement of constitutional rights, such action was not required to complete the Constitution as law in Blackstone's sense.

Again, relying on our commentator: "It may fairly be assumed that the founding fathers did not contemplate a new species of constitutional tort. There is evidence that the transgression of a government officer was regarded as a trespass, in accordance with the vocabulary and outlook of the common law." To regard such transgressions as trespasses is not to limit the corresponding remedy for any manner of abuse to an action in trespass, understood in its strict sense. The term "trespass" in the common-law tradition was ordinarily used in a broader sense "to describe the conduct of a government officer actionable at common law, even though strictly speaking a form of action other than trespass would have been appropriate in the particular case."[18] The framers' reliance upon the remedial institutions of the common law explains why, although many a legal right could be found on the books without a corresponding remedy being specified, Chief Justice Marshall could confidently assert as binding for the American system of law

Blackstone's formulation that "it is a general and indisputable rule, that where there is a legal right, there is also a legal remedy, by suit or action at law, whenever that right is invaded."[19]

It must be conceded that a difficulty in implementation through actions at law would arise if a right created by the Constitution had no common-law counterpart and no appropriate common-law remedy for it could be found to exist. The Fourth Amendment, however, is emphatically free of this problem. The language of the amendment does not purport to create the right to be secure against unreasonable searches and seizures but rather recognizes it as already existing. As was observed by Justice Story, the Fourth Amendment "is little more than the affirmance of a great constitutional doctrine of the common law."[20] It is perhaps more accurate to describe the amendment as an extension of the common law, given that specific warrants were not the rule of the day in the English tradition. In any case, an integral part of that "great constitutional doctrine of the common law" that survived intact was that unreasonable searches and seizures were considered trespasses and that officers of the government who abused their authority in such a manner were liable to those whose persons or property they caused to be invaded.

That this remedial branch of the common law on the subject of search and seizure was well known to the Fourth Amendment's framers cannot be gainsaid. It was central to the controversy over the legality of general warrants, which arose from the circumstances accompanying the crown's arrest of John Wilkes for seditious libel during the reign of George III. That controversy, which spanned the years 1763 to 1765, was precipitated by the search and seizure of the books and papers, and in some instances the persons, of Wilkes and forty-eight other Englishmen under a general warrant. Its fame on this side of the Atlantic was second only to James Otis's attempt to prevent the issuance to customs officers of writs of assistance, which in their oppressive nature were much akin to the general warrants used in England against Wilkes and his comrades. For our purposes, we need only note that every action brought by Wilkes and his associates for the unreasonable searches and seizures was for damages against the officials who issued the warrant and the officers who executed it.

When the common-law origins of the Fourth Amendment are recognized, and it is further observed that the amendment does not create a right but rather acknowledges an existing one, the amendment does not appear to suffer from incompleteness. For the Fourth Amendment to be law in the full sense, it must be understood as requiring an available remedy for violation of the asserted right. The framers assumed that this demand was met by the remedial aspect of the common law regarding unreasonable searches and seizures.

One scholar has suggested that the Fourth Amendment "guarantees that the injured person shall not be denied a cause of action against the trespasser."[21] This position carries the necessary implication that the abrogation by legislative action of civil remedies for illegal searches and seizures would violate the Fourth Amendment and, presumably, due process. According to this view, the civil remedy against errant government officers was given constitutional sanction by the Fourth Amendment and cannot lawfully be abridged.

I would agree that in light of the framers' understanding of the nature of law, the Fourth Amendment must be understood as guaranteeing the availability of a remedy for violations of the Fourth Amendment right; and if Congress should take affirmative action to deny such a remedy, its action would be unconstitutional and void. This is not to say, however, that the Fourth Amendment gives fixed constitutional status to any particular remedy. That the framers assumed that common-law remedies would be used to implement the Fourth Amendment right does not in any way imply that those specific remedies were themselves of constitutional status. Not only could other remedies and sanctions be added by governmental action to the forms of action characteristic of the common-law trespass remedy, in keeping with the general principle that common law must give way to statutory law, Congress could legitimately replace the trespass remedy altogether with a criminal or other action, even an exclusionary rule, provided that an effective means of enforcement, in harmony with the purposes of the Fourth Amendment, continued to be available for unreasonable searches and seizures.

The point to be emphasized is that the framers did not regard the Fourth Amendment as impotent in the absence of remedial legislation. The common-law remedy of trespass historically had been available for unreasonable searches and seizures, and the Fourth Amendment guaranteed that it would continue to be so unless or until the legislature chose to enact an effective substitute.

There is less evidence for the view that the common law understood governmental oppression of individuals to be a public as well as a private wrong, thereby rendering offending officers subject to criminal prosecution by the sovereign power. It is noteworthy, however, that such a view was expressed by Hamilton in *The Federalist* No. 83. Attempting to assuage those who were fearful of oppressive modes of collecting the national revenues, Hamilton argued: "As to the conduct of the officers of the revenue, the provision in favor of trial by jury in criminal cases, will afford the security aimed at. Wilful abuses of a public authority, to the oppression of the subject, and every species of official extortion, are offenses against the government; for which, the persons who commit them, may be indicted and punished according to the circumstances of the case."[22] When Hamilton wrote this, there was no Fourth Amendment, no national Bill of Rights. The laws establishing the public rights and wrongs referred to must, then, have had their source in the body of common law.

If Hamilton's reading of the common law is correct, the Fourth Amendment should be read as affirming both private and public rights, with their corresponding modes of redress. Indeed, it could plausibly be argued that the public nature of the right protected by the Fourth Amendment is indicated by the amendment's language. It speaks of "[t]he right of the people." The natural sense of these words implies that the right is not only personal but also collective or public. My research, however, has not turned up any American case that has treated the violation of the right protected by the common law and the Fourth Amendment as constituting a public crime in the absence of legislation making it so. Hamilton's assumption that willful abuses of a public authority are of a criminal nature does not, then, appear to have found support in common opinion.

Be that as it may, it must be observed that the trespass remedy is not devoid of a public end. So much is manifest in the common-law doctrine that recovery can be had beyond compensation for the injury received. This doctrine of punitive or exemplary damages received its definitive justification, later cited in American cases, in the English Case of General Warrants in 1763. In that case Chief Justice Pratt, later to be Lord Camden, upheld a large damage award for a victim of a trespass by the king's officers. In doing so, he stated: "[A] jury have it in their power to give damages for more than the injury received. Damages are designed not only as a satisfaction of the injured person, but likewise as a punishment to the guilty, to deter from any such proceeding for the future and as a proof of the detestation of the jury to the action itself."[23] Thus, the remedy the founding generation considered appropriate for a violation of the Fourth Amendment right, that of trespass, served a multiplicity of ends: redress, punishment, deterrence, and morality.

Granting, then, that the constitutional right embodied in the Fourth Amendment was intended by its framers to be implemented in the first place by means of the remedial institutions of the common law; the question next arises of which courts of law—state, federal, or some combination thereof—were to be the instruments by which the wronged parties were to be enabled to procure adequate redress.

In defining the limits of the power of the federal judiciary, the Constitution provides that "[t]he judicial Power shall extend to all Cases, in Law and Equity, arising under this Constitution, the Laws of the United States, and Treaties made, or which shall be made, under their Authority" (Art. III, Sec. 2). During the first few decades following the Constitution's ratification, it was a matter of some controversy whether this clause meant to extend the power of the federal courts to common-law cases. As we have indicated, Hamilton understood willful abuses of a public authority to be offenses at common law. Given the fact that Hamilton considered such crimes to be subject to the constitutional requirement for jury trials in criminal cases (Art. III, Sec. 2), it follows that he understood the federal judicial power to extend to common-law crimes. Furthermore, if that power extended to willful abuses of authority viewed as public wrongs, there would seem to be no grounds for denying its extension to such abuses viewed as private wrongs.

But whatever the disposition of the original Constitution toward extending the federal judiciary's power to violations of the common-law right to be secure against unreasonable searches, the ratification of the Fourth Amendment rendered the question practically moot. By incorporating the common-law doctrine regarding searches and seizures into its charter of national existence, the people of the United States gave it constitutional status, thereby placing all cases arising under that law within the limits of the federal judicial power.

It is axiomatic that for the federal judicial power to be able to operate in all cases arising under the Constitution, federal courts must be endowed with appropriate jurisdiction. Article III of the Constitution vests in the Supreme Court original jurisdiction over "all Cases affecting Ambassadors, other public Ministers and Consuls, and those in which a State shall be Party," giving that Court appellate jurisdiction in all other cases "with such Exceptions, and under such Regulations as the Congress shall make" (Art. III, Sec. 2). The existence and jurisdiction of inferior federal courts are left to the discretion of Congress.

The jurisdictional plan of the Constitution has been summarized as follows: "Congress would decide from time to time how far the federal judicial institution should be used within the limits of judicial power; or, stated differently, how far judicial jurisdiction should be left to the state courts, bound as they are by the Constitution as 'the supreme Law of the Land . . . any Thing in the Constitution or laws of any State to the Contrary notwithstanding.'"[24] Today, with our heavy reliance on the federal judiciary as courts of first instance in cases raising federal questions, we have a tendency to forget that throughout our early history, the principal forum for the vindication of constitutional rights was the state court. It is striking that before 1875, Congress deemed it neither necessary nor desirable to provide federal courts with original jurisdiction over cases involving rights claimed under the Constitution. As Charles Warren has pointed out, "large numbers of American statesmen were, from the outset of the Government, in favor of allowing the State Courts to exercise primary, or at least concurrent, jurisdiction in most of the cases to which the Federal judicial power was extended by the Constitution; and they regarded the exercise of the Federal judicial power as chiefly necessary in the appellate tribunal."[25] These statesmen assumed, of course, that the judicial power of the states extended to such cases. Yet it must be said that the pages of the Supreme Court reports reveal quite a variety of opinions regarding whether and to what extent the jurisdiction of state courts extends to cases involving federal rights.

That some confusion would arise from the plan of the Constitution was not unforeseen by its framers. Hamilton wrote:

> The erection of a new government, whatever care of wisdom may distinguish the work, cannot fail to originate questions of intricacy and nicety; and these may in a particular manner be expected to flow from the establishment of a constitution founded upon the total or partial incorporation of a number of distinct sovereignties. 'Tis time only that can mature and perfect so compound a system, can liquidate the meaning of all the parts, and can adjust them to each other in a harmonious and consistent WHOLE.[26]

Wishing to start this process off on the proper foot, Hamilton devoted *The Federalist* No. 82 to the questions posed to the judicial department by the new federal structure and, in particular, to those questions relating to "the situation of the state courts in regard to those causes, which are to be submitted to federal jurisdiction."[27] In that essay, the role envisioned by the Constitutionalists for the state courts in the execution of federal law comes into focus.

What is argued in *The Federalist* No. 82 comes as no surprise to the reader, for it had been presaged in earlier essays. For example, in *The Federalist* No. 16, Hamilton had stated that opposition to the national government by seditious individuals "could be overcome by the same means which are daily employed against the same evil, under the State governments. The Magistracy, being equally the Ministers of the law of the land, from whatever source it might emanate, would doubtless be as ready to guard the national as the local regulations from the inroads of private licentiousness."[28] Again in *The Federalist* No. 27, Hamilton asserted that "[t]he plan reported by the Convention, by extending the authority of the Federal head to the individual citizens of the several States, will enable the government to employ the ordinary magistracy of each in the execution of its laws."[29] While these passages refer to state judicial enforcement of congressional acts, the principle embodied therein also would support state judicial enforcement of federal constitutional law, since state magistrates are "equally the Ministers of the law of the land, from whatever source it might emanate."

An objection occasionally has been raised to this position on the ground that state courts simply lack jurisdiction over those cases to which the judicial power of the United States extends and which "enter into the national policy, affect the national rights, and may compromit [*sic*] the national sovereignty." In Justice Story's words, "[A]s to cases [arising] under the constitution, laws, and treaties of the United States . . . the state courts could not ordinarily possess a direct jurisdiction. The jurisdiction over such cases could not exist in the state courts previous to the adoption of the constitution, and it could not afterwards be directly conferred on them; for the constitution expressly requires the judicial power to be vested in courts ordained and established by the United States."[30] Hamilton, for one, did not entertain so restrictive a view of state jurisdiction.

Hamilton's thesis in *The Federalist* No. 82 regarding state court jurisdiction under the federal Constitution is this: With Madison, Hamilton saw the plan of the Federal Convention as "partly federal, and partly national." As it aims "only at a partial Union or consolidation, the State Governments . . . clearly retain all the rights of sovereignty which they before had and which were not by the act *exclusively* delegated to the United States."[31] Therefore, in regard to the judicial power of the states, the state courts retain all jurisdiction not taken away by the Constitution. Since there is no clause in the Constitution confining causes within federal cognizance to the federal courts, state courts hold concurrent jurisdiction over those that fall within that description of causes of which they previously had cognizance. To these classes of cases, the doctrine of concurrent jurisdiction is "clearly applicable." "It is not equally evident in relation to cases which may grow out of, and be *peculiar* to the constitution . . . : For not to allow the state courts a right of jurisdiction in such cases can hardly be considered as the abridgement of a pre-existing authority." Over such cases, the national legislature may in its discretion give the federal courts exclusive jurisdiction. Nonetheless, not only is it forbidden that the state courts be deprived of any part of their primitive jurisdiction, except as it relates to appeal; "in every case in which they were not expressly excluded by the future acts of the national legislature, they will of course take cognizance of the causes to which those acts may give birth." This is to be inferred from "the nature of the judiciary power, and from the general genius of the system."

> The judiciary power of every government looks beyond its own local or municipal laws, and in civil cases lays hold of all subjects of litigation between parties within its jurisdiction though the causes of dispute are relative to the laws of the most distant part of the globe. Those of Japan not less than of New-York may furnish the objects of legal discussion to our courts. When in addition to this, we consider the state governments and the national governments as they truly are, in the light of kindred systems and as parts of ONE WHOLE, the inference seems to be conclusive that the state courts would have a concurrent jurisdiction in all cases arising under the laws of the union, where it was not expressly prohibited.[32]

Hamilton, then, regarded it as incontestable that the state courts would have jurisdiction over cases arising under the Constitution which involved rights and obligations that were actionable in state courts before the ratification of the Constitution. He also argued the legitimacy of state jurisdiction over cases arising under the Constitution over which there was no preexisting state jurisdiction, provided such jurisdiction was not expressly denied by Congress.

It is not entirely clear whether Hamilton regarded jurisdiction over this latter class of cases to devolve upon state courts sheerly by virtue of the states being parts of one whole, or whether he believed such jurisdiction to be dependent on positive grants by the state legislatures. His words "the state court *would have* a concurrent jurisdiction in all cases arising under the laws of the union, where it was not expressly prohibited" do not indicate a contingent character to that jurisdiction.

For our purposes, however, it is unnecessary to determine whether the Constitution directly grants state jurisdiction over cases to which the federal judicial power extends, absent congressional prohibition. The preexistent nature of the right protected by the Fourth Amendment and the fact that state courts universally possessed jurisdiction over common-law trespasses by government officers place all cases arising under that amendment in the category of cases that "grow out of" but are certainly not "peculiar to" the Constitution. According to Hamilton's analysis, state judicial authority over such cases is unquestionable.

Hamilton's position on state jurisdiction over federal issues was defended by John Marshall in the Virginia Ratifying Convention and, usefully for our purposes, in the context of a discussion of the legal consequences of oppressive behavior by federal collection officers. George Mason instigated the debate by waging an attack on the extent of the judicial power delegated by the Constitution:

> Give me leave to advert to the operation of this judicial power. Its jurisdiction in the first case will extend to all cases affecting revenue, excise, and custom-house officers. . . . "All cases in law and equity arising under this Constitution, and the laws of the United States," take in all the officers of the government. . . . In what predicament will our citizens then be? We know the difficulty we are put in by our own courts, and how hard it is to bring officers to justice even in them. If any of the federal officers should be guilty of the greatest oppressions, or behave with the most insolent and wanton brutality to a man's wife or daughter, where is this man to get relief? If you suppose in the inferior courts, they are not appointed by the states. They are not men in whom the community can place confidence. It will be decided by federal judges.[33]

Marshall responded:

> [H]e says that the officers of the government will be screened from merited punishment by the federal judiciary. The federal sheriff, says he, will go into a poor man's house and beat him, or abuse his family, and the federal court will protect him. Does any gentleman believe this? Is it necessary that the officers will commit a trespass on the property or persons of those with whom they are to transact business? Will such great insults on the people of this country be allowable? Were a law made to authorize them, it would be void. The injured man would trust to a tribunal in his neighborhood [i.e., an

> inferior federal court]. To such a tribunal he would apply for redress, and get it. There is no reason to fear that he would not meet that justice there which his country will be ever willing to maintain.[34]

And besides, Marshall added, "[t]here is no clause in the Constitution which bars the individual member injured from applying to the state courts to give him redress." Thus, according to Marshall, the state courts could try individual actions against federal officers, just as could the federal courts (assuming Congress gave them the appropriate jurisdiction).

In regard to the federal courts, Marshall may have believed with Hamilton that their jurisdiction would reach wrongs at common law, or he may have anticipated federal legislation on this matter. As to state courts, the source of the law could be either positive state law, the common law as it was in force in the states, or, as Marshall made clear in the same discussion, federal law. "The state courts will not lose the jurisdiction of the causes they now decide. They have a concurrence of jurisdiction with the federal courts in those cases in which the latter have cognizance." Therefore, state court jurisdiction over cases arising from the right to be free from unreasonable searches and seizures was assured, both before and after the ratification of the Fourth Amendment.

The framers' view that the state courts would have jurisdiction over cases involving federal rights led one prominent scholar to assert that, "[i]n the scheme of the Constitution, [the state courts] are the primary guarantors of constitutional rights."[35] This is debatable, since many of the leading defenders of the Constitution, including Hamilton and Marshall, believed that Congress would provide the federal courts with the full range of the judicial power, in which case the state courts at most would be partners with the federal judiciary in the enforcement of constitutional rights. As a historical matter, however, the state courts did, indeed, from the beginning function as the "primary guarantors" of constitutional rights.

The reason for this is that the Federal Judiciary Act of 1789, which established the jurisdiction of the federal courts, was the product of a compromise between the Federalists and the Anti-Federalists, "so framed as to secure the votes of those who, while willing to see the experiment of a Federal Constitution tried, were insistent that the Federal Courts should be given the minimum powers and jurisdiction."[36] The Judiciary Act did not confer the entire judicial power on inferior federal courts. Neither the district nor the circuit courts received general jurisdiction over cases arising under the Constitution, laws, or treaties of the United States. Nor were those courts given cognizance of suits or proceedings against federal officers for their conduct in executing the laws, except as the circuit courts were given jurisdiction by reason of diversity of citizenship, and as the district courts were given admiralty and maritime jurisdiction. The intention of the Judiciary Act, then, was, with the exceptions noted, to leave the enforcement of remedies against federal officers to the state courts. National supervision was to be exercised by writ of error from the highest court of the state to the Supreme Court of the United States when the state decision contravened an alleged right or immunity claimed under the federal Constitution or under a federal treaty, statute, or commission.

We are now in a position to summarize the original understanding of how the right to be secure against unreasonable searches and seizures was to be enforced.

Because of the jurisdictional limitations placed by the First Congress on the federal courts, the primary responsibility for redressing violations of the right devolved upon the state courts. Such violations were considered to be trespasses, in conformity with the common-law tradition. Since every right was understood to have a corresponding remedy, the forms of actions appropriate at common law to the various forms of trespass were regarded as available in remedy for wrongful searches and seizures. In such cases, the modes of relief most often invoked would be those for damages, such as an action in trespass or trover, and those for repossession of property unlawfully detained, such as replevin.

As Chief Justice Marshall indicated in *Slocum v. Mayberry*,[37] actions in the state courts for repossession were in some instances, particularly those involving property seized under federal law for supposed forfeiture, contingent on a prior determination by the federal courts of the reasonableness of the seizure. It is not clear whether the same would hold true for actions for damages, since such suits would not impinge on the federal court's jurisdiction over the property. At any rate, there certainly would be no objection to the initiation of a damage action against a federal officer prior to or contemporaneous with federal court proceedings involving the same search and seizure in those cases where the resolution of the damage suit does not depend on the question at issue in the federal proceedings.

There remains one matter still outstanding, however, in this account of the early view of the enforcement of the right protected by the Fourth Amendment. It has been argued here that neither the silence of Congress regarding the implementation of the Fourth Amendment right nor the unavailability of a federal court for redressing that right was understood to affect in any way the existence or availability of a remedy in a suit at law. The remedy was assumed to exist as a matter of right under the Fourth Amendment, and the state courts were commonly understood to have jurisdiction to enforce the remedy. When one turns to the case reports of the first three quarters of the nineteenth century, one finds that in cases alleging a wrongful search or seizure by a federal officer, traditional common-law forms of action associated with trespass were, indeed, without exception, the modes of redress invoked. To those of us weaned on modern procedural law, however, in which it is a settled practice to declare, where relevant, the constitutional source of the right being asserted, it is curious that in these early cases the officer is charged with acting outside his legitimate authority to search or seize, without any reference being made to the fact that the action with which he is charged violates a constitutional right. Often the officer is described as liable "in suit at common law." Does this imply that the right to a remedy in such cases arises under the common law rather than the Fourth Amendment? Does the liability of the federal officer derive not from the Constitution but from a law of less than constitutional stature?

First, it must be observed that it would be erroneous to assume that a trespass by a government officer was not understood by the framers of the Constitution and the Bill of Rights to be a constitutional case. At the very least, the Constitution would bear on the officer's defense. For instance, if a federal officer pleaded a warrant in justification of his action, the Fourth Amendment's requirements for the warrant's issuance would provide the standard of judging the warrant's validity, whether it issued from a state or a federal judicial officer.

Second, one must keep in mind the relationship between the common law and the Constitution.

> [E]ven if the right to recover must be found in the common law, the common law does not, in the United States, have an existence independent of the Constitution. The common law has always absorbed and given effect to interests created by statutes and constitutions in the same way that it has given effect to interests created by judicial decision. If the Constitution is viewed as an integral aspect of the common law, as it ought to be, the dichotomy of Constitution and common law becomes a false one.[38]

This legal phenomenon has been described in this way: "The process of adaptation of the forms of action to serve statutory and constitutional ends was sometimes tortuous, but it was a significant part of the common law system and a reason for its continued vitality. If, in the case of an officer charged with an unconstitutional encroachment, the remedy of trespass or ejectment was deemed to be 'given' by the common law, it was nevertheless the Constitution that determined the outcome."[39] To say that the remedy of trespass in search and seizure cases was deemed to be "given" by the common law is not, however, necessarily to deny that the right to such a remedy would be, under certain circumstances, constitutionally dictated as well. As I have argued, the Fourth Amendment, when viewed in light of its common-law origins and the view shared by the founding generation of the nature of law, requires the availability of an effective remedy or sanction for its violation. In the absence of legislative provision, the available common-law remedy would thereby exist as a matter of constitutional right.

Since the Fourth Amendment is "little more than the affirmance of a great constitutional doctrine of the common law," and since the Founders clearly relied on the remedial institutions of the common law for the implementation of the Constitution, it should not cause surprise that little occasion was found for reference to the Fourth Amendment in suits involving an unreasonable search or seizure. Except for one or two of the amendment's particulars for requiring the issuance of warrants, no difference between it and the common law on the subject existed. Indeed, the common law provided the guidance for the interpretation of the general terms of the amendment. Thus, in conformity with the pleading conventions before the advent of the modern system of code pleading, which had "a foundation in English history wholly unrelated to any attempt to identify the sovereign source of an asserted right in a federal system,"[40] suits "at common law" were considered perfectly adequate to vindicate the Fourth Amendment right.

Unlike the Fifth Amendment, which in its very words refers to the process whereby evidence is introduced in court, the Fourth Amendment is silent on the question of the use of evidence in court. In order to determine the original understanding of the relation of the Fourth Amendment to the admissibility of evidence, therefore, we are justified in looking to the law of evidence as it existed at the time of the ratification of the Fourth Amendment and as it developed during the formative period of our federal judicial history.

Evidence obtained by means of an illegal search and seizure has always been admitted in England and was universally admitted in American courts for more than a century after the Revolution. This rule is documented in the authoritative nineteenth-century work on evidence, Greenleaf's *A Treatise on the Law of Evidence*. Listed there as one of "those doctrines and rules of the Law of Evidence which are common to all the United States" is the following entry:

> Para. 254a. *Evidence admissible, though illegally obtained.*
> It may be mentioned . . . that though papers and other subjects of evidence may have been *illegally taken* from the possession of the party against whom they are offered, or otherwise unlawfully obtained, this is no valid objection to their admissibility if they are pertinent to the issue. The court will not take notice how they were obtained, whether lawfully or unlawfully, nor will it form an issue to determine that question.[41]

So widespread was acceptance of this rule that Professor Wigmore, in his own monumental work on evidence, ventured the observation that the foregoing doctrine "was never doubted until the appearance of the ill-starred majority opinion of *Boyd v. United States*," in 1886.[42]

Professor Wigmore's assertion should not, however, be taken to mean that the issue of the exclusion of evidence obtained through an unreasonable search and seizure had never received the attention of American courts before 1886. It had, and exclusion, at least in regard to controversies of a criminal or quasi-criminal nature, had been consistently and, as far as can be gathered from the available records, unanimously rejected. It appears that the earliest American case that raised the question of the admissibility into evidence of the product of an unlawful search or seizure was that of *United States v. La Jeune* in 1822. This was a case of libel brought against the schooner *La Jeune Eugenie*, which had been seized by a federal officer for being employed in the slave trade. Counsel for the claimants argued inter alia that the officer had no right to search, that therefore the seizure of the vessel was founded on an abuse of power, and finally, that such an abuse "cannot authorize an American Court to use any evidence acquired in virtue of such abuse."[43]

In rejecting this argument, Justice Story, sitting as a circuit judge, articulated the ruling law of evidence vis-à-vis searches and seizures with unsurpassed clarity:

> As to the . . . position, that if there exists no right of visitation and search, there cannot exist any right to use any evidence, which may be discovered by such search, I must be permitted to doubt, if that doctrine, in the full extent of its meaning, can be supported. In the ordinary administration of municipal law the right of using evidence does not depend, nor, as far as I have any recollection, has ever been supposed to depend upon the lawfulness or unlawfulness of the mode, by which it is obtained. If it is competent or pertinent evidence, and not in its own nature objectionable, as having been created by constraint, or oppression, such as confessions extorted by threats or fraud, the evidence is admissible on charges for the highest crimes, even though it may have been obtained by a trespass upon the person, or by any other forcible and illegal means. The law deliberates not on the mode, by which it has come to the possession of the party, but on its value in establishing itself as satisfactory proof. In many instances, and especially on trials for crime, evidence is often obtained from the possession of the offender by force or by contrivances, which one could not easily reconcile to a delicate sense of propriety, or support upon the foundations of municipal law. Yet I am not aware, that such evidence has upon that account ever been dismissed for incompetency.[44]

Curiously, references to Justice Story's statement of the rule are infrequent in subsequent cases where the exclusionary question was raised and are almost nonexistent in the literature on the subject. Notoriety has instead fallen to the opinion of Justice Wilde of the Supreme Judicial Court of Massachusetts who in 1841 addressed the exclusionary issue in the context of a criminal prosecution of a violation of the state's prohibition on the possession or sale of lottery tickets. In *Commonwealth v. Dana* the defendant objected to the admission into evidence of lottery tickets and other materials on the ground that the search warrant under which they were seized had been issued improvidently and was void in law. Justice Wilde, writing for a unanimous court, upheld the admission of the papers primarily on the basis of the validity of the warrant under the fourteenth article of the Massachusetts Constitution, which is akin to the Fourth Amendment to the federal Constitution. Despite the sufficiency of that ruling to dispose of the issue, Justice Wilde offered the following dictum on the exclusionary question:

> If the search warrant were illegal, or if the officer serving the warrant exceeded his authority, the party on whose complaint the warrant issued, or the officer, would be responsible for the wrong done; but this is no good reason for excluding the papers seized as evidence, if they were pertinent to the issue. . . . When papers are offered in evidence, the court can take no notice how they were obtained, whether lawfully or unlawfully; nor would they form a collateral issue to determine that question.[45]

Thus we see that, while Justice Wilde made no reference to Justice Story's opinion in *La Jeune*, his opinion with respect to the question of admissibility was the same: the manner in which evidence was obtained had no bearing on the issue of its admissibility.

Justice Wilde's opinion in *Dana* regarding the admissibility of unlawfully obtained evidence furnished a visible precedent for the latter half of the nineteenth century. It was invoked as authority for like decisions in other state courts and, together with Justice Story's opinion in the *La Jeune* case, was relied on by federal courts to justify the admission of books and papers into evidence, regardless of the legality of their seizure.

That completes our tour of early American jurisprudence regarding the means of enforcing the sacred constitutional right to be secure against unreasonable searches and seizures. I have not had occasion here to comment on the Supreme Court's applications of the Fourth Amendment right and the exclusionary rule to state constitutional systems, phenomena of recent vintage when we take the view from the founding. Whatever one might think of the incorporation of the Fourth Amendment right into the Fourteenth Amendment, the requirements of due process and of nonarbitrary searches and seizures lived in harmony in the thought of the Founders. In that same jurisprudence, however, the exclusionary rule has no life at all.

Notes

1. *Chapman v. United States*, 365 U.S. 610, 618 (1961) (Frankfurter, J., concurring in judgment).

2. J. Landynski, *Search and Seizure and the Supreme Court: A Study in Constitutional Interpretation* (Baltimore:

Johns Hopkins Univ. Press, 1966), p. 42.

3. *See* W. LaFave, *Search and Seizure: A Treatise on the Fourth Amendment*, vol. 1 (St. Paul: West, 1978), p. v.

4. Amsterdam, *Perspectives on the Fourth Amendment*, 58 Minn. L. Rev. 349, 353–54 (1974).

5. Storing, *The Constitution and the Bill of Rights*, in R. Goldwin and W. Schambra, eds. *How Does the Constitution Secure Rights?* (Washington, D.C.: American Enterprise Institute, 1985), p. 24.

6. P. Ford, ed., *Pamphlets on the Constitution of the United States* (rept. New York: B. Franklin, 1971), p. 360.

7. *McClannan v. Chaplain*, 136 Va. 1, 17 (1923), quoting *Watson on the Constitution*, vol. 2 (n.d.), pp. 1417–18.

8. Wechsler, *The Courts and the Constitution*, 65 Colum. L. Rev. 1001, 1006 (1965).

9. Landynski, *Search and Seizure and the Supreme Court*, p. 86.

10. *See* Wilson, *The Origin and Development of the Federal Rule of Exclusion*, 18 Wake Forest L. Rev. 1073 (1982); B. Wilson, *Enforcing the Fourth Amendment: A Jurisprudential History* (New York: Garland, 1986), chaps. 3–5.

11. *United States v. Leon*, 468 U.S. 897, 929 (1984) (Brennan, J., dissenting).

12. *Boyd v. United States*, 116 U.S. 616 (1886). In *Boyd*, the Supreme Court held that to seize personal papers violated the Fourth Amendment and that to use them as evidence violated the Fifth Amendment. It was a somewhat eccentric case which should have been decided on Fifth Amendment grounds alone. In 1914, however, the Supreme Court decided *Weeks v. United States*, 232 U.S. 383, in which the Court held for the first time that a violation of the Fourth Amendment by itself could, in certain circumstances, justify the exclusion of evidence.

13. 5 U.S. (1 Cranch) 137, 163 (1803).

14. W. Blackstone, *Commentaries on the Laws of England* (1765; facsimile ed., Chicago: Univ. of Chicago Press, 1979), 1:55–56.

15. *Bivens v. United States*, 403 U.S. 388, 401 n.3 (1971) (Harlan, J., concurring in judgment).

16. 41 U.S. (16 Pet.) 539, 615–16 (1842).

17. Hill, *Constitutional Remedies*, 69 Colum. L. Rev. 1109, 1131–32 (1969).

18. Ibid., p. 1132.

19. Marbury, 5 U.S. (1 Cranch) at 163 quoting Blackstone, *Commentaries* 3: 23.

20. J. Story, *Commentaries on the Constitution of the United States*, 3d ed. (Boston: C. C. Little and J. Brown, 1858), chap. 44, para. 1902, p. 679.

21. Harno, *Evidence Obtained by Illegal Search and Seizure*, 19 Ill. L. Rev. 303, 307 (1925).

22. J. Cooke, ed., *The Federalist* (Middletown, Conn.: Wesleyan Univ. Press, 1961), No. 83, p. 563.

23. *Wilkes v. Wood*, Lofft 1, 18–19, 98 Eng. Rep. 489, 498–99 (C.P. 1763).

24. Wechsler, *The Courts and the Constitution*, pp. 10005–6.

25. Warren, *Federal Criminal Laws and the State Courts*, 38 Harv. L. Rev. 545, 545 (1925).

26. *The Federalist*, No. 82, p. 553.

27. Ibid., p. 555.

28. Ibid., No. 61, p. 104.

29. Ibid., No. 27, p. 174.

30. *Martin v. Hunter's Lessee*, 14 U.S. (1 Wheat.) 304, 334–35 (1816).

31. *The Federalist*, No. 32, p. 200.

32. Ibid., No. 82, pp. 554–55.

33. J. Elliot, ed., *The Debates in the Several State Conventions on the Adoption of the Federal Constitution*, 2d ed. (Philadelphia: J. B. Lippencott, 1936), 3:524.

34. Ibid., p. 554.

35. Hart, *The Power of Congress to Limit the Jurisdiction of Federal Courts: An Exercise in Dialectic*, 66 Harv. L. Rev. 1362, 1401 (1953).

36. Warren, *New Light on the History of the Federal Judiciary Act of 1789*, 37 Harv. L. Rev. 49, 53 (1923).

37. 15 U.S. (2 Wheat.) 1 (1817).

38. Hill, *Constitutional Remedies*, p. 1159.

39. Ibid., p. 1133.

40. Ibid., p. 1130.

41. S. Greenleaf, *A Treatise on the Law of Evidence*, 14th ed., revised, with large additions, by S. Croswell (Boston: Little, Brown, 1883), vol. 1, sec. 254a, pp. 325–26.

42. J. Wigmore, *A Treatise on the Anglo-American System of Evidence*, 2d ed. (Boston: Little, Brown, 1923), vol. 4, sec. 2184, p. 632.

43. 26 F. Cas. 832, 842 (C.C.D.Mass. 1822) (No. 15, 551).

44. *Id.* at 843–44.

45. 43 Mass. (2 Met.) 329, 337 (1841).

JAMES ETIENNE VIATOR

12. The Fourth Amendment in the Nineteenth Century

It might be appropriate to devote a few moments of reflection to the pertinence of the "original understanding" of search and seizure to contemporary interpretation of the Fourth Amendment. Of course, as every schoolboy nowadays knows, the world of constitutional interpretation is divided, much like our geopolitical world, between two theories, namely, interpretivism and noninterpretivism; but like the geopolitical world, the world of constitutional scholarship is not really so monolithic on either side, which is to say there is interpretivism, and then there is interpretivism. For example, on most workdays, I myself adhere to some denomination or other of interpretivism, but I am not sure exactly what it should be called.

Probably the archetypal interpretivist, and the bête noire of many activist-inclined scholars, is Raoul Berger. He is what might be labeled a "specific intentionalist," or an Interpretivist with a capital I. Briefly, this view declares that the specific intentions of the framers as a whole can both be discovered and also bind us in the way that a command of law binds us. These intentions, the argument goes, set the strict limits to our behavior and the behavior of all those, especially judges, who construe the Constitution. The recent debate between Professor H. Jefferson Powell and Raoul Berger about whether or not the framers were themselves interpretivists really misses the point, however, because their battle is conducted on the *champ clos* chosen by Professor Berger—namely, specific intentionalism.[1] It misses the point because anyone who has spent much time examining the manner in which judges and lawyers in the early national and antebellum eras interpreted the Constitution quickly comes to realize that if they were interpretivists, it was not Raoul Berger's sort of interpretivism they practiced. After all, justices as diverse in political views as Marshall and Story and William Johnson and Roger Taney construed the Constitution without a trace of diffidence induced by the absence of Madison's *Notes*, which did not see the light of day until 1840.[2] But to recognize this is not to give up the game, for the framers were, I believe, interpretivists of another sort.

The men of the founding generation were what might be referred to as teleological or telic interpretivists. That is, they looked to the overarching goals and purposes for which the Constitution was devised and the boundaries it set against not only the judicial will but the wills of all citizens. Thus, to admit that Professor Jefferson Powell is correct—that the men of the founding generation were not Raoul Berger's brand of interpretivists—is not to give up on a "jurisprudence of original intention." It is merely to say that the "original understanding" must be discerned in the manner of Jefferson, Madison, and Marshall.

Lawyers, statesmen, and politicians of the founding era never forgot that it was a constitutive document which had been fabricated in Philadelphia, a document aimed toward the great goals or ends of government: toward, as they would phrase it in the Preamble, the establishing of justice and the securing of the blessings of liberty. And these goals were well-known: the delegates to the Philadelphia Convention knew the proper ends of government, for those ends already had been proclaimed in other constitutive documents, most notably in the ringing pronouncement of equal liberty, and of the capital purpose of government as the protection of the people's equal liberty, contained in the Declaration of Independence's first two paragraphs. In this sense Lincoln was merely, and perfectly, typical of an entire antebellum tradition which read the Constitution in light of the great goals and ends of government enshrined in the Declaration of Independence.[3] It was read that way not just by early national and antebellum lawyers but by almost everyone who ever had occasion to give a speech attempting to explain America's role as a new republic among monarchical nations. It does not take much digging in the patriotic orations and political speeches of nineteenth-century America to discover that the Declaration, not the Constitution, was regarded as the fountainhead of our national political tradition.[4] In short, it was Jefferson's felicitous expression of the proper goals of the civil political order that animated constitutional interpretation and rendered apparent the overarching collective intent of the Founders.

In this methodology, also, was Lincoln the typical nineteenth-century constitutional lawyer, though he was certainly more adept and astute than most. The political thought of the Founding Fathers was constantly adverted to by all sides in antebellum debate, without anyone ever betraying so much as a thought that the specific intentions of the drafters should prevail over what, given the fundamental principles at stake and the language of the Constitution, must have been their understanding of the matter.[5] Antebellum interpreters never confused the proper understanding of the Constitution with the collective specific intent of the fifty-five men at Philadelphia: the proper understanding of the Constitution was to be found by repairing to the Declaration of Independence as the wellspring of the American political tradition. In short, Lincoln was typical of his generation when, in reflecting upon our national purpose at his dedication of the military cemetery at Gettysburg, he announced that governments are instituted to secure the liberty and equal natural rights of mankind and that it is by their adequacy in securing these rights that they are to be judged—and not judged by platonic guardians or aristocrats but by the people themselves, by whom and for whom such republican governments are rightfully instituted.

It is obvious, then, in light of the observations made by Lincoln and others concerning the ends for which the Constitution was drafted, that a crabbed literalism based on the bare words of the Constitution will be as unavailing as a "specific intent" interpretivism. To be sure, we must begin with the language of the document we are interpreting, but one of the chief architects of that document, James Madison, knew that "no language is so copious as to supply words and phrases for every complex idea."[6] This is the authentic voice of the natural-law philosophy held, in one form or another, by most members of the founding generation; for they knew that no constitutional language can be a sufficient guide to a proper civil political order without a keen appreciation of the goals and purposes of the government thereby ordained.

Consider also in this respect Madison's argument in *The Federalist* that the legitimacy of the new Constitution should be assessed "by recurring . . . to the transcendent law of nature and nature's God, which declares that the safety and happiness of society are the objects at which all political institutions aim."[7] The similarity to the Declaration is as striking as it is apparent. Therefore, as long as we have law-school-trained lawyers and law professors pontificating that the Preamble to the Constitution, much less the Declaration of Independence, should not be heard at bar since it is not part of the "real Constitution," I do not think we will soon see the sort of Supreme Court jurisprudence that might grant solace to either conservatives or liberals. But with knowledge of the goals and purposes of government that a careful reading of our great state papers will disclose, there is no reason why modern lawyers and judges cannot espouse an attainable and sensible jurisprudence of original intention through the same sort of telic and flexible interpretivism practiced by the framers.

Guided by the interpretive light provided by Whig history, what Patrick Henry called "the lamp of experience," and the natural-rights tradition embodied in all of our great constitutive documents—whether the state constitutions and bills of rights or the Declaration of Independence—the telic interpretivism of the framers was bound to produce a living document of varying, if not variable, content. Nowhere is this made plainer than in the first century or so of case law interpreting the Fourth Amendment.

The earliest interpretation of the amendment came not from the courts but the first session of the First Congress. The first federal legislation to include a section concerning the techniques of search and seizure was the Collection Act of 1789.[8] The collection bill was first mentioned on April 11, 1789, and a committee was appointed "to prepare and bring in" an act to protect merchants and provide for a customs revenue.[9] The act itself was introduced on May 8, 1789,[10] exactly one month before James Madison introduced the proposals that were later to become the Bill of Rights.[11]

Although it is unclear at exactly what stage of its evolution the search and seizure provisions were added to the Collection Act, its passage occurred at approximately the same time the Fourth Amendment was under consideration: the Collection Act in its final form became law on July 31, 1789, and it was less than a month later that Madison's proposed search and seizure amendment assumed the definitive form in which we now see it as the Fourth Amendment to the Constitution.[12] Hence, because the same legislators were busy working on both proposals, it is not unreasonable to assume that the sorts of searches detailed in the Collection Act provide persuasive evidence of what search and seizure techniques were considered to be reasonable within the meaning of the Fourth Amendment.

Contrary to what might have been expected considering the near sacrosanct status to which *Paxton's Case* and the *Wilkes Cases* had ascended by this time, many states provided, as witnessed by their confederation-era customs and excise statutes, for general searches.[13] The Collection Act mirrored this common state practice in section 24, which declared that "every collector, naval officer and surveyor . . . shall have full power and authority, to enter any ship or vessel in which they shall have reason to suspect any goods . . . subject to duty shall be concealed; and therein to search for, seize, and secure any such goods."[14] Hence this act provided for a warrantless search of vessels and it was of the "general" search species since it permitted one on suspicion to enter "any ship or vessel," not just particular or specific vessels. This clause of the Collection Act of 1789, therefore, should be enough in and of itself to refute anyone who argues that, at least by the original understanding, the reasonableness clause of the Fourth Amendment should be read in tandem with the warrant clause of the Fourth Amendment to declare that the only reasonable searches countenanced by the Fourth Amendment's congressional enactors were those which proceeded under a warrant.

The next provision, the search-under-warrant section of the Collection Act, provided more restraints on government agents, however, and displayed a solicitude for the home that, typical of the era, did not extend to ships. This section declared that if these same collection agents should "have cause to suspect a concealment [of uncustomed goods] in any particular dwelling-house, store, building, or other place, they . . . shall, upon application on oath or affirmation to any justice of the peace, be entitled to a warrant to enter such house, store, or other place (in the day time only) and there to search for such goods."[15] Hence the Collection Act paid homage to the traditional English axiom that "a man's house is his castle" by providing that any search of a building—and, notice, not just a house but a store or other building—was to proceed under a warrant given on oath or affirmation and particularly describing the location to be searched. Moreover, the warrant was to be executed only in the daytime, another orthodox circumscription of the era.

The Collection Act also reflected the narrow contemporary understanding of probable cause, for it provided that the magistrate had to give the warrant once the oath or affirmation of suspicion was made to him. This reflected a late eighteenth-century conception of probable cause which was totally unlike our understanding today. It is commonly said nowadays that the probable cause requirement exists in order that the magistrate might stand as an independent judicial sentry to protect against searches and seizures undertaken merely because of an officer's suspicions. Therefore, the probable cause requirement is the linchpin of the machinery by which judges protect our rights against baseless searches and seizures. This was not, however, the prevalent eighteenth-century understanding, as evidenced by the Collection Act. Once the declaration of suspicion was made under oath or affirmation—and note it was suspicion, and not probable cause, which, as we describe it today, is something more than even reasonable suspicion, viz., a reasonable belief—once this declaration was made, the justice of the peace had no discretion to issue the warrant or not, depending on his independent judicial evaluation of the facts underlying the suspicion. Rather, the swearer was "entitled to a warrant to enter such house, store, or other place . . . and . . . to search for . . . goods."

Hence, if one were a "strict intentionalist" kind of interpretivist, one would necessarily side with those who want to strengthen the hand of law enforcement; for as evidenced by the Collection Act, probable cause may have been nothing more than suspicion of some variety or other (bare or reasonable), and there was no judicial control by an examination into the facts underlying the suspicion: rather, the declaration of suspicion was enough in and of itself to command the issuance of a warrant. But as telic interpretivists, the jurists of the early national era did not insult their constitutional forebears by regarding them as martinets. Hence in the next important cluster of cases, those arising out of the Aaron Burr Conspiracy of the winter of 1806–7, we see a slight evolution in the concept of probable cause, bringing it somewhat closer to our modern notion of probable cause and thus to that same extent somewhat beyond the notion of probable cause contained in the Collection Act of 1789.

The issue in the *Burr* cases was not really search and seizure but probable cause to commit for trial, that is, the same sort of probable cause mentioned in Federal Rules of Criminal Procedure 5.1.[16] Nowadays, this species of probable cause is thought of as being somewhat greater than the probable cause required for the issuance of an arrest warrant, more in the nature of establishing some sort of minimal prima facie case in order to hold the prisoner for trial or for the impaneling of the grand jury. It was precisely this sort of procedure that was at issue in the *Burr* cases; that is, the question was whether there existed probable cause for commitment to trial, rather than for the issuance of an arrest or search warrant.[17]

The cases were, however, treated by contemporary commentators as

Fourth Amendment cases. The commentators and treatise writers who cited *Ex parte Bollman & Swartwout*, and other Burr Conspiracy cases as search and seizure cases doubtless helped elevate Fourth Amendment "probable cause" from some level of suspicion to a more factually grounded belief or conviction of wrongdoing.[18] And what is more, the *Burr* cases demonstrated, contrary to the warrant process outlined in the Collection Act, that the judiciary, in making the probable cause determination, was to stand as an independent sentry guarding the rights of the people against the executive branch—the grasping "hand of malignity," as Marshall referred to Jefferson in *United States v. Burr*, 25 F. Cas. at 12. Thus, when popular and influential commentators such as Thomas Sergeant,[19] Timothy Walker,[20] and Joseph Story,[21] treated *Bollman & Swartwout* as a search and seizure case, and when judges and lawyers adopted their treatment, probable cause advanced toward its modern form—that is, some level of belief or conviction above mere suspicion and evaluated by the judge, who is to make an independent legal determination of the adequacy of the factual base to support the belief.

Now, it is impossible to determine with any certainty whether those who so read Marshall's opinions engaged in a creative misreading of probable cause for their own purposes, or whether they were merely recognizing some dawning notion of probable cause as more than mere suspicion. But what is undeniable is that the opinions in the Burr Conspiracy cases helped foster the notion of judicial sentryship through an independent application of a probable cause standard thought sufficient to guard the liberties of citizens against overbearing executive agents.

Furthermore, the judges and commentators who read the Burr Conspiracy cases as search and seizure opinions, rather than the preliminary examination opinions they actually were, certainly did not do this from sloppiness or the inability to read cases. No one familiar with the numbing exactness necessary to plead a case under the common-law writ system would accuse antebellum lawyers of being sloppy in their reading of cases and legal documents. Rather, I think this reading is typical of the common law–natural law tradition, whereby even constitutional grants are merely declaratory of the law and not, as a legal positivist would say, actually the law. Therefore, when phrases such as "probable cause" are used in one context with more or less the same function and purpose as the same words might have in another context, the lawyer working under the declaratory theory of the common law would simply and surely use the one as a precedent for the other. In other words, they were not loathe to reason and use cases from one area of the law in another area of law if the underlying principles, purposes, and functions were more or less the same. The common law–natural law methodology freed them from the sort of attachment to exact statutory or constitutional compartments to which modern lawyers have been schooled. For the antebellum common-law lawyer, the particular concept declared in the positive enactment was not limited and defined by its context in that particular provision. In short, they never confused *lex scripta* and *jus naturale*, and hence were able to use, flexibly and legitimately, the probable cause from the *Burr* cases as probative for, or even coextensive with, the probable cause of search and seizure.

Although there is much search and seizure law to be found between 1807 and 1886, most of it arose in the states, for by the series of opinions beginning with *Barron v. Baltimore*,[22] and extending through *Smith v. Maryland*,[23] it came gradually to be gospel that the Bill of Rights did not apply to the states.[24] Certainly to determine whether a search and seizure doctrine circumscriptive of government powers was considered essential to a republican form of government will require a close examination of the state cases. But pending completion of such research, one can agree with Telford Taylor that the next case "in which the fourth amendment looms large,"[25] is *Boyd v. United States*, 116 U.S. 616 (1886).

Briefly, the case involved a federal revenue statute which provided for the civil forfeiture of uncustomed goods. The federal government needed plate glass for the construction of a courthouse and confected a sales contract with the firm of Edward A. and George H. Boyd that permitted the Boyds to import a certain quantity of glass duty-free. At issue were twenty-nine cases of glass that the government contended the Boyds had imported in violation of the agreement; therefore, the government needed to establish the value of the glass contained in those twenty-nine cases in order to prove that thirty-five cases imported at a later date by the Boyds were not entitled to an exemption from duties under the agreement and thus should be forfeited to the government under the civil penalties provision of the Customs Act of 1874. The act also provided that in civil forfeiture actions the U.S. attorney could move for, and the court could order, the production and inspection of papers and invoices relating to imports. If those documents were not voluntarily surrendered to the court, the matters to which they related—that is, the allegation of nonpayment of customs duties—were taken to be confessed as true by the defendant.[26]

The Court's answer to this procedure may constitute one of the most extraordinary and unexpected cases in all of American constitutional law. For the Court to declare that the Fourth Amendment applied in this context—that is, a civil forfeiture proceeding—it first had to sidestep an earlier Supreme Court opinion declaring that the Fourth Amendment applied only to criminal proceedings (*see Murray v. Hoboken Land Co.*, 18 Howard 272 [1855]). Justice Bradley did this by declaring the forfeiture proceeding to be quasi-criminal in nature. After sidestepping the doctrine of *Hoboken Land Co.*, the Court next addressed the constitutional question that arose from the compulsory production of the plaintiff's records concerning the imported plate glass.

The first problem to be faced by the Court was the long-standing common-law rule by which a court would not stop to examine the constitutional pedigree of evidence as long as it was otherwise competent. In other words, at common law there was no exclusionary rule. Clearly, then, for the Supreme Court to decide in favor of the Boyds on their main issue on appeal would require a construction of the Fourth Amendment going beyond its mere words or even the common law of evidence. Justice Bradley did just that, relying on Lord Camden's famous opinion in one of the *Wilkes* cases, *Entick v. Carrington*, 19 How. St. Tr. 1029 (1765), which helped the Court on two points.

First of all, Lord Camden had declared that a warrant was not legal except in the search for stolen goods or, presumably, other contraband. Relying on the "mere evidence" rule of Lord Camden's opinion in *Entick v. Carrington* (a principle which was also enshrined in nineteenth-century state cases; *see, e.g.*, *Commonwealth v. Dana*, 2 Met. [Mass.] 329 [1841]), Justice Bradley propounded the first major principle of *Boyd*: namely, that this forced use of papers as evidence in a civil forfeiture proceeding was an unreasonable search and seizure within the meaning of the Fourth Amendment. The second, and more controversial, proposition of the case was Bradley's reading in tandem of the Fourth Amendment and the Fifth Amendment's self-incrimination clause. By slightly misreading the *Entick* opinion (and perhaps even intentionally so, since in quoting *Entick* he left out a crucial sentence), Bradley reached the conclusion that there was such an interrelationship between the two amendments that the customs invoices must be excluded from the forfeiture trial because their introduction at trial would amount to compulsory self-incrimination.[27] The Court thereby in effect discarded the traditional common-law rule for the admissibility of illegally seized evidence.

This prototype of a full-blown exclusionary rule took a while to be incorporated securely within the body of federal Fourth Amendment law, and it clearly was not mandated by the text of the Fourth Amendment or by the search and seizure precedents found in the state reporters; *see, e.g.*, *Dana, supra* (cited by Bradley in *Boyd*). Nevertheless, this part of the *Boyd* opinion, and indeed the whole opinion, can plausibly be seen as part of Attorney General Edwin Meese's "jurisprudence of original intention," as long as we understand constitutional methodology in the same way as did the founding generation.

Contrary to a textual or precedential literalism which would bind the nation to the bare words of the Constitution and the gloss placed on them by the most recent opinions of the Supreme Court, Justice Bradley declared that the fundamental principles of the Fourth Amendment "apply to all invasions on the part of the government . . . of the sanctity of a man's home and the privacies of life" (*Boyd*, 116 U.S. at 630). The Supreme Court in *Boyd* could easily have decided to limit the operative sweep of the Fourth Amendment to the leading evil that it had been designed to remedy, the evil that had come to define the perimeters of the Fourth Amendment through its constant repetition not only in the legal literature of the era[28] but also even in high school history texts and such popular interpretations of American history as the works of George Bancroft[29] and Richard Hildreth[30]—namely, the general search warrant. But instead Bradley chose to ground his decision on the great underlying principles of the Constitution. Relying essentially on only one English case, its American progeny, and the fundamental principles for which the Fourth Amendment was drafted, Justice Bradley did indeed engage in a creative act of constitutional interpretation, but it was the very sort of constitutive creativity that is closely akin to the common law–natural law mode of constitutional interpretation employed by the framers whereby general principles are adapted to the facts of particular, and sometimes novel, cases.

Hence the lesson of the *Boyd* and *Burr* cases goes beyond the mere statement of a legal rule or right. Rather, it is a lesson in constitutional self-government. If we resist the strict logic of legal positivism and use the methods of a natural-law/teleological interpretation, then we will not be reduced, in our modern readings of the Constitution, to a mere mimicry of certain framers' specific intentions or, what would be even worse, a textual literalism or an unthinking obedience to the latest opinions appearing in the U.S. Reports. If we repair to the fundamental equal liberties of man, the guarantee of which was the capital leading purpose for the drafting and ratification of the Constitution, then *Boyd* should be seen as a case comprehended within the meaning of a telic interpretivism as practiced by such able constitutional lawyers as James Madison, John Marshall, and Abraham Lincoln.

Notes

1. *Compare* Powell, *The Original Understanding of Original Intent*, 98 Harv. L. Rev. 885–948 (1985), *with* Berger, *"Original Intention" in Historical Perspective*, 54 Geo. Wash. L. Rev. 296–337 (1986).

2. C. Rossiter, *1787: The Grand Convention* (New York: MacMillan, 1966), p. 332.

3. For a thorough and persuasive argument that the Declaration provided an integral part of the national consensus on political values, see Lutz, *The Declaration of Independence as Part of an American National Compact*, 19 Publius: The Journal of Federalism 41–58 (1989).

4. For a thoughtful and illuminating discussion of the Declaration as the cornerstone of popular antebellum political culture, see Green, *Listen to the Eagle Scream: One Hundred Years of the Fourth of July in North Carolina, 1776–1876*, 31 N. C. Hist. Rev. 295–320, 529–49 (1954); Green, *The Spirit of "76*, 11 Emory University Q. 65–82 (1955).

5. Even the leading Founding Father himself took essentially this view of con-

stitutional construction. *See, e.g.*, James Madison to Spencer Roane, May 6, 1821, James Madison to Thomas Jefferson, June 27, 1823, in G. Hunt, ed., *The Writings of James Madison*, 9 vols. (New York: Putnam, 1900–1910), 9:57–62, 141–43.

6. J. Cooke, ed., *The Federalist* (Middletown, Conn.: Wesleyan Univ. Press, 1961), No. 37, p. 236.

7. Ibid., No. 43, p. 297.

8. Act of July 31, 1789, 1 *United States Statutes at Large* 43 (R. Peters, ed., 1845) (hereinafter cited as Stat.).

9. *See* L. De Pauw, ed., *Documentary History of the First Federal Congress of the United States of America: House of Representatives Journal*, vol. 3 (Baltimore: Johns Hopkins Univ. Press, 1977), pp. 17–18.

10. Ibid., p. 53.

11. Ibid., p. 84.

12. In various proceedings, debates, committee reports, and resolves, the House shaped the phraseology of the Fourth Amendment into its final (and current) form between Aug. 17 and Aug. 24, 1789. *See* B. Schwartz, ed., *The Bill of Rights: A Documentary History*, vol. 2 (New York: Chelsea House, 1971), pp. 1112, 1122–23, 1138; C. Bickford and H. Veit, eds., *Documentary History of the First Federal Congress of the United States of America: Legislative Histories*, vol. 4 (Baltimore: Johns Hopkins Univ. Press, 1986), pp. 35–37.

13. *See, e.g.*, Rum Excise Act of 1783, *Acts and Laws of the State of connecticut* (New London, 1784), p. 211 (providing that whenever "any person" informs a justice of the peace of a violation of the Excise Act, the J.P. "shall forthwith grant a writ" ordering a general search); Impost Act of 1784 and Impost Act of 1786, *Laws of the State of New York*, vol. 2 (Albany, 1886), pp. 17, 321 (providing for general warrants to search for uncustomed goods); Impost Act of 1786, in A. Candler et al., eds., *Colonial Records of the State of Georgia*, vol. 19, pt. 2 (Atlanta, 1916), pp. 507–8 (same); Impost Act of 1783, Nov. sess., 1782, chap. 26, sec. 17, in W. Kilty, ed., *The Laws of Maryland*, vol. 1 (Annapolis, 1799), unpaginated (same); Impost Act of 1784, in W. Clark et al., eds., *The State Records of North Carolina*, vol. 24 (Raleigh, 1912), p. 550 (same); Impost Act of 1783, in T. Cooper and D. McCord, eds., *Statutes at Large of South Carolina*, vol. 4 (Columbia, 1838), p. 576 (same).

14. 1 Stat. at 43.

15. Ibid. at 43.

16. *See, e.g.*, *Ex parte Bollman & Swartwout*, 4 Cranch 75, 125 (1807); *United States v. Burr*, 25 F. Cas. 2, 12 (1807).

17. For brief explications of the common-law commitment process and the preliminary examination, see W. Blackstone, *Commentaries on the Laws of England*, vol. 4 (Oxford, 1769), p. 293; J. Goebel and T. Naughton, *Law Enforcement in Colonial New York: A Study in Criminal Procedure (1664–1776)* (New York: Commonwealth Fund, 1944), pp. 339–41; J. Turner, *Kenny's Outlines of Criminal Law*, 19th ed. (Cambridge: Cambridge Univ. Press, 1966), pp. 582–88.

18. For the level of "reasonable belief," as opposed to "suspicion," required by Chief Justice Marshall before an arrestee could be committed for trial, *see United States v. Burr*, 25 F. Cas. at 12 (declaring that to grant the U.S. attorney's motion to commit Burr for trial, the judge first "should require . . . that

probable cause be shown; and I understand probable cause to be a case made out by proof furnishing good reason to believe that the crime alleged has been committed by the person charged"), and *Ex parte Bollman & Swartwout*, 4 Cranch at 125 (suggesting that there is no probably cause to commit for trial if the suspicion is baseless).

19. *See* T. Sergeant, *Constitutional Law* (Philadelphia: A. Small, 1822), p. 242.

20. *See* T. Walker, *Introduction to American Law* (Philadelphia: P. H. Nicklin and T. Johnson, 1837), pp. 181–82 (citing both *Ex parte Bollman & Swartwout* and *Ex parte Burford*, 3 Cranch 447 [1806] [not a Burr Conspiracy case] as declarative of the proper interpretation of the Fourth Amendment; *Burford*, not unlike *Bollman* and *United States v. Burr*, involved probable cause for a warrant of commitment).

21. *See* Joseph Story, *Commentaries on the Constitution of the United States*, vol. 3 (Boston: C. C. Little and J. Brown, 1833), p. 750 (citing *Ex parte Burford* for the proposition that "to be legal [a warrant and the complaint on which it is founded] must state the name of the party [and] also the time, and place, and nature of the offense with reasonable certainty").

22. 7 Peters 243 (1833) (holding that the "just compensation" clause of the Fifth Amendment does not apply to the states).

23. 18 Howard 71 (1855) (holding that the Fourth Amendment does not apply to the states).

24. *But see, e.g.*, W. Rawle, *A View of the Constitution* (Philadelphia: H. C. Carey and I. Lea, 1825), pp. 123–25 (declaring, in an ipse dixit pronouncement, that the Bill of Rights bound the state governments as well as the federal government).

25. T. Taylor, *Two Studies in Constitutional Interpretation* (Columbus: Ohio State Univ. Press, 1969), p. 53.

26. Act of June 22, 1874, chap. 391, sec. 5, 18 Stat. (pt. 3) 186, 187–88. As Justice Bradley explained in his opinion, the 1874 Customs Act had its genesis in a crucial Civil War revenue measure which was passed at a desperate stage of the struggle to preserve the Union. *See* Act of March 3, 1863, chap. 76, 12 Stat. 737. So desperate was the need for revenue that this was the first federal statute calling for the search and seizure of private papers, invoices, and other written records. *See Boyd*, 116 U.S. at 621–23. Another indication of the desperation underlying this unprecedented search and seizure provision is the fact that on the same day this measure was enacted, Congress also passed a statute both authorizing the president's future suspensions of habeas corpus and approving his prior suspensions. *See* Act of March 3, 1863, chap. 81, 12 Stat. 755; *See also* A. Sutherland, *Constitutionalism in America: Origin and Evolution of Its Fundamental Ideas* (New York: Blaisdell, 1965), p. 412.

As it turned out, the response of Northern businessmen and importers to the search provisions of the Customs Act of 1863 and the similar provisions in the amended versions of this wartime measure (*see* Act of March 2, 1867, chap. 188, sec. 2, 14 Stat. 546, 547 and the Act of June 22, 1874, *supra*) was reminiscent of the response of the Boston merchants to the British writs of assistance involved in *Paxton's Case*. From 1865 through 1874, businessmen from Boston, New York, and other large port cities made repeated attempts to have Congress repeal the search and seizure provisions of these revenue measures. The businessmen failed in this major effort of repeal when the Customs Act of 1874 was passed with the modified search and seizure provision at issue in *Boyd*, whereby federal courts were authorized to grant the government's motion to inspect and to order the production and inspection of records pertinent to the government's civil forfeiture case. Hence, in harmony with the probusiness, antiregulatory trend of late nineteenth-century Supreme Court jurisprudence, *Boyd* may plausibly be regarded as a judicial reversal of the statutory outcome in a warmly contested legislative battle between merchants and the U.S. Treasury Department. *See* Alito, *Documents and the Privilege against Self-Incrimination*, 48 U. Pitt. L. Rev. 27–81, at pp. 31–32, 36 (1986). This is not to say, however, that *Boyd's* protection of "papers and effects" is constitutionally incorrect or suspect, for in every vindication of an individual's constitutional claim, the judiciary reverses a legislative or executive "outcome" as to the contested point.

27. *Boyd*, 116 U.S. at 629–30. At page 629 of his *Boyd* opinion, Bradley quoted a long paragraph from *Entick* which appears at page 1073 of volume 19 of *Howell's State Trials*. The gravamen of this quoted passage was a condemnation of the "general search" warrant because it is based on "mere suspicion" rather than suspicion based on proof and directed toward specific persons and places. Lord Camden condemned the search for "mere evidence" because it was a general, rummaging search which extended to the houses and papers of the innocent as well as the guilty. Lord Camden's linking of the hated "general search" with the "mere evidence" search was made clear in a sentence in the next paragraph of *Entick*—the paragraph left out of Justice Bradley's profuse quotations from *Entick*: "[A]nd if suspicion at large should be a ground of search, especially in the case of [seditious] libels, whose house would be safe?" (19 How. St. Tr. at 1073–74). Thus, the "mere evidence" rule and "general searches" were linked in *Entick*, not "mere evidence" and "self-incrimination" as in *Boyd*. *See also* J. Landynski, *Search and Seizure and the Supreme Court: A Study in Constitutional Interpretation* (Baltimore: Johns Hopkins Univ. Press, 1966), pp. 59–60.

28. *See, e.g.*, Justice Horace Gray's appendix to Josiah Quincy, Jr., ed., *Reports of Cases Argued and Adjudged in the Superior Court of Judicature of the Massachusetts Bay between 1761 and 1772* (Boston: Little, Brown, 1865), pp. 395–540.

29. *See* George Bancroft, *History of the United States*, vol. 4 (New York: Appleton, 1924), pp. 378–79, 414–19.

30. *See* Richard Hildreth, *History of the United States of America*, vol. 2 (New York: Harper, 1849), pp. 498–500. *See also* J. Landynski, *Search and Seizure and the Supreme Court*, p. 60.

Lloyd L. Weinreb

13. The Fourth Amendment Today

Little is more certain about the Fourth Amendment today than that its meaning and its concrete application in the multitude of situations for which it provides a constitutional text are uncertain. Year after year, scholars as well as members of the Supreme Court themselves decry the lack of doctrinal consistency and coherence in Fourth Amendment jurisprudence, the apparent arbitrariness of distinctions that suddenly are given dispositive weight or just as suddenly are dismissed as irrelevant, the disconnectedness of reasoning and result. Such disarray is the more to be regretted, we are reminded, because constitutional doctrine in this area is not only a set of limiting principles; it is also effectively a code of police behavior. Reacting to these criticisms, many people, among them some judges, conclude that to a greater extent than other constitutional provisions, the correct understanding of the Fourth Amendment cannot be based on anything more solid than the interests of those whose views from time to time prevail.

Looking at individual cases as they appear in the reports—whether one compares case with case or compares opposed opinions in the same case—one may find no honest escape from that conclusion. Or looking simply at the general direction of the results from one period to another—the so-called revolution in criminal procedure of the Warren Court and the counterrevolution of the Burger Court—one may see only interests at best or, even less compelling, attitudes, some of which look suspiciously as though they reflect economic and social position. We are not, I think, driven to so disheartening a view. There is disagreement aplenty about the Fourth Amendment. Perhaps it is more often, more insistently expressed than much other disagreement in constitutional law. Beneath the fragmented surface, however, there are powerful, coherent themes, which illuminate the course of decision, bring the debate into focus, and validate it.

There are, first of all, two ways of thinking about the Fourth Amendment. One is that the amendment is a statement of broad principle, which speaks to the fundamental relationship between the individual and the community: roughly, there is a domain of private life within which one's activities are not subject to the shared purposes of the community but are left to the individual himself. The other is that the amendment itself prescribes (implicitly) a detailed set of rules and regulations covering most aspects of official intrusions into our lives. The curiously mismatched language of the amendment's two main clauses gives support to both of these constructions.[1] The first clause provides in sweeping general terms that the government shall not engage in unreasonable searches and seizures. The second clause gives rather precise instructions for the issuance of a search warrant. There is nothing except a comma and a conjunction ("and") to indicate which clause should predominate.

We should not look to the intention of the framers of the Fourth Amendment to resolve this ambiguity, whatever one may think about the significance of that factor in constitutional interpretation generally. For the circumstances in which the amendment was written are different in critical respects from those in which it is applied. Most important, there was not then as there is now a regular body of public officials, charged to maintain public order, who interact with private persons constantly in many of the most routine aspects of daily life. It is that change of circumstance above all which creates the incongruity between the amendment's two clauses, by providing the occasion for a very large number of arrests and searches that necessarily are without a warrant.

Even if that were not so, the dual aspects of the amendment are not idiosyncratic to it but rather are exemplary of opposed traditions of American law. The view of the amendment as broad principle reflects the habit of our thought that transforms every issue of political philosophy into one of constitutional law. The Constitution is our fundamental law in a general as well as a specific sense. So much so, indeed, that at the deepest level, which particular clause of the Constitution one is construing in a particular case may seem almost not to matter, because the issue goes so far beyond anything that could be contained in a few words. Some of the results that the Supreme Court has reached under the Fourth Amendment might, perhaps, be cabined more aptly under the Fifth Amendment's privilege against compulsory self-incrimination or the due process clause. But it is also our habit, nowhere more so than in criminal procedure, to "constitutionalize" rules that seem less than fundamental and to make of the Constitution a statutory code. Driven by lawyer advocates who pursue their arguments to the end, the meaning and application of the law implicate the Constitution, if not at first then at last. The outcome of these divergent habits may be a union of the most abstract principles with the most detailed and concrete applications, by a dubious implication. So it is with the Fourth Amendment.

All agree that the great object of the amendment is to protect an area of life as private, in the particular respect that it is not subject to direct inspection and oversight by government officials, however benign the government's purpose. The privacy at stake covers both being in private—doing what one chooses to do, with whom one chooses, without intrusion—and having in private—preserving what one treasures, or merely possesses, unexposed to the world. Both kinds of privacy enable the individual to constitute himself as the unique person he is. Both are aspects of the fully realized life. And both importantly provide conditions for the realization of the common good as well. The divisive question has been when, in what circumstances for what reasons, the values of privacy give way to another public purpose.

One response to that question proceeds from the premise that the ordinary affairs of ordinary lives—the small incidents and accomplishments that constitute main events for the actors but less subjectively are unimportant and even banal—in and of themselves are the repository of the values that the Fourth Amendment protects. There need be no inquiry into the worth or even the morality of the activity in question; it is enough that it arises out of the human personality. So, in a case involving secret monitoring of conversations, Justice Harlan referred to "that spontaneity—reflected in frivolous, impetuous, sacrilegious, and defiant discourse—that liberates daily life."[2] It follows that a "search and seizure"—every form of governmental intrusion into the private domain—is regarded as extraordinary and constitutionally suspect from the start. The Fourth Amendment declares in effect that the functions of government are not to be carried out on a regular basis by intrusions into private life. Rather, all such intrusions require justification specific to the circumstances. Accordingly, a rule authorizing an intrusion is fashioned to permit the least, and least frequent, intrusion that is practically necessary. Not only must the extent and occasion of a search be considered but also the purpose to be served; if the purpose is uncertain or fairly debatable, the value of privacy is preferred.

Quite a different response is that private activities have value primarily because they serve large public purposes of the community as a whole. What is sought is political debate, intellectual inquiry, creative enterprise; and whatever is trivial from the public perspective is simply that, trivial. Not that ordinary lives are criticized for being ordinary. There is no intention affirmatively to bend the individual to the service of the state; and most of the time, ordinary activities are let alone. But if a legitimate public purpose is served and no public purpose is significantly hindered, the government's invasion of privacy is not especially to be regretted. According to this view, the Fourth Amendment confines official actions covered by it to what is usual, conventionally accepted in fact, and, therefore, in the constitutional term, "reasonable." The amendment does not prohibit this sort of official action generally, insofar as it is accepted as part of community life; it prohibits only what is unusual, in the straightforward sense that it is not ordinary official behavior. Whereas the framework for analysis indicated by the former approach starts from a normative principle that intrusive official action is undesirable and ought to be avoided, according to the latter, the starting point is factual: What is the usual official behavior? The normative legal conclusion is built on that factual foundation; if the behavior is not (too) unusual, it is permitted.

I would not make this difference too stark, for the sake of categorical neatness. Whatever our normative premises, wholly routine aspects of our lives are not likely to call for much justification, if only because they are not singled out for notice. What counts as an intrusion, what are the boundaries of the private domain, are themselves considerably matters of fact. From the other side, whether or not a practice is usual is not without some understood normative qualifications. Usual to whom, and for what? How much detail is it appropriate to build into the situational categories? The notion of the "reasonable" is explicitly, albeit ambiguously, evaluative. Even so, these frameworks help to explain the course of Fourth Amendment jurisprudence, as the more familiar description of decisions simply as liberal or conservative does not. Those are protean labels; and even if we give them their current conventional meanings, they are only descriptive of the results, as if the only thing that mattered was to choose up sides.

Upholding the authority of police to frisk a person in a public place for weapons, the Supreme Court in 1968 limited such authority to circumstances in which an officer could not otherwise safely fulfill his duty as a peace officer. In *Terry v. Ohio*, the Court said that a frisk is not permitted unless there are specific, articulable facts indicating danger to the officer or others and must be limited to averting the danger.[3] The Court did not spend time weighing the privacy that was at stake; it was enough to call for the protection of the Fourth Amendment that privacy was at stake at all.[4] Acknowledging that street encounters between police officers on patrol and private persons are a frequent, multiform phenomenon of urban life, which often intrude minimally on private activities, and that many such encounters are simply beyond judicial regulation, the Court nevertheless limited forceful encounters to what it thought was a practical necessity. Since then, the Court has considerably eased such limitations, without eliminating them altogether.[5] Provided that the police action is neither arbitrary nor excessive in the context of police work generally, it is likely to be upheld.

The rule announced in *Chimel v. California* in 1969 for a search incident to an arrest also illustrates the approach that requires specific justification.[6] Rejecting the earlier rule that when a person is arrested in a private place, the entire premises may be searched as an "incident" of the arrest, the Court reasoned that an arrest legitimates a search only insofar as necessary to prevent the person either from grabbing a weapon or means of escape, which might frustrate the arrest and endanger the arresting officer, or from grabbing evidence and destroying it. On that basis, it limited a search to the area within the arrested person's control, by which it meant actually within his reach. Anything more, the Court said, requires the specific justification of a search warrant. The dissent argued that if the police were already on the premises and had probable cause for a search, the requirement of a search warrant was a pointless interference with effective police work.[7] It is not enough, the majority concluded, that a warrant could be obtained; only if it is in fact obtained, with all the specificity that the warrant clause demands, is the special nature of a search respected. Subsequent cases have enlarged the so-called grabbable area beyond the very narrow range that *Chimel* indicated.[8] The only evident rationale is that police making an arrest do look around for evidence and, within imprecise limits, it is reasonable for them to do so.

As *Chimel* suggests, the warrant clause has been the principal basis of assurance that an invasion of privacy remains the exception rather than the rule. If a warrant is obtained, the formalities of the procedure and the content of the warrant themselves establish that there are special reasons, specific to the situation, for a search. If exceptions to the requirement of a warrant are allowed only in "exigent circumstances" that make it impracticable to obtain a warrant, this framework is fulfilled. The full implications of insistence that an official intrusion on privacy requires extraordinary justification is suggested by the old "mere evidence rule," which has now been discarded.[9] According to that rule, even a warrant is not enough if the purpose of a search is only to seize evidence of a crime. The needs of ordinary criminal investigation are not sufficiently special to justify the extraordinary invasion of privacy. The Court's rejection of the rule in 1967 indicates that so long as the warrant procedure is followed and the occasions for a search are thereby limited, there will be no inquiry into the sufficiency generally of the function to be performed; limitation of the occasions is enough to qualify the search as special.

In the same way, enlargement of the scope of exceptions to the requirement of a warrant, unaccompanied by any other special requirements, has been the vehicle for implementation of the framework that accepts an invasion of privacy in some circumstances as an exercise of the ordinary authority of government. In three areas of police practice, which have a good deal in common, the Supreme Court has adopted this approach. The first is the scope of a search incident to an arrest. As I have mentioned, recent cases have blurred the narrow boundary drawn by the strict notion of search functionally related to an arrest. Persons who are arrested are subject to a full search of the person, including the contents of discrete containers like a wallet or handbag. Beyond that, the immediate vicinity of the arrest evidently may be searched, even if the person is no longer free to grab anything. The clearest illustration of this doctrine and its lack of connection to the explanation given in *Chimel* is the rule that, having arrested the occupant of an automobile, police officers are authorized to search the whole passenger area, including the glove compartment and any unattached containers within the area, like a shopping bag or a piece of luggage.[10] Plainly, such a search can only be made after the person is out of the car and presumably in custody. But if that is so, in most circumstances, the functional reasons for allowing a search just because there has been an arrest are gone.[11] The Court observed that it is desirable to have a "bright line" rule; but it offered no explanation for the line it drew except the conclusion that a search in such circumstances is reasonable.

The second example of expansive police authority concerns the search of automobiles not as an instance of search incident to an arrest but pursuant to an independent rubric, often called the "automobile exception" to the requirement of a warrant. The Supreme Court has enunciated several distinct doctrinal strands, the details of which need not concern us here; together, they have the effect that if police lawfully have custody of a vehicle for an extended period, they can search it thoroughly and examine its contents.[12] The police may impound a vehicle for a wide variety of reasons: because they have probable cause to believe that it contains evidence of a crime, because the driver has been arrested, or because it is parked illegally and has been towed. The functional justifications for a search are similarly various: a prompt search may shorten the period during which the car is impounded; the police may want to protect the contents of the car, or make sure that the contents are not dangerous, or protect themselves against an accusation of theft of the contents. Except in rather special circumstances, such arguments are makeweights at best. Closer to the point, the Supreme Court has frequently observed that the police regularly exercise some control over automobiles for a variety of reasons, such as enforcement of licensing and inspection regulations; furthermore, travel on public roads is less private than activities in private premises.[13] Although the precise reasoning of the Court is clouded by this barrage of explanations, its conclusion is clear. "[T]here is a constitutional difference between houses and cars,"[14] and the privacy of the latter is less than the privacy of the former.

The third example also has a rubric of its own: "jailhouse searches." Persons who are arrested and detained in a cell, however briefly, are subject to a thorough search, which may include whatever ordinary containers they carry on or about their person: certainly a wallet or pocketbook and probably a briefcase or similar small piece of luggage.[15] The justificatory arguments are familiar: protection of the person's property, protection of the person or others lodged in the same cell, and protection of the police from harm or an accusation of theft. Most often, those objectives could be achieved more simply and effectively if the person was allowed to put his possessions into a lock-seal container or they were put into a container for him without being examined. The true explanation for allowing a search of persons who are arrested and detained is that it is a routine practice, which the police and even those who are arrested generally take for granted. That being the case, the search is constitutionally reasonable.

This approach found its baldest and most sweeping expression in *Hudson v. Palmer*, decided in 1984.[16] Referring to the practical necessities of prison administration, a majority of the Supreme Court concluded flatly "that the Fourth Amendment has no applicability to a prison cell."[17] The Court did not pause long to consider whether a more carefully crafted rule would not suffice for day-to-day operation of a prison. It said simply: "We are satisfied that society would insist that the prisoner's expectation of privacy always yield to what must be considered the paramount interest in institutional security."[18]

These conflicting doctrinal results illustrate the different premises about why the Fourth Amendment protects privacy that I stated earlier. In the *Terry* and *Chimel* cases, the Court did not ask whether a frisk of someone whose behavior suggests danger or a search of someone after he is arrested costs much in the way of social utility. Most likely it does not; a loss of privacy in those circumstances, by people in the groups most likely to be affected, is not likely to frustrate our shared political or economic or cultural objectives. The constitutional protection is fully applicable, nevertheless, because the individual, not the community as a whole, is the relevant entity. In contrast, current doctrine concerning the *Terry* and *Chimel* situations as well as the rubrics of automobile and jailhouse searches dismisses almost casually the substantial loss of privacy that the individuals may suffer. Nothing in the fact of being accosted by a police officer or being arrested or even being jailed indicates that one has no concern about exposing what he carries with him to public view. So also, although cars are registered and inspected periodically and others may be able to glance through the windows, considerable privacy remains. The weakness of the functional arguments that the Court has given to support a search in these situations emphasizes its dismissal of the countervailing individual interest in privacy, virtually without any argument at all.

Different as these approaches are, both are deeply rooted in our political tradition. Abstracted from the particular context of the Fourth Amendment, they reflect what are commonly discussed as "rights-based" and "utility-based" theories of liberty and political obligation.[19] Whether or not those labels can be sustained completely abstractly—I am inclined to think they cannot—they express a strong difference of emphasis, which is evident in our public controversies generally. One is not more fixed in our jurisprudence than the other. In particular, defenders of the Warren Court in the 1960s are mistaken to suppose that the decisions of that period establish the correct or "standard" meaning of the Fourth Amendment, so that all decisions since then are sufficiently characterized according to their fit or lack of fit with those precedents. Although, for reasons that I shall explain, I believe that the Supreme Court currently has veered too much toward utility-based results, it has been the peculiar genius of American politics and law to achieve a working harmony between rights and utility which strengthens both.

Despite the contentiousness of the current debate about the Fourth Amendment, we ought not abandon the effort to achieve something like an accord between the opposed positions. We should not expect to find a theory or formula which all will accept and which, once accepted, will be dispositive. Too much often depends on small matters of fact that are themselves uncertain. Furthermore, no formula overcomes disagreement about the competing values: privacy and the public values that privacy serves, on the one hand, and the values, including law enforcement, that oppose privacy, on the other. We ought, however, to work toward a common ground of understanding which makes the outcomes in particular cases intelligible. The reasons that are given to justify a result ought not appear, as too often they do now, as nothing but rationalizations for a decision reached on another, undisclosed basis.

The path to such common ground lies, I think, in more careful, more fully informed attention to the public officials—all but exclusively the police—whose day-to-day actions are directly affected by the rules in question. Because of the prominence of the warrant clause, applications of the Fourth Amendment have largely been guided by the supposition that police practices must either be accepted as they are or rejected and replaced by procedures of another kind altogether, ones that depend on prior application for a warrant solemnly and deliberately issued by a magistrate. The warrant clause, however, was not written with a modern police force in mind. The convenience of the police is not a sufficient public purpose to outweigh the individual value of privacy. Nor does the community's acceptance of a practice, without more, evince such a purpose. The fact that police routinely engage in some form of intrusion into personal privacy as part of the performance of their ordinary duties is not by itself a reason to approve it. At the same time, the rules for concrete application of the Fourth Amendment ought not be fashioned abstractly, as if for a body of "public officials" whose professional characteristics and duties and the circumstances of whose work are either unknown or irrelevant. Responsibility for keeping the peace and general law enforcement having been entrusted to a public agency whose primary characteristics are speed, mobility, and available force, effective performance of that responsibility must often have incidental consequences inconsistent with a magisterial procedure, which should not be considered as a separable event; rather, the consequences are justified, if at all, as circumstantial to the performance of the primary duty.

All three of the doctrines that I discussed previously, which justify an extensive search as a collateral part of regular peacekeeping or investigative work—search incident to an arrest, a car search, and a jailhouse search—are derived mainly from actual police practice. In all three situations, police are currently allowed to examine private, and frequently intimately private, possessions thoroughly and deliberately, without any specific objective, for no greater reason than that they have become accustomed to doing so. Even if one were to accept the (dubious) argument that having a special basis for a search sufficient to sustain a warrant, the police should not be put to the inconvenience of obtaining one, the vast majority of such searches lack even that explanation. The situation provides an opportunity and nothing more. The short and sufficient objection to these searches is that large numbers of people are subjected to a significant intrusion on their privacy for no reason.

Even though the occasion for it is limited, the search should be regarded as a general search, because it has no specific function but rather is in aid of the general functions of government. To reject the rules that authorize such searches does not bar a search which is specifically justified, by an actual emergency or by a warrant. Nor, as I shall urge, does it countermand actions that are a practical necessity for the performance of official duties.

The other side of the matter is that acting often in unpredictable, rapidly changing, and possibly dangerous situations, police cannot be expected always to calibrate their conduct very finely to the precise facts. Even if the particular circumstances are less exigent, they cannot be expected on demand to modify the pattern of behavior appropriate to that type of situation. Not all of the work of the police is of that type, of course; and when it predictably is not, their performance ought to be different. But often enough, conduct of the police has to be considered in light of the situation as a whole and not as a series of discrete functional responses. The reasoning of the *Chimel* case purported to limit a search incident to an arrest to specific functions. Considered in that way, as deliberate action, such a search makes no sense; for it must almost always be the case that if the arresting officers have time to deliberate at all, the person is already in custody and will not grab anything. Considered as an undeliberate, almost reflexive part of the arrest itself, however, looking around for and seizing a potential weapon or the fruits or other evidence of a crime is readily understood. And it may be that, already on the scene to make an arrest, police cannot realistically be expected not to look somewhat beyond the immediate vicinity of the arrest if evidence is likely to be found. Whatever the rules, they will probably do so, not so much to obtain evidence for subsequent use at trial but simply to confirm the arrest. Something similar may be at work in situations covered by the car and jailhouse rubrics, although to a far less extent than the rubrics currently allow. Frank acknowledgment of this undeliberate dimension of police conduct, instead of unconvincing efforts to explain it as carefully considered, functionally justified action, might go a long way toward providing the basis for mutual understanding that we lack. The acknowledgment is troubling, because it suggests that we are not able to have it any way we want, without limit. But even professional behavior, we know, is not so adaptable as that. It does not advance understanding to fashion rules that oblige us to distort the facts lest we have to admit that the rules themselves are inapt for the situations for which they prescribe. Furthermore, an authorization of official action is far less susceptible to indefinite and arbitrary expansion if it has an accurate factual underpinning than if its theoretical limitations are anchored only by the imagination and wishful thinking.

To allow a search on the ground that it is incidental to performance of another official function may seem to accept too easily the view of the Fourth Amendment that makes privacy instrumental to other public values. But I have not suggested that any search ought to be allowed on that basis, whatever the official function may be. It is appropriate to ask whether the purpose that is served by a search outweighs the value, individual or public, of the privacy at stake. The mode of analysis that led to the mere evidence rule is sound, even if the earlier Court's conclusion that criminal investigation does not justify issuance of a search warrant is rejected. In the cases that I have described, the purpose of the search is correctly identified as performance of the primary duty, rather than some purpose dubiously associated with the search itself.

Insofar as the peacekeeping and crime preventive activities of the police are an unexceptional part of life, so also are the incidental invasions of privacy that accompany them, although on one strict view of the matter the rights protected by the Fourth Amendment are in some measure diminished. One could, of course, ask the question whether these general police functions outweigh the loss of privacy they entail. But for better or worse, the conditions of social order now make the maintenance of a police force unavoidable as a practical matter. That is a circumstance not contemplated when the Fourth Amendment was drafted; and for most purposes, recognition of that circumstance and what it imposes accommodates the view that the amendment always requires that searches be justified specially. Provided that justification on these grounds goes no further than the realities of police work truly require, the former view is largely respected.

What I have said up to now indicates how I should resolve the conflict between the Fourth Amendment as protective of the individual values of privacy and as protective of privacy for public purposes. I can give no concrete content to the individual values in question without attending to the community in which we are placed. The notion of an absolute right to privacy derived directly from the abstract idea of a person yields only abstractions too weak to sustain the concrete rights of real persons. We are constituted as the persons we are within the community in which we live. In that sense, the Fourth Amendment does reflect the concrete realities of this community, including its public values. The immediate reference of the amendment, however, is to the individual. It does not depreciate the community's political, social, and economic values to observe that their particular shape is likely to be determined by those whose power in the community is large. They may exercise their power for the general good, as they see it; but the public interest is also, inevitably, the private interest of some more than others. Within the limits that I have described, the Fourth Amendment stands above, not within, that calculation. Even those whose conclusions have seemed to adopt an instrumental view of the amendment would not, I think, disagree.

The decisions of the Supreme Court upholding police authority to search cars have been based very much on the premise that the privacy one has in a car is of less value than the privacy of a home; persons reserve their most significant privacies for the latter. That seems to me substantially inaccurate for a large portion of the population. For many persons, who lack a private place of their own and access to other private places shared only with whom they choose, a car may be the principal means for expression and realization of one's self. The elaborate personalization of cars by decorations, accessories, and the like and the congregating in cars, Sunday outings on crowded highways, and aimless "driving around" not only of teenagers but of adults are familiar aspects of American life. I see no reason why the Fourth Amendment should protect such privacy less than the privacy of a home. Were it otherwise, the protection of the amendment would be too much like a premium on the value of property, which some have and others do not, rather than a right guaranteed to all.

Similarly, instead of concluding that an arrest or detention diminishes a person's interest in privacy, it seems to me that such circumstances are those in which it is most important to confirm his interest. Having already required a person to submit to the authority of the government, the community ought to emphasize that its officials exercise lawful authority and not mere force. The extension of official authority beyond what the situation requires, for no reason other than that the person is, as it were, in the government's hands, is too much like the latter. The Supreme Court's recent rulings in these areas, as in the matter of car searches, considerably favor those in the community who are better off economically and are less likely to be arrested or detained. The unhappy suspicion of unconscious class bias is strengthened by the Court's failure even to acknowledge this aspect of the issues before it.

From the perspective of the individual, the weakness in this respect of current doctrines is not overcome by the fact, if it is a fact, that they are consistent with public policy and fulfill the instrumental approach to the Fourth Amendment. At that point in the debate, the issue is enlarged to the general considerations of liberty and equality out of which we compose a conception of social justice. The Fourth Amendment does finally open out in that way. For myself, referring specifically to the particular issues of privacy with which the amendment is concerned, I do not doubt that social justice requires greater respect for equality, without which the liberty that is protected itself loses its value.

Bicentennials are not an occasion for grumbling. Scarcely anyone has had a kind word recently for the jurisprudence of the Fourth Amendment. I have been none too complimentary myself. It is worth stating clearly that intense as it is, controversy about the Fourth Amendment builds on a secure foundation of settled rights, about which there is no significant disagreement. We do not fear a sudden knock on the door and an unannounced entry, or a secret search of our possessions, or an abduction by officials answerable only to themselves. In countless smaller ways, we take the protections of the Fourth Amendment for granted; and we are not deceived.

All of that we accomplish while at the same time supporting a strong public agency charged to keep the peace, prevent crime, and provide a large range of a general services to the community at large. Although the failings are likely to arrest our attention, the durable achievement is great.

Notes

1. "The right of the people to be secure in their persons, houses, papers, and effects, against unreasonable searches and seizures, shall not be violated, and no Warrants shall issue, but upon probable cause, supported by Oath or affirmation, and particularly describing the place to be searched, and the persons or things to be seized."

2. *United States v. White*, 401 U.S. 745, 787 (1971) (dissenting opinion) (footnote omitted).

3. *Terry v. Ohio*, 392 U.S. 1 (1968).

4. The Court did refer to the individual privacy at stake in rather hyperbolic language. But its discussion of the point did not go much beyond hyperbole. The hyperbole, moreover, was a response to the suggestion the Fourth Amendment was not involved at all. Responding to the suggestion that a brief stop and frisk "is outside the purview of the Fourth Amendment," the Court said: "It must be recognized that whenever a police officer accosts an individual and restrains his freedom to walk away, he has 'seized' that person. And it is nothing less than sheer torture of the English language to suggest that a careful exploration of the outer surfaces of a person's clothing all over his or her body in an attempt to find weapons is not a 'search.' Moreover, it is simply fantastic to urge that such a procedure performed in public by a policeman while the citizen stands helpless, perhaps facing a wall with his hands raised, is a 'petty indignity.' It is a serious intrusion upon the sanctity of the person, which may inflict great indignity and arouse strong resentment, and it is not to be undertaken lightly." 392 U.S. at 16–17 (footnotes omitted).

5. *See, e.g., Brown v. Texas*, 443 U.S. 47 (1979); *Adams v. Williams*, 407 U.S. 143 (1972); *cf. United States v. Sharpe*, 470 U.S. 695 (1985).

6. *Chimel v. California*, 395 U.S. 752 (1969).

7. 395 U.S. 770, 773–75 (opinion of White, J.).

8. *E.g., United States v. Harrison*, 461 F.2d 1127 (5th Cir. 1972); *People v. Fitzpatrick*, 32 N.Y. 2d 499, 300 N.E.2d 139 (1973). *See* the discussion of a search incident to the arrest of the occupant of a car, *infra*.

9. The rule is discussed in *Warren v. Hayden*, 387 U.S. 294 (1967), in which the Court rejected it.

10. *New York v. Belton*, 453 U.S. 454 (1981).

11. There might be a reason to search if other occupants of the car were not arrested or if the person who was arrested was allowed to return to his car after the arrest was completed.

12. *See South Dakota v. Opperman*, 428 U.S. 364 (1976) (inventory search); *Cady v. Dombrowski*, 413 U.S. 433 (1973) (caretaking search); *Chambers v.*

Maroney, 339 U.S. 42 (1970) (probable cause to believe car contains evidence).

13. *E.g.*, *Oppermann*, *supra* note 12.

14. *Chambers*, *supra* note 12, at 52.

15. *United States v. Edwards*, 415 U.S. 800 (1974); *see Illinois v. Lafayette*, 462 U.S. 640 (1983) (station house search).

16. *Hudson v. Palmer*, 468 U.S. 517.

17. *Id.* at 536.

18. *Id.* at 528.

19. To describe the approaches to the Fourth Amendment as "rights-based" and "utility based" is not to suggest, of course, that one ignores utility and the other ignores rights entirely. The doctrines of *Terry* and *Chimel* allow strong public need—utility—to overcome the individual's rights in the specified circumstances. On the other side, however broadly the rules allowing a search are construed, the fact that there are any rules at all confirms that the rights in question are not altogether lost.

Albert W. Alschuler

14. Fourth Amendment Remedies: The Current Understanding

The evil that most directly sparked the Fourth Amendment was the writ of assistance, a document that authorized general searches for goods on which duties had not been paid.[1] In proscribing this historic evil, the framers used broad and general language; they declared the right of the people to be secure in their persons, houses, papers, and effects against unreasonable searches and seizures.

The evil that prompted this declaration, if described too narrowly, does not mark the limits of constitutional protection. Few would contend, for example, that the Fourth Amendment limits only searches by revenue officers.[2] As Anthony Amsterdam once observed, "To suppose [that the framers of the Constitution] meant to preserve to their posterity by guarantees of liberty written with the broadest latitude nothing more than hedges against the recurrence of particular forms of evils suffered at the hand of a monarchy beyond the seas seems . . . implausible in the extreme."[3]

At the same time, people who describe the objects of the Constitution at the grandest level of generality—declaring, for example, that because the framers of the Fourth Amendment sought to protect privacy, the emanations of their language create a right to use contraceptives[4]—tend to reduce constitutional adjudication to a word game. Still more clearly, "noninterpretivists" who declare that their "different experience of life in our polity" entitles them to reinvent constitutional doctrine without significant regard for the text of the Constitution, its history, or its objects[5] challenge the rule of law.

Between errors of excessive particularity and errors of excessive generality lies an area of legitimate choice whose boundaries are uncertain. Calls for adherence to the "original intention" may be unobjectionable, but they do not help much. The boundaries of appropriate judgment cannot be described "in the large"; they must be determined "in the specific" by examining the merits of individual cases. In deciding what rules and remedies will guarantee the right of the people to be secure against unreasonable searches and seizures, judges must judge.

Among the things that did not exist at the time the Fourth Amendment became part of the Constitution were cocaine, heroin, helicopters, magnetometers, drug-detecting dogs, professional police forces, and the exclusionary rule. Changed circumstances have required successive generations of judges to determine without clear guidance from the past what searches and seizures are unreasonable. In resolving this central Fourth Amendment issue, courts have responded to changing cultural norms, changing technologies, changing law enforcement needs, and changing forms of governmental and private organization. For the most part, they have done so without departing from either the spirit or the language of the Constitution—a fact which bespeaks the wisdom and vision of the people who wrote this document.

More specifically, the Supreme Court has come during the past century to view privacy rather than property as the principal value protected by the Fourth Amendment.[6] This development has had two sides. During 1967, the year that the Court first recognized Fourth Amendment protection against nontrespassory electronic surveillance,[7] it also withdrew the amendment's former protection against the seizure of tangible property sought merely as evidence. One wonders how many "interpretivists" would overrule the Court's decision in *Warden v. Hayden*,[8] thereby denying law enforcement the power to seize a murderer's bloody shirt in order to use it as evidence. The framers of the Fourth Amendment apparently would have condemned this seizure of private property as unreasonable even when authorized by a narrowly drawn warrant supported by probable cause.[9]

Changed concepts of substantive protection have led to changed Fourth Amendment remedies. The most obvious remedy for a wrongful deprivation of property is a return of the property, but a return of tangible property cannot remedy a wrongful invasion of privacy. Courts have sought to limit the effects of improper intrusions upon privacy by forbidding the use of wrongfully obtained information. When a law enforcement officer reveals illegally obtained information in court, not only does the officer know things that he or she is not entitled to know, but others—the judge, jurors, and spectators—know these things as well. One sentiment that probably has contributed to the development of the Fourth Amendment exclusionary rule has been the sense that a use of improperly obtained information can aggravate an invasion of privacy and, perhaps, constitute a further invasion.[10]

No one dates the Fourth Amendment exclusionary rule before 1886, the year that the Supreme Court decided *Boyd v. United States*.[11] Nevertheless, earlier reported cases in which courts received unlawfully obtained evidence were infrequent. In the absence of today's extensive governmental regulation of private activity and the emergence of today's public law enforcement agencies, the question of exclusion apparently arose only rarely.

An expansion of the substantive criminal law—particularly the creation of new "victimless" crimes including gambling and alcohol and drug offenses—made intrusions upon privacy more essential to effective law enforcement. The creation and growth of urban police forces, the development of informant systems, and the improvement of police technology facilitated these intrusions upon privacy and some unnecessary intrusions as well. Furthermore, the Balkanization of American law enforcement, with power and responsibility divided among innumerable local police agencies, prompted judicial efforts to control police misconduct—efforts that European nations with more effective administrative controls generally have considered unnecessary. The federal exclusionary rule of *Boyd*, expanded in 1914 by *Weeks v. United States*,[12] was supplemented within fifteen years of *Weeks* by exclusionary rules in twenty-one states,[13] by later federal decisions requiring state courts to exclude evidence obtained by seizures that shocked the conscience,[14] and finally, in 1961, by the Supreme Court's "incorporation" of the Fourth Amendment within the due process clause and its extension of the exclusionary rule to the states.[15]

Too often, protagonists in the controversy over the exclusionary rule have viewed each other's positions with indignation. The rule implements in an incomplete fashion a fundamental remedial principle—that courts should place the victim of a wrong in the position that he or she would have occupied had the wrong not occurred. The rule's grounding in this principle bears not only on its ethical justification but also on the costs that it exacts.

Justice Stewart maintained that the exclusionary rule imposes the same burdens on law enforcement that observance of the Constitution would have imposed in the absence of the rule.[16] Faithful adherence to the Fourth Amendment prevents law enforcement officers from discovering some criminals whom they otherwise would have apprehended. When officers have disregarded constitutional requirements, the exclusion of evidence that they have seized results in the release only of offenders whom the officers probably would not have detected had these officers obeyed the law. Exclusion becomes an issue only when other measures have failed to prevent the wrong. Alternative measures that truly would ensure compliance with the Constitution would leave as many criminals at large.

Justice Stewart's analysis could be pressed too far. The release of a proven murderer seems substantially more troubling than the failure to apprehend a murderer. Sensible people are indeed reluctant to allow known criminals to go free. Nevertheless, Justice Stewart's argument places the issue in perspective. The framers of the Fourth Amendment were willing to incur substantial law-enforcement costs, including the failure to punish some murderers, to preserve our freedom from unreasonable searches and seizures.

Ordinary remedial principles sometimes yield when the victim of a wrong is a wrongdoer himself or herself. Indeed, almost no one would place every victim of an unlawful search in the position that he or she would have occupied had the search not occurred. For example, few would return to a thief a stolen million-dollar painting that the police had discovered illegally in his or her closet. The sentiment that leads even the most enthusiastic proponents of the exclusionary rule to oppose the return of a stolen Rembrandt to a thief leads others to resist exclusion of the Rembrandt at the thief's trial. The moral foundations of opposing views concerning the exclusionary rule are plausible enough that outrage on either side seems unwarranted.

Although few people would press the view that the government should not profit from its wrong to the limit, this view is entitled to consideration and respect. Justice Holmes declared, "I think it a less evil that some criminals should escape than that the Government should play an ignoble part."[17] Over the years the Supreme Court has advanced a variety of nonconsequentialist rationales for the exclusionary rule—the "imperative of judicial integrity,"[18] the argument that seizing evidence is akin to forcing a suspect to supply this evidence in violation of the privilege against self-incrimination,[19] and the assertion that the exclusion of improperly obtained evidence is the Fourth Amendment's "most important constitutional privilege"[20]—part and parcel of the right that the amendment creates. Although one might quarrel with any of these formulations, all reflect a sense that the affirmative use of unlawfully obtained evidence is a form of unjust governmental enrichment. Indeed, the extent to which one accepts the proposition that the government should not profit from its wrong seems more likely to determine this person's position on the exclusionary rule than historical analysis or any assessment of the rule's empirical effects. When an illegal search has uncovered a wrongdoer, either this wrongdoer or the government must receive a benefit which seems undeserved. The principal question posed by the exclusionary rule may be simply which form of unjust enrichment one considers less offensive. A person's judgment on this issue need not go all one way or all the other.

Supreme Court decisions during the past two decades have departed from "rights" theories of the exclusionary rule, asserting that the primary function of the rule is the prevention of future police illegality.[21] Commentators have attributed this change primarily to alterations in the composition of the Supreme Court during and after the Nixon presidency, thereby neglecting its origins in two Warren Court decisions, *Linkletter v. Walker*[22] and *Desist v. United States*.[23] The commentators have implied that the current Court's nearly exclusive focus on the "deterrence function" of the exclusionary rule may be a device for setting the rule up for a kill or for a very substantial restriction.[24] This speculation is supported not only by limitations of the rule that the Court already has announced but also by the Court's repeated claims that the deterrent benefits of the rule are unproved and unprovable.[25] The Court often has appeared to balance what it regards as the rule's certain costs against its assertedly speculative benefits, finding the benefits insufficient in various contexts to justify the rule's application.[26]

Mathematically rigorous proof of the exclusionary rule's behavioral effects may be unattainable, but so is rigorous proof of the beneficial effects of maintaining armaments, educating children, punishing criminals, and exploring space. Insisting upon clear, quantitative proof that costs are matched by benefits might go a long way toward reducing governmental budgets to zero. Evaluating the exclusionary rule on the basis of the sorts of evidence that inform most private and governmental decisions, however, one can fairly describe the exclusionary rule as one of the law's success stories.

It is useful to remember the way things were. In 1961, the year that the Supreme Court decided *Mapp v. Ohio*,[27] it also decided *Monroe v. Pape*.[28] The plaintiffs in this federal civil rights action alleged that thirteen Chicago police officers had broken into their home without a warrant during the early morning hours; had forced the plaintiffs—a suspect, his wife, and their six children—to stand naked in the living room as the officers "ransacked every room, emptying drawers and ripping mattress covers"; then had taken the suspect to a station house, detained him on "open" charges, interrogated him, refused to allow him to call his family or an attorney, and finally, after ten hours, released him without filing charges. Stories still circulating in the Chicago Police Department suggest that the allegations in *Monroe v. Pape* may have reflected the typical behavior of a legendary Chicago police captain, Frank Pape. The plaintiffs in *Monroe v. Pape* prevailed at a jury trial following the Supreme Court's decision. Other stories of the Chicago Police Department a quarter century ago are even more disturbing.[29]

The Chicago Police Department appears to be a different place today—as one of my students, Myron Orfield, discovered when he conducted extensive interviews with twenty-six Chicago narcotics officers. Orfield has permitted me to report some preliminary findings of his study.[30] Without exception, the veteran officers whom Orfield interviewed reported that police procedure had become substantially more professional during their service. One said: "In the past, a police officer's reputation depended simply on being tougher than anyone else on the street. Being tough is still important, but it's no longer the only thing. Knowing the book and following it is as important to an officer's success as anything else."

One need not look far to discover evidence of increased police professionalism elsewhere. Colorado prosecutors have spoken of late-night telephone calls in which police officers sought opinions concerning the legality of proposed searches. William Mertens and Silas Wasserstrom described the responses of two police agencies to a Supreme Court decision forbidding random automobile stops to check drivers' licenses.[31] The Metropolitan Police Department of the District of Columbia formerly had permitted these stops in reliance on local judicial decisions. Within hours of the Supreme Court's ruling, however, the chief of police had issued a telex forbidding the practice. Mertens and Wasserstrom reported that the response of the Delaware State Police was equally impressive.

The causes of increased police professionalism are complex. Nevertheless, police officers themselves—even as they express dissatisfaction with the courts—report that judicial rulings on search and seizure issues are among the forces that have contributed to their improved performance. Surprisingly, none of the Chicago officers whom Orfield interviewed favored abolition of the exclusionary rule (although all of the officers did favor modification of the rule to permit the admission of evidence seized in reasonable good faith).

Discussions of the "deterrence function" of the exclusionary rule probably have led courts and commentators astray, for the rule has not achieved its success primarily through deterrence. In ordinary usage, deterrence does not encompass every technique for restricting or altering behavior; it refers to the process of influencing behavior through fear of punishment.

In frequently quoted language, the opinion in *Elkins v. United States*[32] confounded the concepts of deterrence and behavioral change induced by other methods: "[The] purpose [of the rule] is to deter—to compel respect for the constitutional guaranty in the only effectively available way—by removing the incentive to disregard it."[33] Removing an incentive to disregard the Constitution—withholding a reward—is not the same as imposing a punishment. By itself, excluding unlawfully obtained evidence does not punish or deter; it leaves an officer who has violated the Constitution in no worse position than if he or she had obeyed it.

The "deterrence function" of the exclusionary rule should not be entirely discounted, however, for in conjunction with other practices, the rule may truly deter. Chicago narcotics officers reported that their superiors almost invariably knew when evidence had been suppressed and that these superiors frequently manifested their concern. Indeed, officers who lose even a small number of cases by conducting illegal searches commonly are transferred from the Narcotics Section. Moreover, the lecture that a judge may deliver when he or she suppresses evidence, the gleeful look of a guilty but victorious defendant as he or she leaves the courtroom, and the disappointment that an officer may sense when a case has ended in dismissal may be experienced as punishment.

Nevertheless, the exclusionary rule probably works less through punishment than through the withdrawal of one affirmative incentive for wrongdoing. In *Weeks* the Supreme Court described the evidence that it suppressed as "appropriated" property,[34] and some of the arguments in favor of excluding unlawfully obtained evidence are analogous to the arguments in favor of refusing to receive stolen goods.

An argument of the sort that the Supreme Court has shunted aside in recent years is moralistic. Even were it shown that a person's refusal to receive stolen property would not reduce the incidence of theft, this person should not receive stolen property. A fence who proclaimed, as the Supreme Court has with respect to the exclusionary rule, that "the ruptured privacy of the victims' homes and effects cannot be restored" and that "[r]eparation comes too late"[35] would offer a weak rationalization for his or her conduct. A second reason for refusing to receive stolen property, however, is pragmatic. This refusal removes one incentive for theft and may thereby reduce the incidence of this misconduct. It may do so, moreover, although other incentives for theft remain.

The exclusionary rule apparently does reduce the principal incentive for unlawful searches and seizures. Although other reasons for making these searches and seizures sometimes motivate the police, the officers whom Orfield interviewed reported that they rarely conducted searches unless they intended to use the evidence that they obtained in court. Moreover, Orfield's study suggests the inaccuracy of claims that police officers "count" arrests rather than convictions, that they often do not know that evidence has been suppressed, and that they commonly do not understand the reasons for suppression when they know about it.

The Fourth Amendment exclusionary rule, in conjunction with other practices, may deter, and the rule also reduces one affirmative incentive for wrongdoing. In addition, the rule probably influences conduct in a third and substantially more positive way. Before the development of the exclusionary rule, courts had little occasion to rule on the legality or illegality of police seizures. The constitutionality of these seizures was simply irrelevant to any issue that was likely to come before the courts, and judges gave police officers almost no guidance concerning the propriety of their behavior. The exclusionary rule imposes upon judges the responsibility of developing and articulating Fourth Amendment law; and quite apart from any sanctions or incentives that the rule provides, the repeated articulation of constitutional norms seems likely to have a long-range behavioral effect.

Law probably works less through sanctions than through example and habit formation. The "third degree" has not become less common[36] because courts have developed substantially more effective ways of discovering what happens in the back rooms of police stations. It has not diminished in frequency primarily because lawless officers have feared the discovery of their abuses and the judicial exclusion of evidence that they have obtained. Instead, the primary reason for the relative rarity of the "third degree" as a routine police practice may have been almost the opposite of the one implied by the word "deterrence." Essentially law-abiding officers have accepted the guidance that the law has provided. Along with other social institutions, judicial decisions have contributed to the acceptance of new norms by new generations of police officers.

Critics of the exclusionary rule may have followed too closely Justice Holmes's advice to view the law from the perspective of a "bad man" who wishes only to evade it.[37] From a "bad cop" perspective, it is easy to ridicule the exclusionary rule's supposed deterrent effect.[38] Critics of the rule, however, have been thinking about law in the wrong way. America's experience since *Mapp v. Ohio* suggests that, although the "bad cop" deserves careful attention, the "good cop" merits notice as well.

It is doubtful that the Narcotics Section of the Chicago Police Department would have permitted an outside study of its operations twenty-five years ago. The current supervisors of this section, however, devoted substantial resources and energy to facilitating Orfield's study. These supervisors apparently were proud of what the section had accomplished.

No one has suggested that the Narcotics Section has achieved full compliance with the law. Indeed, three-quarters of the officers whom Orfield interviewed admitted that the police sometimes "shade the facts a little or a lot to establish probable cause when there may not have been probable cause in fact."[39] A slight majority of the officers described judges as "frequently correct" when they disbelieved police testimony.[40]

Police dishonesty may have weakened the exclusionary rule, but this dishonesty has not destroyed it. One reason is that judges have not invariably accepted the officers' stories. Indeed, the frequency with which judges have disbelieved police testimony (even when the officers told the truth) has been one circumstance that has led the Narcotics Section to abandon almost completely the practice of conducting what its officers call "on view" searches—warrantless searches based on the direct observation of narcotics activity on the streets, in bars, or incident to arrests for traffic violations and other crimes.[41] In accordance with a policy formulated by the Narcotics Section's supervisors, its officers now conduct virtually all of their searches only after obtaining judicial warrants. One cannot know whether the Narcotics Section would have adopted this policy if America had never had an exclusionary rule, but one can guess.

Chief Justice Burger and others have suggested the creation of new, more effective damage actions as a substitute for today's exclusionary rule,[42] and damage actions against offending officers undoubtedly were the principal remedy for unlawful searches and seizures at the time that the Fourth Amendment was written.[43] Commentators, however, have tended to dismiss tort remedies as inherently defective. They have observed that the victims of unlawful searches are unlikely to be attractive plaintiffs, that these victims are unlikely to be adequately advised or to have ready access to legal services, that juries imbued with excessive "Support Your Local Police" zeal may refuse to award damages in meritorious cases, and that police officers frequently are judgment-proof.[44] The commentators also have argued that an exclusive reliance on damage remedies would encourage the government to violate constitutional rights whenever it was willing to pay money for the privilege.

These commentators may have gotten things backwards. The principal danger of a more frequent use of damage actions may not be that they would be ineffective or that they would inadequately deter violations of the Fourth

Amendment. The principal danger may instead be that these remedies would overdeter, inhibiting even appropriate law enforcement activity.[45]

A Chicago narcotics detective revealed his mastery of Fourth Amendment law as well as his understanding of the dynamics of police work when he said to Orfield: "Did you see Chief Justice Burger's proposal in *Bivens*? You know, if they ever try that one, we're going to stop doing anything." This conversation prompted Orfield to ask the following question in his interviews: "Some people say a system in which victims of improper searches could sue police officers directly would be better than the exclusionary rule. Is this correct?" Without exception, Orfield's officers answered no. Orfield then asked, "What would be the effect of civil suits for damages on police work?" He gave his respondents four choices: "(a) the police would be more careful, (b) the police would be afraid to conduct searches they should make, (c) there would be no effect, and (d) other." Eighty-six percent of the officers answered that the police would be afraid to conduct searches that they should make.

Law enforcement activity benefits the public, but damage actions of the sort that existed in 1791—actions unqualified by police immunity for good-faith errors—inflict the burdens of excess and mistake on individual officers. This mismatch easily could lead officers to play it safer than they should. So long as a search conceivably might be held illegal, an officer faced with the prospect of damage liability would have little to gain and much to lose by making it. Although governments commonly indemnify officers for financial liability incurred within the scope of their employment, an officer might fear that an action which led to governmental liability also would lead to some form of personal discipline. Indeed, those who would substitute new civil remedies for the exclusionary rule commonly intend this effect.

Recognizing that damage actions judge individual officers and affect their pocketbooks in ways that the exclusionary rule does not, the Supreme Court has made the damage remedy currently afforded by the Constitution and by federal civil right statutes less broad than the Fourth Amendment's substantive guarantees and also less broad than the remedy apparently available in 1791. The Court has afforded immunity to officers who violate the Fourth Amendment while acting in objectively reasonable good faith.[46] Unless the Court were to withdraw this civil immunity, its restriction of the exclusionary rule would leave many violations of the Fourth Amendment without a remedy—a result which apparently would violate an axiom of those who wrote the Fourth Amendment: "[W]here there is a legal right, there is also a legal remedy."[47]

The Fourth Amendment exclusionary rule probably provides more appropriate incentives for compliance with the amendment's guarantees than the remedies afforded at the time of the amendment's adoption. Although the release of known criminals required by the rule provides a plausible ethical basis for opposing it, alternative remedies that would effectively insure compliance with the Fourth Amendment would themselves leave most of these criminal at large. "Rights" theories of the exclusionary rule are not so compelling that reasonable people must accept them, but they rest on a strong ethical foundation and are entitled to respect. Moreover, when one abandons artificial social science conventions and evaluates the exclusionary rule on the basis of the sort of evidence that informs most governmental decisions, the rule appears to have worked well.

The framers of the Fourth Amendment could not have foreseen what mechanisms would prove necessary to keep the amendment's substantive promises in an era of vastly expanded law enforcement activity. The judicial creation of the exclusionary rule reflected changed law enforcement needs and practices as well as changed concepts of substantive Fourth Amendment protection. This judicial action was well within the bounds of legitimate constitutional interpretation. The exclusionary rule has been one of many developments during the past 200 years that have kept our Constitution more than a form of words.[48]

Notes

1. *See* T. Taylor, *Two Studies in Constitutional Interpretation* (Columbus: Ohio State Univ. Press, 1969), pp. 35–41.

2. *See* Meese, *Address: Construing the Constitution*, 19 U.C.D. L. Rev. 22, 23 (1985) ("[T]he Bill of Rights spoke, through the Fourth Amendment, to 'unreasonable searches and seizures,' not merely the regulation of specific law enforcement practices of 1789.").

3. Amsterdam, *Perspectives on the Fourth Amendment*, 58 Minn. L. Rev. 349, 399 (1974).

4. *Cf. Griswold v. Connecticut*, 381 U.S. 479 (1965).

5. *See, e.g.*, Parker, *The Past of Constitutional Theory—And Its Future*, 42 Ohio St. L.J. 223 (1981).

6. *See, e.g.*, *Warden v. Hayden*, 387 U.S. 294 (1967). For an argument that the Supreme Court has failed to protect privacy as much as it should and at the same time has restricted the Fourth Amendment's protection of property, *see* Alschuler, *Interpersonal Privacy and the Fourth Amendment*, 4 N. Ill. L. Rev. 1 (1983).

7. *Katz v. United States*, 389 U.S. 347 (1967); *Berger v. New York*, 388 U.S. 41 (1967).

8. 387 U.S. 294 (1967).

9. *See Entick v. Carrington*, 19 Howell's State Trials 1029, 1073 (1765). A narrow "originalist" view of the Fourth Amendment would severely restrict accepted law enforcement practices in other ways as well. This view might, in fact, bring much of law enforcement to a halt. For example, the framers probably would have condemned today's issuance of search warrants on the basis of the hearsay declarations of unnamed informants, today's arrests without warrants for misdemeanors outside the presence of arresting officers, and today's no-

knock entries to make felony arrests in exigent circumstances.

10. *See* Mertens and Wasserstrom, *The Good Faith Exception to the Exclusionary Rule: Deregulating the Police and Derailing the Law*, 70 Geo. L.J. 365, 377–78 (1981); *Boyd v. United States*, 111 U.S. 616, 630 (1886) (referring to "the sanctity of a man's home and the privacies of life" and declaring, "breaking into a house and opening boxes and drawers are circumstances of aggravation; but any forcible and compulsory extortion of a man's own testimony or of his private papers to convict him of crime is within the condemnation of [English and American law]").

I do not suggest that the development of today's exclusionary rule was an inevitable consequence of an increased emphasis on privacy, only that the substantive and procedural developments were probably related. Just as the restitution of improperly obtained property cannot remedy an invasion of privacy, this restitution cannot remedy every physical trespass. Judges have historically awarded damages to remedy trespasses that cannot be remedied through the restitution of property. In this context, the inadequacy of a restitutionary remedy has not led to an exclusionary remedy. Nevertheless, the nexus between a "seizure" of information and use of this information seems closer than that between a wrongful deprivation of property and a use of evidence derived from this deprivation. A seizure of property can itself be viewed in part as a seizure of information, and this reconceptualization may tend to make an exclusionary remedy more plausible.

Courts have long concluded that individuals cannot gain personal rights in certain sorts of property—contraband and the fruits and instrumentalities of crime. Even when the government has seized this tangible property wrongfully, courts have withheld a restitutionary remedy. As informational privacy grew more important, courts also might have classified some information as "contraband," concluding that individuals have no legitimate claim to the privacy of information concerning their criminal activities. Nevertheless, sentiments concerning the privacy of incriminating information are ambivalent. The Fifth Amendment privilege against self-incrimination, far from viewing incriminating information as less deserving of privacy than other information, affords special protection to this information.

11. 116 U.S. 616 (1886).

12. 232 U.S. 383 (1914).

13. *See* Plumb, *Illegal Enforcement of the Law*, 24 Cornell L.Q. 337, 357 (1939).

14. *See Rochin v. California*, 342 U.S. 1165 (1952).

15. *See Mapp v. Ohio*, 367 U.S. 643 (1961).

16. Stewart, *The Road to Mapp v. Ohio and Beyond: The Origins, Development, and Future of the Exclusionary Rule in Search-and-Seizure Cases*, 83 Colum. L. Rev. 1365, 1392–93 (1983).

17. *Olmstead v. United States*, 277 U.S. 438, 470 (1928) (Holmes, J., dissenting).

18. *See Elkins v. United States*, 364 U.S. 206, 222 (1960).

19. *See Boyd v. United States*, 116 U.S. 616, 630, 633 (1886).

20. *See Mapp v. Ohio*, 367 U.S. 643, 656 (1961).

21. *E.g., Michigan v. DeFillipo*, 443 U.S. 31, 38 n.3 (1979); *Stone v. Powell*, 428 U.S. 465, 492 (1976).

22. 381 U.S. 618 (1965).

23. 394 U.S. 244 (1969). Both *Linkletter* and *Desist* held Fourth Amendment rulings nonretroactive and emphasized the supposed deterrence function of the exclusionary rule. These decisions laid the groundwork for a more complete abandonment of nonconsequentialist justifications for the rule in later years.

24. *See, e.g.*, Kamisar, *Does (Did) (Should) the Exclusionary Rule Rest on a "Principled Basis" Rather than an "Empirical Proposition,"* 16 Creighton L. Rev. 565 (1983).

25. *See, e.g.*, *United States v. Janis*, 428 U.S. 433, 448–54 (1976).

26. *See United States v. Calandra*, 414 U.S. 338 (1974); *United States v. Janis*, 428 U.S. 433 (1976); *Stone v. Powell*, 428 U.S. 465 (1976); *Michigan v. DeFillippo*, 443 U.S. 31 (1979); *I.N.S. v. Lopez-Mendoza*, 468 U.S. 1032 (1984); *United States v. Leon*, 104 S. Ct. 3405 (1984).

27. 367 U.S. 643 (1961).

28. 365 U.S. 167 (1961).

29. Although less extreme, the facts of *Mapp* itself illustrate the frequently rough-and-ready character of law enforcement in 1961.

30. Between the presentation of these remarks and their publication, a large portion of Orfield's study was published as Comment, *The Exclusionary Rule and Deterrence: An Empirical Study of Chicago Narcotics Officers*, 54 U. Chi. L. Rev. 1016 (1987). My remarks, however, include references to portions of Orfield's study that were not included in his published comment.

31. Mertens and Wasserstrom, *The Good Faith Exception to the Exclusionary Rule*, pp. 399–401 (describing the effect of *Delaware v. Prouse*, 440 U.S. 648 [1979]).

32. 364 U.S. 206 (1960).

33. *Id.* at 217.

34. *Weeks v. United States*, 232 U.S. 383, 398 (1914).

35. *Linkletter v. Walker*, 381 U.S. 618, 637 (1965).

36. *Cf.* National Commission on Law Observance and Enforcement, *Report on Lawlessness in Law Enforcement* (Washington, D.C.: GPO, 1931), p. 153.

37. *See* Holmes, *The Path of the Law*, 10 Harv. L. Rev. 458, 459–62 (1897).

38. *See, e.g.*, *Bivens v. Six Unknown Named Agents of the Fed. Bureau of Narcotics*, 403 U.S. 388, 415 (1971) (Burger, C.J., dissenting) (the hope that the exclusionary rule would "give meaning and teeth to the constitutional guarantees" was "hardly more than a wistful dream").

39. When Orfield asked one officer why evidence had been suppressed in a recent case, the officer replied, "It had to do with the way I said 'reached.' I simply said that the suspect 'reached into his pocket' when I should have said that he 'reached into his pocket in an unusual way as if to go for a gun or something.' "

40. In *United States v. Janis*, 428 U.S. 433, 449–50 (1976), the Supreme Court observed, "[A]lthough scholars have attempted to determine whether the exclusionary rule in fact does have any deterrent effect, each empirical study on the subject, in its own way, appears to be flawed." The Court dismissed "response" studies on the ground that they "are hampered by the presence of the respondents' interests" (*id.* at 452–53). When respondents make statements contrary to their interests, however, as

they frequently did to Orfield, their statements gain credibility. Chicago narcotics officers may lie in court; but when they admit this deception in interviews, it seems doubtful that they are lying to the researcher.

41. Lest offenders in Chicago stumble upon this paper and get the wrong idea, I should mention that district officers outside the Narcotics Section continue to conduct "on view" searches.

42. *See, e.g., Bivens v. Six Unknown Named Agents of the Fed. Bureau of Narcotics* 403 U.S. 388 (1971) (Burger, C.J., dissenting); Barnett, *Resolving the Dilemma of the Exclusionary Rule: An Application of Restitutive Principles of Justice*, 32 Emory L.J. 937, 969–85 (1983).

43. *See* Wilson, *Enforcing the Fourth Amendment: The Original Understanding*, 28 Catholic Lawyer 173 (1983).

44. *See* Foote, *Tort Remedies for Police Violations of Individual Rights*, 39 Minn. L. Rev. 493, 499–500 (1955); Note, *Grievance Response Mechanisms for Police Misconduct*, 55 Va. L. Rev. 909, 916–27 (1969).

45. As usual, I may exaggerate. Damage actions might prove ineffective in some situations for the reasons that the commentators have advanced. In other situations, however, damage actions might prove too effective.

46. *See Pierson v. Ray*, 386 U.S. 547 (1967); *Harlow v. Fitzgerald*, 457 U.S. 800 (1982).

47. *See*, W. Blackstone, *Commentaries on the Laws of England* (London, 1765–69) 3:*23; *Marbury v. Madison*, 5 U.S. 137, 163 (1803); Wilson, *Enforcing the Fourth Amendment*, pp. 175–77. Current law also appears to contravene this original understanding. In cases in which officers acting in objectively reasonable good faith have violated the Fourth Amendment without seizing material that they propose to use as evidence, neither an exclusionary remedy nor a damage award is available under federal law. Moreover, some states have abrogated the common-law rule that denied civil immunity to governmental officers who made unlawful searches and seizures. *See, e.g.*, Ill. Rev. Stat. chap. 85, sec. 2–202, 2–203 (1985). Moreover, state trespass actions do not reach all police conduct that violates the Fourth Amendment. *See Bivens v. Six Unknown Named Agents of the Fed. Bureau of Narcotics*, 403 U.S. 388, 392–94 (1971). Finally, in light of the absolute civil immunity of judges for wrongful official actions, the ruling in *United States v. Leon*, 104 S. Ct. 3405 (1984), leaves most judicial violations of the Fourth Amendment without a potential remedy.

48. *Cf.* Bradford P. Wilson, chapter 11, *supra*.

V.

DUE PROCESS AND THE ADMINISTRATIVE STATE

CHRISTOPHER WOLFE

15. The Original Meaning of the Due Process Clause

The debate over the proper way to interpret the U.S. Constitution has expanded in recent years to include a position once widely considered by most well-known scholars to be dead. That is the position that the Constitution ought to be read as it was written. According to this position, for example, the very legitimacy of an act of judicial review depends on courts resting such an act on the firm ground of the Constitution as it was originally understood by its framers and ratifiers.

Of all the phrases in the Constitution that have been invoked to justify judicial voiding of legislative and executive acts, none can match the historical record of the due process clause. Indeed, until the explosion of equal protection law under the Warren Court and its successor, no clause could even come close to the dominance of constitutional law by due process cases. It has been regarded by most modern scholars as the greatest of the Constitution's "majestic generalities."

My thesis in this chapter is simple. It is that virtually all of the constitutional law built on the due process clause is built upon air, since the original meaning of the due process clause was rather narrow. At the same time, I want to make some points about how "original meaning" should be understood.

The Conflict over Original Intention

What exactly does "original intention" mean? It may seem obvious at first glance that it means "what the Constitution was understood to mean by those who framed it," but the issue is more complicated. First, for the record, it must be pointed out (with Madison) that the document should be understood not simply in light of the intention of the framers but in light of those for whom it was framed.[1]

Coming from the Convention which produced it, by itself, the Constitution had no authority. Its authority was derived from its ratification by the people of the United States, in the various state ratifying conventions. Ultimately, Madison traced the question of the authority of the Constitution back to the Declaration of Independence: the people have the right to establish, and to alter, government in order to achieve the goal of protecting the fundamental rights of man, among them life, liberty, and the pursuit of happiness.[2]

Because these principles were so widely accepted in American political life, the framers should be assumed to have stated their meaning in plain language, and normally there should be no conflict between the Constitution as understood by its framers and the Constitution as understood by its ratifiers. Of course, it is an empirical question open to argument whether this assumption is true. Should there be a conflict, the Constitution is authoritative in the sense in which it was understood by those for whom it was written. But the burden of proof rests upon those who would contend that the Constitution was understood by its ratifiers differently from the way it was written by its authors.

Second, when we speak of "original meaning" or "original intention," we have in mind what the meaning of the document is—what its words mean, taken separately and as a whole, and their fair implications. This original intention concerns the principles embodied in the document, which can be distinguished from the expectations of the framers as to how the principles would be applied in concrete cases. What the Constitution ratified was not the expectations but the principles.

At the same time, the burden is strongly on those who would contend that expectations widely shared by the authors and ratifiers of the Constitution are not necessary implications of the document. After all, constitutional principles are frequently formulated by generalizing from specific problems or abuses, and those problems or abuses are often a significant source of light on the meaning of the general principles, at least where there is virtually universal agreement on the particular problems that gave rise to a provision. The presumption, then, should be that contemporaneous understandings of the application of a provision which are generally shared by those proposing it are proper applications of it.

Nonetheless, one can imagine a situation in which expectations—perhaps even widely shared expectations—do not correspond with the intrinsic requirements of the principles of the document. For example, it cannot be properly contended—as it was by at least one of the congressmen voting for the Fourteenth Amendment—that its protections against racial discrimination apply to blacks but not to Chinese.[3] Nor could it properly be contended that the First Amendment's guarantee of free exercise of religion applies to Protestants (or Christians) but not to Catholics (or Jews or Mohammedans), as some in the founding generation argued.[4]

The "original intention" or meaning of the Constitution, then, is to be found in the principles embodied in the document, as its language was understood by those for whom it was framed. This brings us to another question, which is related to the second point above. How are we to arrive at an understanding of these principles of the document? To what do we turn in order to discover the original intention? The answer is that we turn first and primarily to the words of the document, read as a whole, and only secondarily to "extrinsic," historical sources of evidence. (While the word "only" deliberately minimizes the extrinsic sources, it should be noted that the statement implicitly accepts them as a possible subordinate source.)

The central reason for this is that the only absolutely clear basis for authority which we have is the ratification vote that was taken in regard to the words of the document itself. We cannot know with the same certainty that anyone's opinion about the meaning of the document was meant to be given authority. To rely on extrinsic sources of the meaning of the document as the primary source would be to undercut the clarity and certainty that are such an essential element of the rule of law. Moreover, the language of the document inevitably will be our only guide in many cases, since the framers (and ratifiers) will not have thought of an increasing number of problems arising over time.

Even in regard to the language of the document, however, certain historical considerations are essential. The words are to be understood as they were understood by those for whom they were written, and therefore we must know what those understandings were. This implies the necessity of recourse to some study of the founding era (and of those which produced amendments), especially the explanations of constitutional provisions by those who proposed them. Such study is a kind of cross-check to insure that the words as we understand them today have the same meaning as when they were adopted.[5]

In some cases, historical sources may be of greater importance because it is possible that certain words or phrases employed in the Constitution may be "terms of art" or technical terms (especially legal terms). In those cases, still, the point is to ascertain how the provisions were understood by those for whom they were framed. While in one sense there is a departure from the ordinary or popular usage, in another sense one can argue that the technical meaning was precisely the ordinary sense of such terms.

With these qualifications, however, one must emphasize that the leading figures of early constitutional interpretation placed primary emphasis on construction of the words of the document itself in their constitutional interpretation. One important piece of evidence for this argument is their treatment of the records of the Convention of 1787. Great figures of American constitutional interpretation such as John Marshall did not use the records of the Convention to any significant extent but concentrated on an analysis of the document itself. Now, one response to this is that Madison's notes of the Convention were not available until after his death, i.e., not until about half a century after the ratification of the Constitution. But this begs the question. Why was it that Madison did not publish them earlier? Why did only Madison take notes, on his own initiative, apart from the record (of votes only) in the formal Journal? The answer is clear: it was the text of the document, not the debates behind it, that was regarded as authoritative—again, that was what the people had before them when they ratified the Constitution.

There are a number of interrelated and overlapping reasons why there has been an unfortunate shift of emphasis from the reading of the document to examining extrinsic historical sources for its intent. First, many people read the document less carefully today and therefore jump too quickly to the conclusion that the words of the document provide little, or at least insufficient, guidance. Second, in some cases where the document is genuinely unclear, there is a natural tendency to try to clear up the uncertainty by recourse to historical evidence of intent; this may create a disposition or habit of looking for extrinsic evidence even where the words are clearer. Third, the modern assumption that judges have the right and duty to interpret (or, more accurately, give definite content to) the Constitution and to exercise judicial review even in cases where the document is unclear—especially certain key provisions of the Constitution that are today assumed to be very vague or ambiguous—encourages reliance on extrinsic sources as a hedge against subjective judicial opinions.

It would be wrong simply to reject extrinsic sources of evidence of the meaning of the Constitution. Where the evidence is clear and decisive, it often can serve especially to confirm a fair reading of the document. This is the usual way in which it was employed by Marshall, for instance. Yet extrinsic sources have to be used with great care, because it is possible to jump to wrong conclusions in using such data and because it often is difficult to show that evidence is really determinative as to the intention of the framers and ratifiers, taken not individually but as a whole.[6] These limits suggest that even when extrinsic evidence is considered, there will be a gradation of authority involved. Where there is greater evidence that a statement about the meaning of a provision was generally shared, it has more weight. Therefore, for instance, a public statement explicitly intended to explain the meaning of a constitutional provision during the ratification process and coming from an acknowledged leader of the forces supporting the ratification (e.g., *The Federalist*) will have more weight than, say, a disputed after-the-fact statement of what a provision means in the context of a political debate many years afterwards by a person who was an opponent of the Constitution. Yet even in the former case, there is no certainty that the evidence is dispositive; in fact, it is rather clear that on some points *The Federalist* was flat wrong (e.g., Hamilton's statement in No. 77 on the removal power, assuming that senatorial approval would be necessary).

To the extent that the framers were good draftsmen, it would never be the case that extrinsic sources of evidence would clearly show that a provision was intended to mean something contrary to or different from a fair reading of the document. Of course, that is an empirical question, and assertions that the framers had failed that way would have to be addressed case by case. (I doubt that such a case exists.) More likely, however, might be a case where a plausible but disputable case built on extrinsic sources differs from a plausible but disputable case built on a fair reading of the document itself. I believe, for the reasons given above, that the framers would tend to give preference in such cases to the fair reading of the document itself. (A separate case, on which I will reserve comment until later in this chapter, is what the framers would say about the exercise of judicial review in plausible but doubtful cases—whether built upon reading the document or extrinsic historical sources.)

It is this approach to constitutional interpretation which I shall draw on as I make an effort to ascertain the original meaning of the due process clause of the Fifth Amendment. It will turn out to be a relatively typical case of constitutional interpretation: a cursory reading of the document will reveal several possible meanings, of which one is strongly suggested by a more careful reading in context; historical sources will provide some basis for several positions but generally support the fairest reading of the text.

The Original Meaning of Due Process: The Words

Fifth Amendment due process was quite limited in scope. The key phrase is "due process of law." What does the wording suggest? "Process," especially process of law, normally would be taken to mean some kind of legal proceedings or legal procedure. That is, some kind of legal process must be followed before depriving someone of life, liberty, or property.[7]

With respect to this procedural content of due process, there are several major different interpretations, which flow from different answers to the question, What is due process of law? What is the criterion or reference point for what is "due" or owed a person?

The narrower interpretation would be that a person has a right to that process which is due to a person under the law. What is due a person is the legal process that is specified by the law (common law and statutes). The broader interpretation would be that a person has a right to just or proper legal procedure, i.e., what is necessary to guarantee fairness as a matter of natural rights or natural law. This interpretation would be a significant limit on the legislature as well as the executive and judiciary, unlike the narrower interpretation.[8]

Another interpretation would lie in between the first two. The law which would be the norm for due process would be the 1789 law. This would make it a limit on the legislature, since the source of this law would be something other than the legislature itself, but it would also give it a more clear-cut or specified source, since the common law is a definite received body of doctrine whose content can be established with less controversy than the natural law.[9] The wording by itself, then, suggests several possibilities.

Turning from the words of the particular provision to its context, the Bill of Rights has at least some rough order—it is not a mere grab bag of rights.

I. Substantive Rights
- A. I: Freedom of Religion (establishment prohibited and free exercise guaranteed)
  Freedom of Speech, Press
  Freedom of Assembly and Petition for Redress of Grievances
- B. II: The Right to Bear Arms
- C. III: Limitations on Quartering of Soldiers in Citizens' Homes

II. Procedural Rights
- A. IV: Freedom from Unreasonable Searches and Seizures (including requirements for warrants)
- B. V: Rules Governing Proceedings against Life, Liberty, and Property (applicable especially to pretrial matters)
  1. Grand jury requirement;
  2. Double jeopardy prohibition;
  3. Self-incrimination prohibition, due process;
  4. Just compensation requirement
- C. VI: Procedural Rights of Individual Once Charged with a Crime
  1. Speedy and public trial, by impartial local jury, notice of accusation;
  2. Confrontation of witnesses;
  3. Compulsory process for defendant's witnesses and assistance of counsel for defense
- D. VII: Trial by Jury in Civil Cases
- E. VIII: No Excessive Bail, Excessive Fines, or Cruel and Unusual Punishments

III. A Rule of Construction regarding the Bill of Rights
- A. IX: Enumeration of Some Rights Not to Deny or Disparage Others

IV. Relation of State Powers to Those of the Government Established by the Constitution
- A. X: Powers Not Delegated to the United States or Prohibited to States Are Reserved to the Individual States, or the People.[10]

There is some roughness in the organization (as is common with committee work), but that should not obscure the existence of a basic structure. Due process is in a section generally concerned with procedural matters. Within that section it is in the second of five amendments, and within that one it is the second half of the third of four sections (separated by semicolons). This placement—it is buried in the midst of a number of specific rights—suggests rather strongly that due process is a fairly limited right rather than a broad general one. On its face, it makes quite unlikely the very broad form of procedural due process, according to which it is a general guarantee of fair or just legal process. Such a broad guarantee would have been singled out as a separate amendment (like trial by jury in civil cases) or at least placed at the beginning or, more likely, the end of the procedural guarantees.

The placement also casts doubt on the interpretation of the due process clause as a perpetual guarantee of the whole 1789 common-law legal process as a limit on all three branches of government. Such an interpretation would appear to be a variant of the very broad interpretation (the natural law—at least as regards legal procedure—approach), with this difference: the natural law guarantees would be assumed to have been comprehensively and permanently embodied in the common-law, as it stood in 1789.

The interpretation most supported by the placement is the narrower one: one is guaranteed that process which is specified by law. The common law would be the source of this law, for the most part, but it would not be the standard in such a way as to proscribe legislative modifications thereof. (Whether there are any limitations on legislative modifications of common law legal procedure may be a more difficult question—this narrower interpretation seems to leave the legislature free, but an interpretation based more on the 1789 common law would probably impose some limits, as the discussion of *Murray* below indicates. I only note here, again, that such limitations would not be very general, or otherwise the due process clause assumes a breadth which its placement tends to deny.)

There is another important aspect of the context of the due process clause which suggests that it has a (relatively) narrow meaning. The other provisions of the Bill of Rights include many specific procedural guarantees, e.g., grand jury, double jeopardy, self-incrimination, trial by jury, notice and hearing, confrontation of witnesses, assistance of counsel. If due process were a general guarantee that includes all of these, then those provisions were redundant or superfluous and would not have been included. The fact that they were included suggests that due process was not understood to cover them, i.e., was very narrow or covered them only in the sense that they were part of the standing law at the time of the framing of the Bill of Rights (a standing law subject to modification through the ordinary lawmaking process).[11]

Redundancy is thus avoided, and the clause is given an intelligible content if it is interpreted as a reference to the standing laws regarding legal procedure (i.e., the common law of the courts, as modified by the legislature).

This interpretation is sometimes criticized for guaranteeing something that is obvious. What is essential to remember is that many obvious rights have been violated throughout history. English history provided the framers with numerous examples of tyrannical acts of Parliament or the king (and their agents) depriving particular individuals or groups of life, liberty, and property without legal procedure according to the standing law. Moreover, the purpose of the Bill of Rights was primarily to quiet the fears of opponents to the national government by cautionary explanations. Many Federalists, such as Madison, argued that the Bill of Rights was not strictly necessary but that it was a prudent measure to calm Anti-Federalists fears.

The Original Intention of Due Process: History

One of the most important facets of the historical evidence on the meaning of the due process clause of the Fifth Amendment is what was not said. First, there was hardly any debate or controversy about the due process clause in the congressional discussion of the Bill of Rights or in the state ratification of the Bill of Rights. Second, there was very little use of the Fifth Amendment due process clause for the first century of its existence. The first major Supreme Court case defining it did not come until 1856.[12] Both of these facts strongly suggest that due process did not have a broad meaning.

What was its historical meaning at the time of the adoption of the Fifth Amendment? Its origin was taken to be the Magna Charta provision that no freeman would be imprisoned, dispossessed, banished, or destroyed "except by the lawful judgment of his peers or by the law of the land." A later reissue of the Charter (in 1354 by Edward III) used "due process of law" in place of "by the law of the land." The phrases seemed to be identified with each other by Sir Edward Coke, who defined due process as requiring "indictment and presentment of good and lawful men, and trial and conviction in consequence." Keith Jurow, in a fascinating article, "Untimely Thoughts: A Reconsideration of the Origins of Due Process of Law," shows that this assumed equivalence is quite doubtful.[13] In fact, due process was a very narrow right associated with use of the proper writ to bring an accused person before a court.

More evidence of the narrow meaning of due process in English law at the time of the founding can be found in Sir William Blackstone's *Commentaries on the Laws of England.* In Book IV, he discussed public wrongs and the method of punishing them. His outline of this part of the book is:

VI. The method of punishment, wherein of
- 1. The Several Courts of Criminal Jurisdiction
- 2. The Proceedings There
    - 1. Summary
    - 2. Regular; by
        - 1. Arrest
        - 2. Commitment and Bail
        - 3. Prosecution; by
            - 1. Presentment
            - 2. Indictment
            - 3. Information
            - 4. Appeal

4. Process
5. Argument and its Incidents
6. Plea, and Issue
7. Trial, and Conviction Etc.

Note that process is something between the initial prosecution (presentment or indictment) and the arraignment. In this chapter (IV, 24) Blackstone identified this process with due process of law: "for the indictment cannot be tried unless he personally appears, according to the rules of equity in all cases, and the express provision of statute Edw. III, 3 in capital ones, that no man shall be put to death without being brought to answer by due process of law." The two-page discussion that follows indicates: (1) that "due process" consisted in using the proper writ to bring before the court a person who was indicted without being present, and (2) that this was the usual time to transfer certain cases from inferior courts to the Court of King's Bench. It is clear, then, that for Blackstone "due process of law" was an extremely narrow matter.

Blackstone's authority is not determinative, however. His *Commentaries* were published in England in 1765–69 and had just become available in America at the time of the Revolution. Older commentators such as Coke were probably still the more frequently cited authorities, even by the time of the First Congress, which passed the Bill of Rights.

Early American legal commentators give a broader reading to due process, following Coke in identifying it with the Magna Charta provision that the king will not take or imprison or dispossess or outlaw or exile any freeman "except by the lawful judgment of his peers or by the law of the land." Hamilton cited Coke in defining New York State's law of the land clause in 1786: it means "due process of law, that is . . . *by indictment or presentment of good and lawful men*, and trial and conviction in consequence."[14] Kent also cited Coke,[15] as did Story, who summarized the clause more broadly when he concluded: "So that this clause in effect affirms the right of trial according to the process of proceedings of the common law."[16]

What remains ambiguous is Story's statement on the relation of the "proceedings of the common law" to the legislature. It is clear from Hamilton that the legislature is limited by the clause: it cannot authorize wholesale arbitrary punishment of a class of people (Tories, in that particular case) without a legal determination of guilt beforehand: the legislature "cannot, without tyranny, disfranchise or punish whole classes of citizens by general descriptions, without trial and conviction of offenses known by laws previously established, declaring the offense and prescribing the penalty."[17] But this seems to be a reference to legislative attempts to impose penalties directly, without permitting a regular course of judicial proceedings. But what of more properly legislative acts: e.g., a modification of common-law procedure by general rules of laws? There is nothing to suggest that the forms of the common law of 1790 were engraved in the Constitution, beyond such legislative modification, by the Fifth Amendment due process clause. (If that was what the framers had intended, it would not have been difficult to say that—but they did not.) That is, "common law" could have been (likely was) understood as "the prevailing law," i.e., the law of the courts, as codified and/or modified by statute. Whatever were the legal procedures guaranteed by the standing law had to be accorded people before punishing them, by deprivation of life (capital punishment), liberty (jail), or property (fine). It is as if the framers of the Fifth Amendment were saying: "In addition to these specific rights we have mentioned, which are constitutionally guaranteed beyond legislative modification, the other rules of legal proceedings in effect at a given time—whatever they may be—are also to be accorded persons before punishing them."

The Meaning of Due Process: Early Precedents

The first major due process case defining the due process clause was *Murray's Lessee v. Hoboken Land Improvement Co.*, Howard 272 (1856). Justice Curtis's opinion for a unanimous Court argued that this clause is a limit on the legislature: Congress cannot make any process "due process of law" merely by its will. What then are the criteria for due process? They are (1) the Constitution's provisions and (2) "[t]hose settled usages and modes of proceeding existing in the common and statute law of England, before the emigration of our ancestors, and which are shown not to have been unsuited to their civil and political condition by having been acted on by them after the settlement of this country." Since the kind of distress warrant at issue in this case was clearly provided for in the common law, Curtis's discussion needed to go no further. He did not need to address himself to the possible issue of the validity of some legislative modification of common-law legal procedure.[18]

When pointing to the common law, did Curtis mean that its usages and proceedings as of 1789 were "locked into" the Constitution by the Fifth Amendment due process clause? It is not possible to answer this question with certitude, but given the very nature of the common law, it seems unlikely. First, the common law throughout its history showed itself to be very adaptable to new circumstances, and accordingly it was continually developed and modified rather than fixed in all its facets. This flexible development of the common law would not be possible if it were absolutely fixed in its form in a given year.[19] Second, the common law—Coke's efforts to the contrary notwithstanding—was subject to statutory modification by Parliament. This traditional legislative discretion would be eliminated if the common-law procedural guarantees as of 1789 were made permanent, subject to alteration only by constitutional amendment.

If Curtis did not mean to say that the 1789 common law legal procedures became fixed by means of Fifth Amendment due process, then what did he mean? Perhaps, as Crosskey suggested, he would say that legislative modifications of the common law were legitimate but subject to the power of the courts "to pass on the 'reasonableness' and essential 'fairness' of any legislative innovations on Common Law,"[20] with (I would add) the customary deference the courts owe legislative judgments. Or perhaps, as the Court itself was to suggest in *Hurtado v. California*,[21] the common-law legal procedure's principles were constitutionally protected, while the "forms" were subject to legislative modification (as long as the principles or purposes of the older forms were adequately preserved by the new forms). The common-law protections might be guaranteed through different forms, but they could not be abolished altogether.

The placement of the due process clause indicates, I think, that Curtis's reading of the clause expands it vis-à-vis its original intent. Even this broader reading of the due process clause, however, should be understood in light of an important characteristic of early judicial review: it was limited by the traditional understanding that in the absence of clear constitutional commands, "reasonable" legislative opinions as to the constitutionality of legislation precluded judicial review. Had Curtis's interpretation prevailed down until the present day, due process law would be a much smaller section of contemporary casebooks.

The Case for a Broader Due Process

If the evidence, both interpretive and historical, suggests so strongly a narrow meaning for the due process clause (relative to its amorphous boundaries today), how can one account for the change? That puzzled Justice Samuel Miller too, who in *Davidson v. New Orleans*, 96 U.S. 97 (1878), noted:

> It is not a little remarkable, that this provision has been in the Constitution of the United States, as a restraint upon the authority of the Federal Government, for nearly a century, and while, during all that time, the manner in which the powers of that Government have been exercised has been watched with jealousy, and subjected to the most rigid criticism in all its branches, this special limitation upon its powers has rarely been invoked in the judicial forum or the more enlarged theater of public discussion. But while it has been a part of the Constitution as a restraint upon the power of the States, only a very few years, the docket of this Court is crowded with [such] cases. . . . There is here abundant evidence that there exists some strange misconception of the scope of this provision as found in the Fourteenth Amendment.[22]

The question, then, must be asked again: Why, despite such strong evidence of the relatively narrow character of this clause, was it able to be transformed as it has been into a blank check for judicial notions of justice, in the area of procedural due process and especially in the area of substantive due process, as exemplified today by the privacy cases such as *Griswold v. Connecticut* and *Roe v. Wade*? The answer is complicated, but there is at least a partial explanation.

There did exist in early American courts, especially at the state level, a string of cases which gave a broader reading to "due process of law" by emphasizing the last word especially. If the law under which one is being deprived of life, liberty, or property turns out not to be a law really—if it lacks some essential element of law—then it might be argued that such a law violated the due process clause and that punishment under it (deprivations of life, liberty, and property) was invalid, prohibited.

What is "law"? Whatever the exact definition, there was widespread agreement that it had to be general—not, for example, a decree as to particular persons. (This suggests the reasoning behind the prohibition of bills of attainder.) This characteristic of law—its generality—was lacking in an action such as arbitrarily taking property from A and giving it to B. In this way, some early state court decisions were able to invoke the due process clause of the state constitutions (or the law of the land clause, which was generally considered to be its equivalent) to protect property rights against "arbitrary legislative deprivation."

For example, in *University of North Carolina v. Foy*[23] the North Carolina courts held unconstitutional a legislative repeal of an earlier grant of land to the university, invoking the law of the land clause. The property rights could be taken away from the trustees only after the judiciary "in the usual and common form" pronounced them guilty of some acts that would justify forfeiture of their rights.

Likewise, in *Dartmouth College v. Woodward*, Daniel Webster cited New Hampshire's law of the land provision (again, widely regarded as equivalent to due process) in this way: "By the law of the land is most clearly intended the general law; a law which hears before it condemns; which proceeds upon inquiry, and renders judgment only after trial." This sounds procedural, but it was used to attack the New Hampshire legislature's unilateral altering of Dartmouth College's charter on the grounds that these acts were "particular acts of the legislature, which have no relation to the community in general, and which are rather sentences than laws."[24]

In New York both the law of the land and the due process clauses were held to be violated by a law which permitted individuals to condemn the property of others in order to build private highways, in *Taylor v. Porter*.[25] Eminent domain was legitimate only when used for public purposes. In the absence of a public purpose, property could be taken only when the normal judicial channels had ascertained guilt of a kind which justified the deprivation.[26]

On the federal level, there are several factors which could be invoked to support this reading. First, in the wording and placement of words in the

Constitution itself there is something suggestive. While most of the amendments of the Bill of Rights are broadly procedural (IV–VIII), and the due process clause is found in the middle of these amendments, and while the Fifth Amendment itself is largely a collection of procedural guarantees (such as grand jury indictment, double jeopardy, and self-incrimination), still there is something rather less procedural about the last clause of the Fifth Amendment, which immediately follows the due process clause: namely, the just compensation clause. This provided that private property could not be taken for public purposes unless just compensation were to be given for it. This might be read to deal not with procedure but with the substance of law as it affects property rights, since it would preclude a legislative act authorizing the taking of private property for public purposes without just compensation (and also, presumably, a law authorizing the taking of private property for private purposes). Thus interpreted, this clause might provide a less rigorously procedural context for the foregoing due process clause and support a less procedural application of it.

I might add that I do find this reasoning particularly persuasive. A better explanation for the placement of the just compensation clause is that the wording of the due process clause suggested the idea of arbitrary deprivations of property, and so the substantive provision dealing with that issue was included next. Perhaps it was a precaution to prevent due process from being read as a barrier to the power of eminent domain, by pointing out that private property could be taken under some circumstances. More importantly, for establishing the context, the due process clause is connected with the self-incrimination clause—only a comma separates them—rather than with the just compensation clause—a semicolon comes between them. And recurring to our earlier analysis of the broad context, why include a broad substantive guarantee against arbitrary government action in this place?

Second, another factor at the federal level supporting a broader reading of due process is the flirtation with "natural justice judicial review" in Marshall's opinion in *Fletcher v. Peck*,[27] which contains (among other things) reasoning relative to the nature of the law. The argument is essentially that depriving certain people of their land is a judicial act rather than a legislative one.

> It may well be doubted whether the nature of society and of government does not prescribe some limits to the legislative power. . . . To the legislature all legislative power is granted; but the question, whether the act of transferring the property of an individual to the public, to be in the nature of the legislative power, is well worthy of serious reflection. It is the peculiar province of the legislature to prescribe general rules for the government of society; the application of those rules to individuals in society would seem to be the duty of other departments.[28]

Marshall suggests that the legislature is limited by such intrinsic requirements of law. This line of reasoning contributed to the origin of substantive due process as well, I believe.

Such "natural justice judicial review" (i.e., judicial review apart from the language of the document itself) did exist at the founding, but I believe that it was an anomaly (which helps to explain why it died out). In Marshall's case, I would point out that he uses rather tentative language in *Fletcher*, which suggests some ambivalence, and that he abandoned this approach—though it would seem to be just as applicable and Webster used it in his argument to the Court—in *Dartmouth College v. Woodward*, preferring the clearer-cut contract clause argument.

Third, there is a dictum in an early Supreme Court case to support this view. Justice Johnson wrote the opinion for the Court in *Bank of Columbia v. Okely* and gave a brief but broad reading of Maryland's law of the land clause, widely regarded as equivalent to the due process clause (following Coke). These words, he said "were intended to secure the individual from the arbitrary exercise of the powers of government, unrestrained by the established principles of private rights and distributive justice."[29]

Justice Johnson's ideas on private rights and the Constitution were, however, generally idiosyncratic. This can be seen best by examining his long note to his opinion in *Satterlee v. Matthewson*, arguing that the most important protection for private rights in the Constitution was the ex post facto law prohibitions of Article I, Sections 9 and 10. The Supreme Court over his objections had consistently maintained its earlier interpretation of those clauses, confining them to criminal law.[30]

Substantive due process, then, does have some (relatively tenuous) roots in the federal level in the traditional era. On the state court level these principles developed rather earlier, and in 1856 the New York State Court of Appeals used them to strike down a law which forbade the sale of liquor (except for medicinal purposes) in *Wynehamer v. N.Y.* The judges explicitly disavowed a straightforward natural justice basis for their opinion and argued that certain legislative actions could not be taken "even by the forms which belong to due process of law."[31]

Only a year later, in the *Dred Scott* case, we see the only significant pre–Civil War use of substantive due process on the federal level. Even here the precedent is not strong. The reliance on substantive due process occurs in Taney's plurality (three of the seven justices) rather than a Court opinion. Even in Taney's opinion it is referred to only once, and not in any developed way: "An act of Congress which deprives a citizen of the United States of his liberty or property merely because he came himself or brought his property into a particular territory of the United States and who had committed no offense against the law could hardly be dignified with the name due process of law."[32] Of course, having a precedent like *Dred Scott* did not lend much weight to a doctrine in the wake of the Civil War.

So there is some historical evidence which could be used to support a broader reading of the due process clause.[33] Besides the reasons noted above, which limit the weight of some of these arguments, I would emphasize three facts. First, this historical evidence comes well after the founding, for the most part, and this limits the weight one should attach to it. Relying on such evidence is only legitimate to the extent that it can be shown that it was simply a continuation of ideas prevalent earlier, when the Constitution was being written. But the evidence—perhaps especially the absence of cases of a similar type earlier in constitutional history—suggests the contrary.

Second, I would reemphasize once more the placement of the due process clause. Were the due process clause intended to be what some have argued it to be—a general prohibition of arbitrary legislation—then it is very difficult to explain its position in the Bill of Rights.

Third, again there is the absence of debate or discussion about the due process clause in the Congress that passed the Fifth Amendment and (insofar as we have information about them) the state legislatures that ratified it. If the clause had been intended to be the broad guarantee against arbitrary government that it is alleged to be, it is extremely unlikely—indeed, it is inconceivable—that this would be the case.

A Final Consideration

One last point to be made involves a return to more general considerations of constitutional interpretation and judicial review. Defenders of an expansive due process clause typically try to muster some evidence that due process is a broad guarantee against arbitrary government action and conclude that—given their evidence and the contrary evidence that suggests a narrower meaning—the clause is a "majestic generality" and must be left to the courts to "interpret."

The sifting of the evidence above, however, suggests that the most minimal conclusion one could draw is that the due process clause is not clearly either a general guarantee against arbitrary action or even a general guarantee of procedural fairness. (A less crabbed evaluation of the evidence seems to me to suggest overwhelmingly that it is no more than a guarantee of the judicial proceedings appropriate under the standing law.) Under the traditional rationale for judicial review, judges were not to employ one particular interpretation of a provision to override a legislative enactment which was based on an interpretation of the provision that was at least as plausible (not merely on a first glance, of course, but after careful interpretation). This defense was rooted in the ground for judicial review: it was not judges applying their own will but only judges applying the will of the people in the Constitution. Unless the judges had a clear basis for judicial review in the Constitution, they had no authority to strike down an act.[34]

The main argument against this position is that it would make judicial review very infrequent and thus an ineffective bulwark protecting constitutional rights. My response to this is first, that judicial review was not necessarily expected to be frequent; second, that even infrequently used judicial review can serve a useful function (since its benefits include not only the acts that are overturned but also those that are forestalled); and third, that the Founders looked not only to the judiciary but also and perhaps especially to the political process to vindicate constitutional rights. Whether this approach to judicial review is an adequate one may, of course, be debated. Whatever its merits, though, I think it can be shown to be the prevailing view among the Founders of American government. All debates over the "original intention" of particular provisions of the Constitution must be carried on in light of this more fundamental aspect of original intention.

In light of this understanding of judicial review, it is fair to assume that the due process clause would not be a legitimate ground for many exercises of judicial review. The only acts that would clearly violate it would be acts that deprive people of life, personal liberty, or property without according them the procedures guaranteed by the standing (common and state) law. Confining constitutional law to this original understanding of the due process clause would, of course, dramatically curtail judicial power in the American regime as we know it today. Whether such an original intention ought to be the norm of present Supreme Court decisions—especially in light of the disruption of precedent it would cause—is a question which must be confronted even by those who generally favor "original intent" as the norm of constitutional interpretation. But especially in this bicentennial era, it is at least desirable for us to confront the issue, rather than being ignorant of its existence.

Notes

1. Madison to Thomas Ritchie, Sept. 15, 1821, to John G. Jackson, Dec. 27, 1821, in G. Hunt, ed., *The Writings of James Madison* 9 vols. (New York: Putnam, 1900–1910), 9:72, 74.

2. G. Wills, ed., *The Federalist Papers* (New York: Bantam Books, 1982), No. 40, pp. 200–201.

3. Higby of California, *Congressional Globe*, 39th Cong., 1st Sess., 1056.

4. So, for example, the First Amendment cannot be limited to protecting the religious liberty of Christians on the grounds of what Justice Story said was the "real object of the First Amendment," namely, "not to countenance, much less to advance, Mahometanism, or Judaism, or infidelity, by prostrating Christianity; but to exclude all rivalry among Christian sects, and to prevent any national ecclesiastical establishment which should give to a hierarchy the exclusive patronage of the national government" (quoted from R. Cord, *Separation of Church and State: Histor-*

ical Fact and Current Fiction [New York: Lambeth, 1982], p. 13). Note that I am not contending that Justice Story himself would have so limited it, but I do believe that some of the founding generation might have.

5. Madison discusses this in a letter to Henry Lee, June 25, 1824, in Hunt, *Writings of Madison*, 9:191.

6. One of the best discussions of the difficulties of ascertaining original intent through extrinsic sources is a long footnote by Justice Story (responding to Jefferson) in his *Commentaries on the Constitution of the United States* (Boston: Hilliard, Gray, 1833), 3:389.

7. The only other possible reading of "process" would seem to be that the law according to which one is deprived of life, liberty, or property must have been established by the appropriate lawmaking process. But to say that the law must really be a law, at least in this sense, seems trivial. Nor would this interpretation fit what seems to be the order of the Bill of Rights—see *infra*.

8. The narrower interpretation would limit the legislative power only in the sense that the legislature could not itself move to deprive a particular person of life, liberty, or property without the legal procedure guaranteed by the standing law. It would leave the legislature free to modify the general law regarding legal procedure.

9. The common law could be considered to be guaranteed in two possible senses: either the specific, determinate law of 1789 or at least the general principles underlying the 1789 common law (leaving open the possibility of new forms of procedure being acceptable as long as they continue to guarantee the general principles).

10. Parts of the above outline are from R. Perry, ed., *Sources of Our Liberties* (Chicago: American Bar Foundation, 1959), pp. 427–29. Leaving out the other two proposed amendments, passed by Congress but rejected by the states, does not disturb the order. The two rejected amendments (at the head of the list approved by Congress) differed from the others considerably; one regulated the size of the House and the other regulated congressional increases in compensation.

11. The argument that due process includes all of the guarantees of the Bill of Rights and more would also give the due process clause a raison d'être, but is not compatible with the placement or supported by historical evidence. An alternative argument that it contains the more fundamental parts of Bill of Rights guarantees, or some of them, as well as other rights, also creates problems explaining the placement and has no historical evidence to support it.

12. *Murray v. Hoboken Land Improvement Co.* 59 U.S. 272 (1856), described *infra*.

13. 19 Am. J. of Legal Hist. 265 (1975).

14. Letter of Phocion, in H. Lodge, ed., *The Works of Alexander Hamilton* (New York: Putnam, 1904), 4:232.

15. C. Kent, *Commentaries on American Law* (New York, 1826), P. IV, Lecture 24 (citing Story as well).

16. Story, *Commentaries on the Constitution* 3:38, sec. 1789.

17. Lodge, *Works of Hamilton* 4:232.

18. As W. Crosskey pointed out in *Politics and the Constitution* (Chicago: Univ. of Chicago Press, 1953), 2:1109. The quality of Crosskey's treatment of the Constitution is erratic, but his discussion of due process's original intent is very profitable reading, though I think he rejects narrower interpretations of it too easily (at 2:1104).

19. Nor is this evolutionary view of the common law merely a twentieth-century reading, although the philosophical foundations for legal change may have been different in earlier writers. A traditional discussion of the adaptability of the common law appears, for example, in James Wilson's *Lectures on Law* (1792), in R. McCloskey, ed., *The Works of James Wilson*, 2 vols. (Cambridge: Belknap, 1967), 1:335, 353–54.

20. Ibid., p. 1108.

21. *Hurtado v. California*, 110 U.S. 516 (1884).

22. *Davidson v. New Orleans*, 96 U.S. 97, 104 (1878).

23. *University of North Carolina v. Foy*, 2 Hayward (N.C.) 310 (1804).

24. *Dartmouth College v. Woodward*, 4 Wheaton 518, 581 (1819).

25. *Taylor v. Porter*, 4 Hill (N.Y.) 140 (1843).

26. These cases and many others are discussed in E. Corwin, *Liberty against Government* (Baton Rouge: Louisiana State Univ. Press, 1948), chap. 3.

27. *Fletcher v. Peck*, 6 Cranch 87 (1810).

28. 6 Cranch 89, 135–36.

29. *Bank of Columbia v. Okely*, 4 Wheaton 235, 244 (1819).

30. *See* 2 Peters 380, 414, and note.

31. *Wynehamer v. New York*, 13 NY 378 (1856); Corwin, *Liberty against Government*, pp. 101–10. Most other state courts rejected this reasoning.

32. *Dred Scott*, 19 Howard 393, 450 (1857).

33. Other evidence that might be cited for a broader view would draw on English constitutional history, giving weight especially to various historical meanings and uses of the Magna Charta. *Cf.* F. Strong, *Substantive Due Process of Law* (Durham, N.C.: Carolina Academic, 1986). This argument is subject to many of the same objections (e.g., from the placement of the clause in the Bill of Rights) and also seems to lack support from the time of the framing of the Bill of Rights itself. Professor Strong's book, for instance, leaps from English history to nineteenth-century American history with hardly any discussion of the founding or the text of the Constitution itself.

34. On this and other questions regarding the approach to judicial review characteristic of the early or traditional era of American constitutional history, see C. Wolfe, *The Rise of Modern Judicial Review* (New York: Basic Books, 1986), pt. 1.

VI.

PRIVATE PROPERTY, THE TAKINGS CLAUSE, AND DUE PROCESS

HARRY N. SCHEIBER

16. The "Takings" Clause and the Fifth Amendment: Original Intent and Significance in American Legal Development

The Fifth Amendment's "takings" clause, which casts the mantle of constitutional protection over private property rights when government acts to expropriate under the power of eminent domain, poses a special problem for the historian of original intent. This problem consists of the strange configuration of Fifth Amendment history in the pattern of our constitutional development: this amendment was not, in fact, a prominent or even very explicit feature of constitutional debate and action in the founding era. Moreover, for a long period after the founding, the focus of the legal historian's attention must shift away from the national government altogether: The heart of the story is not in what the Constitution writers and ratifiers, Congress, or the federal courts did; it is, instead, in how the constitutions and courts of the states dealt with this aspect of our law. And therefore much of what I will have to say here will concern the early history of eminent domain in a process of legal and constitutional change which featured the states as prominent actors in the drama.

"Original intent" is a slippery and treacherous concept no matter which provision of the Constitution we are concerned to understand. Some of the document's language is, of course, unequivocal and deals with matters in a positive and unambiguous way—for example, that the Congress shall consist of two houses and should meet once in every year, or that money should be drawn from the Treasury only in consequence of appropriations. But most of the Constitution's phrases and concepts are susceptible to divergent interpretations by reasonable persons. Moreover, when we seek "intent," do we mean the intent of the person who moved the language in the Convention or in one of the ratifying bodies in which Bill of Rights provisions were proposed? Or the intent of the person who introduced a provision in Congress? Or the collective intent (if one can imaginably be conjured) of all the members of state legislatures who voted on the proposed amendments? "Intentions of the Founders," therefore, is not so easy to ascertain as it sounds.[1]

The Fifth Amendment poses even more difficulties than the other Bill of Rights provisions because it was not part of "The Larger Original Understanding," as I term it—the understanding that comprised the original document of 1787 plus the proposed amendments that were drafted and put forward by the ratifying states in 1787–88. The ratifying conventions' proposals for Bill of Rights amendments took the form of recommendations and petitions; but in fact they were expectations, reflecting firm political promises. Hence the Bill of Rights was integrally a part of the initial understanding, fulfilled when James Madison made congressional approval and submission of the amendments a first order of business as the new government went into operation.[2] Madison introduced what became the Fifth Amendment, apparently drafting it on his own.

Yet the takings clause deals with property, no doubt of that. And there had been a vigorous and richly textured discussion concerning property in the great Convention itself: the relationship of private property ownership and its relationship to republicanism, its function in representation, its protection through the Article I, Section 10 limitations on state enactment of ex post facto laws or laws impairing the obligation of contract. One would be surprised had it been otherwise, after all. These were eighteenth-century political men; and educated persons of that era were keenly aware of property ownership and its claims, the interplay of property and political consent and allegiance, the place of property in political theory from Locke's writings to their own time.[3] They were also well versed in the maxims of the common law, a law profoundly protective of quiet possession and concerned with the proper legal boundaries of governmental and private action against property owners' claims. They knew and despised the depredations of the Stuart kings in their disregard of parliamentary prerogatives in regard to life, liberty, and property of the political opposition. All these were core elements of political consciousness and the lexicon of political values well known to them. This is important to remember as we try to reconstruct the milieu and the intellectual context of the takings clause in the Bill of Rights.[4] Only a few years before the Convention, in fact, a wave of confiscation had swept the colonies as the property of loyalists was seized and disposed of by the revolutionary state governments.[5] Moreover, takings had long been an instrument of government action in normal times, both in Great Britain and in the American colonies.[6]

At first blush, then, it is rather surprising that neither in the Convention nor in the state ratifying conventions was the expropriation of property by government the subject of explicit debate. Since this was the case, however, we have to resort to some informed speculation on the matter. Four facets of the problem, four points of inquiry, seem to me worth pursuing briefly here: Madison's own view, the specific language of the takings clause, the history of takings in the Anglo-American experience with government to then, and, finally, the takings concept as it had been developed in legal thought and in the larger framework of received political ideas that prevailed in the new Republic.[7]

First, we have the testimony from Madison himself as to what he had in mind with regard to the Bill of Rights generally. (Even if we could read his mind or accept as entirely accurate his explanation, this would not amount to "original intent," but it is an important dimension of the history by any standard.) Madison seems to have taken up the role of republican schoolmaster;[8] for as he explained before Congress in proposing the amendments, he believed that the Bill of Rights would serve the highly useful function of educating the public: Though the guarantees in his proposed amendments might appear to be only "paper barriers," Madison declared, still they would "have a tendency to impress some degree of respect for them, to establish the public opinion in their favor, and rouse the attention of the whole community." Thereby, the Bill of Rights would be yet one more obstacle in the way of tyranny—in sum, "one means to control the majority from those acts to which they might otherwise be inclined" and to guard against "an exercise of undue power" by the national government and its officialdom.[9]

Second, we have the language of the takings clause itself, and its context in the Fifth Amendment, to give us some guidance on what kind of "exercise of undue power" it sought to guard against, either from the people (through Congress) or the government's executive officers: "[N]or shall private property be taken for public use, without just compensation."

The phrase "for public use" qualifies the word "taken," but only as a descriptive qualifier—it is not, at least not on the face of it, a limitation, self-enforcing or otherwise. Earlier colonial charters of liberties had used the phrase "pressed or taken for any public use or service," and the like; it was tautological, as it were, that if government took property it was for public use.[10] As I hope to make clear later in this essay, however, in the hands of nineteenth-century judges the concept of "public use" quickly became a limitation—for these judges interpreted it as a limiting concept derived from natural and civil law.

The phrase "without just compensation" comes to the heart of things. Clearly there is room for some honest disagreement in most instances as to what constitutes a "just" recompense; and, as it proved, there was even room for disputing whether a tangible payment of money or other valuable consideration was the minimal element of compensation. But still, the language meant at a minimum that an American republic's equivalent of the king's armies could not march up and down the countryside, or through the commercial towns, taking what they needed in the way of property for the government's purposes; and the civilian officialdom would be likewise constrained. The essence of Magna Charta's phrase, repeated in the 1628 Petition of Right, that "no free man shall be . . . disseised . . . or in any way destroyed . . . except by the lawful judgment of his peers and by the law of the land"[11] was captured in this language, no less than in the magnificent clause that stood alongside the takings clause regarding deprivation of "life, liberty, and property" and the necessity for "due process."

The historic bridge was built across the Atlantic and raised up scarcely more than a decade after the 1628 Petition in the Massachusetts Body of Liberties (1641), which included the phrases that "no mans goods or estaite shall be taken away from him, nor any way indammaged under color of law or Countenance of Authoritie, unless it be by vertue or equitie of some express law of the Country warranting the same."[12] The plain words of William Penn in 1675, that it was a fundamental maxim of English law and the birthright of English subjects that they have "an ownership, and undisturbed possession: that what they have is rightly theirs, and no body's else,"[13] expressed an idea which extended through such provisions in colonial documents and early state bills of rights, and through the takings clause, to the danger of arbitrary seizures by government under the new Constitution.

Several of the state constitutions in force prior to adoption of the 1787 federal Constitution contained provisions prohibiting deprivation of life, liberty, and property without due process or "except by law of the land,"[14] language easily interpreted as subsuming and altogether incorporating the "takings" clause provision.[15] The Northwest Ordinance and the Massachusetts Constitution each included, side by side, a takings provision with a more general "life, liberty, and property" provision such as is found in the federal Constitution's Fifth Amendment.[16] As for Madison: Whether in accord with his political motives (for he made satisfying the dissident states and factions in the ratification fight a primary consideration in drafting the amendments) in a quest to mollify and quiet all fears[17] or else, instead, intending to read his lesson in republican faith more clearly, he took the path of placing both provisions, side by side, in his draft amendment. And so it has come down to us.

Third, as still another facet of the problem of original meaning and intent, we have the history of takings in the Anglo-American experience with government to that time.

Professor Stoebuck's exhaustive research in the statutes, in a splendid article on history and theory of eminent domain in America, has shown that certainly in regard to highways construction the colonies had devised a number of means for taking the necessary rights of way (and sometimes also the construction materials), all of which were in a direct line of development to nineteenth-century eminent domain practice. There was, to be sure, a mingling of "easement" concepts with takings of palpable physical property, and also there were reservations in some land grants as to percentages that might be taken without specific compensation (an advance discount, as it were, understood as part of the transfer) or as to takings of that land which had not been improved when a road must be cut. For all the technical complexity of language and rules, however, takings were an element of government transport building.[18] It could not have been otherwise, since the possibility of a single owner, in the absence of the eminent domain power, standing in the way of a road or other line of communications left the door open for blackmail. One cannot doubt that this sort of activity by government was in the mind of those who voted on the Fifth Amendment language when, with its takings clause, it went before Congress and then to the states.

I would embroider in one particular, however, the tapestry that Stoebuck has blocked out so fully. There were also milldam statutes in several colonies that involved private landowners who wished to build millraces and thereby flood private lands held by others, granting to them the power to take such property in accord with prescribed procedural limitations and on payment of compensation to be determined by juries or courts. Far more than some other types of law that scholars sometimes adduce, mistakenly I think, as precedents of eminent domain,[19] these milldam laws bespoke communal needs and the material prosperity and growth of the commonwealth as legitimating canons that warranted the extraordinary use of state power.[20] As such, they stood in a direct line down to the sort of takings that were involved in much of state law in the nineteenth century; but it seems most doubtful that Madison and others in the 1789 amendments debate believed that an equivalent problem would arise in operation of the national government. As for the western territories under direct federal control, they were already under the protection of provisions for taking in the Northwest Ordinance that were, if anything, much more stringent than what is found in the takings clause of the Fifth Amendment.[21]

Finally, we need to consider perhaps the most important element of all in the original understanding—a historically important element since the nineteenth-century judges who shaped takings law made it so: This was the status of the concept of "takings," along with the corollary issues of compensation and public use, in legal thought and the larger framework of received ideas down to the 1790s. The writers in natural law and civil law all made the argument that the eminent domain (takings) power was an inherent attribute of sovereignty. Drawing upon Vattel, Pufendorf, Grotius, and others from the natural law and civil law traditions, the legal scholar J. B. Thayer wrote in his essay of 1856, the first American treatise on eminent domain, that:

> [The power] attaches to the State as the right of property attaches to man; it is, so to speak, one of the natural rights of the State, and its sources lie nowhere else than in the fountain-head of government itself.
>
> . . . It is not, then, any common or technical doctrine of the

> law . . . but a sovereign right, coeval with the State itself[,] . . . a right whose sanction lies not in the authority of the State, or in human reason, like that of the law, but rather in that which is the source of the authority of the State; to wit, a necessity in the nature of man; and this is nothing less than the appointment of the Deity itself—for as the State originates in this transcendent necessity, so do all its inherent, essential rights, of which this is one.[22]

If the demands and character of basic sovereignty required that the eminent domain power inhere in government's armory of rights and authority, then what of the sturdy tradition in English common law—so solicitous of quiet possession—and in the constitutional law of England and the colonies that made (in Justice Patterson's words, in the 1795 case of *Van Horne's Lessee*) "the preservation of property . . . a primary object of the social compact"? What of Lockean precepts, and the linkage of property ownership to personhood, the claims that one's freedom from arbitrary invasion of his or her property was a basic element of liberty?[23]

Some way had to be found to accommodate and reconcile the security of property rights with what Justice Patterson freely admitted was a "despotic power . . . [that] exists in every government." The solution lay in a requirement, as the natural and civil law theorists contended, that compensation be paid—that the person who was singled out for special loss of tangible property must be made whole (to the extent possible, given that no amount of money might be enough, in the owner's mind and heart): that the owner's value in money terms be restored. If eminent domain was an attribute of sovereignty and was "founded on necessity,"[24] then it also was a power tempered with equity and concern to protect (as one nineteenth-century counsel asserted) against a regime in which we "hold our property [only] at the will of the legislature."[25]

If we are to understand what followed in American constitutional development, we have to hold firmly in mind this dual foundation, this dual understanding, of eminent domain takings. For in the century that followed, notions of vested rights, sacred property claims against government, and economic liberty certainly prevailed on many critical occasions in the federal and state courts. Indeed, the trend, in that respect, gives solid support to the idea that American legal culture generally embodied a robust respect for vested property rights.[26] But so too did an alternative view prevail at critical junctures: it was the notion of sovereignty, embedded in which was the idea that eminent domain was an integral and necessary power of all governments, entitled to the support that the law could give it in order that government might function effectively.

At this celebration of the Constitution's bicentennial, we are prone, often, to think entirely in terms of the glorious defense of individual rights and liberties, including property rights, that were provided for by the

Constitution, including especially its Fifth Amendment. But so far as the takings clause was concerned, all that I have said to this point about original intent and significance has to be seen from an entirely different historical perspective: from a perspective which suggests the possibility of sovereignty's claims, with the government's necessities or exigencies—or even the government's "convenience"—warranting takings of a variety probably not foreseen at all in 1789. We need to envision a scenario, in sum, in which claims of "the public," through their government, prompted a variety of actions that ended in what the Supreme Court candidly termed "injustice and oppression" against property owners—but which neither the state courts nor the federal high court deemed unconstitutional.[27]

If Madison and his colleagues—Federalist and Anti-Federalist alike—regarded their legacy in the 1780s as one that would defend property unambiguously and trigger a kind of automatic justice in regard to compensation for takings, they proved sadly wrong. (Whether the result was right or wrong, just or unjust, is another question: I am concerned with their accuracy in prophecy and prediction.) How and why they apparently proved so wrong is what we need to explore now.

The course of takings law almost to the end of the nineteenth century was, as I have said, in the hands mainly of the state courts. The die was cast for this when the Fifth Amendment was written in language that apparently applied only to the national government, not the states: the latter were left to rely upon their own constitutions for the protection their citizens wanted in takings actions. Whether or not the Fifth Amendment was an encapsulation of "higher law" and so applicable generally, and enforceable by federal judicial authority against the states, was for a long time, however, something of an open question—a question left open by Chief Justice Marshall's adversions and resort to natural law concepts in such instances as his opinion in the land fraud case of *Fletcher v. Peck*.[28]

If it was Marshall and his property-minded conservative colleagues who left the question open, however, it was the same Marshall Court that closed the door firmly in the case of *Barron v. Baltimore*, in 1833. The Court decided in *Barron* the foursquare issue of whether the Fifth Amendment applied to the states; and the answer was a definitive negative.[29] It was not until 1848 (in *West River Bridge v. Dix*) that the Supreme Court decided a takings compensation case, as opposed to cases involving inverse-condemnation claims. In *West River Bridge*, the Court declared that "private rights vested under the government . . . are, by necessary implication, held in subordination to [the eminent domain] power, and must yield in every instance to its proper exercise."[30] The Court endorsed a very broad view of how far the power went—that the state might properly take any sort of property when "the interest, or even the expediency, of the State" was the objective.[31] No recourse to the federal Constitution was available.

This was a truly ominous doctrine to conservatives—hardly comforting to those such as Daniel Webster, who tried to reargue the failed *Charles River Bridge* cause when he appeared in the 1848 *West River Bridge* case, contending that unless the Court stepped in, the states would be left free to exercise "unlimited despotisms over the private citizens."[32] Webster's worst fears on this score must have seemed to him well warranted when, two years later, in a case out of Illinois, a ferry owner's property was taken and a pitifully inadequate sum paid the owner. The Supreme Court denied redress, stating it was the responsibility of state courts, not the federal bench, "to protect their citizens from injustice and oppression of this description."[33]

Surely few American lawyers or jurists of any prominence in the mid-nineteenth century would have taken exception to Justice Story's much-quoted view (stated in an 1829 opinion) that "the fundamental maxims of free government seem to require that the rights of personal liberty and private property should be held sacred" so that it would be manifestly unconstitutional for "a legislative act to transfer the property of A to B," that is, from one private party to another.[34] But it was another matter to take from A and transfer to the government itself, or even to a private agent of the government with quasi-public status (for example, to a bridge or railroad company). In such cases, it was left to the states to deal with any injustices or "oppression."

And how did the states deal with it, then? One must take account of a critical dichotomy: There was the law as it was formulated formally—what Justice Holmes called the "law in books"; and then there was the reality beneath the law—"the law in action."

The formalities—what may be called the emergent theory of eminent domain in state law—lead us back immediately to the Fifth Amendment. For occasionally distinguished judges and lawyers did argue or act on the theory that the Fifth Amendment limitations applied to the states. The takings and due process clauses, they contended, were embodiments of a higher law which was universally applicable; hence in the absence of a state constitutional provision limiting government in takings cases, the Fifth Amendment and the natural law were to be applied as legitimating judicial review to assure equity.[35]

Beyond Fifth Amendment considerations, the state courts developed important formal concepts that would take their place at the center of takings law in future years (and down to our own day). Briefly summarized, these formal developments in doctrine were: (1) "Public use" (or "public purpose," an alternative construct) was found to be not a tautological phrase but instead a positive limitation on government's power to take (thus addressing the problem of giving land of A to B under guise of eminent domain). (2) In accord with Vattel and other writers and consistent with the property doctrines of the common law, "compensation" was interpreted as a requirement. This was so whether the compensation phrase was written into the applicable state constitution or included (as it was in the Fifth Amendment) as an ostensibly descriptive phrase. In sum, as the New York court ruled in an early milldam case involving inverse condemnation: "Private property may, in many instances, be appropriated to public use; but such appropriations are constitutional, legal, and justifiable only when a fair and just equivalent is awarded to the owner of property thus taken."[36] Finally, (3) the state courts interjected due process specifically into takings law, many of them raising the issue of procedural fairness in determination of both public use and (more especially) justice of compensation.[37] In its most elaborate form, this concern with due process also raised complex inverse condemnation issues, involving courts' review of actions by the legislature not strictly takings but alleged to have the effect of takings.[38] In this last respect, the early nineteenth-century state judiciary began to forge the outlines and structure of a basic question which still remains at the very center of American public law, a question which vexes today's adjudication of Fifth Amendment takings issues: the problem of when a police power regulation violates due process so as to constitute an effective taking—that is, the problem of defining an inverse condemnation.[39]

Thus, we find that the state judiciary elaborated in the antebellum years in a very full and impressive way the conceptual problems associated with takings, both as to procedure and as to substantive limitations and meanings. In their advancement of formal legal theory, they demarcated vividly and most usefully the border between the rights of sovereignty and the equities of liberty in property ownership. They successfully isolated and defined the "takings issue" as one that involved the police power/eminent domain line that differentiated state actions requiring compensation from those actions which (because they guarded the state or the public from harm) carried no compensation requirement.[40] All this was accomplished without significant participation by the U.S. Supreme Court, which opted out in 1833 and affirmed sweeping discretion in the states in the two further decisions of 1848 and 1850.

But how well, then, did the state judiciary do on these things as a matter of "law in action," rather than in the theory that we find in "law in books"? What was the actual substance of protection for property in takings, and what was the real-life meaning of that conceptual line between police power and eminent domain as it was drawn by the states' constitution writers, legislators, and courts?

My own research and the research of others on historic American eminent domain policies and law in the states and on the practical consequences of the legal development reveals a picture which departs significantly from what the emerging theory suggested.[41] Even while doctrines were being constantly voiced that theoretically limited eminent domain takings most strictly, in the ways already mentioned, judges in fact were regularly lending sanction to harsh practices. It is not too much to conclude that in reality the states engaged in the systematic extraction of involuntary subsidies from persons on whom the costs of so-called public enterprises fortuitously fell. Not only did courts characteristically interpret "public use" or "public purpose" in ways that were virtually synonymous with legislative determination; in addition, they generally applied the compensation requirement in ways that left the taking agency or enterprise (public or, when power was devolved, private) free of substantial judicial review so long as minimal procedures were prescribed and followed. Although the legal historian Tony Freyer has found that in the Middle Atlantic states the courts and juries handed down many judgments on compensation that seem to have required payment of true market value, I think the balance of evidence that we have for some other jurisdictions indicates that in the courts of those states the market value was rarely paid.[42]

Indeed, courts overtly—though not without controversy—narrowed drastically the very concept of a "compensable taking" so as to exclude altogether nearly all forms of consequential, incidental, or indirect damages. Among the most dramatic effects in reducing entrepreneurial or state costs was the widespread practice of prescribing "offset" calculations, so that the estimated benefits to a landowner of the enterprise taking his or her property would be deducted from the calculated costs of the expropriated property.[43] Courts also contrived subsidiary technical doctrines that cut even further into property owners' protection against uncompensated or badly compensated takings. Thus once eminent domain proceedings were approved, the standard common-law remedies (suits for trespass, ejectment, or nuisance) became unavailable to property owners. Also, once a private activity was ruled eligible for eminent domain power under a state's law, courts threw a similar blanket of tort immunity over their actual operations (for example, as to smoke or noise from railroad trains). More generally, in most jurisdictions the rule emerged that for any compensation whatever to be due, a "physical taking" of tangible property must be involved.[44]

In sum, while the Fifth Amendment–style due process and takings provisions of state constitutions were prominent in the rhetoric of antebellum judicial doctrine, they were at least equally conspicuous for the ingenuity with which courts side stepped them or refashioned them as subsidies for selected enterprises, both governmental and private.[45] Whether because the society as a whole gave enormous priority to economic growth or, instead, because prevailing elites and/or majorities had their way with it—and whichever propertied interests, in a given situation, were winners and losers in eminent domain redistribution—the burden of actual practice was in stunning contrast to theory.[46]

At least one prominent critic has argued that the Hughes Court of the 1930s, when it renounced substantive economic due process, put traditional property rights in a dustbin.[47] If so, that same dustbin was already filled with the artifacts of property claims from an earlier period of American legal history, when the Fifth Amendment was written into the fabric of American constitutional doctrine but the states wove a different pattern over it in ways that bespeak the great discretion they enjoyed in the era of dual federalism.[48]

The bicentennial celebration of 1987–93 and accompanying scholarly efforts to reflect on the Constitution quite properly take the founding period of the Convention and Bill of Rights as one main focus, and they take dramas from the present day (with images of police car lights flashing and the like, to emphasize what individual rights really mean to an individual citizen) as another focus. As the history of the takings clause suggests, however, we need to give some sustained attention to the 198 years in between if we are to give a faithful reading of constitutional meanings and patterns. These intervening 198 years need our best thought if we are to capture for our own day and for tomorrow the meaning of "constitutionalism," its limits and its potential, as opposed to narrower concerns with the Supreme Court or the Founders in their oracular roles.[49]

And so I would close with the reminder that with reference to the takings clause any commentary on "original intent" requires a full analysis of the Fourteenth Amendment, how it was framed, the meaning of its phraseology, and its parlous course in the legislatures and the courts from 1868 to our own day. Analysis must consider also the renewed fusion of Fifth Amendment jurisprudence and federal review with eminent domain and takings questions in the states. Attention to this interesting history will, if nothing else, serve as a salutary reminder of how constitutional change has its ironies and its challenges to lawyers who pay lip service, at least, to consistency of doctrine. Former Attorney General Meese and others who have been so adamant in their criticism of incorporation of the Bill of Rights into the Fourteenth Amendment will be reminded that the first of the Bill of Rights limitations to be swept in and applied to the states through incorporation by the Supreme Court, nearly a century ago, was not a search and seizure, church-state, free speech, or right to counsel or some other criminal matter but a good sound property question: none other than the takings clause of the Fifth Amendment.[50]

One does not hear Meese's voice, or that of others raised so angrily recently against the "judicial activism" connected with Fourteenth Amendment jurisprudence, sounding out against this incorporation move that swept property rights in eminent domain cases back in under the protective wing of the Court and the federal Constitution! Yet if we wish to give full measure to the history of the takings clause, we do well to remember how for Madison, at least, rights in property and the citizen's "property in rights" were two sides of the same coin. We also ought to remember well how both federal and state judges who were committed to a robustly activist style, during two distinct stages of American legal history, dramatically refashioned the law of takings in the pursuit of sharply divergent policy goals and opposed ideological premises.

Notes

1. For an attempt to recapture original intent with regard to federalism and its values in 1787, *see* my own essay, *Federalism and the Original Understanding*, in *American Law and the Constitutional Order*, ed. L. Friedman and H. Scheiber (Cambridge: Harvard Univ. Press, 1978). *See also* the provocative discussion in F. McDonald, *Novus Ordo Seclorum: The Intellectual Origins of the Constitution* (Lawrence: Univ. Press of Kansas, 1985).

On the takings clause specifically, Treanor, *The Origins and Original Significance of the Just Compensation Clause of the Fifth Amendment*, 94 Yale L.J. 694 (1985) is an excellent overview of evidence and analysis (hereafter cited as Treanor, *Just Compensation Clause*).

The vagaries and pitfalls of "original intent" are a main theme of contemporary legal and constitutional scholarship, and there are as many recipes for solving the problems as there are commentators. An inquiry into "intent" and "interpretation" can well begin with such works as Sandalow, *Constitutional Interpretation*, 79 Mich. L. Rev. 1033 (1981); Hurst, *The Role of History*, in *Supreme Court and Supreme Law*, ed. E. Cahn (Bloomington: Indiana Univ. Press, 1954), pp. 55–59; Curtis, *The Role of the Constitutional Text*, ibid., pp. 64–70; Brest, *The Fundamental Rights Controversy: The Essential Contradictions of Normative Constitutional Scholarship*, 90 Yale L.J. (1981); and J. Choper, *Judicial Review and the National Political Process: A Functional Reconsideration of the Role of the Supreme Court* (Chicago: Univ. of Chicago Press, 1980). Madison himself, as well as others of the founding generation, late in life warned in sternest terms of the dangers of relying on post hoc interpretation of "original intent" in defining standards of constitutionality.

2. Thus New York's ratification was approved with language stating it was done "in confidence" that proposed Bill of Rights amendments would "receive an early and mature consideration." The New York version was one of several forms in which the ratifying states expressed the enlarged understanding. In the Reagan presidency commentators on "original understanding," including President Reagan himself and his attorney general, and the latter's high-ranking staff members, made an unfortunate practice of frequently adverting to the original understanding in terms that set the Bill of Rights apart from the terms of analysis. They also did so to even more grievous effect with the post–Civil War amendments, including the Fourteenth—as though they were generally, but especially the Fourteenth, intrusive and essentially alien elements of the larger system of constitutional ideals and values.

On the dynamics of ratification in relation to the amendments, see R. Rutland, *The Birth of the Bill of Rights* (Chapel Hill: Univ. of North Carolina Press, 1955), and, *inter alia*, documents and commentary in B. Schwartz, ed., *The Bill of Rights: A Documentary History* (New York: Chelsea House, 1971).

3. Stanley Katz reminds us of this important if manifest dimension of the

context when he writes of the Revolutionary generation that "the right to property was an unquestioned assumption. . . . To assert this is merely to assert that they were 18th-century men," but beyond that they regarded property ownership as "one of the bases of republic government" (Katz, *Thomas Jefferson and the Right to Property in Revolutionary America*, 19 J. L. and Econ. 469–70 [1976]).

4. *See, generally*, studies by scholars such as Gordon Wood and Bernard Bailyn; and also, R. Smith, *Liberalism and American Constitutional Law* (Cambridge: Harvard Univ. Press, 1985).

5. *See, e.g.*, "A Freeholder" [John Jay], *A Hint to the Legislature of the State of New York* (1778), reprinted in P. Kurland and R. Lerner, eds., *The Founders' Constitution*, 5 vols. (Chicago: Univ. of Chicago Press, 1987), 5:312–13, in which Jay protested against the impressment by the military of horses, teams, and carriages "without the Intervention of a civil Magistrate, and without any Authority from the Law of the Land." It was the "undoubted right and unalienable Privilege of a Freeman," Jay declared, "not to be divested, or interrupted in the innocent use, of Life, Liberty or Property, but by Laws to which he has assented, either personally or by his Representatives. This is the Corner Stone of every free Constitution, and to defend it from the Iron Hand of the Tyrant of Britain, all America is now in arms."

6. We have as yet no full-scale historical study of eminent domain either in Britain or colonial North America, but Professor Stoebuck has done exhaustive research in the statutes and provided the fullest available analysis. *See* Stoebuck, *A General Theory of Eminent Domain*, 47 Wash. L. Rev. 553ff. (1972). Treanor's discussion (in *Just Compensation Clause*) relies upon the Stoebuck article for background in the colonial period but offers as a caveat that Stoebuck relied too much upon the highways statutes—which by any standard are certainly the principal body of evidence for colonial practice—to the exclusion of any other form of evidence. Those other forms, as they are suggested by Treanor, consist, however, of qualifying clauses or assumptions in land grants requiring actual settlement or improvement to prove the claims; evidence that such grants were rescinded does not, in my view and, I take it, in Professor Stoebuck's, constitute good cause to consider them "confiscatory" or "expropriative" in any sense comparable to the highway takings policy or eminent domain as we know it. They are a contract-fulfillment issue, and nothing more ought to be squeezed out of them. None of this is to fault very seriously, however, Treanor's excellent discussion, which fills an important gap in our thinking about what he terms "original significance."

7. On "received ideas" and the idea of a republican system or framework, *see especially* B. Bailyn, *The Ideological Origins of the American Revolution* (Cambridge: Belknap, 1965).

8. Apologies to Professor Ralph Lerner, who has written on the federal courts as "republican schoolmasters."

9. Madison's speech, reprinted in B. Schwartz, *The Bill of Rights* 5:1029–30. *See also* the discussion in Treanor, *Just Compensation Clause*, pp. 710–12.

10. *See* note 12 *infra*.

11. Magna Charta, chap. 39; Petition of Right (1628) reprinted in Schwartz, *The Bill of Rights* 1:20.

12. Reprinted in Schwartz, *The Bill of Rights* 1:72. In addition the Body of Liberties, chap. 8, provided that no goods or cattle be taken "for public use or service" except on act of the legislature and on payment of "such reasonable prices and hire as the ordinarie rates of the Countrie do afford."

13. Quotation from W. Penn, *England's Present Interest Considered*, (1675), in Schwartz, *The Bill of Rights* 1:158.

14. *E.g.*, Maryland Decl. of Rights, 1776, in ibid., p. 282. For a full discussion of the early state constitutional provisions, see Grant, *The "Higher Law" Background of the Law of Eminent Domain*, 6 Wis. L. Rev. 67–85 (1930–31).

15. "Law of the land," as a concept incorporating the just compensation idea, had a long and complex history. I deal very briefly with some of it, *infra*; but *see*, *inter alia*, Haines, *Judicial Review of Legislation in the U.S. and the Doctrines of Vested rights and of Implied Limitations on Legislatures*, 2 Tex. L. Rev. 257, 387 (1924); and Howard, *The Road from Runnymede* (Charlottesville: Univ. Press of Virginia, 1968).

16. The Northwest Ordinance provision made the public use concept more of a precise limitation, it would appear, reading: "No man shall be deprived of his liberty or property but by the judgment of his peers, or the law of the land; and should the public exigencies make it necessary for the common preservation to take any person's property, or to demand his particular services, full compensation shall be made for the same" (quoted in Treanor, *Just Compensation Clause*, p. 707n.).

17. Bringing in the two remaining states and "remov[ing] remaining inquietudes" were among the four objectives that Madison jotted down in his notes for the speech introducing and moving the amendments in 1789 (Schwartz, *The Bill of Rights* 5:1042; *see also* Madison's speech, ibid., 5:1024).

18. Stoebuck, *General Theory*, *passim*.

19. *See* comment on Treanor, *Just Compensation Clause*, who accepted some of these contentions of other scholars, *supra*, note 6.

20. *See* my full study of nineteenth-century doctrine: Scheiber, *The Road to Munn: Eminent Domain and the Concept of Public Purpose in the State Courts*, 5 Perspectives in American History 327–402 (1971) (rept. in B. Bailyn and D. Fleming, eds., *Law in American History* [Boston: Little, Brown, 1971], pp. 327–402).

See on the milldam statutes of Massachusetts, O. and M. Handlin, *Commonwealth, a Study of the Role of Government in the American Economy: Massachusetts, 1776–1861*, rev. ed. (Cambridge: Belknap, 1969), and W. Nelson, *Americanization of the Common Law: The Impact of Legal Change on Massachusetts Society, 1760–1830* (Cambridge: Harvard Univ. Press, 1975). Nor were milldam flooding rights for entrepreneurs given only in the northern colonies. *See*, *e.g.*, the act regarding water mills, Virginia Assembly, Acts in Force, 1758 (22 Geo. II [1748] cap. 26).

21. *See* note 16, *supra*.

22. Thayer, *The Right of Eminent Domain*, n.s. 9 Monthly Law Reporter 242 (1856).

23. On the Lockean tradition, *see* Stoebuck, *General Theory*; the classic study by C. MacPherson, *The Political Theory of Possessive Individualism* (Oxford: Clarendon, 1964); Fellman, *Property in Colonial Political Theory*, 16 Temp. U.

L.Q. 388 (1942); and Smith, *Liberalism and American Constitutional Law.*

24. Judge Ruffin, in *Raleigh and Gaston Railroad Co. v. Davis*, 2 Dev. and Batt. 451, 458 (No. Carolina, 1837).

25. Argument, in *Scudder v. Trenton Del. Falls Co.*, 1 N.J. Eq. 694 (1832). On the foundations in legal theory of the takings problem, *see* esp. Sax, *Takings and the Police Power*, Yale L.J. 74 (1964); also, Masnerus, *Public Use, Private Use, and Judicial Review in Eminent Domain*, 58 N.Y.U. L. Rev. 409–15 *et passim* (1983).

26. I acknowledge here the very useful commentary by Professor James B. Ely, on my original presentation of this paper at Vanderbilt, that I have given insufficient attention to the question of basic mores of the legal culture. *See* note 43, *infra*.

27. *See* text at notes 29, 31–32, *infra*.

28. 10 U.S. 87 (1810). *See* B. Wright, *The Contract Clause of the Constitution* (Cambridge: Harvard Univ. Press, 1938).

29. *Barron v. Mayor of Baltimore*, 32 U.S. 243 (1833). For later use of eminent domain arguments in the *Charles River Bridge* case and other landmark cases, *see* Scheiber, *Road to Munn*. The decision in *Barron v. Mayor of Baltimore* was of a piece with other decisions of the early nineteenth century, including some major decisions of the nationalistic Marshall Court. *See* discussion in Scheiber, *Federalism and the American Economic Order, 1789–1910*, 10 L. and Soc. Rev. 57–118 (1975).

30. *West River Bridge Co. v. Dix*, 6 How. 507 (U.S. 1848).

31. A concept drawn from the decision of the New York chancellor, in an 1831 decision. 6 How. 507 at 535.

32. *See* discussion of Webster in Scheiber, *Road to Munn*, pp. 379–80, and also Maurice Baxter's full and excellent biographical study of Webster and constitutional law.

33. *Mills v. St. Clair County*, 8 How. 569, 584 (1850).

34. *Wilkinson v. Leland*, 2 Pet. 627 (U.S. 1829) at 658. On Story's jurisprudence, *see* the judicial biography by K. Newmyer, *Supreme Court Justice Joseph Story* (Chapel Hill: Univ. of North Carolina Press, 1985).

35. *See* Scheiber, *Road to Munn*, p. 360ff.; Treanor, *Just Compensation Clause*, pp. 714–15.

36. *People v. Platt*, 17 Johns 195, 216 (1819).

37. *See* Grant, *The "Higher Law" Background.*

38. Scheiber, *Road to Munn*, p. 337ff.

39. *See* McCutcheon and Stoebuck, chapter 17, *infra*, for both analysis of the contemporary situation and citation of current literature.

40. Scheiber, *Road to Munn*, pp. 337ff., 360ff.

41. *See* ibid. Relevant materials are also in two other articles of mine: Scheiber, *Property Law, Expropriation, and Resource Allocation by Government: The United States, 1789–1910*, 33 J. Econ. Hist. 33 (1973); and *Public Rights and the Rule of Law in American Legal History*, 72 Calif. L. Rev. 217–51 (1984).

42. Freyer, *Reassessing the Impact of Economic Domain in Early American Economic Development*, 1981 Wis. L. Rev., 1236–86.

On Ohio, *see* H. Scheiber, *Ohio Canal Era: A Case Study of Govern-*

ment and the Economy (Athens: Ohio Univ. Press, 1969); on California, Scheiber and McCurdy, *Eminent Domain Law and Western Agriculture*, 49 Agric. Hist. (1975). M. Horwitz, in *The Transformation of American Law, 1790–1860* (Cambridge: Harvard Univ. Press, 1977), makes much of subsidy effects but argues that they fell mainly on the lower orders of society, which I do not think is necessarily true, and does not cite any hard evidence of damage awards and their probable relationship to market values. *See* my commentary in Scheiber, "Public Rights and the Rule of Law."

43. Scheiber, *Road to Munn*, pp. 364–65; *see also* L. Levy, *The Law of the Commonwealth and Chief Justice Shaw* (Cambridge: Harvard Univ. Press, 1954), pp. 130–35; and Comment, *Eminent Domain: Set-off of Benefits against Damages*, 43 Iowa L. Rev. 303 ff. (1958). For some evidence on an important Old Northwest state, *see* Scheiber, *Ohio Canal Era, passim.*

44. Particularly grievous was the New York doctrine that only damages appraised and paid at the time of a taking were compensable. *Steele v. Western Inland Nav. Co.*, 2 John. 283 (New York, 1807). *See also* Cormack, Legal Concepts in Cases of Eminent Domain, 41 Yale L.J. 221–61 (1931–32).

45. In a commentary on this chapter, when it was presented in an earlier version at Vanderbilt University, Professor James Ely raised the interesting point that even with eminent domain law running against vested rights, still the "legal culture" must be seen as deeply concerned with the protection of property. This is so, I am certain; but the issue constantly turned on what constituted "protection," and here I am in accord with the Hurst view that dynamic rather than static, "vested" rights were preferred when conflicts arose. And these conflicts often turned on the uses of eminent domain and distribution of costs through the takings process.

In New Jersey in the mid-1840s it was still optional with courts as to whether highway takings should be compensated at all.

46. I have offered my own views on the "winners and losers" issues—and the contention of some scholars that courts were consciously and perhaps even conspiratorially favoring new enterprises over "old property" and the rich over the poor and dispossessed, a view that I think is dramatically oversimplified—in my *Public Rights and the Rule of Law*.

47. As said by Judge Oakes in his Washington lecture, *"Property Rights" in Constitutional Analysis Today*, 56 Wash. L. Rev. 608 (1981).

48. On dual federalism and the range of autonomy in the states, *see* Scheiber, *Federalism and the American Economic Order, 1789–1910. See also* Selvin, *The Public Trust Doctrine in American Law and Economic Policy, 1789–1920*, 1980 Wis. L. Rev. 1403–42; and Rose, *The Comedy of the Commons: Custom, Commerce, and Inherently Public Property*, 53 U. Chi. L. Rev. 711–81 (1986).

49. *See* Scheiber, *American Constitutional History and the New Legal History: Complementary Themes in Two Modes*, 68 J. Am. Hist. 337–50 (1981).

50. The case was *Chicago, Burlington and Quincy RR v. Chicago*, 166 U.S. 226. *See* discussion in H. Abrahams, *Freedom and the Court: Civil Rights and Liberties in the United States*, 4th

ed. (New York: Oxford Univ. Press, 1982), pp. 33–34. *Also see* Note, *The Public Use Limitations on Eminent Domain*, 56 Yale L.J. 599 (1949); and Scheiber, *The Jurisprudence—and My Theology—of Eminent Domain in American Legal History*, in E. Paul, ed., *Property, Liberty, and the Constitution* (Albany: State Univ. of New York Press, 1989).

Melody B. McCutcheon and
William B. Stoebuck

17. Current Understandings of the Takings Clause

Introduction

Elsewhere in this volume, Professor Harry N. Scheiber shows us that the original meaning of the eminent domain or takings clause of the Fifth Amendment is known only circumstantially, owing to a lack of evidence of the drafters' specific intent. In the ensuing 200 years many applications of the clause have become clear by dint of numerous judicial decisions. Routine condemnation actions are to gain the physical use of land, usually through the taking of either an easement or a fee simple estate. Governmental appropriation to its own use of any estate in land is an exercise of the eminent domain power.[1] We know that any compulsory physical occupation of land, even a slight encroachment, by governmental authority is a compensable taking.[2] Flooding by the backwaters from a public dam constitutes the de facto taking of a flowage easement.[3] Extinction of an easement by governmental occupation of the servient tenement falls under the clause.[4] Overflight of aircraft from a public airport at very low altitudes works the taking of an easement through airspace.[5]

As governmental interference with an owner's use and enjoyment of land becomes less physical, there is increasing question about whether a taking has occurred. In several categories of cases there is physical governmental activity that does not physically touch the owner's land. Examples are cases in which activities of a governmental entity interfere with an owner's access to an abutting public way[6] or with a riparian owner's rights to reach or use an adjoining stream.[7] There is less agreement in such cases about whether a nontrespassory taking has occurred than when government physically touches the owner's land. More confusing and still in a developing stage are decisions on whether governmental activity that causes nuisance-type interferences, such as noise from nearby jet aircraft landing at a public airport and odors from sewage disposal plants, may work a "condemnation by nuisance."[8]

Of all the ways government may interfere with an owner's use of land, the way that has the least physical impact is the governmental regulation of land uses. Zoning and many other forms of regulation, including the many recent environmental regulations, more or less diminish the landowner's property rights of use and enjoyment without touching the land in the slightest. Since rights of use and enjoyment are a large portion of the sticks in the bundle of rights we call real property, the owner may contend that a regulation which substantially reduces those rights is a taking of property under the Fifth Amendment. The extent to which that is so is today the most pressing question in eminent domain law; it has become synonymous with the phrase "the taking issue." There is a considerable body of Supreme Court law on the issue, pieces in a puzzle not yet finished. Even as this chapter is written, an important decision has just filled in a major section of the mosaic.[9]

The taking issue will be explored with reference to two separate questions: (1) What is a taking? and (2) What is the remedy for a taking? Relevant cases applicable to each question are considered. The analysis culminates with commentary on two very recent Court decisions on these questions.

What Is a Taking?

For sixty-five years the Supreme Court's favored analysis to test the validity of land-use regulations has been the taking doctrine. This doctrine arises from the Fifth Amendment's prohibition against the taking of property for public use without just compensation.

The taking analysis is traced to Justice Holmes's 1922 majority opinion in *Pennsylvania Coal Co. v. Mahon.*[10] Pennsylvania's Kohler Act prohibited coal mining that caused the surface to subside under a dwelling. This prohibition prevented the coal company from making any use of the underground layer of coal it owned in the vicinity of Mahon's house. According to the Court, this regulation was a taking under the Fifth Amendment because it went "too far." The regulation went too far because it destroyed all the rights of use and enjoyment the mineowner had in the severed estate in the coal. The Court acknowledged that whether a taking occurred was a matter of degree turning on the particular facts of each case. Notwithstanding the reference to compensation in the Fifth Amendment, however, the remedy selected by the Court was invalidation of the statute, the same remedy that would be given for a due process violation.

Justice Brandeis's dissent in *Mahon* argued essentially for the doctrine in *Mugler v. Kansas.*[11] *Mugler* is the leading authority for the view that regulatory measures cannot be takings. In *Mugler*, the Court reviewed a Kansas statute against the brewing of beer which forced the defendant to close his brewery. The Court said that exercises of the police power that validly preserved the public health, safety, or welfare were never takings. Reference to preserving the public health, safety, or welfare is, in this context, tautological, because a regulation which failed to serve some such purpose would be void for lack of due process. So, it may simply be said that *Mugler* stands for the proposition that police power regulations cannot be takings.

The Holmes-Brandeis split reveals a clear dichotomy between *Mahon* and *Mugler*. Under *Mahon*, a police power regulation amounts to a taking if it goes "too far" in diminishing the regulated landowner's property rights. *Mugler* stands for the proposition that no exercise of the police power is a taking; police power is one thing, eminent domain another. Despite this dichotomy, the Court has never cast aspersions upon *Mugler*, and the case continues to be favorably cited by all sides of the Court, 100 years later, in the most recent taking challenges considered by the Court.[12] In keeping *Mugler* alive, rather than making a choice between two competing doctrines, the Court apparently feels it can reconcile it with *Mahon*. Nonetheless, throughout the years *Mahon*'s "too far" test has been the staple of individual analysis despite the vitality of conflicting doctrine in *Mugler*.

The "too far" test originated with *Mahon*, and ever since the unresolved question has been, How far is "too far"? The facts in *Mahon* suggest that the diminution in use was total because of the single-use nature of the severed stratum of coal. However, the Court did not explicitly rest its holding that a taking had occurred on the fact that there was total loss of use.

Moreover, since *Mahon*, and continuing to the present, the Court has repeatedly said that a land-use regulation can at some point become so severe that it constitutes an eminent domain taking. Doubt remains as to whether a viable judicial formula exists for determining when a taking has occurred. When is something less than a total loss a taking? Because of the persistence of the conflict between *Mugler* and *Mahon* and the inconsistency of the Court's decisions, the issue remains muddled. The early cases on the takings issue set the pattern of continued confusion.

A number of decisions suggest that severe but not total deprivation of use will withstand a takings challenge. These opinions roughly establish that a diminution in value of as much as 75 to 85 percent will not be considered "too far." The first case to note a particular percentage factor was *Village of Euclid v. Ambler Realty Co.*,[13] decided in 1926. This was also the first Supreme Court decision to consider the constitutional validity of a zoning ordinance. The appellant landowner sought an injunction against enforcement of the ordinance, based upon the potential harm that future buyers of his property might be deterred by the zoning restrictions. The Court upheld the ordinance as a legitimate exercise of the police power, despite the alleged 75 percent reduction in the value of the land.[14]

A severe regulation was also upheld in *Goldblatt v. Town of Hempstead*.[15] The ordinance in that case prohibited excavating below the water table and required excavations below that level to be refilled. The appellant had to cease the mining operation on his land as a result of the regulation. Since the Court found the record to be insufficient to show specific adverse effects on the value of the property for other uses, whether the particular regulation was a taking was not analyzed in detail. In its discussion of previous takings cases, the Court once again stated that a regulation which is too onerous may be a taking. The Court also noted that a comparison of before and after property values was "by no means conclusive."[16] Just what would be conclusive or too onerous was left unresolved.

Both *Euclid* and *Goldblatt* uphold severe land-use regulations. Nonetheless, the Court cautions us, particularly in *Goldblatt*, that not all such regulations will be sustained. Yet the decisions in two other early cases suggest that even a total diminution in value will withstand challenge when the circumstances are particularly compelling. For example, in *Miller v. Schoene*,[17] the Court addressed the state-mandated destruction of the plaintiff's cedar trees, because they produced cedar rust that was fatal to apple trees. Apple trees were an important crop in Virginia, whereas the cedar trees in question were not valued for lumber. The Court characterized the state as having to choose between the preservation of one class of property over another class. Despite acknowledging that exercise of the choice destroyed one class of property to save another, the Court held the statute to be valid. Citing *Mugler* and other cases, the Court stated: "And where the public interest is involved preferment of that interest over the property interest of the individual, to the extent even of its destruction, is one of the distinguishing characteristics of every exercise of the police power which affects property."[18] *Mahon* had been decided just six years earlier, but the Court's opinion in *Miller* contains no reference to *Mahon*. Although "total destruction" is arguably going "too far," the Court seemed persuaded by the compelling nature of the problem faced by the state and the lack of alternative options for the state to exercise.

In *United States v. Central Eureka Mining Co.*,[19] the government restriction is once again easier to reconcile under *Mugler* than with *Mahon*. In *Central Eureka Mining* a wartime government order prohibiting operation of all gold mines was held not to be a taking. This result is surprising, given that one particular industry was singled out for regulation. In addition, the government had a "dominant" purpose to induce experienced miners into war-related work rather than the nonessential mining of gold. The Court's analysis centered upon the fact that the government did not take physical possession of the mines. Without acknowledging the conflict, the Court cited *Mugler* and also asserted the general notion that a regulation can so diminish the value of property as to constitute a taking. Once again, the compelling nature of the governmental objective seems to have persuaded the Court to uphold a very severe regulation.

More recent cases have displayed a similar tendency to uphold severe regulations without clarifying how far is "too far." The *Penn Central*[20] decision of 1978 epitomizes the historical confusion regarding the taking analysis. *Penn Central* involved New York City's designation of Grand Central Station as a historic site, thus preventing Penn Central, its owner, from adding an office tower building above the terminal. To soften the blow, the city offered Penn Central transferable development rights that might be used upon other sites, including some Penn Central owned. New York's

Court of Appeals, following the analysis it developed in *Fred F. French Investing Company v. City of New York*,[21] had treated the case as a due process case and had decided the regulation was not so severe as to cause it to be invalid.

In the Supreme Court, the due process theory was ignored; Justice Brennan's opinion, signed by justices Stewart, White, Marshall, Blackmun, and Powell, considered the case only as a takings case. In a long decision, the Court reviewed its many prior decisions on takings, as well as some due process decisions, and sorted out factors and approaches that had been used. Instead of identifying and trying to resolve inconsistencies that exist among some of those decisions, the majority seemed to treat them as alternatives, depending upon various factors. The Court acknowledged that historically it had faced considerable difficulty in stating a workable test in this area. Rather than trying to develop such a test in this case, though, the Court merely concluded that there was no "single, simple" test. Nonetheless, *Mahon*'s "too far" test was prominently mentioned and seems to be the theory that best suited the facts.

Under none of the approaches the majority described had a taking occurred: the landmark ordinance did not interfere with the present use of the property, which the appellants admitted was capable of earning a reasonable return.[22] Thus, they did not have to consider the effect of the transferable development rights, either whether they might prevent a taking or constitute just compensation if there was a taking. Justice Rehnquist's dissent, signed by Chief Justice Burger and Justice Stevens, concluded that the historic site designation had caused a taking, apparently in the *Mahon* sense, and that the case should be remanded for determination of whether the transferable development rights were valuable enough to be just compensation.

In 1980 the Supreme Court again forestalled a definitive taking test in *Agins v. City of Tiburon*,[23] up on appeal from a decision of the California Supreme Court.[24] Justice Powell's unanimous opinion simply reduced the facts of the case so that no taking occurred. At issue was a City of Tiburon zoning ordinance which limited a land developer to building somewhere between one and five homes on a five-acre tract of choice view land. The developer alleged that the ordinance left "no beneficial use" of the land. Though the case was up on the allegations of the complaint, on a motion to dismiss, the Supreme Court looked behind the complaint and noted that the developer had not applied for or received a final permit for the number of homes he could build. Five homes, considering the value of the land for luxury homes, would not have been very restrictive, but perhaps a limit of one would have been. In any event, the Court merely considered the ordinance on its face and easily determined it did not constitute a taking. Though the opinion exhibits some confusion about the taking doctrine,[25] it appears to contemplate *Mahon*'s "too far" test as the standard.

As the previous review of cases suggests, we have never had a definitive test of when a land-use regulation went "too far." A few cases upheld a regulation despite a specific finding that the diminution in value was in the 75 to 85 percent range. Other cases did not rely on a specific percentage figure but rather weighed the governmental interest at stake versus the reduction in value to the landowner. In *Penn Central* the Court openly abandoned any effort to state a definitive test and relied on the fact that the landowner continued to have an economically viable use of his land. *Agins* similarly suggests that the ability to make at least some use of one's property will thwart a takings challenge.

Although one reviewing these decisions could hold out hope for a definitive test, a 1987 Supreme Court decision suggests this would be a futile effort. In *Keystone Bituminous Coal Association v. DeBenedictis*,[26] the Court had an opportunity to revisit its original takings analysis in *Mahon*, because of the similarity between the regulations in both cases. The appellants argued that *Mahon* was controlling and dictated a holding that the act resulted in a taking. The Court in a 5-to-4 opinion instead distinguished *Mahon* and held that no taking had occurred. This case is of particular importance, since it is the first one since the "no single test" pronouncement in *Penn Central* where the Court has directly tried to answer the "what is a taking" question.

Keystone involved a taking challenge by several coal companies to a state act which required that 50 percent of the coal beneath certain structures be kept in place for surface support. The Court's treatment of *Mahon* was a curious surprise. Initially, the opinion seems to confine the *Mahon* holding to the "particular facts" of that case[27] and then declares that the discussion in *Mahon* of the general validity of the regulation was an "advisory opinion" out of character with Justice Holmes's usual opinions.[28] This is startling treatment of the "too far" test that has been the mainstay of taking analysis for sixty-five years. The dissent remonstrates at the majority's cavalier treatment of *Mahon* and suggests the "too far" test should have dictated a taking.

To go further, the *Keystone* opinion does not even apply *Mahon*'s "too far" test. Rather, the Court states that "two factors . . . are integral parts of our takings analysis."[29] Citing *Agins* and *Penn Central*, these two factors leading to a conclusion that a regulation is a taking are: (1) the land-use regulation does not substantially advance a legitimate state interest, or (2) the regulation denies economically viable uses of an owner's property.[30] In *Keystone* the Court found that the state act in question was designed to prevent a significant threat to the public welfare. This is to be contrasted with the Kohler Act in *Mahon*, which was characterized as having been enacted solely for the benefit of the class of private surface owners who had released their right to support.

As for the diminution-in-value component, the Court stated that its test required a comparison between the value that has been taken from the property with the value that remains in the property. The Court also referenced but did not explain an additional part of the analysis, consideration of "investment-backed expectations."[31] Reference to this factor is hard to reconcile with *Penn Central*'s focus on the present, remaining use of the land and the rejection of the claim that a taking occurred because the landowner might not be able to construct an office building "addition" to Grand Central Terminal.

Nonetheless, the Court concluded in *Keystone* that there had been an insufficient showing of diminution in value. Unlike the *Mahon* finding that the act made the mining of coal commercially impractical, there was no claim in *Keystone* that the appellant's mining operations or specific mines were unprofitable as a result of the regulation. The appellants claimed that the regulation required them to leave approximately 27 million tons of coal in place; since they could not mine this coal, they alleged it had been "taken." Although acknowledging this burden, the Court refused to consider that coal as a separate segment of property. Analogizing to setback requirements affecting a small portion of a total parcel, the Court instead focused on the totality of coal owned by the appellants. Considered in this light, this adverse "treatment" of less than 2 percent of the appellants' coal was not the taking of a "separate parcel of property."[32] The dissent took issue with this focus and noted that the effect of the regulation was a total destruction in an identifiable segment of property.

The *Keystone* opinion is also of interest because of its puzzling allusions to some sort of previously undefined "nuisance" component of takings analysis. The Court stressed the importance of the "nature of the State's action"[33] and started off by citing *Mugler*'s stance that a legitimate land-use regulation is not a taking because the state acts to protect the public welfare from an injurious private use of property. Without pausing to note the inconsistency between *Mugler* and subsequent cases applying *Mahon*, the Court went on to discuss both *Miller* and *Goldblatt* as nuisance cases. The Court commented that it has been hesitant "to find a taking when the state merely restrains uses of property that are tantamount to public nuisances."[34] In the broadest of terms, the Court seems to suggest that police power actions inevitably involve restrictions on private property and that such restrictions will not be considered takings because private property owners get "compensating" advantages in terms of an enhanced public welfare. The dissent picked up on this sidelight and expressed alarm that, viewed through the majority's eyes, every regulation could be justified as beyond the reach of a taking challenge. The dissent, written by Chief Justice Rehnquist, took direct aim at this "nuisance exception."

The majority's mention of nuisance law played an unclear role in its holding that no taking had occurred. Can one infer from this that a complete taking is permitted if the regulation can be cast as a nuisance restriction? Or does the Court's insistence that the coal left in place in Keystone, despite its considerable quantity, cannot be considered a separate property interest decide the issue without reference to nuisance law? The Court seems to have rejected *Mahon*'s "too far" test, and yet not to have replaced it with anything more definitive. The Court described the two factors it relied on in deciding the issue but then strayed into the area of nuisance law for no clear reason. The result from *Keystone* is, once again, confusion as to when a regulation will be considered a taking. The test, as stated in *Keystone*, is relatively clear, but its application in that case muddies the waters. The outcome may very well be that a federal taking challenge is no real deterrent to government regulation, since the Court seems willing to resurrect *Mugler* and (almost) to bury *Mahon*. It is hard to imagine how severe a regulation would have to be to convince the U.S. Supreme Court that a taking had occurred. Litigation at the state level would seem the more likely outlet, since some state courts are willing to find a taking at a lower threshold level.

The second recent Supreme Court decision of interest is *Nollan v. California Coastal Commission*.[35] *Nollan* does not precisely involve a land-use regulation. It is a case in which, as a condition to granting a demolition and rebuilding permit to a homeowner whose land fronted on a public beach, the coastal commission required, without payment, the dedication of a public easement across the applicant's lot, running parallel to (not at right angles to) the beach. In a 5-to-4 decision, the Supreme Court held this to be a compensable taking. Justice Scalia's majority opinion conceded some matters that considerably narrow the decision's scope. The commission argued that no compensation was due for the easement because it was to alleviate a problem the applicant's proposed house would create, mainly by blocking the public's view of the beach. In fact, they argued, the permit might have been denied outright to protect the public's view. The majority opinion concedes that, if necessary to protect the public's view, the permit might have been denied or it might have been granted upon the condition that the owner dedicate an easement running down to the beach. However, Justice Scalia pointed out, an easement running parallel to the beach would do nothing to alleviate the alleged view problem, so that on the facts there was not a close enough "fit" between the public problem and the proposed solution. Justice Brennan's dissent complains that the majority insisted upon too close a "fit." Thus, the holding that there was a taking is narrowed to depend upon a precise set of facts. One gets the impression that this narrowing was necessary to hold together the five-justice majority.

The due process clause of the Fourteenth Amendment has a great deal of affinity to the taking issue.[36] Since *Pennsylvania Coal Co. v. Mahon* came down, a particularly severe land-use regulation may, on account of its severity, be challenged as either a taking or a denial of substantive due process. Language in the most recent Supreme Court decisions appears to create an even further overlap between the taking and due process challenges. The line between the two constitutional limitations has become quite muddled.

Lawton v. Steele[37] has been called by the Supreme Court its classic decision on due process protection of property rights.[38] Its teaching is that a regulation on the use and enjoyment of property denies due process, and so is void, either if the regulation serves no legitimate public purpose, or if, balancing a purpose it does serve against the degree of regulation on the property owner, it is "unduly oppressive" on that owner. Therefore, a regulation which serves no public purpose, that is, no purpose that it is any legitimate function of government to serve, is void. *Nectow v. City of Cambridge*[39] is the leading Supreme Court decision for this proposition in the zoning context. It seems likely that a majority, if not all, of the present Court accepts the proposition that a land-use regulation which serves no legitimate public purpose denies due process and is void. This will be called the first part of *Lawton v. Steele*'s due process test.

The second part of *Lawton* emphasizes the degree to which a regulated owner's use and enjoyment of his property are diminished. We now assume that the regulation to some extent does serve a legitimate public purpose. Considering and balancing the protection the public receives from the regulation, is the diminution of the owner's property rights so great that the regulation is "unduly oppressive"? It takes no extended discussion to see that *Lawton*'s phrase, "unduly oppressive," looks much like *Pennsylvania Coal v. Mahon*'s phrase, "too far." It is in this area that there has been an obvious overlap between the due process and taking theories since *Mahon* came down. In addition, certain passages in the Supreme Court's recent opinion in *Keystone Bituminous Coal Association v. DeBenedictis* suggest that a balancing of public need versus extent of regulation of a landowner may now play a role in the "too far" taking issue.[40]

One of the imponderables of Supreme Court jurisprudence is the extent to which *Lawton*'s second part still has vitality in that Court.[41] It is not unusual for a state court to invalidate a land-use regulation on the due process ground that it is too harsh or, as often put, that it denies all profitable use of land or simply that it is unreasonable. But in the Supreme Court, so-called economic due process reached its apogee in 1905 in *Lochner v. New York*,[42] which invalidated a New York statute setting working hours for bakers on the broad ground that it denied employers due process. The *Lochner* era, when economic legislation could be overturned on a broad policy basis, came to an end in New Deal days. Justice Stone's famous footnote 4 in *United States v. Carolene Products Co.*[43] in 1938 took the position, still accepted in Supreme Court jurisprudence, that due process protection of economic interests has a much narrower scope than that of certain personal liberties. Though *Lochner* has not been formally overruled, it remains in an eclipsed state. It is clear that the Supreme Court has no inclination to return to the *Lochner* era.[44]

It is not clear, however, that due process protection against land-use regulations, in *Lawton v. Steele*'s second sense, is entirely dead. During the 1970s and 1980s, several Supreme Court developments related to that question have suggested the theory may have some continuing vitality. These items of evidence have been detailed elsewhere and will not be repeated here,[45] but special note should be taken of *Moore v. City of East Cleveland.*[46] In this 1977 decision the Court invalidated part of a zoning ordinance on due process grounds in what must be *Lawton*'s second sense. However, the decision is a narrow and somewhat confusing one[47] and involves what the Court viewed as regulatory intrusion on rights of privacy and of the family. Moreover, the Supreme Court has long evinced a preference for the taking analysis in cases of severe land-use regulations. This was particularly apparent in *Penn Central Transportation Co. v. City of New York*,[48] involving the validity of the New York City regulation that designated Grand Central Station a historic site. The New York Court of Appeals had analyzed the case as one of substantive due process,[49] but the Supreme Court, ignoring that ground, considered it only as a taking case. A fair summary of the status of *Lawton v. Steele*'s second part is that while it is not dead as a constitutional limitation on land-use regulations, it has a very limited scope, it largely overlaps *Mahon*'s "too far" test, and the taking analysis is preferred.

Now we must return to *Lawton v. Steele*'s first part: a regulation on property rights which serves no legitimate public purpose denies due process. This is *Nectow v. City of Cambridge*, and it appears to have the allegiance of today's Supreme Court, as already noted. Traditionally there has been no overlap between this kind of due process limitation and taking theory. The very recent Supreme Court taking decisions, however, have created confusion and appear to have created an overlap. Justice Stevens's opinion for the Court in *Keystone Bituminous Coal Association v. DeBenedictis*[50] suggests that a land-use regulation might be a taking if it did not serve a "public purpose" or the "public interest." He does this in a discussion in which, citing *Mugler v. Kansas* as principal authority, he suggests the defect of the statute in *Pennsylvania Coal Co. v. Mahon* was not simply that it went "too far" but that it served private rather than public purposes. That is a novel reading of *Mahon*. But again Chief Justice Rehnquist does somewhat the same thing in his majority opinion in *First English Evangelical Lutheran Church v. County of Los Angeles*[51] where he recognizes the possibility that a regulation, otherwise a taking, might not be a taking if it was a "safety" regulation. Justice Stevens's suggestion is that a regulation, not otherwise a taking, may become a taking if it serves no public purpose; Chief Justice Rehnquist suggests a regulation, otherwise a taking, may be excused if it serves a high enough public purpose. These are statements at opposite ends of a spectrum, but it is the same spectrum: whether a taking occurs depends upon the degree of public purpose it serves. That is the core due process proposition in *Lawton v. Steele*'s first part. Whether intentionally or inadvertently, *Keystone* and, to some extent, *First English* appear to have created an overlap between *Mahon* and *Lawton*'s first part, where no overlap existed before.

The interrelationship between *Mahon*'s taking theory and *Lawton*'s due process doctrine is now very confused; it is hard to follow the threads. *Lawton*'s first proposition, that a regulation denies due process if it serves no legitimate public purpose, appears to have continuing vitality. However, the very recent Supreme Court taking decisions appear to have insinuated questions about the public purpose of a regulation into the taking analysis. *Lawton v. Steele*'s second proposition, turning on a balancing of public purpose against how "oppressive" a regulation is on the person regulated, appears to be of quite limited force in the Supreme Court, though it often is a ground of decision in state courts. There has always, since *Mahon* was decided, been an obvious overlap between its "too far" test and *Lawton*'s question of "unduly oppressive." Balancing a degree of public protection against extent of regulation may now play a role in the taking analysis, as it does in due process doctrine. It is not clear whether the overlaps and blending in the Supreme Court's taking and due process jurisprudence are inadvertent, or whether the Court means entirely to subsume due process into the taking theory. Theoretically it is possible, though pragmatically it is doubtful, that due process might replace the taking doctrine. In any event, now more than ever, the two constitutional limitations on land-use regulations occupy the same ground.

What Is the Remedy If There Is a Taking?

It would be an entirely logical assumption that the remedy for a regulation found to be a taking would be compensation to the landowner; this, it would seem, is what the Fifth Amendment requires. However, the result in *Mahon* was invalidity of the regulation, rather than an award of just compensation for the taking that had occurred. For many years after, the Supreme Court decisions assumed, without discussing, that invalidation was the appropriate remedy.

In the decade of the 1970s, several decisions from the California Court of Appeals and from the federal northern district of California began to recognize another remedy, compensation, which they called "inverse condemnation."[52] With this the government entity must pay just compensation for the period commencing on the date the regulation first effects the taking and ending, if at all, on the date the government entity chooses to rescind or otherwise amend the regulation. However, the California Supreme Court absolutely rejected this formula in *Agins v. City of Tiburon*.[53] In *Agins* the court held that compensation was not an appropriate remedy for a regulatory taking, but rather that invalidation of the regulation was the only acceptable remedy.

The U.S. Supreme Court found that no taking had occurred when it reviewed the California Supreme Court decision in *Agins.*[54] The Court took note of California's sharp rejection of the compensation remedy but simply observed that since there was no taking, it did not have to consider the question of appropriate remedy. However, that question had been broached and would explode in the Court's next takings decision.

In *San Diego Gas & Electric Co. v. City of San Diego,*[55] the Supreme Court added the first significant addition to its regulatory taking jurisprudence since *Mahon.* The case was complicated procedurally. San Diego had imposed restrictive regulations upon a tract of several hundred acres the gas and electric company owned, allegedly freezing large parts of it from useful development. California's trial court had awarded compensation for a taking under the inverse condemnation doctrine, and a California appeal court had affirmed a monetary award, though reducing the amount. Upon appeal to the California Supreme Court, which had by then rendered its decision in *Agins,* that court remanded to the court of appeal with instructions to follow *Agins,* i.e., to strike the compensation award. In this posture the U.S. Supreme Court granted certiorari from the appeal court.

The Supreme Court's decision was contained in a plurality opinion written by Justice Blackmun, joined by Chief Justice Burger and justices White and Stevens. Justice Rehnquist concurred separately in an opinion which will be noted further in a moment. Justice Blackmun's opinion simply concluded that because the California appeal court had contemplated a remand to the trial court for determination of some further facts, the state action was not complete. Thus, the Supreme Court did not have jurisdiction because the action was not "final" under 28 USC section 1257. There was no significant discussion of the taking question. Once again, the Court postponed progress, or at least four justices did.

But progress there was in Justice Brennan's dissenting opinion, signed by justices Stewart, Marshall, and Powell. In a lengthy, sweeping, heavily documented opinion, they first concluded that because California had foreclosed any possibility of the compensation or inverse condemnation remedy, that aspect of the case was ripe for determination. Justice Brennan then spelled out in detail the remedy he would apply, the compensation or inverse condemnation remedy. He flailed California's decision in *Agins v. City of Tiburon.* This remedy would apply to a regulation which caused a taking under the *Mahon* test. In this circumstance the court would award the landowner temporary compensation (measured generally by diminution in rental value caused by the regulation) up to the date of the judgment. Then the regulating governmental entity would be given a choice whether to repeal the offending regulation or to keep it. If it repealed the regulation, no further remedy would be due. If it chose to keep the regulation, then permanent compensation would be awarded (generally measured by the diminution in market value, which would, of course, subsume the amount of temporary compensation).

As noted above, Justice Rehnquist specially concurred in the plurality opinion. With difficulty, he concluded that the case was not ripe for Supreme Court decision on the merits. In doing so, however, he commented that he agreed with "much of what is said in the dissenting opinion." At the time, one wondered, of course, how much is "much," but we now know[56] that Chief Justice Rehnquist accepts the Brennan compensation remedy, as first articulated in *San Diego Gas*.

After *San Diego Gas* it could be said that the Supreme Court had two theories before it. In both, *Mahon*'s "too far" test defined whether a regulation had caused a taking. If it had, the supposition in *Mahon* and in the many cases citing it in the Supreme Court and in many other courts, was that the remedy was invalidation of the offending regulation. Justice Brennan's remedy would be compensation under the formula he spelled out. These remedies are, of course, mutually exclusive.

The *San Diego Gas* dissent prompted great interest in the future approach the Court might take toward a remedy for a taking. There followed several intervening years of speculation as to what a true majority of the Court might do. During these years some federal courts and several state appellate courts adopted the Brennan formula, perhaps assuming (correctly, as it turned out) that it was the Court's majority position.[57] However, intervening Supreme Court opinions showed that the high Court itself was not yet ready to reach this conclusion.

In *Williamson County Regional Planning Commission v. Hamilton Bank*,[58] the Court in 1985 postponed a definitive doctrine, as it had done in *Agins*. The Sixth Circuit had determined that compensation was due under Justice Brennan's formula for a change in subdivision regulations which denied the developer "economically viable" use of its land. The Court remanded the case on prematurity grounds, but in stating its reasons for the case being premature, the plurality disclosed some of its thinking on the remedy issue. As one alternative reason the case was premature, the Court said the land developer had failed to pursue a Tennessee state inverse condemnation remedy which would, if successfully pursued, have provided "adequate compensation for the taking."[59] Thus, the plurality seems implicitly to have put their imprimatur on a taking compensation doctrine that is "adequate," whatever that means.

The 1986 decision in *MacDonald, Sommer & Frates v. Yolo County*[60] is another subdivision regulation case in which a taking was alleged. Since the case came up through the California courts, the compensation or inverse condemnation remedy had been denied because of the California Supreme Court's decision in *Agins v. City of Tiburon*.[61] The majority opinion refused to decide on the merits on the familiar ground that the case was premature. In a dissenting opinion, Justice White, joined by Chief Justice Burger, wanted to decide the case and made it clear they wanted to decide it on the basis of Justice Brennan's taking compensation theory. In another dissent, Justice Rehnquist, joined by Justice Powell, was willing to conclude on the basis of the complaint that a taking had occurred but did not want to decide if the compensation remedy was required until, upon remand, the California courts had had an opportunity to address that question.

The string of cases postponing a decision on the remedy issue—*Agins*, *Hamilton Bank*, and *Yolo County*—heightened suspicion that a majority of the Court had not yet made up its mind to adopt the Brennan compensation remedy. Observers of the Court's takings decisions began to despair at the lack of resolution. Finally, the Court ended years of suspense with its June 1987 decision in *First English Evangelical Lutheran Church v. County of Los Angeles*.[62]

The *First English* case provides a clear answer to the remedy question: when governmental regulations have resulted in a taking, subsequent invalidation of the regulation by the government cannot relieve it of the duty to provide compensation for the period during which the taking was effective.[63] The six-justice majority frames the question as follows: Does the Fifth Amendment require payment of compensation for "temporary" regulatory takings? One suspects that the question is stated this way because it obviously folds into the answer provided by the Brennan formula: temporary or permanent, a taking requires compensation.

The procedural posture of *First English* invoked the rule of the California Supreme Court decision in *Agins*. In *First English*, the appellant challenged an interim ordinance preventing construction in designated flood protection areas. The appellant's church camp, in a canyon along a creek, had been destroyed by a flood. Los Angeles County adopted an interim ordinance which prohibited any rebuilding. The complaint alleged a denial of all use of the land, alleged a taking, and sought to recover damages for the "inverse condemnation." There was no prayer for invalidation of the ordinance. The trial court granted the motion to strike the allegation, relying on the California Supreme Court ruling in *Agins*, which eliminated the possibility of a compensation remedy. The California Court of Appeal affirmed, and the California Supreme Court refused to hear an appeal. Before the U.S. Supreme Court, the allegations of denial of all use and of a taking were assumed to be true. Although the dissent urged more scrutiny of this allegation and believed that no taking had occurred, the majority placed the case in exactly the posture it needed to resolve the remedy issue.

The Court's unequivocal holding is that temporary compensation is due for a regulatory taking. California's decision in *Agins* was held inconsistent with the Fifth Amendment. Thus, the compensation remedy is binding upon state as well as federal courts as a matter of federal constitutional law.

In reaching its decision, the majority found "substantial guidance" from cases where the government has only temporarily exercised its right to use private property.[64] As the dissent points out,[65] however, those cases all involve physical occupation or use; they do not involve regulatory takings, which is clearly a more difficult area of analysis. The majority seems to lump together that which had been carefully recognized as separate in prior decisions. In this respect the dissent may be correct that the majority is ignoring a basic distinction which has been followed since *Mahon*.[66]

Despite the clarity of the holding in *First English*, there remains some confusion about the "nuisance exception" first discussed explicitly in *Keystone*. In discussing the California courts' treatment of the case, the majority in *First English* notes in passing that they "have no occasion to decide . . . whether the county might avoid the conclusion that a compensable taking had occurred by establishing that the denial of all use was insulated as a part of the State's authority to enact safety regulations."[67] The dissent focuses on this point when stating its view that the Court's precedents would require a finding that the county's flood regulations "cannot" constitute a taking.[68] The three dissenters' view is that when government imposes "these types of health and safety regulations," compensation is inappropriate.[69]

Justice Stevens, writing for the dissent in *First English* and for the majority in *Keystone*, seems to believe that certain exercises of the police power are immune from a takings challenge, which is an echo of the Court's statements in *Mugler*. Asserting in *Keystone* that the statute in *Pennsylvania Coal Co. v. Mahon* was invalid because it served private purposes, not public welfare, he seems to suggest that a regulation would not be a taking if it did serve the public welfare.[70] Moreover, Chief Justice Rehnquist's opinion for the Court in *First English* contains a negative suggestion that "safety" regulations might not be considered takings.[71] The two justices, who have opposing views on the taking question in the Court's most recent opinions, seem to be pursuing a similar idea, though public welfare is a broader concept than safety. In any event, there is a suggestion that regulations that serve a strong public purpose may not be takings at all. As far as *First English* is concerned, the California courts have ample room to decide as a fact that no taking has occurred. Perhaps this is just where the Court wishes to leave the taking question for now. Compensation is due under the Brennan formula if—but only if—a taking has occurred. As far as the Supreme Court's interpretation of the Fifth Amendment is concerned, it appears that a land-use regulation must be extremely restrictive before it must be held to be a taking. Even then, it may be that a sufficient justification in the public safety or welfare will save the most restrictive regulation. State courts would not be required to find a taking at a lower threshold of restriction. On the other hand, a state court would be free to find a taking at a lower threshold, certainly if it put its decision under its own state constitution.[72] That puts the taking ball into the court of the state courts.

Conclusions

In the history of the Fifth Amendment's eminent domain clause, the critical judicial functions have been to define what acts of government cause a taking of property. Over the years the tendency has been for the courts to have to consider whether less and less physical interferences with private property are takings.

The least-physical governmental activities that may cause takings are regulations on the use and enjoyment of land, such as zoning and other environmental regulations. When, even whether, exercises of the police power may cause takings is the current frontier of eminent domain law, notably in the U.S. Supreme Court. That Court's first consideration of the question came in 1887 in *Mugler v. Kansas.*[73] Stated most simply, the decision in *Mugler* stands for the proposition that police power regulations on land use, while they may be void by denying substantive due process under the Fourteenth Amendment, cannot amount to Fifth Amendment takings. Yet, in 1922 in *Pennsylvania Coal Co. v. Mahon,*[74] the Court declared void a regulation which apparently totally denied an owner the use of its land, announcing the doctrine that a land-use regulation which goes "too far" in diminishing rights of use and enjoyment is a Fifth Amendment taking. The obvious inconsistency between *Mugler* and *Mahon*, never acknowledged by the Supreme Court, continues and is perpetuated in the latest Court decisions, which try to bridge the gap between them.[75]

Justice Holmes's decision in *Pennsylvania Coal Co. v. Mahon* begins the current era, in which a land-use regulation may be a taking; it is, as the Court has said, the origin of American regulatory takings jurisprudence.[76] Countless state court decisions have applied *Mahon*'s test, vague as it is, to determine if land-use regulations are or are not takings. In the Supreme Court, though *Mahon* has been cited and purportedly applied many times, it can still be said that the Court has found no regulation other than the one in *Mahon* itself to amount to a taking.[77] In cases such as *Village of Euclid v. Ambler Realty Co.*[78] and *Goldblatt v. Town of Hempstead,*[79] though they involved severe land-use regulations, no takings were found. State appellate court decisions, however, have exhibited a broader range of applications of the *Mahon* test; it is not unusual for a state court to strike down a zoning or other land-use regulation as a taking.[80] Thus, while *Mahon* was given cramped application in its own Court, it found more fertile ground in the state courts.

With the Supreme Court's decision in *San Diego Gas & Electric Co. v. City of San Diego,*[81] or more precisely with Justice Brennan's dissent, *Mahon*'s taking question bifurcated. *Mahon* had said, without discussion, and it had subsequently been assumed, that the remedy for a regulatory taking was invalidation of the offending land-use regulation. This, incidentally, is the same remedy as for a regulation which denies due process, compounding the confusion that exists over a regulation which is a taking and a similar regulation which denies due process. Justice Brennan's dissent, for the first time in a Supreme Court opinion, described and argued strongly for a different remedy, temporary compensation from the time the regulation became a taking until trial if the governmental entity repealed it or permanent compensation if they elected to retain it. What will be called here the Brennan compensation formula is sometimes called inverse condemnation. Three justices signed Justice Brennan's dissent, and Justice Rehnquist, though finally concurring with the majority not to consider the case on the merits, indicated he agreed with "much" of what Justice Brennan said. In two subsequent Supreme Court decisions, though they were inconclusive on the merits, there were further straws in the wind, indicating that a majority of the justices probably agreed with the Brennan formula.[82] It was widely speculated that this would prove true.

Thus, after *San Diego Gas* there were two taking questions. First, did a given land-use regulation amount to a taking—did it, in Justice Holmes's words in *Pennsylvania Coal Co. v. Mahon*, go "too far"? Second, if a regulation was held to amount to a taking, was the proper remedy invalidation or the Brennan compensation formula?

The Supreme Court's 1987 decision in *First English Evangelical Lutheran Church v. County of Los Angeles*[83] answers the second question definitively. If a regulation causes a taking, the Fifth Amendment to the U.S. Constitution, which is directly binding upon the federal government and is binding upon the states through the Fourteenth Amendment, requires compensation.[84] Justice Brennan's compensation formula is the law of the land.

On the first question above, the test for when a regulation goes "too far" and becomes a taking, we have advanced only a little since *Mahon*. *First English* does not help, as, in the procedural posture of the case, the Supreme Court simply assumed a taking had occurred. However, two other 1987 decisions, chiefly *Keystone Bituminous Coal Association v. DeBenedictis*[85] and to some extent *Nollan v. California Coastal Commission*,[86] shed some light on the matter. Analysis of these decisions shows an apparent narrowing of *Mahon*'s scope, if, indeed, *Mahon* ever had a wide scope.

Keystone reverted at some length to old *Mugler v. Kansas*, citing the passage that, if understood literally, means a regulation cannot be a taking. Justice Stevens's majority opinion suggested that the problem in *Mahon* was that the prohibition on coal mining served no public purpose but only protected private owners against subsidence. Of course, if that were so—if the regulation served no public purpose—it would be void because it denied due process.[87] Moreover, Justice Holmes's language in *Mahon* about a regulation's being a taking, which scholars and judges have generally supposed to be the heart of the decision, was labeled an "advisory opinion."

The regulation in *Keystone* bore a superficial resemblance to the one in

Mahon: both were Pennsylvania restrictions on coal mining, designed to prevent subsidence of the surface. But the two regulations were factually distinguishable and were distinguished in one section of the majority opinion. The Court might have stopped there. However, as described in the preceding paragraph, the majority seemed to go out of its way to criticize and to weaken *Mahon*, as Chief Justice Rehnquist noted pointedly in his dissenting opinion. Yet he himself, in his opinion for the Court in *First English Evangelical Lutheran Church v. County of Los Angeles*, cited *Mugler v. Kansas* as authority for a passing suggestion that a land-use regulation which totally prevented all use might not be a taking if enacted as a safety regulation. Many regulations, the ones in *Keystone* and *Mahon* and even the floodway ordinance in *First English* itself, might be considered by some to be safety measures.

The Supreme Court's current decisions intensify the previous suspicion that the Court holds a very restricted view of *Mahon*'s "too far" test. *Mugler v. Kansas* is very much alive and is relied upon by different segments of the Court. In an apparent attempt to reconcile *Mugler* and *Mahon*, the suggestion is repeatedly made that a land-use regulation might deny an owner all use of his land and yet not be a taking if it protected the public safety. There is even a suggestion in *Keystone* that *Mahon*'s regulation might have been constitutional if it had served a public purpose. The majority in *Keystone* labeled *Mahon*'s "too far" test an "advisory opinion." How can we but say that *Mahon* has a very narrow compass in the U.S. Supreme Court? In the present state of affairs, it will take a most extreme land-use regulation to convince the Supreme Court that a taking has occurred. Apparently it will have to be a regulation which denies an owner all or nearly all use of his land and a regulation which does not protect the public safety.

And so the Supreme Court has left the regulatory taking issue in this posture: Only a most extreme regulation will, as a matter of federal constitutional law, require a court to find that a taking has occurred. State courts are free to find a taking at a less extreme level of regulation than the Supreme Court requires; certainly they are permitted so to find under their state constitutions.[88] However, if a court finds a taking, compensation, according to the Brennan formula, is required under the Constitution. Perhaps after decades of uncertainty, this is just where the Supreme Court wishes to leave the taking issue for now.

Notes

1. *See United States v. General Motors Corp.*, 323 U.S. 373 (1945).

2. *Loretto v. Teleprompter Manhattan CATV Corp.*, 458 U.S. 419 (1982).

3. *Pumpelly v. Green Bay Co.*, 80 U.S. (13 Wall.) 166 (1871).

4. *United States v. Welch*, 217 U.S. 333 (1910).

5. *Griggs v. Allegheny County*, 369 U.S. 84 (1962); *United States v. Causby*, 328 U.S. 256 (1946).

6. *See* Stoebuck, *The Property Right of Access versus the Power of Eminent Domain*, 47 Texas L. Rev. 733 (1969). The Supreme Court has hardly spoken to the loss-of-street-access question. *See Sauer v. City of New York*, 206 U.S. 536 (1907); *Chicago v. Taylor*, 125 U.S. 161 (1888) (Illinois law).

7. *See* Stoebuck, *Condemnation of Riparian Rights: A Species of Taking without Touching*, 30 La. L. Rev. 394 (1970). Supreme Court decisions on riparian rights, of which there are a number, are complicated and in some confusion because of the so-called navigation servitude doctrine (*id.* at 419–32).

8. *See* Stoebuck, *Condemnation by Nuisance: The Airport Cases in Retrospect and Prospect*, 71 Dick. L. Rev. 207 (1967). The Supreme Court has yet to speak to the question of whether there may be a condemnation by nuisance.

9. *First English Evangelical Lutheran Church v. County of Los Angeles*, 482 U.S. 304, 107 S. Ct. 2378 (1987).

10. 260 U.S. 393 (1922).

11. 123 U.S. 623 (1887).

12. *See Keystone Bituminous Coal Ass'n v. DeBenedictis*, 480 U.S. 407, 107 S. Ct. 1232, 1244 (1987); *First English Evangelical Lutheran Church v. County of Los Angeles*, 482 U.S. 304, 107 S. Ct. 2378 (1987); *Nollan v. California Coastal Comm'n*, 483 U.S. 825, 107 S. Ct. 3141 (1987).

13. 272 U.S. 365 (1926). *See also Hadacheck v. Sebastian*, 239 U.S. 394 (1951), which upheld a regulation causing an 87½ percent reduction in land value.

14. 272 U.S. 365, 384 (1951).

15. 369 U.S. 590 (1962).

16. *Id.* at 594.

17. 276 U.S. 272 (1928).

18. *Id.* at 279–80.

19. 357 U.S. 155 (1958).

20. 438 U.S. 104 (1978).

21. 39 N.Y.2d 587, 385 N.Y.S.2d 5, 350 N.E.2d 381 (1976).

22. 438 U.S. at 129.

23. 447 U.S. 255 (1980).

24. *Agins v. City of Tiburon*, 24 Cal. 3d 266, 157 Cal. Rptr. 372, 598 P.2d 25 (1979).

25. In particular, Justice Powell's opinion cited *Nectow v. City of Cambridge*, 277 U.S. 183 (1928), as a taking case. *Nectow* has always been recognized as a leading substantive due process decision.

26. 480 U.S. 470, 107 S. Ct. 1232 (1987).

27. *Id.* at 1236.

28. *Id.* at 1241.

29. *Id.* at 1242.

30. *Id.*

31. *Id.* at 1246.

32. *Id.* at 1249.

33. *Id.* at 1244.

34. *Id.* at 1245.

35. 483 U.S. 825, 107 U.S. 3141 (1987).

36. The basic framework of analysis for this section on takings and substantive due process was developed in Stoebuck, *San Diego Gas: Problems, Pitfalls, and a Better Way*, 25 J. Urban & Contemp. L. 3 (1983), and in Stoebuck, *Police Power, Takings, and Due Process*, 37 Wash. & Lee L. Rev. 1057 (1980).

37. 152 U.S. 133 (1894).

38. *Goldblatt v. Town of Hempstead*, 369 U.S. 590 (1962), called *Lawton v. Steele* "classic."

39. 277 U.S. 183 (1928).

40. *See especially* 480 U.S. 470, 107 S. Ct. 1232, 1242–45 (1987).

41. The present summary of the status of *Lawton v. Steele*'s "second part" is based particularly upon the much fuller development of that subject in Stoebuck, *San Diego Gas*, pp. 23–34. This article is primary authority for statements made here.

42. 198 U.S. 45 (1905).

43. 304 U.S. 144, 152 n. 4 (1938).

44. *See* Justice Powell's comment to that effect in his opinion for the Court in *Moore v. City of East Cleveland*, 431 U.S. 494 (1977), and Justice Marshall's dissent in *City of Cleburne v. Cleburne Living Center*, 473 U.S. 432, 105 S. Ct. 3249 (1985).

45. *See* Stoebuck, *San Diego Gas*, pp. 26–32.

46. 431 U.S. 494 (1977).

47. The distinction between *Moore* and *Village of Belle Terre v. Boraas*, 416 U.S. 1 (1974), is exceedingly fine. The Court's attempt to distinguish its then recent decision in *Belle Terre* is not wholly convincing.

48. 438 U.S. 104 (1978).

49. *See Penn Central Transp. Co. v. City of New York*, 42 N.Y. 2d 324, 397 N.Y.S. 2d 914 366 N.E. 2d 1271 (1977).

50. *See especially* 480 U.S. 470, 107 S. Ct. 1232, 1242 (1987).

51. *See especially* 482 U.S. 304, 107 S. Ct. 2378, 2384–85 (1987).

52. *Agins v. City of Tiburon*, 80 Cal. App. 3d 225, 145 Cal. Rptr. 476 (1978); *Eldridge v. City of Palo Alto*, 57 Cal. App. 3d 613, 129 Cal. Rptr. 575 (1976); *vacating Eldridge v. City of Palo Alto*, 51 Cal. App. 3d 726, 124 Cal. Rptr. 547 (1975); *Turner v. County of Del Norte*, 24 Cal. App. 3d 311, 101 Cal. Rptr. 93 (1972) (dictum). *Accord, Arastra Limited Partnership v. City of Palo Alto*, 401 F.Supp 962 (N.D. Cal. 1975), *vacated*, 417 F.Supp. 1125 (N.D. Cal. 1976); *Dahl v. City of Palo Alto*, 372 F.Supp. 647 (N.D. Cal. 1974).

53. 24 Cal. 3d 266, 157 Cal. Rptr. 372, 598 P.2d 25 (1979), *aff'd*, 477 U.S. 255 (1980).

54. 447 U.S. 255 (1980).

55. 450 U.S. 621 (1981).

56. *See First English Evangelical Lutheran Church v. County of Los Angeles*, 482 U.S. 304, 107 S. Ct. 2378 (1987), in which Chief Justice Rehnquist wrote the majority opinion upholding the compensation remedy.

57. *See Corrigan v. City of Scottsdale*, 149 Ariz. 538, 720 P.2d 513 (1986); *Schwartz v. City of Flint*, 426 Mich. 295, 395 N.W. 2d. 678 (1986); *Zinn v. State*, 112 Wis. 2d 417, 334 N.W. 2d 67 (1983); *Rippley v. City of Lincoln*, 330 N.W. 2d 505 (N.D. 1983); *Sheerr v. Township of Evesham*, 184 N.J. Super. 11, 445 A.2d 46 (1982); *Burrows v. City of Keene*, 432 A.2d 15 (N.H. 1981).

58. 473 U.S. 172 (1985).

59. *Id.* at 3122.

60. 477 U.S. 340, 106 S. Ct. 2561 (1986).

61. 24 Cal. 3d 266, 157 Cal. Rptr. 372, 598 P.2d 25 (1979).

62. 482 U.S. 304, 107 S. Ct. 2378 (1987).

63. *Id.* at 2384.

64. *Id.* at 2387.

65. *Id.* at 2395.

66. *Id.*

67. *Id.* at 2384–85.

68. *Id.* at 2391.

69. *Id.* at 2392.

70. *See Keystone Bituminous Coal Ass'n v. DeBenedictis*, 480 U.S. 470, 107 S. Ct. 1232, 1242–45 (1987).

71. *See First English Evangelical Lutheran Church v. County of Los Angeles*, 482 U.S. 304, 107 S. Ct. 2378, 2384–85 (1987).

72. *See PruneYard Shopping Center v. Robins*, 447 U.S. 74 (1980).

73. 123 U.S. 623 (1887).

74. 260 U.S. 393 (1922).

75. *See First English Evangelical Lutheran Church v. County of Los Angeles*, 482 U.S. 304, 107 S. Ct. 2378 (1987); *Keystone Bituminous Coal Ass'n v. DeBenedictis*, 480 U.S. 470, 107 S. Ct. 1232 (1987).

76. *See First English Evangelical Lutheran Church v. County of Los Angeles*, 482 U.S. 304, 107 S. Ct. 2378, 2386 (1987).

77. The statement in text is believed to be still correct, though narrowly so since two very recent decisions. In *First English Evangelical Lutheran Church v. County of Los Angeles*, 482 U.S. 304, 107 S. Ct. 2378 (1987), because the case came to the Court on the granting of a motion to strike a claim, the Court assumed the land-use regulation had caused a total deprivation of use and that it was a taking. *Nollan v. California Coastal Comm'n*, 483 U.S. 825, 107 S. Ct. 3141 (1987), where the Court did find a taking, did not involve precisely a regulation but the dedication of an easement which was required as a condition to the granting of a demolition-building permit. However, from the opinion it is not clear whether the Court sharply observed the regulation-dedication distinction.

78. 272 U.S. 365 (1926).

79. 369 U.S. 590 (1962).

80. *See, e.g.*, the leading zoning case of *Arverne Bay Constr. Co. v. Thatcher*, 278 N.Y. 222, 15 N.E.2d 587 (1938).

81. 450 U.S. 621 (1981).

82. *See MacDonald, Sommer & Frates v. Yolo County*, 477 U.S. 340, 106 S. Ct. 2561 (1986) (especially dissents by Chief Justice Burger and justices Powell, Rehnquist, and White); *Williamson County Regional Planning Comm'n v. Hamilton Bank*, 473 U.S. 172 (1985).

83. 482 U.S. 304, 107 S. Ct. 2378 (1987).

84. *First English* makes amply clear that the Brennan compensation formula is binding upon the states. The Court announced that California's decision in *Agins v. City of Tiburon*, 24 Cal.3d 266, 157 Cal. Rptr. 372, 598 P.2d 25 (1979), which had laid down the rule that compensation could not be awarded for a regulatory taking, was contrary to the Fifth Amendment.

85. 480 U.S. 470, 107 S. Ct. 1232 (1987).

86. 483 U.S. 825, 107 S. Ct. 3141 (1987).

87. *See Nectow v. City of Cambridge*, 277 U.S. 183 (1928). *See also San Diego Gas & Elec. Co. v. City of San Diego*, 450 U.S. 621, 656 n. 23 (1981) (Brennan, J., dissenting).

88. *See PruneYard Shopping Center v. Robins*, 447 U.S. 74 (1980).

VII.

CONFESSIONS, THE SELF-INCRIMINATION CLAUSE, AND DUE PROCESS

Ralph Rossum

18. "Self-Incrimination": The Original Intent

> Our forefathers, when they wrote this provision into the Fifth Amendment, had in mind a lot of history which has been largely forgotten today.
>
> Judge Calvert Magruder
> *Maffie v. United States*
> 209 F.2d 225, 237 (1954)

This chapter explores the original understanding of what we call today the self-incrimination clause of the Fifth Amendment. It is essential at the outset to observe, however, that the Fifth Amendment does not use the term "self-incrimination." Rather, it says: "No person . . . shall be compelled in any criminal case to be a witness against himself." Unlike certain other reformulations of constitutional provisions, such as "separation of church and state" for the establishment clause and "freedom of expression" for "the freedom of speech, or of the press," this reformulation is narrower than the constitutional guarantee itself. A person can be a witness against himself in ways that do not incriminate him. He can, in a criminal case, injure his civil interests or disgrace himself in the public mind. Thus, unlike their popular reformulation, the words of the amendment would seem to protect not only against self-incrimination but also against any disclosures that would expose one to civil liability or infamy. Likewise, since the words of the amendment refer not to the accused but rather to persons generally, they would also seem to apply not only to criminal defendants but also to witnesses and would seem to shield them against exposure to public obloquy. Thus, despite its title, this chapter focuses on the guarantee's original formulation as found in the Fifth Amendment, not on its widely used reformulation. It explores what those who included this guarantee in the Constitution originally intended for it to mean.

The Constitution drafted by the Federal Convention during the summer of 1787 was described by its principal architect, James Madison, as the complete remedy for the diseases of republican government. Marked as it was by the framers' new understanding of separation of powers and federalism and operating as it did over a large, differentiated, commercial republic, the Constitution was, Madison believed, the means of "secur[ing] the public good, and private rights, against the danger of a [tyrannical majority], and, at the same time, [of] preserv[ing] the spirit and form of popular government."[1] Madison, for one, saw no need for a bill of rights, as the Constitution itself was, by virtue of its institutional design, a full defense of liberty. Neither, apparently, did his fellow delegates. Over three months passed before it even occurred to anyone at the Federal Convention to suggest a bill of rights, and when George Mason proposed on September 12 (just five days before the Convention adjourned) that the Constitution be prefaced by a bill of rights, his motion was defeated by a vote of ten states to none.[2]

During the ratification struggle, however, pressure mounted to add a bill of rights which would include, among other provisions, the right against self-incrimination. In Pennsylvania, the second state to ratify the Constitution, the Anti-Federalist minority of the state ratifying convention criticized the Constitution for failing to include a bill of rights and argued that it should be ratified only on the condition that certain amendments be approved. Included in one of their conditional amendments was a prohibition "in all capital and criminal prosecutions" against compelling a man "to give evidence against himself."[3] (Interestingly, they proposed that this prohibition—as well as the requirements of notice and hearing, the right to be heard personally and by counsel, the rights to confrontation and compulsory process, and the right to a speedy trial by a jury of one's peers—be made applicable "as well in the federal courts as in those of the several States.") By a vote of 46 to 23, however, the Federalist-dominated convention rejected the minority's propositions and refused even to enter them into the journal of the convention or the reporter's account of the debates. Nonetheless, the minority succeeded in publishing their *Address and Reasons of Dissent* privately, which was reprinted from Boston to Richmond.

Massachusetts was the sixth state to ratify and the first to do so with recommended amendments. While one of its Anti-Federalist spokesmen, Abraham Holmes, criticized the Constitution for failing "to prevent Congress from passing laws which shall compel a man, who is accused or suspected of a crime, to furnish evidence against himself," only one criminal procedural amendment was in fact formally proposed—one that would require indictment by grand jury.[4] While every state thereafter recommended amendments to the Constitution, it was only the last four to ratify that included comprehensive bills of rights in their recommendations. Thus, Virginia recommended a bill of rights modeled closely after Virginia's Declaration of Rights of 1776; Section 8 in both documents stated in identical language that in no "capital or criminal prosecutions" can a man "be compelled to give evidence against himself."[5] New York followed and passed a proposed bill of rights that, inter alia, declared that "in all criminal prosecutions, the accused . . . should not be compelled to give evidence against himself."[6] Apparently greatly influenced by Virginia's actions, the New York convention recommended this provision notwithstanding its absence in New York State's own constitution.[7] North Carolina included among its proposed amendments a comprehensive bill of rights which was identical to that proposed by the Virginia Ratifying Convention.[8] And Rhode Island included in its proposed bill of rights a self-incrimination clause identical to that found in the Virginia Declaration of Rights; however, since its ratification came after the First Congress had already drafted the Bill of Rights, its recommendations were too late to be of any influence.[9]

The importance attached to the protection against self-incrimination by the state ratifying conventions paralleled the importance of this protection in the state constitutions themselves. With independence, all the states with the exception of the corporate colonies of Rhode Island and Connecticut framed new constitutions. Following Virginia's lead, seven of these eleven states annexed separate bills of rights to them. Every one of these states protected the right against self-incrimination and essentially in the language of Section 8 of Virginia's Declaration of Rights. In its entirety, that section declared:

> That in all capital or criminal prosecutions a man hath a right to demand the cause and nature of his accusation, to be confronted with the accusers and witnesses, to call for evidence in his favor, and to a speedy trial by an impartial jury of twelve men of his vicinage, without whose unanimous consent he cannot be found guilty, nor can he be compelled to give evidence against himself; that no man be deprived of his liberty, except by the law of the land or the judgment of his peers.[10]

The self-incrimination clause of Section 8 was quite narrow; read literally and in context, it applied only to a criminal defendant at his trial. Nonetheless, the six other states that also annexed separate bills of rights to their constitutions followed its basic formulation. Pennsylvania adopted Section 8 verbatim, save for adding to it the right to be represented by counsel.[11] Delaware made its self-incrimination clause an independent section rather than placing it among the enumerated rights of the criminally accused; moreover, by declaring "That no Man in the Courts of common Law ought to be compelled to give Evidence against himself," it extended the right to witnesses as well as defendants and to civil cases as well as criminal prosecutions.[12] Maryland likewise broadened the right to include witnesses and civil cases; it then qualified the right, however, by providing for exceptions to it "in such cases as have been usually practiced in this State, or may hereafter be directed by the Legislature." As a consequence, a man could be required to give evidence against himself if a pardon or grant of immunity against prosecution exempted him from the penal consequences of his disclosures. North Carolina followed Virginia's Section 8.[13] Massachusetts modified Section 8 slightly and provided that the accused should not be compelled "to accuse, or furnish evidence against himself," as did New Hampshire.[14]

Leonard W. Levy, in his definitive *Origins of the Fifth Amendment*, argues that George Mason, author of the Virginia Declaration of Rights, could not have said what he meant when he drafted the self-incrimination clause of Section 8. It seems to apply only to the criminally accused at his trial; yet, Levy asserts, if that is all it means, it is superfluous.[15] There was no need to protect the accused at his trial, for under the common law he was not permitted to give testimony, whether for or against himself. His interest in the case disqualified him from testifying on the theory that what he would say would be unreliable.[16] Permitting a defendant to testify in his own behalf was a nineteenth-century reform which began in the state courts in Maine in 1864 and in the federal courts by an act of Congress in 1878.[17] Since at the time of the Virginia Declaration of Rights a defendant could neither be placed on the stand by the prosecution nor even take the stand in his own defense, Levy concludes that Mason and his colleagues in the Virginia legislature "failed to say what they meant" when they drafted Section 8. He insists that they did not intend their words to be "anything but a sonorous declamation of the common-law right of long standing."[18]

This common-law right was *nemo tenetur seipsum accusare* (no one is bound to accuse himself). It was a legitimate defense which could be invoked by every individual,[19] not merely against the courts and judicial inquiries but against all of government; it protected witnesses no less than defendants and protected both equally from the threats of criminal liability, civil exposure, and public obloquy.

There are a number of problems with Levy's interpretation. The first is, of course, the obvious problem that Mason and his colleagues in Virginia—and the delegates to the other state assemblies who employed Section 8 as a model for their own self-incrimination clauses—simply did not say what Levy insists they meant, despite repeated opportunities on their part to do so. Levy wants the self-incrimination clauses to be understood as embodying "the still evolving common law of the matter rather than a rule of fixed meaning."[20] He wants them to be empty vessels into which judges are able to pour whatever new and changing meaning they wish. Since the states' self-incrimination clauses did not say what Levy wishes they had said, he is faced with a difficulty, which he attempts to remove by discrediting the credentials of the authors of these clauses. He accuses George Mason of "bad draftsmanship," "careless[ness]," and "thoughtlessness" and those who modeled their work on Virginia's Declaration of Rights of imitation "that verged on ineptness."[21]

Because it conflicts with his overall understanding of what the Bill of Rights and the role of the courts should be, Levy never takes seriously the possibility that Mason and the others meant exactly what they said. He argues that because under prevailing judicial practice criminal defendants were not permitted to testify, any interpretation of the self-incrimination clause of Section 8 that confined it to a defendant at his trial reduced it to a "meaningless gesture."[22] This argument, however, fails to consider what would happen if prevailing judicial practice were to be altered and if defendants were either permitted (as eventually they were) or required to testify. At that juncture, the clause is no longer meaningless. Levy does not consider that the clause may have been added by Mason not to end some current abuse but simply to provide a floor of constitutional protection above which the common law was free to operate but below which it could not go. He also fails to discuss why, consistent with his interpretation, Mason and the others would have wished to constitutionalize all of the common law on the subject, thereby precluding statutory refinements and modifications by the popular branches.

A second problem also exists with Levy's interpretation that the states intended their various self-incrimination clauses to incorporate the whole scope of the common-law concept that "no one is bound to accuse himself." Even when such states as Delaware and Maryland expanded upon Virginia's Section 8 and extended the protection against giving evidence against oneself to witnesses as well as to parties and in civil as well as criminal cases—thereby conforming more closely to Levy's interpretation—states such as North Carolina, Massachusetts, and New Hampshire[23] that drafted their bills of rights after Delaware and Maryland did clearly failed to appreciate that these expansions achieved more fully the ends Levy insists they all had, for they instead reverted to Virginia's phraseology.

This leads directly into a third problem. Even those states that expanded upon Virginia's Section 8 stopped far short of "decla[ming] the common-law right of long standing." Both Delaware and Maryland confined the right to courts; neither made it applicable against all of government. Moreover, in the case of Maryland, the right was expanded but also qualified so that a man could be required to give evidence against himself if pardoned or given a grant of immunity. This qualification clearly exposed the defendant or witness to civil liability and to public disgrace and reproach.

A fourth and final difficulty with Levy's interpretation of the states' self-incrimination clauses is that he fails to consider them in relation to the other provisions of Virginia's and the other states' bills of rights. Levy regards *nemo tenetur seipsum accusare* as the linchpin of all rights secured under the common law—in sixteenth- and seventeenth-century England, it was. However, under the constitutions of the states, the protection against self-incrimination was simply one right among many; it did not have the burden of supporting all the others.

Levy closely links the right not to give evidence against oneself to "freedom of speech and religious liberty. It was, in its origins, unquestionably the invention of those who were guilty of religious crimes such as heresy, schism, and nonconformity, and, later, of political crimes such as treason, seditious libel, and breach of parliamentary privilege." He declares that it was intended to be not so much a "protection of the guilty, or even the innocent, but a protection of freedom of expression, of political liberty, and of the right to worship as one pleased."[24] Levy is entirely correct to do so. The origins of the right can be traced to the struggles between Anglicanism and Puritanism, between Parliament and the crown, between freedom of conscience and suppression of heresy, between the accusatory and the inquisitional system of procedure, and between the common law and its canon and civil rivals.

These issues all came together in the use of the oath ex officio by prerogative courts—particularly by the ecclesiastical Court of High Commission. The High Commission, an instrument of the crown used to maintain religious uniformity under the Anglican establishment, relied upon the inquisitorial process of the canon law and the oath ex officio to achieve its results. Individuals suspected of nonconformist opinions would be summoned before it and required to take an oath to answer truthfully all interrogatories. If they refused to take the oath or, having taken it, refused thereafter to answer the questions asked, they could be sentenced for contempt and invited to Star Chamber proceedings. If they took the oath and then lied, they could be convicted of perjury. If they took the oath and responded truthfully, they risked implicating themselves and others of religious and political crimes. Common lawyers of the Puritan party seeking a means by which to extricate nonconformist victims of the High Commission from the bind in which they found themselves, began to develop the bold argument that the oath was unconstitutional because it violated Magna Charta. This argument received a positive reception from Sir Edward Coke, named chief justice of the Common Pleas in 1606, and his colleagues in the common-law courts, who issued a series of writs of prohibition staying the High Commission's proceedings based on precedents and inferences from Magna Charta.[25]

While the struggle between the common-law and canon-law systems continued and while the powers of the High Commission and the Star Chamber in fact reached their peak in the 1630s, dramatic changes were soon to occur as a result of Lilburne's trial and its aftermath. In his 1637 trial for printing and importing heretical and seditious books, John Lilburne, a Puritan agitator, refused to take the oath ex officio, declaring: "I am not willing to answer you to any more of these questions, because I see you go about by this examination to ensnare me. . . . Of any other matter that you have to accuse me of, I know it is warrantable by the law of God, and I think by the law of the land, that I may stand upon my just defence and not answer to your interrogatories." He was condemned by the Council of the Star Chamber to be whipped and pilloried for his "boldness in refusing to take a legal oath," and his sentence was executed in April 1638. However, when the Long Parliament, dominated by the Puritan party and common lawyers, came to power in 1640, it proceeded to condemn his sentence as "illegal and most unjust, against the liberty of the subject and the law of the land and Magna Carta," granted him £3,000 in reparations, abolished the Star Chamber and High Commission, and prohibited the ecclesiastical courts from administering any oath obliging one "to confess or accuse himself or herself of any crime."[26] The actions of the Long Parliament thus reinforced the opinions of Lord Coke and figured prominently in the eventual victory of freedom of conscience over suppression of heresy, of limited government over arbitrary rule, of the accusatorial over the inquisitional system of procedure, and of the common law over the civil and canon law.

Opposition to the oath ex officio ended in the common-law right of a person to refuse to give evidence against himself. Recognition of this right was crucial in securing political and religious liberty in England. Levy stresses this point and another as well: recognition of this right was also crucial in the emergence of those criminal procedural rights designed to ensure a fair trial for the criminally accused. As he says, *nemo tenetur seipsum accusare*

> harmonized with the principles that the accused was innocent until proved guilty and that the burden of proof was on the prosecution. It was related to the idea that a man's home should not be promiscuously broken into and rifled for evidence of his reading and writing. It was intimately connected to the belief that torture or any cruelty in forcing a man to expose his guilt was unfair and illegal. It was indirectly associated with the right to counsel and the right to have witnesses on behalf of the defendant, so that his lips could remain sealed against the government's questions or accusations.[27]

For Levy, the right of a person not to accuse himself is inextricably intertwined with the rights of political liberty, religious freedom, and criminal procedure. He perceives any narrowing of the common-law right against self-incrimination as an inevitable narrowing of these other rights as well. His insistence that the self-incrimination clauses of the states' bills of rights were genuine but inelegant attempts to incorporate the entire scope of the common-law right is therefore understandable. If the states' bills of rights were, in fact, devoid of any specific acknowledgment and protection of these other rights, Levy's interpretation might be defensible. However, the states' bills of rights were hardly deficient in this respect. Virginia's Declaration of Rights, for example, protected against unreasonable searches and seizures, preserved trial by jury, provided for the rights of confrontation and compulsory process, guaranteed freedom of the press, and ensured free exercise of religion.[28] These rights, and others, did not depend at all upon the right against self-incrimination but were independently affirmed and protected. Other states went further still in their bills of rights, with Pennsylvania providing for right to counsel,[29] Delaware protecting against excessive fines and bails and cruel or unusual punishments,[30] and New Hampshire proscribing double jeopardy.[31]

Levy fails to give adequate attention to the explicit protections in the states' bills of rights of these other rights—he forces these protections off to the wings by giving the center stage exclusively to the right against self-incrimination. As a consequence, he is led to misconstrue the intentions of Mason and his Virginia colleagues when they drafted Section 8 and of those in the other states who employed its phraseology in their own bills of rights. He is led to read into their self-incrimination clauses far more than they intended or than their words can sustain. What he does to those who drafted the states' bills of rights, he does as well to James Madison. He attributes to Madison the same intention he attributes to them, for he contends that Madison, when he proposed a series of amendments in the First Congress that eventually became the Bill of Rights, likewise sought, through the self-incrimination clause he included, to "incorporate" into the U. S. Constitution the "whole scope" of rights associated with the common-law maxim of *nemo tenetur seipsum accusare*.[32]

There is some evidence to support Levy's contention that Madison intended to draft a comprehensive self-incrimination clause—though not, it must be stressed, because he saw it as a means of protecting other rights. In his original proposal, he placed this right in a miscellaneous article that read: "No person shall be subject, except in cases of impeachment, to more than one punishment or trial for the same offence; nor shall be compelled to be a witness against himself; nor be deprived of life, liberty, or property, without due process of law; nor be obliged to relinquish his property, where it may be necessary for public use, without a just compensation."[33] Madison did not qualify the clause in any way—he did not place it in an amendment enumerating the procedural rights of the criminally accused and did not restrict it to criminal defendants, to criminal proceedings, or even to judicial proceedings. He seems to have intended it to apply to any governmental inquiry and to any incriminating or injurious testimony that would expose one to criminal liability, civil penalty, or public disgrace. Yet, and this contradicts Levy's contention, when Representative John Laurence from New York proposed in the Committee of the Whole that the clause "be confined to criminal cases" only and moved an amendment to that effect, it passed without objection, not even from Madison, despite the fact that the amended clause now excluded from its protection parties and witnesses in civil and equity suits as well as witnesses before nonjudicial governmental proceedings. Levy finds Madison's failure to object to this narrowing of the self-incrimination clause "bewildering,"[34] but it is not. It is understandable in the light of his understanding of the relationship to the Constitution of the Bill of Rights in general and of the self-incrimination clause in particular.

Madison was initially suspicious of any bill of rights—he viewed them as "parchment barriers" and remarked that "experience proves the inefficacy of a bill of rights on those occasions when its control is most needed."[35] He argued strenuously against any efforts to add a bill of rights so long as the Constitution remained unratified. As he wrote to George Eve in 1789: "I freely own that I have never seen in the Constitution as it now stands those dangers which have alarmed many respectable Citizens. Accordingly, whilst it remained unratified, and it was necessary to unite the States in some one plan, I opposed all previous alterations as calculated to throw the States into dangerous contentions, and to furnish the secret enemies of the Union with an opportunity of promoting its dissolution."[36]

Once the Constitution was ratified, however, Madison became the principal sponsor of the Bill of Rights. The answer to his apparent change of heart can be found in a letter he wrote to Thomas Jefferson: "I have never thought the omission (of a bill of rights) a material defect, nor been anxious to supply it even by *subsequent* amendment, for any other reason than that it is anxiously desired by others. I have favored it because I supposed it might be of use, and, if properly executed, could not be of disservice."[37]

In the same letter to Jefferson, Madison noted: "It is a melancholy reflection that liberty should be equally exposed to danger whether the Government have too much or too little power." He believed that the Constitution that the Federal Convention had drafted struck the proper balance. It was based on recent improvements in the "science of politics" that made it possible for the Convention to devise a government "of a more perfect structure"[38]—one marked by a new kind of separation of powers and federalism and operating over an extended republic.[39] That constitution would be the means of securing the liberties of the people not only from the tyrannical excesses of the majority—i.e., from too much governmental power—but also from the ravages of imbecility and anarchy—i.e., from too little governmental power. Madison also believed that a bill of rights, if properly framed, would not jeopardize but in fact could help preserve that balance. It could thwart attempts by the Anti-Federalists to revise the basic structure and powers of the new federal government. "We have in this way," he candidly confessed to the House of Representatives, "something to gain, and, if we proceed with caution, nothing to lose."[40]

Madison labored persistently on behalf of the Bill of Rights not because he thought it essential but because others did. In much the same way that the Constitution he helped to design channels and directs the self-interest and passions of the citizenry in directions that serve the public good and happiness, so, too, Madison channeled the public's desire for a bill of rights into a set of amendments that gave "satisfaction to the doubting part of our fellow-citizens" without "endangering any part of the Constitution, which is considered as essential to the existence of the Government by those who promoted its adoption."[41] On June 8, 1789, Madison addressed the House of Representatives and introduced a series of amendments that he proposed be adopted as the Bill of Rights. It is significant that in this crucial speech

Madison never argued on behalf of these amendments in his own name. He proposed these amendments, he said, so that "those who had been friendly to the adoption of this Constitution may have the opportunity of proving to those who were opposed to it that they were as sincerely devoted to liberty and a Republican Government, as those who charged them with wishing the adoption of this Constitution in order to lay the foundation of an aristocracy or despotism." Madison insisted that those who believed that the Constitution was deficient because it lacked a bill of rights were "mistaken," but, he continued, "there is a great body of the people falling under this description, who at present feel much inclined to join their support to the cause of Federalism, if they were satisfied on this one point." Accordingly, he urged the Congress "not to disregard their inclination, but, on principles of amity and moderation, conform to their wishes, and expressly declare the great rights of mankind secured under this Constitution." Madison's words here are of decisive importance; he saw the Bill of Rights as expressly declaring rights already secured under the Constitution, not as protecting rights that the Constitution somehow placed in jeopardy. A bill of rights would, he argued, reassure "a great number of our fellow-citizens who think these securities necessary." It would "satisfy the public mind that their liberties will be perpetual."[42]

The people wanted a bill of rights, and even though there was no need for it, Madison was prepared to give it to them—but only if it was "properly executed." Only then could there be "something to gain" and "nothing to lose." Thus, Madison proposed amendments that were "of such a nature as will not injure the Constitution."[43] He did not seek to alter the structure of the federal government (by imposing, for example, a council on the president, as many Anti-Federalists wanted). Neither did he seek to restrict its powers (by prohibiting standing armies, the granting of monopolies, or suspension of the writ of habeas corpus as Jefferson urged).[44] These measures would have undermined the constitutional scheme and sapped the vigor and capacity of the government. Rather, he sought measures that restated the principles of, and rights already secured by, the Constitution. Thus, the rights spelled out in what became the first eight amendments merely restated rights Madison believed were secured by separation of powers, federalism, and the operation of an extensive commercial republic.[45] Among these rights was the right of a person not to be a witness against himself. The structure of government established by the Constitution would ensure that the government would not violate this right; consequently, Madison did not object to Representative Laurence's amendment to narrow Madison's original language. All any language would do is declare—more or less comprehensively—this right already secured not by parchment barriers but rather by the Constitution's institutional design.

It should be noted that one of Madison's proposals did represent an attempt to improve substantially the original constitutional design; interestingly, however, it was directed against the states. Madison proposed that "[n]o State shall violate the equal rights of conscience, or the freedom of the press, or the trial by jury in criminal cases."[46] Madison described this amendment as "the most valuable amendment in the whole list."[47] It was rejected by the Senate, but it reflected Madison's long-standing belief that the principal threat to liberty was not the new federal government but the tyrannical excesses and incapacity of the state governments. The state governments were not yet improved by the framers' new science of politics; moreover, given their small size, they would never be able to duplicate fully the federal Constitution's "more perfect structure." It is for these reasons that Mason and the other authors of the states' bills of rights could not be as complaisant as Madison was concerning the actual wording of their self-incrimination clauses. These clauses were included in the states' bills of rights not merely to declare a right already secured by institutional contrivance but to secure that very right in the first place.

Madison saw nothing in the amendments he proposed "that can endanger the beauty of the Government in any one important feature, even in the eyes of its most sanguine admirers." Thus, he appealed to the members of Congress to embrace them, declaring that "if we can make the Constitution better in the opinion of those who are opposed to it, without weakening its frame, or abridging its usefulness in the judgment of those who are attached to it, we act the part of wise and liberal men to make such alterations as shall produce that effect."[48]

He also proposed that these amendments be incorporated into the body of the Constitution itself. He proposed, for example, that the miscellaneous article containing the self-incrimination clause be placed at the end of Article I, Section 9. He declared that "there is a neatness and propriety in incorporating the amendments into the Constitution itself; in that case the system will remain uniform and entire; it will certainly be more simple, when the amendments are interwoven into those parts to which they naturally belong."[49] The Constitution and the Bill of Rights had, for him, the same objective—the latter merely declared the rights that the former secured. He saw no need to introduce a distinction between them, which he feared placing the amendments elsewhere would do. Madison, however, lost on this point. Roger Sherman argued that the amendments should be added at the end of the Constitution—to attempt to "interweave" these amendments into the Constitution itself would, he warned, "be destructive of the whole fabric. We might as well endeavor to mix brass, iron, and clay."[50] George Clymer agreed; he argued that the amendments should be kept separate so that the Constitution "would remain a monument to justify those who made it; by a comparison, the world would discover the perfection of the original, and the superfluity of the amendments."[51]

The Congress ultimately agreed with Sherman and Clymer, but the results have not been what Clymer predicted. By placing the amendments at the tail of the Constitution, a significance has been given to the Bill of Rights in general and to the self-incrimination clause in particular that neither Madison nor the other members of the First Congress intended. Moreover, Madison's understanding of the relationship of the Constitution to the Bill of Rights has been obscured. Madison regarded the Constitution as the fundamental protector of the public's rights and liberties—securing them from both the threats of too much governmental power (tyranny) and too little (imbecility and anarchy). He also viewed the Bill of Rights as expressly declaring the rights that the Constitution secured. In contemporary constitutional law, however, the Bill of Rights tail has come to wag the constitutional dog. Clymer's reason for appending the amendments at the end of the Constitution has been turned on its head, with the original Constitution now regarded as a "superfluity"—when not an actual threat—to the protection of rights and with "perfection" now ascribed to the Bill of Rights—or more specifically, to activist judges interpreting its provisions.

To understand the original intention of those who drafted the Fifth Amendment's self-incrimination clause, one must clearly address the common-law maxim of *nemo tenetur seipsum accusare* and the great constitutional struggles in sixteenth- and seventeenth-century English history that gave it birth. One must also focus on constitution making in the states and on the dynamics of the process by which the U.S. Constitution was ratified. Most importantly of all, however, one must appreciate the framers' understanding of the relationship of the entire Bill of Rights to the Constitution.

In an address at the dedication of the Bill of Rights Room at the U.S. Subtreasury Building in New York City on August 9, 1964, Justice John Marshall Harlan observed that "we are accustomed to speak of the Bill of Rights . . . as the principal guarantee of personal liberty. Yet it would surely be shallow not to recognize that the structure of our political system accounts no less for the free society we have." The framers, he continued, "staked their faith that liberty would prosper in the new nation not primarily upon declaration of individual rights but upon the kind of government the Union was to have." One cannot understand the original intention of the self-incrimination clause until one understands what Justice Harlan meant by these words.

Notes

1. J. Cooke, ed., *The Federalist* (Middletown, Conn.: Wesleyan Univ. Press, 1961), No. 10, p. 61.

2. M. Farrand, ed., *The Records of the Federal Convention of 1787*, 4 vols. (New Haven: Yale Univ. Press, 1911–37), 2:587–88.

3. J. McMaster and F. Stone, eds., *Pennsylvania and the Federal Constitution, 1787–1788* (Philadelphia, 1888), p. 461.

4. J. Elliot, ed., *The Debates in the Several State Conventions on the Adoption of the Federal Constitution as Recommended by the General Convention in Philadelphia in 1787*, 5 vols. (Philadelphia: Lippincott, 1863), 2:111, 177.

5. Ibid., 3:658.

6. Ibid., 1:328.

7. L. Levy, *The Origins of the Fifth Amendment: The Right against Self-Incrimination* (New York: Oxford Univ. Press, 1968), p. 420. One should be hesitant to attribute hypocrisy to the New York delegates because they sought protections against the federal government that they did not seek to secure against their own state government. Under the common law, New York had a long tradition of providing for the protection against "self-incrimination," while, as the Anti-Federalist delegate Thomas Tredwell observed, "we are ignorant whether . . . [the proceedings of the federal courts] shall be according to the common, civil, the Jewish, or Turkish law" (Elliot, *Debates* 2:400).

8. Elliot *Debates* 4:243.

9. Ibid., 1:334.

10. F. Thorpe, ed., *The Federal and State Constitutions, Colonial Charters, and Other Organic Laws of the States, Territories, and Colonies Now or Heretofore Forming the United States of America*, 7 vols. (Washington, D.C.: GPO, 1909), 7:3813.

11. Ibid., 5:3083.

12. P. Kurland and R. Lerner, eds., *The Founders' Constitution*, 5 vols. (Chicago: Univ. of Chicago Press, 1987), 5:6.

13. Thorpe, *The Federal and State Constitutions* 3:1688, 5:2787.

14. Ibid., 3:1891, 4:2455. Vermont, technically an independent republic from 1776 until its entry into the union in 1791, also annexed a separate bill of rights to its constitution and included in it language modeled after Section 8 of Virginia's Declaration of Rights (ibid., 6:3741).

15. Levy, *Origins of the Fifth Amendment*, p. 407.

16. L. Levy, *Right against Self-Incrimination*, in *Encyclopedia of the American Constitution*, ed. L. Levy, K. Karst, and D. Mahoney, 4 vols. (New York: Macmillan, 1986), 3:1570. A defendant was permitted, however, to tell his story unsworn in a final statement to the court.

17. Ibid.

18. Levy, *Origins of the Fifth Amendment*, pp. 407, 409.

19. It was a "fighting right"; unless invoked, it offered no protection.

20. Levy, *Right against Self-Incrimination*, p. 1574.

21. Levy, *Origins of the Fifth Amendment*, pp. 407, 409, 411. It must be owned that Levy does at one point conclude that "for all their faults, the state bill of rights adopted before the federal Bill of Rights were achievements of the first magnitude compared to anything in the past, on either side of the Atlantic" (ibid., p. 412).

22. Levy, *Right against Self-Incrimination*, p. 1570.

23. To these states, the independent republic of Vermont can also be added. *See* note 14, *supra*.

24. Levy, *Right against Self-Incrimination*, p. 1572.

25. *See* J. Wigmore, *The Privilege against Self-Crimination: Its History*, 15 Harv. L. Rev. 610, 621–24 (1902).

26. Ibid., p. 625, and Levy, *Right against Self-Incrimination*, p. 1571.

27. Levy, *Right against Self-Incrimination*, p. 1572.

28. Thorpe, *Federal and State Constitutions* 7:3812–14.

29. Ibid., 5:3082–84.

30. Kurland and Lerner, *The Founders' Constitution* 5:5–6.

31. Thorpe, *Federal and State Constitutions* 4:2453–2457.

32. Levy, *Origins of the Fifth Amendment*, p. 423.

33. Speech in the House of Representatives, June 8, 1789, in *Annals of Congress*, vol. 1 (Washington, D.C.: Gales & Seaton, 1834), p. 434.

34. Levy, *Origins of the Fifth Amendment*, p. 425.

35. Madison to Thomas Jefferson, Oct. 17, 1788, in G. Hunt, ed., *The Writings of James Madison*, 9 vols. (New York: Putnam, 1900–1910), 5:271–75.

36. Madison to George Eve, Jan. 2, 1789, ibid., p. 319.

37. Madison to Thomas Jefferson, Oct. 17, 1788, ibid., pp. 271–72.

38. *The Federalist*, No. 9, p. 51.

39. *See* R. Rossum and G. Tarr, *American Constitutional Law: Cases and Interpretation*, 2d ed. (New York: St. Martin's, 1987), pp. 9–18, for an account of how the framers' new understanding of separation of powers, federalism, and the extended republic contributed to their solution of the rival defects of republican government: majority tyranny on the one hand and democratic imbecility on the other.

40. Speech in the House of Representatives, June 8, 1789, in *Annals of Congress* 1:450.

41. Ibid., pp. 449, 450.

42. Ibid., pp. 449, 450.

43. Ibid., p. 449.

44. Jefferson to James Madison, Dec. 20, 1787, in J. Boyd et al., eds., *The Papers of Thomas Jefferson* (Princeton, N.J.: Princeton Univ. Press, 1950—), 12:440.

45. The same argument can also be made for what became the Ninth and Tenth Amendments. The Ninth Amendment merely stated that other rights in addition to those already specifically enumerated were also protected by these same institutional arrangements. The Tenth Amendment met the objection Madison himself had raised to a bill of rights that its presence would suggest that the federal government was one of reserved rather than delegated powers and, again, was wholly consistent with the original constitutional scheme.

46. Speech in the House of Representatives, June 8, 1789, in *Annals of Congress* 1:452.

47. Speech in the House of Representatives, Aug. 17, 1789, ibid., p. 784.

48. Speech in the House of Representatives, June 8, 1789, ibid., p. 459.

49. Speech in the House of Representatives, Aug. 13, 1789, ibid., p. 736. *See* Madison to Alexander White, Aug. 24, 1789, in Hunt, *The Writings of Madison* 5:418: "It became an unavoidable sacrifice to a few who knew their concurrence to be necessary, to the dispatch if not the success of the business, to give up the form by which the amendments when ratified would have fallen into the body of the Constitution, in favor of the project of adding them by way of appendix to it. It is already apparent I think that some ambiguities will be produced

by this change, as the question will often arise and sometimes be not easily solved, how far the original text is or is not necessarily superceded, by the supplemental act."

50. Speech in the House of Representatives, Aug. 13, 1789, in *Annals of Congress* 1:734–35.

51. Ibid., p. 737.

STEPHEN J. SCHULHOFER

19. Reconsidering *Miranda* and the Fifth Amendment

Few decisions of the Warren Court have attracted as much attention and as much controversy as its 1966 ruling in *Miranda v. Arizona.*[1] *Miranda* relied upon the Fifth Amendment privilege against compulsory self-incrimination to impose limits on custodial police interrogation. The Court was vilified for "handcuffing the police" and for "favoring the criminal forces over the peace forces" in this country. Recently the *Miranda* decision has become the focus of renewed debate. Critics argue not only that the *Miranda* decision was legally incorrect and socially unwise but also that the Court stepped far outside its proper adjudicatory function and engaged in an illegitimate act of legislation. These claims of illegitimacy are fueled by the elaborate, rulelike character of *Miranda* requirements. Attorney General Edwin Meese, for example, attacked *Miranda* for "its prescription of a detailed, code-like set of rules for police conduct—the sort of rules more properly devised by the legislative or executive branches of government."[2] Because the Court stepped beyond the appropriate limits of the judicial function, these critics assert, *Miranda* should be overruled.

Talk about overruling *Miranda* ignores the fact that *Miranda* contains not just one holding but a series of complex and important interpretations of the Fifth Amendment. One could subdivide them in various ways, but three important and conceptually distinct steps were involved in the Court's decision. First, the Court held that informal pressure to speak—that is, pressure not backed by legal process or any formal sanction—can constitute compulsion within the meaning of the Fifth Amendment. Second, *Miranda* held that this element of informal compulsion can be satisfied by any questioning of a suspect in custody, no matter how short the period of questioning may be. Third, *Miranda* held that a series of precisely specified warnings is required to dispel the compelling pressure of custodial police interrogation. The third step, the series of particularized warnings, poses some obvious problems of legitimacy. But the core of *Miranda* is located in the first two steps. I want to begin by considering these first two holdings in depth.

The Court's first holding was that compulsion, within the meaning of the Fifth Amendment, can include informal pressure to speak. Note first that there is not the slightest doubt about the legitimacy of the Court's settling this question by adjudication. The Fifth Amendment says that no person shall be "compelled" to be a witness against himself. According to one school of thought, this word referred only to formal legal compulsion. It is a normal act of judicial interpretation for a court to consider the meaning of the word "compelled" and to decide whether it extends to informal pressures.

A much more important problem is to determine whether the Court's decision on this point was correct on the merits. In *Bram v. United States*,[3] decided in 1897, the Court had relied on the Fifth Amendment to suppress a statement made in the course of a brief custodial interrogation, but *Bram* was repudiated shortly afterwards, and for the next sixty years the Court frequently and consistently held that the Fifth Amendment privilege was inapplicable to police interrogation. Because the suspect was under no legal obligation to speak, the argument ran, there was no compulsion in the relevant Fifth Amendment sense of the term. Confessions obtained by "breaking the suspect's will" were called involuntary and held inadmissible under the due process clause, which was conceived as a distinct and more flexible constitutional restraint.

In rejecting this view and holding the Fifth Amendment applicable to informal compulsion, *Miranda* undoubtedly departed from a long line of precedent. Nonetheless, this first step in the *Miranda* analysis was the appropriate interpretation of the constitutional command. Although the early history of the privilege is clouded and ambiguous, it seems clear that the privilege was intended primarily to bar pretrial examination by magistrates, the only form of pretrial interrogation known at the time. The reasons for concern about that form of interrogation under formal process apply with even greater force to questioning under compelling informal pressures. As Professor Edmund Morgan showed almost forty years ago, "The function which the police have assumed in interrogating the accused is exactly that of the early committing magistrates, and the opportunities for imposition and abuse are fraught with much greater danger. . . . Investigation by the police is not judicial, but when it consists of an examination of the accused, it is quite as much an official proceeding as the early English preliminary examination before a magistrate, and it has none of the safeguards of a judicial proceeding."[4] Other leading experts on the law of evidence concur in Morgan's assessment. Thus, Professor John McNaughton, writing almost thirty years ago, noted that virtually all the policies underlying the Fifth Amendment privilege "apply with full force to insure that police in informal interrogations not have the right to compel self-incriminatory answers. . . . Answers should not be compelled by police."[5]

Not only do history and policy suggest the implausibility of restricting the Fifth Amendment to purely formal pressures, but the Court's decisions concerning activities other than police interrogation make clear that no tenable line can be drawn between formal and informal compulsion. In fact,

Miranda's first holding was strongly foreshadowed by *Griffin v. California*,[6] in which the Court held that prosecutorial comment upon a defendant's failure to testify at trial violated the privilege by making its assertion costly. Of course, any compulsion involved in *Griffin* did not flow from formal process or any legal obligation to speak. The objection to the comment was that it increased (indirectly) the chances of conviction. To be sure, the state lent its approval (indirectly) to that consequence by declining to bar this kind of jury argument. But what gave *Griffin* its point were the real-world consequences of the prosecutorial behavior, not the very attenuated sense in which the state had brought to bear either formal process or any official sanction. If a requirement of formal compulsion remained at all after *Griffin*, it surely had been stretched paper thin.

I submit that after all the textual, historical, and practical arguments are pursued, for the Court to have held that compulsion within the meaning of the Fifth Amendment requires the use of formal legal process and does not extend to other state-created pressures to speak would have been not only formalistic but analytically untenable.

Miranda's second major step was the holding that any custodial interrogation, even one police question, involves enough informal pressure to constitute compulsion within the meaning of the Fifth Amendment. Again, notice that there is no doubt about the legitimacy of settling this issue by judicial interpretation. The question of what pressures constitute compulsion unavoidably confronts the Court in cases involving loss of a job, a moment of silence, the menacing look of a person in authority, and countless other situations. There is nothing inherently improper or even unusual about deciding such questions in the course of adjudication. It is worth mentioning here that even Justice White, in the course of his sometimes bitter dissent in *Miranda*, emphasized that it was appropriate and indeed inevitable for the Court to address and decide this kind of question.

On the merits, is the Court's second holding sound? This issue admits of much more doubt than the first one. One difficulty here arises from the emphatically per se character of the Court's holding. But before addressing this problem, we must first be clear about the standard that would apply, in the absence of a per se rule, to determine the kinds of interrogation that are compelling within the meaning of the Fifth Amendment. The concerns that gave rise to the Fifth Amendment focused on Star Chamber inquisition tactics such as the rack and thumbscrew, but compulsion cannot be conceived so narrowly. Fifth Amendment compulsion can perhaps be identified more naturally with the due process standard of voluntariness under the Fourteenth Amendment. By this approach a person would be compelled for Fifth Amendment purposes when his will is overborne by pressure, whether physical or psychological. This conception of the Fifth Amendment test appears to be a common one, and some of the Court's recent decisions make explicit the connection between compulsion and the old due process standard. In *Oregon v. Elstad*, for example, the Court said that an actual violation of the Fifth Amendment (as distinguished from a mere presumption of compulsion) occurs only when there is "physical violence or other deliberate means calculated to break the suspect's will."[7]

If this is indeed what Fifth Amendment compulsion requires, then *Miranda*'s second step involved a seemingly superfluous change in the wording of the governing test, followed by a glaring non sequitur in the application of that test to the facts. The Court replaced involuntariness (the due process touchstone) with compulsion (an identically defined Fifth Amendment criterion) but then found compulsion in circumstances that countless decisions had found consistent with voluntariness, circumstances which no conceivable stretch of the imagination could view as breaking the suspect's will. Thus, if compulsion is properly equated with the due process prohibition against breaking the will, *Miranda*'s second holding not only departs from numerous precedents but appears unjustified and even incomprehensible in terms of the applicable constitutional standard.

The question, however, is whether Fifth Amendment compulsion can indeed be equated with the due process rule against the use of "deliberate means to break the suspect's will." It is readily understandable that terms so similar in ordinary usage, "involuntary" and "compelled," can get confused with one another, even by lawyers. The equation of compulsion with breaking the will is taken for granted by many commentators and can be supported by incidental language in several recent Supreme Court decisions. Nonetheless, this concept of compulsion involves a fundamental misunderstanding of settled Fifth Amendment principles and, if taken seriously, would make nonsense of the privilege against self-incrimination.

A threat to discharge a public employee, for example, will render any resulting statement "compelled." Yet no one could suggest that such a threat "breaks the will" of the employee; he simply faces the unpleasant choice between silence and his job. Similarly, under the *Griffin* case previously discussed, a comment on the defendant's silence at trial is held impermissible because it makes exercise of the privilege costly; no one could suggest that the prospect of this disadvantage breaks the defendant's will. In some quarters, these applications of the Fifth Amendment privilege remain controversial; if breaking the will is the appropriate standard, then these rules can be dismissed as wrong. But consider one clearly uncontroversial application—a contempt statute subjecting a defendant to fine or six month's imprisonment for refusal to testify. If the Fifth Amendment means anything, it means that a witness properly claiming a potential for self-incrimination cannot be punished under such a statute; the fine or imprisonment constitutes clear compulsion in the Fifth Amendment sense. Even a $100 fine for silence is undeniably improper. Yet no one would suggest that such a penalty "breaks the will," and we regularly impose much more severe sanctions upon recalcitrant witnesses not in a position to claim the privilege.

The upshot is that Fifth Amendment compulsion cannot be limited to breaking the will. At the other extreme, it cannot be satisfied by any inconvenience resulting from failure to testify. Disabilities or pressures that have the effect of discouraging silence but are not imposed for that reason may be permissible, though *Griffin* and the employment discharge cases suggest that any such generalization may be overbroad. In any event, pressure imposed for the purpose of discouraging silence constitutes prohibited "compulsion" whether or not it "breaks the will." This is the clear teaching of the Fifth Amendment's core applications to compulsion by legal process, and this presumably uncontroversial principle is probably sufficient for purposes of bringing police interrogation into a Fifth Amendment focus. The policy served by the amendment is not limited to preventing inhuman degradation or breaking the will but extends to all governmental efforts intended to pressure an unwilling individual to assist as a witness in his own prosecution.

For this perspective, *Miranda* is not directly in conflict with the numerous due process voluntariness cases decided before 1966. *Miranda* does overrule the implicit holding of these cases that the Fifth Amendment is inapplicable to informal compulsion; but with respect to the degree of pressure sufficient to constitute compulsion, these cases are simply silent. In holding in various contexts that police did not "break the will" of various suspects, the Court did not hold that the police had avoided pressuring individuals to speak. Indeed, it was quite evident in every one of the voluntariness cases that the police had deployed significant pressure for the purpose of getting recalcitrant suspects to talk. Under the due process approach, such conduct was considered permissible if it was not so extreme as to "shock the conscience." Even express promises of benefit, designed to overcome silence, had been allowed if they did not break the suspect's will.[8]

The one pre-*Miranda* precedent that is relevant to determining the degree of interrogation pressure permissible for Fifth Amendment purposes is *Bram*. There, in the course of a brief interview the interrogator had suggested, "If you had an accomplice, you should say so, and not have the blame of this horrible crime on your own shoulders."[9] The Court found this statement sufficient by itself to establish a Fifth Amendment violation. The Court held that the statement "might well have been understood as holding out an encouragement that by [naming an accomplice] he might at least obtain a mitigation of the punishment for the crime. . . . 'the law cannot measure the force of the influence used or decide upon its effect upon the mind of the prisoner, and, therefore, excludes the declaration if any degree of influence has been exerted.'"[10]

It is this Fifth Amendment standard, never considered controversial in the context of formal pressures, that underlies the *Miranda* Court's second holding. Custodial interrogation brings psychological pressure to bear for the specific purpose of overcoming the suspect's resistance to talk, and it is therefore inherently compelling within the meaning of the Fifth Amendment.

But even if the *Miranda* decision is supportable so far, further difficulty arises from the per se character of the Court's holding. The problem is that the Court in *Miranda* held that an officer's very first question involved compulsion. Defenders of *Miranda* would note that even the initial question could have a compelling character under some circumstances. Imagine a young suspect in a stabbing case, arrested late at night, transported to a police station far from his home, and then brought to an interrogation room at one or two o'clock in the morning. Imagine that the suspect has no knowledge of his rights, that he believes the police are entitled to demand answers from him, and that a powerfully built, square-jawed investigator enters the room, glares hostilely at him, and asks, "Where did you get that knife?" The defendant's answer, following just these few seconds of interrogation, can plausibly be seen as compelled by fear of mistreatment, or more simply by expectations of unrelenting interrogation, or more simply yet by the utterly natural assumption that he is obliged to answer—that when the interrogator, a person in authority, asks a question, the official is legally entitled to a response.

But, of course, an example of this kind is inadequate to support *Miranda*'s crucial second step. The Court did not just hold that a brief period of interrogation can involve compulsion. The Court held that the initial question, in the briefest possible period of interrogation, necessarily will involve compulsion. To test the propriety of the Court's holding we have to go further and imagine whether there is any case in which the defendant's first answer would not be compelled. What if the defendant is not young and inexperienced, the interrogator is not powerfully built and square-jawed, and the suspect actually knows his rights. What if the suspect, a middle-aged professor who spends his life teaching the subject of criminal procedure, knows perfectly well that he is entitled to remain silent and that no formal penalties can be imposed upon him for refusing to talk. Is it plausible to say that even this knowledgeable and sophisticated suspect has been compelled to speak, compelled by the very first question?

In thinking about this issue, it is useful to remember that under any realistic assessment of the circumstances, even the sophisticated, knowledgeable suspect faces considerable state-created pressure to talk. If he knew the law, he would know that the police cannot subject him to thirty-six hours of uninterrupted interrogation, that they have to give him reasonable breaks, and that they can't hold him for two or three weeks without permitting him to make a phone call. But the sophisticated suspect, precisely because he would know the law, would have other grounds for anxiety. He would know that under the due process approach, the police were explicitly permitted to deploy considerable pressure and that they could subject him to extended periods of interrogation, day and night. He would also know that if he didn't talk, his silence would count against him. In fact, it is still true today that post-arrest silence can be used for impeachment purposes if the detained suspect has not received *Miranda* warnings.[11] Our pre-*Miranda* law professor would know that refusal to respond to police questions would subject him to a penalty in the event of trial, and police interrogators were trained to get this point across to any suspect sufficiently knowledgeable to attempt to invoke his rights.[12]

Beyond these problems is a more basic difficulty. Even if our sophisticated law professor knew his rights and all their ramifications, he would need to know whether the police know his rights. Indeed, if he had had even the most remote acquaintance with realistic studies of the law-in-action, he would know that custodial interrogation occurs outside the view of any disinterested observer and that the police who conduct it are a close-knit, supportive community. He would know that for perfectly understandable reasons, conscientious officers, intent on solving brutal crimes, sometimes lost their tempers and that instances of physical abuse, though not the norm, often surfaced in the case reports. I submit that even the sophisticated law professor, if he found himself suspected of crime, would be under considerable pressure to cooperate with the police, to try to get them on his side by telling what he knew or what he thought he could safely disclose, rather than standing confidently on his right to remain silent. So it is by no means implausible for the Court to have said that any questioning, even a few seconds of custodial interrogation, is inherently compelling.

One might argue, however, that my examples still do not go quite far enough. One might say that my examples still depend on introducing elements of fear, anxiety, and so on. What justification is there for the Court's holding that such elements necessarily must be present in every custodial police interrogation? Surely one can imagine a case in which the professor knows his rights but is ignorant of the existence of abuses, in which he tells all in response to the first question, not because of any sense of pressure but simply because he really wants the truth to come out. Because such a case conceivably could exist, and because the Court's per se rule would require finding a violation of the Fifth Amendment even in that case, some critics conclude that the Court's second holding is prophylactic, that the Court did not simply interpret the meaning of compulsion but rather replaced the no-compulsion rule with a different and much broader prohibition. Professor Joseph Grano, for example, suggests that the Court could properly have adopted a presumption of coercion in cases of custodial police interrogation but that principles of judicial legitimacy require that any such presumption be rebuttable, that the state remain free to produce evidence showing an absence of compulsion in the particular case.[13] By making the presumption irrebuttable, Grano argues, the Court in effect rewrote the Constitution and established a different substantive standard for determining when confessions are admissible.

In evaluating this kind of challenge to the use of conclusive presumptions and related forms of prophylactic rules, we must remember first that these aids to adjudication are a pervasive feature of judicial decision making in nearly all fields of law. In the antitrust area, for example, we have rules that conclusively presume that certain kinds of agreements constitute unreasonable restraints of trade.[14] In constitutional law, we have prophylactic rules that conclusively presume abridgment of freedom of speech from the mere possibility that certain kinds of statutes will deter the exercise of first amendment rights.[15] The Court has held that the required separation of church and state is violated in some contexts by the mere risk that state-sponsored programs can be used for religious indoctrination, even when the risk has never materialized.[16] In areas closer to the subject at hand, the Court has held, in a ruling rarely if ever questioned by critics of *Miranda*, that an indigent's need for appointed counsel in a felony prosecution will be conclusively presumed, regardless of evidence about his own maturity, background, and education.[17] Similarly, under the due process voluntariness test preferred by critics of *Miranda*, the Court held as early as 1944 that a few extreme forms of police pressure would trigger a conclusive presumption of involuntariness, regardless of the suspect's maturity, stamina, or physical condition.[18] While in recent years the Supreme Court has tended to prefer constitutional tests that turn on all the circumstances, the contemporary Court not only has reaffirmed the prophylactic rules just mentioned but also, in response to its own perceptions of the problems of adjudication, has created some new presumptions that amount to reverse prophylactic rules. The Court has ruled, for example, that a police officer's search of the rear seat of a car, incident to the arrest of an occupant, will be conclusively presumed reasonable, regardless of evidence that in the particular case the suspect may have been handcuffed or far removed from the car and regardless of evidence about whether any other legitimate basis to search was actually present.[19]

One must look closely at these prophylactic rules in order to see whether they are appropriate for the context in which the Court has applied them. But there is nothing inherently improper or illegitimate about a rule just because it embodies a conclusive presumption.

Against this background, we can now return to the criticism of *Miranda*'s holding that any police interrogation of a suspect in custody is inherently compelling. The proper question to ask here is whether an irrebuttable presumption is an appropriate adjudicatory tool in this particular context. This is a question with a history, and the *Miranda* Court came to it after decades of experience with case-by-case assessment of the totality of the circumstances. Whatever logic may suggest about the rigidity of conclusive presumptions, experience had shown that the flexible due process test created problems not only for suspects facing interrogation but for the courts and for the police themselves.[20] Although the shift from due process to the Fifth Amendment approach greatly reduced the permissible degree of pressure and ostensibly eliminated the basis for balancing the need for a confession against the suspect's right to silence, other difficulties of the due process approach remained. The voluntariness test had left lower courts without adequate adjudicatory standards and thus created disproportionate demands for case-by-case review in the Supreme Court and in lower federal courts hearing habeas corpus petitions. This situation in turn generated costly friction between state and federal courts. The problems of judicial review also meant that in practice, intense interrogation pressures and unseemly forms of manipulation were inadequately controlled. The case-by-case approach even failed to prevent, and in subtle ways actually encouraged, illegal physical brutality. As Professor Wigmore perceptively noted, "The exercise of the power to extract answers begets a forgetfulness of the just limitations of that power. The simple and peaceful process of questioning breeds a readiness to resort to bullying and to physical force and torture."[21] Finally, and most significantly, case-by-case review left the police themselves without adequate guidance. Faced with a reticent suspect who might finally be starting to crack, were the police supposed to give him some rest or to keep up the tension and pressure? The due process approach in effect told the police to do both.

To put these problems in perspective, we have to think about how often, after meticulous evaluation of all the circumstances, a genuine absence of compulsion is likely to be found. Police interviews are tension-filled matters under the best of circumstances. Such interviews in the absence of counsel, in the heavily police-dominated circumstances of the custodial environment, are filled with tension in spades. And the tensions are created for the very purpose of overcoming the suspect's unwillingness to talk. Indeed Professor Grano himself candidly recognizes as much (in another article): "[D]istinctions can be made in terms of perceived offensiveness among tactics designed to increase the suspect's anxiety. The point remains, however, that all such tactics, whether or not 'offensive,' are intended to increase the pressure—the compulsion—on the suspect to confess. The 'inherent compulsion' of custodial interrogation would be present if an untrained, uniformed officer questioned the suspect in the stationhouse receiving room."[22] The notion that an isolated, unwarned suspect facing custodial interrogation is not under great state-created pressures to talk can only be the flimsiest of fictions.

Are such pressures sufficient to constitute compulsion? *Griffin v. California*, previously mentioned, is suggestive here as well. Justice Stewart, dissenting in *Griffin*, complained that the Court had "stretche[d] the concept of compulsion beyond all reasonable bounds."[23] A few critical commentators agree. But *Griffin*, decided over only two dissents, remains good law and has been reaffirmed and extended by lopsided majorities in the Burger Court.[24] If a comment on silence generates excessive pressure for the defendant to speak at trial (even though the comment adds only marginally to inferences the jury will draw anyway), can we plausibly say that a police officer's demand for information, addressed to the isolated suspect in custody, does not involve excessive pressure? Since an adverse inference from silence also lies in the background for refusing the police officer's demand, a finding of compulsion here has to be an easy a fortiori case so long as *Griffin* remains on the books.

Finally, add to the analysis the fact that naive, emotionally unstable suspects outnumber, by massive proportions, the few well-educated, psychologically sophisticated suspects who already know their rights and that reliable evidence about what actually occurs in the interrogation room can come only from the police themselves. Under all these circumstances, is it any wonder that the Court, exasperated after years of case-by-case adjudication, finally did adopt a prophylactic rule? I submit that a conclusive presumption of compulsion is in fact the only responsible reaction to the problems of the voluntariness test, to the rarity of cases in which significantly compelling pressures are truly absent, and to the overwhelming adjudicatory costs of case-by-case decision making in this area. Indeed, in any ranking of the litigation problems that properly demand some form of prophylactic rule, the problem of determining compulsion in the context of incommunicado custodial police interrogation wins the prize hands down.

To summarize, then, one has to say that *Miranda*'s second step, like its first, not only was an unquestionably legitimate act of adjudication, but was, on the merits, a sound and well-supported interpretation of the Fifth Amendment.

This brings us to *Miranda*'s third step, its panoply of "code-like rules," with the requirement that the suspect receive a complex, fourfold warning of his rights. Here the complaints about judicial legislation seem to have some force. But before dwelling on those complaints, we should first focus on the effect of *Miranda*'s detailed package of rules. Do the warnings handcuff the police? In fact, we can now see that their function is precisely the opposite. If the Court was correct in the first two steps of its analysis, and I submit that it was, then far from handcuffing the police, the warnings work to liberate the police. *Miranda*'s much maligned rules actually work to sanitize the interrogation process and to permit the officer to continue questioning his isolated suspect, the very process that the Court's first two holdings find, most persuasively, to be a violation of the Fifth Amendment.

The Court's theory with respect to the warnings was that they could "dispel" the inherently compelling atmosphere of police interrogation. But there is great room for doubt about that theory. Indeed, the *Miranda* opinion itself lays out the reasons why that theory is hopelessly unrealistic:

> The circumstances surrounding in-custody interrogation can operate very quickly to overbear the will of one merely made aware of his

> privilege by his interrogators. . . . A once-stated warning, delivered by those who will conduct the interrogation, cannot itself suffice to [assure an unfettered choice between silence and speech] among those who most require knowledge of their rights. . . . Even preliminary advice given to the accused by his own attorney can be swiftly overcome by the secret interrogation process. *Cf. Escobedo v. Illinois*, 378 U.S. 478, 485, n.5.[25]

This, from the *Miranda* Court itself, shows how dubious is the notion that police-initiated warnings can dispel the compulsion. But in any event the fundamental point for present purposes is that *Miranda*'s detailed warnings, whether justified or not, unquestionably serve, and were from the outset designed to serve, the function of permitting custodial police interrogation to continue. As Justice Rehnquist recognized, writing for the Court in *Michigan v. Tucker*, the purpose of the warnings is "to help police officers conduct interrogations without facing a continued risk that valuable evidence would be lost."[26]

The *Miranda* decision, in short, was a compromise. As things have turned out, *Miranda* accomplished a great deal at surprisingly little cost. *Miranda* provides reaffirmation of our symbolic commitment to limited government, it provides a measure of reassurance and dignity to arrested suspects, and by reducing the permissible level of interrogation pressure, it gives suspects questioned in the station house at least some of the safeguards that we extend to suspects questioned in public in formal legal proceedings. At the same time, *Miranda* has posed surprisingly few barriers to effective law enforcement. In fact, nearly every empirical study undertaken since *Miranda* shows that clearance rates and confession rates have been essentially unaffected by the decision.[27] If there are any new data to the contrary, one would expect that police departments, which have had all the statistics in hand for years, would have made the information public long ago. Chief Justice Burger, commenting on his unwillingness to overrule *Miranda*, undoubtedly offered a sound assessment on this point when he wrote that "[t]he meaning of *Miranda* has become reasonably clear and law enforcement practices have adjusted to its strictures."[28]

Whether *Miranda* represents the best possible compromise is a different and more difficult question. Those who do not like *Miranda*'s code-like rules and would strip them from the opinion will be left with the much more stringent principle that the isolated suspect in custody cannot be questioned at all. Those who would replace the *Miranda* code with a different set of procedures must be prepared to justify those procedures not on the basis of law enforcement needs but on the basis of the written constitutional mandate. That will inevitably mean more rather than less protection for the suspect.

For those who would remain faithful to the Constitution, the important question is not, Which compromise? Rather, it is the question of why compromise is justified at all. Undoubtedly there are times when the Fifth Amendment is hard to live with. But even if interrogation under the *Miranda* rules had posed practical problems (and it has not), the Court could not simply decide to give the green light to police use of compelling pressure. The Court cannot amend the Fifth Amendment and should not be asked to do so. From that perspective, the proper critique of *Miranda* is not that it handcuffs the police but that it did not go quite far enough. *Miranda*'s safeguards deserve to be strengthened, not overruled.

Notes

1. *Miranda v. Arizona*, 384 U.S. 436 (1966).

2. Meese, "Square Miranda Rights with Reason," *Wall Street Journal*, June 13, 1986, p. 22.

3. *Bram v. United States*, 168 U.S. 532 (1897).

4. Morgan, *The Privilege against Self-Incrimination*, 34 Minn. L. Rev. 1, 27 (1949).

5. McNaughton, *The Privilege against Self-Incrimination*, in *Police Power and Individual Freedom*, ed. C. Sowle (Chicago: Aldine, 1962), pp. 223, 237–38.

6. *Griffin v. California*, 380 U.S. 609 (1965).

7. *Oregon v. Elstad*, 105 S. Ct. 1285, 1295 (1985); *United States v. Washington*, 431 U.S. 181, 188 (1977).

8. *Stein v. New York*, 346 U.S. 156 (1953). This remains the rule today in cases in which only the due process voluntariness test applies. *Miller v. Fenton*, 796 F.2d 598, 608–9 (3d Cir., 1986).

9. 168 U.S., at 539.

10. *Id.* at 565, quoting 3 *Russell on Crimes* (6th ed.) at 478.

11. *Fletcher v. Weir*, 455 U.S. 603 (1982).

12. Before *Miranda*, a well-known manual for police interrogators advised the following response to the suspect who invokes his right to silence: "Joe, you have the right to remain silent. That's your privilege. . . . But let me ask you this. Suppose you were in my shoes and I were in yours . . . and I told you, 'I don't want to answer any of your questions.' You'd think I had something to hide" (F. Inbau and J. Reid, *Criminal Interrogation and Confessions* [Baltimore: Williams and Williams, 1962], p. 111).

13. Grano, *Prophylactic Rules in Criminal Procedure: A Question of Article III Legitimacy*, 80 Nw. U.L. Rev. 100 (1985).

14. *E.g., U.S. v. Sacony-Vacuum Oil Co.*, 310 U.S. 150 (1940).

15. *E.g., Gooding v. Wilson*, 405 U.S. 518 (1972).

16. *E.g., Grand Rapids School Dist. v. Ball*, 473 U.S. 373 (1985); *Aguilar v. Felton*, 473 U.S. 402 (1985). *See* generally *Lemon v. Kurtzman*, 403 U.S. 602, 619 (1971) (Burger, C.J.).

17. *Gideon v. Wainwright*, 372 U.S. 335 (1963).

18. *Ashcraft v. Tennessee*, 322 U.S. 143 (1944).

19. *New York v. Belton*, 453 U.S. 454 (1981).

20. For discussion, *see* Schulhofer, *Confessions and the Court*, 79 Mich. L. Rev. 865, 867–77 (1981).

21. J. Wigmore, *Evidence*, 3d ed. (Boston: Little, Brown, 1940), 8:309.

22. Grano, *Selling the Idea to Tell the Truth*, 84 Mich. L. Rev. 662, 674 (1986).

23. 380 U.S., at 620.

24. *E.g.*, *Carter v. Kentucky*, 450 U.S. 288 (1981).

25. 384 U.S., at 469–70.

26. *Michigan v. Tucker*, 417 U.S. 433, 443 (1974).

27. *See* Schulhofer, *Reconsidering Miranda*, 54 U. Chi. L. Rev. 435, 455–60 (1987).

28. *Rhode Island v. Innis*, 446 U.S. 291, 304 (1980) (Burger, C.J., concurring).

VIII.

CRUEL AND UNUSUAL PUNISHMENT

Raoul Berger

20. The Cruel and Unusual Punishments Clause

Few chapters in the annals of the Supreme Court more clearly exemplify its ongoing revision of the Constitution than its curb on death penalties under the aegis of the cruel and unusual punishments clause of the Eighth Amendment. A leading critic of death penalties, Hugo Bedau, wrote that "[u]ntil fifteen years ago, save for a few mavericks, no one gave any credence to the possibility of ending the death penalty by judicial interpretation of constitutional law."[1] "Save for a few eccentrics and visionaries," he remarked, the death penalty was "taken for granted by all men . . . as a bulwark of social order."[2]

A prominent activist member of the Texas faculty, who also is opposed to death penalties, Sanford Levinson, considers it a "devastating problem" that "both the Fifth and Eighth Amendments specifically acknowledge the possibility of a death penalty. They require only that due process of law be followed before a person can be deprived of life."[3] The very same framers who adopted the Bill of Rights enacted the act of April 30, 1790,[4] which made a number of offenses punishable by death, implying that capital punishment was untouched by the Bill of Rights. In his 1791 Lectures, Justice James Wilson, second only to Madison as an architect of the Constitution, said, "The crime of willful and premeditated murder is and has been punished by death . . . this is unquestionably a crime for which it ought to be inflicted."[5]

The phrase "cruel and unusual punishments" had been borrowed from the English Bill of Rights of 1689. In the 100-year interval before the adoption of our 1789 Bill of Rights, England's "Bloody Code" punished more than 250 offenses with death.[6] The death penalty was also a familiar sanction of colonial law. Thus the phrase "cruel and unusual punishment" had acquired a familiar content. It has long been a canon of construction that when the draftsmen employed common-law terms, the common-law "definitions," said Justice Story, "are necessarily included as much as if they stood in the text" of the Constitution.[7] Whatever may be the meaning of "cruel and unusual," one thing it unquestionably did not mean was the death penalty unless it was accompanied by cruelties.[8]

To escape from this history the Court fabricated a doctrine that the Eighth Amendment must draw its meaning from society's "evolving sense of decency."[9] Death, said Justice Brennan, "stands condemned as fatally offensive to human dignity"[10] and is therefore a "cruel and unusual punishment." No such doctrine obtained in England or the colonies. Blackstone wrote that some punishments "fix a *lasting stigma* on the offender by slitting the nostrils, or branding on the hand or cheek," other punishments "consist principally in their *ignominy* . . . such as whipping . . . the pillory, the stocks, and ducking stool."[11] Lord Camden, who had been chief justice of the Court of Common Pleas, referred in 1791 to the punishments that might be inflicted such as "loss of ears, whipping, or any other *disgrace*."[12] Infliction of ignominy and disgrace are at war with a solicitude for "human dignity." Such punishments were common in colonial law[13] and continued after the Revolution. The federal act of April 30, 1790, made whipping part of the punishment for "stealing or falsifying records."[14] A 1791 Massachusetts statute provided that highway robbers should be burned on the forehead or hand;[15] and as late as 1823 Nathan Dane noted the punishments of "pillory, branding or whipping."[16] The punishments of "whipping and standing in the pillory" were abolished by the federal act of February 28, 1839.[17] These acts prove that the Founders contemplated the continuing availability of common-law punishments, and that these were left in place by the Bill of Rights.

But, it may be argued, does not the "evolving sense of human dignity" call for a reinterpretation—actually for a revision—of the cruel and unusual clause? That "evolving sense" is a figment of the imagination. Recently the *New York Times* reported that "opponents of the death penalty, acknowledging the overwhelming public, political and legal support for the death penalty, are . . . saying that they expect it to be a long time before public attitudes can be changed."[18] Justice Brennan recently acknowledged that his "is an interpretation to which a majority of my fellow Justices—not to mention, it would seem, a majority of my fellow countrymen—does not subscribe. On this issue, the death penalty, I hope to embody a community striving for human dignity for all, though perhaps not yet arrived."[19] Baldly stated, he stubbornly insists on cramming his morals down the throats of a people who do not share his views.

Assume, contrary to the fact, that there is an "evolving sense of human dignity" at play which does not authorize the Court to revise the Constitution. Hamilton, the foremost proponent of judicial review, wrote in *The Federalist* No. 78: "Until the people have, by some solemn and authoritative act [amendment] annulled or changed the established form, it is binding upon themselves collectively, as well as individually; and no presumption, or even knowledge of their sentiments, can warrant their representatives in a departure from it, prior to such an act."[20]

Activists rely on *Weems v. United States* for recognition of a "proportionality principle in the Eighth Amendment,"[21] i.e., the punishment must be proportioned to the crime. No such principle existed in the post-1689 period. The theft of a few shillings was punishable by death, and Lord

Ellenborough inveighed in 1813 against repeal of that statute.[22] It was repealed by statute in 1827,[23] not set aside by a court. With good reason did Chief Justice Edward White dissent in *Weems*, being joined by Justice Holmes: "That in England it was nowhere deemed that any theory of proportional punishment was suggested by the bill of rights or that a protest was thereby intended against severity of punishments, speaking generally, is demonstrated by the practice which persisted in England as to punishing crime from the time of the bill of rights to the time of the American Revolution."[24]

My own study of English history convinced me that White cannot be controverted. When the Court stated in *Solem v. Helms* that "when the Framers of the Eighth Amendment adopted the language of the English Bill of Rights, they also adopted the principle of proportionality,"[25] it correctly reiterated the long-held view that the content of the Constitution's common-law terms is to be sought in English practice. But its proportionality statement is ahistorical. The framers were far from adopting a principle of proportionality; that is evidenced by the act of April 30, 1790, which made murder, forgery, and counterfeiting of public securities punishable by death.[26] Capital punishment for forgery is by no means proportional to death for murder.

A word as to the impact of the Fourteenth Amendment. Stephen Gillers of New York University, who vigorously criticizes my views, concedes that the proposition that the amendment "was not intended to invalidate capital punishment" is "uncontested."[27] Let me supply a few reasons. Hamilton had assured the New York Ratification Convention that "the States have certain independent powers, in which their laws are supreme, for example, in making and executing laws concerning the punishment of certain crimes, such as murder, theft, etc., the States cannot be controlled."[28] State jurisdiction, Madison wrote in *The Federalist*, was to be "inviolable,"[29] as was nailed down by the Tenth Amendment. James Wilson, chairman of the House Judiciary Committee, assured the framers gathered in the Thirty-ninth Congress that "[w]e are not making a general criminal code for the States."[30] Louis Henkin concluded that the amendment "did not withdraw from the states the principal administration of criminal justice."[31] Surveying the postamendment scene, Justice Miller rejected a construction which would subject states "to the control of Congress, in the exercise of powers universally conceded to them" in the absence of "language which expresses such a purpose too clearly to admit of doubt." And he said, "Our statesmen have still believed that the existence of the states with power for domestic and local government . . . was essential to the working of our complex form of government."[32]

It remains to comment on the Court's insistence that juries must observe judicially prefabricated standards of sentencing, whereby it has created a logjam on death row, with postponement of the execution of undoubted murderers for ten years or more. Consider first issues of fact. Very early Lord Matthew Hale stated that "of such matters of fact they are the only competent judges . . . if the judge's opinion must rule the matter of fact, the trial by jury would be useless."[33] An issue of fact, wrote our own Justice James Wilson, a leading framer, "belongs exclusively to the jury"; it is the juror's "exclusive province to determine."[34] An English commentator, William Forsyth, wrote in 1852: "The law throws upon them the whole responsibility of ascertaining facts in dispute, and the judge does not attempt to interfere with the exercise of their unfettered discretion in this respect."[35] Such discretion is manifestly curtailed by prefabricated standards for the exercise of their discretion, as Chief Justice Thomas Cooley, renowned commentator on the Constitution, declared: "[T]he jury must be left to weigh the evidence . . . by their own tests. They cannot properly be furnished for this purpose with balances that leave them no discretion."[36] For, as repeatedly appears in the records, the matter was left to the "conscience" of the jury, and their verdict, wrote Lord Bacon, "was considered as a kind of gospel."[37]

Pure questions of law, on the other hand, were for the court; but a problem was posed by mixed questions of law and fact, which general verdicts in criminal cases involved.[38] On this issue the English cases were divided. They were canvassed at great length in *Sparf & Hansen v. United States* (1895),[39] apparently a case of first impression. The majority, led by Justice Harlan, espoused the view of Lord Mansfield's school, that here too judges were judges of the law. Opposed to that view was that of Lord Camden's camp, whose position was defended by Justice Horace Gray in a seventy-two-page dissent. Gray, I heard at first hand from Professor Felix Frankfurter, was one of the ablest historians on the bench; and Mark deWolfe Howe, after commenting on Gray's dissent, observed: "There can be no question but that he made important contributions to knowledge of the legal past in a number of his judicial opinions."[40] Wherever I went behind Gray's statements, I found them solidly anchored. Gray examined opinions of the jury rights school, Bacon, Hale, Vaughan, Somers, Holt, and Camden,[41] adding the earl of Chatham (the elder Pitt), Charles James Fox, the younger Pitt, and Thomas Erskine.[42] He considered the opposition, Kelynge, Scroggs, Jeffreys, Raymond, Hardwick, and Mansfield.[43]

That conflict of opinion led in no small part to Fox's Libel Act in 1791, which declared that the views of the Camden school were the law. Lord Loughborough, for many years chief justice of Common Pleas, said during the debate: "[T]he bill was a declaratory bill . . . to declare and explain what was understood to be . . . the law of the land."[44] The bill itself was entitled "An act to remove doubts respecting the functions of juries in cases of libel."[45] Loughborough stated that as chief justice he "had ever deemed it his duty in cases of libel, to state the law as it bore on the facts, and to refer the combined considerations to the jury," whose "decision was final."[46] So too, Lord Camden, who likewise had served as chief justice of Common Pleas, declared during the debates that "the judge should interpose nothing but his advice; if he attempted to control them, there was an end to trial by jury. Indeed there was no legal power to control them."[47] The jury, he affirmed, "had an undoubted right to form their verdict themselves according to their consciences . . . if it were otherwise, the first principle of the law of England would be defeated or overthrown."[48] Those views were adopted in the "declaratory" Fox's Libel Act;[49] and they were considered to be the prevailing rule in criminal cases.[50]

Justice Gray also examined the early American cases and concluded that in this country, "from the time of its settlement until more than half a century after the Declaration of Independence, the law as to the rights of juries, as generally understood and put in practice, was more in accord with" the Camden than the Mansfield school.[51] So much is conceded by Justice Harlan: "The language of some judges and statesmen in the early history of the country, implying that the jury were entitled to disregard the law as expounded by the courts, is perhaps to be explained by the fact that 'in many of the States the arbitrary temper of colonial judges, holding office from the Crown, had made independence of the jury in law as well as in fact of popular importance.'"[52]

Constraints of space permit only a few illustrations. John Adams, writing in 1771, stated, "whenever a general verdict is found, it assuredly determines both the fact and the law. . . . [I]t is an absurdity to suppose that the law would oblige them to find a verdict according to the direction of the courts, against their own opinion, judgment and conscience." It is the juror's duty "to find the verdict according to his own best understanding, judgment and conscience, though in direct opposition to the direction of the court."[53] Few judges have been as thoroughly grounded in constitutional history as James Kent. In 1804, in a New York case that evenly divided the court,[54] he expressed

> a firm conviction that this court is not bound by the decisions of Lord Raymond and his successors. . . . Those opinions are repugnant to more ancient authorities which had given the jury the power, and with it the right, to judge of the law and fact, when they were blended by the issue, and which rendered their decisions in criminal cases, final and conclusive. . . . Some of the judges treated the [Raymond] doctrine as erroneous, and the Parliament at last, declared it an innovation [in Fox's Libel Act], by restoring the trial by jury in cases of libel, to that ancient vigor and independence, by which it had grown so precious to the nation, as the guardians of liberty and life, against the power of the court, the vindictive persecution of the prosecutor, and the oppression of the government.[55]

Other early pronouncements set forth by Gray richly confirm his conclusion that for forty years after adoption of the Constitution this was the prevailing view.[56] When Justice Harlan summarily brushed such early statements aside, he overlooked that such contemporaneous constructions carry greater weight than later views to the contrary.[57]

For the Founders, trial by jury was a central pillar of the society they sought to erect, and as Kent shows, it was considered a shield from judicial oppression exemplified by Scroggs and Jeffreys. Like other state constitutions, that of North Carolina of 1776 declared that "the ancient mode of trial by jury ought to remain sacred and inviolable."[58] James Iredell referred in the North Carolina Ratification Convention to trial by jury as "that noble palladium of liberty."[59] In marked contrast to the two express provisions for trial by jury in the Constitution, no mention was made of judicial review—a suspect innovation which on several occasions had spurred movements in the fledgling states for removal of judges.[60] Of this the framers were aware, so that Hamilton was constrained to assure the ratifiers that of the three branches, "the judiciary is next to nothing."[61] It borders on the inconceivable to attribute to the Founders an intention to leave their "noble palladium" at the mercy of judges whom, according to James Wilson, they had regarded with "aversion and distrust."[62] To the contrary, the "Federal Farmer" assured the ratifiers that "by holding the jury's right to return a general verdict in all cases sacred," "[w]e secure to the people at large their just and rightful control in the judicial department."[63]

Chief Justice Burger correctly stated on behalf of a plurality of four in 1978 that "[t]he Court has never intimated prior to *Furman* that discretion in sentencing offended the Constitution."[64] In 1931 the Ninth Circuit Court of Appeals said that "[t]he discretion of the jury is unlimited and unrestricted."[65] Certainly the cruel and unusual clause does not demand a departure from that practice. It was concerned solely with the nature of the punishment, not with the process whereby the sentence is reached.[66] History, I submit, confirms the Court's judgment in *McGautha v. California* that it is "quite impossible to say that committing to the untrammelled discretion of the jury to pronounce life or death in capital cases is offensive to anything in the Constitution."[67] The fact is that judicial interference with that discretion violated the jury's constitutional prerogative. For, as a common-law attribute of trial by jury, such discretion, like the right to challenge jurors, is embodied in the Constitution and therefore immune from judicial governance.

Notes

1. H. Bedau, *The Courts, the Constitution, and Capital Punishment* (Lexington, Mass.: Lexington Books, 1977), p. 118.

2. Ibid., 12. Chief Justice Burger stated, "In the 181 years since the enactment of the Eighth Amendment, not a single decision of this Court has cast the slightest shadow of a doubt on the constitutionality of capital punishment" (*Furman v. Georgia*, 408 U.S. 238, 280 [1972], dissenting opinion).

3. S. Levinson, "Wrong but Legal," *Nation*, Feb. 26, 1983, p. 248.

4. 1 Stat. 117 (1st Cong., 2d Sess. 1790).

5. R. McCloskey, ed., *The Works of James Wilson*, 2 vols. (Cambridge: Belknap, 1967), 2:661.

6. *McGautha v. California*, 402 U.S. 183, 281 (1971).

7. *United States v. Smith*, 18 U.S. (5 Wheat.) 153, 160 (1820). *See also Ex parte Grossman*, 267 U.S. 87, 108–9 (1925). For additional citations, *see* R. Berger, *Death Penalties: The Supreme Court's Obstacle Course* (Cambridge: Harvard Univ. Press, 1982), pp. 61–65.

8. In the Virginia Ratification Convention, Patrick Henry said that our ancestors "would not admit tortures or cruel and barbarous punishments" (J. Elliot, *The Debates in the Several State Conventions on the Adoption of the Federal Constitution*, 2d ed. [Washington, D.C.: U.S. Congress, 1836], 3:447). Edmund Pendleton likewise pointed out that "cruel punishment, such as torture . . . shocking to human nature" had been discarded (ibid., p. 294).

9. *Trop v. Dulles*, 356 U.S. 116–22 (1958), plurality opinion.

10. *Furman v. Georgia*, 408 U.S. 238, 305 (1972).

11. W. Blackstone, *Commentaries on the Laws of England* (London: A. Strahan, 1765–69), 4:377.

12. Quoted by Justice Horace Gray in *Sparf & Hansen v. United States*, 156 U.S. 51, 136 (1895), dissenting opinion.

13. For citations, *see* Berger, *Death Penalties*, p. 118 n. 129.

14. *Supra* note 4.

15. R. Perry, *Sources of Our Liberties* (Chicago: American Bar Foundation, 1978), p. 237.

16. 2 *Dane's Abridgement* 569, 570, quoted in *Ex parte Wilson*, 114 U.S. 417, 428 (1885).

17. Chap. 36, sec. 5; 5 Stat. 322.

18. *New York Times*, Aug. 19, 1985, p. A-13. "Capital punishment is very popular all over the country" (Sherrill, "Death Row on Trial," ibid., Nov. 13, 1983 [Magazine], p. 80).

19. *The Great Debates: Interpreting Our Written Constitution* (Washington, D.C.: Federalist Society, 1986), pp. 11, 24.

20. *The Federalist* No. 78, p. 509 (Mod. Lib. ed. 1937).

21. *Weems v. United States*, 217 U.S. 349 (1910); Gillers, *Berger Redux*, 92 Yale L.J. 731, 742 (1983).

22. Quoted *Furman v. Georgia*, 408 U.S. 238, 246 n. 9 (1972).

23. *Id.*

24. *Weems v. United States*, 217 U.S. 349, 393 (1910).

25. *Solem v. Helms*, 103 S. Ct. 3001, 3007 (1983).

26. 1 Stat. 113–15 (1st Cong., 2d Sess.).

27. Gillers, *Berger Redux*, p. 740.

28. Elliot, *Debates* 2:362.

29. *The Federalist*, No. 39, p. 249 (Mod. Lib. ed. 1937).

30. *Cong. Globe* 1120 (39th Cong., 1st Sess., 1866).

31. Henkin, "Voice of a Modern Federalism" in *Frankfurter: The Judge*, ed. Wallace Mendelson (New York: Reynal, 1964), p. 99.

32. *Slaughter-House Cases*, 83 U.S. (16 Wall.) 36, 78, 82 (1872).

33. 2 M. Hale, *Pleas of the Crown* 312, 313, quoted by Justice Gray, 156 U.S. at 118–19.

34. McCloskey, *Works of Wilson* 2:540, quoted by Justice Harlan, 156 U.S. at 69.

35. W. Forsyth, *History of Trial by Jury* 262, 282 (1852), quoted by Justice Harlan, 156 U.S. at 88.

36. *People v. Garbutt*, 17 Mich. 9, 27–28 (1868).

37. Quoted by Justice Gray, 156 U.S. at 117.

38. McCloskey, *Works of Wilson* 2:540.

39. *Sparf & Hansen v. U.S.*, 156 U.S. 51, 64 (1895).

40. M. Howe, *Justice Oliver Wendell Holmes: The Proving Years* (Cambridge: Belknap, 1963), p. 116. He "was quite properly conceived to be a legal historian of exceptional competence" (ibid.).

41. 156 U.S. at 142.

42. *Id.* at 131 (Chatham), 133 (Fox and Pitt), 133 (Erskine).

43. *Id.* at 142.

44. 29 *Parliamentary History of England* 731 (1817). Camden "did not apprehend that the bill had a tendency to alter the law, but merely to remove doubts that ought never to have been entertained" (ibid., p. 732, quoted by Justice Gray, 156 U.S. at 137).

45. Quoted by Justice Gray, 156 U.S. at 134.

46. Quoted *id.* at 137.

47. 29 *Parliamentary History of England*, 731.

48. Ibid., p. 1536.

49. Justice Willes had dissented in *Dean of St. Asaph's Case*, 21 Howell State Trials 847, on the ground that the jury had the right on the general issue to decide the law. Subsequently Lord Blackburn observed in the House of Lords that the Fox Libel Act had adopted Willes's view (*Capital and Counties Bank v. Henty*, 4 App. Case. 741, 755, quoted by Justice Gray, 156 U.S. at 133–34).

50. In the course of the debate, Charles James Fox said it was known "that it was the province of the jury to judge of the law and fact; and this was the case not of murder only, but of felony, high treason and of every other criminal indictment" (29 *Parliamentary History of England* 564, 565, 597, quoted by Justice Gray, 156 U.S. at 136).

In *The King v. Burdett*, 4 B & Ad. 95, 131, 132, Justice Best said of the Fox Libel Act, "Judges are in express terms directed to lay down the law as in other cases. In all cases the jury may find a general verdict; they do so in cases of murder and treason, but there the judge tells them what is the law, though they may find against him . . . and this is plain from the words of the statute." (*id.* at 131, 132, quoted by Justice Gray, 156 U.S. 141). On appeal Chief Justice Abbott said that the statute was intended "to declare that they should be at liberty to exercise their own judgement upon the whole matter in issue, after receiving there upon the opinion and directions of the judge" (*id.* at 145–47, 183, 184, quoted by Justice Gray, 156 U.S. at 141).

51. 156 U.S. at 142.

52. 156 U.S. at 89.

53. J. Adams, *Works* (Freeport, N.Y.: Books for Libraries Press, 1969), 21: 253–55, quoted by Justice Gray, 156 U.S. at 143–44.

54. *People v. Croswell*, 3 Johns Cas. 337 (1804).

55. *Id.* at 375, 376, quoted by Justice Gray, 156 U.S. at 149. So too, in the Trial of John Fries for treason (1800), Justice Chase stated, "It is the duty of the court . . . in all criminal cases to state their opinion of the law arising on the facts; but the jury are to decide . . . in all criminal cases, both the law and the facts, on their consideration of the whole case" (quoted by Justice Gray, 156 U.S. at 162).

Earlier, in *Georgia v. Brailsford*, 3 Dall. 1 (1794), Chief Justice Jay stated to the jury, "it is presumed that juries are the best judges of the facts; it is, on the other hand, presumable that the court are the best judges of law. But still both objects are lawfully within your power of decision" (*id.* at 3–5). Among the other justices present were two framers, Wilson and Paterson, and a ratifier, Iredell (156 U.S. at 156).

56. 156 U.S. at 168.

57. Justice William Johnson referred in 1827 to the "presumption that the contemporaries of the Constitution have claim to our deference . . . because they had the best opportunity of informing themselves of the understanding of the framers of the Constitution, and of the sense put upon it by the people when it was adopted by them" (*Ogden v. Saunders*, 25 U.S. [12 Wheat.] 212, 190). *See also Stuart v. Laird*, 5 U.S. (1 Cranch) 299, 309 (1803). Justice Gray was aware of the weight attached to this rule (156 U.S. at 169), if Justice Harlan was not.

58. Article XIV in B. Poore, *The Federal and State Constitutions, Colonial Charters, and Other Organic Law of the United States* (1877), 2 vols. (New York: B. Franklin, 1973), p. 1410.

59. Elliot, *Debates* 4:148; *see* Hamilton's tribute in *The Federalist*, No. 83, p. 543 (Mod. Lib. ed. 1937).

60. R. Berger, *Congress v. the Supreme Court* (Cambridge: Harvard Univ. Press, 1969), pp. 38–43.

61. *The Federalist*, No. 78, p. 504 (Mod. Lib. ed. 1937).

62. The judiciary "were derived from a different foreign source . . . they were directed to foreign purposes. Need we be surprised that they were objects of aversion and distrust?" (McCloskey, *Works of Wilson* 1:292–93).

63. H. Storing, *The Complete Anti-Federalist* (Chicago: Univ. of Chicago Press, 1981), p. 19.

64. *Lockett v. United States*, 438 U.S. 586, 598 (1978).

65. *Smith v. United States*, 47 F.2d 518, 520 (9th Cir. 1931).

66. The point was made by Chief Justice Burger, *Furman v. Georgia*, 408 U.S. 238, 399 (1972); and by Justice Rehnquist, *Gardner v. Florida*, 430 U.S. 349, 371 (1977). Speaking on behalf of the Court in *Powell v. Texas*, 392 U.S. 514, 531 (1968), Justice Thurgood Marshall said, "The primary purpose of a [cruel and unusual] clause has always been considered, and properly so, to be directed at the method and kind of punishment imposed."

67. *McGautha v. California*, 402 U.S. 183, 207 (1971).

Jack Greenberg

21. Against the American System of Capital Punishment

Over and over, proponents of the death penalty insist that it is right and useful. In reply, abolitionists argue that it is morally flawed and cite studies to demonstrate its failure to deter. Were the subject not so grim and compelling, the exchanges would, by now, be tiresome.

Yet all too frequently, the debate has been off the mark. Death penalty proponents have assumed a system of capital punishment which simply does not exist: a system in which the penalty is inflicted on the most reprehensible criminals and meted out frequently enough both to deter and to perform the moral and utilitarian functions ascribed to retribution. Explicitly or implicitly, they assume a system in which certainly the worst criminals, Charles Manson or a putative killer of one's parent or child, for example, are executed in an evenhanded manner. But this idealized system is not the American system of capital punishment. Because the goals that our criminal justice system must satisfy are not being met—deterring crime, punishing the guilty, acquitting the innocent, avoiding needless cruelty, treating citizens equally, and prohibiting oppression by the state—America simply does not have the kind of capital punishment system contemplated by death penalty partisans.

Indeed, the reality of American capital punishment is quite to the contrary. Since at least 1967 the death penalty has been inflicted only rarely, erratically, and often upon the least odious killers, while many of the most heinous criminals have escaped execution. Moreover, it has been employed almost exclusively in a few formerly slaveholding states, and there it has been used almost exclusively against killers of whites, not blacks, and never against white killers of blacks. This is the American system of capital punishment. It is this system, not some idealized one, that must be defended in any national debate on the death penalty. I submit that this system is deeply incompatible with the proclaimed objectives of death penalty proponents.

Here is how America's system of capital punishment really works today. Since 1967, the year in which the courts first began to grapple in earnest with death penalty issues, the death penalty has been frequently imposed but rarely enforced. Between 1967 and 1980, death sentences or convictions were reversed for 1,899 of the 2,402 people on death row, a reversal rate of nearly 80 percent.[1] These reversals reflected, among other factors, a 1968

Supreme Court decision dealing with how juries should be chosen in capital cases,[2] a 1972 decision declaring capital sentences unconstitutional partly because they were imposed arbitrarily and "freakishly,"[3] and a 1976 decision holding mandatory death sentences unconstitutional.[4] Many death sentences were also invalidated on a wide variety of commonplace state-law grounds, such as hearsay rule violations or improper prosecutorial argument.

This judicial tendency to invalidate death penalties proved resistant to change. After 1972, in response to Supreme Court decisions, many states adopted new death penalty laws, and judges developed a clearer idea of the requirements that the Court had begun to enunciate a few years earlier. By 1979 the efforts of state legislatures finally paid off when John Spenkelink[5] became the first person involuntarily[6] executed since 1967.[7] Nevertheless, from 1972 to 1980, the death penalty invalidation rate declined to "only" 60 percent.[8] In contrast, ordinary noncapital convictions and sentences were almost invariably upheld.[9]

Today, the death row population has grown to more than 1,600 convicts. About 300 prisoners per year join this group, while about 100 per year leave death row, mainly by reason of judicial invalidations but also by execution and by death from other causes.[10] Following Spenkelink's execution, some states began to put some of these convicted murderers to death. Five persons were executed involuntarily in 1983, twenty-one in 1984, and fourteen in 1985.[11] Nevertheless, the number of actual executions seems to have reached a plateau. The average number of executions in the United States hovers at about twenty per year.[12] Yet even if this number doubled, or increased fivefold, executions would not be numerous either in proportion to the nation's homicides (approximately 19,000 per year)[13] or to its death row population (over 1600).[14]

One reason for the small number of executions is that the courts continue to upset capital convictions at an extraordinarily high rate, albeit not so high as earlier. Between January 1, 1982, and October 1, 1985, state supreme courts invalidated 35 percent of all capital judgments. State post-appellate processes undid a few more. The federal district and appeals courts overturned another 10 percent, and during a recent term the Supreme Court reversed three of the four capital sentences it reviewed. Altogether, about 45 percent of capital judgments that were reviewed during this period were set aside by one court or another.[15] One index of the vitality of litigation to reverse executions is that while legal attacks on capital punishment began as a coordinate effort by civil rights lawyers, they now come from a variety of segments of the bar.[16]

States not only execute convicted killers rarely, but they do so erratically. Spenkelink's execution, the nation's first involuntary execution since 1967, did not augur well for new systems of guided discretion designed to produce evenhanded capital justice in which only the worst murderers would be executed. Spenkelink was a drifter who killed a traveling companion who had sexually abused him. The assistant attorney general of Florida in charge of capital cases described him as "probably the least obnoxious individual on death row in terms of the crime he committed."[17]

The current round of invalidations highlights the erratic imposition of the death penalty. These invalidations have been based largely on grounds unrelated to the heinousness of the crime or the reprehensibility of the criminal.[18] Thus, the most abhorrent perpetrators of the most execrable crimes have escaped the penalty on grounds wholly unrelated to moral desert—for example, because defense counsel, the prosecutor, or the judge acted ineffectively or improperly on some matter of evidence. By contrast, criminals far less detestable by any rational moral standard—like Spenkelink, "the least obnoxious individual on death row"—have gone to their deaths because their trials "went well."[19] Of course, when errors occur in securing a death penalty, the sentence should be invalidated, particularly because "there is a significant constitutional difference between the death penalty and lesser punishments."[20] The corollary of this imperative is that the current system of capital punishment violates a central tenet of capital justice—that the most reprehensible criminals deserve execution, and others deserve lesser sentences.

It is troubling as well that the current level of executions has been attained only by using expedited procedures that undermine confidence in the fairness of the death penalty process. Recent executions have occurred during a period in which some federal judges, frustrated with the slow pace of capital justice, have taken extraordinary measures to expedite capital cases in federal courts. For example, the Fifth Circuit has quickened habeas corpus appeals in capital cases by accelerating the dates of arguments and greatly compressing the time for briefing cases.[21] Increasingly, the Supreme Court has encouraged this hurry-up justice. The Court has not only denied stay applications,[22] but it has also vacated stays entered by lower courts[23] in cases in which stays would have been routine in earlier times.[24] In sum, the recent invalidation rate seems unlikely to change significantly, thereby perpetuating the current system of erratic and haphazard executions.

Of course, one major difference exists between the period 1982 to 1985 and earlier years: increasingly, the death penalty has been concentrated geographically, not applied evenly across the United States. In the most recent period, there were forty-three involuntary executions.[25] Quite strikingly, all occurred in the states of the Old Confederacy. Thirty-four of the forty-three were in four states, and more than a quarter were in a single state, Florida, with thirteen.[26] In all but four cases, the defendants killed white persons.[27] In no case was a white executed for killing a black person.[28]

Why are there so few executions? Convictions and sentences are reversed, cases move slowly, and states devote relatively meager resources to pursuing actual executions. Even Florida, which above all other states has shown that it can execute almost any death row inmate it wants to, has killed only 13 of 221 inmates since 1979, 12 since 1982. (It now has 233 convicts on death row.)[29] Outside the former slaveholding states, more than half the states are now abolitionist either de jure (fourteen states) or de facto (five states have no one on death row).[30] Moreover, past experience suggests that the execution level will not go very high. Before the 1967–76 moratorium, the number of executions exceeded fifty only once after 1957—fifty-six in 1960.[31] At that time there were fewer abolitionist states and more capital crimes. This experience suggests that executions will not deplete the death row population.

The limited number of actual executions seems to me to reflect the very deep ambivalence that Americans feel about capital punishment. We are the only nation of the Western democratic world that has not abolished capital punishment.[32] By contrast, countries with whose dominant value systems we ordinarily disagree, like the Soviet Union, China, Iran, and South Africa, execute prisoners in great numbers.[33]

We have a system of capital punishment which results in infrequent, random, and erratic executions, one that is structured to inflict death neither on those who have committed the worst offenses nor on defendants of the worst character. This is the "system"—if that is the right term—of capital punishment that must be defended by death penalty proponents. This system may not be justified by positing a particularly egregious killer like Charles Manson. Our commitment to the rule of law means that we need an acceptable general system of capital justice if we are to have one at all. However, the real American system of capital punishment clearly fails when measured against the most common justifications for the infliction of punishment: deterrence and retribution.

If capital punishment can be a deterrent greater than life imprisonment at all, the American system is at best a feeble one. Studies by Thorsten Sellin[34] showed no demonstrable deterrent effect of capital punishment, even during its heyday. Today's death penalty, which is far less frequently used, is geographically localized, and is biased according to the race of the victim, cannot possibly upset that conclusion. The forty-three persons who were involuntarily executed from 1982 to 1985 were among a death row population of more than 1,600 condemned to execution out of about 20,000 who committed nonnegligent homicides per year. While 43 percent of the victims were black,[35] the death penalty is so administered that it overwhelmingly condemns and executes those who have killed whites.

Very little reason exists to believe that the present capital punishment system deters the conduct of others any more effectively than life imprisonment.[36] Potential killers who rationally weigh the odds of being killed themselves must conclude that the danger is nonexistent in most parts of the country and that in the South the danger is slight, particularly if the proposed victim is black. Moreover, the paradigm of this kind of murderer, the contract killer, is almost by definition a person who takes his chances like the soldier of fortune he is.[37]

But most killers do not engage in anything like a cost-benefit analysis. They are impulsive, and they kill impulsively. If capital punishment is to deter them, it can do so only indirectly: by impressing on potential killers a standard of right and wrong, a moral authority, an influence on their superegos which, notwithstanding mental disorder, would inhibit homicide. This conception of general deterrence seems deeply flawed because it rests upon a quite implausible conception of how this killer population internalizes social norms. Although not mentally disturbed enough to sustain insanity as a defense, they are often highly disturbed, of low intelligence, and addicted to drugs or alcohol. In any event, the message, if any, that the real American system of capital punishment sends to the psyches of would-be killers is quite limited: you may in a rare case be executed if you murder in the deepest South and kill a white person.[38]

The consequences of the real American system of capital justice are no more favorable as far as retribution is concerned. Retributive theories of criminal punishment draw support from several different moral theories that cannot be adequately elaborated here. While some of the grounds of retribution arguments resemble the conscience-building argument underlying general deterrence theory,[39] all retribution theories insist that seeking retribution constitutes a morally permissible use of governmental power. To retribution theorists, the death penalty makes a moral point: it holds up as an example worthy of the most severe condemnation one who has committed the most opprobrious crime.

As with many controversies over moral issues, these purely moral arguments may appear to end any real possibility for further discussion. For those who believe in them, they persuade, just as the moral counterarguments persuade abolitionists. But discussion should not end at this point. Those who claim a moral justification for capital punishment must reconcile that belief with other moral considerations. To my mind, the moral force of any retribution argument is radically undercut by the hard facts of the actual American system of capital punishment. This system violates fundamental norms because it is haphazard and because it is regionally and racially biased. To these moral flaws, I would add another: the minuscule number of executions nowadays cannot achieve the grand moral aims that are presupposed by a serious societal commitment to retribution.

Some retribution proponents argue that it is the pronouncement of several hundred death sentences followed by lengthy life imprisonment, not the actual imposition of a few executions, that satisfies the public's demand for retribution. Of course, the public has not said that it wants the death penalty as it exists—widely applicable but infrequently used. Nor, to the best of my knowledge, is there any solid empirical basis for such a claim.

Like other statutes, death penalty laws are of general applicability, to be employed according to their terms.[40] Nothing in their language or legislative history authorizes the erratic, occasional, racially biased use of these laws. But my objections to this argument go much deeper. I find morally objectionable a system of many pronounced death sentences but few actual executions, a system in which race and region are the only significant variables in determining who actually dies. My objection is not grounded in a theory which posits any special moral rights for the death row population. The decisive point is my understanding of the basic moral aspirations of American civilization, particularly its deep commitment to the rule of law. I cannot reconcile an erratic, racially and regionally biased system of executions with my understanding of the core values of our legal order.

Death penalty proponents may respond to this argument by saying that if there is not enough capital punishment, there should be more. If only killers of whites are being executed, then killers of blacks should be killed too; and if many sentences are being reversed, standards of review should be relaxed.[41] In the meantime, they might urge, the death penalty should go on. But this argument is unavailing because it seeks to change the terms of the debate in a fundamental way. It seeks to substitute an imaginary system for the real American system of capital punishment. If there were a different kind of system of death penalty administration in this country, or even a reasonable possibility that one might emerge, we could debate its implications. But any current debate over the death penalty cannot ignore the deep moral deficiencies of the present system.[42]

This debate about whether we should have a death penalty is a matter on which the Supreme Court is unlikely to have the last say now or in the near future. Yet, the Court's decisions have some relevance. The grounds that the Court has employed in striking down various forms of the death penalty resemble the arguments I have made. Freakishness was a ground for invalidating the death penalty as it was administered throughout the country in 1972.[43] Rarity of use contributed to invalidation of the death penalty for rape[44] and felony murder[45] and to invalidation of the mandatory death penalty.[46] That constitutional law reflects moral concerns should not be strange: concepts of cruel and unusual punishment, due process, and equal protection express contemporary standards of decency.

Moreover, the whole development of the Fourteenth Amendment points to the existence of certain basic standards of decency and fairness from which no state or region can claim exemption. One such value is, of course, the racially neutral administration of justice. No one disputes that one of the Fourteenth Amendment's central designs was to secure the evenhanded administration of justice in the southern state courts and that the persistent failure to achieve that goal has been one of America's greatest tragedies. We cannot be blind to the fact that actual executions have taken place primarily in the South and in at least a racially suspect manner. In light of our constitutional history, the race-specific aspects of the death penalty in the South are profoundly unsettling.

Given the situation as I have described it, and as I believe it will continue so long as we have capital punishment, one could argue that the death penalty should be declared unconstitutional in all its forms. But the Court is unlikely to take that step soon. Only ten years have passed since the type of death statute now in use was upheld, and some states have had such laws for an even shorter period. Thirty-seven states have passed laws showing they want some sort of death penalty. Public opinion polls show that most Americans want capital punishment in some form. Having only recently invalidated one application of the death penalty in *Furman v. Georgia* in 1972, the Court is unlikely soon to deal with the concept wholesale again. But if the way capital punishment works does not change materially, I think that at some point the Court will declare the overall system to be cruel and unusual. If this prediction is correct—and it is at least arguably so—an additional moral factor enters the debate. Is it right to kill death row inmates during this period of experimentation? There is, of course, an element of bootstrapping to my argument: exercising further restraint in killing death-sentenced convicts reinforces arguments of freakishness and rarity of application. But unless one can assure a full and steady stream of executions, sufficient to do the jobs the death penalty proponents claim that it can do, there is no further reason to kill any one at all.

Notes

1. These statistics and the pre-1981 experience with the death penalty are reviewed more extensively in Greenberg, *Capital Punishment as a System*, 91 Yale L.J. 908, 917–18 (1982).

2. *See Witherspoon v. Illinois*, 391 U.S. 510 (1968). On the erosion of *Witherspoon, see Wainwright v. Witt*, 105 S. Ct. 844 (1985), and the perceptive comment in *The Supreme Court, 1984 Terms*, 99 Harv. L. Rev. 120 (1985).

3. *Furman v. Georgia*, 408 U.S. 238, 293 (1972) (Brennan, J., concurring).

4. *See Woodson v. North Carolina*, 428 U.S. 280 (1976).

5. *See Spinkellink v. State*, 313 So.2d 666 (Fla. 1975), *cert. denied*, 428 U.S. 911 (1976). Spenkelink's name was misspelled by many of the courts that considered his case. *See Spinkellink v. Wainwright*, 578 F.2 582, 582 n. 1 (5th Cir. 1978); Greenberg, *Capital Punishment as a System*, p. 913 n. 27.

6. I call an execution "involuntary" if the defendant has contested actual implementation of the death penalty. Conversely, a "voluntary" execution is one in which the defendant at some point has voluntarily ceased efforts to resist.

7. This statistic was derived from NAACP Legal Defense and Educational Fund, *Death Row U.S.A.* (Washington, D.C., 1986), p. 4, and Greenberg, *Capital Punishment as a System*, p. 913. Other statistics set forth in this article, including the number and location of

death-sentenced prisoners, whether they have been executed, and their race and the race of their victims, have been obtained from the *Death Row U.S.A.* data bank (on file at the NAACP Legal Defense and Educational Fund in New York), which was computerized in 1984–85. *Death Row U.S.A.* is frequently used as an authoritative source by courts, *see, e.g., Godfrey v. Georgia*; 446 U.S. 420, 439 nn.7 & 8 (1980); the media, *see, e.g., U.S. News and World Report,* May 11, 1981, p. 72; and scholars, *see, e.g.,* Gillers, *Deciding Who Dies,* 129 U. Pa. L. Rev. 1, 2 n. 2 (1980).

8. *See* Greenberg, *Capital Punishment as a System,* p. 918.

9. *For example,* in the federal court system during the year ending June 30, 1980, 28,598 defendants were convicted while only 4,405 convicted defendants filed appeals. Of these appeals, only 6.5 percent prevailed. Thus, while not all defendants appealing were convicted during the year surveyed, one can estimate that about 1 percent of all criminal convictions handed down during that year (290 out of 28,598) were upset on appeal. *See* Administrative Office of the U.S. Courts, *1980 Annual Report of the Director,* pp. 2 (table 2), 51 (table 10), 97. State court experience is similar. *See* Greenberg, *Capital Punishment as a System,* p. 918 and n. 65.

10. *See* NAACP Legal Defense and Educational Fund, *Death Row U.S.A.,* p. 1; *Death Row U.S.A.* data bank.

11. *See* NAACP Legal Defense and Educational Fund, *Death Row U.S.A.,* p. 4. Between Jan. 17, 1977, and March 1, 1986, there were eight voluntary executions. Five were in states outside the South. At least seven were of killers of whites; in the eighth case, the race of the victim was unknown (*see id.*).

12. *See id.*

13. *See* Federal Bureau of Investigation, U.S. Dept. of Justice, *Uniform Crime Reports, Crime in the United States 1984* (Washington, D.C., 1985) (18,692 murders in 1984).

14. *See* NAACP Legal Defense and Educational Fund, *Death Row U.S.A.,* p. 1.

15. These statistics on reversals have been derived from the *Death Row U.S.A.* data bank. While 45 percent of judgments reviewed during this period were reversed, the cases involved sentences which in some instances had been imposed before Jan. 1, 1982.

16. The NAACP Legal Defense and Educational Fund, of which I was director counsel until 1984 and which commenced the attacks on capital punishment, has participated in virtually none of the state cases that invalidated death penalties and in very few of the recent federal cases. The American Bar Association Board of Governors, however, approved an effort to obtain $150,000 for a postconviction death penalty representation project in December 1983, and the Florida legislature enacted a law to furnish counsel on postconviction death penalty proceedings (*see* Fla. Stat. Ann. sec. 27,7001 [West Supp. 1986]).

17. Adler, *Florida's Zealous Prosecutors: Death Specialists,* Am. Law., Sept. 1981, p. 36.

18. *See Death Row U.S.A.* data bank (reporting grounds of reversal). Because most invalidations occur in state courts, proposed legislation that would make federal habeas corpus more difficult for prisoners (*see, e.g.,* S. 238, 99th Cong., 1st Sess., 131 *Cong. Rec.* S481–82 [daily ed. Jan. 22, 1985]) would have only marginal effect.

19. Because the invalidations rest on a wide variety of grounds, no single doctrinal shift, or even a small number of shifts, is likely to result in a lower reversal rate.

20. *Beck v. Alabama*, 447 U.S. 625, 637 (1980).

21. *See Barefoot v. Estelle*, 463 U.S. 880, 886–92 (1983).

22. *See Dobbert v. Wainwright*, 105 S. Ct. 34 (1984) (6–3 decision).

23. *See Wainwright v. Adams*, 104 S. Ct. 2183 (1984) (5–4 decision); *Woodard v. Hutchins*, 464 U.S. 377 (1984) (5–4 decision) (per curiam).

24. *Cf.* Marshall, *Remarks on the Death Penalty Made at the Judicial Conference of the Second Circuit*, 86 Colum. L. Rev. 1, 6–7 (1986) (observing that expedited procedures deny defendants the ability to present their claims properly); "Marshall Assails Death Penalty Plea Process," *New York Times*, Sept. 7, 1985, p. A24, col. 1.

25. *See* NAACP Legal Defense and Educational Fund, *Death Row U.S.A.*, p. 4.

26. Ibid. There were eight in Texas, seven in Louisiana, and six in Georgia. The remainder were in Virginia, three; North Carolina and South Carolina, two; and Alabama and Mississippi, one.

27. Ibid.

28. Ibid. The race-of-victim factor is examined in detail in Gross, *Race and Death: The Judicial Evaluation of Evidence of Discrimination in Capital Sentencing*, 18 U.C.D. L. Rev. 1275 (1985). Killers of whites are clearly sentenced to death more frequently than killers of blacks (ibid. at 1318–19). The legal significance of the discrepancy is, however, under consideration by the Supreme Court and therefore not settled. *See McCleskey v. Kemp*, 753 F.2d 877 (11th Cir. 1985) (en banc), *petition for cert. filed* (U.S. May 28, 1985) (No. 84–6811). The principal issues are whether it is necessary to demonstrate that the discrepancy is a consequence of a pattern of intentional discrimination, whether it is necessary to demonstrate an intent to discriminate in the particular case, and how large a discrepancy must be shown to constitute a violation of the equal protection and cruel and unusual punishment clauses.

29. *See* NAACP Legal Defense and Educational Fund, *Death Row U.S.A.*, p. 8.

30. West Virginia is the only southern state that is abolitionist (ibid., p. 1).

31. *See* H. A. Bedau, *Background and Developments*, in *The Death Penalty in America*, 3d ed., ed. H. Bedau (New York: Oxford Univ. Press, 1982), p. 25. There were twenty-one executions in 1962 and one in 1966 (ibid.).

32. *See* Greenberg, *Capital Punishment as a System*, p. 925. The European Convention of Human Rights has been amended to prohibit the death penalty in peacetime (*see* Protocol No. 6 to the Convention for the Protection of Human Rights and Fundamental Freedoms Concerning the Abolition of the Death Penalty, April 28, 1983, Council of Europe, 22 I.L.M. 539). The consequence of the amendment is that parties to the treaty who ratify may not reinstitute the death penalty without repudiating the entire treaty, a move which would have undesirable political consequences.

33. *See* Greenberg, *Capital Punishment as a System*, p. 925; "When Peking Fights Crime, News Is on the Wall," *New York Times*, Jan. 28, 1986, p. A2, col. 3.

34. Sellin's studies of deterrence are reviewed in L. Klein, B. Forst, and V. Filatov, *The Deterrent Effect of Capital Punishment: An Assessment of the Evidence*, in Bedau, *The Death Penalty in America*, pp. 139–40. The work of Isaac Ehrlich, who arrived at contrary conclusions, is reviewed in the same essay (ibid., pp. 140–42). The authors conclude that Ehrlich's findings are seriously flawed and not persuasive (ibid., pp. 157–58).

35. *See* Bedau, *Volume and Rate of Murder*, ibid., pp. 39, 43.

36. In the sense of specific deterrence or incapacitation, of course, the forty-three who were put to death indeed have been deterred. But those serving life sentences or terms of years, of course, occasionally kill. That fact would not be accepted as grounds for having sentenced them to death in lieu of the original prison term. Recidivism by convicted murderers and killings by prisoners generally are discussed in Bedau, *Recidivism, Parole, and Deterrence*, ibid., p. 173, and Wolfson, *The Deterrent Effect of the Death Penalty upon Prison Murder*, ibid., p. 159, respectively. Wolfson concludes: "Given that the deterrent effect of the death penalty for prison homicide is to be seriously doubted, it is clear that management and physical changes in the prison would do more than any legislated legal sanction to reduce the number of prison murders" (ibid., p. 172).

37. It might be argued that even the rare execution is dramatic and unduly publicized and consequently has great effect. Ironically, the slight increase in the number of executions in the past few years has robbed them of much dramatic effect.

38. As to an asserted salutary influence on the healthy mind, tending to cause it to shun lethal violence, one can only respond that no evidence has been offered. Religious, social, moral, and noncapital legal requirements all teach us not to murder. If the death penalty were needed as an incremental influence to persuade noncriminals to abjure killing, there would be elevated murder rates in abolitionist states and nations; these have not been demonstrated.

39. The reply to this argument is the same as to the arguments that the death penalty deters by teaching not to kill. Retribution is also said to have another utilitarian by-product distinct from a Kantian eye-for-an-eye justification: it satisfies demands for vengeance, preventing retaliatory killing. Yet, during the period of no executions (1967–77) and in the overwhelming number of states that have abolished the death penalty, have not sentenced anyone to death, or have not carried out executions, it is difficult to find an instance of vengeance killing, although during this time there have been perhaps 360,000 murders (about 20,000 per year for eighteen years).

It is also argued that, particularly for those who have been close to the victim, who are members of his or her family, or who are fellow police officers, or for those members of the public who somehow feel an identification with the deceased, the death penalty provides personal satisfaction, repaying in some measure the loss they felt in the death of the victim. This hardly justifies the present system.

40. A few death penalty proponents say that the death penalty is the only way of "assuring" life imprisonment for the worst criminals. Recognizing that most death sentences have turned into interminable prison sentences, they say this is preferable to sentences of life imprisonment from which convicts may be

released on parole. But human ingenuity can fashion a sentence of life without parole. The death sentence following extensive litigation, amounting to life sentence for most while executing only a few, is an inefficient way of achieving the purpose of life imprisonment. And again, this sort of life-sentencing process is not what the death penalty laws contemplate.

41. This argument can be made by those who would defend the death penalty on deterrence grounds, as well as by those who rely upon retribution concepts.

42. Some death penalty proponents argue that the erratic quality of the capital sentencing system and its racial bias are characteristic of the criminal justice system generally. But while such a condition may or may not be tolerable when it results in imprisonment, it hardly justifies killing convicts.

43. *Furman v. Georgia*, 408 U.S. 238, 293 (1972) (Brennan, J., concurring).

44. *Coker v. Georgia*, 433 U.S. 584, 594–97 (1977).

45. *Enmund v. Florida*, 458 U.S. 782, 792–96 (1982).

46. *Woodson v. North Carolina*, 428 U.S. 280, 292–303 (1976).

WILLIAM BRADFORD REYNOLDS

22. The Death Penalty Is Not Cruel and Unusual Punishment

Capital punishment deserves special attention in any analysis of our Constitution. After all, capital punishment was of sufficient importance to our Founding Fathers to merit specific mention within the four corners of the Constitution. And it should command no less respect today as an important feature of our criminal justice system.

Responding to certain heinous crimes by putting to death the criminal is plainly no latter-day idea. Well before the birth of our nation, the death penalty had been imposed on criminals who committed particularly offensive acts against society. And certainly since then, we have generally regarded capital punishment as neither cruel nor unusual for a carefully defined category of criminal conduct.

Yet this long-accepted form of criminal punishment came under intense attack in the 1960s and 1970s, as did many other traditional concepts of the role of punishment in our society. Spearheaded by a small cadre of committed abolitionists, this challenge, for a time, made some inroads into traditional public support for the death penalty. While it bears noting that few states repealed their death penalty statutes during the period, the decline in public support for the death penalty was trumpeted by some social and political commentators as signifying the dawning of a more humane era in American criminal justice.

In 1958 the Warren Court had already proclaimed, in *Trop v. Dulles*, that the Eighth Amendment would be interpreted according to the "evolving standards of decency that mark the progress of a maturing society."[1] Measured against these conveniently imprecise standards, critics of capital punishment aggressively asserted that the death penalty fell woefully short. In fact, argued the critics, putting society's worst enemies to death was a barbaric practice, evidencing "deep-seated sadistic instincts," as Justice William Douglas expressed it. Such a practice was presumably unworthy of a nation entering the Age of Aquarius.

Armed with this Supreme Court standard and fueled by inflammatory rhetoric, the opponents of capital punishment marched boldly and concertedly through the decade of the 1960s and into the 1970s, gaining some followers along the way. Their march culminated in the landmark decision of *Furman v. Georgia*,[2] a 5–4 decision which packed a precedent-busting wallop—enough, apparently, to retire to the sidelines the long-standing death penalty statutes of thirty-nine states and the federal government.

It is not unfair to say, I think, that the diffuse collection of concurring opinions in *Furman v. Georgia* contained no coherent principle. It was the effervescence of a lighter-than-air jurisprudence which perhaps comported well with the times but served both the people and the Constitution poorly.

To the extent that there is a holding in *Furman*, it is largely an imputed, constructive one which goes like this—sentencing procedures that permit arbitrary and freakish imposition of the death penalty violate the spirit at least of the Eighth Amendment's prohibition against "cruel and unusual" punishment.[3]

On the other hand, *Furman*'s apparent attempt to abolish the death penalty for all time fell short of its mark. Since 1972 thirty-eight states and the federal government have reaffirmed their commitment to the death penalty by enacting capital sentencing procedures responsive to *Furman*. And, today, support for capital punishment is overwhelming. A recent Associated Press poll shows that 86 percent of the American public supports the death penalty for murder, while only 11 percent are opposed; the support is both massive and broadly based.

The road back to sensible criminal jurisprudence in this area has been anything but smooth. To be sure, since 1972 the Court has beaten a continued, if erratic, retreat from the abolitionist view, until today *Furman* and its progeny are, to put it most graciously, of limited precedential value. As capital punishment expert George Smith has written, "[S]tarting with *Gregg v. Georgia* and its four 1976 companion cases, the Supreme Court's decisions over the past decade have cleared the way for the resumption of capital punishment as an accepted and institutionalized component of criminal law enforcement."[4] Thus, to borrow again from Smith's excellent monograph *Capital Punishment 1986: Last Lines of Defense*, the Court has concluded that:

> —The death penalty itself does not constitute cruel and unusual punishment under the Eighth Amendment.
> —Each new conviction for a capital crime need not be compared with all preceding convictions for the same category of offense to assure that imposition of the death penalty is "proportional" to that offense.
> —Mandatory capital sentences for all forms of murder are impermissible, but death sentences passed after individualized balancing of aggravating and mitigating factors are sustainable.
> —There is no constitutional requirement that only juries may decide whether the death penalty can be imposed, and, in fact, judges may override a jury recommendation for a life sentence and impose the death penalty.
> —And no particular standard of proof (such as "proof beyond a

> reasonable doubt") is required to govern the death-sentencing determination of whether aggravating circumstances outweigh mitigating circumstances.[5]

Yet numerous judicially created obstacles still remain to fair, effective, and timely administration of the death penalty. Since the Court decided the *Gregg*[6] quintet of cases in 1976, only 67 prisoners have been executed. At the end of 1985, some 1,600 prisoners were under sentence of death in thirty-two states.[7] And state courts steadily continue to hand down death sentences.

Repeatedly, the Court has performed eleventh-hour logical and procedural gymnastics in response to a parade of last-minute writs of habeas corpus, petitions for stay of execution, and other applications for review, which have left the death penalty in a state of disarray. Such was the case of *Darden v. Wainwright*.[8] At issue was a stay of execution for a man, who beyond a doubt had robbed a woman, sexually assaulted her, shot her husband between the eyes while she looked on, and then shot and attempted to kill a sixteen-year-old boy who came to her aid. After first denying a stay of execution, the Court—only a few hours later—reversed itself and granted certiorari. Chief Justice Berger was so frustrated by his brethren that he penned this memorable dissent:

> In the twelve years since petitioner was convicted of murder and sentenced to death, the issues now raised in the petition for certiorari have been considered by this Court four times, and have been litigated before no fewer than 95 federal and state court judges. Upon review of the petition and the history of this case, I conclude that no issues are presented meriting plenary review by this Court. Because we abuse our discretion when we accept meritless petitions presenting claims that we rejected only hours ago, I dissent.[9]

Like the former chief justice, most Americans are understandably losing patience with the sort of conduct displayed by the Court in *Darden*. For such cases do not involve good faith, meritorious efforts to prevent miscarriages of justice. No one takes exception to legitimate appeals by convicted capital defendants who can demonstrate that they failed to receive the full benefit of the process due under law. But in the overwhelming majority of such appeals, due process is not what is at issue—not at all. Instead, we are all too regularly witnessing frivolous, last-ditch maneuvers by lawyers and judges who philosophically oppose the imposition of the death penalty in every case—no matter how well-established the guilt of the criminal, no matter how serious the crime, no matter how fair the trial, and no matter how deserved the punishment.

Opponents of the death penalty regularly accuse the American public of being "barbaric" and "sadistic" for demanding capital punishment for criminals whose crimes can only be described as themselves barbaric and sadistic. They deride a belief strongly held by most Americans—i.e., that a person may knowingly and willfully commit an act or acts so evil, so outrageous, so injurious to individuals and society that the only appropriate, the only just punishment is the death penalty. Cold-blooded murder and treason against the United States leap immediately to mind.

Ultimately, the policy and legal arguments against capital punishment stem from a particular moral aversion to this kind of punishment. It is not an argument which attempts to persuade us that the death penalty can today reasonably be called "unusual"; its historical acceptance since well before our founding and its regular use since then preclude that assertion. Nor is a serious effort made to convince us that society today regards capital punishment as "cruel"; too many know better. Rather, the reasoning put forth is that a more decent, more humane, and more enlightened society of the future will ultimately come to the view that the death penalty—however administered—falls short of "the constitutional ideal of human dignity." That prognosis for the future is the excuse for resisting any imposition of the death penalty now.

Those so intent on thwarting implementation of capital punishment until the day of true enlightenment finally dawns do a grave injustice to the text and history of the Constitution. On a more practical level, their position either ignores or rejects the two solid policy reasons on which society has always relied for imposing the ultimate sanction.

The first of these, the one most commonly heard and debated, is that the death penalty acts as a forceful and effective deterrent. Notwithstanding the refusal of critics to accept this proposition, we know scientifically as well as intuitively that punishing heinous crimes with the death penalty does in fact discourage similar acts by others. Indeed, one new study of the deterrent effect of executions indicates that each additional execution deters fifteen murders. This finding was recently published in the *Bulletin* of the New York Academy of Medicine by Stephen Layson, a professor of economics at the University of North Carolina at Chapel Hill.[10] Professor Layson combined rigorous and sophisticated statistical analysis with the most recent data on homicide to prove the deterrence theory in general and the deterrent power of the death penalty in particular. His conclusions will not easily be upset.

Moreover, Professor Layson's results accord with common sense. We all know that the greater the penalty for a crime, the greater also will be the number of persons who will weigh the payoff against the risk and find their incentive to commit that crime insufficient. I doubt seriously, for example, that acts of espionage and treason against the United States would be nearly so attractive to those receiving money or sexual favors for the disclosure of top secrets to foreign governments if the swift and lasting response of our criminal justice system was death to the traitors.

And even if this deterrent impact does not reach all persons, it is undeniably 100 percent effective on that group demonstrably most in need of deterrence—the repeat offenders. All too often murderers have had their lives spared only to kill or attempt to kill again. Many who fall into this category are serving long prison terms and strike prison guards or fellow inmates. Others kill again after serving their time, or escaping, or even while on temporary release.

Eddie Simon Wein was such a murderer. Wein was sentenced to death in Los Angeles Superior Court in 1957. Instead of being executed, he was released from prison eighteen years later to live in West Los Angeles. Within months, he began to attack and kill women in the area. Fortunately for other potential victims, his apprehension was swift. He was convicted in 1976 of first-degree murder of one woman, attempted murder of another, and numerous sexual offenses. Clearly, this tragic loss and scarring of lives would have been avoided had Eddie Wein been executed as originally decreed.

The second argument for the death penalty, heard far less often, is actually the more persuasive one. In fact, taken alone it is decisive. I am speaking of the moral and practical necessity of retributive punishment. In some instances capital punishment is not only morally permissible but morally compelled: morally compelled, that is, if we believe that life has any moral content whatsoever; morally compelled, if we believe life has any purpose and meaning; morally compelled, if we believe there is some truth or principle greater than man himself.

Most law-abiding citizens abhor crime of any sort. Crime is wrong, reprehensible, and, for most, wholly unacceptable. But some crimes take us beyond the purely unacceptable to a fundamental outrage that the basic norms of any civilized community have been irretrievably transgressed. Vicious, cold-blooded murder is such a crime. So is treason. And so is espionage that puts the security of our country at risk. Such crimes arouse our most intense feelings. They understandably make us extremely angry—as well they should; indeed, for most law-abiding citizens, angry to the depths of their souls.

It is not just the heinous crime that arouses such feelings; it is also the criminal, the perpetrator of these despicable acts, that deservedly receives our wrath. The overwhelming urge to pay back the criminal—to avenge the victim and to exact the price of justice from the wrongdoer—is shared by most Americans. The fancy word for this is "retribution." It is a normal, healthy feeling, and one that, among others, makes us human and sets us apart from mere animals. Indeed, if we should ever stop feeling anger (strong, deep, disturbing anger) at senseless, premeditated crimes of violence against individuals or society, we ourselves will have then surrendered a measure of our own humanity. For our anger displays a certain, essential level of caring for our fellow human beings. It shows that we are not indifferent to the fate of those who share—or who once did share—life with us. The desire in these terms for retribution against those who criminally violate others in society is a positive individual and community response. Indifference to the criminal's fate is, by contrast, a sign of moral decay and decline.

Professor Walter Berns has written perhaps the single best statement of why we must have the death penalty. His book is entitled simply *For Capital Punishment*. In it he quotes J. F. Stephen, an early penologist, on the point I have been making. "Criminals should be hated," wrote Stephen, "and the punishments inflicted on them should be so constructed as to give expression to that hatred."[11] Of course, what Stephen wrote was a truth which was set down a very long time ago in the moral and religious writings of our ancestors. These writings—the Bible, the Talmud, and other religious works, not to mention the treatises on philosophy and ethics of the ancient Greeks and Romans—have given our civilization much of its unique character. Stephen, notes Professor Berns, "saw that the connection between punishment and . . . general prevention [of crime] is anger. Anger is the passion that recognizes and cares about justice."[12]

To be sure, there are some who arrogantly maintain that righteous anger has no place in a proper scheme of punishment. We are too sophisticated and civilized for that now, they assert. They thus would have us avert our eyes, for example, from the suffering of an eleven-year-old boy who was bludgeoned from his bicycle with a drill bit, stuffed into a car trunk, and then repeatedly molested.[13] And they urge detached indifference to the victims of three men who drove to a baseball park to, in their own words, "see if we could find a girl to rape." Finding young Carlotta Hartness and her boyfriend, these men proceeded to kill her boyfriend, repeatedly rape her, force her into oral sodomy, take target practice at her head, and hours after killing her, return to mutilate her body.

Rather than joining with shocked communities in outrage and anguish, the opponents of capital punishment side in such cases with the sadistic murderers at the time of reckoning. With the trial over and guilt proved beyond a reasonable doubt, they rush tirelessly to file contrived briefs on behalf of the convicted, offering constitutional arguments that mock the integrity of our great charter. Think not of the due process rights denied the poor victim, they argue; what is more important, they claim, is some technical defect in the already oversolicitous process already afforded the criminal. Let not your outrage at the heinous crime affect your judgment, they urge; for, to take the life of one who has anointed himself the high-priest executioner of other innocent members of society is nonetheless "cruel and unusual" punishment.

To this circle of advocates, the gentlest response is simply to point out that their moral sense is tragically dislocated. A society that feels no righteous anger when such lurid crimes are committed—or worse, is forced to squelch that anger in meting out punishment—has surrendered a measure of its civilized character. In the process, the intolerable gains a degree of respectability; grave wrongs are too readily excused; and in time human life does not count for very much.

Happily, the overwhelming majority of Americans has flatly rejected the course charted by those intent on outlawing the death penalty. They understand that to love good means to hate evil; that to uphold the law means to punish the criminal in proportion to his transgression; and that to justly impose punishment on the criminal strengthens the commitment to abide by the law. As Professor Berns points out, a system of law and punishments that says only that it is not in the interests of a man to commit a crime—and does not impute blame, moral culpability—will soon disintegrate into lawlessness. His exact words are worth repeating: "Once people are no longer governed by their morals . . . they will soon enough discover the secret of how to evade the laws. In short, deterrence will work only if the threat of punishment is combined with the conviction that the forbidden acts are not only illegal and therefore punishable but immoral."[14]

In sum, if punishment is to educate the public civically, as it should, then it must in part be a punishment of "just deserts" and retribution. Put another way, deterrence should not be the sole purpose and standard of punishment, as some would argue. This is so, let me emphasize again, because focusing on deterrence alone would allow the public to lose sight of the immorality of crime. A theory of penology which determines the punishment of one criminal by its likely effect on the potential crimes of others—and nothing more—is inadequate. Justice imposed on a criminal without anger is a hollow reckoning; it is justice in name only. Likewise, justice without retribution is not justice, it is mere calculation.

And so, we are left with a truth as old as man himself: Anger and retribution are irreducible, irreplaceable parts of true justice. But we must be ever vigilant that our anger and retribution are matched to the crime that inspires them and that they are visited on the offender in such a way as to affirm the sanctity of life, of liberty, and of property.

If we are to endure as a democratic society, we must constantly reinforce in the public a respect for the rule of law. As a child learns character from the example of his parents or mentors, so a society learns law-abidingness from the daily example set in its system of justice. There the values of our nation are on display for every citizen to see.

That is why it is so critically important that our system of punishments have a moral foundation which extends beyond simple self-interest. That is why we must have retributive justice. That is why we must have capital punishment—to deal with those crimes that mock human dignity and the value of life itself. For no other penalty, not even life imprisonment with no possibility of parole, is adequate to repay the sort of crimes that I have described. Some crimes deserve death, and nothing else will quench our righteous anger, or vindicate our humanity, or inspire sufficiently profound respect or reverential fear of the law and the underlying moral order. Serving justice at times demands imposing the ultimate sanction.

Judicious and just use of the death penalty is an awesome responsibility. But it is one that must be met. And it cannot be met simply by looking away from heinous crimes, their victims and their perpetrators. For should we allow ourselves to look the other way, we will have turned our backs on the good and moral and just society that we should ever endeavor to be.

Notes

1. *Trop v. Dulles*, 356 U.S. 86 (1958).

2. *Furman v. Georgia*, 408 U.S. 238 (1972).

3. Media General–Associated Press random sampling of 1,251 adults from across the country, Nov. 7–14, 1986.

4. G. Smith, *Capital Punishment 1986: Last Lines of Defense* (Washington, D.C.: Washington Legal Foundation, 1986), p. 2.

5. Ibid.

6. *Gregg v. Georgia*, 428 U.S. 153 (1976); *Jurek v. Texas*, 428 U.S. 262 (1976); *Proffitt v. Florida*, 428 U.S. 242 (1976); *Woodson v. North Carolina*, 428 U.S. 280 (1976); and *Roberts v. Louisiana*, 428 U.S. 325 (1976).

7. *Capital Punishment, 1985*, Bureau of Justice Statistics Bulletin (1985). The exact number was 1,591, all for murder.

8. *Darden v. Wainwright*, 54 U.S.L.W. 4734 (June 23, 1986).

9. *Id.*, at 4740.

10. S. Layson, vol. 62, No. 5, Bulletin of New York Academy of Medicine 589 (2d ser., 1986).

11. W. Berns, *For Capital Punishment* (New York: Basic Books, 1979), p. 152.

12. Ibid.

13. *Wainwright v. Witt*, 53 U.S.L.W. 4108 (Jan. 21, 1985).

14. Berns, *For Capital Punishment*, p. 139.

IX.

THE SIXTH AMENDMENT AND THE RIGHT TO CRIMINAL JURY TRIAL

William E. Nelson

23. The Jury and Consensus Government in Mid-Eighteenth-Century America

The Pervasive and Undifferentiated Role of Colonial Courts

Courts were vital to mid-eighteenth-century colonial government, for that government, unlike our own, had no ubiquitous bureaucracy with clear chains of command reaching upward to central political authorities. Because there was no modern bureaucracy, the judiciary and the officials responsible to it (e.g., sheriffs) were the primary link between a colony's central government and its outlying localities. The judiciary alone could coerce individuals by punishing crimes and imposing money judgments. In some colonies, such as Virginia, the judiciary was virtually the whole of local government, but even in colonies where other officials were available, the nonexistence of doctrines of official immunity rendered those officials subject to judicial control. As one of John Marshall's contemporaries observed, "[o]ther departments of the Government" may have been "more splendid," but only the "courts of justice [came] home to every man's habitation."[1]

The vital role of the courts in colonial government did not, however, mean that government performed only functions which we today would classify as judicial. Colonial government regulated its subjects' lives in pervasive detail; government in the Age of Mercantilism sought to insure not only the physical and economic but the moral and social well-being of its subjects.[2] The courts, as a vital part of the government, maintained order, protected life and property, apportioned and collected taxes, supervised the construction and maintenance of highways, issued licenses, and regulated licensees' businesses. Through administration of the settlement law, which permitted localities to exclude undesired newcomers, and the poor law, which made localities liable for the support and hence the general well-being of all who were born and raised in a locality and all newcomers who were not excluded, the legal system fostered community self-definition and a sense of community responsibility for inhabitants.[3] Indeed, in some colonies, the courts of general sessions of the peace, which possessed basic criminal, administrative, and some minor forms of civil jurisdiction, also performed the executive and even the legislative functions of local government.[4]

The work of the courts, in sum, was of an undifferentiated, pervasive character. The undifferentiated character of that work was important for present purposes because it obscured distinctions between legislation, administration, and adjudication drawn by political theorists. Despite Montesquieu's early statement of the modern doctrine of separation of powers,[5] Americans as late as the 1780s generally regarded the courts as part of the executive and did not routinely distinguish the judiciary as an independent branch which exercised only judicial functions: they did not, that is, distinguish law from politics. As one tract observed, "Government is generally distinguished into three parts, Executive, Legislative and Judicial, but this is more a distinction of words than things. . . . [H]owever we may refine and define, there is no more than two powers in any government, viz., the power is only a branch of the executive, the CHIEF of every country being the first magistrate."[6]

The pervasive character of the courts' work was important because it placed the courts, which are today at the periphery of governmental activity, at the core instead. It insured that men like John Marshall who learned the ways of government in the Revolutionary era would be familiar with the manner in which courts functioned. And it requires, if we are to understand the background and training of the generation of the Founding Fathers, that we too study the workings of mid-eighteenth-century courts and of their most important agency, the jury.

The Law-finding Power of Juries

Although judges with the multifarious duties of mid-eighteenth-century courts were prominent local leaders, they were leaders who had power only to guide, not to command. For juries rather than judges spoke the last word on law enforcement in nearly all, if not all, of the eighteenth-century American colonies. Except in equitable actions, which were nonexistent in some colonies and narrowly limited in the rest, judges could not enter a judgment or impose a penalty without a jury verdict. And, in the cases in which they sat, eighteenth-century juries, unlike juries today, usually possessed the power to determine both law and fact.

Although the common law of eighteenth-century England recognized several devices for controlling jury findings of law and fact, mid-eighteenth-century American courts appear not to have used them extensively in either civil or criminal cases. One device apparently in use in England was special pleading and the exclusion from evidence of all matters immaterial to the special plea. Special pleading had the capacity of framing a single, simple factual question for the jury which the jury could decide without passing upon the law, since the court's prior determination of the legal sufficiency of proffered pleas resolved all questions of law before a case was given to the jury.[8] But there is no evidence that special pleading was widely used in colonial America, except perhaps in early eighteenth-century Maryland.[9]

Litigants usually preferred to try cases not under a special plea but under a plea of the general issue, so called because it imported an absolute and general denial of every allegation and put all the allegations in issue before the jury. When the general issue was pleaded, juries did not confront only evidence directly relevant to a single issue, but instead heard evidence on several issues and during deliberation had to decide how those issues related to each other.[10] Thus, jurors found not only facts but also the legal consequences of facts; that is, absent other restrictions they decided the law. The result was that although special pleading had the potential to reduce the power of juries to determine law as well as fact, its disuse in colonial America prevented it from attaining that potential.

A second common-law device to control juries' findings of law was the special verdict, by which a jury merely stated its factual conclusions without expressing any opinion about which party should win. The court then applied the law to the facts and rendered judgment. This procedure was not especially effective in controlling the law-finding powers of colonial American juries, however, since all the litigants had to agree to it. Any party could as a matter of right demand a general verdict in which the jury applied the law to the facts.[11] When it was used, counsel on both sides usually would draft notes for the verdict that the jury then rendered; but even then the verdict could be entered on the record only if objections by counsel for both litigants were resolved to their mutual satisfaction. Litigants probably used special verdicts chiefly in complex factual cases where both sides were at least as interested in a judicial declaration of law for their future guidance as in a resolution of the pending dispute.[12] In typical cases, especially if one of the parties anticipated that the jury would render a favorable general verdict, special verdicts were rare.

Furthermore, it was not clear that an unwilling jury could be forced to return a special verdict even if both parties desired one. John Adams, for instance, denied that juries were "under any legal or moral or divine Obligation to find a Special Verdict where they themselves are in no doubt of the Law."[13] The Maryland Provincial Court apparently shared that view, for after the jury in *Smith's Lessee v. Broughton*[14] returned a general verdict in favor of the defendant even though the court, with both parties' consent, had instructed it to find a special verdict, the Maryland court rejected the plaintiff's argument that the jury's disobedience warranted an arrest of judgment.[15]

Some scholars believe that the demurrer to the evidence and the compulsory nonsuit, somewhat similar and overlapping procedures, were also available to prevent juries from applying law to facts.[16] Although either party could claim through a demurrer to the evidence that his opponent's evidence was insufficient to support an allegation, it appears that defendants demurred more commonly than plaintiffs, often claiming at the close of a plaintiff's affirmative case that the evidence did not support the cause of action.[17] When such demurrers were interposed, the judge, circumventing the jury, would rule on the legal sufficiency of the plaintiff's evidence. According to an early nineteenth-century case in South Carolina, the nonsuit similarly lay "wherever it appears that the evidence is insufficient to make out the plaintiff's case, or where there is a total failure of proof necessary for that purpose." In such a case, a trial court was directed to grant a defense motion for nonsuit "whether the plaintiff consent or not."[18]

However, neither the compulsory nonsuit nor the demurrer to evidence effectively reined jury power in eighteenth-century America. Before 1800, published reports include no case in which the compulsory nonsuit was used to prevent a jury from determining an issue of law otherwise before it.[19] The demurrer to evidence, though extant in five states, similarly failed to keep cases away from the jury because procedural disadvantages discouraged its use.[20]

Thus, due to the apparent infrequency of special pleading and the ineffectiveness of demurrers to the evidence and procedures for compulsory nonsuits and special verdicts, juries usually must have returned general verdicts in lawsuits not decided by default. In the absence of modern procedural devices such as judicial instructions on law and evidence and the practice of setting aside verdicts contrary to law or evidence, this meant that juries in both civil and criminal cases were usually called upon to find both law and fact. Although these modern devices were in use in England by the time of *Bright v. Eynon*[21] and *Appleton v. Sweetapple*,[22] neither device was an effective instrument for jury control in pre-Revolutionary America.

Instructions to the jury were ineffective for several reasons. First, it appears that in many cases instructions were brief and rudimentary. In Massachusetts lawyers could and did assume that jurors were "good judges of the common law of the land,"[23] since "[t]he general Rules of Law and common Regulations of Society, under which ordinary Transactions arranged themselves, . . . [were] well enough known to ordinary Jurors."[24] Accordingly juries might be directed that as to many matters, they "need[ed] no Explanation [since] your Good Sence & understanding will Direct ye as to them."[25] In Connecticut the court merely summarized the opposing claims without commenting on the law involved in the case,[26] while in New Hampshire one judge told a jury "to do justice between the parties not by any quirks of the law . . . but by common sense as between man and man."[27] Likewise, in one criminal case in colonial New York, Chief Justice Mompesson informed the jury that "there are some points [of law] I am not now prepared to answer,"[28] while in another case the court informed the jury only that the evidence from the prosecution's witnesses seemed "so ample, so full, so clear and satisfactory" that it should convict the prisoner "if you have no particular reasons in your own breast, in your own consciences to discredit them."[29] Similarly, in South Carolina civil litigation in the 1780s, one jury was instructed "to find a general verdict, or a special one, . . . as they thought proper,"[30] while another jury was told "to give what they thought reasonable" in "damages."[31] In other cases, no instructions were given at all; in Virginia, for example, according to one commentator, there were "numerous cases" in which the jury "retired without a word said by the court upon the subject" of the case.[32]

Instructions were also ineffective because they were often contradictory. One potential source of contradiction was counsel, who on summation could argue the law as well as the facts, at least in Georgia, Massachusetts, New York, Pennsylvania, South Carolina, and Virginia, and probably in other colonies for which no direct evidence is available. Most confusing of all was the court's seriatim charge. Nearly every court in eighteenth-century America sat with more than one judge upon the bench, and it appears to have been the general rule for every judge who was sitting to deliver a charge if he wished to do so. Perhaps the most revealing case is *Georgia v. Brailsford*, where the Supreme Court of the United States sat in 1793 with a Philadelphia jury in an original action brought by the state of Georgia against the defendant Brailsford. There Chief Justice John Jay, reporting perhaps upon his understanding of the general state of American law, told the jury that it was "fortunate on the present, as it must be on every occasion, to find the opinion of the court unanimous" and to have the court "entertain no diversity of sentiment" and "experience . . . no difficulty in uniting in the charge."[33] Such unanimity was not always the case. In both Massachusetts and South Carolina there are examples from the Revolutionary period of judges giving conflicting instructions to juries,[34] and as late as 1803 Alexander Addison, a common pleas judge in Pennsylvania, was successfully impeached for refusing to permit other judges on his court to address juries.[35] Only in Maryland does the routine practice by counsel of preserving exceptions to objectionable instructions suggest that trial judges were required to deliver a single, correct set of instructions or face the prospect of reversal for error.[36]

Of course, whenever jurors received conflicting instructions, they were left with power to determine which judge's interpretation of the law and the facts was correct. Even when the court's instructions were unanimous, however, juries could not be compelled to adhere to them. Once jurors had received evidence on several factual issues and on the parties' possibly conflicting interpretations of the law, a court could compel them to decide in accordance with its view of the case only by setting aside any verdict contrary either to its statement of the law or to the evidence. By the 1750s English courts, upon motion of the losing party, would set aside such a verdict and order a new trial,[37] but most eighteenth-century American jurisdictions did not follow English practice.

In Massachusetts *Erving v. Cradock*[38] made clear the court's lack of jurisdiction to set aside a verdict contrary to its instructions. Similarly, the Connecticut Supreme Court in the 1780s denied several new-trial motions on the ground that "[i]t doth not vitiate a verdict, that the jury have mistaken the law or the evidence: for by the practice of this state, they are judges of both."[39] The Massachusetts and Connecticut rule appears to have been followed throughout New England.[40] Maryland and Virginia also followed the same practice. In Maryland, the provincial court denied one motion in arrest of judgment which alleged that the "Jury [had] reject[ed] law, reason, and evidence"[41] and another motion for a new trial even though the jury had failed to follow instructions given by the court with the consent of both counsel.[42] In Virginia the leading case was the *Parson's Cause*,[43] although an earlier case had also declined to set aside a verdict which the defendant claimed was contrary to the law.[44]

The same rule also appears to have been followed in four other states, although the evidence is somewhat less clear. In *Proprietor v. Keith*,[45] a seventeenth-century Pennsylvania prosecution for seditious libel, the court left to the jury all issues of law and fact, including the question whether the publication was actually seditious. In a 1773 civil case in Pennsylvania, the reporter made special note of the fact that "it was agreed by counsel, that the opinion of the court should be conclusive to the jury"[46]—a note implying that the opinion would not have been conclusive absent the agreement. In another case the reporter noted that "the jury were of the same opinion" as the court,[47] thereby suggesting that juries might sometimes have been of a different view. In South Carolina motions for new trials on the ground that verdicts were against the law were made on four reported occasions in the 1780s and denied without exception, although the courts noted the special circumstances of each case and never articulated a general rule concerning the jury's power to determine the law.[48] In Georgia the Constitution of 1777 barred judges from interfering with the jury's power to determine the law,[49] while New Jersey did the same by statute in 1784.[50] Both these provisions probably confirmed preexisting colonial practice.

Only in New York does evidence exist that judges and other informed commentators believed that a court could grant a new trial if the jury in a civil matter ignored the law, and nearly all this evidence arises from a single 1763 case, *Forsey v. Cunningham*.[51] The supreme court denied a new-trial motion in *Forsey*, but several of the justices and Lieutenant Governor Cadwallader Colden all subsequently contended in letters that courts could set aside verdicts that were against law or evidence.[52] The apparent inconsistency between the justices' statements and their action in *Forsey* can be resolved in several ways,[53] but whatever the inconsistency, it does not appear that colonial New York courts routinely granted new trials in civil cases. Indeed, acting as counsel in his own cause, Robert Livingston in 1784 denounced the new-trial motion as a "new-fangled doctrine of Lord Mansfield" and added that "no single authority" was to be found in its support, in a case of a trial at bar, by a struck jury, in term time."[54] Other lawyers writing about New York practice in that and the next decade still spoke with confusion about the relative powers of court and jury,[55] and as late as 1800 judges did not fully agree that they could set aside a verdict against law or evidence.[56] In criminal cases, of course, *King v. Zenger* established the power of juries to determine law as well as fact,[57] although convictions were set aside in a few cases because juries misapplied the law.[58]

Thus, the various eighteenth-century procedural devices for controlling the power of the jury were only infrequently used and partially effective. It accordingly seems safe to conclude that juries in most, if not all, eighteenth-century American jurisdictions normally had the power to determine law as well as fact in both civil and criminal cases. Statements of contemporary lawyers, moreover, buttress this conclusion; Zephaniah Swift of Connecticut and Robert Treat Paine of Massachusetts said that "[t]he jury were the proper judges, not only of the fact but of the law that was necessarily involved"[59] in each case; that the "Jury ha[d] a right to do as they please[d]";[60] and that "no verdicts . . . [were] thrown out."[61]

Even more telling, perhaps, are statements by three of the most eminent lawyers in late eighteenth-century America—John Adams, Thomas Jefferson, and John Jay. In the early 1770s Adams observed in his diary: "It was never yet disputed, or doubted, that a general Verdict, given *under the Direction of the Court* in Point of Law, was a legal Determination of the Issue." Adams argued that even a verdict contrary to the court's directions should stand, for it was "not only . . . [every juror's] right but his Duty in that Case to find the Verdict according to his own best Understanding, Judgment and Conscience, tho in Direct opposition to the Direction of the court."[62] In 1781–82 Thomas Jefferson painted an equally broad picture of the power of juries over the law in his *Notes on Virginia*. "It is usual for the jurors to decide the fact, and to refer the law arising on it to the decision of the judges," Jefferson wrote. "But this division of the subject lies with their discretion only. And if the question relate to any point of public liberty, or if it be one of those in which the judges may be suspected of bias, the jury undertake to decide both law and fact."[63] As late as 1793 John Jay, sitting as chief justice of the United States, informed a civil jury that while the court usually determined the law and the jury found the facts, the jury nevertheless had "a right to take upon yourselves to judge of both, and to determine the law as well as the fact in controversy." "[B]oth objects," Jay concluded, "are lawfully, within your power of decision."[64]

Shared Values as the Basis of Eighteenth-Century Law

That eighteenth-century juries often decided cases after receiving rudimentary, conflicting, or no instructions from the court suggests that many jurors came to court with preconceptions about the substance of the law. This point was explicitly made in the 1788 Connecticut case of *Pettis v. Warren*.[65] In a black slave's suit for freedom, one juror was challenged for having a preexisting opinion "that 'no negro, by the laws of this state, could be holden a slave.'" Affirming the trial court's overruling of the challenge, the Connecticut Supreme Court held that "[a]n opinion formed and declared upon a general principle of law, does not disqualify a juror to sit in a cause in which that principle applies." Indeed, the court observed that the jurors in every case could "all be challenged on one side or the other, if having an opinion of the law in the case is ground of challenge,"[66] since, as John Adams had once noted, "[t]he general Rules of Law and common Regulations of Society . . . [were] well enough known to ordinary Jurors."[67] Jurors, the Connecticut court believed, were "supposed to have opinions of what the law is," since they sat as "judges of law as well as fact."[68]

One might infer further that jurors came to the court with similar preconceptions about the law, at least as it applied to disputes that frequently came before them. Indeed, one cannot escape this inference without abandoning all efforts to understand how eighteenth-century government functioned. If jurors came to court with different and possibly conflicting opinions about substantive law, one would expect to find, first, that juries had difficulty reaching unanimous verdicts and that mistrials due to hung juries were correspondingly frequent and, second, that different juries at different times would reach different, perhaps inconsistent verdicts, thereby making the law so uncertain and unpredictable that people could not plan their affairs. In fact, no such evidence exists. On the contrary, the available evidence suggests that juries had so little difficulty reaching verdicts that they often heard and decided several cases a day.[69] No one in the mid-eighteenth century complained about the inconsistency of the jury verdicts, and as soon as such complaints were heard in the century's last decade,[70] the system of jury law-finding began to disintegrate.[71]

Although we have no direct evidence, most men probably did not desire to serve as jurors.[72] At a time of difficult travel, few men would have cared to attend court sessions, and those who did probably were pursuing business interests from which jury duty was an unwelcome distraction. In short, there is every reason to think that eighteenth-century citizens avoided jury duty as eagerly as citizens today and that the chore was therefore distributed among as much of the eligible population as could be conscripted.[73] Although some groups (notably women, blacks, servants, religious dissenters, and anyone who did not own land or pay taxes) may have been systematically excluded from juries, it does not seem unreasonable to infer that juries contained a random and representative cross section of the remaining population.[74]

That conclusion suggests a final inference. If juries in fact mirrored the white, male, landowning, and taxpaying population and if upon coming to court nearly all jurors shared similar ideas about the substance of the law, then perhaps a body of shared ideas about law permeated a large segment of the population of every territory over which a court that sat with a jury had jurisdiction. Colonial government may have been able to derive policies from and otherwise function on the basis of those shared values.

Those who live amid the twentieth-century cacophony of conflicting interests may find it difficult to imagine how a government acting only in the absence of serious conflict could ever function effectively. The eighteenth-century Anglo-American world, however, was sufficiently different from our own so that government in that era might have so functioned.

Several differences should be noted. First, the primitive character of the economy meant that most communities could afford only a few salaried officeholders.[75] Indeed, many men did not have enough wealth and time even to participate in elections "without manifest injury to their crops."[76] As a result, competition for local leadership positions was often understandably slight,[77] and local governments lacked substantial salaried bureaucracies that could enforce decisions. Part-time police officials such as deputy sheriffs and constables enforced government decisions, so long, that is, as they did not contravene the wishes of neighbors with whom they had close economic and social ties.[78] The ultimate enforcement body—the militia—was merely the community itself organized as a quasi-military body which would, of course, not act against the community's wishes. Colonial economic conditions, in short, reduced conflict and competition in local politics and precluded the rise of coercive institutions that might have been used by one portion of a community seeking to promote its interests at the expense of others.

Second, colonial American communities differed tremendously. Religion remained important in eighteenth-century life, and America could afford room for almost any religious community.[79] Religious differences were not the only ones among the communities. Important economic differences also existed, for while most communities were agricultural, some were either mercantile or chiefly engaged in fishing. Finally, inarticulable differences in life-style and ambience distinguished communities, as any visitor of the restored colonial towns of Sturbridge, Massachusetts, and Williamsburg, Virginia, can see, or as any reader of the diaries of eighteenth-century travelers like Dr. Alexander Hamilton can learn.[80]

Colonials did not find it especially difficult to change their residence from one community to another. Benjamin Franklin, for example, moved from Boston to Philadelphia with relative ease,[81] while thousands of colonial Americans found the move from established towns to the frontier not at all insuperable.[82] As a result, most colonials who dissented from their own community's conception of right and justice could move without great difficulty to a more congenial community. Newly arriving immigrants were also able to identify and settle in communities that welcomed their religious beliefs, life-styles, and economic skills.[83] The tendency of people to live in communities they found congenial was important, particularly because it enabled communities to retain their identity by facilitating the departure of those whose personal ethical codes would have diluted that identity.

But while colonial Americans could readily move between communities, they generally seem not to have established the kind of sustained intercommunity contact likely to produce conflict. American communities had long since abandoned schemes of subjugating each other or seizing each other's wealth; the Dutch of Manhattan and the Puritans of Long Island, for example, learned how to coexist when they each abandoned thoughts of conquest and developed their primary social and economic communication with their respective compatriots in the Hudson Valley and in New England rather than with each other.[84] The availability of land,[85] which made territorial quarrels unnecessary, and the lack of a developed transportation and communication network, which made sustained contact difficult, also help account for the infrequency of disputes between communities. Geographically proximate communities were thus able to remain distinct,[86] to pursue their own conception of right, and to avoid intercommunity disputes that legal institutions dependent on local community support would have been incapable of resolving.[87]

Finally, colonial politics existed within an established constitutional structure which colonials could not control. Parliament, in which colonials had no direct voice, alone possessed the power to decide many fundamental social and economic issues, and for the first sixty years of the eighteenth century it was willing to abide by decisions reached in the preceding century that were often favorable to the colonies. Thus, much of the grist for genuine political conflict was removed from the realm of imperial politics; absent a radical restructuring of the Anglo-American system, there was simply no point in building a political organization around the issue of whether, for example, Anglicans would be tolerated in Massachusetts[88] or whether Americans would be free to trade with French Canada without restriction.[89]

Provincial politics were not radically different. Americans controlled their colonial legislatures, but they could not effectively enact legislation that significantly altered the structure of colonial society since such legislation would almost always be vetoed by a colonial governor or by London.[90] As a result, colonial legislation usually consisted of mere administration: raising and appropriating small amounts of tax money, distributing the even smaller amounts of government largess, and legislating as necessary to keep the few governmental institutions functioning.[91] While provincial political conflict commonly occurred, it rarely involved important social issues.[92] Of course, occasional conflicts grew from religious differences, such as the division in Pennsylvania politics between Quaker and anti-Quaker parties, and from the rivalry between seaboard and backcountry areas, such as the 1740s land-bank dispute in Massachusetts and the 1760s Regulator movement in the Carolinas.[93] But since these disputes could not be locally resolved within the British power structure, they quickly degenerated into mere personal and factional conflicts between men seeking personal advancement.[94] Provincial political conflict may have been widespread, but as shrewdly observant colonial political writers vehemently announced, it departed from the ideal polity of consensus[95]—a polity which may have existed in many eighteenth-century local communities.

Taken together, these facts may have helped to sustain a political order in colonial America radically different from the political order of America today. The stable imperial constitution combined with primitive colonial economies to remove most social and economic issues from imperial and provincial politics. Before Independence, most newly arising socioeconomic conflicts were resolved and new socioeconomic decisions taken at the local level. The primitiveness of the colonial economy had another influence: by keeping the social elite small and depriving it of effective military and bureaucratic power necessary to coerce the people at large, the colonial American economic system denied colonial leaders the opportunity to exploit their localities in their own self-interest. Colonial leaders generally had to govern and resolve social tensions according to values commonly accepted in their localities. Finally, the real differences between localities and the ease with which people could move to a community whose ideas they shared preserved each community's distinct identity. As a result, the colonial American polity may on the whole have consisted of a series of local communities whose inhabitants jointly defined standards of right and justice and insured that the community lived by those standards.

Notes

This chapter is adapted and reprinted, with permission, from William E. Nelson, *The Eighteenth-Century Background of John Marshall's Constitutional Jurisprudence*, 76 Mich. L. Rev. 893 (1978).

1. *See* P. Bonomi, *A Factious People* (New York: Columbia Univ. Press, 1971), pp. 145, 227; C. Sydnor, *Gentlemen Freeholders* (Chapel Hill: Univ. of North Carolina Press, 1952), pp. 83–84, 86–93; *Annals of Congress*, vol. 18 (Washington, D.C.: Gales & Seaton, 1834), p. 110 (remarks of Sen. Hillhouse).

2. For example, Parliament passed the Navigation Acts to increase the wealth of the entire empire (*see generally*, O. Dickerson, *The Navigation Acts and the American Revolution* [Philadelphia: Univ. of Pennsylvania Press, 1951]; L. Harper, *The English Navigation Laws* [New York: Octagon Books, 1939]), and colonial legislatures passed inspection acts to promote the sale of colonial products abroad (*see* J. Goebel and T. Naughton, *Law Enforcement in Colonial New York* [New York: Commonwealth Fund, 1944], p. 41 n. 201; O. Handlin and M. Handlin, *Commonwealth*, rev. ed. [Cambridge: Belknap, 1969], pp. 64–65).

3. *See* Bonomi, *A Factious People*, p. 36 n. 27; R. Ireland, *The County Courts*

in Antebellum Kentucky (Lexington: Univ. Press of Kentucky, 1972), pp. 18–31; W. Nelson, *Americanization of the Common Law*, p. 15; C. Sydnor, *American Revolutionaries in the Making* (New York: Free Press, 1965), pp. 80–85; M. Creech, *Three Centuries of Poor Law Administration* (Chicago: Univ. of Chicago Press, 1936), pp. 8–75; J. Benton, *Warning Out in New England* (Freeport, N.Y.: Books for Libraries Press, 1970), pp. 9, 118–21.

4. *See* Ireland, *The County Courts in Antebellum Kentucky*, p. 18; Nelson, *Americanization of the Common Law*, p. 15; Sydnor, *American Revolutionaries in the Making*, p. 80; Bockelman, *Local Government in Colonial Pennsylvania*, and Carr, *The Foundations of Social Order: Local Government in Colonial Maryland*, in B. Daniels, ed., *Town and County* (Middletown, Conn.: Wesleyan Univ. Press, 1978), pp. 91–93, 216–21. Local courts had fewer powers, however, in New York and South Carolina (*see* Bonomi, *A Factious People*, pp. 35–36; M. Sirmans, *Colonial South Carolina* [Chapel Hill: Univ. of North Carolina Press, 1966], pp. 250–52).

5. For a discussion of Montesquieu, see M. Vile, *Constitutionalism and the Separation of Powers* (Oxford: Clarendon Press, 1967), pp. 76–97.

6. *Four Letters on Interesting Subjects* (Philadelphia, 1776), p. 21.

7. *See* Katz, *The Politics of Law in Colonial America*, 5 Perspectives in American History 257, 262–65 (1971); Nelson, *Americanization of the Common Law*, p. 21.

8. *See* Nelson, *Americanization of the Common Law*, pp. 21–22 and sources cited therein.

9. Litigants in Massachusetts rarely continued special pleading beyond defendant's initial plea and the plaintiff's joinder of issue or joinder in demurrer (*see* ibid., p. 23), and the published colonial cases suggest that special pleading was also rare in Pennsylvania and Virginia. The only special pleading case reported in pre-Revolutionary Pennsylvania, *Swift v. Hawkins*, 1 Dall. 17 (Pa. 1768), involved merely a joinder of issue to a plea of payment in a writ of debt. No cases of special pleading are recorded in T. Jefferson, ed., *Reports of Cases Determined in the General Court of Virginia from 1730 to 1740; and from 1768 to 1772* (Charlottesville: O. F. Carr, 1829), the only volume of pre-Revolutionary Virginia cases.

10. A plea of the general issue did not frame a single, precise factual question for two reasons. First, a typical complaint alleged several facts, all of which a general denial put in issue. Second, courts did not restrict the parties (as they did in the case of a special plea) to proof only of facts tending to verify their allegations. The test of admissibility of evidence under the general issue was not relevance to a single factual question but whether as a matter of law the proposed evidence ought to constitute a good defense to the plaintiff's action (Nelson, *Americanization of the Common Law*, pp. 22–23).

11. *See generally* Henderson, *The Background of the Seventh Amendment*, 80 Harv. L. Rev. 289, 307–10 (1966); L. Wroth and H. Zobel, eds., "Introduction" to *Legal Papers of John Adams*, vol. 1 (Cambridge: Belknap, 1965), p. xlvii.

12. This is at least my sense after an extensive, albeit unsystematic, search of Massachusetts courts from the mid-eighteenth century.

13. Wroth and Zobel, *Legal Papers of John Adams* 1:230.

14. 1 H. & McH. 33 (Md. Provincial Ct. 1714). As recorded, the disposition of the case is ambiguous and subject to misinterpretation if read in isolation. Because the final entry in *Broughton* is "[j]udgment on the verdict of nonsuit," the case has been read to grant a compulsory nonsuit "by implication" (Henderson, *Background of the Seventh Amendment*, p. 301 n. 25). In fact, this literal reading of the entry is impossible: the verdict in *Broughton* was for the defendant, the plaintiff was the moving party, and a plaintiff could not nonsuit himself (*see* note 17, *infra*). Thus, the phrase "[j]udgment on the verdict of nonsuit" in *Broughton* probably indicates the entry of judgment for defendant, as dictated by the verdict, despite the plaintiff's motion in arrest of judgment on the ground that the jury's general verdict violated the agreement of the parties. An evaluation of the case found in the index to the volume further confirms this conclusion.

15. For a New York case in which a jury returned a general verdict after the parties had agreed on a special one, *see Brown v. Clock* (N.Y. Sup. Ct. 1695).

16. *See* Henderson, *Background of the Seventh Amendment*, 80 Harv. L. Rev. 289, 300–301, 304–5 (1966).

17. Although a plaintiff could theoretically demur to a defendant's evidence (*see Kissam v. Burrell*, Kirby 326, 328 [Conn. Super. Ct. 1787]; *Smith v. Steinbach*, 2 Cai. Cas. 158, 171 [N.Y. 1805]; *Lessee of the Proprietary v. Ralston*, 1 Dall. 18, 18 [Pa. Sup. Ct. 1773]), he rarely advanced his interest by doing so.

18. *Hopkins v. De Graffenreid*, 2 S.C.L. (2 Bay) 441, 445 (1802). English authority existed for nonsuiting a plaintiff even after a jury had rendered a verdict in his favor if a nonsuit would have been appropriate prior to submission of the case to the jury. *See, e.g., Abbot v. Plumbe*, 1 Dougl. 216, 99 Eng. Rep. 141 (K.B. 1799); *Bird v. Randall*, 1 Bl.W. 373, 96 Eng. Rep. 210 (K.B.), *reargued*, 1 Bl.W. 387, 96 Eng. Rep. 218 (K.B. 1762).

19. The only states in which nonsuit cases have been found are Maryland, New Jersey, New York, Pennsylvania, and South Carolina (*see* Henderson, *Background of the Seventh Amendment*, p. 301). In Maryland, the earliest reported case occurred in 1802 (*see Webb's Lessee v. Beard*, 1 H. & J. 349 [Gen. Ct. 1802]).

20. As the Pennsylvania Supreme Court implied in *Hurst v. Dippo*, 1 Dall. 20 (Pa. 1774), the demurrer to the evidence as "disused" in most colonies. The most severe disadvantage was that the demurrant had to admit all the facts shown in the evidence against him and all adverse inferences that could be drawn from those facts.

21. 1 Burr. 390, 2 Keny. 53, 96 Eng. Rep. 1104 (K.B. 1757). For the English practice on rejection of jury verdicts, see generally Henderson, *Background of the Seventh Amendment*, pp. 311–12; Note on the Development of the Right to a New Trial in England, in J. Goebel and J. Smith, eds., *The Law Practice of Alexander Hamilton: Document and Commentary* (New York: Columbia Univ. Press, 1964–81), vol. 3.

22. 3 Dougl. 137, 140–41, 99 Eng. Rep. 579, 580 (K.B. 1782).

23. James Sullivan to Elbridge Gerry, Dec. 25, 1779, Massachusetts Historical Society, *quoted in* Nelson, *Americanization of the Common Law*, p. 26.

24. Wroth and Zobel, *Legal Papers of John Adams* 1:230.

25. Grand Jury Charge (1759), Cushing Papers, box 1, Massachusetts Historical Society, *quoted in* Nelson, *Americanization of the Common Law*, p. 26.

27. *See* Howe, *Juries as Judges of Criminal Law*, 52 Harv. L. Rev. 582, 601 (1939).

28. *See* G. Wood, *The Creation of the American Republic, 1776–1787* (Chapel Hill: Univ. of North Carolina Press, 1969), p. 297.

28. *Queen v. Makemie* (1707), in P. Force, ed., *Tracts . . .*, 4:44, no. 4, *quoted in* Goebel and Naughton, *Law Enforcement in Colonial New York*, p. 666.

29. *King v. Hughson* (1741), Horsmander Papers, box 120, New-York Historical Society Library, *quoted in* Goebel and Naughton, *Law Enforcement in Colonial New York*, p. 667.

30. *Pledger v. Wade*, 1 S.C.L. (1 Bay) 35, 36 (1786).

31. *Eveleigh v. Administrators of Stitt*, 1 S.C.L. (1 Bay) 92, 92 (1789). *See also Liber v. Executors of Parsons*, 1 S.C.L. (1 Bay) 19 (1785).

32. *Commonwealth v. Garth*, 3 Leigh 761, 773, 30 Va. 825, 838 (General Ct. 1831) (Leigh's amicus curiae brief). *See also* Nelson, *Americanization of the Common Law*, p. 26.

33. 3 U.S. (3 Dall.) 1, 4 (1794).

34. *See Pateshall v. Apthorp*, Quincy 179 (Mass. 1765); *Bromfield v. Little*, Quincy 108 (Mass. 1764); *Hanlon v. Thayer*, Quincy 99 (Mass. 1764); *Derumple v. Clark*, Quincy 38 (Mass. 1763); *Jackson v. Foye*, Quincy 26 (Mass. 1762); *Cooke v. Rhine*, 1 S.C.L. (1 Bay) 16 (1784).

35. In one Pennsylvania case, the reporter noted that "[t]he Court were unanimous and clear in their opinions" (*Boehm v. Engle*, 1 Dall. 15, 16 [Pa. 1767]). We may infer that such unanimity was worthy of mention.

36. *See, e.g.*, *Coursey v. Wright*, 1 H. & McH. 394 (Md. Provincial Ct. 1771); *Joce's Lessee v. Harris*, 1 H. & Mc.H. 196, 197 (Md. Provincial Ct. 1754); *Crow's Lessee v. Scott*, 1 H. & Mc.H. 182, 184 (Md. Provincial Ct. 1751).

37. *See* text at notes 21–22, *supra*.

38. Quincy 553 (Mass. 1761). On the new trial motion in Massachusetts, see also Nelson, *Americanization of the Common Law*, pp. 27–28.

39. *Wittner v. Brewster*, Kirby 422, 423 (Conn. Super. Ct. 1788). In addition, see *Carpenter v. Child*, 1 Root 220 (Conn. Super. Ct. 1790); *Pettis v. Warren*, Kirby 426 (Conn. Super. Ct. 1788); *Taylor v. Geary*, Kirby 313 (Conn. Super. Ct. 1787); *Wickham v. Waterman*, Kirby 273 (Conn. Super. Ct. 1787); *Woodruff v. Whittlesey*, Kirby 60 (Conn. Super. Ct. 1786).

40. Howe, *Juries as Judges of Criminal Law*, p. 591.

41. Keech's *Lessee v. Dansey*, 1 H. & McH. 20, 21 (Md. Provincial Ct. 1704).

42. *Smith's Lessee v. Broughton*, 1 H. & McH. 33 (Md. Provincial Ct. 1714). *See* note 14, *supra*. *But see Miller's Lessee v. Hynson*, 1 H. & McH. 84 (Md. Provincial Ct. 1734), where the jury attached an erroneous conclusion of law to its special factual findings. Under these circumstances, the court set the verdict aside and ordered a new trial.

43. Reverend James Maury sued in *Parson's Cause* to collect that portion of salary which the defendant, through Patrick Henry, claimed was barred by an act of the House of Burgesses. The court instructed the jury that the bur-

gesses' act, which had been subsequently disallowed by the Privy Council, was void ab initio and hence that the plaintiff deserved his full salary, but when the jury awarded damages of one penny, the court denied Maury's motion for a new trial on the ground that the verdict contradicted the evidence (James Maury to John Camm, Dec. 12, 1763, in J. Fontaine, *Memoirs of a Huguenot Family* [Baltimore: Geneological Publishing Co., 1867], pp. 418–24 [discussing *Parson's Cause* (1763)]).

44. *Waddill v. Chamberlayne*, Jeff. 10 (Va. 1735). It is unclear, however, whether the court agreed with the jury or believed that it lacked the power to dismiss a jury verdict.

45. *Reported in* S. Pennypacker, *Pennsylvania Colonial Cases* (Philadelphia: R. Welsh, 1892), p. 117. *See* Testimony of Judge Edward Tilghman, *in Report of the Trial of the Honorable Samuel Chase* (New York: Da Capo Press, 1970), p. 27.

46. Anonymous, 1 Dall. 20, 20 (Pa. 1773).

47. *Lessee of Albertson v. Robeson*, 1 Dall. 9 (Pa. 1764). In *Boehm v. Eagle*, 1 Dall. 15, 16 (Pa. 1767), the reporter said that the "jury was conformable to [the court's] opinion." And in *Lessee of the Proprietary v. Ralston*, 1 Dall. 18, 19 (Pa. 1773), the reporter plainly implied that the jury was determining the law when "[a] verdict passed for the plaintiff, by which the sense of the jury was that the non-performance of conditions of settlement, did not void the grant." *Cf. Hurst v. Dippo*, 1 Dall. 20, 21 (Pa. 1774).

48. *Steel, qui tam v. Roach*, 1 S.C.L. (1 Bay) 62 (1788); *Bourke v. Bulow*, 1 S.C.L. (1 Bay) 49 (1787); *Pledger v. Wade*, 1 S.C.L. (1 Bay) 35 (1786); *Mounier v. Meyrey*, 1 S.C.L. (1 Bay) 24 (1785). *See also White v. McNeily*, 1 S.C.L. (1 Bay) 11, 12 (1784), where the jury's apportioning of damages among joint tortfeasors "was at first doubted as a deviation from the old common law rule . . . [that the] jury could not sever." The court, "upon mature consideration," sanctioned the verdict, but it is unclear whether the court recognized the jury's power to decide law or simply considered the jury's verdict a better rule.

49. Ga. Const. of 1777, sec. 411.

50. An Act for regulating and shortening the Proceedings in the Courts of Law, 1784 N.J. Laws, ch. 32, sec. 14. New Jersey's act prohibited trial courts from vacating jury verdicts but did make verdicts subject to reversal by the court of error.

51. N.Y. Sup. Ct., 1763.

52. *See* the statements of judges Jones and Livingston in "Report of the Case between Forsey and Cunningham," *New-York Gazette; or, The Weekly Post-Boy*, Jan. 31, 1765, at 1, col. 3, and at 2, col. 1; Cadwallader Colden to the Earl of Halifax, Dec. 13, 1764, in E. O'Callaghan, ed., *Documents Relative to the Colonial History of the State of New York*, vol. 7 (Albany: Weed, Parsons and Co., 1856), pp. 682–84.

53. Possible explanations for the New York Supreme Court's action in *Forsey* are (1) that the court did not consider the verdict to be against law or evidence and hence would not set it aside on that ground, or (2) that the court did consider the verdict to be against evidence but held the granting of a new trial under such conditions to be an act of discretion which it chose not to exercise in the instant case.

54. J. Kent, An Address Delivered be-

fore the Law Association of the City of New York (Oct. 21, 1836), in (pts. 1–2) 1 Colum. Jur. 110, 122, at 123 (1885).

55. *Compare* Goebel and Smith, *The Law Practice of Alexander Hamilton* 1:60, 118, *and* W. Wyche, *A Treatise on the Practice of the Supreme Court of Jurisdiction* 2d ed., 1784 (New York: Arno, 1972), pp. 168, 176.

56. In the two cases of *Wilkie v. Roosevelt*, 3 Johns. Cas. 66 (N.Y. Sup. Ct. 1803); 3 Johns. Cas. 206 (N.Y. Sup. Ct. 1802), judges Thompson, Radcliff, and Kent ruled in favor of a new trial; Chief Judge Lewis and Judge Livingston dissented. The *Wilkie* juries clearly expressed their feelings on the issue of vacating verdicts by thrice defying the court's instructions; after the third trial the litigants accepted the jury's perverse verdict. The case is discussed in Goebel and Smith, *The Law Practice of Alexander Hamilton* 2:228–31.

57. *See* Goebel and Naughton, *Law Enforcement in Colonial New York*, pp. 239–40, 278–79, 588–89, 666, 669; *see, e.g., People v. Barrett*, 1 Johns. 66 (N.Y. Sup. Ct. 1806).

58. *See* Goebel and Naughton, *Law Enforcement in Colonial New York*, pp. 278–79; *see, e.g., People v. Townsend*, 1 Johns. Cas. 104 (N.Y. Sup. Ct. 1799).

59. Z. Swift, *A System of the Law of the State of Connecticut* (New York: Arno, 1795–96), 1:410, 2:257–59.

60. *Lyon v. Cobb* (Bristol County Ct. of C.P. 1769), *quoted in* Nelson, *Americanization of the Common Law*, p. 28 (argument of counsel).

61. *Quincy v. Howard* (Bristol County Ct. of C.P. 1770), *quoted in* Nelson, *Americanization of the Common Law*, p. 28 (argument of counsel).

62. Wroth and Zobel, *Legal Papers of John Adams* 1:230.

63. T. Jefferson, *Notes on the State of Virginia*, ed. J. Randolph (1853), p. 140.

64. *Georgia v. Brailsford*, 3 U.S. (3 Dall.) 1, 4 (1794).

65. Kirby 426 (Conn. Sup. Ct. 1788).

66. *Id.*, at 427.

67. Wroth and Zobel, *Legal Papers of John Adams* 1:230.

68. Kirby at 427.

69. Wroth and Zobel, "Introduction," *Legal Papers of John Adams* 1:xlvii. Most extant eighteenth-century court records show that courts rarely met for terms exceeding several days and that they often disposed of more than 100 cases during those terms, many of them by jury verdicts.

70. *See* M. Horwitz, *Transformation of American Law* (Cambridge: Harvard Univ. Press, 1977), p. 28; Nelson, *Americanization of the Common Law*, p. 165; Swift, *System of Law for the State of Connecticut* 2:257–59.

71. Between 1790 and 1820 courts in nearly every state for which evidence exists began to grant motions for new trials in civil cases where juries returned verdicts contrary to law, instructions, or evidence.

72. Under eighteenth-century law, jurors were selected by one of several largely random processes: they were chosen by lot from a list of freeholders, elected by the voters of the jurisdiction, or summoned by the sheriff from among the bystanders at court.

73. The one available local study indicates, in fact, that between one-fourth and one-third of all adult males served on juries. *See* Nelson, *Introductory Essay: The Larger Context of Litigation in*

Plymouth County, 1725–1825, in D. Konig, ed., *Legal Records of Plymouth County, 1686–1859*, vol. 1 (Wilmington: M. Glazier, 1978), p. 25.

74. *Cf.* C. Williamson, *American Suffrage* (Princeton, N.J.: Princeton Univ. Press, 1960), pp. 20–39, which concludes that between one-half and three-fourths of all adult white males were qualified to vote in most localities in eighteenth-century America.

75. Virginia justices, for example, received neither salary nor fee for their services (Sydnor, *Gentlemen Freeholders*, p. 84). The fees paid to Massachusetts judges and judicial officers were not particularly high either (*see* Wroth and Zobel, "Introduction" to *Legal Papers of John Adams* 1:lxix–lxxi).

76. Freeholders' Appeal to the Governor, *quoted in* Sydnor, *Gentlemen Freeholders*, p. 33.

77. That local officials had to be compelled by law to serve evinces the lack of competition for many local offices, (*see* Nelson, *Americanization of the Common Law*, p. 38; *cf.* Greenberg, *The Effectiveness of Law Enforcement in Eighteenth-Century New York*, 19 Am. J. Legal Hist. 173, 174–86 [1975] [finding qualified men willing to serve as law enforcement officers was difficult]). At times, even legislative elections were not competitive (*see* Bonomi, *A Factious People*, p. 190).

78. *See* Greenberg, *The Effectiveness of Law Enforcement*, pp. 175–79; Nelson, *The Legal Restraint of Power in Pre-Revolutionary America: Massachusetts as a Case Study, 1760–1775*, 18 Am. J. Legal Hist. 7–9, 30–32 (1974).

79. Puritan communities prevailed, of course, in New England, as Anglican communities did throughout the South, but Dutch Calvinists established communities in New York. Quakers settled in Pennsylvania, and Baptists and Presbyterians scattered communities along the frontier. Other sorts of Protestant communities also existed, as well as Roman Catholic communities in Maryland and even a Jewish community in New York. *See* H. Grinstein, *The Rise of the Jewish Community of New York, 1654–1860* (Philadelphia: Jewish Publication Society of America, 1945); H. Browne, *Catholicism in the United States*, in *The Shaping of American Religion*, eds. J. Smith and A. Jamison (Princeton, N.J.: Princeton Univ. Press, 1961), pp. 72, 74–75.

80. *See* Alexander Hamilton, *Gentlemen's Progress*, ed. C. Bridenbaugh (Chapel Hill: Univ. of North Carolina Press, 1948).

81. *See* C. Van Doren, *Benjamin Franklin* (New York: Viking, 1938), pp. 37–44.

82. C. Grant, *Democracy in the Connecticut Frontier Town of Kent* (New York: Columbia Univ. Press, 1961), pp. 28–103, discusses one example of the ease of settlement. In particular, Grant shows that in the twenty-two years following Kent's founding in 1738, 772 different men bought land in the town, 61 percent of whom took up residence (ibid., p. 56).

83. News of the different colonies' willingness to receive immigrants filtered back to Europe in vast quantities. *See* M. Hansen, *The Atlantic Migration, 1607–1860* (Cambridge: Harvard Univ. Press, 1940), pp. 32–52; Conway, *Welsh Emigration to the United States*, in 7 Perspectives in American History 175, 185–88 (1973).

84. *See* D. Fox, *Yankees and Yorkers* (New York: New York Univ. Press, 1940), pp. 57–151.

85. *See* Hansen, *The Atlantic Migra-*

tion, p. 45. Until the middle of the eighteenth century, even the smaller and older colonies like Connecticut had free land on which new towns could be founded (*see* Grant, *Democracy in the Connecticut Frontier Town of Kent*, pp. 3–11).

86. *See* C. Nettels, *The Emergence of a National Economy, 1775–1815* (New York: Holt, Rinehart, and Winston, 1962), pp. 38–40.

87. *See* Bonomi, *A Factious People*, pp. 24–28.

88. Pressure from London forced Massachusetts to treat Anglicans as a separate denomination exempt from religious taxation. *See* C. Bridenbaugh, *Mitre and Sceptre: Transatlantic Faiths, Ideas, Personalities, and Politics, 1689–1775* (New York: Oxford Univ. Press, 1962), pp. 73–74.

89. The Navigation Acts, of course, prohibited trade between the colonies and French Canada. *See* note 2, *supra*.

90. For example, English authorities overrode Massachusetts's land-bank legislation. *See* J. Schutz, *William Shirley, King's Governor of Massachusetts* (Chapel Hill: Univ. of North Carolina Press, 1961), p. 40.

91. *See* Nelson, *Americanization of the Common Law*, p. 14.

92. *See generally* B. Bailyn, *The Origins of American Politics* (New York: Knopf, 1968); S. Katz, *Newcastle's New York* (Cambridge: Belknap, 1968), pp. 44–58; Schutz, *William Shirley, King's Governor of Massachusetts*.

93. *See* J. Hutson, *Pennsylvania Politics, 1746–1770* (Princeton, N.J.: Princeton Univ. Press, 1972), p. 130; *see* Schutz, *William Shirley, King's Governor of Massachusetts*, pp. 37–40; *see* R. Brown, *The South Carolina Regulators* (Cambridge: Belknap, 1963), pp. 38–63.

94. *See* Hutson, *Pennsylvania Politics*, pp. 130–77; Schutz, *William Shirley, King's Governor of Massachusetts*, pp. 48–57, 62–63.

95. *See* Bailyn, *The Origins of American Politics*, pp. 64–65.

Ronald J. Allen

24. Unexplored Aspects of the Theory of the Right to Trial by Jury

There was a time—quite a long time, in fact—when members of the legal profession viewed legal institutions as self-contained, virtually hermetically sealed organisms whose purposes could be ascertained and furthered by internal self-examination. This was a time when doctrine reigned supreme, and its grip extended over the entire domain ranging from those engaged in the most mundane practice to those engaged in the most theoretical speculations about the legal system. To be sure, the realists during the early part of this century mounted an assault upon the traditionally narrow way of conceiving of the legal system. Their efforts did not much shake the legal system loose from the narrow conception of legal reality, however, and in any event the realists were soon overwhelmed by the resurgence of positivism with its primary message that "the rule's the thing, while all else is secondary."[1] The pervasiveness of the narrow conception of the legal system is captured in an extraordinary way in a recent article by Judge Richard Posner:

> Such was the atmosphere of the Harvard Law School when I was a student. With a handful of exceptions . . . the faculty believed, or at least appeared to believe, that the only thing law students needed to study was authoritative legal texts—judicial and administrative opinions, statutes, and rules—and the only essential preparation for a legal scholar was the knowledge of what was in those texts, and the power of logical discrimination and argumentation that came from close and critical study of them. The difference from Langdell's day—a difference that was the legacy of Holmes and the legal realists—was that law now was recognized to be a deliberate instrument of social control, so that one had to know something about society to be able to understand law, criticize it, and improve it. The "something," however, was what any intelligent person with a good general education and some common sense knew; or could pick up from the legal texts themselves (viewed as windows on social custom); or, failing these sources of insight, would acquire naturally in a few years of practicing law: a set of basic ethical and political values, some knowledge of institutions, some acquaintance with the workings of the economy.[2]

The narrow conception of the law has come increasingly into disfavor in the last two decades for a number of reasons. The first, and perhaps most important, is the increasing democratization of virtually all institutions in the United States, including legal institutions. On the one hand, this is the inevitable result of the reach of the law extending further and further into everyday affairs. As that occurs, the law not only affects but is affected by everyday life, and thus its insularity is reduced. On the other hand, the democratization of the legal system is simply another example of the increasing skepticism with which claims of privilege are met in our society. Doctors no longer behave in a dictatorial fashion toward their patients; rather, they explain in detail the treatment options that are available and assist the patient in choosing. The claims of organized religion to superior access to wisdom and godliness carry less and less weight, as the Catholic church in the United States in particular is learning to its regret these days as a result of the lay revolt against its teaching on various issues. And our public leaders are scrutinized in a manner which would have been unthinkable twenty years ago. Similarly, the legal system, and its claims of special privilege, are subject to increasingly intense scrutiny by the lay public and by its representatives in the legislative branches of government. "Tort reform" is the most current, but by no means the only example of exogenous forces being brought to bear upon the legal system.

There are other factors at play, as well. Related academic disciplines have expanded their reach and provided insightful analyses of legal institutions. Economics, literary theory, and philosophy are the disciplines most in vogue right now, but political theory, psychology, game theory, history and sociology, among many others, have made and are continuing to make important contributions to our understanding of legal institutions. The interdisciplinary barriers between law and related disciplines are breaking down, and an educated lawyer must now have a thorough grounding in subject matters that a short time ago would have been viewed at least as unnecessary for, if not alien to, the study of law.

What, one might wonder, does any of this have to do with the right to trial by jury? After all, the great battles between the economists and their adversaries are being fought over such issues as antitrust policy and the nature of the tort system, not over much that has to do with provisions in the Bill of Rights providing for jury trials. Similarly, philosophy and political theory have been brought into the debate over competing conceptions of the constitutional vision, and their implications have not reached the level of such housekeeping matters as the form of trial.

While the right to trial by jury, in both its Sixth and Seventh Amendment forms, may be primarily a matter of housekeeping, it has certain intriguing aspects that make it ripe for consideration from the broader perspective evident in much legal scholarship today. It is one of our most democratic institutions and thus may sustain, and in any event is certainly quite compatible with, the continuing democratization of the country. More intriguing still, the right to trial by jury occupies one of the important intersections of law and common affairs. Its existence requires that the isolation of the law be broken by mandating that outcomes in trials be determined by individuals extraneous to the system. Consequently, the law must explain itself to such individuals and is affected by the decisions that they reach.

Those decisions, presumably, are the product of the values and the thought processes individual jurors bring to their task. But saying that opens up the institution of trial by jury to the probing eyes of all the law's sister disciplines. What, exactly, are the values that jurors bring to their task? How should they affect the outcome of cases? Should jurors bring those values to the fore in deliberations, or should they be encouraged to suppress their personal values and apply instead the values of the legal system as explained to them by judges? Does it, in any event, make sense to talk about the jurors' "suppressing" their own values? How does rational thought progress if not from a stable matrix formed from the experiences and beliefs of particular individuals? What does it mean to "deliberate," and how does it occur? Or does it matter how it occurs? Is this an issue which is better left unexamined? What if we discovered, for example, that the views of women are less forcefully presented in juries with a mix of males and females than they would be in a group composed of all females? Would that matter?

There are, in short, numerous issues integral to the right to trial by jury that may be enlightened from a perspective extraneous to the law, and indeed work is proceeding on many of these issues. In addition to arguing that lawyers have much to learn from other disciplines about the implications of the right to trial by jury, I will be making the related point that the failure to think carefully about this right, employing all the tools available within our culture, has resulted in the legal system reaching some curious positions if not making outright mistakes. The deep structure of my argument, though, should by now be clear. The right to trial by jury poses fundamental questions about the nature and structure of the legal system.

I want to explore briefly two areas. The first is the nature of evidence, and the second is the nature of deliberation.

Beginning an analysis which is supposed to focus on the right to trial by jury with an inquiry into the nature of evidence may seem a bit odd, but I think that it is the best place to begin. Under the current conception of trial by jury, jurors are to hear evidence and decide cases based upon that evidence. Thus, the nature of evidence is a crucial variable underlying the right to have a trial by jury based upon that evidence.

Crucial it may be, but perhaps you are thinking that it is not terribly difficult. After all, evidence is that which the parties produce at trial, and basing their deliberation upon what is produced—and only what is produced—the jurors are to decide the case. Such is the standard conception of evidence. But how convincing or powerful a concept is it? Take a somewhat crude but nonetheless interesting example. When witnesses testify at trial, they normally do so through the spoken word. To understand what the witness says, one must understand what the words mean that the witness is employing. Yet, the meaning of the various words spoken by witnesses will rarely itself be the subject of evidence at trial. How, then, is it possible for the jurors to decide the case based solely upon what is produced as evidence? Obviously, it is not possible. Instead, the matrix of decision must include the language skills of the jurors, and only in the unusual case will the language of witnesses be the subject of inquiry at trial. This recognition, though, requires a significant modification of the general principle that the jury decides based only upon what is produced at trial.

Press the matter further. Suppose a witness testifies that the light was red when the defendant's car went through it, and suppose further that the case is one of negligence premised upon the running of a red light. Does this testimony establish the plaintiff's case so that a decision in the plaintiff's favor can now be rendered? Of course not, but why not? The answer, of course, is that for an untold number of reasons this testimony may be false, which here means not consistent with objective reality. How is a jury to know whether the testimony is true or false? Again, the answer seems obvious, but its obviousness hides a profound point. The jury will judge this testimony in light of the jury's experience and background. Does the witness appear to know what the word "red" means? Is there anything about this witness that suggests he is lying? Was he squirming on the stand, or does he have an interest in the case? Does his testimony make sense, which means, of course, make sense from the perspective of the jury? And, of course, the opposing side must have an opportunity to demonstrate that the witness is in error for one reason or another. That will be done by the presentation of further evidence that, like the evidence of the plaintiff, will be assessed in light of the jurors' background and experience in life.

Like language, the jury's experience and perspective are crucial variables in determining the effect of the words that a witness speaks at trial, and like language, they will not be the subject matter of evidence themselves. In fact, jurors are typically instructed to take their experience into account in deciding cases and to exercise judgment. Yet another large qualification must now be added to the principle that the jury is to decide the case based upon what is produced at trial. What is produced at trial is but the tip of a very large iceberg, and while important, it is no more so than the great bulk of the iceberg lying below the surface. Indeed, has not our basic conception of evidence been thrown into doubt? Our initial conception focused on the act of producing something at trial, yet we are driven to see evidence not as a thing produced at trial but instead as the result of an interactive process between what is produced at trial and the jury. Evidence, in other words, is whatever influences a jury on propositions material to a case. What will influence a jury, however, is a function of how what is produced at trial is analyzed by each juror in light of his or her background and experience.

Interestingly enough, the law recognizes this point. It does so by permitting the parties to litigate a case at virtually whatever level of generality they like. Thus, if the plaintiff in our hypothetical was concerned that the jury may doubt whether the witness knows the difference between red and green, evidence may be produced on the matter, and so on. In such a fashion, the parties may decide to particularize the case more or less. The more they particularize the case, the larger the tip of the iceberg becomes; and the less they particularize the case, the smaller the tip remains.

Redefining the concept of evidence as we have done poses some very difficult problems directly related to the concept of trial by jury. If evidence is whatever influences a jury, the only way to know whether something is evidence or not is to present it to the jury and see what happens. If that is so, however, it makes a substantial portion of the law of evidence obsolete, including what many consider its most important aspect, the requirement of relevancy.

Another aspect of the theory of the legal system is that only relevant evidence is admissible, and the judge determines relevancy as an initial matter. Relevancy, in turn, is defined as evidence that increases or decreases the chance of some legally operant (material) proposition being true. If, however, we can only know the effect of evidence by observing how the jury responds to it, what warrant is there for judges to exclude evidence from trial? Relevancy can only be determined in light of what a jury does; what a judge thinks, ironically, is irrelevant.

There seems, then, to be a substantial incompatibility between the roles of the judge and the jury. This incompatibility stems from the interesting fact that we apply quite different epistemological theories to these two actors in the legal system. Juries are based upon a relativistic or communitarian theory of knowledge. What is true—or at least what is true for purposes of after-the-fact determinations, an important qualifier—is determined by community consensus. Knowledge emerges, in a sense, from shared norms and the community structure. This, by the way, is not a new idea. During the period of Jacksonian democracy, considerable strictures were placed upon the judiciary, in particular in the states, with respect to fact-finding. This was done explicitly because of the concern that judges, being an elite, would bring their peculiar perspectives to bear upon the fact-finding process. Thus, even if only unconsciously, fact-finding would be skewed toward the values and views held by an elite body. To discourage that from happening, fact-finding by individuals drawn from an ever widening pool was required, and the judges' ability to affect the process of fact-finding was seriously reduced. At a very early time in our history, then, we recognized in the context of right to trial by jury what philosophers of science such as Ernest Nagel and Thomas Kuhns and students of epistemology such as Richard Rorty, Mary Douglas, and W. V. Quine have pressed upon us during this century, that knowledge emerges from community discussion and consensus.

We apply a quite different theory of knowledge to judges, however. There is only one ground that can justify permitting judges to exclude evidence on relevancy grounds, and that is that by doing so accuracy in outcome is advanced. Whether the doctrinal reason for exclusion is lack of probative value, waste of time, or any of the several other criteria, the basis for exclusion is factual accuracy. The admission of a bit of evidence is a waste of time, for example, only when its admission will not influence the jury toward a factually accurate outcome. Yet note the stringent conditions that must be satisfied before a judge can exclude evidence upon this or any other ground. The judge must first know what the correct outcome in a trial is. Second, he or she must accurately gauge how the jurors will react to this bit of evidence in light of how they have reacted and will react to all the other evidence in the case.

There are two problems with this view. The first is that it requires the judge to make decisions that no human is competent to make. The second is that it fundamentally rejects the epistemological basis of trial by jury by replacing the communitarian norms bolstering it with an objective theory of knowledge of the sort found in older writers such as Berkeley, and to some extent in the writings of Max Planck and Mortimer Adler. In this view, the universe is knowable by human effort, and knowledge corresponds to what exists in fact.

I do not intend to mediate between these views. I intend only to highlight their incompatibility and to demonstrate some of the inconsistencies that have emerged in the treatment of these related institutions. The first such inconsistency I have already mentioned. From the point of view of the theory of juries, there is no warrant for judges excluding evidence. In addition, there is no warrant for a jury being consigned to a passive role. The theory underlying trial by jury leads in the direction that the jury should be an active participant in the evidentiary process by informing the parties of what it wants to hear. After all, it is that body that will decide the significance of evidence in light of its background and experience. Accordingly, as a matter of efficiency if nothing else, that body should be in a feedback relationship with the parties in which evidence is received by the jury and feedback given to the parties will generate in turn more evidence in light of the jury's reaction to the first offer (something, I might add in an effort to establish that I have not entirely gone off the deep end, somewhat akin to some descriptions of certain Continental systems).[3]

Of course, if we are not convinced by all this communitarian stuff and believe that the world really is concrete and knowable, and further believe that judges have a relative advantage over juries in appraising the conflicting stories of litigants, then why have juries?

This basic conflict between the theory of judges and the theory of juries, and the underlying conflict as to whether truth is objective or emanates from human beings, also spills over into the decision of cases. A perfect example is the recent decision by the Supreme Court in *Pope v. Illinois*.[4] The question in *Pope* was whether the jury should be instructed to employ community standards in deciding the third prong of the *Miller v. California*[5] test of obscenity, which requires the trier of fact to determine whether the litigated work, taken as a whole, lacks serious literary, artistic, political, or scientific value. The Court said: "The proper inquiry is not whether an ordinary member of any given community would find serious literary, artistic, political, or scientific value in allegedly obscene material, but whether a reasonable person would find such value in the material, taken as a whole."[6]

This standard is virtually incomprehensible; and if it is not incomprehensible, it is inordinately silly. Jurors for the most part will be voluntary members of the community from which they are drawn and presumably will generally share the values of that community. To the extent that is true, the values of the reasonable person from a community and community values will be virtually identical. Thus, as the dissent pointed out, the Court seems to be asking for a juror to find that "ordinary" members of his or her community are not reasonable.[7] To be sure, there is within communities room for reasonable disagreement about matters, including artistic value, but that raises more problems than it resolves. First, how does one know how large a segment of the population must hold a view for it to be reasonable? In a footnote, the Court said, "Of course . . . the mere fact that only a minority of a population may believe a work has serious value does not mean the 'reasonable person' standard would not be met."[8] Similarly, the dissent suggested that the First Amendment applies if "some reasonable persons could consider it as having serious . . . value."[9] What if it is a minority of one—the author of the disputed work, for example—is that enough to make the judgment reasonable? Or, better yet, what if the author does not think so highly of the work, but some not yet extant being might? Indeed, who is to know how tastes may change over time? The point is, of course, if one goes from a presumably majoritarian community standard to a standard based upon the views of a real or hypothetical minority, one has to know both how to identify the relevant minority as well as how large a minority counts to make views held by those individuals reasonable.

Perhaps this numerical approach to the question is not the proper way to proceed, however, and there is another possibility. Rather than determining the size of the group thinking that a work has value, the jury could decide if anybody held such a view and then decide if the person so holding that view is "reasonable." How would the jury do that, though? The only way in which the jury could judge the reasonableness of some person is to judge that person by reference to some standard, and absent an instruction to the contrary, the standard employed will be the background and experience of the jurors, a background and experience which together with that of other community members forms the community standards that the Court was trying to avoid.[10]

Where did the Court go wrong? I cannot say for certain, of course, but my sense is that it failed to recognize that it was attempting to fashion a substantive rule designed to increase the protection for literary works by manipulating the thought processes of jurors. In other words, it appears as though the Court believes that obscenity is an objective fact which exists independently of communities, but it is attempting to provide First Amendment protection through the mechanism of community decision making. The two are incompatible. If obscenity is a fact with a concrete reality, then its attributes need to be defined and provided to the fact finder. If obscenity is a value of a community, then the only question is what is the relevant community. Had the Court, and more to the point the lawyers for the parties, attended more carefully to the underlying epistemological concerns, this mistake might have been avoided.

I wish to turn my attention now quite briefly to the second general area that I intend to discuss, which is the nature of deliberations. It has always struck me as somewhat remarkable that there is virtually no law related to the deliberative process of juries. It is remarkable because the deliberative process is one of the most crucial aspects of trial by jury, and for that reason alone one would think that there would be periodic attempts to regulate it in one fashion or another. To the contrary, though, there is a uniform rule in this country that what goes on in the jury room is inviolate from both ends. We don't instruct the jury on how to deliberate, and we don't inquire into how they did so when they have finished.

The traditional approach to deliberations certainly is supported by weighty considerations. There is a great value in having a black box into which we can pour our problems and out of which we can get decisions. Nonetheless, I wonder if that black box should remain inviolate even from advancing knowledge that may raise serious concerns about the nature of the deliberative process. It is one thing to impose a blanket imposition of inquiry or direction on an institution when there is no reason to doubt its fairness (even if there is no reason but experience to trust it), but it is another to do so when data begin to collect that cast some doubts on the matter. In my judgment, such data have begun to collect, although they have for the most part been studiously ignored to date by the legal system. The most striking data have to do with the interactions of males and females in small groups, and it is to that issue that I will direct my remarks.[11]

Suppose you wanted to construct a deliberative process which involved widespread participation, the goal being to involve all the members of the relevant group. Suppose further that you discovered that within the relevant group there were at least two identifiable subgroups who tended to approach problems from quite different perspectives and thus tended to appraise the same evidence in quite different ways, frequently drawing different inferences. Perhaps your initial thought would be that such a finding reconfirms the value of your primary goal of encouraging widespread participation by the group. Since you define the group as a single unit and want a group decision, that decision should be an amalgam of the constituent parts of the group. Thus, to the extent there are different ways of approaching problems within the group, open and thorough deliberations are to be encouraged in order to obtain a decision which emerges from the blending of the various views. Indeed, so far it sounds like this is a prescription for trial by jury. But what if you found out it doesn't work this way? What if you found out that one of those two groups tends to be overly deferential to the other, or at least does not pursue its own views as aggressively? Or, what if you found out that one group tends to speak considerably less when in contact with the other group than they would if deliberating by themselves? Would you view such matters as problems to be corrected? If so, we must modify trial by jury, because there is very good evidence that men and women react to each other in ways along the lines I have sketched out.

Psychologists who have done mock jury studies have found that men make considerably more contributions to deliberations than women,[12] a finding consistent with the implication of research done in the field of small-group dynamics: "studies show that men speak more often at greater length, and are more likely to interrupt other speakers than women. One effect of this male behavior is that women's silences lengthen as men interrupt, overlap, or give a delayed or minimal response to the female speaker. One obvious way to maintain power in a group is to monopolize and control discussion. Those who have the power can do the talking; those who lack power must do the listening."[13] In the context of juries, the male exercise of control is furthered by the selection of the foreman, who is virtually always a male.

If the gender bias were just a gender bias carrying with it no secondary consequences, it would be bad enough, but there are secondary consequences here. Men and women tend to interact differently, have differing perspectives on the same event, and share those perspectives in differing ways. Data show, for example, that men tend to overestimate a witness's ability to identify a suspect more than women do, women tend to recall better than men information about female victims, and women attempt more than men to accommodate differing points of view among members of a group.[14] Most important of all, in all female groups the more active speakers attempt to draw out the more reticent, whereas in all male groups the more active participants end up ignoring the less active, and "[i]n mixed groups . . . the women consistently [become] more silent."[15] Thus, an important perspective on reality may be lost or slighted in jury deliberations.

I cannot here rehash all the wonderfully complex findings that the social sciences are now generating, but it is becoming increasingly well documented, and it certainly seems intuitively correct, that jurors do not undergo mystical transformations when they enter the jury room. Rather, they take a good part of their cultural baggage with them. In many respects they may do precisely what we want them to do, but do we want matters of social hierarchy and status to affect deliberations over facts? Should certain segments of society have their views overrepresented on juries as they are in other aspects of life? Or, should we attempt to compensate for such matters in some way?

We could, for example, instruct jurors on small-group dynamics, and by doing so encourage the more aggressive to pay more attention to the less aggressive among them. We could actively encourage the selection of women as foremen. Or, as my wife suggested, who is both a woman and a lawyer, we could even affect the environment within which jurors deliberate. Apparently jury rooms invariably have rectangular tables, but rectangular tables are both a sign of and conducive to hierarchy. Those in authority sit at the ends of such tables, and those who are more submissive sit elsewhere. Jury studies have found, for example, that men almost always sit at the end of the tables, and the women sit in the middle.[16] Why not use circular tables? Indeed, why not use circular tables and encourage the jury periodically to canvass the views of each member by going around the table?

One reason we may not want to do so is that it would inject what some might call artificialities into the jury process, and if an artificiality is anything that differs from what would occur if some variable is not influenced, then indeed such proposals would be guilty of the charge. Nonetheless, the same would be true of any variable at any time. Before the jury room is furnished, it has neither a circular nor a rectangular table. Before the jury is instructed, it has no instructions. Before the jury enters the room, it is appropriate, it seems to me, to think about whether we want to encourage or discourage its members from mirroring society in all respects.

There are numerous issues still to be considered that would emphasize the fact that the jury system is a crucible for the development of knowledge in our society. For example, consider the remarkable strains on the system imposed by the recent development of toxic tort litigation and the resultant epidemiological studies relevant to causation. How are such issues to be resolved, and can juries be expected to be able to provide rational answers in such cases? If not, how is such a conclusion to be rationalized with the increasing democratization of our institutions? Indeed, on the one hand, the Federal Rules of Evidence come along and eliminate virtually all barriers to the admission of evidence, and on the other hand, Judge Weinstein comes along in the Agent Orange litigation and refuses to give a very important, controversial, and complex case to the jury.[17] I am not suggesting either the Federal Rules or Judge Weinstein was wrong, but only that we should think about this issue and many others as well, and in doing so we should employ whatever tools we are fortunate enough to find, regardless of whether they traditionally have been found in the workshop of the law or elsewhere.

Notes

1. *See, e.g.*, H. L. A. Hart, *The Concept of Law* (Oxford: Clarendon, 1961).

2. Posner, *The Decline of Law as an Autonomous Discipline, 1962–1987*, 100 Harv. L. Rev. 761, 763 (1987).

3. *See, e.g.*, Langbein, *The German Advantage in Civil Procedure*, 52 U. Chi. L. Rev. 823 (1985). It is not clear to me, however, whether such descriptions can be taken at face value. *See* Allen, Koeck, Riechenberg, and Rosen, *The German Advantage in Civil Procedure: A Plea for More Details and Fewer Generalities in Comparative Scholarship* 82 Nw. U.L. Rev. 705 (1988).

4. *Pope v. Illinois*, 107 S. Ct. 1918 (1987).

5. *Miller v. California*, 413 U.S. 15 (9173).

6. *Id.* at 1921.

7. *Id.* at 1926 (Stevens, dissenting).

8. *Id.* at 1921 n.3.

9. *Id.* at 1927.

10. Which may explain why Stevens just gives up the effort and concludes that the state cannot criminalize the possession of "obscene" material (*id.* at 1927).

11. I am indebted to the excellent student note, *Gender Dynamics and Jury Deliberations*, 96 Yale L.J. 593 (1987), for having been the catalyst to my thoughts on this problem.

12. Ibid., pp. 595–96.

13. Ibid., pp. 597–98.

14. Ibid., pp. 601–3.

15. Ibid., p. 603.

16. Ibid., p. 595.

17. *In re* "Agent Orange" Product Liability Litigation, 611 F. Supp. 1267 (E.D.N.Y. 1985).

X.

THE SIXTH AMENDMENT AND THE RIGHT TO COUNSEL

William Gangi

25. The Sixth Amendment, Judicial Power, and the People's Right to Govern Themselves

> No authority shall on any pretense be exercised over the people or members of this state but such as shall be derived from and granted by them.
>
> Constitution of the State of New York (1777)

In 1641 the good people of Massachusetts specified in their Body of Liberties that "no man shall be forced by torture to confesse any crime against himself or any other unlesse it be in some capital case, where he is first fullie convicted by cleare and sufficient evidence to be guilty, after which if the cause be of that nature, that it is very apparent there be other conspiratours, or confederates with him, then he may be tortured, yet not with such tortures as be barbarous and inhumane."[1]

To the modern ear the rights mentioned do not offer much protection. They contain too many conditions—too many compromises. But that view fails to appreciate that the rights specified presupposed the authority of citizens and their representatives to think about, discuss, and determine public policy. That right—to self-government—was at the heart of the American Revolution, and it preceded and was considered superior to any individual right.[2] It is the right of self-government that has been and now is being eroded by the Supreme Court of the United States.[3]

Under English rule, any absolute individual rights were procedural; such rights were those considered necessary to protect citizens from traditional executive and judicial abuses.[4] Substantive absolute rights against the English Parliament did not exist. Furthermore, once the colonialists won the war for American independence, any absolute rights against a state or the federal legislature would have, in effect, amounted to rights against the citizens of those states, thus inhibiting their ability to respond to unforeseen circumstances.[5] Abusive legislative decisions were subject to electoral accountability.

When our forefathers subsequently proposed and ratified a system of government, as we might expect, the written document that they called a constitution also contained no absolute rights, and when two years later, the Bill of Rights was ratified, it contained essentially the procedural protections associated with English history.[6] Indeed, both documents purposely utilized phrases having long common-law histories, and because of those histories, citizens of the several states were familiar with their meanings. That fact is precisely what gave comfort to those who had opposed the Constitution's ratification and why those who had opposed a bill of rights before ratification could now assent. In sum, by ratification these common-law meanings became constitutionalized, protected from the ordinary legislative power of the Congress to modify.[7]

This chapter contends that if we can clearly discern what the framers meant by a particular clause, judges are bound to respect that meaning. Such a position admittedly contains considerable difficulties, but I suggest that such difficulties are more easily surmounted than the issues created by the contrary view. For that contrary view raises questions such as what is a written constitution, and whether the framers' design—government by the people—can be abandoned legitimately without obtaining the people's consent. Before returning to those issues, let us turn to the Sixth Amendment.

Until 1695 those accused of felonies in England, including treason, were not allowed counsel at all.[8] In that year, however, Parliament not only granted defendants the right to "retain counsel [in treason cases], but [also] . . . provided that the court must appoint counsel . . . upon the request of the accused."[9] These were harsh times. Most felonies committed throughout the seventeenth and eighteenth centuries were capital offenses. Nevertheless, not until 1836 did the English Parliament extend the right to counsel as we know it today to all felony defendants. Despite the absence of a statutory requirement, however, for nearly two centuries on their common-law authority judges have extended the right to counsel on a case-by-case basis.[10]

In the American colonies legislatures took a more active role in securing the right to retain counsel, preferring statutory protection to judicial discretion.[11] Furthermore, in several colonies "courts appointed counsel where a capital crime was charged and the accused requested it,"[12] thereby going beyond what the English Parliament at the same time was providing its citizens.[13]

After the American Revolution and before the adoption of the Constitution, in the words of Justice Roberts, the thirteen sovereign states "exhibit[ed] great diversity."[14] Thus, apparently no state afforded the right to counsel constitutional status, and for those that addressed the issue, the right apparently consisted only of "the right to retain counsel of one's own choice and at one's own expense."[15] States, as indicated in Justice Roberts's remarks, subsequently remained free to define the right as their citizens saw fit even after adoption of the Sixth Amendment to the U.S. Constitution because that amendment—from the time of its adoption until the 1960s—applied only against the federal government.[16]

In 1791 federal courts came under the Sixth Amendment provision specifying that "in all criminal prosecutions, the accused shall enjoy . . . the assistance of counsel for his defense."[17] The evidence demonstrates that for the framers of that amendment, it had a very narrow meaning—the simple right to retained counsel—nothing more.[18] That conclusion is further supported by two occurrences. On the day before the Sixth Amendment was proposed, Congress passed a statute permitting use of retained counsel in federal courts.[19] Even more significant, seven months before the amendment's ratification, Congress provided for assigned counsel where a person is "indicted of treason or other capital crime." From these two statutes Professor William Beaney concluded that for Congress "the Sixth Amendment was irrelevant . . . to the subject of appointment of counsel." In sum, the amendment guaranteed only the right to retained counsel, while congressional statutes went further, not only extending the right to match English practice—assignment in treason cases—but authorizing assignment in all capital cases.[20] After the amendment was adopted, however, no one suggested that Congress was obliged to assign counsel in all felony cases, and in fact Congress never did.[21]

Please remember that until the mid-1960s in federal courts, as a matter of constitutional law, neither the Fifth nor the Sixth Amendment applied to police interrogation since those clauses did not become operative until a criminal trial or criminal prosecution commenced,[22] and that did not occur until arraignment.[23] Instead, with respect to police interrogation, in both federal and presumably state courts, common or statutory law governing confession admissibility applied.[24] Rules of evidence, however, did not enjoy constitutional statute, and for more than a century after the adoption of the Bill of Rights, the sole issue with respect to police interrogation was whether an obtained confession was "voluntary."[25] In fact as late as 1955 Professor David Fellman could state that "an accused does not have a constitutional right to the assistance of a lawyer during the police interrogation following arrest, and the overwhelming weight of authority holds that a confession is not necessarily bad because it was made without the advice of counsel."[26]

Not until 1938 in *Johnson v. Zerbst*[27] did the Supreme Court rule that the Sixth Amendment required assignment of counsel in all capital cases. The *Johnson* case in turn was based on the 1932 case of *Powell v. Alabama*.[28] There Justice Sutherland "applied to the states through the due process clause of the Fourteenth Amendment the same requirement which a federal statute had since 1790 imposed on federal courts in capital cases."[29] I contend, however, that the Supreme Court in *Powell* exceeded its authority. In confusing statutory and constitutional rights, the Court majority illegitimately imposed upon the American people the justices' "deep concern for the rights of all criminal defendants."[30] Neither opinion cites credible evidence to support two implicit contentions: (1) that the Court is authorized to elevate rights from statutory or common law to constitutional status, or (2) that those who framed the Fourteenth Amendment intended any other definition of due process to apply against the states than had applied against the federal government through the Fifth Amendment.

In fact, in *Powell*[31] Sutherland explicitly circumvents traditional interpretative rules of construction that provide that enumeration excludes the nonmentioned.[32] Sutherland acknowledges its pertinence,[33] but instead of submitting to its dictates he counters with the statement that "the Hurtado case does not stand alone."[34] He then cites two groups of precedents. The first group alludes to substantive economic rights cases,[35] while the second group[36] consists of cases more familiar to the modern reader. This division—the economic and personal liberty double standard—Professor Kutler later would call the "new faith," wherein after 1936 the Court deferred to Congress in the definition of economic rights but took an active role for itself in the expansion of personal liberties.[37]

Thus, the *Powell* and *Johnson* cases demonstrate only this: that by the 1930s the newest variation of progressivist principles was beginning to be injected into constitutional law. However these principles are expressed—whether in terms of "fundamental principles of liberty and justices,"[38] or "ordered liberty,"[39] or "methods that commend themselves to a progressive and self-confident society"[40]—none are traceable to the intentions of the framers; therefore, none should enjoy constitutional stature. Judges have no authority to impose such standards on Congress or the states, and Sutherland's defense amounts to an early version of what Professor Yale Kamisar eventually defended as the "time lag argument"[41]: an earlier judicial abuse cited to justify a subsequent one. On the contrary, I contend that if cited precedents do not rest on the framers' intentions, or do not establish upon what authority the court makes law, then the precedents cited, as well as the opinion being challenged, become suspect.[42]

That is about as far as I wish to trace the development of the Sixth Amendment. After the 1930s the Sixth Amendment right to counsel, common-law confession rule, and Fifth Amendment compulsory self-incrimination cases become intertwined with Fourth Amendment exclusionary rule cases in the Supreme Court's dialectic march to the fantasy world of *Miranda v. Arizona*.[43]

All citizens and agents of the government are bound by the clearly discernible intentions of those who framed and ratified the Constitution and subsequent amendments. Judicial review is legitimate, intended by the framers to impede executive or legislative overreaching or attempts to reduce the protection afforded by the meaning the common-law terms had when they were elevated to constitutional status.[44] But judicial review is not an unlimited power to rewrite the text. Publius summed it up nicely: "until the people have, by some solemn and authoritative act, annulled or changed the established form, it is binding upon themselves collectively, as well as individually; and no presumption, or even knowledge of their sentiments, can warrant their representatives in a departure from it prior to such an act."[45]

Conceived thusly, judicial review is a tool given to judges by the framers to remind the majority's presently elected representatives of the limited power granted to them by a past extraordinary majority. The authority of the justices stems from the conveyance of the intentions of those who framed and ratified relevant provisions, not their personal intellect. That is the meaning "constitutionalism" had for the framers of the Constitution, the Bill of Rights, and the Fourteenth Amendment.[46] If that understanding has changed, the American people are entitled to know by what "solemn and authoritative act" they "annulled or changed the established form" of their government. When did the American people give up self-government in favor of rule by judges? The framers believed judges possessed no special expertise for public policy making.[47]

Given the above views, won't the Constitution become inflexible, unable to adapt to changing circumstances? Not at all! Our tradition is one of legislative adaptation to changing circumstances.[48] For example, as we have seen, although the Sixth Amendment guaranteed only retained counsel, Congress provided assigned counsel in treason and capital cases. The Constitution guarantees only that the right to retained counsel not be ordinarily denied. Similarly, while I contend that the Supreme Court cannot as a matter of constitutional law legitimately require assignment of counsel in federal courts to all defendants charged with felonies, Congress is not thereby prevented from so requiring. Indeed, if Congress wishes, it might provide that counsel be assigned in all misdemeanor cases, regardless of ability to pay, and that that right shall commence either once an investigation begins to focus on the accused or the accused's freedom of action is limited in any significant way.[49]

But unless judges establish that any requirements they impose can be located in the clear intentions of those who framed relevant constitutional provisions, they do not have the authority to inhibit the people's representatives from addressing public policy matters as they see fit. If some citizens believe that ought to be a law, they must convince their fellow citizens of their cause. If other citizens believe statutory laws provide inadequate security from abuse, they must do what their ancestors did to obtain the constitutional protections presently enjoyed: use the amendment process. To counter with the argument that both the legislative and amendment processes are cumbersome not only fails to address the legitimacy issue but reveals ignorance of our history and constitutional structures.[50] They are willing to gamble that the good results obtained will not undermine the constitutional structure. And who authorized such risk taking? No one.

Freedom to decide public policy questions is on the other side of the coin demanding submission to the framers' intentions. The framers never authorized the judiciary to adapt the Constitution to changing circumstances or to create minority rights—only to guard original intent. Judicial review was not intended as an alternative to the legislative power. It was but one device to protect citizens from the natural tendency of democratic republics to majority tyranny. But being in the minority on public policy issues is not tyrannical in the constitutional sense simply because in the eyes of that minority—including a majority of Supreme Court justices—the rights extended or the public policies adopted are not as broad or as humane or as just as either group think they ought to be. Bluntly put, no judge as a matter of constitutional law can legitimately impose on the people even the most just or moral proscriptions. As a human being and citizen I might applaud those proscriptions, I might even prefer them to the ones offered by the framers, but their imposition by the judiciary is not what republicanism is about, it is not what our tradition is all about, and it certainly is not what constitutional law is about.[51] In the words of James Wilson: "laws may be unjust, may be unwise, may be dangerous, be destructive, and yet not be so unconstitutional as to justify the judge in refusing to give them effect."[52]

Before addressing three myths that sustain abusive judicial power today, let me discuss another problem which pervades contemporary scholarship. Contemporary scholars cannot talk definitively about constitutional provisions because we often lack a good understanding of what the people in the several states did before, during, and after adoption of both the federal and state constitutions and bills of rights.[53] At one time I thought all it took was curiosity, extensive reading, and a logical mind. But over the past twenty years I have learned that facts are not self-interpreting and that unless one reexamines original sources, earlier scholars might have unintentionally misinterpreted the facts.[54] Many were weaned on progressivist assumptions and that often biased their factual interpretations to reflect an implicit faith in progress—in nutshell form, the alleged movement from a closed to an open society.[55] Hence for the last fifty years justices have been basing their opinions on an alleged knowledge of historical evolution. Although the dreams they dreamed, like those of their laissez-faire predecessors, were fantasies,[56] these dreams hindered if not prevented accurate interpretation of every Bill of Rights provision that I have researched, including of course, the Sixth Amendment.[57] It is in this context that I explicitly state what has been thus far implied: identifying rights abuses and providing remedies are legislative tasks and/or ones reserved to the people by Article VI of our Constitution.[58] Having said that, let me briefly describe three myths that today support abusive judicial power and inhibit representative institutions from addressing public policy questions.[59]

The first myth believes the framers considered the three branches of government equal and coordinate. Nonsense! As Madison stated, "in republican government, the legislative authority necessarily predominates."[60] Contemporary supporters of judicial power, however, paint an entirely different picture. They assert that unlike legislators concerned with reelection, judges can do what is appropriate even if it lacks majority support.[61] That view is diametrically opposed to those held by the framers. The problem today thus is both an arrogant judiciary and legislators who avoid taking responsiblity for difficult public policy choices.[62]

The second myth assumes that the adoption of the Bill of Rights elevated individual rights above the people's right to self-government. Put another way—that the Bill of Rights consisted of absolute bars against legislative policy-making. Again, nonsense.[63] The Bill of Rights applied only against the federal government; more important, even after its adoption Congress engaged in policy-making. While Congress could not breach—abridge is an excellent term to convey the point[64]—specific common-law meanings, it was otherwise free to do what it pleased.[65] I already demonstrated that the Sixth Amendment did not preclude additional legislative protections. Similarly, when Congress successfully passed the Alien and Sedition Acts, members argued the acts actually afforded greater protection than that provided by the First Amendment.[66]

The final and most pervasive contemporary myth is, however, the belief that those who framed the Fourteenth Amendment intended in whole or in part to apply the first eight amendments to the states.[67] Whatever the choice of implementation—the due process or equal protection clauses, total or selective incorporation—those interpretations lack historical support. Imposition on the states of First, Fourth, Fifth, Sixth, and Eighth Amendment rights, whatever their policy merits, rests on no more substantial foundation then did imposition of economic rights favored by the laissez-faire.[68] Thus, unfortunately, today much of law school constitutional law training rests upon a foundation of sand, convenient ignorance, or, worse, abandonment of historical truth for the sake of good results.[69]

In sum, those today claiming the existence of rights in our Constitution often cannot locate them in our tradition or in the consent of the governed; and in turning to the judiciary to secure those rights, they have asserted and taken refuge in an illegitimate power. The judicial lawmaking of Holmes and Cardozo[70] has grown to the functional equivalent of arguing that we fought World War I to keep the world safe for judicial oligarchy. Judges increasingly make major public policy decisions and leave to the people's representatives the trivial task of implementing them. Instead of self-government, we have what Raoul Berger aptly calls *Government by Judiciary*.[71]

For several generations now attorneys and legislators have been trained in an alien tradition—that of judicial power. Those expected by the framers to guard the constitutional law tradition have abandoned it. Surely law students must suspect something amiss when in one class they learn how to protect from judicial interference their client's intent to leave all earthly possessions to the family cat, but in their constitutional law class they learn the justices may ignore even the framers' clearest intentions? As a result of a century of illegitimate judicial lawmaking, original common-law constitutionalized protections have become intertwined with newer more fashionable terminology—initially liberty of contract language but now such things as penumbras and emanations,[72] expectations of privacy,[73] walls of separation,[74] and on and on. But when this latest progressivist bubble bursts, can you be sure that the next court majority will not also sweep away the original protections afforded by the framers?[75] Upon what possible ground can you protest?

The situation is getting even more ominous. Shortly we may find, on the one hand, some citizens passionately committed to particular rights like abortion, speech, or privacy. They sincerely believe that those rights are part of our tradition. Will they be prepared to fight to preserve them? On the other hand, some citizens will passionately believe that the judiciary abuses its authority, renders self-government incompetent or ineffective, and undermines the legitimacy of the Republic. Will they be prepared to fight to resecure the right to govern themselves? In sum, we might have before long the classical ingredients for civil war.

The framers' intentions are the only neutral principles we possess. We may have to change portions of the Constitution, but that is why the amendment process was provided. Various public policy issues may have to be fought on the state level unless and until a national consensus is reached. States must again return to being experimental laboratories.[76] We can and must deconstitutionalize much of contemporary constitutional law and regain for the American people their most precious right—that of self-government—a most appropriate task in this bicentennial year.

Notes

1. W. Kendall and G. Carey, *The Basic Symbols of the American Political Tradition* (Baton Rouge: Louisiana State Univ. Press, 1970), p. 52.

2. "[T]he rights of all individuals will be safest if *first* the rights of the people are assured, and above all the right of the people to *govern themselves*, that is, the very right that . . . emerg[ed] in America from the Mayflower Compact; through the Body of Liberties" (ibid., p. 66). "[T]he representative assembly is supreme . . . in the sense that no other *political* authority can challenge or gainsay it" (ibid., p. 71).

3. *See e.g.*, R. Berger, *Death Penalties: The Supreme Court's Obstacle Course* (Cambridge: Harvard Univ. Press, 1982).

4. Kendall and Carey, *Basic Symbols*, pp. 51–52.

5. Publius made it very clear that a statement of rights, equivalent to the Magna Charta or Petition of Right, has "no application to constitutions, professedly founded upon the power of the people and executed by their immediate representatives and servants." Referring to the Preamble to the Constitution, he concluded: "Here is a better recognition of popular rights than volumes of those aphorisms which make

the principal figure in several of our State bills of rights and which would sound much better in a treatise of ethics than in a constitution of government" (J. Madison, A. Hamilton, and J. Jay, *The Federalist Papers*, ed. C. Rossiter [New York: New American Library, 1961], No. 84, p. 513). Publius was equally frank about power: "It rests upon axioms as simple as they are universal; the *means* ought to be proportioned to the *end*; the persons from whose agency the attainment of any *end* is expected ought to possess the *means* by which it is to be attained." On the important matters he was most frank: "These powers [of common defense] ought to exist without limitation, *because it is impossible to foresee or to define the extent and variety of national exigencies, and the correspondent extent and variety of the means which may be necessary to satisfy them.* The circumstances that endanger the safety of nations are infinite, and for this reason no constitutional shackles can wisely be imposed on the power to which the care of it is committed. This power ought to be coextensive with all the possible combinations of such circumstances; and ought to be under the direction of the same councils which are appointed to preside over the common defense" (ibid., No. 23, p. 153).

6. *See generally*, ibid., No. 84 (addition of a bill of rights unnecessary and dangerous). The Bill of Rights had been proposed, lest one forget, by opponents of the Constitution who feared federal power. After ratification of the Constitution was secured, the Federalists sought to reassure opponents that even the limited powers granted the federal government would be exercised within the context of familiar procedures. *See* Gangi, *The Exclusionary Rule: A Case Study in Judicial Usurpation*, 34 Drake L. Rev. 35, 41 n. 15 (1985).

7. "The Founders resorted to a written Constitution the more clearly to limit delegated power, to create a fixed Constitution; and an important means for the accomplishment of that purpose was their use of common law terms of established and familiar meaning" (Berger, *Death Penalties*, p. 61). "[A]s Justice Story stated . . . the common law 'definitions are necessarily included, as much *as if they stood in the text of the Constitution*'" (ibid., quoting *United States v. Smith*, 18 U.S. 5 [Wheat] 153, 160 [1920]).

The above does not foreclose difficulties of interpretation. For example, grants of power may be approached somewhat differently than prohibitions. The former demand deference of the judiciary to the legislative branches while the latter required judicial vigilance. Such vigilance, however, does not constitute a right to expand. *See* additional comments in Gangi, *The Supreme Court: An Intentionist's Critique*, 28 Catholic Lawyer 252, 306–8 n. 283 (1983).

8. W. Beaney, *The Right to Counsel in American Courts* (Ann Arbor: Univ. of Michigan Press, 1955), p. 9. As Professor Beaney describes it, the right to retained counsel "illogically" existed in misdemeanor cases (e.g., libel, perjury, battery) and crimes of a political nature under the jurisdiction of the Star Chamber. In the latter, counsel was "mandatory" (ibid., pp. 8–10). For reasons stated later (*see comments* accompanying notes 53–57, *supra*), I am uncomfortable with characterizations such as "illogically" since they often demonstrate the researcher's inability to grasp the thought processes of his subject. Professor Beaney does make a stab at it ("the state's interest was apparently deemed so slight that it could afford [in misdemeanor cases] to be considerate

toward defendants" [ibid., p. 8]), but I would be cautious in placing great weight on such judgments.

9. Ibid., p. 9. Beaney notes that this gesture resulted largely from the "frequent alternations of political power which characterized" England at the time and "which made treason a likely concomitant of a political career for many who felt themselves 'loyal' and decent citizens." For some time I have been doubtful of the modern assumption that concern for criminal defendants was a primary motivation for the proposal of the Bill of Rights. *See* Gangi, *The Exclusionary Rule*, pp. 98–99. *Cf.* Beaney, *The Right to Counsel*, pp. 17–18.

10. Beaney, *The Right to Counsel*, p. 9. Despite the fact that no statutory basis existed, "in many cases the court of its own volition, and without pretending to change the rule, permitted counsel to argue points of law" (ibid.). The exercise of such power, absent contrary statute law, is usually within the judge's common-law authority.

11. Ibid., pp. 25, 15–18. *See also, Note, An Historical Argument for the Right to Counsel during Police Interrogation*, 73 Yale L.J. 1000, 1030–31 (1964).

12. Beaney, *The Right to Counsel*, p. 18.

13. *See* text accompanying notes 9–11, *supra*. I suspect that in part the American Revolution was fought to protect the "rights of Englishmen," which in fact were practiced in America but not in England.

14. *Betts v. Brady*, 316 U.S. 455, 467 (1941). Justice Roberts commented: "In the light of . . . common law practice . . . constitutional provisions to the effect that a defendant should be 'allowed counsel' . . . were intended to do away with the rules which denied representation . . . but were not aimed to compel the State to provide counsel for a defendant" (id., at 466). *See also* Beaney, *The Right to Counsel*, p. 21 ("no uniform practice," "Diversity of policy"). Beaney notes that the colonialists had "greater distrust of government" and since they had a "greater opportunity to indicate that distrust in legislative form . . . [it] may go far to explain the widespread statutory concern in the colonies over the right to counsel and the absence of any substantial change in actual judicial procedure." He then concludes that "[a]s yet we have insufficient evidence upon which to base any claim that the American practice was in sharp contrast to the English. Advance there was, but in many ways it was a technical advance" (ibid., pp. 21–22).

Of course, what comes to mind is the awkward situation colonialists found themselves in when they tried to assert the rights of Englishmen, only to find that the rights granted in the colonies may have exceeded those in the mother country. But don't get distracted by the specific content of those rights—concentrate on the right to make them—the right to self-government.

15. Beaney, *The Right to Counsel*, p. 21. Only two states made provision for appointed counsel. In New Jersey appointed counsel was provided "by statute" and in Connecticut the right existed "by practice" (ibid.). In neither case, therefore, was the right to appointed counsel a constitutional one.

Justice Roberts summarized the situation thusly: "Rhode Island had no constitutional provision on the subject until 1843, North Carolina and South Carolina had none until 1868. Virginia has never had any. Maryland, in 1776, and New York, in 1777, adopted provisions to the effect that a defendant accused of crime should be 'allowed' counsel. A constitutional mandate that the accused should have a right to be heard by himself and by his counsel was adopted by Pennsylvania in 1776, New Hampshire in 1774, by Delaware in 1782, and by Connecticut in 1818. In 1780 Massachusetts ordained that the defendant should have the right to be heard by himself or his counsel at his election. In 1798 Georgia provided that the accused might be heard by himself or counsel, or both. In 1776 New Jersey guaranteed the accused the same privileges of witnesses and counsel as their prosecutors 'are or shall be entitled to'" (ibid., p. 465).

16. *Barron v. Mayor and City Council*, 32 U.S. (7 Pet.) 243 (1833).

17. U.S. Constitution, Amendment VI.

18. It may be "impossible" to know with certitude "the intentions of Congress" since we have no record of what transpired (Beaney, *The Right to Counsel*, p. 24). I contend, however, that when the information provided by Beaney is considered along with (a) an understanding of what the Bill of Rights and division of powers between the federal government and the states did and did not provide, (b) appropriate canons of construction, and (c) the contemporaneous and subsequent actions by Congress and the states, Beaney's somewhat reluctant conclusion that the Sixth Amendment right was confined to retained counsel is irrefutable. Surely it represents a conclusion beyond reasonable doubt.

19. Ibid., p. 28 (the statute provided that "the parties may plead and manage their own causes personally or by the assistance of counsel"). This provision was contained in the very significant Judiciary Act of 1789, wherein Congress exercised powers granted it in Article III: "In all other Cases . . . the Supreme Court shall have appellate Jurisdiction . . . with such Exceptions, and under such Regulations as the Congress shall make" (U.S. Constitution, III, 2.2). Presumably these measures were taken to allay the fears of Anti-Federalists that traditional rights would not be respected in federal courts.

20. Beaney, *The Right to Counsel*, p. 28.

21. Professor Beaney comments: "The ratification of the Sixth Amendment was not followed by statutory changes, and the acts of 1789 and 1790 remained the sole guides to the legal import of the Sixth Amendment until 1938. Story described the right contained in the Sixth Amendment as 'the right to have counsel employed for the prisoner,' and Cooley permitted the phrase to stand as Story had written it. If there had been any general understanding that federal courts were required by the Sixth Amendment to appoint counsel in other than capital cases, *which were covered by the 1790 act*, it seems remarkable that these two astute observers failed to say so" (ibid., pp. 28–29).

22. The Fifth Amendment provides: "No person . . . shall be compelled in any criminal case to be a witness against himself" (U.S. Constitution, Amendment V). The compulsion prohibited referred to that of a legal nature, to put one on oath, not physical coercion. *See* Pittman, *The Fifth Amendment: Yesterday, Today, and Tomorrow*, 42 A.B.A.J. 509, 510 (1956). *See also Brown v. Mississippi*, 297 U.S. 278, 285 (1936).

23. *An Historical Argument*, p. 1005.

24. *Wilson v. United States*, 162 U.S. 613 (1896) (confession found voluntary despite fact that defendant was in custody, manacled, and questioned by a commissioner who neither apprised him of his right to counsel nor was he

represented by same). *See generally*, J. Wigmore, *A Treatise on the Anglo-American System of Evidence in Trial in Common Law* (Boston: Little, Brown, 1940), pp. 232–46, and W. Gangi, *The English Common Law Confession Rule and Early Cases Decided by the United States Supreme Court*, Information Report Series, No. 205 (Chicago: American Judicature Society, 1973).

25. Until *Lisenba* (*Lisenba v. California*, 314 U.S. 219 [1941]) "voluntary" probably meant trustworthy. *See* Gangi, *The English Common Law Confession Rule*, pp. 5–8. *See also* Gangi, *The Inbau-Kamisar Debate: Time for Round 2?*, 12 W. St. U.L. Rev. 117, 142–43 (1984) (the original purpose of the confession rule was the admission of reliable evidence [ibid., p. 143 n. 148]). Even a staunch defender of defendant rights such as Yale Kamisar agrees that reliability was the original purpose of the common-law confession rule. *See* Y. Kamisar, *Police Interrogation and Confessions: Essays in Law and Policy* (Ann Arbor: Univ. of Michigan Press, 1980), pp. 254–55 n. 49. *See also* comment at note 22, *infra*.

26. Fellman, *The Right to Counsel under State Law*, 1955 Wis. L. Rev. 281, 292.

27. *Johnson v. Zerbst*, 304 U.S. 458 (1938) ("The Sixth Amendment withholds from federal courts, in all criminal proceedings, the power and authority to deprive an accused of his life or liberty unless he has or waives the assistance of counsel" [*id.*, at 463]). Professor Beaney characterizes Justice Black's statement as a "new rule" (Beaney, *The Right to Counsel*, p. 42) and comments: "There was no feeling before 1938 that defendants who pleaded guilty, or those who failed to request counsel, had a constitutional right to be advised and offered counsel, or that a conviction without counsel was void. History denied such a meaning to the counsel provision of the Sixth Amendment, and no responsible authority, scholarly or judicial, had held it to be within the scope of the Amendment" (ibid., pp. 32–33).

28. *Powell v. Alabama*, 287 U.S. 45 (1932). Defendants, black, were charged with assaulting whites, including two women (*see id.*, at 49–52). Beaney comments that "Justice Sutherland carefully limited the decision to the facts in the case" (Beaney, *The Right to Counsel*, p. 34). Justice Sutherland stated: "In a capital case where the defendant is unable to employ counsel, and is incapable adequately of making his own defense because of ignorance, feeble-mindedness, illiteracy, or the like, it is the duty of the court whether requested or not, to assign counsel for him as a necessary requisite of due process of law" (*Powell v. Alabama*, 287 U.S. 45, 71 [1932]).

29. Beaney, *The Right to Counsel*, p. 34. I object to Beaney's characterization, omitted in the text, of the Court as "merely" having elevated a statutory requirement to a constitutional one. The Court's reasoning fails because of what Beaney elsewhere notes: "If Congress in 1790 had chosen to strengthen a weak constitutional requirement by a more generous statute where capital offenses were involved, it had obviously decided against extending this treatment to non-capital cases" (ibid., p. 38). Furthermore, if the Court can elevate statutory protections to constitutional ones, it simultaneously and proportionately contracts the people's right to govern themselves. It places restrictions on their ability to make policy decisions without their consent. The people are bound to respect the intent of ratifiers—not the justices.

30. Ibid., p. 34.

31. *Powell v. Alabama, supra* note 28, at 65–66. Justice Sutherland notes that "[i]n the face of the reasoning of the *Hurtado* [*Hurtado v. California*, 110 U.S. 516 (1884)] case, if it stood alone, it would be difficult to justify the conclusion that the right to counsel, being thus specifically granted by the Sixth Amendment, was also within the intendment of the due process of law clause" (*Powell v. Alabama, supra* note 28, at 66).

32. *See* Gangi, *Judicial Expansionism: An Evaluation of the Ongoing Debate*, 8 Ohio N.U.L. Rev. 1, 9 (1981); Gangi, "*O What a Tangled Web We Weave . . . ,*" 19 The Prosecutor, pp. 15, 17–18 (1986). The framers of the Constitution were both aware of canons of construction and used them, including the one noted in the text. Publius noted: "Specification of particulars is an exclusion of generals" (*see The Federalist*, No. 41, p. 263). For a general discussion, *see* text and comments accompanying notes 57–66 in Gangi, "*O What a Tangled Web.*" Professor Beaney noted: "Nor does the Fifth Amendment due process clause furnish any guidance. . . . Apart from the logical difficulty in arguing that a broader right to counsel should be included under the vague term 'due process,' when a more explicit provision was available, the concept of due process was limited, at least until 1850, to its historic meaning 'law of the land'; the law of the land, as Cooley explained, required procedural safeguards comparable to those extended at common law. . . . [T]here was no common-law precedent which called for the appointment of counsel except in treason cases. Thus, the requirement that due process of law be observed could add nothing to the right to counsel granted by the Sixth Amendment" (Beaney, *The Right to Counsel*, p. 29).

33. *Powell v. Alabama, supra* note 28, at 65–66.

34. *Id.*, at 66.

35. *Id.*, citing *Chicago, Burlington & Quincy R. Co. v. Chicago*, 166 U.S. 266, 241 ("private property taken for public use without justice compensation, was violation of the due process of law required by the Fourteenth Amendment, notwithstanding that the Fifth Amendment explicitly declares that private property shall not be taken for public use without just compensation"). Justice Sutherland was a transitional justice, approving the infusion of both economic and personal liberties into the Constitution. Beaney comments: "The eloquence of Justice Sutherland (whose economic predilections caused American liberals to tag him as a reactionary) in discussing the right of an indigent accused to make his defense by counsel had had an influence far beyond the facts and the holding in the particular trial" (Beaney, *The Right to Counsel*, p. 34).

36. *Powell v. Alabama, supra* note 28, at 67, citing "*Gitlow v. New York*, 268 U.S. 652, 666; *Stromberg v. California*, 283 U.S. 359, 368; *Near v. Minnesota*, 283 U.S. 697, 707."

37. Kutler, *Raoul Berger's Fourteenth Amendment: A History or Ahistorical*, 6 Hast. Const. L.Q. 511, 513 (1979). *See also* Gangi, *Judicial Expansionism*, pp. 40–42 (double standard).

38. *Herbert v. Louisiana*, 272 U.S. 312, 316 (1926), cited in *Powell v. Alabama, supra* note 28, at 67.

39. *Palko v. Connecticut*, 302 U.S. 319, 325 (1937) (Justice B. Cardozo).

40. *McNabb v. U.S.*, 318 U.S. 332, 344 (1943) (Justice Frankfurter).

41. Y. Kamisar, *Is the Exclusionary Rule an "Illogical" or "Unnatural" Inter-*

pretation of the Fourth Amendment, 62 Judicature 67, 74 (1978).

42. Gangi, *The Exclusionary Rule*, pp. 94–95.

43. *Miranda v. Arizona*, 384 U.S. 436 (1966). *See* Gangi, *"O What a Tangled Web,"* p. 20.

44. *See* Gangi, *Judicial Expansionism*, pp. 10–14, and Gangi, *"O What a Tangled Web,"* pp. 16–17.

45. *The Federalist*, No. 78, p. 470.

46. A unanimous 1872 Judiciary Committee Report noted: "In construing the Constitution we are compelled to give it such interpretation as will secure the result which was intended to be accomplished by those who framed . . . and adopted it. . . . A construction which should give . . . [a] phrase . . . a meaning different from the sense in which it was understood and employed by the people when they adopted the Constitution, would be as unconstitutional as a departure from the plain and express language of the Constitution. . . . A change in the popular use of any word employed in the Constitution cannot retroact upon the Constitution, either to enlarge or limit its provisions. . . . Judge Thomas Cooley . . . wrote: 'The meaning of the Constitution is fixed when it is adopted, and it is not different at any subsequent time. . . . [T]he object of construction, as applied to a written constitution, is to give effect to the intent of the people in adopting it'" (quoted in Berger, *"Government by Judiciary": Judge Gibbons' Argument Ad Hominem*, 59 B.U.L. Rev. 783, 785 n. 12 [1979] [Citations omitted]).

47. Elsewhere I have stated: "An expanded judicial role requires members of the judiciary to become experts on topics ranging from anatomy to zoology—to presume an expertise sufficient to resolve differences of opinions within each field, as well as to evaluate periodic challenges to essential assumptions therein. The intentionist recognizes that such expertise is inherently presumptuous and leads to the probability that members of the judiciary will substitute personal preferences for those of the Framers or legislators. The judiciary's responsibility is to guard constitutionalized principles and not to decide the common good where those principles are not at issue. In summary, the intentionist believes that it is quite enough for a judge to be required to have constitutional competency and to exercise judicial power prudently. The Constitution did not burden members of the judiciary with more. On the historical record, the intentionist believes the Framers were correct, for experience has taught that when members of the judiciary do not so confine themselves, they have become neither competent nor prudent" (Gangi, *The Exclusionary Rule*, p. 302). *See also* DuPont, *No Matter What You Think About—, The Constitution Should Not Be Compromised*, Legal Backgrounder (Washington Legal Foundation), June 26, 1987, pp. 1, 6–7 (Court contributed to segregation and economic recession and depression).

48. *See generally* W. Hurst, *Dealing with Statutes* (New York: Columbia Univ. Press, 1982), p. 4 (primary task of legislatures is to adapt society to changing circumstances), and Choper, *The Supreme Court and the Political Branches: Democratic Theory and Practice* 122 U. Pa. L. Rev. 810 (1974).

49. Some of the language in the text, of course, is borrowed from *Escobedo v. Illinois*, 378 U.S. 1, 490 (1964) ("investigation . . . has begun to focus") and *Miranda v. Arizona*, 384 U.S. 436, 467

(1966) ("freedom of action . . . any significant way").

50. *See* Gangi, *Judicial Expansionism*, pp. 37–39. *See also* Choper, *The Supreme Court and the Political Branches* (critique of democratic process difficult to sustain).

51. Gangi, *Judicial Expansionism*, pp. 59–62. Professor Berger states: "Nowhere in the Constitution or its history is there an intimation that judges were given a power of attorney to fashion unenumerated 'minority rights' in order to remedy 'injustice, *as they perceive it*'" (Berger, *The Scope of Judicial Review: An Ongoing Debate*, 6 Hast. Const. L.Q., 527, 605 [1979] [citations omitted]). *See* Bridwell, *The Federal Judiciary: America's Recently Liberated Minority*, 30 S.C.L. Rev. 467 (1979), and Carey, *Separation of Powers and the Madisonian Model: A Reply to the Critics*, 72 Am. Pol. Sci. A. J. 151 (1978) (purpose of separation of powers was to thwart governmental tyranny—not to thwart majority rule or to protect minority interests).

52. As quoted in Berger, *The Scope of Judicial Review*, p. 628.

53. "Unless we can see a *correspondence* between the symbols we have in hand and the people's action in history, the symbols we have in hand do not in fact represent that people, and we must look a second time for the symbols that do in fact represent them" (Kendall and Carey, *Basic Symbols*, p. 26). Today we are faced with two difficulties: (1) obtaining an accurate historical record—e.g., on the Sixth Amendment, and (2) convincing others that history (intent) is relevant to constitutional law. These issues are discussed elsewhere. *See* Gangi, *The Exclusionary Rule*, pp. 60–63. Scholars today consider history irrelevant because of arguments I group under the title: "The Past Is Dead—The Constitution Living." *See* Gangi, *Judicial Expansionism*, pp. 18–22.

54. *See* Gangi, *The Supreme Court*, pp. 285–87.

55. *Cf.* sources accompanying note 53, *supra*, with Gangi, *The Exclusionary Rule*, pp. 88, 105; Gangi, *Judicial Expansionism*, pp. 65–67; G. Gilmore, *The Ages of American Law* (New Haven: Yale Univ. Press, 1977); and A. Bickel, *The Supreme Court and the Idea of Progress* (New York: Harper & Row, 1970). Regarding particulars *see, e.g.*, R. Cord, *Separation of Church and State: Historical Fact and Current Fiction* (New York: Lambeth, 1982) (Supreme Court distorts the framers' First Amendment establishment and free exercise of religion clauses); Berger, *Death Penalties* (Supreme Court distorts the framers' Eighth Amendment cruel and unusual punishment clause); L. Levy, *Legacy of Suppression* (Cambridge: Belknap, 1960) (Supreme Court distorts First Amendment freedom of speech and press clauses).

56. *See* Voegelin, *Wisdom and the Magic of the Extreme: A Mediation*, S. Rev. 235 (Spring 1981).

57. For example, the infusion of progressivist criteria in one of the cited works, *An Historical Argument for the Right to Counsel during Police Interrogation*, rendered it largely unusable. Professor Beaney's work (*The Right to Counsel*) also periodically does the same thing, but you can spot it much easier, and as far as I can tell, he never fails to relate the traditional understanding. Many contemporary scholars no longer bother to master the traditional understanding; hence, it is slipping out of the consciousness of the bar.

58. Article VI of the Constitution refers to the amendment procedures.

59. In another piece I provide the reader with a list of some fourteen erroneous assumptions. *See* Gangi, *The Exclusionary Rule*, pp. 90–118.

60. *The Federalist*, No. 51, p. 322.

61. *See* Gangi, *The Supreme Court*, pp. 264–68 (supporters of contemporary judicial power assume the failure of democratic government).

62. *See, e.g.*, Bridwell, *The Federal Judiciary*, and Choper, *The Supreme Court and the Political Branches*.

63. *See* Gangi, *Judicial Expansionism*, pp. 39–41.

64. Publius, for example, uses the term "abridged" when discussing the right of legislatures to provide trial by jury in civil cases. I conclude, similarly, that with respect to the First Amendment, Congress can pass laws it believes proper as long as they do not abridge the original constitutionalized common-law meaning: no prior censorship or licensing of press. (I'd go further and suggest that those conditions apply to peacetime.) *See* Gangi, *"O What a Tangled Web,"* p. 40 n. 64.

65. When the framers did not approve of the common-law meaning, they specifically used other language: e.g., two witnesses in treason cases. *See* Berger, *Death Penalties*, p. 63. Congress did the same thing when it extended the common-law meaning of retained counsel constitutionalized by the Sixth Amendment. *See* text accompanying notes 19–21, *supra*. Professor Berger details Congress's rejection of the common law privilege of benefit of clergy (able to read) as providing an exemption from the death penalty (*Death Penalties*, p. 42).

66. Section 3 of the Alien and Sedition Act provided: "That if any person shall be prosecuted under this act, for the writing or publishing of any libel aforesaid, it shall be lawful for the defendant, upon the trial of the cause, to give in evidence in his defense, the truth of the matter contained in the publication charged as a libel. And the jury who shall try the cause, shall have the right to determine the law and the fact, under the direction of the court, as in other cases" (W. Swindler, *Sources and Documents of United States Constitutions* 2d ed. [Dobbs Ferry, N.Y.: Oceana Publications, 1982], p. 482). Neither truth as a defense nor jury determination of the law (whether what was published qualified as sedition under the law) was part of First Amendment protections.

67. *See* Henkin, *Selective Incorporation in the Fourteenth Amendment*, 73 Yale L.J. 74, 77 (1963); Berger, *Death Penalties*, p. 16.

68. *See* Gangi, *The Exclusionary Rule*, pp. 123–25.

69. *See* Gangi, *Judicial Expansionism*, pp. 62–63 n. 472. *See also* Gangi, *The Exclusionary Rule*, p. 131 n. 545 ("The sharp eye of the . . . lawyer becomes . . . demurely averted").

70. C. Wolfe, *The Rise of Modern Judicial Review* (New York: Basic Books, 1986), pp. 223–29.

71. R. Berger, *Government by Judiciary* (Cambridge: Harvard Univ. Press, 1977). The recent Supreme Court case that paves the way for "judicial taxation" is simply one of the more interesting applications.

72. *Griswold v. Connecticut*, 381 U.S. 479, 484 (1965).

73. *Katz v. United States*, 389 U.S. 347, 350–51 (1967).

74. *Everson v. U.S.*, 330 U.S. 1, 16 (1947).

75. *See* Gangi, *The Inbau-Kamisar Debate*, pp. 135–42, and Gangi, *The Supreme Court*, pp. 310–14.

76. "It is one of the happy incidents of the federal system that a . . . State may . . . serve as a laboratory; and try novel social and economic experiments." *New State Ice Co. v. Liebmann*, 285 U.S. 262, 280, 311 (1931) (Justice Brandeis, dissenting).

KATHLEEN F. BRICKEY

26. The Current Understanding of the Sixth Amendment Right to Counsel

In today's law enforcement environment, Sixth Amendment right to counsel issues have as much to do with lawyers' fee arrangements as they do with the rights of lawyers' clients. If you were to ask criminal lawyers across the country what the major concern of the criminal defense bar is today, you would be told that the most pressing concern is an "intolerable Sixth Amendment crisis"[1] created by governmental intrusions into the attorney-client relationship. The government has at its disposal an expanding array of statutes and procedures that alter the attorney-client relationship and implicate the Sixth Amendment right to counsel, you would learn.

If you then asked these lawyers to catalog the offending practices, the litany would read as follows.

Item one. The practice of issuing subpoenas to attorneys, summoning them to provide the grand jury with financial information that relates to their clients.[2] The government wants to know the amount of the fee paid for the lawyer's representation, the manner in which it was paid (i.e., was it a large amount of cash), and the identity of the payor (i.e., is your client carrying around all of this cash, or did you obtain it from some third-party benefactor).

The reason the government seeks fee information from the lawyer is item two. The Racketeer Influenced and Corrupt Organizations Act (RICO)[3] and the Continuing Criminal Enterprise statute (CCE)[4]—require forfeiture of assets acquired directly or indirectly through specified racketeering and drug activities.[5] Fee information the government obtains from lawyers thus may provide evidence that their clients have assets subject to forfeiture. To compound the problem, a prosecutor who decides to seek forfeiture of those assets may obtain a pretrial restraining order which prevents the client from transferring them to anyone—including his lawyer—and may notify the lawyer that all tainted assets, including those already paid as a fee for legal services, may be forfeited upon the client's conviction.

Item three is a relatively new provision in the Internal Revenue Code, known as Section 6050I. Section 6050I requires every person who receives more than $10,000 in cash in connection with a trade or business to file a report with the Internal Revenue Service.[6] The regulations that implement Section 6050I make clear that service providers—including lawyers—are engaged in a trade or business for purposes of the reporting requirement.[7] Thus, a lawyer may be required to inform the government that client X paid him $100,000 in cash on the fourth of July.[8]

And what if the lawyer has reason to know that some or all of the fee is derived from the client's criminal activity? That brings us to item four. A new federal money-laundering statute[9] makes it a crime to engage knowingly in a monetary transaction with a financial institution if the amount of the transaction exceeds $10,000 and the funds are derived from specified criminal activity.[10] Thus, if the lawyer knows that the source of the client's money is illicit, he cannot deposit the $100,000 fee in the bank without committing a crime.

This money-laundering statute provides a useful vehicle for bringing the right to counsel issues more sharply into focus. The constitutional controversy this particular law has generated revolves around the question whether the Sixth Amendment requires that legitimate attorneys' fees be exempted from its reach.

Those who argue that attorneys' fees must be exempted do so on the ground that otherwise the statute would impermissibly chill the attorney-client relationship. If fees were not exempt, the argument runs, the money-laundering statute would make lawyers reluctant or even unwilling to represent entire categories of defendants whose alleged criminal activity could taint the money used to pay their legal fees. In addition, lawyers would be exposed to the risk that they might have to reveal client confidences in order to prove they did not know they were dealing with criminally derived property. Last but not least, the statute would create conflicts of interest for criminal defense lawyers, whose fear of prosecution might inhibit thorough investigation of their clients' cases.[11]

The money-laundering statute may trigger these concerns in two distinct contexts: (1) the case in which a lawyer knows at the time of payment that the fee is paid in crime-related assets, and (2) the case in which a lawyer takes the fee not knowing that it is derived from criminal activity but learns during the course of the representation that she has been paid with the fruits of criminal activity.

The Sixth Amendment issues will vary, depending on which of these two contexts confronts us. The second category of cases clearly raises a host of substantial constitutional and ethical concerns.[12] But we must first address the threshold questions that arise when a lawyer knowingly accepts crime-related money as a fee, for the answers could moot the remaining issues. If criminal defendants were held to be constitutionally entitled to use tainted assets to pay their legal fees, for example, attorneys' fees would be exempt from the reach of the statute. In that event, it would make no difference whether (or when) a lawyer learned that a fee had been paid with the proceeds of crime. Hence, the threshold question to the right to use what both lawyer and client know are the fruits of crime to pay the lawyer's fee.

Hypothetical case A illustrates how the issues may arise. A lawyer reads in the newspaper that a local bank was robbed of $45,000 the preceding day. The newspaper account indicates that the bank teller who handed over the bag of loot gave the robber more than he asked for—"bait" money treated with a chemical which would turn orange within a few hours.

The next day a new client comes to the lawyer's office, tells the lawyer that he is a suspect in the robbery, and asks the lawyer for help. The lawyer agrees to represent the suspect for $15,000 but tells him that the fee must be paid in advance. "No problem," says the client, who produces a suitcase full of cash. Predictably, the bills have a distinctly orange tinge.

At this point the lawyer balks. "Look," the lawyer says, "I don't want this money. You'll have to pay the fee with some other assets." "You must be kidding," replies the client. "If I had that kind of dough to start with, I wouldn't have robbed a bank."

May the lawyer accept the fee with impunity?[13] The elementary question this case raises is whether the Sixth Amendment guarantees the suspect the right to use robbery proceeds to employ counsel to defend him.

In view of the way courts dealt with this issue before the forfeiture and money-laundering laws appeared on the scene, the facts of this hypothetical pose an unappealing Sixth Amendment case. In less exotic contexts, courts have seemed less troubled by the notion that wrongdoers should not benefit from their wrongdoing. Courts have held that neither the attorney-client privilege, the Fifth Amendment privilege against self-incrimination, nor the Sixth Amendment right to counsel entitles a client accused of criminal wrongdoing to use his lawyer as a depositary for fruits, instrumentalities, and evidence of crime.[14]

The attorney-client privilege does not protect fruits and instrumentalities of crime because it extends only to confidential communications made for the purpose of obtaining legal advice.[15] Despite the client's fear that the effects of disclosure of his fee arrangement might reveal incriminating information, courts have concluded that "[p]rofessionally competent and informed advice can be rendered by an attorney even though he or she must disclose that a fee was a gem suspected to have been recently stolen, currency with certain serial numbers, or a sum far in excess of the client's reported income."[16] To erect a shield against disclosure of such information would, in the courts' view, create "considerable temptation to use lawyers as conduits of information or of commodities necessary to criminal schemes or as launderers of money."[17] Thus, delivery of criminal evidence to a lawyer does not place it beyond the reach of the law.[18]

Nor does the client's Fifth Amendment privilege against self-incrimination protect fruits and instrumentalities of crime. A lawyer who obtains evidence from a client must comply with a subpoena to produce the evidence unless the client could have refused to produce it on Fifth Amendment grounds and the evidence was transferred to the attorney for the purpose of obtaining legal advice—i.e., it was protected by the attorney-client privilege.[19]

And what about the Sixth Amendment? Are fruits and instrumentalities of crime possessed by the lawyer protected by the client's Sixth Amendment right to counsel? No. Although lawyers may be privileged not to testify about the origin of their fees, lawyers' refusal to accept robbery proceeds as legal fees will not implicate a suspect's Sixth Amendment rights,[20] even if the suspect otherwise cannot retain private counsel. The Sixth Amendment grants the accused an absolute right to have counsel assist in his defense[21] and a qualified right to counsel of his choice.[22] The accused is entitled to employ counsel of choice if he can afford it or to be represented by appointed counsel if he cannot.[23]

In hypothetical case A our robbery suspect is financially unable to pay a lawyer to represent him. He has offered to pay not his money but money that belongs to the bank. He has no property in the money that he can lawfully pass to the lawyer.[24] If he has no other assets, he is indigent. If he is indigent, he is constitutionally entitled to appointed, but not retained, counsel.

A second reason these facts pose an unappealing Sixth Amendment case is that federal and state laws uniformly criminalize the knowing receipt of stolen property—including robbery proceeds.[25] These statutes do not condone a lawyer's receipt of stolen property to protect a client from the consequences of his crime[26] or to satisfy a legal fee.[27] Yet, it has never been thought that the failure to exempt attorneys' fees under these receiving statutes violates a robbery suspect's Sixth Amendment right to counsel. Indeed, knowingly taking or secreting fruits and instrumentalities of crime has long been recognized as both an independent criminal offense[28] and "an abuse of a lawyer's professional responsibility."[29] A lawyer may not accept stolen property as a fee because "[t]he privilege to practice law is not a license to steal."[30]

That brings us to hypothetical case B. In this case, it will be harder for the lawyer to tell which of the client's assets are criminally derived because the client is under investigation not for robbery but for trafficking in drugs. During the preceding year, however, the lawyer had represented another drug defendant and had learned that cocaine was the new client's only steady source of income. When the client comes to pay the advance retainer, he brings a suitcase full of $20 bills.

What does the lawyer do in this case? Under these circumstances the lawyer would be charged with knowledge that the money is drug-related.[31] But receipt of the $15,000 fee with that knowledge would not violate the money-laundering statute, because the statute does not penalize the receipt of tainted assets. It limits, instead, what the receiver can do with them. Here the lawyer can spend $15,000 in cash or deposit the cash in the bank—but not all at once. It would be a crime under the money-laundering statute to knowingly deposit more than $10,000 in crime-related assets.[32] So in this case we have inconvenienced the lawyer—perhaps not enough to keep him from representing the suspect, but perhaps so.

Now consider case C. The same drug suspect wants to pay the lawyer not in cash but with an airplane purchased (no doubt) with drug money. The suspect executes a power of attorney in favor of the lawyer for the purpose of transferring title to the plane but demands that the transfer of title occur in the Bahamas.[33] After the title is transferred, the lawyer advertises the plane and ultimately sells it for $140,000. The purchaser tenders a certified check for the full amount.

At this point, what should the lawyer do? He has no need for a $140,000 airplane. But if he accepts the check, he cannot deposit it with knowledge that it is derived from proceeds of the client's drug-related activities. And it would be unseemly to demand that a legitimate buyer pay the purchase price in cash. Hence, the attorney may decline to represent the suspect because the lawyer cannot lawfully obtain beneficial use of the fee. So until the prospective client is able to locate another buyer, or a lawyer who wants an expensive plane, or a dishonest lawyer, he will be unable to retain private counsel.

In a variation, case D, the drug dealer finds a legitimate buyer for the plane. The dealer then offers to endorse over a check drawn payable to him by the buyer. The lawyer still cannot deposit the check knowing that it is derived from the proceeds of a crime. Nor can the lawyer advise the client to cash the check, because that would be advising him to commit a money-laundering offense. So once again, the lawyer will not accept the client's fee.

All four cases are similar. In each, the lawyer knows that the fee is criminally derived, and his knowledge is gained from objective or external factors, not through the client's privileged communications. Unlike case A, however, the lawyer in cases B, C, and D is permitted to take the fee. But the money-laundering statute limits the manner in which the lawyer may dispose of the fee in case B and prevents meaningful disposition of it in cases C and D. Thus, in each of these cases the statute may operate as an economic disincentive to represent the client and may stymie the client's efforts to retain private counsel.

The critical question is whether this statutory economic disincentive is constitutionally distinguishable from other kinds of financial embarrassment that may dissuade private counsel from taking the case. Although the issue has yet to be litigated under the money-laundering statute, it closely parallels the basic question in attorneys' fee forfeiture cases arising under RICO and CCE. The root problem is that the client does not have sufficient untainted assets to pay counsel. When the reason for his inability to pay is that the assets are subject to forfeiture, should the court exempt an amount sufficient to pay a reasonable attorney's fee to protect the suspect's Sixth Amendment right to counsel of choice?[34]

Courts in these cases are concerned about the possible *in terrorem* effect that attorneys' fee forfeitures will have on the availability of private counsel. Because lawyers will be reluctant or unwilling to represent a defendant with knowledge that at the end of the trial their fees may be forfeited,[35] the argument runs, the defendant may be denied the right to counsel of his choice.

The right to counsel of choice is not, of course, absolute. It may be subsumed by important governmental interests—as, for example, the fair and efficient administration of justice.[36] Thus, the question in the forfeiture cases is the extent to which the government's interest in depriving wrongdoers of the economic base that enables them to engage in ongoing criminal activity justifies infringing their right to choose and retain private counsel.

In the view of most courts, the defendant's Sixth Amendment interests outweigh the government's interest in depriving drug dealers and racketeers of their economic power base, unless the transfer of assets to an attorney occurs as part of a sham or fraud.[37] When the assets are transferred in payment for legitimate legal services, according to the courts, the government's interests do not override the individual's right to use his property to retain private counsel, even if the assets ultimately prove to be tainted by the individual's criminal conduct.[38] Because the government cannot directly prevent drug and racketeering defendants from retaining counsel to defend them, it should not be permitted to accomplish indirectly—by threatening forfeiture—what it cannot directly do.[39]

Although this has been the prevailing view in the district courts, whether it will withstand appellate scrutiny remains to be seen. Indeed, a review of the brief but tortuous history of the reported court of appeals decisions reveals that the law is in an unusual state of disarray.

The Fifth Circuit was the first to rule on the point. In *United States v. Thier*,[40] the court declined to rule on the constitutionality of attorneys' fee forfeitures but found, as a matter of statutory construction, that assets needed to pay reasonable and bona fide legal fees are exempt from forfeiture. *Thier* arose in the context of a pretrial restraining order which froze all of the defendant's monies. In a subsequent case, *United States v. Jones*,[41] the court applied its holding in *Thier* to a postconviction claim by Jones's attorneys, who were seeking payment of their legal fees from property that had been ordered forfeited. The court again held that assets to pay reasonable attorneys' fees are exempt from forfeiture. A portentous concurrence, however, noted the author's acquiescence only because he was bound by *Thier*. "If I were free to do so," the concurring judge wrote, "I would follow the recent en banc opinion of the Fourth Circuit" that reached a contrary conclusion.[42] The Fifth Circuit subsequently agreed to reconsider *Jones* en banc.[43] At this writing, the en banc decision has yet to be announced.

The Fourth Circuit opinion to which the concurrence in *Jones* refers is *In re Forfeiture Hearing as to Caplin & Drysdale*.[44] A panel of the court had earlier held in *United States v. Harvey*[45] that the forfeiture statute applies to attorneys' fees but that such application is unconstitutional because it violates the Sixth Amendment right to counsel of choice. Although agreeing that the statute applies to attorneys' fees, the en banc court reversed on the ground that the panel erred in finding a constitutional right to use illicit assets to pay attorneys' fees. A petition for certiorari has been filed and, at this writing, is pending a determination by the Court.[46]

The Second Circuit ventured into the fray in *United States v. Monsanto*. A panel of the court held that attorneys' fees are not exempt from forfeiture and that the Sixth Amendment does not require their exemption.[47] After rehearing the case en banc, the court reversed the panel and held, per curiam, that the defendant is entitled to "access to restrained assets to the extent necessary to pay legitimate (that is, non-sham) attorneys' fees" to defend the criminal charge and that such fees are exempt from forfeiture.[48] Unfortunately, however, no majority of the court could agree on a rationale for this holding. Thus, the Second Circuit points us to a result without a reason.[49] At this writing, the time for filing a petition for certiorari has not expired.

The Tenth Circuit has also fueled the controversy on this issue. In *United States v. Nichols*,[50] a three-judge panel held that the forfeiture statute does not exempt attorneys' fees from forfeiture and that failure to exempt them does not deny the Sixth Amendment right to counsel of choice. Predictably, one judge dissented. Although he agreed that the statute does not exempt attorneys' fees from forfeiture, he would find the statute unconstitutional to the extent that it prevents a defendant from employing counsel to defend against the charge.[51]

And what accounts for such extraordinary judicial indecision on this point? Courts in the forfeiture cases are concerned that if threatened forfeiture of the means to pay counsel makes the defendant constructively indigent, he will be relegated to appointed counsel. The full impact of this deprivation cannot be measured, the courts tell us, until we consider the difference between retained and appointed counsel.

First, there is the question of adequacy. Question: "Did you have a lawyer when you went to court?" Answer: "No, I had a public defender."[52] Courts in the forfeiture cases are concerned that RICO and CCE defendants may be denied the effective assistance of counsel if they are required to forgo the luxury of a privately retained lawyer. This concern is not so much an indictment of the competency of public defenders as it is a recognition of the limited resources available to them.[53]

Second, courts are concerned about the question of timing. Our hypothetical client is under investigation. He has not been formally charged with a crime. Indeed, the grand jury has yet to be convened. But he wants guidance from counsel now, during the early stages of the investigation, to insure that his interests are protected throughout the whole process. If we relegate him to appointed, rather than retained, counsel, he is not yet eligible for an appointed lawyer under the Criminal Justice Act. The Act grants him a statutory right to appointed counsel only upon the following conditions: (1) he must be charged with a felony or a misdemeanor; or (2) he must be arrested and entitled by law to representation by an attorney; or (3) the Sixth Amendment must require the appointment of counsel.[54]

Now we are getting somewhere. Linger over the third condition, for it goes to the heart of the problem. Our hypothetical client will be eligible for appointed counsel under the Criminal Justice Act when the Constitution requires that counsel be made available to him.

And when will that be? The Sixth Amendment right to counsel provides the accused the assistance of an expert at confrontational stages of a prosecution to insure the accused a fair trial. The right to counsel attaches at "critical"[55] or "trial like" stages of a "criminal prosecution,"[56] not at preliminary stages of an investigation. This constitutional right is enjoyed only by "the accused" and is provided "for his defence."[57] "Of course, . . . it may well be true that in some cases preindictment investigation could help a defendant prepare a better defense."[58] But, as the Supreme Court observed, the controlling cases " have never suggested that the purpose of the right to counsel is to provide a defendant with a preindictment investigator."[59] The Court has found "no reason to adopt" such a "novel interpretation of the right of counsel."[60]

Thus, notwithstanding the legitimacy of the concerns voiced in the forfeiture cases, those concerns are not, by and large, addressed by the Sixth Amendment. A generalized concern that a suspect would be better off if he was represented by counsel while under investigation does not implicate Sixth Amendment rights.

To return, then, to the defense bar's concern in the money-laundering context, established Sixth Amendment principles do not support the call for a blanket exemption of attorneys' fees from the reach of the statute. Although the statutory limitation on a lawyer's ability to launder large amounts of tainted money through a financial institution may impede a prospective client's efforts to retain private counsel, it does not inevitably implicate the client's Sixth Amendment rights. To invoke the right to counsel on the mere possibility of prejudice—as courts in the forfeiture cases have done—is, in truth, "to wrench the Sixth Amendment from its proper context."[61]

Afterword

In 1989 the Supreme Court directly addressed the Sixth Amendment issues explored in this chapter. In *United States v. Monsanto*,[62] the Court held that the RICO and CCE forfeiture provisions are sufficiently broad to reach assets a defendant intends to use to pay attorneys' fees. In a companion case, *Caplin & Drysdale, Chartered v. United States*,[63] the Court held that application of these forfeiture provisions to attorneys' fees does not impermissibly burden the Sixth Amendment right to counsel.

The high Court stressed that while the Sixth Amendment guarantees criminal defendants the right to employ private counsel if they can afford it, the Constitution does not guarantee impecunious defendants the right to counsel of choice. It only assures that criminal defendants are entitled to assistance of counsel. Thus, if the defendant has no available assets to employ counsel of choice, the defendant is entitled representation by court-appointed counsel, but no more. In consequence, *Monsanto* and *Caplin & Drysdale* place RICO and CCE defendants who have only forfeitable assets to pay their attorneys' fees on the same constitutional footing as indigent defendants.

The clear implication of the Court's holdings in *Monsanto* and *Caplin & Drysdale* is that Congress possesses broad authority to separate criminals from the proceeds of their crimes. Congress may directly burden a RICO or CCE defendant's ability to retain counsel through the simple expedient of declaring the fruits of his crime subject to forfeiture. That the Court found no constitutional infirmity in preventing the use of tainted assets in the forfeiture context bodes ill for the argument that, as applied to attorneys' fees, the money-laundering statute impermissibly chills the Sixth Amendment right to counsel.

Notes

1. *NACDL to Congress: Reform Section 1957*, Nat'l A. of Crim. Def. Law. Washington Digest, May 20, 1987, No. 6 at 1, col. 2.

2. *See, e.g., United States v. (Under Seal)*, 774 F.2d 624 (4th Cir. 1985), *cert. denied*, 106 S. Ct. 1514 (1986); *In re Grand Jury Subpoena Duces Tecum Dated January 2, 1985 (Simels)*, 767 F.2d 26 (2d Cir. 1985); *In re Grand Jury Subpoena Served upon Doe*, 759 F.2d 968 (2d Cir. 1985); *In re Grand Jury Matters*, 751 F.2d 13 (1st Cir. 1984); *In re Grand Jury Subpoena Duces Tecum (Shargel)*, 742 F.2d 61 (2d Cir. 1984); *In re Ousterhoudt*, 722 F.2d 591 (9th Cir. 1983).

3. Racketeer Influenced and Corrupt Organizations Act, 18 U.S.C. sec. 1961–68 (1982 & Supp. III 1985).

4. 21 U.S.C. sec. 848 (1982 & Supp. III 1985).

5. 18 U.S.C. sec. 1963; 21 U.S.C. sec. 853.

6. 26 U.S.C. sec. 6050(I) (Supp. III 1985).

7. 26 C.F.R. sec. 1.6050I-1 (1987).

8. *See generally* Du Mouchel and Oberg, *Defense Attorney Fees: A New Tool for the Prosecution*, 1986 U. Det. C.L. Rev. 57.

9. 18 U.S.C.A. sec. 1957 (Supp. 1987).

10. The laundry list is lengthy, but it includes the racketeering and drug offenses discussed above. The list of offenses is contained in a companion money-laundering statute, 18 U.S.C.A. sec. 1956 (Supp. 1987).

11. *See* Franklin, *Fee Tale—Money Laundering Guidelines Worry the Defense Bar*, N.Y.L.J., May 14, 1987, p. 5, col. 2; Tarlow, *RICO Report*, 11 Champion 35 (Feb. 1987). At one point in time the House version of the bill contained a provision exempting bona fide attorneys' fees (*see* H.R. Rep. No. 855, 99th Cong., 2d Sess., pt. 1 at 1, 14 [1986]), but that provision was eliminated by a conference committee (132 *Cong. Rec.* E3821, E3822 [daily ed., Nov. 6, 1986] [statement of Rep. McCollum]).

12. Some of those concerns are addressed in recently issued Justice Department Guidelines. Under the Guidelines, an attorney who accepts tainted property as a bona fide fee for representation in a criminal matter should not be prosecuted under the money-laundering statute unless the government has proof beyond a reasonable doubt that the lawyer actually knew the illegal origin of the specific asset and unless the evidence proving the lawyer's knowledge does not consist of confidential communications between the lawyer and the client during the course of the representation (U.S. Dept. of Justice, U.S. Attorneys' Manual sec. 9–105.400 [May 12, 1988]).

13. Assuming the lawyer accepts the cash as a retainer, what will he do with it? He certainly would not go around town paying for groceries and buying gasoline with obviously marked money. Instead, at some point in time he would want to deposit the money in an escrow account and—if questioned about its source by law enforcement authorities—assert the attorney-client privilege. "You cannot require me to tell you about the money," the lawyer would say, "because disclosing what I know might incriminate a client or reveal a client confidence."

14. *See, e.g., State v. Dillon*, 93 Idaho 698, 710, 471 P.2d 553, 565 (1970).

15. *Fisher v. United States*, 425 U.S. 391, 403 (1975). Although payment of a fee is a necessary prerequisite to obtaining legal advice, disclosure of the fee does not inhibit communication of information the attorney needs to represent the client. *In re Grand Jury Subpoena Served upon Doe*, 781 F.2d 238, 247–48 (2d Cir. 1986). *Cf. State v. Olwell*, 394 P.2d 681, 684 (Wash. 1964) (criminal evidence does little, if anything, to aid the lawyer's preparation of the client's defense). Thus, even though a transfer of a fee to an attorney—including the fruits of the client's crime—is made for the purpose of employing the attorney to give legal advice, the fee information is generally not considered privileged.

16. *In re Shargel*, 742 F.2d 61, 63 (2d Cir. 1984). *See also In re January 1976 Grand Jury (Genson)*, 534 F.2d 719 (7th Cir. 1976) (affirming lawyer's contempt citation for refusing to comply with subpoena ordering him to surrender money received as a fee from clients suspected of bank robbery).

17. *In re Shargel*, 742 F.2d 61, 64 (2d Cir. 1984).

18. *People v. Investigation into a Certain Weapon*, 448 N.Y.S. 2d 950, 963 (1982). *See also People v. Superior Court*, 192 Cal. App.3d 32, 237 Cal. Rptr. 158 (1987) (defense counsel who obtains possession of physical evidence related to criminal charge against client must turn it over to police or prosecu-

tor); *People v. Meredith*, 29 Cal.3d 682, 631 P.2d 46, 175 Cal. Rptr. 612 (1981) (attorney has duty not to remove or alter physical evidence so as to prevent prosecutor from discovering it); *State v. Dillon*, 93 Idaho 698, 471 P.2d 553 (1970) (attorney-client privilege does not entitle attorney to act as depository for or to suppress criminal evidence); *People v. Nash*, 110 Mich. App. 428, 313 N.W.2d 307 (1981) (attorney has duty to turn evidence over to prosecution).

Once a lawyer obtains criminal evidence from his client, however, the lawyer may refuse to reveal its source on the ground that to do so would violate the attorney-client privilege. *People v. Nash*, 110 Mich. App. 428, 313 N.W.2d 307 (1981).

19. *Fisher v. United States*, 425 U.S. 391, 402 (1975). Even if the evidence is not subject to subpoena because it is testimonial in nature, it nonetheless remains subject to seizure under the Fourth Amendment because neither attorney nor client is required to authenticate it or aid in its discovery. *Anderson v. Maryland*, 427 U.S. 463, 473–74 (1976).

20. *See Clutchette v. Rusher*, 770 F.2d 1469, 1472 (9th Cir. 1985); *Morrell v. State*, 575 P.2d 1200, 1207 (Alaska 1978); *Anderson v. State*, 297 So.2d 871, 875 (Fla. App. 1974); *State v. Green*, 493 So.2d 1178, 1182, 1184 (La. 1986). *Cf. In re January 1976 Grand Jury*, 534 F.2d 719 (7th Cir. 1976) (For purposes of this appeal from a lawyer's contempt citation, "[w]e express no opinion as to whether the suspects having chosen to make [the lawyer] a witness to their crime [by paying their fee with robbery proceeds], if such should subsequently prove to be the fact, may properly invoke the Sixth Amendment to bar his eyewitness testimony at trial.").

21. Under current Supreme Court interpretation, the right to counsel is absolute for all offenses except misdemeanors and petty offenses that do not result in the imposition of a sentence of imprisonment. *Scott v. Illinois*, 440 U.S. 367, 373–74 (1979).

22. *See, e.g., Urquhart v. Lockhart*, 726 F.2d 1316, 1319 (8th Cir. 1984); *United States v. Cicale*, 691 F.2d 95, 106 (2d Cir. 1982); *Linton v. Perini*, 656 F.2d 207, 209–12 (6th Cir. 1981), *cert. denied*, 454 U.S. 1162 (1982). For a discussion of the origins of and limitations on the right to counsel of choice, *see* Brickey, *Forfeiture of Attorneys' Fees: The Impact of RICO and CCE Forfeitures on the Right to Counsel*, 72 Va. L. Rev. 493, 506–10 (1986).

23. *See* Brickey, *Forfeiture of Attorneys' Fees*, p. 504 n. 49.

24. *In re Ryder*, 263 F. Supp. 360, 369 (E.D. Va. 1967).

25. *See, e.g.*, 18 U.S.C. sec. 659 (1982); 18 U.S.C. sec. 2113(c) (1982); 18 U.S.C. sec. 641 (1982); Model Penal Code sec. 223.6 (P.O.D. 1962).

26. *In re Ryder*, 263 F. Supp. 360, 369 (E.D. Va. 1967) (lawyer took robbery proceeds with intent to return them to bank after client's trial).

27. *United States v. Scruggs*, 549 F.2d 1097 (6th Cir. 1977).

28. *See United States v. Scruggs*, 549 F.2d 1097 (6th Cir. 1977) (upholding conviction of lawyer for knowingly possessing, concealing, and disposing of robbery proceeds accepted as a fee and for obstruction of justice); *United States v. Cameron*, 460 F.2d 1394 (5th Cir. 1972) (reversing lawyer's conviction of receiving stolen property because of erroneous jury instruction; lawyer ac-

cepted robbery proceeds as a fee); *Laska v. United States*, 82 F.2d 672 (10th Cir.), *cert. denied*, 298 U.S. 689 (1936) (upholding conviction, as accessory to kidnapping, of lawyer who accepted ransom as a fee and advised client how to launder remaining ransom money); *State v. Wolery*, 348 N.E.2d 351, 362 (Ohio 1976) (upholding conviction of lawyer for receiving stolen property, where some of property appears to have been used to satisfy lawyer's fee); *State v. Harlton*, 669 P.2d 774 (Okla. 1983) (lawyer convicted of crime of concealing weapon used in a crime suspended from practice). *But see Commonwealth v. Stenhach*, 514 A.2d 114 (Pa. 1986) (vacating lawyer's conviction for hindering prosecution and tampering with evidence on ground that statutes were unconstitutionally vague as applied to attorneys during representation of criminal defendants).

Cf. In re January 1976 Grand Jury (Genson), 534 F.2d 719 (7th Cir. 1976) (affirming lawyer's contempt citation for refusing to comply with subpoena ordering him to surrender money received as fee from client suspected of bank robbery); *State v. Olwell*, 394 F.2d 681 (Wash. 1964) (reversing attorney's contempt citation for refusing to produce material evidence of a crime because subpoena was defective in that it required attorney to testify about matters confided by client).

29. *In re Ryder*, 381 F.2d 713, 714 (4th Cir. 1967) (suspending lawyer from practice for taking possession of stolen weapon with intent to conceal it until after client's trial). *Cf. People v. Laska*, 109 Colo. 389, 126 P.2d 500 (1942) (per curiam) (refusing to reinstate lawyer who was disbarred following conviction for accepting kidnapping ransom money); *People v. Laska*, 105 Colo. Rep. 426 (1940) (disbarring attorney in same case); *State v. Harlton*, 669 P.2d 774 (Okla. 1985) (suspending lawyer convicted of concealing evidence).

30. *Laska v. United States*, 82 F.2d 672, 677 (10th Cir. 1936) (lawyer accepted ransom as a fee).

31. *Cf. United States v. Werner*, 160 F.2d 438, 441–42 (2d Cir. 1947) ("The receivers of stolen goods almost never 'know' that they have been stolen, in the sense that they could testify to it in a court room. . . . But that the jury must find that the receiver did more than infer the theft from the circumstances has never been demanded.").

32. The money-laundering statute also prohibits him from exchanging the $20s for $100 bills or $1,000 bills into $50s in large quantities. Any transaction with a bank (or a money launderer) must be structured in amounts less than the jurisdictional amount. The lawyer must, in addition, report the receipt of the cash to the IRS under section 6050I.

Although structuring transactions in amounts of less than $10,000 to avoid reporting requirements imposed under the Currency and Foreign Transactions Reporting Act is a crime, the money-laundering law is not a reporting statute, and it does not expressly proscribe breaking up the deposits.

33. *See United States v. Long*, 654 F.2d 911 (3d Cir. 1981).

34. *See United States v. Thier*, 801 F.2d 1463, 1477 15th Cir. 1986 (Rubin, J., concurring), *modified*, 809 F.2d 249 (1987); *United States v. Harvey*, 814 F.2d 905, 927 (4th Cir. 1987); *United States v. Nichols*, 654 F. Supp. 1541, 1559 (D. Utah 1987); *United States v. Estevez*, 645 F. Supp. 869, 871–72 (E.D. Wis. 1986).

35. *Harvey*, 814 F.2d at 921; *United States v. Badalamenti*, 614 F. Supp.

194, 197 (S.D.N.Y. 1985); *United States v. Bassett*, 632 F. Supp. 1308, 1316–17 (D. Md. 1986).

36. *See* note 22, *supra*.

37. *United States v. Monsanto*, No. 87–1397, slip op. at 4746 (2d Cir. July 1, 1988); *Harvey*, 814 F.2d at 924, 927; *United States v. Badalamenti*, 614 F. Supp. 194 (S.D.N.Y. 1984); *United States v. Rogers*, 602 F. Supp. 1332 (D. Colo. 1985). *But cf. United States v. Thier*, 801 F.2d 1463, 1474 (5th Cir. 1986), *modified*, 809 F.2d 249 (1987).

38. *Harvey*, 814 F.2d at 927.

39. *Id.* at 924. As a Fourth Circuit panel recently admonished in *United States v. Harvey*: "The right to counsel . . . [protects] the guilty as well as the innocent. It must certainly have been created, therefore, on the assumption—indeed with the sure knowledge—that in exercising the primary right to privately retained counsel, ill-gotten gains might be used by defendants who would ultimately be found guilty" (*id.* at 924–25). Curiously—or perhaps not so curiously—the court neglected to explain just what transforms an expectation that criminal defendants will pay legal fees with the fruits of their crimes into a constitutional right to do so.

In any event, let us consider the implications of the *Harvey* court's—and the Sixth Amendment framers'—"sure knowledge" that, from time immemorial, criminal defendants have used ill-gotten gains to pay their lawyers. Does this mean that the Sixth Amendment guarantees our hypothetical robber a constitutional right to pay counsel with the robbery proceeds? No, according to the court. And why not? Because, the court tells us, when the government seizes a bank robber's loot, "the government seizes property manifestly that of someone other than the accused and for preservative purposes" (*id.* at 926). "The financial plight that may result to an accused from sequestration of contraband," the court continues, "is simply of a piece with that resulting from other vagaries of life that may make it impossible to hire private counsel" (*id.*). But when the government attempts to sequester other ill-gotten gains to which "no third party has a superior claim" (*id.*), it is attempting to do indirectly what it cannot directly do—that is, to prevent the defendant from attaining counsel of his choice.

The distinction apparently rests, then, on title of the assets, not on their unlawful acquisition. But query whether this is a rational baseline to draw. What if the client was not a bank robber but was, instead, a bank teller who enriched himself at the bank's expense? If he has stolen the money out of the till, he has committed larceny. *See, e.g., United States v. Clew*, 4 F.Cas. 700 (C.C. Wash. 1827) (No. 14,819). He has unlawfully taken money from the bank's possession but—like the robber—has acquired no title to the money. If, on the other hand, the teller has pocketed money handed over by a customer without first placing it in the till, he has committed embezzlement. *See, e.g., Kramer v. State*, 116 Ala. App. 456, 78 So. 719, *cert. denied*, 201 Ala. 700, 78 So. 719 (1918). He has, by misappropriating something lawfully in his possession, unlawfully acquired title to the property. *See* W. LaFave and A. Scott, *Criminal Law*, 2d ed. (St. Paul, Minn.: West Publishing Co., 1986), secs. 8.1–8.6, sec. 8.8(a).

Are the embezzler and the thief on equal constitutional footing? Or is the embezzler—but not the thief—constitutionally entitled to retain counsel with the fruits of his crime because he wrongfully acquired ownership, and not mere possession? Surely the framers of the

Sixth Amendment would not have entrusted the contours of so important a constitutional right to the vagaries of theft law.

So perhaps the court meant something else. Perhaps the court's reference to third parties who have a superior claim to the property related not so much to the concept of title as it related to the concept of entitlement. As between the robber and the bank, the bank is entitled to the property. The same would undoubtedly be true with respect to embezzled funds, irrespective of the question of title.

But consider the possibilities. Suppose the client has been running a profitable boiler-room securities operation which specializes in selling worthless securities. He is charged with mail and wire fraud (18 U.S.C. secs. 1341, 1343 [1982]). As between the securities seller and his defrauded customers, the customers are entitled to their hard-earned money. Would the Fourth Circuit say that under these circumstances the government could therefore seize the fraudulently obtained monies—"for preservative purposes"—without implicating the seller's constitutional right to counsel? Although one cannot be sure of the outcome, the tenor of the panel's opinion suggests that the court would not have been receptive to seizure or sequestration of assets if that action would prevent the defendant from hiring counsel to defend him. *See Harvey*, 814 F.2d at 926.

The distinction the Fourth Circuit draws, then, is tenuous at best. Although the en banc opinion rejected the panel's distinction between illicit drug proceeds and the robber's loot, it did not fully address the implications of that distinction. The en banc opinion dismissed the distinction on the ground that it would not always be true that robbery proceeds were manifestly the property of someone other than the robber. Instead, "the robber may have deposited the proceeds in his own account or otherwise disguised them. Similarly, the assets sought to be forfeited . . . may well be 'manifestly' illicit, as is the case where the defendant has piles of cash and no records of any legitimate income whatsoever" (*Caplin & Drysdale*, 837 F.2d at 645). *But see United States v. Nichols*, 841 F.2d 1485, 1510 (10th Cir. 1988) (Logan, J., dissenting) (when bank and accused robber fight over ownership of funds, they do so under traditional common-law property concepts; government's interest in forfeitable assets differs in that it is grounded in public policy, not property rights).

40. 801 F.2d 1463 (5th Cir. 1986), *modified*, 809 F.2d 249 (1987).

41. 837 F.2d 1332 (5th Cir. 1988).

42. *Id.* at 1337.

43. 844 F.2d 215 (5th Cir. 1988).

44. 837 F.2d 637 (4th Cir. 1988) (en banc).

45. 814 F.2d 905 (4th Cir. 1987).

46. No. 87–1729, 56 U.S.L.W. 3821 (April 11, 1988).

47. 836 F.2d 74 (2d Cir. 1987).

48. No. 87–1397, slip op. at 4746 (2d Cir. July 1, 1988) (en banc) (per curiam).

49. Or, viewed differently, the court gave an abundance of reasons, none of which carried the day. In addition to the per curiam opinion of the court, eight separate concurrences and dissents were filed. *See id.* at 4746 (concurring opinion of Chief Judge Feinberg, joined by judges Oakes and Kearse); *id.* at 4750 (dissenting opinion of Judge Mahoney, joined in part by judges Cardamone and Pierce); *id.* at 4766 (opinion of Judge Cardamone, joined by Judge Pierce,

concurring in part and dissenting in part); *id.* at 4768 (opinion of Judge Pratt, concurring in part and dissenting in part); *id.* at 4771 (opinion of Judge Pierce, joined by Judge Cardamone, concurring in part and dissenting in part); *id.* at 4772 (concurring opinion of Judge Winter, joined by judges Meskill and Newman); *id.* at 4786 (opinion of Judge Miner, joined by Judge Altimari, concurring in part and dissenting in part); *id.* at 4788 (concurring opinion of Judge Oakes).

50. 841 F.2d 1485 (10th Cir. 1988).

51. *Id.* at 1509 (Logan, J., dissenting). *Cf. United States v. Unit No. 7 and Unit No. 8 of Shop in the Grove Condominium*, No. 87–2499, slip op. at 3, 15 (8th Cir. Aug. 5, 1988) (holding, under facts of case, that government's effort to deprive defendant of assets needed to pay reasonable attorney's fee impermissibly conflicted with Fifth and Sixth Amendments).

52. *See Did You Have a Lawyer When You Went to Court? No, I Had a Public Defender*, Yale Rev. L. & Soc. Act., Spring 1971, at 4.

53. *See, e.g., United States v. Rogers*, 602 F. Supp. 1332, 1349 (D. Colo. 1985).

54. 18 U.S.C. sec. 3006A(a) (1982).

55. *See Gilbert v. California*, 388 U.S. 263 (1967); *United States v. Wade*, 388 U.S. 218 (1967).

56. *See Gerstein v. Pugh*, 420 U.S. 103 (1975); *United States v. Ash*, 413 U.S. 300 (1973).

57. "In all criminal prosecutions, the accused shall enjoy the right . . . to have the Assistance of Counsel for his defence." U.S. Constitution, Amendment VI.

58. *United States v. Gouveia*, 467 U.S. 180, 191 (1984).

59. *Id.*

60. *Id.*

61. *Id.* (case involving unsuccessful argument for extension of the Sixth Amendment right to counsel), quoting *United States v. Marion*, 404 U.S. 307, 321–22 (1971) (referring to the Sixth Amendment right to speedy trial).

62. 109 S. Ct. 2657 (1989).

63. 109 S. Ct. 2646 (1989).

XI.

THE SEVENTH AMENDMENT AND THE RIGHT TO CIVIL JURY TRIAL

Morris S. Arnold

27. A Historical Inquiry into the Right to Trial by Jury in Complex Civil Litigation

Readers of recent law reviews and reports will not need to be told that in the last few years a very considerable controversy has arisen over the availability of jury trial in complex civil cases.[1] In all the commentary addressed to this issue it seems to have escaped remark that there is nothing very new in attempts by certain interests to avoid jury trial. For instance, well over a century ago *Hunt's Merchants' Magazine* lamented the "frequent inability of jurors to agree" in commercial cases.[2] In part because "merchants tended to believe that in cases involving complex commercial issues . . . a single judge was likelier to understand the case and thus be more reliable than a jury," they "preferred whenever possible to bring suit in equity."[3] We are today witnessing a recrudescence of such efforts.

Some who argue that juries need not be employed in complicated civil litigation maintain that juries are incapable of rendering intelligent and informed verdicts in complex cases; hence the remedies at law are inadequate,[4] and equitable jurisdiction is appropriate.[5] Because all the authorities seem to agree that the right to jury trial in the federal courts is to be determined, at least in part, by reference to the practices contemporaneous with the adoption of the Seventh Amendment in 1791,[6] proponents of the "complexity exception" have attempted to discover a historical foundation for their theory. They purport to find in eighteenth-century English law a well-established head of equity jurisdiction which allowed the defendant, as well as the plaintiff, to insist on avoiding jury trial in cases involving complicated facts.[7] This chapter will attempt to show that this view is misconceived in a number of important and fatal ways: not only is it a view at odds with the current of American legal thought in the late eighteenth century, it is also without general support in the English authorities of that age.[8]

Justice Story wrote in an opinion early in the nineteenth century that the common law alluded to in the Seventh Amendment was "[b]eyond all question . . . not the common law of any individual state, (for it probably differs in all), but it is the common law of England, the grand reservoir of all our jurisprudence."[9] This statement has been understood to mean that the right to jury trial in the federal courts should be determined solely by reference to the eighteenth-century English practice.[10] In fact, however, the exact question involved in the case before Story was whether federal courts should apply the Massachusetts practice of giving a right to jury trial on appeal. Story's dictum thus has no bearing on our inquiry, for we are not concerned with what sort of jury trial the Constitution would require in a case conceded to be at law; our question is rather where the boundary between legal and equitable jurisdiction lay at the time of the adoption of the Seventh Amendment.

Although our focus is different from Story's, it is nevertheless true that the line between law and equity may have been drawn differently from colony to colony; we know, for instance, that in the Confederation period, equity procedure differed somewhat from place to place.[11] Yet the variety of colonial and state practice in the latter part of the eighteenth century is relevant to the question of the scope of the Seventh Amendment right in at least three ways. First, and most important, it exposes to view the sentiment for and attachment to trial by jury that Americans had in the nascent period of the nation. That special affection for the jury ought to be viewed as relevant not just to the fact that jury trial was "preserved" in the Constitution; it is relevant as well to interpreting the scope of the actual provision, for it gives the right granted an aura and the Constitution a meaning they would not otherwise have if the institution of jury trial had been regarded more or less indifferently. Second, especially in those places in which the English brand of common law was consciously regarded as the model to emulate, the American practice in 1791 is some evidence of what Americans thought the English practice was. Third, the U. S. Supreme Court has itself stated that the Seventh Amendment "guaranty has always been construed to mean a trial in the mode and according to the settled rules of the common law, including all the essential elements recognized in this country and England when the Constitution was adopted."[12] In an inquiry intended to uncover the original understanding of those who drafted and ratified the Seventh Amendment, eighteenth-century American attitudes toward courts of equity cannot therefore be unimportant. A short review of what can be discovered about these matters will thus be attempted.

In *The Federalist* No. 83, Alexander Hamilton revealed himself to be something of an admirer of equitable jurisdiction. Discussing the proposal for a constitutional provision regarding jury trial, he predicted that "to extend the jurisdiction of the courts of law to matters of equity . . . will tend gradually to change the nature of the courts of law, and to undermine the trial by jury, by introducing questions too complicated for a decision in that mode."[13] But there is every reason to think that Hamilton's views on this matter, as on some others, were somewhat idiosyncratic. Indeed, Professor Katz has said that "[f]ew American politicians of the colonial era would have seen equity law and chancery courts in such a favorable light."[14] Katz went on to note that "no colonial legal institution was the object of such sustained and intense political opposition as the courts dispensing equity law."[15]

Virtually absent from the colonies in the seventeenth century, regular courts of equity existed in only five of the thirteen original states in 1791;[16] and in the eighteenth century equity courts found themselves in the center of a storm of controversy. Much of this opposition was of a political character, focusing on the power to create such courts and the authority to appoint their members, rather than the content of equity doctrine.[17] But much of the opposition was also due to the unavailability of a jury in regular chancery practice.[18] Indeed, in some of the apparently political opposition to equity, opposition which emphasized the centralized character of equity in contrast to the decentralized trials of the common law, it is right to see an affection for the rough and tumble of *nisi prius* verdicts in preference to a decision by one man alone. Juries were often regarded as more than a mode of trial: They were instruments of local government as well.

In New York a good deal of the opposition to equity courts was due to the lack of jury trials in those forums.[19] In the early part of the century an enormous stir was occasioned by the litigation between Governor William Cosby and Rip Van Dam over which of them was entitled to the salary and perquisites of the governorship.[20] When Cosby, through the power of his office, maneuvered the controversy into the court of exchequer, many thought that he had done so in order to avoid a jury trial.[21] Moreover, Cosby's creation of a court of equity was perceived as motivated by a desire to deprive the colonists of their right to trial by jury;[22] and some complained that "trials by juries are taken away when a governor pleases."[23] Thus in early eighteenth-century New York the popular association of equity with arbitrary power may be readily established, and in the 1760s the right to trial by jury was even more strenuously asserted and insisted upon in the controversy over equity courts.[24]

It would, in fact, be extremely surprising if the opposition to chancery were not in some measure directly linked to the colonists' high regard for the jury. As in medieval England,[25] juries in eighteenth-century America had much more power to decide questions both of law and fact than do modern ones. This has been documented best in the case of Massachusetts,[26] but there is good reason to believe that the Massachusetts experience in this respect was not unlike that in most American colonies.[27] Most of the jury-control techniques that modern lawyers take for granted were simply unknown in early American practice,[28] and other technical devices that have as their aim and effect the control of the jury were unavailable as well. For instance, special pleading, the purpose of which is partly to circumscribe the jury's scope of operation and thus to limit its discretion, was extremely rare.[29] Many important eighteenth-century Americans recognized that this gave juries the power and authority to decide law; indeed, they applauded that capacity. John Adams, using a metaphor which tells us a great deal about the natural-law orientation of early Americans, said that the common law was known to all "and imbibed with the Nurses Milk and first Air."[30]

Professor Nelson's description of the effect of this view of the law is worth quoting at length:

> Lawyers thus believed that juries should have the power to find law, apparently so that they could serve when needed as a restraint on judicial power. The law-finding power of juries had a number of consequences, however, that appear to have been unanticipated. One set of consequences arose out of the fact that law found by juries to fit the circumstances of individual cases has great potential for flexibility, for records of jury determinations of points of law are seldom preserved, and hence those determinations do not become precedents with a binding effect on future juries. In each case, a jury is free, if justice requires, to reach the same result reached by other juries in analogous cases in the past; if, on the other hand, justice requires departure from past verdicts, the jury is free so to depart. Moreover, no record is kept of such departures, and therefore legal change and development are imperceptible; men have the valuable illusion of legal stability. Explicit rules of law, such as the rules of pleading considered above, remain unchanged, while substantive law is still extremely flexible in its ability to adapt itself to social needs in individual cases. The broad power of juries to find law thus gave the legal system real flexibility while simultaneously giving the illusion of stability—two values that are important in doing justice in individual cases and in convincing litigants that justice has been done them.
>
> The law-finding power of juries also made possible adherence to the doctrine that judges—the agents of a potentially arbitrary executive—ought to follow precedent and so not alter the rules of law. For, as we have seen, the vast power of juries in general left judges with only a few rather simple law tasks, such as instructing juries and deciding pleading motions, which could be mechanically performed by looking to precedent.
>
> Most important, perhaps, the law-finding power of juries meant that the representatives of local communities assembled as jurors generally had effective power to control the content of the province's substantive law. Because of the power of juries, the legal system could not serve as an instrument for the enforcement of coherent social policies formulated by political authorities, either legislative or executive, whether in Boston or in local communities, when those policies were unacceptable to the men who happened to be serving on a particular jury. The ultimate power of juries thus raises the question whether the judgments rendered in the courts on a day-to-day basis were a reflection more of law set out in statute books and in English judicial precedents or of the custom of local communities.[31]

A distinguished historian of English law lately has noticed that legal systems which delegate law-finding functions to laymen cannot be anxious about producing a systematic substantive law, since they give professionals so few occasions to review the legal significance of facts.[32] The allowance of such large latitude to laymen is jurisprudentially significant because it seems to reveal a society at home with the notion that law and right are changeless truths discoverable by lawyers and laymen alike. In such a world law is a fact like any other: all that is necessary for the resolution of a dispute is for intelligent and moral people, free from the temptations of corruption, to apply their minds to it in a reasonably diligent fashion.

This is exactly the way the common law was conceived of in eighteenth-century America,[33] and this view of the law and of the capacity of jurors had an impact on procedures in those eighteenth-century American tribunals hearing equitable matters. Practice before many of them took on a definite common-law cast. Chancery jurisdiction and practice in early America still awaits its historian, and until the records of the various jurisdictions become more readily accessible, general conclusions in this area are a little hazardous. Some relevant items may be advanced with confidence, however, and they indicate a bias in favor of juries even in suits in equity.

In Massachusetts general equitable relief was unavailable in any of the courts until almost one hundred years after the adoption of the Seventh Amendment.[34] During the colonial period acts were passed granting certain kinds of specific equitable powers to law courts: in 1693 jurisdiction to chancer bonds was given; in 1698 and 1735 power to relieve against forfeiture by mortgagors was granted; and in 1713 and 1719 jurisdiction was conferred over redemption of lands after sale under an execution.[35] In all these cases trial was by jury, and in 1791 no matters of fact material to equitable issues were tried other than by jury.[36]

It is well known that Thomas Jefferson favored the use of juries in chancery courts as authoritative determiners of the facts. In a proposed constitution for Virginia that he composed in 1776, Jefferson urged that "[a]ll facts in causes, whether of Chancery, Common, Ecclesiastical, or Marine law, shall be tried by a jury."[37] Another Jefferson draft of 1783 contained a similar recommendation.[38] The reports of George Wythe, America's first law professor, indicate that juries were used in the Virginia High Court of Chancery to fix the value of the thing in dispute[39] or to determine the boundaries of real estate that was the subject of litigation.[40] Under this procedure the chancery court would "direct an issue to be tried" by a jury in a common-law court and order a report on the result to be sent up for scrutiny.[41] While the use of juries in equity courts in England was not unknown, the frequency of resort to them, and the kinds of occasions on which resort would be had, was evidently larger in Virginia. This was clearly the case in Kentucky; a recent study of the federal court that sat there beginning in 1789 has revealed frequent use of juries in equity cases.[42] The same can be said of Georgia in this period; that state "allowed trial by jury in some causes which by tradition belonged to the equity side of the bench."[43] A North Carolina statute enacted in 1782 had the same aim and effect.[44]

William Penn, referring to the happy condition of the Indians in Pennsylvania, noted in 1683 that they "are not disquieted with bills of lading and exchange, nor perplexed with chancery suits."[45] And it is perhaps in Pennsylvania that one encounters the most extensive use of juries in chancery proceedings. There, except for a brief period in the eighteenth century, equity was administered entirely in the courts of law.[46] Without chancery courts, it fell "to the lot of Pennsylvania," William Rawle said in 1868, "through necessity, to have blended together, in a single tribunal, equitable principles and equitable jurisdiction, and to have dispensed those *principles* through the medium of common law forms."[47] One of the short-lived acts creating courts of equity in Pennsylvania demonstrates how careful one must be in interpreting historical evidence of the times. In 1711 the common-pleas judges were empowered to sit as a court of equity four times yearly, with instructions to observe "as near as may be, the rules and practices of the high court of chancery in Great Britain."[48] Without more, this would lead to the conclusion that a jury would not ordinarily be employed. But the act went on to provide that "when matters of fact should arise in the hearing of any cause, the court should first refer them to issue and trial before the Common Pleas, before proceeding to decree in equity."[49]

The lack of equitable remedies in Pennsylvania meant that the common-law courts had to improvise when persons sought enforcement of equitable rights. Thus Horace Binney could say that this difficulty "taught us how to clothe a large body of equity principles in the drapery of the law."[50] For instance, if specific performance was sought, a substitute for an injunction had to be found, so eighteenth-century Pennsylvania courts granted "conditional damages, so large in amount, that the defendant finds it to his advantage to yield to the plaintiff the equity which is the subject of the suit."[51] A case decided in 1791 nicely illustrates the use of this device.[52] If specific performance of a land-sale contract was sought, then ejectment, a real action at common law offering specific recovery of the realty, was made available;[53] likewise, replevin could effect the recovery of a chattel owed.[54] And so, "by an ingenious and liberal use of . . . common law methods,"[55] the common-law courts of Pennsylvania fashioned equitable remedies for the vindication of equitable rights.

As noted before, early American chancery records have not yet been fully mined for the information they may contain, and general statements are therefore somewhat difficult. But it is nevertheless clear that no case of that period yet printed indicates a willingness on the part of the chancellor to assume jurisdiction because of a matter's alleged unsuitability for trial before a jury. It is true that after the Seventh Amendment was passed, nineteenth-century courts occasionally claimed that the basis for jurisdiction over suits for accounting in equity was the impracticality of trying them before a jury.[56] But no eighteenth-century American court, so far as we can tell, so held. A South Carolina case initiated in 1717,[57] asking for an accounting in a partnership setting, has indeed been cited as an example of equity jurisdiction's being premised upon the complexity of the facts.[58] Examination of the pleadings, however, reveals an entirely different basis for the jurisdiction: the need for the discovery and subpoena power of equity that was unavailable in the common-law courts. Plaintiff concluded her bill for equitable relief as follows:

> All which Actings and doeings of the said Francis LeBrasseur [the defendant] are contrary to all Equity and good Conscience and Ministers Fresh occasion of Sorrow and Affliction to your Oratrix's late great Misfortunes well known to this Honourable Court In tender Consideration whereof and for that your Oratrix is wholly remediless in the premisses at the Common Law for that your Oratrix cannot by any Action at Law Compel the said Francis LeBrasseur to produce his said Books of Accounts and Consequently cannot Ascertain her Damages to a Jury occasioned by the said LeBrasseur his breach of the Covenant of the aforesaid Indenture of Copartnership nor can your Oratrix Sufficiently prove at Common Law the said Collaterall Verbal Agreement or the Stock advanced by your Oratrix pursuant thereunto or the proffits accrewing to your oratrix therefrom without Sight Perusal and Examination of said Books of Accounts. . . . Where fore . . . May it please your Honours to Grant unto your Oratrix the Writt of subpena to be Directed to the said Francis LeBrasseur . . . and Alsoe to Grant unto your Oratrix the Writt of Duces tecum to be directed to the said Francis LeBrasseur requiring him at a Certain Day to bring in and Deposit in this Honourable Court all the said Old partnership Books of Accounts . . . And all papers Minuments and Writings relating to the said Copartnership.[59]

Nowhere does the bill mention the complicated character of the case. Indeed, even if one was to discover in the eighteenth-century archives a case in which equitable jurisdiction rested on complexity, it would prove only that complexity was a basis for providing an equitable remedy at the option of the plaintiff. It would not even suggest the possibility that a plaintiff seeking a legal remedy proper to the circumstances could be enjoined from doing so.

In a recent article on suits at common law in eighteenth-century England, Lord Devlin has argued that the chancellor sometimes would intervene in complex cases "to prevent a purely legal claim from being tried by jury"[60] and that "[t]he English judicial attitude toward putting such a task upon a jury has been unchanged over two centuries."[61] The abandonment of the jury in England in recent times is a fact too notorious to dispute,[62] but, with respect, the assertion that significant antecedents of this attitude existed in a much earlier period is not easily maintained. Indeed, only two cases are cited in favor of this proposition, and examination reveals them to be much too frail to support the large reliance placed upon them. *Towneley v. Clench*,[63] a chancery suit decided by Ellesmere in 1603, is the first such case, and, although quite interesting, it is terribly obscure. The short report as Cary has it follows:

> *Inter* Tomley and Clench, it appeared by testimony of ancient witnesses speaking of sixty years before, and account books and other writings, that Francis Vaughan, from whom Tomley claimed, was *mulier* [*i.e.* legitimate]; and Anthony, from whom Clench claimeth, was a bastard; and the possession had gone with Tomley fifty years. In this case the Lord Egerton not only decreed the possession with Tomley, but ordered also that Clench should not have any trial at the common law for his right till he had shewed better matter in the Chancery, being a thing so long past; it rested not properly in notice *de pais*, but to be discerned by books and deeds, of which the Court was better able to judge than a jury of ploughmen, notwithstanding that exceptions were alleged against those ancient writings; and that for the copyhold land, the verdict went with Clench upon evidence given three days before Serjeant Williams that Anthony was *mulier* (31st May, 1 Jacob. 1603).[64]

In order to understand why it is so difficult to interpret this report with real confidence, it is first necessary to recall the nature of early seventeenth-century reporting. Reports in this period were in no sense "official"; indeed, official reports would not appear in England or America until well after the Seventh Amendment was adopted.[65] Until then, the books printed as "reports" could have had several different original purposes: they might have been, as in the medieval yearbook tradition, the notes of students present in court;[66] or they might have been the notes of counsel or judges participating in the litigation.[67] In no sense were they complete: not every case was reported, and not every aspect of reported cases received attention. Rarely was there anything resembling the opinions of modern American law reports. Most likely this was because the breadth of the jury's power over results left professionals few opportunities to speak on the legal significance of facts. Not until the early nineteenth century did anxiety over the power and authority of judges produce demands for official reports. Before then, the idea of stare decisis was simply not well established in substantive matters and the need for control of judge and jury was not a cause for great concern.[68]

Against this background the relatively unscientific and imprecise character of early reports is easy to understand. The reporter in *Towneley v. Clench* does not even bother to tell us the exact nature of the bill initiating the suit. A first reading of the case suggests that it might well belong to a class of land cases that equity began to entertain in the sixteenth century because one party was withholding "deeds and evidences" from the other;[69] those cases seem to be prototypes of that head of equity jurisdiction grounded on the availability of discovery in chancery. One could also speculate—and there is nothing in the meager report to indicate otherwise—that the case was brought evoking the *quia timet* jurisdiction of equity. In light of these alternative possibilities, it seems highly unwarranted, simply on the evidence of the report in Cary, to take the unprecedented view that the basis for equity jurisdiction was the complexity of the case.

A search of the early chancery records in the Public Record Office in London[70] has now revealed the actual basis for invoking equitable jurisdiction in *Towneley v. Clench*. The bill recites that Bedolph, a codefendant, had taken the plaintiff's "evidences of title" from the plaintiff's servant by force. These evidences came into the possession of the defendant Clench, making it impossible for the plaintiff's lessee to defend against an ejectment suit which Clench's lessee brought at law.[71] The bill also mentions the difficulty that most of the pertinent witnesses were in the islands of Guernsey and Jersey. It explains further that the defendant claimed by virtue of the right of his wife Mary Clench,[72] who claimed through Anthony Vaughan, the bastard son of Sir Hugh Vaughan, and that the plaintiff claimed as the devisee of Sir Hugh's legitimate son Francis. The plaintiff therefore prayed a subpoena.[73] Within two weeks the defendant answered, setting out the claim of title that the plaintiff had attributed to him but denying that Anthony was a bastard.[74] Three months later Francis Bacon, on behalf of the plaintiff, informed that his client had been in peaceable possession for forty years and that the defendant was claiming through Anthony, who was "known to have been a bastard."[75] The court issued a temporary injunction against the ejectment proceedings at law "until the matter should be determined in Chancery."[76] The next month the defendant successfully requested an order requiring the plaintiff to find a surety for the mesne profits.[77]

There followed some procedural skirmishing that lasted more than a year. Then in May 1602 the defendant Clench moved that the injunction be lifted "since the principal question is whether Anthony Vaughan was a bastard, which is meet to be tried at common law."[78] In June the court denied the motion, partly on the ground that the "plaintiff does not wholly insist on the point of bastardy but upon some other question."[79] Final judgment was not rendered until almost a year later, on May 31, 1603. The decree stated as a finding of fact that Anthony was a bastard, born to Dame Blanch, the last wife of Sir Hugh, before they were married and during his prior marriage to Dame Anne Hungerford, whereas Francis, through whom the plaintiff claimed, was a legitimate son of Sir Hugh and Dame Blanch.[80] The court indicated that this finding was supported by much evidence. First, the court rolls from several manors of presentments made in the time of Queen Mary stated that Francis had been found heir to George the eldest (legitimate) son of Hugh despite the fact that depositions of witnesses read in court indicated that Anthony was much older than George. Second, Sir Hugh's will entailed the lands first to George, then to Francis, and then to Anthony; this was taken as circumstantial evidence that Anthony was not legitimate. The court's conclusions are worthy of full quotation:

> [T]herefore, and because it appeareth that the possession of the said lands hath for the space of about fifty years gone and continued with the said Francis Vaughan and with plaintiff who claims from him, and that the plaintiff's evidences concerning the said lands were by force and violence taken away by the said Bedolph [a codefendant] from the plaintiff's servant as he was carrying them in the open street, and the same were shortly after brought to the said Clench by the said Bedolph, whereby it is supposed the plaintiff may be disabled to maintain his title at the common law, *It Is Ordered Adjudged and Decreed by This Court* that the plaintiff . . . hold . . . the possession of the manors, lands and tenements . . . until better matter shall be showed in this Court to the contrary.[81]

A number of interesting and pertinent observations are made possible by this new evidence on the nature of the dispute in *Towneley v. Clench.* For one thing, it is significant that the plaintiff at no time made the claim that equitable jurisdiction rested on the complexity of the case. Indeed, the facts seem remarkably simple. The difficulty, as the record reveals, was that legal process in the law courts was inadequate for Towneley in two ways: first, there was no subpoena power to compel the production of the purloined documents; second, there was no power to compel witnesses to appear. The first difficulty could be overcome in equity by ordering a return of the documents, although Towneley seems never to have accomplished this; the second evidently was overcome by taking the depositions of the pertinent witnesses. Thus the obvious basis for jurisdiction was the superior process available in equity.

Moreover, the decree itself does not mention the supposed inferiority of jury trial as a reason for denying the defendant his right to sue at common law. It mentions only the plaintiff's apparent right and the fact that the defendant had contrived to render the plaintiff's defense at law impossible. When the decree says that the injunction will be lifted only if "better matter shall be showed," the meaning is clear: the defendant has possession of the relevant documents, and he can come forward with them if he believes them helpful to his cause. The decree proceeds on the assumption that the relevant evidence was being withheld, not that it would be too complex for the jury if it was made available. Thus, the records of the proceedings indicate that the official reasons for denying the defendant his ordinary recourse to law were unremarkable, routine, and wholly unrelated to the mode of trial afforded by the common-law courts.

Even if we assume that Ellesmere made the condescending statement attributed to him by Cary,[82] it does not follow that the chancellor meant to create a new font of equity jurisdiction grounded in complexity. One needs to recall that in this period the jury was still said to possess an investigative function and might be expected to come to court with some knowledge of the facts. This suggests that Ellesmere can be understood to have found simply that cases requiring notice of ancient facts are not suitable for jury trial.[83] According to this interpretation, Ellesmere's objection that a "jury of ploughmen" might not be the most competent body to examine and understand account books and writings is thus beside the point. In any case, the law courts would soon attempt to overcome such objections by making the interpretation of most documents a matter of law.

In the days before they became official, law reports often featured asides from those who were doing the reporting. This was an old tradition, and sometimes some fairly unflattering remarks about judgments were preserved. At the end of the report of *Towneley v. Clench*, the reporter, said to be William Lambert,[84] indicated his surprise over, and disagreement with, Ellesmere's conclusion. He implied that the decision could not be supported because the evidence relied upon was controverted by Clench, and he pointed out, moreover, that Clench had only recently won a judgment for copyhold land on the same evidence. The record of the case supports the reporter on this point by revealing that the court actually quieted the title to this land in Clench on his motion.[85] In any event, Ellesmere's novel opinion was apparently never regarded as authority later, and there is no evidence that its principles, whatever they might have been, were ever again invoked. Indeed, *Towneley v. Clench* is so obscure that it had entirely escaped the notice of most commentators until recently, when it became necessary to ransack the old books in search of a distinguished parentage for what is really a relatively new idea—that a jury may be denied a plaintiff on the ground that the case is "too complex." The most recent scholarly look at the clash between law and equity in the seventeenth century does not even so much as mention the case.[86]

Finally, in assessing the significance of Ellesmere's remark, one needs to keep in mind that the Lord Keeper's imperious style was not regarded as something worthy of emulation by his successors. His hostile and competitive feelings toward the law courts of the age, and in particular his difficulties with Coke, have not left his memory entirely unblemished. In the years following his time as chancellor, law and equity learned to accommodate each other, and the condescending attitude toward juries attributed to Ellesmere by Cary would not have won the approval of succeeding generations.

The second English case said to support the view that equity would claim exclusive jurisdiction over complex cases is *Blad v. Bamfield*,[87] decided by Lord Nottingham in 1674. Bamfield and other Englishmen brought common-law actions against Blad, a Dane, for seizing goods from their ships plying the waters of Iceland. Blad brought suit in chancery to stay the proceedings at law, alleging that the king of Denmark had by patent granted him a monopoly which the defendants had violated. Bamfield replied that such a patent, if proved, would be illegal and a breach of a recent treaty. In granting Blad's prayer for a permanent injunction, the Lord Chancellor noted that the case properly belonged to chancery because it was a trespass on the high seas, and chancery had admiralty jurisdiction; an action at common law would mean that the court would have to "pretend to judge of the validity of the king's letters patent in *Denmark*, or of the exposition and meaning of the articles of peace."[88] Moreover, he counted it "monstrous and absurd" to allow a "common jury" to "try whether the *English* have a right to trade in *Iceland*."[89] This case stands for the simple proposition that suits involving foreign relations ought to be tried in prerogative courts: it is not the complexity of the case that renders it unsuitable for trial in a common-law forum but the source of the rights claimed. Today, of course, there would be no reason why such cases could not be submitted to juries: ample jury-control techniques exist so that complicated matters of foreign and domestic law may ultimately be ruled on by judges.[90] Certainly there is no longer any concept like that of a prerogative court which stands in the way. On any reading, the case gives slim support to the view that complexity is a reason for withdrawing a case from a jury.

It is true that the claim was made in the nineteenth century that certain cases, including those involving accounts, belonged to the concurrent jurisdiction of law and equity because they were in some sense "complex." So Justice Story, a champion of equity who, as a young Massachusetts legislator, introduced an abortive bill to create a chancery court there,[91] complained early in that century of the difficulty of trying commercial cases to juries.[92] It may well be that Story's objection to jury trials in such cases was that the jury might have difficulty in understanding the matters in issue; we have seen that in this period such claims were being made.[93] But the original extension of equity into the accounting area could not have been on this ground because juries did not try accounts anyway; they merely determined whether the defendant ought to be put to an accounting before auditors. Indeed, Blackstone attributes the entry of equity into the area of accounting to the availability of discovery in equity courts.[94] In any case, accounting is an obvious area for equity to occupy: it usually involves relationships that entail fiduciary obligations, and even the old legal action of account recognized that fact in determining amounts due from accountants.[95]

In 1791, the year of the adoption of the Seventh Amendment, James Wilson delivered his famous law lectures at the University of Pennsylvania. Noting the virtual demise of the action of account at law, he laid that decline to the action's complexity. But it was not the jury's inability to understand that gave him concern. He explained:

> Accounts never were, by the course of the common law, brought to trial before a jury. To a jury, indeed, the general question—ought the party to account—was submitted for its determination. But the adjustment of the accounts was submitted to auditors, instead of being tried by a jury. If, upon any article in account, the auditors cannot agree; or, if agreeing, the parties are not satisfied; then, upon each point, so litigated, a separate and distinct issue may be taken, and that issue must be tried by a jury. In this manner, a hundred issues may be joined in the same cause, and tried separately by as many juries; but the general statement of the disputed accounts still remains before the auditors, and by them the general result from the whole must be formed and ascertained. This mode of liquidating accounts judicially at common law, is obviously exposed to many disadvantages and delays; and, for this reason, the action of account has, in a great measure, fallen into disuse. In England, the parties in unsettled and litigated accounts have recourse to chancery; in Pennsylvania, to arbitrators, or to jurors acting in the character of arbitrators.[96]

Wilson offered these remarks to demonstrate why the action was only rarely chosen by plaintiffs; nowhere does he suggest that trial by jury was not available at the plaintiff's option.

A diligent search of the available sources has not revealed any evidence of an eighteenth-century American or English belief that complexity was a ground for the exercise of equitable jurisdiction. In the nineteenth century statements to that effect can be discovered, but their lineage is in no sense ancient or otherwise distinguished. On the contrary, there is ample evidence that the jury was revered in most of the American colonies, so much so that jury trial found a regular place in chancery, a practice which would have raised eyebrows in England. Finally, even if one were to concede the existence of an eighteenth-century head of equitable jurisdiction premised on complexity, it nevertheless would be true that the cases said to support it give no indication at all of a jurisdiction which is exclusive. There thus seems to be no good historical foundation for the argument that plaintiffs may be denied the right to a jury trial because their cases are complex. As I have noted, such arguments are hardly new; but it is only recently that they have come to be countenanced in the courts.[97]

Notes

This chapter first appeared as Morris Arnold, *A Historical Inquiry into the Right to Trial by Jury in Complex Civil Litigation*, 128 U. Pa. L. Rev. 829 (1980) and is reprinted with permission.

1. *E.g.*, *In re* U.S. Financial Sec. Litig., 609 F.2d 411 (9th Cir. 1979); *Zenith Radio Corp. v. Matsushita Elec. Indus. Co.*, 478 F. Supp. 889 (E.D. Pa. 1979), interlocutory appeal granted, No. 79–

2540 (3d Cir. Sept. 20, 1979) (argued Feb. 14, 1980); Devlin, *Jury Trial of Complex Cases: English Practice at the Time of the Seventh Amendment*, 80 Colum. L. Rev. 43 (1980); Comment, *The Right to an Incompetent Jury: Protracted Commercial Litigation and the Seventh Amendment*, 10 Conn. L. Rev. 775 (1978); Note, *The Right to a Jury Trial in Complex Civil Litigation*, 92 Harv. L. Rev. 898 (1979); Note, *Jury Trials in Complex Litigation*, 53 St. John's L. Rev. 751 (1979); Note, *Preserving the Right to Jury Trial in Complex Civil Cases*, 32 Stan. L. Rev. 99 (1979) (and cases cited therein at 99 n. 2); Note, *The Right to Trial by Jury in Complex Litigation*, 20 Wm. & Mary L. Rev. 329 (1978); Campbell, *A Historical Basis for Banning Juries*, Nat'l L. J., Feb. 11, 1980, at 17, col. 1.

2. DeForest, *Trial by Jury in Commercial Cases*, 35 Hunt's Merchants' Mag. 302, 304 (1856).

3. T. Freyer, *Forums of Order: The Federal Courts and Business in American History* (Greenwich, Conn.: JAI Press, 1979), pp. 40–41.

4. This argument confuses improbability with impossibility. For a remedy at law to be inadequate, the just remedy must be unavailable to the plaintiff. For example, an award of money damages would be inadequate for the disappointed purchaser of land, because no two pieces of real property are alike. The just remedy—an order transferring the property—would be impossible to obtain in a court of law; hence the available remedy would be inadequate.

However limited the capacity of a jury to understand issues in complex litigation, a just remedy at law is not unavailable to the plaintiff. Although the limitations of the jury may indeed render a just and adequate remedy less probable than if the suit were tried in equity, that remedy is nevertheless always a possible one.

The suggestion that the jury's lack of sophistication operates to deny the plaintiff an adequate remedy at law is really a complaint about denial of due process, dressed in the formality of the rules of pleading. A plaintiff seeking damages is certainly in the right court, and properly before a jury. Whether a jury is the best possible trier of fact is an issue unrelated to the adequacy of the remedy.

5. *See, e.g.*, Devlin, *Jury Trial of Complex Cases*.

6. "In Suits at common law, where the value in controversy shall exceed twenty dollars, the right of trial by jury shall be preserved, and no fact tried by a jury, shall otherwise be re-examined in any Court of the United States, than according to the rules of the common law." U.S. Constitution, Amendment VII. *See, e.g.*, Wolfram, *The Constitutional History of the Seventh Amendment*, 57 Minn. L. Rev. 639, 639–40 (1973).

7. Devlin, *Jury Trial of Complex Cases*, p. 72 *et seq*.

8. This chapter assumes, without addressing, the correctness of the view that the scope of the Seventh Amendment right to jury trial is determined by the distinction between legal and equitable claims as it existed in 1791.

9. *United States v. Wonson*, 28 F. Cas. 745, 750 (C.C.D. Mass. 1812) (No. 16,750).

10. *See* Wolfram, *The Constitutional History of the Seventh Amendment*, pp. 639–42. "No federal case decided after *Wonson* seems to have challenged this sweeping proclamation; perhaps later judges have hesitated to appear to be

the kind of intractable person that would require Mr. Justice Story to elaborate on the obvious" (*id.*, at 61).

11. *See* J. Goebel, *History of the Supreme Court of the United States*, vol. 1 (New York: Macmillan, 1971), pp. 580–89.

12. *Continental Ill. Nat'l Bank & Trust Co. v. Chicago, R.I. & Pac. Ry.*, 294 U.S. 648, 669 (1935).

13. A. Hamilton, J. Jay, and J. Madison, *The Federalist*, ed. Benjamin Wright (Cambridge: Belknap, 1961), p. 528.

14. Katz, *The Politics of Law in Colonial America: Controversies over Chancery Courts and Equity Law in the Eighteenth Century*, in D. Fleming and B. Bailyn, eds., *Law in American History*, (Boston: Little, Brown, 1971), p. 257.

15. Ibid., pp. 257–58.

16. Goebel, *History of the Supreme Court* 1:580.

17. W. Rawle, *Equity in Pennsylvania* (Philadelphia, 1868), pp. 53–54; Katz, *The Politics of Law in Colonial America*, pp. 282–83.

18. L. Friedman, *A History of American Law* (New York: Simon and Schuster, 1973).

19. Smith and Hershkowitz, *Courts of Equity in the Province of New York: The Cosby Controversy, 1732–1736*, 16 Am. J. of Legal Hist. 1, 60 (1972), pp. 36–37.

20. *See generally* Katz, *The Politics of Law in Colonial America*, pp. 277–82; Smith and Hershkowitz, *Courts of Equity in the Province of New York*.

21. Smith and Hershkowitz, *Courts of Equity in the Province of New York*, p. 19 n. 49.

22. Ibid., pp. 31–32.

23. *New York Weekly Journal*, No. 23, Apr. 8, 1734, reprinted in J. Alexander, *A Brief Narrative of the Case and Trial of John Peter Zenger*, ed. S. Katz (Cambridge: Belknap, 1963), pp. 134–36, Appendix. *See* Smith and Hershkowitz, *Courts of Equity in the Province of New York*, p. 40 & n. 100.

24. Smith and Hershkowitz, *Courts of Equity in the Province of New York*, p. 50.

25. *See generally* Arnold, *Law and Fact in the Medieval Jury Trial: Out of Sight, Out of Mind*, 18 Am. J. of Legal Hist. 267 (1974).

26. *See generally* W. Nelson, *The Americanization of the Common Law* (Cambridge: Harvard Univ. Press, 1975), pp. 21–30, 165–71.

27. Nelson, *The Eighteenth Century Background of John Marshall's Constitutional Jurisprudence*, 76 Mich. L. Rev. 893, 904–17 (1978).

28. Nelson, *Americanization of the Common Law*, pp. 21–28.

29. Ibid., 21–23.

30. L. Wroth and H. Zobel, eds., *Legal Papers of John Adams* 3 vols. (Cambridge: Belknap, 1965), p. 230.

31. Nelson, *Americanization of the Common Law*, pp. 28–29.

32. S. Milsom, *Historical Foundations of the Common Law* (London: Butterworths, 1969), pp. 26–38.

33. *See* M. Horwitz, *The Transformation of American Law, 1780–1860* (Cambridge: Harvard Univ. Press, 1977), pp. 4–9.

34. *See generally* Curran, *The Struggle for Equity Jurisdiction in Massachusetts*, 31 B.U.L. Rev. 269, 269 (1951); Woodruff, *Chancery in Massachusetts*, 5 L.Q. Rev. 370, 383–84 (1889), re-

printed in 9 B.U.L. Rev. 168, 181–82 (1929).

35. Woodruff, *Chancery in Massachusetts*, p. 376 n. 2, rept. in 9 B.U.L. Rev. 174 n. 26.

36. *See* the historical discussion by Justice Hammond in *Parker v. Simpson*, 180 Mass. 334, 349–59, 62 N.E. 401, 406–7 (1902).

37. T. Jefferson, "A Bill for new modelling the form of government, & for establishing the fundamental principles thereof in future" (before June 13, 1776) (third draft of Jefferson's proposed Virginia Constitution), in J. Boyd et al., eds., *The Papers of Thomas Jefferson* (Princeton, N.J.: Princeton Univ. Press, 1950—), 1:362.

38. M. Tachau, *Federal Courts in the Early Republic: Kentucky, 1789–1816* (Princeton, N.J.: Princeton Univ. Press, 1978), p. 180, n. 32.

39. *Ross v. Pleasants, Shore & Co.*, Wythe 10, 22, 24 (Va. 1790) (commentary on opinion and decree of the Court of Appeals, which reversed the decree of the High Court of Chancery) (value of tobacco exchanged for land); *Hinde v. Pendleton*, Wythe 354, 357 (Va. Ch. 1791) (value of slaves auctioned fraudulently).

40. *Southall v. M'Keand*, Wythe 95, 97–98 (Va. Ch. 1791) (summary of proceedings), *rev'd in relevant part*, 1 Va. (1 Wash.) 337 (1794).

41. For an example of the phrase, *see* Wythe 98.

42. Tachau, *Federal Courts in the Early Republic*, pp. 179–82.

43. Friedman, *A History of American Law*, p. 131.

44. Ibid. (citing chap. 11, 1782 N.C. Laws).

45. William Penn to the Free Society of Traders, Aug. 16, 1683, in R. Proud, *History of Pennsylvania*, vol. 1 (Philadelphia: Zachariah Poulson, 1797), pp. 246, 255.

46. Liverant and Hitchler, *A History of Equity in Pennsylvania*, 3 Dick. L. Rev. 156, 162, 165 (1933).

47. Rawle, *Equity in Pennsylvania*, p. 2.

48. An Act for Establishing Courts of Judicature in this Province, Feb. 28, 1711, chap. 168, sec. 25, 2 Pa. Stat. (1682–1801), at 301 (repealed 1713), quoted in Rawle, *Equity in Pennsylvania*, p. 16.

49. Rawle, *Equity in Pennsylvania*, p. 17.

50. H. Binney, An Eulogium upon the Hon. William Tilghman, Late Chief Justice of Pennsylvania, Oct. 13, 1827 (address to the Bar of Philadelphia), in 16 Serg. & Rawl. 439, 449 (Pa. 1827).

51. A. Laussat, *An Essay on Equity in Pennsylvania* (Philadelphia, 1826), p. 48.

52. *Clyde v. Clyde*, 1 Yeates 92 (Pa. 1791).

53. Rawle, *Equity in Pennsylvania*, pp. 61–62.

55. Laussat, *Essay on Equity in Pennsylvania*, p. 57.

56. *E.g.*, *President of the Farmers' & Mechanics' Bank v. Polk*, 1 Del. Ch. 167, 175–76 (1821): "Is this such a case that the parties should be decreed to account? Upon that point I have no doubt. These transactions are so complicated, so long and intricate, that it is impossible for a jury to examine them with accuracy. They will require time, assiduous attention and minute investigation, and are involved in so much confusion and difficulty that no other

tribunal, by reason of the forms of proceeding of the courts of law, can afford the plaintiff a remedy."

See Ludlow v. Simond, 2 Cai. Cas. 1, 52 (New York 1805) ("The settlement of accounts, if they are in any degree long or complex, is improper, if not impracticable for a jury."). For discussion of difficulties in accounting cases, see text accompanying notes 92–96 *infra*.

57. *Bill of Complaint, Wright v. LeBrasseur* (filed Sept. 23, 1717), reprinted in A. Gregorie, ed., *Records of the Court of Chancery of South Carolina, 1671–1779* (Washington, D.C.: Am. Hist. Assoc., 1950), p. 208.

58. The editor of the case states that the basis for seeking equitable jurisdiction here was that a jury was "entirely unfitted to deal with the complexities of facts usually involved in such an accounting," but there is nothing whatever in the case to support this assertion (ibid., p. 47).

59. Bill of Complaint, ibid., pp. 216–17.

60. Devlin, *Jury Trial of Complex Cases*, p. 74.

61. Ibid., p. 76.

62. *See, e.g.*, J. Baker, *An Introduction to English Legal History* (London: Butterworths, 1979).

63. *Clench v. Tomley*, Cary 23, 21 Eng. Rep. 13 (Ch. 1603). The report in Cary reverses the parties and misspells the plaintiff's name.

64. *Id.*

65. *See generally* W. Daniel, *The History and Origin of the Law Reports* (London: Wildy and Sons, 1884).

66. *See* Baker, *An Introduction to English Legal History*, pp. 152–53; F. Maitland, ed., "Introduction" to *Year Books of Edward II*, vol. 1, Selden Society, vol. 17 (London, 1903), pp. ix, xiii.

67. *See* Baker, *An Introduction to English Legal History*, pp. 153–58; J. Dawson, *The Oracles of the Law* (Ann Arbor: Univ. of Michigan Law School, 1968), p. 76. Many of the cases reported by Coke were of this variety.

68. This is one theme of Dawson, *The Oracles of the Law*, chap. 1 *passim*.

69. Edith Henderson of the Harvard Law School very kindly suggested this possibility to me.

70. Professor J. H. Baker of Cambridge very kindly made the search of the records for me and furnished me with abstracts and transcripts on which the following discussion is based. All quotations, unless otherwise noted, are from his notes, which are paraphrases of the original records in modern English spelling. A copy of his notes is on file with the *University of Pennsylvania Law Review*.

71. Bill on behalf of Francis Towneley, *Towneley v. Clench* (sworn Jan. 24, 1600 [i.e., 1601]), Public Record Office, London, C2/Eliz/T3/60.

72. The defendant was Thomas Clench of Lincoln's Inn.

73. P.R.O. C2/Eliz/T3/60 (Jan. 24, 1600 [i.e., 1601]).

74. Answer of Thomas Clench, *Towneley v. Clench* (sworn Feb. 7, 1600 [i.e., 1601]), P.R.O. C2/Eliz/T3/60.

75. P.R.O. C33/99, fol. 462v (May 7, 1601); ibid., C33/100, fol. 450.

76. Ibid.

77. P.R.O. C33/99, fol. 672 (June 16, 1601).

78. P.R.O. C33/102, fol. 584 (May 17, 1602).

79. P.R.O. C33/102, fol. 674v (June 14, 1602).

80. P.R.O. C33/103, fol. 681 (May 31, 1603).

81. Ibid. (spelling modernized by Professor Baker; *see* note 70, *supra*).

82. *See* text accompanying note 64, *supra*. Professor Baker was unable to locate any report of the case other than that made by Cary.

83. Hence Cary's report says, speaking of the critical event in the case: "being a thing so long past; it rested not properly in notice *de pais*" (*Towneley v. Clench*, Cary 23, 21 Eng. Rep. 13 [Ch. 1603]). This rationale, of course, can have no application to modern juries.

84. J. Wallace, *The Reporters*, 4th ed. (Boston: Soule and Bugbee, 1882), p. 469.

85. P.R.O. C33/99, fol. 672 (June 26, 1601).

86. *See generally* L. Knafla, *Law and Politics in Jacobean England* (Cambridge: Cambridge Univ. Press, 1977).

87. 3 Swan. 604 (App.), 36 Eng. Rep. 992 (Ch. 1674).

88. *Id.* at 607, 36 Eng. Rep. p. 993.

89. *Id.*

90. *See* Note, *Preserving the Right to Jury Trial in Complex Civil Cases*, pp. 116–20.

91. Curran, *The Struggle for Equity Jurisdiction in Massachusetts*, p. 274.

92. J. Story, *Commentaries on Equity Jurisprudence Section* (Cambridge: Harvard Univ., 1835), p. 451.

93. *See* notes 2 and 3, *supra*, & accompanying text.

94. W. Blackstone, *Commentaries on the Laws of England*, vol. 3 (Oxford: Clarendon, 1768), p. 437.

95. Chief Justice Belknap, for example, expressed the view that a receiver who did nothing to make his receipts productive "will be charged for reasonable profits." *Hastynges v. Beverley*, Y.B. Pasch. 2 Rich. 2 (1379), reprinted in M. Arnold, ed., *Year Books of Richard II* (London, 1975), pp. 121, 122.

96. R. McCloskey, ed., *The Works of James Wilson*, 2 vols. (Cambridge: Belknap, 1967), p. 492.

97. *See ILC Peripherals v. IBM Corp.*, 458 F. Supp. 423 (N.D. Cal. 1978); *Bernstein v. Universal Pictures, Inc.*, 79 F.R.D. 59 (S.D.N.Y. 1978); *SEC v. Associated Minerals, Inc.*, 75 F.R.D. 724 (E.D. Mich. 1977); *In re U.S. Financial Sec. Litig.*, 75 F.R.D. 702 (S.D. Cal. 1977), rev'd, 609 F.2d 411 (9th Cir. 1979); *Jones v. Orenstein*, 73 F.R.D. 604 (S.D.N.Y. 1977); *In re Boise Cascade Sec. Litig.* 420 F. Supp. 99 (W.D. Wash. 1976).

XII.

ORIGINAL INTENT AND THE NINTH AMENDMENT

CHARLES J. COOPER

28. Limited Government and Individual Liberty: The Ninth Amendment's Forgotten Lessons

A lecture on the Constitution, like a sermon, should begin with the text, the scriptures themselves. Our text today is the Ninth Amendment, which provides: "The enumeration in the Constitution, of certain rights, shall not be construed to deny or disparage others retained by the people."[1] To many, no doubt, it is unfamiliar. I venture to say that the Ninth Amendment, unlike the First and Fourth Amendments, could not be paraphrased, let alone quoted accurately, by a majority of lawyers practicing today.

The obscurity of the amendment is undeserved, however, for it expresses two of the most basic propositions of our constitutional law: that the federal government is one of delegated powers, and that the enumeration of those powers is a guarantee that the American people enjoy unenumerated, and therefore innumerable, rights against the federal government.

The relationship between the rights of the people and the powers of the federal government may be unfamiliar to readers of recent Supreme Court opinions, but it was central to the framers' concept of republican government. The framers believed that the enumerated powers of the federal government and the retained rights of the people were reciprocally related. By delegating legislative power over certain subjects to the federal government, the people consented to abide by the laws enacted by the federal government that pertained to those subjects. However, as to those subjects over which the federal government had no delegated legislative power, the people retained the right, vis-à-vis the federal government, to do as they pleased. For example, because the federal government had no delegated authority to make laws concerning conveyances of real property, the people retained the right, as against the federal government, to convey land as they wished. The Ninth Amendment is a rule of constitutional construction designed to protect residual rights that exist by virtue of the fact that the federal government has only limited powers.[2]

The Ninth Amendment has recently been rediscovered by many judges and constitutional scholars. An examination of the cases and literature on the subject, however, suggests that those who wish to revive the Ninth Amendment today are not interested in reviving a basic principle of our constitutional jurisprudence; instead, they seek to employ the Ninth

Amendment to increase the control of the federal judiciary over every aspect of our lives.

During the last fifty years, the federal judiciary has enlarged its power through expansive and sometimes extravagant constructions of the Constitution. This expansion of federal power through the judiciary has been limited only by the language of the constitutional provisions enumerating specific rights. Anyone familiar with the Supreme Court's interpretation of the commerce clause or the due process clause understands that the wording of many of the Constitution's provisions is none too constraining.[3] Nevertheless, since it is difficult to transform even the right to due process of law into the right to housing or to a particular standard of living without doing violence to the language of the Constitution, most judges, if not most academicians, shrink from the challenge. Therefore, to bring rule by the judiciary to its final perfection, one must find in the Constitution a provision which can be construed as a grant of unenumerated rights, the content of which will be determined by the federal judiciary and enforced against the states. The logical candidate for this role is the Ninth Amendment, with its reference to unspecified "other [rights] retained by the people."[4]

The Ninth Amendment received its most famous judicial exposition in *Griswold v. Connecticut*,[5] where the Supreme Court held that a Connecticut statute criminalizing the use of contraceptives could not constitutionally be applied to married couples. Justice Goldberg, concurring in *Griswold*, relied upon the Ninth Amendment in arguing that the Connecticut statute infringed upon the fundamental "right of privacy in the marital relation."[6] In the same vein, Justice Douglas suggested a few years later that "the right of the people to education or to work or to recreation . . . , like the right to pure air and pure water, may well be rights 'retained by the people' under the Ninth Amendment."[7]

Even conservative scholars look to the Ninth Amendment for a grant of unenumerated rights. For instance, Stephen Macedo, in his booklet *The New Right v. The Constitution*, argues that the Ninth Amendment explicitly calls upon the judiciary to engage in "principled judicial activism" based upon "sound moral thinking . . . and . . . our political tradition."[8] He seems to have in mind a jurisprudential revival of the line of cases exemplified by *Lochner v. New York*.[9]

As the balance of my chapter will seek to demonstrate, these interpretations turn the Ninth Amendment on its head. The rights protected by the Ninth Amendment derive from the absence of a power delegated to the federal government, not against the states. The history of the Ninth Amendment compels this conclusion.

Most nonlawyers would be surprised to learn that the Constitution signed by the framers 200 years ago did not include a bill of rights. And they would probably be shocked to discover that the framers paid scant attention to individual rights during the four months that they were convened in Philadelphia. Throughout the summer of 1787, the delegates devoted most of their energies and attention to the structure and powers of the national government. The first reference to a federal bill of rights was not made until August 20, almost three months after General Washington had called the Constitutional Convention to order. Charles Pinckney, the twenty-nine-year-old South Carolinian, submitted a detailed bill of rights to the Committee of the Whole. His propositions, which included many of the freedoms later incorporated into the first eight amendments, were referred to the Committee of Detail without debate or consideration.[10]

Apparently, the Committee of Detail did not believe that the Constitution needed a bill of rights, for the issue was not raised again until the last week of the Convention. Then, on September 12, George Mason suggested that the Constitution be prefaced with a bill of rights. The Virginian argued that a declaration of rights would "give great quiet to the people." As the principal author of Virginia's Declaration of Rights, Mason assured his fellow delegates that the Convention could prepare a federal bill of rights in a matter of hours by using the state declarations of rights as models. Evidently persuaded by Mason's arguments, Elbridge Gerry of Massachusetts moved that a bill of rights be added to the Constitution, and the motion was seconded by Mason. At this point, Roger Sherman of Connecticut rose to argue against a federal bill of rights. Sherman thought that a federal bill of rights would be redundant because the rights of the people already were protected adequately by state constitutions. Mason responded that the state bills of rights would provide no protection from the new national government because, under the proposed Constitution, federal law would be supreme. The Convention nevertheless rejected Gerry's motion to include a bill of rights in the Constitution. In fact, the rejection of the motion was unanimous, Mason having failed to convince even his fellow Virginians of the merit of his position.[11]

Given that Roger Sherman's reliance upon state constitutions was so obviously wrong, it may seem puzzling that the Convention rejected Mason's proposal. Later in the same week, however, some light was shed on the more likely reason that lay behind the delegates' vote. On September 14, Pinckney and Gerry moved to insert a clause in the Constitution which would declare "that the liberty of the Press should be inviolably observed." At this point, Sherman again voiced an objection, but this time he argued that such an amendment was unnecessary because "[t]he power of Congress does not extend to the press." The delegates, apparently agreeing with Sherman, defeated the motion.[12]

Just three days later the Convention met for the last time and the Constitution was signed. Mason and Gerry refused to affix their signatures to the document, in large part because it did not include a bill of rights.[13]

These two men, along with others who came to be known as Anti-Federalists, continued to attack the Convention's failure to adopt a bill of rights throughout the ratification debates.

In order to understand fully the purpose of the Ninth Amendment, one must be familiar with the nature of the debate over the ratification of the Constitution. The Federalists, led by Alexander Hamilton, James Madison, and James Wilson, opposed a federal bill of rights for two reasons: they believed that a bill of rights was unnecessary, and, more importantly, they believed that it was dangerous. On the other hand, the Anti-Federalists, led by George Mason and Elbridge Gerry, asserted that a bill of rights was essential to safeguard individual rights. Both sides agreed, however, that there were certain fundamental rights of the people that could not be abridged by the national government.

The Federalists believed that a bill of rights was unnecessary because the structure of the national government adequately protected the rights of the people. Their structural argument was premised on the notion that the national government would be one of enumerated, and therefore limited, powers. The people were protected by virtue of the fact that the federal government in most cases would lack the power to act in a manner which might affect their civil liberties.

The Federalists' theory is perhaps best illustrated by the position that they took on the proposed amendment protecting freedom of the press. They argued that such an amendment was unnecessary because the national government lacked the power to control the press in the first instance. James Wilson, the famed Pennsylvania lawyer and one of the foremost opponents of a federal bill of rights, asked: "[W]hat control can proceed from the federal government to shackle or destroy that sacred palladium of national freedom?" He conceded that an amendment would be necessary if "a power similar to that which ha[d] been granted [to Congress] for the regulation of commerce, had been granted to regulate literary publications."[14] However, since Congress lacked the power to regulate the press, the proposed amendment to the Constitution would be superfluous. Alexander Hamilton viewed the issue in precisely the same manner. Writing in support of ratification, he asked: "Why, for instance, should it be said that the liberty of the press shall not be restrained, when no power is given by which restrictions may be imposed?"[15]

It is important to remember, of course, that the structure of the national government under the Constitution protects more than just freedom of the press and other individual rights that might be deemed to be fundamental. The structure chosen by the framers also established the right of individuals, vis-à-vis the national government, to do anything that the newly constituted government lacked the power to prevent them from doing. The framers were well aware of this fact when they chose to grant the national government only specifically enumerated powers. As General Washington, the president of the Convention, wrote to his friend Lafayette: "The people evidently retained every thing which they did not in express terms give up."[16]

Quite apart from the question of whether an express enumeration of individual rights was a necessary safeguard against government encroachment, the framers of the original Constitution elected against such an enumeration because of the danger of omission. James Wilson explained the matter succinctly to the Pennsylvania Ratifying Convention: "If we attempt an enumeration [of rights], every thing that is not enumerated is presumed to be given. The consequence is, that an imperfect enumeration would throw all implied power into the scale of the government, and the rights of the people would be rendered incomplete." Wilson thought that "an omission in the enumeration of the powers of government is neither so dangerous nor important as an omission in the enumeration of the rights of the people."[17]

Thus, as Wilson's statement makes clear, the Federalists feared that the enumeration of rights might imply that the national government had the power to abridge any right not expressly preserved. The framers' belief that the people retained the right, vis-à-vis the federal government, to do anything that the national government lacked the delegated power to prevent them from doing, created a body of rights which was virtually limitless. No one could hope to catalogue all of these rights, and Wilson was indignant at the suggestion that such a task should have been undertaken in the Constitutional Convention. During the ratification debates he exclaimed: "Enumerate all the rights of men! I am sure, sir, that no gentleman in the late Convention would have attempted such a thing."[18]

The Federalists' fear of a bill of rights can perhaps be illustrated by considering a hypothetical situation in which a law professor importunes one of his first-year students to purchase a BMW sedan for him during the student's summer trip to Europe. The professor, who is involved in the Critical Legal Studies movement, has only a fuzzy recollection of "black letter" law, but he nonetheless sets about drawing up the necessary papers. He first drafts an instrument which grants the student the power to acquire a new BMW on his behalf. Although this power of attorney does not expressly forbid the student from acting as the law professor's agent on other matters, the law professor is adequately protected. Under the ancient canon of construction *expressio unius est exclusio alterius*, the expression of one thing means the exclusion of another.[19] Therefore, the explicit mention of the student's authority to purchase the car firmly implies that the student lacks the authority to act with respect to other matters. The instrument that the professor has drafted would be called a special power of attorney.

Before the law professor gives the student this special power of attorney, however, he discusses the matter with his wife, who is the Anti-Federalist of the family. Not surprisingly, she is a little wary of placing so much trust in any student, particularly a first-year law student. The wife suggests that the student might purchase, on the professor's behalf, 500 kegs of beer in Bavaria. The professor at first shrugs off his wife's suggestion because he realizes that the instrument that he has drawn up cannot logically be construed as authorizing the student to take such an action. But the more he thinks about the matter, and about this particular student, the more concerned he becomes. Because he decides it is better to err on the side of caution, the professor amends the original instrument to provide expressly that the student lacks the authority to purchase beer on his behalf. After making this change, the professor gives the student the power of attorney and bids him farewell.

A few weeks later the professor receives the following telegram from the student: "Congratulations on your recent acquisition of a BMW sedan, per your specifications. *Stop.* Car shipped to Baltimore, as directed. *Stop.* While in Germany, also got great deal for you on Mercedes Benz convertible 450SL. *Stop.* Handles great, and ladies here in Paris love it. *Stop.* Wish you were here." The law professor is outraged that the student, while acting as his agent, has purchased two cars. He immediately takes a copy of the power of attorney to his colleague, a contracts professor, who notes that the original agreement would have made it clear that the student's authority was limited to the acquisition of a BMW sedan. The amendment that was made as an extra precaution, however, made the agreement ambiguous. Because the amendment stated that the student did not have the power to purchase beer, it could be argued that the student was authorized to take any other action as the professor's agent. This hypothetical captures fairly well the Federalists' fear of a bill of rights. James Iredell of North Carolina, one of the leading Federalists, said that the grant of authority to the national government could "be considered as a great power of attorney, under which no power can be exercised but what is expressly given."[20]

The Federalists clearly believed that if specific limitations were placed on this "power of attorney," it might follow by implication that the federal government had the power to take any action that was not inconsistent with these explicit prohibitions.

In many states, including Virginia, the Constitution was ratified only on explicit assurances that the First Congress would propose a bill of rights, and the desirability of amending the Constitution was debated in the House of Representatives of the First Congress. One of my favorite statements during these debates concerned the necessity for a constitutional amendment explicitly protecting the right of peaceable assembly. Congressman Sedgwick of Massachusetts objected to such an amendment on the ground that "it is a self-evident, inalienable right which the people possess . . . [and] that never would be called in question." Sedgwick argued that if the House was going to "descend to such minutiae," it may as well "have gone into a very lengthy enumeration of rights; they might have declared that a man should have a right to wear his hat if he pleased; that he might get up when he pleased, and go to bed when he thought proper; but [I] would ask the gentleman whether he thought it necessary to enter these trifles in a declaration of rights, in a Government where none of them were intended to be infringed."[21]

Despite the opposition to a bill of rights by Federalists such as Representative Sedgwick, the first ten amendments were adopted by Congress in 1789 and ratified by the states two years later. The first eight amendments, of course, positively disable Congress from enacting certain kinds of legislation. The Ninth Amendment, on the other hand, was not intended to grant any additional rights to the people. Instead, it was crafted specifically to respond to the concern that an enumeration of rights retained by the people would imply that the enumeration was exhaustive.

In introducing his proposal for a bill of rights on the floor of the House, Madison stated:

> It has been objected also against the bill of rights, that, by enumerating particular exceptions to the grant of power, it would disparage those rights which were not placed in that enumeration; and it might follow, by implication, that those rights which were not singled out, were intended to be assigned into the hands of the General Government, and were consequently insecure. This is one of the most plausible arguments I ever heard urged against the admission of rights into this system; but I conceive, that it may be guarded against. I have attempted it, as gentlemen may see by turning to the last clause of the fourth resolution.[22]

The final clause of the resolution to which Madison was referring was framed as follows:

> The exceptions here or elsewhere in the constitution, made in favor of particular rights, shall not be so construed as to diminish the just importance of other rights retained by the people, or as to enlarge the powers delegated by the constitution; but either as actual limitations of such powers, or as inserted merely for greater caution.[23]

Since the framers understood that delegated powers and retained rights were two sides of the same coin, the clause in Madison's proposal negating any implied purpose "to diminish the just importance of other rights retained by the people" was entirely redundant to the clause negating any intent "to enlarge the powers delegated by the Constitution." Neither clause added anything of substance to the other.

Accordingly, the meaning of the Ninth Amendment was not changed when Madison's original proposal was amended by the House to delete reference to delegated powers. Indeed, the congruence of meaning between Madison's original proposal and what ultimately became the Ninth Amendment was confirmed by Madison himself in a letter to George Washington. Madison was advising President Washington of Edmund Randolph's opposition to Virginia's ratification of the Ninth Amendment. Governor Randolph had argued against the enlargement of delegated powers rather than a preservation of retained rights. Madison found Randolph's point "altogether fanciful." As he put it, "[i]f a line can be drawn between the powers granted and the rights retained, it would seem to be the same thing, whether the latter be secured by declaring that they shall not be abridged, or that the former shall not be extended. If no line can be drawn, a declaration in either form would amount to nothing."[24]

Thus Madison stated clearly that the wording of his original proposal and the Ninth Amendment were merely two complementary ways of saying the same thing—namely, that with respect to any field of endeavor over which the national government lacked delegated power, the American people retained the right, vis-à-vis the national government, to do as they please.

A few years after the ratification of the Bill of Rights, James Madison employed the principle of the Ninth Amendment to argue against the Alien and Sedition Acts of 1798, which made it a crime to write or utter anything that would tend to bring officials of the federal government into disrepute. The Virginia and Kentucky legislatures circulated resolutions objecting to such laws. In support of the Virginia resolution, Madison drafted a detailed committee report which included a demonstration of the constitutional infirmity of the Sedition Act. Madison's analysis still stands as one of the all-time best examples of the correct—and now largely forgotten—way to approach illegitimate exercises of the federal power.

Madison began his attack on the constitutionality of the Sedition Act by asking whether Congress had been given authority to legislate on the subject at hand. Since no authority to regulate the press appears on the face of the Constitution, defenders of the legislation had sought to find it implied. Their primary argument was based on some of the more general language in the Constitution: the preamble, the clause empowering Congress to collect taxes and "to pay the Debts and provide for the common Defence and general Welfare," and the clause allowing for such laws as are "necessary and proper" to suppress insurrections.[25] Madison demonstrated that to read these constitutional provisions to allow a measure like the Sedition Act would render the Constitution's specific enumeration of federal powers quite illusory: "[I]t must be wholly immaterial whether unlimited powers be exercised under the name of unlimited powers, or be exercised under the name of unlimited means of carrying into execution limited powers."[26]

Only in the second section of his analysis did Madison turn to the First Amendment. For Madison, the discussion of the First Amendment merely supplemented his main point, that Congress lacked the delegated power to regulate subversive speech.[27]

Unfortunately, many judges today have forgotten about the first step in Madison's two-pronged analysis. Modern judicial opinions dealing with alleged violations of individual rights by the federal government rarely even allude to the question of whether the government has the delegated power to take the challenged action. Instead, such opinions typically assume the existence of federal power and then look to see whether some provision of the Bill of Rights prohibits its exercise.

A good example of this backward approach is the Supreme Court's 1976 opinion in *Buckley v. Valeo*.[28] In that case, the Court upheld provisions of the Federal Election Campaign Act that impose (1) a $1,000 limitation on contributions to a single candidate, (2) a $5,000 limitation on contributions by a political committee to a single candidate, and (3) a $25,000 limitation on total contributions. The Court's holding was premised solely on its finding that these provisions did not "directly imping[e] upon the [First Amendment] rights of individual citizens . . . to engage in political debate and discussion."[29] Although the Court's First Amendment analysis is questionable, what is even more striking about its opinion is its utter failure to consider whether Congress had the authority under Article I of the Constitution to enact this statute. Without any analysis whatsoever, the Court announced that "[t]he constitutional power of Congress to regulate federal elections is well established and is not questioned by any of the parties in this case."[30] If the Court had analyzed the issue in Madisonian fashion—if it had examined the language, structure, and history of the various constitutional provisions dealing with federal elections—its conclusion regarding Congress's regulatory power could not have been stated so confidently.[31] *Buckley* illustrates well the way in which judges have ignored the Ninth Amendment and thereby slighted the innumerable individual rights that each of us has vis-à-vis the federal government.

As I mentioned earlier, a number of judges and constitutional scholars are also distorting the original meaning of the Ninth Amendment in another way in order to increase the influence of the federal judiciary. These jurists and law professors argue that the Ninth Amendment protects some individual rights from encroachment by the states. It is clear, however, that the framers intended the Ninth Amendment to govern only the relationship between the American people and the national government. Indeed, it would be nonsensical to apply the Ninth Amendment to the states. The rights retained under the amendment are defined by the limits of the federal government's enumerated powers. To apply the same limits to the states would deprive them of the bulk of their police powers.[32]

The proper interpretation of the Ninth Amendment can be best illustrated by examining a number of well-known Supreme Court cases. First, let us look at a case I mentioned earlier, *Griswold v. Connecticut*,[33] where the Court held that a Connecticut statute prohibiting the use of contraceptives could not constitutionally be applied to married couples. Justice Goldberg's concurring opinion, which relied heavily upon the Ninth Amendment, asserted that the right of a married couple to use contraceptives was protected because it was rooted in the traditions and [collective] conscience of our people."[34] In dissent, Justice Black pointed out that "the scientific miracles of this age have not yet produced a gadget which the Court can use to determine what traditions are rooted in the '[collective] conscience of our people.'"[35] Like Justice Black, I believe that although the Connecticut statute was "offensive,"[36] it did not violate the Ninth Amendment. It is important to remember, however, that Justice Goldberg was wrong only because a state statute was at issue. There is a constitutional right to marital privacy protected by the Ninth Amendment, but this right exists only against the federal government. The American people have a Ninth Amendment right, vis-à-vis the federal government, to use whatever contraceptive devices they choose because Congress is without delegated power to legislate in this area.[37]

Similarly, in *Roe v. Wade*,[38] the Supreme Court invalidated certain state law restrictions on a woman's ability to secure an abortion under the due process clause of the Fourteenth Amendment. I believe that *Roe* was incorrectly decided, for substantive due process restrictions on state legislative authority are no more justified in the privacy area than in an economic context. I do believe, however, that a federal statute restricting abortions would be unconstitutional. Such a statute would violate the Ninth Amendment because Congress does not have any delegated power to regulate abortions.[39]

In *Bowers v. Hardwick*,[40] the most important recent decision involving privacy rights, the Court held up Georgia's antisodomy statute. The Court decided that the due process clause of the Fourteenth Amendment did not grant homosexuals a right, vis-à-vis the states, to engage in sodomy. Perhaps the most interesting aspect of the case is that Professor Laurence Tribe of the Harvard Law School sought to challenge the Georgia statute on the basis of the Ninth Amendment. According to Professor Tribe, the Ninth Amendment "signifies that, even if a particular right is unenumerated, the Constitution's textual guarantee of liberty limits the power of government at least to the extent of requiring an articulated rationale by government for an intrusion on the person and the home as pervasive as Georgia's sodomy law."[41]

The Court did not embrace Professor Tribe's argument, which was first raised in the petition for rehearing. The Ninth Amendment claim raised in *Bowers* is nevertheless noteworthy, for it illustrates the inherently open-ended and subjective nature of any theory of unenumerated rights enforceable against the states. Any exercise of the state's police power can be challenged as a violation of some "unenumerated" constitutional right, and judges must discern the existence and contours of such a right without traditional materials of constitutional adjudication (the text, structure, and history of the Constitution) to guide their inquiry and thus constrain their judgment. A Ninth Amendment claim against federal action, however, is determined by the extent of the federal government's enumerated powers, which in turn requires judicial inquiry into the traditional materials of constitutional adjudication. Accordingly, had *Bowers* involved a federal antisodomy statute, Professor Tribe's Ninth Amendment claim would have been well taken, because the government has no delegated power to regulate in this area.

I hasten to emphasize that the proper application of the Ninth Amendment would by no means insure results pleasing to conservatives. Most conservatives, for example, would approve of the outcome of the Court's decision in *Pierce v. Society of Sisters.*[42] Certainly, I do. There the Court invalidated an Oregon statute requiring parents to send their children to public school. Although I find the statute appalling, I do not believe that the Court was correct in holding it a violation of due process. As I have already stated, Lochneresque substantive due process, even in the service of a good cause, has no place in our constitutional jurisprudence. More importantly for our purposes, the Ninth Amendment is not available to invalidate a state (as opposed to a federal) statute requiring parents to send their children to public school. The same may be said about *Meyer v. Nebraska,*[43] where the Court held unconstitutional a state statute prohibiting the teaching of modern foreign languages to children who had not completed the eighth grade. Neither the due process clause of the Fourteenth Amendment nor the Ninth Amendment justifies this holding.[44]

In closing, I return to the point that judicial acceptance of modern theories concerning the meaning of the Ninth Amendment would have deeply regrettable consequences, no matter how laudable and pleasing the result of any particular case may be. First, many constitutional rights enforceable against the federal government under the Ninth Amendment are now largely ignored. A proper interpretation of the Ninth Amendment would restore these forgotten liberties. Second, modern theorists of both the right and the left seek to use the Ninth Amendment as the basis for the creation of fundamental rights against the states. These arguments represent the culmination of the modern era's movement to judicial supremacy at the expense of democratic self-government. The Ninth Amendment does not specify what rights it protects other than by its reference to the enumerated powers of the federal government. Therefore, a rights theory based on this amendment will contain, as Justice Black observed in his *Griswold* dissent,[45] no principle whatsoever to guide the judiciary in deciding whether state legislation should be invalidated. The contemporary battle over the Ninth Amendment's interpretation thus represents in its starkest form the struggle between a jurisprudence informed by fidelity to the framers' constitutional framework and a jurisprudence controlled by whatever faction can get five votes on the Supreme Court.

Notes

1. U.S. Constitution, Amendment IX.

2. Similarly, the Tenth Amendment reserves to the states, or to the people, all sovereign powers not delegated to the federal government or otherwise prohibited by the Constitution. Thus, the Ninth and Tenth Amendments operate in a parallel fashion: the Ninth Amendment reserves to the people the right to be free of federal regulation in all areas to which the federal government's enumerated powers do not extend. Obviously, the Ninth Amendment concerns only the relationship between the citizen and the federal government, not the state government. The Ninth Amendment cannot be understood to establish a right to be free of state (as opposed to federal) regulatory powers since the Tenth Amendment expressly reserves to the state the power to regulate in precisely those areas.

3. Domestic Policy Council, U.S. Executive Office of the President, *The Status of Federalism in America* (Washington, D.C., Nov. 1986), pp. 18–51.

4. *See* note 2, *supra*, and accompanying text.

5. 381 U.S. 479 (1965).

6. *Id.* at 499 (Goldberg, J., concurring).

7. *Palmer v. Thompson*, 403 U.S. 217, 233–234 (1971) (Douglas, J., dissenting).

8. S. Macedo, *The New Right v. The Constitution* (Washington, D.C.: Cato Institute, 1986), p. 43.

9. 198 U.S. 45 (1905) (invalidating a state law regulating the hours of work).

10. M. Farrand, ed., *The Records of the Federal Convention of 1787*, 4 vols. (New Haven: Yale Univ. Press, 1911–37), 2:340–42.

11. Ibid., pp. 587–88.

12. Ibid., pp. 617–18.

13. Governor Randolph was the only other delegate in attendance on Sept. 17, 1787, who refused to sign the Constitution (ibid., p. 649).

14. M. Jensen, ed., *The Documentary History of the Ratification of the Constitution*, vol. 2 (Madison: State Historical Society of Wisconsin, 1976), p. 168.

15. A. Hamilton, J. Madison, and J. Jay, *The Federalist*, ed. C. Rossiter (New York: New American Library, 1961), pp. 513–14.

16. J. Fitzpatrick, ed., *The Writings of George Washington*, vol. 29 (Washington, D.C.: GPO, 1933), p. 478.

17. J. Elliot, ed., *The Debates in the Several State Conventions on the Adoption of the Federal Constitution*, 4 vols. (New Haven: Yale Univ. Press, 1986), 2:436–37.

18. Ibid., p. 454 (statement of J. Wilson at the Pennsylvania Ratifying Convention, Dec. 4, 1787).

19. *Black's Law Dictionary* 521 (5th ed. 1979).

20. J. Elliot, *Debates*, 4:148 (statement of J. Iredell at the North Carolina Ratifying Convention, July 28, 1788).

21. *Annals of Congress*, vol. 1 (Washington, D.C.: Gales & Seaton, 1834),

pp. 759–60. In response, Congressman Page of Virginia argued that "a man has been obliged to pull of his hat when he appeared before the face of authority; people have also been prevented from assembling together on their lawful occasions, therefore it is well to guard against such stretches of authority, by inserting the privilege in the Declaration of Rights."

22. Ibid., p. 456.

23. Ibid., p. 452.

24. Madison to G. Washington, Dec. 5, 1789, in G. Hunt, ed., *The Writings of James Madison*, 9 vols. (New York: Putnam, 1900–1910), 5:432.

25. U.S. Constitution, Preamble and Article I, sec. 8, cls. 1, 15, 18.

26. J. Elliot, *Debates* 4:568.

27. Ibid., pp. 569–80.

28. 424 U.S. 1 (1976).

29. *Id.* at 58.

30. *Id.* at 13. The Court's dearth of analysis is undoubtedly due in part to the fact that there is nothing in the text of the Constitution granting Congress the power to place restrictions on contributions to a political candidate.

31. *See* Cooper, *The First Amendment, Original Intent, and the Political Process*, 10 Harv. J. L. & Pub. Pol'y 15 (1987).

32. *See* note 3, *supra*.

33. 381 U.S. 479 (1965).

34. *Id.* at 493 (Goldberg, J., concurring) (quoting *Snyder v. Massachusetts*, 291 U.S. 97, 105 [1934]).

35. *Id.* at 519 (Black J., dissenting).

36. *Id.* at 507 (Black, J., dissenting).

37. Justice Holmes once quipped that "[c]ommerce depends upon population, but Congress could not, on that ground, undertake to regulate marriage and divorce" (*Northern Sec. Co. v. United States*, 193 U.S. 197, 402 [1904] [Holmes, J., dissenting]). Although the Supreme Court's commerce clause decisions make it difficult to imagine an area beyond the regulatory grasp of Congress (*see, e.g., Garcia v. San Antonio Metro. Transit Auth.*, 469 U.S. 528 [1985]; *Wickard v. Filburn*, 317 U.S. 111 [1942]), few would maintain that the modest limit on Congress's delegated powers recognized by Holmes has been toppled.

38. 410 U.S. 113 (1973).

39. This statement, of course, must be qualified in the context of federal funding regulations. Congress can constitutionally restrict the use of federal funds to secure abortions; *see Harris v. McRae*, 448 U.S. 917 (1980) (Hyde Amendment violates neither the due process clause of the Fifth Amendment nor the establishment clause of the First Amendment).

40. 106 S. Ct. 2841 (1986).

41. Respondent's Petition for Rehearing, p. 9, *Bowers v. Hardwick*, 106 S. Ct. 342 (1986).

42. 268 U.S. 510 (1925).

43. 262 U.S. 390 (1923).

44. *See also Moore v. City of East Cleveland*, 431 U.S. 494 (1977) (city ordinance making it a crime for a grandmother to live with her grandson violates the due process clause of the Fourteenth Amendment).

45. 381 U.S. 479, 520 (1965) (Black, J., dissenting) (a broad interpretation of the Ninth Amendment would "make of this Court's members a day-to-day constitutional convention").

EDWARD J. ERLER

29. The Ninth Amendment and Contemporary Jurisprudence

The importance of the Ninth Amendment for contemporary jurisprudence was dramatically displayed in the confirmation hearings before the Senate Judiciary Committee on the nomination of Judge Robert Bork to the Supreme Court. Almost the only topic that aroused any interest was the right to privacy. There was much discussion about the *Griswold* case and the role of the Court in articulating "unenumerated" rights. Judge Bork, of course, deplored the Court's creation in that case of what he called "a generalized right to privacy." When pressed as to whether he thought the Connecticut law banning the use of contraceptives for married couples should have been struck down, Judge Bork was unequivocal. It was, he said in agreement with Justice Stewart's dissent in *Griswold*, an "uncommonly silly law." Judge Bork told the Senate Judiciary Committee that he believed the Connecticut law could have been struck down without resort to the creation of an undefined (and undefinable) right to privacy that was not rooted in any text of the Constitution.

When pressed, Judge Bork suggested that the Fourteenth Amendment's due process clause might have been a better vehicle, the reasoning being that the Connecticut law deprived married couples of a protected liberty. Judge Bork immediately realized that he had misspoken and retreated from this ill-advised answer, saying that the due process suggestion was perhaps not a good idea because it relied on what Justice Black in his dissent in *Griswold* had called "natural law due process philosophy." The due process solution, Judge Bork recanted, would allow the same unfettered discretion to judges as the generalized notion of a right to privacy.

Judge Bork was in something of a dilemma: "There may be an equal protection question here," he said, "but I haven't thought it through. I suppose an argument could be constructed on equal protection grounds, but I will have to think about it." This colloquy points to the problem most scholars and judges have in trying to understand the question of unenumerated rights posed by the Ninth Amendment. Unless Judge Bork was simply being disingenuous before the committee, he demonstrated his inability (or unwillingness) to grapple with what has become the jurisprudential question of our time. His opponents on the committee were even less able to grasp the issues of constitutional interpretation involved in the Ninth

Amendment. Yet they had the advantage. Judge Bork had allowed himself to be put on the defensive by conceding the moral (and rhetorical) high ground to his detractors. They were able to portray themselves as the defenders of rights against the assaults of Bork and his epigones. It was impossible for Bork to regain the high ground because he was unwilling to argue the moral superiority of the constitutionalism of the framers. Judge Bork believed that an argument derived from the text of the Constitution, rather than its principles, was sufficient.[1]

The political attack upon Bork had been prepared some years in advance by academics. In 1981 Charles Black, always on the leading edge of academic fashionableness, declared that it was a matter of utmost urgency for the nation to adopt "at long last" the Ninth Amendment. Black reasoned that "[w]e need the Ninth Amendment, for the sake of honesty and for the sake of utility."[2] Presumably, Professor Black was not unmindful of the fact that the Ninth Amendment had been adopted in 1791. No doubt, in his mind the fact that the amendment had fallen into seeming desuetude in the intervening years was proof that it had never been adopted. Black was calling for "contemporary" ratification. Contemporary ratification was an urgent necessity because it was, in his view, dishonest to continue to extend the due process and equal protection clauses into areas of ambiguous or doubtful legitimacy. This could be remedied by the adoption of the Ninth Amendment since, in Black's view, that amendment would serve to legitimate a variety of measures that could not be justified even under the most expansive reading of the so-called open-textured clauses of the Constitution.

The extension and expansion of rights under the aegis of the Ninth Amendment could be justified by what Black calls "the analogical and structural modes of inference." This "open Ninth Amendment approach" sets up "an atmosphere *hospitable* to the establishment of unnamed rights" that are "closely analogous or functionally similar to a named right."[3] And the hospitality of the Ninth Amendment is so great that it can be transformed into a veritable "foundation of law."[4]

Professor Black gives some very instructive examples of the structural and analogical derivation of rights. It is rather disingenuous, Black argues, to attempt to justify any prohibition against discrimination based on sex through the equal protection clause. Even though that provision refers to "persons," the history of the Fourteenth Amendment ties it closely to race, and sex is not the same as race although it may be analogous. In any case, the structural derivation is missing since "it would be laughable" to insulate women against discrimination based on "the Carolene Products footnote."[5] Here, then, is a perfect example of how the capacious confines of the Ninth Amendment might be used to establish reserved rights. Resort to the Ninth Amendment avoids a host of problems that arise under the Fourteenth Amendment. It renders irrelevant the interpretive baggage that surrounds equal protection analysis, such as whether sex is a "suspect classification" or only subject to an intermediate level of scrutiny. Under the Ninth Amendment the right to be free from discrimination based on sex could be protected directly and would almost certainly establish an effects test as the measure of discrimination.[6]

Although unacknowledged by Black, Justice William Douglas was the inventor of the argument from structure and analogy. Douglas has used the doctrine to reach some remarkable—if not indeed bizarre—conclusions. Fortunately, the most egregious of these conclusions—with the notable exception of *Griswold*—were never accepted by a majority of the Court. In his dissent in *Palmer v. Thompson* (1971),[7] Douglas brought the argument from structure and analogy to its logical reductio ad absurdum. *Palmer* was a controversial decision. Instead of obeying an order to integrate its swimming pools, the city of Jackson, Mississippi, closed all its public swimming facilities, citing the need to maintain order and fiscal considerations. Justice Black, writing for the majority, declined to inquire into the city's motives for closing the pools. The real question, Black noted, is "whether black citizens in Jackson *are* being denied their constitutional rights when the city has closed the public pools to black and white alike."[8] Since the Fourteenth Amendment creates no obligations for the states to provide public swimming facilities, Black concluded, the equal protection clause is not offended when all are denied access equally: "Should citizens of Jackson or any other city be able to establish in court that public, tax-supported swimming pools are being denied to one group because of color and supplied to another, they will be entitled to relief. But that is not the case here."[9]

Justice Douglas, however, found Ninth Amendment grounds to object to the majority's decision. Douglas conceded that the actions in question did not directly violate the Fourteenth Amendment. They may, however, fall within the "penumbras" of, not only the Fourteenth Amendment but the Thirteenth and Fifteenth as well. And those rights that fall within the penumbras of these amendments "should be in the category of those unenumerated rights protected by the Ninth Amendment. If not included, those rights become narrow legalistic concepts which turn on the formalism of laws, not on their spirit."[10] Douglas did suggest some of the "penumbral" rights that might be claimed on this occasion, implying that the assertion of these rights was the appropriate means of rendering the Constitution "modern." There is, of course, not a word in the Constitution, unlike many modern constitutions, concerning the right of the people to education or to work or to recreation by swimming or otherwise. Those rights, like the right to pure air and pure water, may well be rights "retained by the people" under the Ninth Amendment. May the people vote them down as well as up?[11] In Douglas's irrefragable logic the question posed was merely rhetorical. Others have extended Douglas's logic, suggesting that the Ninth

Amendment should be read to incorporate the United Nation's Declaration of Rights—presumably including the right to a vacation.[12]

In Professor Black's vision (and that of Justice Douglas), the job of articulating the substance of the Ninth Amendment's unenumerated rights falls to the courts. Since the judiciary is isolated from the majoritarian political process, it can insulate those rights against the depredations of self-interested majorities.[13] This does not present a problem for democratic theory, Black reasons, because the Congress has the power to control the appellate jurisdiction of the courts.[14] As long as the political or representative bodies of government allow the courts to indulge in the task of enumerating unenumerated rights, as apparently they have done by not invoking their power under the exceptions clause, then the Court cannot be accused of acting the part of "virtual representative," although it must occasionally do so to protect the rights of "discrete and insular minorities" from the acts of hostile majorities.

Black, of course, is not serious. He knows as well as anyone that the exceptions clause will never be an effective check upon the power of the courts. Indeed, it is precisely the collusion of the courts and Congress that Black expects to complete the creation of the centralized administrative state. Congress has been quite content to leave the most controversial policy decisions (e.g., affirmative action, busing, school prayer, etc.) to the courts. As John Marini remarks, "the situation today is this: Congress controls the administrative details of politics through the bureaucracy it created, and the judiciary reigns supreme in the realm of politics or regarding general policy matters. In terms of constitutional government, this arrangement has prevented the true sovereign—the American people—from exercising its decisive political role."[15] The recent decision in *Morrison v. Olson* (1988)[16] indicates the extent to which the Supreme Court is willing to cooperate with Congress in its incursions upon the executive branch.

One scholar, however, did seem to take Black's argument seriously, although it is difficult to believe that he was not being facetious or naive. In any case, this scholar faulted Black for his attempt to legitimize the Court's role under the Ninth Amendment by invoking the exceptions clause as a democratic limit to the power of the courts. It is counterproductive, this scholar contends, to publicize and invite the use of a constitutional power (the very constitutionality of which is suspect) which might diminish the Court's power to articulate new rights under the guise of numerating the unenumerated. This scholar is not troubled, as Black pretends to be, by a bad conscience concerning the legitimacy of courts in a constitutional democracy. It seems that a new consciousness—not deterred by questions of constitutional legitimacy—must accompany the newly found judicial activism occasioned by the readoption of the Ninth Amendment.[17]

It is very difficult—nay, impossible—to imagine that the framers of the Ninth Amendment could ever have contemplated such a transmogrification of their handiwork. In the First Congress, Madison supported the inclusion of a bill of rights as a matter of political expediency: it will be "highly politic for the tranquility of the public mind, and the stability of the Government, that we should offer something . . . to be incorporated in the system of Government, as a declaration of the rights of the people."[18] It was not a simple matter, however, to accomplish the task in a way which would "not injure the constitution."[19] The Ninth Amendment was the principal instrument designed by Madison to prevent such injury.

As everyone seems to know, Madison proposed the Ninth Amendment in part to overcome a defect that was inherent in all attempts at enumerating rights: the fact that any enumeration would be read as exhaustive under the rule of construction that the inclusion of one thing necessarily means the exclusion of another. From this point of view, every enumerated right would be a disparagement of an unenumerated one, precisely because every unenumerated right by implication would be given over to the government rather than being retained by the people. James Wilson had stressed this point in the Pennsylvania Ratifying Convention in countering objections that the Constitution contained no bill of rights. "A bill of rights annexed to a constitution, is an *enumeration* of the powers reserved. If we attempt an enumeration, every thing that is not enumerated, is presumed to be given. The consequence is, that an imperfect enumeration would throw all implied power into the scale of the government, and the rights of the people would be rendered incomplete."[20] Madison made the same point in introducing the amendments to the Constitution in the First Congress:

> It has been objected also against a bill of rights, that, by enumerating particular exceptions to the grant of power, it would disparage those rights which were not placed in that enumeration; and it might follow, by implication, that those rights which were not singled out, were intended to be assigned into the hands of the General Government, and were consequently insecure. This is one of the most plausible arguments I have ever heard urged against the admission of a bill of rights into this system; but I conceive, that it may be guarded against. I have attempted it, as gentlemen may see by turning to the last clause of the fourth resolution [the Ninth Amendment].[21]

Madison, of course, always considered a bill of rights superfluous.[22] He, like Hamilton, believed that "the Constitution is itself, in every rational sense, and to every useful purpose, A BILL OF RIGHTS."[23] The idea that an enumeration of rights was superfluous in a constitution of merely delegated powers was precisely the idea that Madison intended to express in the Ninth Amendment.

The principal danger of a bill of rights, however, was not that the list of enumerated rights would be read as an exhaustive list of rights, but that the specific prohibitions would be construed as grants of power. From this point of view the addition of a bill of rights was not simply superfluous but positively dangerous. As Hamilton explained in *The Federalist Papers*, a bill of rights

> would contain various exceptions to powers which are not granted; and, on this very account, would afford a colorable pretext to claim more than were granted. For why declare that things shall not be done which there is no power to do? Why, for instance, should it be said that the liberty of the press shall not be restrained, when no power is given by which restrictions may be imposed? I will not contend that such a provision would confer a regulation power; but it is evident that it would furnish, to men disposed to usurp, a plausible pretense for claiming that power.[24]

Thus, every exception expressed in terms of the rights of the people implied that, in the absence of the explicit limitation, government would have the power to act. This conveys the impression that the mass of sovereign power belongs to government and that the people's liberties reside only within the interstices of the exceptions to power that they have fashioned for themselves.

Those who insisted upon the addition of a bill of rights never seemed to grasp the importance of the new constitutionalism that was proposed by the Convention. Rather, they took as their models the great charters of English liberty, such as Magna Charta and the English Bill of Rights.[25] But these documents had no relevance to a system of government that was derived from the "consent of the governed." As Hamilton pointed out,

> bills of rights are, in their origin, stipulations between kings and their subjects, abridgments of prerogative in favor of privilege, reservations of rights not surrendered to the prince. . . . It is evident, therefore, that, according to their primitive signification, they have no application to constitutions, executed by their immediate representatives and servants. Here, in strictness, the people surrender nothing; and as they retain everything they have no need of particular reservations.[26]

Constitutional government, therefore, means that the people retain the mass of sovereign power and delegate only certain portions of that sovereignty in the form of enumerated powers to the government. Specific reservations of power (or rights) are thus superfluous at best. The power of government is defeated, not by the assertion or enumeration of rights, but by devices (primarily the separation of powers and the federal relationship) that insure that government exercises only those powers which the people have delegated to it.[27] As Justice Scalia acerbically noted in his recent dissent in *Morrison v. Olson*, "[w]ithout a secure structure of separated powers, our Bill of Rights would be worthless, as are the bills of rights of many nations of the world that have adopted, or even improved upon the mere words of ours."[28]

Madison's first version of the Ninth Amendment referred to a reservation of rights as well as a restriction on powers: "The exceptions here or elsewhere in the constitution, made in favor of particular rights, shall not be so construed as to diminish the just importance of other rights retained by the people, or as to enlarge the powers delegated by the constitution; but either as actual limitations of such powers, or as inserted merely for greater caution."[29] The two aspects of rights and powers are necessary counterparts. As Madison wrote to Washington in December, 1789, "If a line can be drawn between the powers granted and the rights retained, it would seem to be the same thing, whether the latter be secured, by declaring that they shall not be abridged, or that the former shall not be extended."[30] Madison's original version of the Ninth Amendment, of course, appeared in final form as two amendments, the Ninth as a reservation of rights and the Tenth as a reservation of powers. A reservation of rights would be ineffective without the clear recognition that a reservation of rights cannot be construed as a grant of powers. Thus both amendments are declaratory of relations already established in the Constitution.[31]

The reservation of rights in the Ninth Amendment must be read as an affirmation that the federal government is a government of limited powers and can legitimately exercise only those powers delegated to it or those which are a necessary and proper inference from the delegated powers. The Ninth Amendment is necessary because the very fact of enumerating rights implies a grant of power to the federal government. It is thus never necessary to specify the unenumerated rights protected by the Ninth Amendment since the burden of justifying the exercise of governmental power rests with those who are exercising the power to justify that exercise in terms of some delegated power. It is in this sense that the Ninth Amendment provides a rule of construction. It provides the rule for construing the Bill of Rights in a manner which is not inconsistent with the principles of the Constitution: even though the natural implication of an enumeration of rights is to construe the enumeration as exhaustive, that must never be done; even though the natural implication is to read every enumerated right as a disparagement of every unenumerated right, this must never be done; even though the natural implication is to treat every exception as implying a grant of power to the federal government, that must never be done. As a recent report published by the Justice Department's Office of Legal Policy states, "the Ninth Amendment is a rule of construction that creates no rights, but makes clear that those rights of the people not surrendered by the delegation of limited powers to the federal government are retained by the people, whether or not explicitly mentioned elsewhere in the Constitution."[32]

This is not, of course, the view of the matter that fashionable commentators—and I daresay the courts—hold today. They are more apt to view the federal government as possessing plenary power to act except where some right retained by the individual or by the people can defeat that power. These advocates of judicial activism seek to convert a reservation of unenumerated rights into a grant of unexpressed power on the part of the federal judiciary to define and enforce those rights. We find it necessary today to manufacture rights—either by listing those implied in the "penumbras formed by emanations" from various provisions of the Bill of Rights or by specifying those unenumerated rights reserved in the Ninth Amendment—in order to defeat the exercise of government power. But this is precisely what the Ninth Amendment was designed to guard against. The burden does not rest on the people to enumerate retained rights but on the government to justify the exercise of power in terms of some delegated (or enumerated) power. It is the impulse to define the unenumerated rights to defeat government power that has led to the intrusive use of government power not derived from any provisions of the Constitution. It is our belief today that the federal government has the power to do everything except intrude upon fundamental rights. Yet the Ninth Amendment was an attempt to reaffirm that the federal government is one of limited, delegated powers and that the mass of power or sovereignty was retained by the people. As Madison remarked, "rights . . . are reserved by the manner in which the federal powers are granted."[33] This is the exact idea that the Ninth Amendment was intended to convey. It is precisely when the Ninth Amendment appears moribund that it is working in the manner that its framers intended. Those who wish to define the unenumerated rights—whether by analogy or some functional or structural construction—are simply disparaging the rights guaranteed by the Ninth Amendment.

A good example—one that even the ideological liberals should be able to understand—of how rights might be disparaged by enumeration was given by Madison in a letter to Thomas Jefferson written in October, 1789: "[T]here is great reason to fear that a positive declaration of some of the most essential rights could not be obtained in the requisite latitude. I am sure that the rights of Conscience in particular, if submitted to public definition would be narrowed much more than they are likely ever to be by an assumed power. One of the objections in New England was that the Constitution by prohibiting religious tests opened a door for Jews, Turks, & infidels."[34] Again, in Madison's view, the greatest protection for rights was not their enumeration in a bill of rights but in well-constructed government that was limited to the exercise of delegated powers. The Supreme Court reflected

Madison's understanding as late as 1947 when in *United Public Workers v. Mitchell* it rejected a Ninth Amendment claim.[35] The Court delineated the proper mode of construing both the Ninth and Tenth Amendments:

> The powers granted by the Constitution to the Federal Government are subtracted from the totality of sovereignty originally in the states and the people. Therefore, when objection is made that the exercise of a federal power infringes upon rights reserved by the Ninth and Tenth Amendments, the inquiry must be directed toward the granted power under which the action of the Union was taken. If granted power is found, necessarily the objection of invasion of those rights, reserved by the Ninth and Tenth Amendments must fail.[36]

The important idea here is that a claim against the exercise of government power does not depend upon the plausibility of the "right" being asserted but upon whether or not the government has the delegated power to act, or whether the exercise of power is necessarily and properly implied from a delegated power.

Griswold v. Connecticut (1965)[37] changed this calculus and began the modern era of the Ninth Amendment. Since *Griswold*, the Ninth Amendment has almost become the exclusive argument of last resort in constitutional cases. It has been invoked for fanciful as well as frivolous reasons.[38] Strictly speaking, of course, *Griswold* was not a Ninth Amendment case—or was so only tangentially. Justice Douglas's majority opinion listed the Ninth Amendment, along with the First, Third, Fourth, and Fifth, as containing "specific guarantees . . . [that] have penumbras, formed by emanations [that] create zones of privacy."[39] Since the Connecticut statute banning the use of contraceptives among married couples entrenched upon "a relationship lying within the zone of privacy created by several fundamental constitutional guarantees," it was offensive to the Constitution. There is something of an air of mystery about Douglas's lack of specificity. If the right of privacy was derived in part from the emanations of the Third and Ninth Amendments, are those particular emanations applicable to a state law? The Third Amendment has never been incorporated, and the Ninth Amendment as a rule of construction cannot—any more than the Tenth Amendment—be incorporated.

Douglas chose this line of reasoning in order to avoid "a wide range of questions that implicate the Due Process Clause of the Fourteenth Amendment."[40] Substantive due process was the hallmark of the "Old Court," and Douglas wanted to disassociate himself in every way from that discredited doctrine. In a statement drawing its intellectual sustenance from *Carolene Products*, Douglas disdainfully declared that "[w]e do not sit as a super-legislature to determine the wisdom, need, and propriety of laws that touch economic problems, business affairs, or social conditions."[41] But since the present case involved "an intimate relation of husband and wife" falling within the zone of privacy, the Court can become a "super-legislature." The "presumption of constitutionality" is not accorded legislation when it touches upon fundamental individual liberties deemed "to be within a specific prohibition of the Constitution, such as those of the first ten amendments, which are deemed equally specific when held to be embraced within the Fourteenth."[42] But as Justice Black pointed out in his dissent, Douglas's opinion, despite his protestations to the contrary, was bottomed on the due process clause. It otherwise made no sense whatsoever. Black believed that complete deference to the state legislature—whether the issue "was personal rights" or "economic rights"—was the only sure way to avoid substantive due process (or "Lochnerizing" as the current technical term has it).[43]

The interesting Ninth Amendment analysis was adumbrated in Justice Goldberg's famous concurring opinion. He proposed a marriage between the Fourteenth Amendment's due process clause and the Ninth Amendment. Goldberg protested that he was not "turning somersaults with history" in stating that "the Ninth Amendment simply lends strong support to the view that the 'liberty' protected by the Fifth and Fourteenth Amendments from infringement by the Federal Government or the States is not restricted to rights specifically mentioned in the first eight amendments."[44] Further, Goldberg continued, established due process jurisprudence is adequate for determining which of the unenumerated rights are "fundamental" (presumably some unenumerated rights are therefore not "fundamental").

The mistake of Goldberg's analysis, of course, resides in the impulse to define an unenumerated right in order to defeat the exercise of a governmental power. Rather, the thrust of the analysis should be to test the exercise of power in the light of the powers delegated to government. If this were a question of the federal government's power to prohibit the use of contraceptives among married couples, there would be no doubt about its unconstitutionality. But since *Griswold* involved a state law, the matter is somewhat more complicated. The government of the state of Connecticut, no less than that of the United States, is one of delegated powers. The people retain ultimate sovereignty and thereby retain unenumerated rights. The question, then, is whether the Connecticut Constitution authorized the state legislature to act in the manner it did. Prior to the adoption of the Fourteenth Amendment, this would have been entirely a matter for determination by the state of Connecticut, and it is still today as long as there are no federal constitutional questions involved.[45] The question that must be openly confronted, however, is whether or not the prohibition on the use of contraceptives deprived married couples of liberty in violation of the due process clause of the Fourteenth Amendment. This is a question that neither liberals nor conservatives wish to debate openly (the one side not wanting to be accused of "Lochnerizing," the other not wanting to risk the onus of engaging in "natural law due process philosophy"). Yet, the resolution of this question can take place on the level of constitutional debate—it is a constitutional question and does not (and should not under a proper interpretation of the Ninth Amendment) involve an attempt on the part of the Supreme Court to articulate unenumerated rights.

Justice Stewart, in his dissent in *Griswold*, characterized the Connecticut statute as "an uncommonly silly law."[46] This was one point upon which the whole Court agreed. An "uncommonly silly law" is presumably one that lacks rationality or reasonable purpose. But the existence of an irrational law brings into question the very possibility of the rule of law. To the framers of the Constitution at least, the rule of law was identical with the rule of reason. For whatever else the rule of law may mean, it requires that principle or reason rather than human fiat or will be the informing agent of the law. James Wilson in his justly famous "Lectures on Law" delivered at Philadelphia College in 1790–91 put reason at the center of the definition of law: "Law is called a rule," he said, "in order to distinguish it from a sudden, a transient, or a particular order: uniformity, permanency, stability, characterize a law."[47] In the same vein, the authors of *The Federalist Papers* often used "reason" and "law" as interchangeable terms.[48] And for the framers generally, it was precisely the presence or absence of the rule of law (or perhaps due process of law) that distinguished constitutional government from despotic government.[49] Certainly no member of the *Griswold* Court would disagree that an arbitrary and capricious law was unconstitutional.[50] But there was considerable disagreement about whose reason was authoritative in determining which laws are arbitrary or capricious.

Justice Black—in an opinion shared by Stewart—argued that the Connecticut legislature should prevail, regardless of whether the law was reasonable. Black went even further:

> I do not believe that we are granted power by the Due Process Clause or any other constitutional provision or provisions to measure constitutionality by our belief that legislation is arbitrary, capricious or unreasonable, or accomplishes no justifiable purpose or is offensive to our own notions of "civilized standards of conduct." Such an appraisal of the wisdom of legislation is an attribute of the power to make laws, not of the power to interpret them. The use by federal courts of such a formula or doctrine or whatnot to veto federal or state laws simply takes away from Congress and States the power to make laws based on their own judgment of fairness and wisdom and transfers that power to this Court for ultimate determination—a power which was specifically denied to federal courts by the convention that framed the Constitution.[51]

This is not the first time such sentiments in favor of legislative deference have been expressed on the Court. Justices Holmes and Brandeis were proponents of this point of view, Brandeis advocating that the states be left to serve as laboratories for "novel social and economic experiments."[52]

But Justice Goldberg rightly pointed out that such experimentation could never be allowed to innovate upon the fundamental liberties of the people. Simple majoritarianism, whether at the state or federal level, is not sufficient for the rule of law or for constitutional government. The question of majority faction dominated the writings of the framers. As Madison noted, republican government required the transformation of numerical majorities into constitutional majorities, majorities that were capable of ruling in the interest of the whole rather than merely in the interest of the part (the majority). As Madison remarked in *The Federalist Papers*, "it is of great importance in a republic not only to guard the society against the oppression of its rulers, but to guard one part of the society against the injustice of the other part."[53] Thomas Jefferson expressed this same idea in his First Inaugural: "All, too, will bear in mind this sacred principle, that though the will of the majority is in all cases to prevail, that will to be rightful must be reasonable; that the minority possess their equal rights, which equal law must protect, and to violate would be oppression."[54] Thus the authority of the majority is legitimate only to the extent that its will is reasonable—that is, as long as its decisions are directed toward the rule of law understood as the equal protection of equal rights. According to Jefferson—and I daresay this was the view of the founding generation—this is the sacred principle of republican government. "An *elective despotism,*" Jefferson mused, "was not the government we fought for."[55] Jefferson, however, was never so sanguine as to think that the majority would always be reasonable. Thus it was necessary to include in the Constitution institutional arrangements—principally representation and the separation of powers—designed to refine the public will or to check it on those occasions when it overstepped constitutional boundaries.

What then is the role of the courts in this calculus of republican government? "It is . . . rational to suppose," Hamilton wrote in *The Federalist* No. 78, "that the courts were designed to be an intermediate body between the people and the legislature in order, among other things, to keep the latter within the limits assigned to their authority."[56] An independent judiciary is necessary to insure the legislature's—and the people's—adherence to the Constitution when an intrepid sense of its own strength inspires it to ignore the supreme law of the land. As Hamilton noted, "the people commonly *intend* the PUBLIC GOOD. This often applies to their very errors. But their good sense would despise the adulator who should pretend that they always *reason right* about the *means* of promoting it." Yet it is "the reason alone of the public, that ought to control and regulate the government."[57] It is the principal task of the judiciary to defend the reason of the public (expressed in constitutional form) against all assaults.

Chief Justice Marshall expounded this point of view in *Marbury v. Madison* (1803) when he described the Constitution as "paramount law" derived from the "supreme will" of the people that was superior to the Constitution itself.[58] Whenever the legislature contravenes the supreme will of the people, it is necessary for the Supreme Court to defend the sovereignty of the people against the temporary will of the legislature. This is not a usurpation of the right of the people to act through their elected representatives but a vindication of the "original right" of the people to establish the "fundamental principles" of their own governance by confining the legislature to the exercise of delegated powers. It was this reasoning that led Hamilton to remark that "the courts of justice are to be considered as the bulwarks of a limited Constitution against legislative encroachments."[59] This does not mean, of course, that the courts can substitute their will for the "supreme will" of the people or constitute themselves as "a day to day constitutional convention."[60] But the framers were acutely aware of the fact that in a republic the greatest danger of usurpation would arise from the legislative branch, not from the executive or judicial branch.[61] Even as a member of the First Congress debating the amendments to the Constitution, Madison emphatically stated that the greatest precautions "must be levelled against the legislative, for it is the most powerful, and most likely to be abused, because it is under the least control."[62]

The natural home of majority faction was, of course, the states. It was in the states, Madison noted, "that measures are too often disregarded in the conflicts of rival parties, and that measures are too often decided, not according to the rules of justice and the rights of the minor party, but by the superior force of an interested and overbearing majority."[63] An extensive federal republic embracing a multiplicity of interests offered some hope that constitutional majorities would be formed. But debate over the precise nature of the federal relationship in the "partly national, partly federal" republic that emerged from the Convention was not resolved (at least in principle) until the Reconstruction Amendments.

There can be little doubt that the Fourteenth Amendment was intended to change the federal relationship in important ways.[64] Most importantly, it defined state citizenship as derivative from federal citizenship, and by adding prohibitions against the states of the kind found in Article I, Section 10, it established the United States as the principal enforcer of civil rights. Conservative scholars insist that the provisions of the Fourteenth Amendment must be read narrowly. Raoul Berger, for example, argues that the Fourteenth Amendment was intended by its framers to be no more extensive than the (in his view narrowly limited) Civil Rights Act of 1866. Among a host of other considerations, Berger chooses to ignore statements such as those of John Bingham, the principal drafter of the Fourteenth Amendment in the House ("the James Madison of the Fourteenth Amendment" as he has been called) when he remarked on May 10, 1866, that

> [t]here was a want hitherto, and there remains a want now, in the Constitution of our country, which the proposed amendment will supply. What is that? It is the power in the people, the whole people of the United States, by express authority of the Constitution to do that by congressional enactment which hitherto they have not had the power to do, and have never even attempted to do; that is to protect by national law the privileges and immunities of all the citizens of the Republic and the inborn rights of every person within its jurisdiction whenever the same shall be abridged or denied by the unconstitutional acts of any state.[65]

The protection of the "inborn rights of every person" hardly sounds like an intention to protect only against "statutory discrimination with respect to the rights enumerated in the Civil Rights Act."[66] Thaddeus Stevens, a Radical Republican leader in the House, was more pointed when he introduced the amendment in the House on behalf of the Joint Committee on Reconstruction, May 8, 1866: "I can hardly believe that any person can be found who will not admit that every one of these provisions is just. They are all asserted, in some form or other, in our DECLARATION or organic law. But the Constitution limits only the action of Congress, and is not a limitation on the States. This amendment supplies that defect, and allows Congress to correct the unjust legislation of the States . . . Some answer, 'Your civil rights bill secures the same things.' That is partly true."[67] The clear implication of the last statement is that the Fourteenth Amendment was more extensive than the Civil Rights Act of 1866; read in the light of the earlier reference to the Declaration of Independence as the "organic law" for the amendment, there can be little doubt that it is a mistake to interpret the Fourteenth Amendment in the narrow manner suggested by Berger. The natural-law principles of the Declaration, not the Civil Rights Act of 1866, are the authority for the Fourteenth Amendment.

Is there a Fourteenth Amendment due process argument that can be brought to bear in deciding the constitutionality of the Connecticut statute which is narrow enough to rescue Judge Bork from his seemingly unresolvable dilemma? I believe there is. The laws of the state of Connecticut give legal recognition to the institution of marriage. The state of Connecticut almost certainly cannot do otherwise, although there is no specific provision in the Constitution that would prevent it from abolishing marriage. In any case, Connecticut's defense of its prohibition on the use of contraceptives among married couples was to strengthen the marriage relationship by discouraging extramarital relationships. This is, of course, a legitimate purpose falling clearly within the state's police powers. But the means chosen to accomplish this end is destructive of the liberty that is a necessary and essential element of marriage. From any point of view, it is unreasonable or irrational to allow the means to destroy the end. Connecticut's recognition of the institution of marriage means, ipso facto, the recognition of the liberties without which marriage itself could not exist. The antiuse statute must therefore fall of its own weight—it is simply irrational and capricious. As Justice Harlan noted in his dissenting opinion in *Poe v. Ullman* (1961), "[i]t is one thing when the State exerts its power either to forbid extramarital sexuality altogether, or to say who may marry, but it is quite another when, having acknowledged a marriage and the intimacies inherent in it, it undertakes to regulate by means of the criminal law the details of that intimacy."[68] It is the choice of means, in Harlan's analysis, not the choice of the end, that violates due process.

The advantage of the due process analysis is that it does not attempt to articulate an unenumerated right but restricts the notion of the liberty being protected to that liberty which is a necessary part of the legally sanctioned marriage relationship. The majority in *Griswold*, however, chose to "articulate" an independent right to privacy which, once established, became subject to constructions required by other provisions of the Constitution. Thus, in *Eisenstadt v. Baird* (1972),[69] the Court was confronted with the question of whether or not unmarried couples fell within the penumbra of privacy created by *Griswold*. *Griswold* had only spoken of the "sacred" intimacies of the marriage relationship. Under *Eisenstadt*, however, equal protection considerations were at issue. As Justice Brennan observed in unmistakable tones of labored tergiversation:

> If under Griswold the distribution of contraceptives to married persons cannot be prohibited, a ban on distribution to unmarried persons would be equally impermissible. It is true that in Griswold the right of privacy in question inhered in the marital relationship. Yet the marital couple is not an independent entity with a mind and heart of its own, but an association of two individuals each with a separate intellectual makeup. If the right of privacy means anything, it is the right of the *individual*, married or single, to be free from unwarranted governmental intrusion into matters so fundamentally affecting a person as the decision whether to bear or beget a child.[70]

This reasoning was again used in the abortion case to insulate the fundamental right to privacy—now understood to mean the right to decide whether or not to procreate—from state invasion.

This definition of privacy was pressed to its natural limits in *Hardwick v. Bowers* (1986), a case involving consensual sodomy. Obviously the decisive privacy question was not governed by the individual decision of whether or not to procreate. The federal court of appeals, in finding the Georgia antisodomy statute unconstitutional, noted that while private, consensual acts of homosexuality are "not procreative," nevertheless "[f]or some, the sexual activity in question . . . serves the same purpose as the intimacy of marriage"[71] and for this reason was protected by the Ninth and Fourteenth Amendments. The court of appeals not only struck down the

Georgia law but it attempted to repeal nature as well. The court of appeals had obviously been influenced by Professor Black's argument from structure and analogy.

The Supreme Court, however, overturned the court of appeals, ruling that the practice of sodomy did not fall within the scope of the fundamental right of privacy. The Court considered and rejected a due process challenge to the Georgia statute. Justice White, writing for the majority, sardonically remarked that "no connection between family, marriage, or procreation on the one hand and homosexual activity on the other has been demonstrated, either by the Court of Appeals or by respondent."[72] But, as the dissent pointed out, it was the exclusive reliance on due process grounds (beginning with the question "Is there a right to sodomy?") that defeated the court of appeals. Had the court begun with the question of what belongs within the zone of privacy, as the dissent urged, it would have been difficult to find a rationale as to why sodomy did not fall within that zone. It was, as the dissent vehemently pointed out, therefore unnecessary to consider Ninth Amendment arguments or equal protection arguments.

The dissent would have relied on the right of privacy to protect the absolute right of autonomy in intimate relationships. As Justice Blackmun noted, "[t]he fact that individuals define themselves in a significant way through their intimate sexual relationships with others suggests, in a Nation as diverse as ours, that there may be many 'right' ways of conducting those relationships, and that much of the richness of a relationship will come from the freedom an individual has to *choose* the form and nature of these intensely personal bonds."[73] What defeated the assertion of the right to sodomy in the *Bowers* case was a due process argument. The Court did not allow itself to be dragged into the hopeless position of trying to determine the limits (if any) of the right of privacy. Understood as the absolute autonomy of the individual, there can be no limits to what may be legitimately claimed in the name of privacy. It is true that due process arguments have the potential to be (and are) abused by the courts. But this is true of every judgment that is made by a court. The possibility of mistaken judgments should not be an argument for no judgments. This is almost the argument made by Black's dissent in *Griswold*.

The Court in *Bowers* also deferred to the state legislature, arguing that the Georgia statute could be struck down only if it impinged upon a fundamental right. But, by the same token, a state statute permitting consensual homosexuality would infringe upon the same fundamental rights that were at stake in the *Griswold* case. The instance of a state statute permitting sodomy would probably be beyond the reach of the courts, but an argument based on the principles of republican government could be constructed to defeat such a statute. Homosexuality, no less than slavery, is incompatible with the principles of republicanism. Jefferson described the practice of slavery as "a perpetual exercise of the most boisterous passions" which made both master and slave unfit to be citizens of a republic.[74] But much the same can be said of the practice of homosexuality. The exercise of a "right" without reciprocal responsibilities—as in the case of slavery and homosexuality—is not consistent with the rule of law.[75]

There is no doubt that the "fundamental right to privacy" has become a permanent part of our constitutional jurisprudence. Whether based on due process considerations or the Ninth Amendment, it represents the attempt to do what the Ninth Amendment was intended to prevent—the articulation of unenumerated rights. The general consensus of academic commentators is that the right to privacy must be understood in terms of an absolute right to "personal autonomy." As *Bowers* demonstrates, the Supreme Court has not yet accepted that interpretation, although the continued assault on the part of intellectuals and law professors to do so probably bodes ill for the future. The regime that will be created by resort to an "open Ninth Amendment" is not likely to be the regime of constitutional government that Madison and the rest of the framers envisioned. If Professor Black is successful in founding the regime of the "open-textured" Ninth Amendment, we will have a dramatic demonstration of what it means to disparage rights by enumerating unenumerated rights.

Notes

1. *See* Robert Bork, *Tradition and Morality in Constitutional Law*, Francis Boyer Lectures on Public Policy (Washington, D.C.: American Enterprise Institute, 1984), pp. 8–9.

2. C. Black, *Decision according to Law* (New York: Norton, 1981), p. 44. The extent to which fashion plays a role in academia is indicated by the not entirely facetious quarrel about who was the first to call for the "adoption" of the Ninth Amendment (*see* ibid., n. 48).

3. Ibid., pp. 48, 50. It is significant that Black here speaks of the "establishment," not the articulation of rights, reserved to the people.

4. Ibid., p. 44 n. 47.

5. Ibid., p. 61.

6. *See* Erler, *The Equal Rights Amendment and the Disproportionate Impact Standard: The Impact of the Equal Rights Amendment*, Hearings before the Subcommittee on the Constitution, 98th Cong., 1st and 2d Sess., 1984, p. 893.

7. 403 U.S. 217 (1971).

8. *Id.* at 226.

9. *Id.* at 227.

10. *Id.* at 239.

11. *Id.* at 233–34.

12. Paust, *Human Rights and the Ninth Amendment: A New Form of Guarantee*, 60 Cornell L. Rev. 231 (1975).

13. J. Choper, *Judicial Review and the National Political Process* (Chicago: Univ. of Chicago Press, 1983), p. 68. *See* Erler, *Sowing the Wind: Judicial Oligarchy and the Legacy of Brown v. Board of Education*, 8 Harv. J. L. & Pub. Pol'y. 399–426 (1985).

14. Black, *Decision according to Law*, pp. 18 n. 2, 26–27, 80–81.

15. Marini, *The Political Conditions of Legislative-Bureaucratic Supremacy*, 6 Claremont Review of Books 7 (1988).

16. *Morrison v. Olson*, 487 U.S. 654, 108 S. Ct. 2597 (1988).

17. VanAlstyne, *Slouching toward Bethlehem with the Ninth Amendment* 91 Yale L.J. 207 (1981).

18. *Annals of Congress*, vol. 1 (Washington, D.C.: Gales & Seaton, 1834), pp. 439–40; *see also* pp. 429, 432, 442, 448, 704, 732–33.

19. Ibid., p. 108.

20. J. Elliot, *The Debates of the Several State Conventions on the Adoption of the Federal Constitution*, 2d ed. (Washington, D.C.: U.S. Congress, 1836), 2:435–36.

21. *Annals of Congress* 1:439.

22. *See* ibid., p. 441.

23. A. Hamilton, J. Madison, and J. Jay, *The Federalist Papers*, ed. C. Rossiter (New York: New American Library, 1961), No. 84, p. 515.

24. Ibid., pp. 513–14.

25. *See* Erler, *The Great Fence to Liberty: The Right to Property in the American Founding*, in E. Paul and H. Dickman, eds., *Liberty, Property, and the Foundations of the American Constitution* (Albany: State Univ. of New York Press, 1989), pp. 48–50.

26. *The Federalist*, No. 84, p. 513.

27. *See* Erler, *The Constitution and the Separation of Powers*, in L. Levy and D. Mahoney, eds., *The Framing and Ratification of the Constitution* (New York: Macmillan, 1987), pp. 151–66.

28. *Morrison v. Olson*, 487 U.S. 654, 108 S. Ct. 2597, 2622 (1988) (Scalia, J., dissenting).

29. *Annals of Congress* 1:435.

30. Madison to George Washington, Dec. 5, 1789, in R. Rutland et al., eds., *The Papers of James Madison* (Chicago: Univ. of Chicago Press and Charlottesville: Univ. Press of Virginia, 1962—), 12:459. In the Pennsylvania Ratifying Convention, James Wilson did point to a significant difference when he remarked that "an omission in the enumeration of the powers of government is neither so dangerous nor important as an omission of the enumeration of the rights of the people" (Elliot, *Debates* 2:436).

31. *See* Berger, *The Ninth Amendment*, 66 Cornell L. Rev. 1 at 2–3 (1980). "The two [amendments] are complementary: the ninth deals with *rights* 'retained by the people,' the tenth with *powers* 'reserved' to the states or the people. As Madison perceived, they are two sides of the same coin."

32. U.S. Department of Justice, Office of Legal Policy, *Wrong Turns on the Road to Judicial Activism: The Ninth Amendment and Privileges or Immunities Clause* (Washington, D.C., 1987), p. 2.

33. Madison to Thomas Jefferson, Oct. 17, 1788, in Rutland, *Papers of Madison* 11:297.

34. Ibid.

35. 330 U.S. 75 (1947).

36. *Id.* at 95–96. *See also Ashwander v. T.V.A.*, 297 U.S. 288, 330–31 (1937).

37. 381 U.S. 479 (1965).

38. *See* U.S. Dept. of Justice, *Wrong Turns on the Road to Judicial Activism*, pp. 5–6.

39. *Griswold*, at 484.

40. *Id.* at 481.

41. *Id.* at 482.

42. *U.S. v. Carolene Products Co.*, 304 U.S. 144, 152 n. 4 (1938).

43. *Griswold*, at 522.

44. *Id.* at 493.

45. *See* Erler, *Independence and Activism: Ratcheting Rights in the State Courts*, 4 Benchmark 55–66 (1988).

46. *Id.* at 527.

47. James Wilson, "Of the General Principles of Law and Obligation," in R. McCloskey, ed., *The Works of James Wilson*, 2 vols. (Cambridge: Belknap, 1967), 2:100.

48. *See*, e.g., *The Federalist*, No. 78, p. 468 (A. Hamilton), No. 44, p. 285 (J. Madison), No. 81, p. 484 (A. Hamilton).

49. *See* Erler, *Natural Right in the American Founding*, in J. Barlow, L. Levy, and K. Masugi, eds., *The American Founding* (New York: Greenwood, 1988), pp. 210–13.

50. One distinguished jurist has, however, written this remarkable statement: "[L]aws need not be rational means toward some specific end . . . most constitutions impose no obligation on lawmakers or on the people themselves to enact only rational laws" (Linde, *E. Pluribus—Constitutional Theory and State Courts*, 18 Ga. L. Rev. 165, 187, 195 [1984]).

51. *Griswold*, at 513; in his separate dissent, Justice Stewart remarked that it was not appropriate for the courts to "substitute their social and economic beliefs for the judgment of legislative bodies who are elected to pass laws" (*id.* at 540).

52. *New State Ice Co. v. Liebmann*, 285 U.S. 262, 280, 311 (1932).

53. *The Federalist*, No. 51, p. 323.

54. M. Peterson, ed., *Thomas Jefferson: Writings* (New York: Viking, 1984), pp. 492–93.

55. Ibid., p. 245.

56. *The Federalist*, No. 78, p. 467.

57. Ibid., No. 71, p. 432, No. 49, p. 317.

58. *Marbury v. Madison*, 5 U.S. (1 Cranch) 137, 176 (1803).

59. *The Federalist*, No. 78, p. 469.

60. *Griswold*, at 520 (Black, J., dissenting).

61. *The Federalist*, No. 48, pp. 309–10.

62. *Annals of Congress* 1:437.

63. *The Federalist*, No. 10, p. 77; *see inter alia* M. Farrand, ed., *The Records of the Federal Convention of 1787*, 4 vols. (New Haven: Yale Univ. Press, 1911–37), 1:27, 254, 2:76.

64. *See* Erler, *The Fourteenth Amendment and the Protection of Minority Rights*, 1987 B.Y.U. L. Rev. 977 (1987).

65. *Congressional Globe*, 39th Cong., 1st Sess., 2542 (1866).

66. R. Berger, *Government by Judiciary: The Transformation of the Fourteenth Amendment* (Cambridge: Harvard Univ. Press, 1977), p. 176.

67. *Congressional Globe*, 39th Cong., 1st Sess., 2458 (1866).

68. *Poe v. Ullman*, 367 U.S. 497, 553 (1961) (Harlan, J., dissenting).

69. 405 U.S. 438 (1972).

70. *Id.* at 453.

71. *Hardwick v. Bowers*, 760 F.2d 1202, 1212 (1985).

72. *Bowers v. Hardwick*, 478 U.S. 186, 106 S. Ct. 2841, 2844 (1986).

73. *Id.* at 2851.

74. T. Jefferson, *Notes on the State of Virginia*, Q. XVIII, in M. Peterson, *Thomas Jefferson: Writings*, p. 288. *See* West, *The Rule of Law in The Federalist*, in C. Kessler, ed., *Saving the Revolution: The Federalist Papers and the American Founding* (New York: Free Press, 1987), p. 176.

75. *See* Jaffa, *Judicial Conscience and Natural Rights: A Reply to Professor Ledewitz*, 11 U. Puget Sound L. Rev. 219, 252–53 (1988).

XIII.

ORIGINAL INTENT AND THE TENTH AMENDMENT

Eugene W. Hickok, Jr.

30. The Original Understanding of the Tenth Amendment

> Each state retains its sovereignty, freedom and independence, and every Power, Jurisdiction and right, which is not by this confederation expressly delegated to the United States.
>
> Articles of Confederation
> Article 2

> The powers not delegated to the United States by the Constitution, nor prohibited by it to the States, are reserved to the States respectively, or to the people.
>
> Constitution of the United States
> Amendment X

The purpose of this chapter is to outline briefly the original understanding of the Tenth Amendment to the Constitution of the United States. By "original understanding" I mean the general understanding of the Tenth Amendment held by those who were instrumental in the framing and ratification of the Constitution of 1787 and who served in the First Congress that proposed the first several amendments to the Constitution.

Obviously, uncovering the original understanding of any clause or provision of the Constitution is a difficult and cumbersome task. At the very least it requires a comprehensive analysis of a mountain of historical evidence. Certainly, therefore, a comprehensive analysis of the original understanding is beyond the scope of this chapter. It is possible, however, to outline the broad parameters within which the Founders of this Republic approached some agreement on the proper allocation of governing responsibility between the central government and the governments of the several states and then to determine how the Tenth Amendment reflects that agreement.

In order to understand what the Tenth Amendment was intended to mean when it was proposed and ratified, it is necessary to consider what the framers of the Constitution meant by federalism. The delegates to the Federal Convention of 1787 were just that, delegates. They attended the meetings in Philadelphia that summer as representatives of their states. The Convention had been called to consider revisions to the Articles of Confederation, not to create a new government. Indeed, there were some who withdrew from the Convention because they felt their fellow delegates were going beyond their mandate by writing a new constitution. The fact that a new constitution was created in order to form a "more perfect union" should not overshadow the fact that the delegates were not creating a government from scratch. It was the hope of the framers that the new government would indeed be better than what they had experienced under the troubled Articles. The hope was that the union that they created would indeed be "more perfect" than the "league of friendship" that had been established under the Articles. But with the possible exception of Alexander Hamilton, all of the delegates brought to the deliberations in Philadelphia a concern for the interests and security of their state as well as a desire to make whatever adjustments seemed needed in order to improve upon the very defective system of government that existed under the Articles.

While it is something of an overstatement to describe the Constitution of 1787 as nothing but the product of political compromise, it is safe to say that the federal character of that Constitution—the allocation of governing responsibility between the central government created by the Constitution and the governments of the several states—was hammered out through compromise. No other issue dominated the deliberations that summer as much as this. At one point, the debate became so heated that some feared compromise was impossible and that the Convention would have to adjourn without reaching a consensus. But, in the end, largely through the sage advice of Benjamin Franklin, cooler heads prevailed and compromise and consensus were achieved.[1] However, it is important to bear in mind that it was a compromise. The new Constitution that was signed in September 1787 reflected the concerns of those who sought to protect and maintain the authority of the states as well as those who felt the demands of good government required that the states and the citizens delegate some authority to a central government. Federalism as it emerged in 1787 was, therefore, one of the novel inventions of the new Constitution. Nothing like it had been seen before.

At the time of the Convention there were recognized to be two principles for organizing government. On the one hand, there was a unitary or centralized system, in which the power of government was concentrated in a central authority which possessed all sovereignty. On the other hand, there was a federal or confederal system in which the power of government was possessed by independent sovereign states that might form a central agency for the purposes of coordination and alliance only. Great Britain served as a model of a unitary or centralized system. The Articles of Confederation epitomized a federal system. The debate that transpired in Philadelphia revolved around these two models and the degree to which either could guarantee responsible government in a country as large as the United States.

Those who embraced federalism or confederalism brought to the deliberations both the advantages and disadvantages of the experience of government under the Articles of Confederation. Under the Articles the states were sovereign. The central authority was weak and possessed only those powers that were given it by the states. It was a system which emphasized the sovereignty of the states, reinforcing state interests and prejudices and making cooperation and coordination among states quite difficult to obtain. Moreover, most of the states were experiencing serious internal problems, thus contributing to the sense that something had to be done to improve upon the existing system.

Early into the deliberations of the Convention, Edmund Randolph of Virginia proposed his Virginia Plan, which was regarded by most of the delegates to be radically national in character. There was no mistake about it. Randolph's original resolution had stated that "the articles of Confederation ought to be so corrected and enlarged, as to accomplish the objects proposed by their institution; namely, common defense, security of liberty and general welfare." But at the suggestion of Gouverneur Morris, he substituted language that left little room for conjecture about the truly national character of the plan he proposed: "Resolved that a Union of the States merely federal will not accomplish the objects proposed by the articles of confederation, namely common defense, security of liberty, and general welfare and that a national Government ought to be established consisting of a supreme Legislative, Executive and Judiciary."[2]

The Virginia Plan changed the terms of the debate for the remainder of the summer. It was adopted almost immediately, thereby putting the defenders of a federal system on the defensive. Randolph had proposed a truly national system, and so the true federalists had to work to ensure that Randolph's plan contained some federal characteristics. As Martin Diamond tells us: "The opponents of a purely national government found themselves unable to defend the pure federal principle. The simple nationalists remained such in principle, while the pure federalists implicitly found themselves forced to acknowledge the inadequacy of the federal principle. Now the question was between those still advocating a purely national plan and those who, having abandoned a purely federal scheme, were determined only to work some federal features into the final outcome."[3] The compromise which surfaced toward the end of the summer, then, was a compromise that provided for a national system with federal characteristics. As James Madison stated in *The Federalist Papers*, the Constitution "is, in strictness, neither a national nor a federal Constitution, but a composition of both."[4]

What we today refer to as a federal system of government was for the framers of the Constitution a product of compromise between those who favored a purely confederal system and those who favored a purely national system. The partisans of confederation had viewed nationalism as incompatible with individual liberty. The proponents of nationalism viewed confederation as incompetent. What both groups wanted was a system which would be competent but not pose a threat to the rights and liberties of the people. The federal character of the Constitution, then, was understood to be the essential compromise that would achieve that end.

Of course, the great challenge left to the framers of the Constitution, as well as to succeeding generations of Americans, was to determine the exact nature of the federal compromise created in Philadelphia. The federal system created by the Constitution only provided the broad parameters of the allocation of powers between the central government and the states. The exact distribution of those powers—the determination of what government has responsibility in what areas—was not decided in 1787. Indeed, this continues to be one of the fundamental questions of constitutional interpretation. In a way, it can be said that the Constitutional Convention forced us to seek to resolve that issue. And probably no issue so preoccupied the defenders and opponents of the new Constitution as much as defining what federalism did indeed mean.

Alexander Hamilton writes in *The Federalist Papers* that "the task of marking the proper line of partition between the authority of the general and that of the State governments" was an arduous one.[5] For Hamilton, however, the answer could be found in a reliance upon the written document combined with the recognition that states mattered. Hamilton, an ardent nationalist, was convinced that "two sovereignties cannot co-exist with the same limits," but that did not imply that the states could not exercise independent authority independently of the central government.[6] Speaking at the New York Ratification Convention, Hamilton argued that the assertion "that two supreme powers cannot act together is false. They are inconsistent only when they are aimed . . . at one indivisible goal."[7] In other words, the states were quite sovereign in their spheres of governing responsibility, and the central government was quite sovereign in its sphere of governing responsibility. That, indeed, was the nature of the compromise that had allowed for the creation of the Constitution. Moreover, it was a necessary compromise because citizens quite naturally feel a loyalty to and interest in states. "The early connections we have formed, the habits and prejudices in which we have been bred, fix our affections so strongly that no future objects of association can easily eradicate them."[8]

James Madison, also a nationalist at the Convention, although somewhat restrained in his nationalist's fervor later in his life, likewise argued that the states retained an important hold over the sentiments of the people and the lion's share of the powers of government under the new Constitution. According to Madison, "The State governments will have the advantages of the federal government" primarily because the national government will be dependent upon the states, and the citizens will in all probability side with the states in any dispute between the states and the central government. "The State governments may be regarded as constituent and essential parts of the federal government; whilst the latter is nowise essential to the operation or organization of the former," Madison states in *The Federalist Papers*. Indeed, Madison goes on to argue that "each of the principal branches of the federal government will owe its existence more or less to the favor of the State governments."[9]

James Wilson of Pennsylvania, considered by some to have been second only to Madison in his influence during the Convention, argued during the Pennsylvania Ratification Convention much the same thing. For Wilson, federalism meant the states and the central government could exist in harmony together, each exercising authority independently of the other. "Are disputes between the general government and the state governments to be necessarily the consequence of inaccuracy? I hope, sir, they will not be the enemies of each other, or resemble comets in conflicting orbits, mutually operating destruction; but that their motion will be better represented by that of the planetary system, where each part moves harmoniously within its proper sphere, and no injury arises by interference or opposition."[10]

But it was Madison himself who provided a more direct analysis of the sphere of responsibility allocated to each government. Drawing the line between the states and the central authority would indeed be difficult, he acknowledged, but that did not mean a line could not be drawn.

> The powers delegated by the proposed Constitution to the federal government are few and defined. Those which are to remain in the State governments are numerous and indefinite. The former will be exercised principally on external objects, as war, peace, negotiation, and foreign commerce; with which last the power of taxation will, for the most part, be connected. The powers reserved to the several States will extend to all the objects which, in the ordinary course of affairs, concern the lives, liberties, and properties of the people, and the internal order, improvement, and prosperity of the State.[11]

What emerges from the debate over the federal character of the new Constitution is an argument of form and scope. Initially, the opponents and supporters of the new government differed about the feasibility of a system of government in which sovereignty is divided among governments. Was such a system practical, or would it quickly degenerate due to feuds among contending governments? A second debate, more important than the first and continuing today, revolved around how to divide powers up among those governments. This debate was resolved, for the moment, by referring to the government created by the new Constitution as a limited government of enumerated powers only or, as Madison put it, a government whose powers are "few and defined." This argument, coupled with the fact that the populous recognized the deficiencies of the system they were currently living with, was enough to attract the support needed to ratify the Constitution. But the opponents to the Constitution continued to press their fears after the document was ratified, arguing that it was necessary to clarify the limited nature of the national government and secure the "liberties" of the states.

The Constitution was ratified in June 1788. By the spring of 1789, the sixty-five members of the first House of Representatives and the members of the Senate began to arrive in New York. Significant constitutional issues confronted them almost from the outset. During the deliberations from April 1789 to March 1791, two kinds of constitutional questions dominated the proceedings. The first related to the task of forming a government under the new Constitution, and the second to that of securing individual rights and the sovereignty of the states under the Constitution. Although related, the two tasks differed in a very fundamental way. As the members of Congress considered the creation of the executive branch and the judiciary, they debated not only how government shall function but what government shall do. As they debated amending the Constitution to secure individual and state liberties, the perspective was different. The members emphasized what government shall not do. They were engaged in charting that sphere of activity which would be immune to government intrusion. And this was a pressing concern for the Congress, for the opponents to the Constitution had made it clear during the ratification struggle that the new Constitution had to be amended before they would pledge their ongoing support. The members of Congress understood that the future of the government depended upon their proposing amendments. Representative John Page made it perfectly clear: "Unless you take early notice of this subject, you will not have power to deliberate. The people will clamor for a new Convention; they will not trust the House any longer."[12] James Madison, as he introduced amendments and revision to the Constitution, also reminded his colleagues of the concerns some had about the new Constitution. "It cannot be a secret to the gentlemen in this House that, notwithstanding the ratification of this system of Government by eleven of the thirteen United States, in some cases unanimously, in others by large majorities, yet still there is a great number of our constituents who are dissatisfied with it, among whom are many respectable for their talents and patriotism and respectable for the jealousy they have for their liberty, which, though mistaken in its object, is laudable in its motive."[13]

Madison was referring, of course, to the arguments that had been mounted at the various state ratification conventions in favor of adding a bill of rights to the Constitution. At each convention arguments had been advanced on behalf of those who feared the new Constitution lacked specific guarantees against the encroachment by the government upon the liberties of the people and sovereignty of the states. Writing in 1788, the "Federal Farmer" argued, for example, that "[i]f a nation means its systems, religious or political, shall have duration, it ought to recognize the leading principles of them in the front page of every family book." The supporters of the Constitution argued that the new government was limited, reasoned the

"Federal Farmer," so it was not inconsistent to include in the Constitution of that new government a statement or series of statements that made explicit its limited character and would "establish in the minds of the people truths and principles which they might never otherwise have thought of, or soon forgot."[14]

The arguments for a bill of rights need not concern us here. It is enough to point out that the argument for a statement securing the sovereignty of the states was advanced within the greater argument for a bill of rights. The primary concern was, quite predictably, the degree to which the people could find comfort in a constitution in which the notion of reserved powers was implied rather than explicit. In other words, wasn't it necessary to state clearly the fact that the powers of the new government were limited to those enumerated in the Constitution and that all other governmental powers remained in the states? As the "Federal Farmer" put it: "To make declaratory articles unnecessary in an instrument of government, two circumstances must exist; the rights reserved must be indisputably so, and in their nature defined; the powers delegated to the government, must be precisely defined by the words that convey them, and clearly be of such extent and nature as that, by no reasonable construction, they can be made to invade the rights and prerogatives intended to be left in the people."[15]

The Constitution needed to be revised, according to its more vociferous critics, in order to make explicit what was only implicit as it was ratified. The only way to guarantee a limited national government was to place explicit limits on the power of the new national government. This was the motivation behind an amendment proposed by James Iredell at the North Carolina Ratifying Convention:

> Each state in the Union shall respectively retain every power, jurisdiction, and right, which is not by this Constitution delegated to the Congress of the United States, or to the departments of the general government; nor shall the said Congress, nor any department of the said government, exercise any act of authority over any individual in any of the said states, but such as can be justified under some power particularly given in this Constitution; but the said Constitution shall be considered at all times a solemn instrument, defining the extent of their authority, and the limits of which they cannot rightfully in any instance exceed.[16]

The ability effectively to limit the powers of the national government strikes to the very root of federalism. The same debate that had so consumed the energies of the delegates in Philadelphia would command the attention of the members of Congress. On June 8, 1789, James Madison recommended to the House of Representatives that it consider the need for adding to the Constitution a number of provisions which some of the state ratification conventions had cited as essential but missing from the document. The provisions were not discussed in the House until August. On August 18 Thomas Tudor Tucker of South Carolina proposed to amend Madison's ninth proposition—which stated: "The powers not delegated by the constitution, nor prohibited by it to the States, are reserved to the States respectively"—by adding the prefix, "all powers being derived from the people" and inserting "expressly" so that the provision read "the powers not expressly delegated by this Constitution." Madison objected, arguing as he had in *The Federalist Papers* that it was impossible and imprudent to attempt to "confine a Government to the exercise of express powers" and that it was necessary to allow for "powers of implication," otherwise the Constitution would have to descend to minutiae. Tucker rose to defend his proposition, arguing that "expressly" did not really narrow the powers of the government; "he thought every power to be expressly given that could be clearly comprehended within any accurate definition of the general power." Tucker's motion failed.

Within the week Elbridge Gerry offered the same proposal. It was defeated 32 to 17. With some final changes offered by Sherman, the ninth proposition—what was to become the Tenth Amendment—was adopted without debate.[17]

The argument advanced by Tucker was important to determining the meaning of the Tenth Amendment. According to Madison, the central government was indeed one of limited and enumerated powers. But since it was impossible to define adequately the scope of those powers incident to those enumerated in the Constitution, it was dangerous to use the term "expressed." He was making a distinction, therefore, between a government of delegated powers and a government of expressly delegated powers. Both would be limited, for sure. But the latter would be far more limited than the former. The Tenth Amendment provided for a government of delegated powers.

The Tenth Amendment, according to Joseph Story, "is a mere affirmation of what, upon any just reasoning, is a necessary rule of interpreting the constitution."[18] Some have argued that it is a "truism"; it states only that all is retained which has not been surrendered. It is at least this. But it seems accurate to argue as well that the purpose of the Tenth Amendment was "to put the obvious beyond peradventure."[19] It states in bold terms the fundamental demarcation of governing power that was at the very center of the debate over the Constitution. Moreover, as Raoul Berger points out, "to diminish the Tenth Amendment as merely 'declaratory' is likewise to vitiate the supremacy clause and the necessary and proper clause, for each, Hamilton wrote in No. 33 of the *Federalist*, was merely declaratory."[20]

It is correct to assert, as Joseph Story did, that the "sole design" of the Tenth Amendment was "to exclude any interpretation, by which other powers should be assumed beyond those, which are granted."[21] It is, in other words, a reaffirmation that ours is a constitution of limited powers. Madison's concern had been that the term "expressly" would have been a bar to the use of necessary and proper means to carry out granted powers. Removing that bar only ensured the central government would be able to act effectively to carry out its powers. It did not provide the vehicle by which the government could exercise powers not delegated to it or create new powers. The Tenth Amendment, as proposed and ratified, is, as one observer has stated, "a political bargain, key terms of which assumed the continuing vitality of the states as prime law makers in most affairs."[22]

Notes

1. Franklin, the eldest of the delegates, provided guidance to the Convention on more than one occasion. It was Franklin who urged his colleagues to rise above their "partial social interests" so that some consensus might be achieved. On June 28 Franklin called for "prayers imploring the assistance of Heaven, and its blessings on our deliberations" and reminded his colleagues that the world watched to find out whether governments could be established by "Human Wisdom" or if it must be left "to chance war and conquest." *See* J. Madison, *Notes of Debates in the Federal Convention of 1787*, ed. A. Koch (Athens: Ohio Univ. Press, 1966), pp. 209–10.

2. Ibid., p. 34.

3. M. Diamond, "What the Framers Meant by Federalism," in R. Goldwin, ed., *A Nation of States* (Chicago: Rand McNally, 1974), p. 32.

4. A. Hamilton, J. Madison, and J. Jay, *The Federalist Papers*, ed. C. Rossiter (New York: New American Library, 1961), No. 39, p. 246.

5. Ibid., p. 227.

6. M. Farrand, ed., *The Records of the Federal Convention of 1787*, 4 vols. (New Haven: Yale Univ. Press, 1911–37), 1:258.

7. J. Elliot, *The Debates of the Several State Conventions on the Adoption of the Federal Constitution* (Washington, D.C.: U.S. Congress, 1854), 2:335–56.

8. Ibid., pp. 266, 354.

9. *The Federalist*, No. 45, pp. 290–91.

10. Elliot, *Debates* 2:481–82.

11. *The Federalist*, No. 45, pp. 292–93.

12. *Annals of Congress*, vol. 1 (Washington, D.C.: Gales & Seaton, 1834), p. 429.

13. Ibid., p. 442.

14. *See Federal Farmer*, No. 16, written Jan. 20, 1788, in P. Kurland and R. Lerner, eds., *The Founders' Constitution*, vol. 5 (Chicago: Univ. of Chicago Press, 1987), p. 402.

15. Ibid.

16. Elliot, *Debates* 4:248.

17. *Annals of Congress* 1:761–68.

18. J. Story, *Commentaries on the Constitution of the United States*, vol. 3 (Boston: C. C. Little and J. Brown, 1833), sec. 1900–1901.

19. R. Berger, *Federalism: The Found-*

er's Design (Norman: Univ. of Oklahoma, 1987), p. 80.

20. Ibid., p. 81.

21. Story, *Commentaries*, vol. 2, sec. 1808.

22. W. Hurst, *The Legitimacy of the Business Corporation in the Law of the United States*, cited in Berger, *Federalism*, p. 87.

PAUL J. MISHKIN

31. The Current Understanding of the Tenth Amendment

In the first half of this century, the focal issue of Tenth Amendment law was its impact on Congress's power to regulate interstate commerce: assuming an act of Congress to be authorized by that enumerated power, did the Tenth Amendment impose a further, independent curb in the name of preserving the power of the states to make laws governing the subject matter. That issue, and that concept of the Tenth Amendment, ended in 1941. In *United States v. Darby*, the Supreme Court firmly decided in the negative, asserting that the amendment merely stated "a truism that all is retained which has not been surrendered."[1]

That question involved federal laws regulating private transactions in or affecting interstate commerce. The contemporary issues of the meaning of the amendment in this latter half of the century bear on a different dispute about the nature of American federalism: Congress's ability under the commerce power to command states as such—to give binding orders to state (and local) governments. As the Court put it more recently, "While the Tenth Amendment has been characterized as a 'truism,' . . . it is not without significance. The Amendment expressly declares the constitutional policy that Congress may not exercise power in a fashion that impairs the States' integrity or their ability to function effectively in a federal system."[2]

The dispute over that "constitutional policy" has been a churning one. In 1976, explicitly overruling a then eight-year-old case,[3] the Court pronounced that the Tenth Amendment prohibited the federal government from invading "traditional state functions." Nine years later, after several intervening cases, the Court in 1985 abandoned that course and held that the Tenth Amendment—and its underlying policy—did not impose any affirmative, judicially enforceable limits on federal intrusion into state matters. Protection of state sovereignty henceforth would be left to the processes and structure of the federal government itself, saving the remote possibility of a violation of the Tenth Amendment only if the "national political process" failed. Both these decisions were by vote of 5–4, and dissenters in the more recent case explicitly looked forward to the possible overruling of the latest overruling.

The fundamental issue is, then, far from resolved. To lay the groundwork for consideration of how it might and should be dealt with hereafter requires a look first at the ways in which the Court has dealt with the problems that have been presented to it, leading up to its most recent pronouncement. With that background, we can examine that pronouncement and suggest directions that future development might take.

In 1976 the Court departed sharply from the earlier notion that the Tenth Amendment did not provide any affirmative protection of states' rights. It held, in a 5–4 decision in *National League of Cities v. Usery*,[4] that the federal regulation of minimum wage and maximum hour provisions under the Fair Labor Standards Act (FLSA) for state employees violated the Tenth Amendment. A number of states and cities had brought suit claiming that the application of FLSA to state employees violated that amendment. The regulation of minimum wage and maximum hour provisions was well within Congress's power under the commerce clause. Thus, there was no disagreement as to whether Congress could regulate analogous private employers under FLSA. The cities' and states' main argument was that the act as applied to them violated the Tenth Amendment.

The Court agreed with them. It stated that there had never been any doubt that the federal government's power to invade the "sovereignty of the state" was limited. However, for the first time it sought to define where those limits lay. It noted that FLSA regulated the "States as States" and that the power to determine the wages and hours of its employees in carrying out state governmental functions was "essential to [the states'] separate and independent existence." It also noted that forcing the states to comply with federal overtime and minimum wage requirements would cause the states to incur substantial costs and force them to cut back their programs. The act displaced state policies regarding the manner in which the states structured their traditional governmental services. In short, without providing any explicit guidelines as to which functions of a state were within the protected area and which were not, the Court held that Congress had infringed excessively on the states' traditional functions.

While establishing a fundamental role for the Tenth Amendment, *National League of Cities* left a good deal up in the air. Though the majority opinion's general conceptual structure was fairly clear, crucial terms were left undefined. Moreover, beyond that, the justice who cast the fifth vote to make a majority wrote separately to say that he understood the Court opinion (and joined it on this understanding) as adopting "a balancing approach" which would uphold federal power in other cases "where the federal interest is demonstrably greater and where state facility compliance with imposed federal standards would be essential."

The Court did not have occasion to return to the principles it laid down in *National League of Cities* until 1981, in *Hodel v. Virginia State Mining & Reclamation Association, Inc.*[5] In that case, a group of coal companies, a city in Virginia, and the state of Virginia brought suit alleging that the Surface Mining Control and Reclamation Act, an act of Congress, violated the Tenth

Amendment. Congress had passed the act to "establish a nationwide program to protect society and the environment from the adverse effects of surface coal mining operations." The act provided, among other things, that the coal-mining companies had to return some sites to their "approximate original contour." The plaintiffs argued that regulation of mining operations within the states interfered with the states' "traditional governmental function" of regulating land use.

Hodel actually involved the older, easier problem of federal regulation aimed at private activity, rather than at the states as such. But the Court used the occasion to distill a three-part test from the somewhat vague language of *National League of Cities*. First, the challenged statute had to regulate the "States as States." Second, the federal regulation had to address matters that were indisputably "attribute[s] of state sovereignty." Third, the federal statute had to impair directly the states' ability to "structure integral operations in areas of traditional governmental functions." The Court also made clear that this was to be a conjunctive test: "[A] claim that congressional commerce power legislation is invalid under reasoning of *National League of Cities* must satisfy *each* of [the] three requirements."[6] Moreover, even if the first three requirements were met, the statute would not violate the Tenth Amendment if the nature of the federal interest advanced justified state submission.

The Court rejected the challenge because the act did not regulate the "States as States." It noted that the act only governed the activities of individuals and businesses. As such, Congress had plenary power to regulate their activities under the commerce clause. The state had argued that under the *National League of Cities* test, the regulation governed the "States" because it let the state governments regulate surface coal mining in their own states only if they did so in conformity with the federal standard. Essentially, they argued, this forced the states to adopt and enforce the federal criteria rather than their own and thus deprived states of freedom to make their own decisions. The Court rejected this argument because the federal government had the power to preempt state regulation of private activity and because the state always had the option of simply not regulating at all. In short, the Court affirmed that its new tack on the Tenth Amendment would not have any effect on the well-established preemption doctrine. Because the states were given a choice either to regulate in conformity with the federal standard or not to regulate at all, the Court was not faced with the question of whether the Tenth Amendment would be violated if the state were compelled to enforce a federal regulation. It answered this question in part in *FERC v. Mississippi*.

In that case,[7] decided a year after *Hodel*, the Court was faced with the question of whether the Tenth Amendment was violated if the "Federal Government attempt[ed] to use state regulatory machinery to advance federal goals." The question arose in the context of a congressional act designed to combat the nationwide energy crisis, the Public Utility Regulatory Policies Act (PURPA). Three sections of the act were challenged. One required the states' regulatory authorities to implement certain standards promulgated by the Federal Energy Regulatory Commission (FERC). The Court found that an acceptable way for a state to accomplish this was simply to undertake to adjudicate disputes between parties that arose under PURPA. This, the Court reasoned, was the "very type of activity customarily engaged in by the Mississippi Public Service Commission." Analogizing to cases in which the state courts have been directed to hear federal claims, the Court found no Tenth Amendment violation in this section of the act.

Likewise, it rejected the claim that another section of the act that forced the states to consider various energy-saving suggestions set down in PURPA violated the Tenth Amendment. Again analogizing to cases in which the judiciary of the states was enlisted to further federal ends, the Court found no violation. It also relied on the fact that the act only mandated consideration of the standard; it did not require the states to adopt any of the suggested standards. It characterized the federal mandate to consider Congress's suggestions as a condition on the states' continued regulation of the area. Given that the federal government could have preempted state participation in this area altogether, imposing a condition did not violate the Tenth Amendment. It was of no consequence that the condition was an affirmative one, that is, directing the states to take certain action. Again, the Court noted that the state could abandon the task of regulating in this area altogether even though it recognized that as a practical matter this was not a viable option because Congress had not provided a federal plan for utility company regulation in the event the state chose this option.

Finally, the Court rejected without much discussion the argument that a section of the act mandating that the states follow certain procedures in considering the federal suggestions violated the Tenth Amendment. It stated that requiring certain procedural minimums was constitutional if Congress could force the states to consider proposals in the first place. It stated that these requirements did not "compel the exercise of the State's sovereign powers, and did not purport to set standards to be followed in all areas of the state commission's endeavors."

A year later, in *EEOC v. Wyoming*,[8] the Court again upheld a congressional act against a Tenth Amendment challenge. Congress had amended the Age Discrimination in Employment Act (ADEA) to apply to state employees. Thus, the states were not allowed to discriminate against an employee on the basis of age, except where age is a bona fide occupational qualification. Wyoming claimed that the act as applied to the states violated the Tenth Amendment. The Court held that it did not, because it did not "directly impair" the states' ability to operate their traditional governmental functions. It found this case different from *National League of Cities* because it did not force the state to abandon the policy underlying its mandatory age-fifty-five retirement law, namely to assure the physical preparedness of its workers. The act only meant that Wyoming would have to carry out that policy on an individual basis, rather than with a blanket rule. The Court noted that Wyoming's policy was "not overridden entirely, but is merely being tested against a reasonable federal standard." Furthermore, Wyoming had claimed no interest as important as that claimed in *National League of Cities*. Thus, rather than looking at whether the act invaded a traditional state function, the Court found that it did not significantly invade what might well be a traditional governmental function. Justice Stevens's concurrence argued that *National League of Cities* should be overruled, foreshadowing what was to come two years later.

Less than ten years after embarking on these uncharted waters, the Supreme Court in 1985 in *Garcia v. San Antonio Metropolitan Transit Authority*[9] abandoned what it had laid down in *National League of Cities*. Instead, the protection of state sovereignty was to be found in the structure of the federal government, rather than in a judicially enforced substantive limitation.

Garcia involved a challenge to the FLSA, the very act which *National League of Cities* had declared violative of the Tenth Amendment as applied to public employees and the same act involved when Justice Stone dubbed the Tenth Amendment a "truism." The challengers alleged that application of FLSA to employees of a public mass-transit authority violated the protection of state sovereignty guaranteed by the Tenth Amendment. Instead of analyzing the problem under the *Hodel* three-part test, the Court overruled *National League of Cities* by a 5–4 vote. The majority found it impossible to give any working definition of a "traditional governmental function." Neither a historical approach nor use of adjectives such as "integral" or "unique" or "necessary" gave any principled content to which type of state activities were protected from federal intrusion by the Tenth Amendment. Having rejected the *National League of Cities* approach, the Court turned to reconsider the problem underlying Tenth Amendment debate: Given that there are some areas of state sovereignty into which the federal government may not intrude, how is it possible to give a meaningful definition of what those areas are?

Unable or unwilling to come up with a good definition of "state sovereignty," the Court announced that "the principal means chosen by the Framers to ensure the role of the States in the federal system lies in the structure of the Federal Government itself."[10] In other words, the fact that senators were originally elected by state legislatures and representatives were elected by voters qualified and organized in districts by the states meant that Congress could be trusted not to intrude lightly into areas of state sovereignty. The Court cited from *The Federalist Papers* and other "early" sources to support the notion that the framers intended the structure itself to work as a limit on the federal invasion of exclusively state areas.

Valid as this history and line of reasoning may be, it does not follow that the power of judicial review under *Marbury v. Madison* is not also an intended safeguard for the state rights preserved by the Constitution. But the majority went on to decide that the structure of the federal system was the method by which state sovereignty should be protected. The only possible limit it saw on this virtually complete abdication of judicial review was in the event of "possible failings in the national political process." How such a failing might be identified was left undefined, and it seems clear that the majority contemplated with equanimity that the stated possibility might never become an operative concept.

The essential core of the majority opinion in *Garcia* is that it is simply too difficult for a court to draw the line identifying what state functions warrant protection from routine federal intrusion under the commerce clause. Although the opinion may exaggerate the line-drawing problem, there is no doubt that it is real. But that cannot be the whole story. "Drawing lines" is precisely what courts—and the Supreme Court, in particular—are in the business of doing. The argument that a particular line is too difficult to draw is essentially a holding that the issue, or the interests involved, are not important enough to warrant the effort in trying. The majority opinion in *Garcia* never quite addresses this point head-on, preferring instead to emphasize, and even overstate, the various difficulties. But it is undoubtedly true that it does not place great importance on the preservation of state autonomy.

One indication of this is the ease with which the majority accepts the institutional arrangements built into the structure of the federal government as sufficient in themselves to preserve the states' role. It is ironic that the Court discovers the total importance of these "safeguards" now. For it is undoubtedly true that these safeguards were far stronger in prior times, when the Court did not relinquish its role in enforcing constitutional protection of federalism. Indeed, as has been said,

> a good argument can be made [—a convincing one in my judgment—] that a variety of structural and political changes occurring in this century have combined to make Congress particularly *insensitive* to state and local values.
>
> Thus, in terms of structure, Congress did at one time reflect state values: Senators were chosen by their state legislatures and, the 15th Amendment notwithstanding, the states controlled the composition of the electorate. As early as 1913, state structural preponderance was weakened by the ratification of the 17th Amendment and the direct popular election of United States Senators. However, it was not until a half-century later that the combined impact of the four voting amendments, the *Voting Rights Act*, and the Supreme Court's reapportionment decisions resulted in a state structural influence more mythical than real.

> Perhaps even more significant has been the gradual decline in the political influence of state and local interests at the national legislative level. Brought about in large measure by the weakening of the local party organization and the technological unshackling of the national media, that decline is both manifested in and exacerbated by the individual members of Congress: "The past 25 years have brought enormous changes in the types of persons elected to the Senate and House, and in the techniques used in their successful campaigns. The core element in this transformation has been the decline in importance of state party organization, itself a product of several related forces—the effect of money on politics, the changing use of media in campaigns, the phenomenon of celebrity success in politics, and the substitution of welfare state programs for the community service functions of the neighborhood political organization. The consequences are varied, but clearly point in one direction. As Senators and members of the House develop independent constituencies among groups such as farmers, businessmen, laborers, environmentalists, and the poor, each of which generally supports certain national initiatives, their tendency to identify with state interests and the positions of state officials is reduced."[11]

Thus the Court's withdrawal from any active role in protection of states from federal overbearing effectively puts total reliance upon other federal institutions at a time in history when those institutions are least likely to be innately responsive to state constituencies or concerns (and there is no reason to expect the long-term trend to be any different in the future).

Moreover, the Court's abdication is not neutral as to the operation of those other federal institutions but actually will weaken further their functioning as safeguards. The prime importance of the Court's continuing as active potential protector of state sovereignty is not particularly in its invalidation of federal legislation in individual cases. Such invalidation can be very important on isolated occasions. But even that is not as crucial as the continual influence of the Court in shaping communal consideration of federalism and the value of the states. Public debate on constitutional matters, even in the houses of Congress, ordinarily follows the Court's formulation of the issues. Thus the Court sets the terms of discourse. If the Court ceases to address the importance of the states and the protection of their sovereignty, it no longer provides an authenticated vocabulary or imprimatur of legitimacy for constitutional debates. Under those conditions, it becomes even less likely than otherwise that these issues will be perceived and addressed as constitutional values in the committees and halls of Congress or the executive branch.

What is ultimately missing in the perspective of the Court's majority is a recognition of the contemporary importance of federalism and of the states as such. Even the dissenting opinions do not sufficiently supply that deficiency. One finds an expressed concern about the effects which different doctrine might have on the "States as laboratories." Yet it is true that economic and social changes have rendered that concept much less relevant than in the past. Experimentation now often begins at the national level. Similarly, the related concept of federalism as a means of providing individuals with choice among different legislative programs is also not itself a forceful justification of the value of autonomous states. To the extent that such choice requires moving one's home or business, the occasions and actual possibilities of its exercise, though real enough at times, do not seem sufficient in themselves to justify an elaborate institutional structure.

But the political functions of a real and strong federalism have become, if anything, more important than in the past. By political functions, I mean the functions of state (and local) governments as bulwarks of pluralism and of liberty. The states have a role as autonomic power centers—and thus power bases—that are not subject to hierarchical control from the center. They can thus sustain and reflect interests at odds with those having hegemony at the national level, in the media and in Congress. These differing interests may at times be a function of local conditions; e.g., an area of high unemployment may value jobs ahead of reducing air or water pollution (by closing a factory). But they may also simply be a function of the fact that states have different constituencies and thus provide bases for the rise of independent politicians and candidates with views diverging from the dominant national constituencies. States also provide, in their own government and in more local units, opportunities for active participation in politics, which helps evoke and sustain citizen activity and involvement in the public life.

The preservation of state autonomy—or "sovereignty" or "integrity"—to an extent sufficient to provide insulated, alternative power bases is important even in the regular course of affairs. It provides the means by which ideas, programs, and candidates different from those dominant at the national level can emerge, develop, and acquire strength. That autonomous base could be crucial to the maintenance of freedom if a crisis swept "a man on a white horse" to power in Washington. Similarly, the values of direct citizen involvement and participation to the maintenance of a culture of democracy and a spirit of liberty can be important in both ordinary times and crisis.[12]

State autonomy—by whatever label—is essential for the realization of these advantages. But it is not easy to identify what features of state government or functions must be protected in order to maintain that autonomy. Some surely must be. But identifying specific features, rather than just an aggregate, is a much more difficult task. Yet it is not impossible—and the effort is certainly worth making. Scholarly studies may contribute, and the common-law processes of the courts may help distill important essences. The very fact of judicial attention and effort will itself contribute to the perceived status and value of autonomous state and local government.

Identification of the contemporary value of the states in our federal system would serve to reinforce the historical arguments and would provide important reasons and motivation to seek to draw the doctrinal line that would realize the purposes of the Tenth Amendment. Sophisticated elaboration of the contemporary function of the states also would provide a basis for developing the substance and appropriate content of those doctrinal lines. It would not render the lines immediately pellucid or answer all questions posed even in simpler cases. But it would provide the reasons and the basis for a new common-law development of the appropriate constitutional meaning of the Tenth Amendment.

All of this, of course, argues for overruling *Garcia*—or, at the very least, enlarging enormously upon the tiny "process" opening left by the majority opinion here. The structural issues at stake are great enough, and the flux in the authorities here and in the Court in general strong enough, that that possibility is neither entirely unlikely nor inappropriate.

Notes

1. *United States v. Darby*, 312 U.S. 100, 124 (1941).

2. 421 U.S., at 547 n.7 (1975).

3. *Maryland v. Wirtz*, 392 U.S. 183 (1968).

4. *National League of Cities v. Usery*, 426 U.S. 833 (1976).

5. *Hodel v. Virginia State Mining & Reclamation Association, Inc.* 452 U.S. 204 (1981).

6. 452 U.S. at 287.

7. *FERC v. Mississippi*, 456 U.S. 742 (1982).

8. *EEOC v. Wyoming*, 460 U.S. 223 (1983).

9. *Garcia v. San Antonio Metropolitan Transit Authority*, 469 U.S. 528 (1985).

10. 469 U.S. at 550. For elaboration of this theme, *see* J. Choper, *Judicial Review and the National Political Process* (Chicago: Univ. of Chicago Press, 1980), pp. 175–84, and Wechsler, *The Political Safeguards of Federalism: The Role of the States in the Composition and Selection of the National Government*, 54 Colum. L. Rev. 543 (1954); both relied upon in the Court's opinion.

11. Advisory Commission on Intergovernmental Relations, *Regulatory Federalism: Policy, Process, Impact, and Reform* (Washington, D.C., 1984), pp. 50–51, quoting internally Kaden, *Politics, Money, and State Sovereignty: The Judicial Role*, 79 Colum. L. Rev. 847 (1979).

12. For a sophisticated development of these themes and related ones, see Rapaczynski, *From Sovereignty to Process: The Jurisprudence of Federalism after Garcia*, 1985 Sup. Ct. Rev. 341; Nagel, *Federalism as a Fundamental Value: National League of Cities in Perspective*, 1981 Sup. Ct. Rev. 81.

Case Index

Subject Index